CARIBBEAN HIKING

A hiking and walking guide
to thirty of the most popular islands

CARIBBEAN HIKING

A hiking and walking guide
to thirty of the most popular islands

by

M. TIMOTHY O'KEEFE

MENASHA RIDGE PRESS
Birmingham, Alabama

Disclaimer

The information contained in this book should be current for years to come. However, storms and hurricanes can change walking and hiking conditions in the Caribbean overnight. At the same time, neither the author nor the publisher assumes responsibility or liability for any errors or omissions that may have occurred. If you spot any, please let us know; and please keep us informed of any changes you may encounter on your hikes. Your suggestions for subsequent editions are also sought.

Hiking, like many outdoor activities, has inherent risks that are the responsibility of the hiker. Be careful. Walk good.

Copyright © 2001 by M. Timothy O'Keefe
All rights reserved
Manufactured in the United States of America
Published by Menasha Ridge Press
Distributed by The Globe Pequot Press
First edition, first printing

Library of Congress Cataloging-in-Publication Data
O'Keefe, M. Timothy.
    Caribbean hiking: a hiking & walking guide to 30 of the most popular islands/by M. Timothy O'Keefe
        p. cm.
    ISBN 0-89732-389-0 (alk. paper)
    1. Hiking—Caribbean Area—Guidebooks. 2. Caribbean Area—Guidebooks. I. O'Keefe, M. Timothy. Caribbean afoot! II Title

GC199.44C27 O54 2001
917.2904'53—dc21

                                                              2001031605
                                                                      CIP

Cover design by Grant M. Tatum
Text design by Rachel Crutchfield
Maps by Steve Jones and M. Timothy O'Keefe
Cover photo by M. Timothy O'Keefe
All other photos by M. Timothy O'Keefe

Menasha Ridge Press
P.O. Box 43673
Birmingham, AL 35243
www.menasharidgepress.com

DEDICATION

This book is dedicated to Karl Wickstrom and the late Bill Hallstrom of Florida Sportsman Magazine. Time may have sent us on different paths, but without you both my own journey might never have begun.

Old West Indian Saying: *"If you play with dog, dog bites you."*
Translation: *"Don't take needless risks."*

TABLE OF CONTENTS

ACKNOWLEDGMENTS

This book would not exist without the help of many people in the United States and the Caribbean region. I am particularly fortunate to have two friends who aided tremendously: Lee Elliott applied her artistic talents to the map making. She was even crazy enough to tackle the first edit of the first edition and, like me, was amazed and slightly terrified to watch the project take on a life of its own. Thanks, Sis! Charlanne Fields was responsible for the detail in the Guadeloupe and Martinique chapters—she translated much of the local hiking information which was available only in French. Thanks, Charlanne, for sticking with it after it turned out to be a far more prodigious task than either of us imagined. On the islands themselves I'm indebted to:

- Dominica: Superintendent David Williams of the National Parks & Forestry Division; Ken Dill of Ken's Hinterland Tours; and Henry Shillingford.
- Dominican Republic: Dr. Lynne Guitar of Santo Domingo; Tricia Thorndike de Suriel and Richard Weber of Iguana Mama.
- Grenada: Guides Denis Henry and Telfor Bedeau.
- Guadeloupe: Berry Gerard of the Forest Station at Matouba.
- Jamaica: Peter Bentley and the staff at Maya Lodge.
- Martinique: Jos Nosel of the National Parks and the Azimut guide service.
- Nevis: Elmeader Prentiss and Sylvester Pemberton.
- Puerto Rico: Forestry technician Roberto Rijos of the Caribbean National Forest; Miguel Canals of the Guanica Dry Forest Reserve; Arnold Benus at Copamarina Beach Resort.
- St. Kitts: Greg Pereira of Greg's Safaris.
- St. Lucia: Guide Martial Simon of Soufrière, the staff of Anse Chastanet, and the Forestry Department guides.
- Tobago: Forester William Trim and Game Warden Newton George.
- Trinidad: Guide Tony Poyer and the staff of the Asa Wright Nature Centre.
- U.S. Virgin Islands: On St. John, Supervising park ranger Schuler Brown of the National Park Service and Scott McDowell of Thunder Hawk Trail Guides; on St. Croix, environmentalist Olassie Davis and the staffs of the St. Croix Environmental Association and St. Croix Heritage Tours.

My heartfelt appreciation to the people at Menasha Ridge Press: my editors Leslie Cummins (Caribbean Afoot!), Bud Zehmer and Russell Helms (Caribbean Hiking); and publisher Bob Sehlinger, who first listened to the proposal for the book over the phone when he didn't know me from Adam. Thank you for letting me do this book my way.

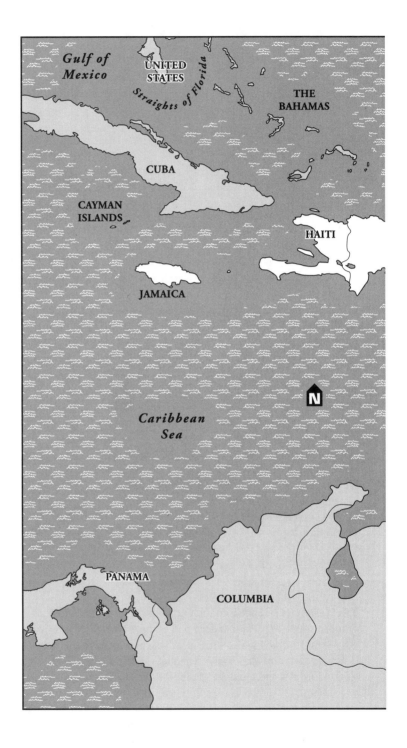

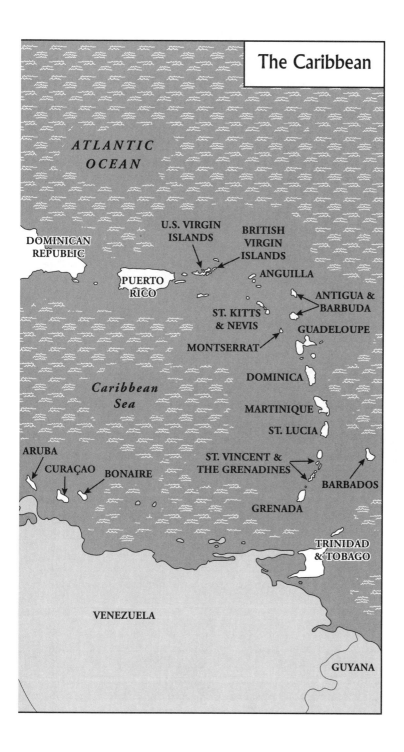

The Caribbean

ATLANTIC
OCEAN

DOMINICAN
REPUBLIC

U.S. VIRGIN
ISLANDS

BRITISH
VIRGIN
ISLANDS

ANGUILLA

PUERTO
RICO

ANTIGUA &
BARBUDA

ST. KITTS
& NEVIS

GUADELOUPE

MONTSERRAT

Caribbean
Sea

DOMINICA

MARTINIQUE

ST. LUCIA

ARUBA

CURAÇAO

BONAIRE

ST. VINCENT &
THE GRENADINES

BARBADOS

GRENADA

TRINIDAD
& TOBAGO

VENEZUELA

GUYANA

LIST OF MAPS

P R E F A C E

Old West Indian Proverb: "Crab walks too much, he loses his claw.
He does not walk, he does not get fat."

Translation: "While it may be risky to go adventuring, it is also
unproductive and unrewarding to be too cautious and stay at home."

You haven't really experienced the Caribbean until you know what an island tastes like, what it sounds like, what it smells like, and how it feels—including its mud and thorns.

A beach offers the briefest glimpse of any of this, and beachside is where most tourists spend their time. As lovely as Caribbean beaches are, they usually are the least interesting and most uncomfortable parts of an island. Consider where the wealthy sugar planters of centuries ago built their great houses. With their vast fortunes, they could have claimed any spot of land, including prime beach frontage. Instead, they chose the higher, cooler elevations where the plant life and wildlife are at their most diverse. They realized it was the interior of the islands, in the hills and valleys, that you find the best of the Caribbean.

And the best way to experience it is by walking and hiking. Spend just half a day away from the beach exploring the interior of an island and I'll wager your vacation will be doubly rewarding. You may find yourself returning to the Caribbean more often and choosing where to go based on an island's walking and hiking opportunities, not just its beaches.

Here are almost 400 hikes and walks to try.

I N T R O D U C T I O N

Old West Indian Proverb: *"See me is one, come live with me is the other."*
Translation: *"Don't be taken in by first appearances."*

Although locals have been doing it for centuries, hiking and walking in the Caribbean are still in their infancy as far as tourism goes. With a new enthusiasm for ecotourism, Caribbean governments are recognizing that walking and hiking paths—on the beaches, through the rain forests, and across the high mountain peaks—are among the West Indies' greatest natural attractions. Walkers and hikers are becoming an important force in the conservation of the Caribbean's natural resources, because trees, plants, and animals in their native habitat are precisely what visitors want to see.

Until the first version of this book was published a number of years ago, it was difficult to obtain precise information on the walking and hiking opportunities in the West Indies. The first edition was the earliest attempt to bring together the best city walks and mountain hikes on the most popular islands in a clear and comprehensive way. And now *Caribbean Afoot!* is back, with a new title, completely updated, and expanded with walking maps of all the major port cities and detailed descriptions of rain forest and mountain hikes—almost 400 in all.

The information in this book is based both on first-hand experience and local contact with each island's most knowledgeable experts. This is not an armchair guide written by a cube dweller. But because most of the descriptions are subjective, it's possible you might hate a hike that I enjoyed. Or you might like one that didn't particularly impress me. I have tried to tell why I liked or disliked a particular city or trail (or island) so you will be aware of the basis and bias of my opinions.

Bear in mind that conditions change dramatically according to the season and weather. A pleasant walk I took during a dry period may be a hellish nightmare in the rainy season, when hiking trails are slick and slippery. The same considerations apply to the city walks, which also will be affected by the company you keep and whether you get along with the locals. No walk is exactly the same twice.

Storm damage can totally change the face of an island, often permanently. Trails once popular become impassable. Furthermore, clearing trails will be the last item on the agenda for a society struggling to restore electrical power, reopen roads, and restore life to normalcy. It still takes 12 to 21 days for a letter to travel the short distance from the U.S. mainland to many islands. With mail service that slow, you get an idea of how rapidly island governments will be able to respond to a crisis. The plain fact is that many islands are too poor to be able to take efficient and prompt action. I would advise waiting 6 to 12 months before visiting any island severely damaged by a hurricane or tropical storm if hiking and walking are your main objectives.

For most of the hikes and walks, you'll notice that length, time, and difficulty information for each description is provided to offer a quick idea of what to expect. In some instances, length is omitted because the precise distance is unknown, even to locals. Distance is deceptive anyway: What is more important is how long the walk is likely to take. The estimates supplied are for an average walker stopping to smell the flowers or watch the birds. If anything, the given walking times are more likely to be overestimated than underestimated.

The reverse is true of the difficulty of each hike or walk; consider these ratings the absolute minimum. Although weather conditions can dramatically increase a hike's difficulty, nothing, except perhaps the installation of escalators, is likely to make any of the walks any easier.

Here is how the difficulty scale applies:

Level 1: Easy, with level walking or with very little climbing. Anyone capable of walking should be able to finish the described hike in the length of time given.

Level 2: Some ascents and descents, but nothing you shouldn't anticipate on a walk in the forest almost anywhere.

Level 3: Expect to sweat (or perspire, if you prefer). Stamina and good balance are essential to enjoy this kind of hike, as are appropriate shoes designed for serious walking and climbing. Anyone in average physical condition should find these trails just a good stretch of the legs.

Level 4: Time to get serious about the amount of exertion you're willing to expend. A fair amount of stamina is required because of the distance or the terrain: probably muddy and slippery and/or steep in many parts, and may require some scrambling. Only those in good physical condition will probably enjoy this hike.

Level 5: A gut buster. Requires extreme, sustained effort. Do not attempt a hike of this level unless you are in excellent physical condition. Expect this to be demanding, challenging, possibly even dangerous in spots, depending on conditions. Any hike rated a 5+ is bound to demand all of your attention and skill. Being part mountain goat is a definite asset.

Hikes rated with a difficulty from 3 to 5 require good, nonskid walking shoes. The quality of your footwear has a lot to do with how much walking you do—as opposed to stumbling and falling and sliding on your butt.

Level 3–5 hikers should:

- Use backpacks so their hands will be free to clutch and grab tree roots, vines, or other vital flora not to fall off the mountainside.
- Carry food and water to sustain energy.
- Not be hungover or high.
- Always go prepared for rain above 1,800 feet.

Oh, yes: Caribbean mud is almost impossible to get out of white socks. Prepare to sacrifice those that you wear to the spirits of the Arawaks and Caribs.

THE CARIBBEAN'S TOP TEN HIKES

The walks and hikes covered by this guide are so diverse it is difficult to choose the top ten. I chose the following because they are unusual and interesting, not necessarily because they're tough. The first one listed, however, could be used in an Ironman competition.

1. **Dominica: The Valley of Desolation and the Boiling Lake Hike.** A seven-hour round-trip marathon up and down the mountains of Dominica to what seems like a prehistoric setting from the beginning of time. Sulfur crystals color the ground; steam vents through cracks in the earth; and streams run black. The Boiling Lake is one of the world's largest boiling lakes. Tough and memorable, there's nothing like this hike anywhere. Far and away the Caribbean's best hike, get into condition for this one and take a guide. At least one tourist has died on the trail. (See p. 90)

2. **Guadeloupe: La Soufriere Summit Hike.** Much less effort required to climb to the summit of an active volcano whose last major eruption was in 1976. Vegetation was destroyed but it's now coming back. A stunning display of all the colors of green. A naturalist guide is essential to appreciate this hike. (See p. 175)

3. **Dominican Republic: Pico Duarte Ascent.** At 10,700 feet, this is the Caribbean's highest peak. Because of the extreme distance between the main camp sites, the hike requires a blistering pace more akin to a run than a walk. For this reason, some people make part of the ascent on foot and part on the back of a mule. The mountain scenery is striking and well worth the effort. The real lure is to stand on the region's tallest mountain. (See p. 113)

4. **Jamaica: Blue Mountain Peak Hike.** Leave your bed at 2 a.m. and walk 7 miles and 3,500 feet up to the peak of Blue Mountain (7,402 feet high) in time to catch the sunrise (assuming it's not raining or cloudy). The entire experience, especially climbing Jacob's Ladder and stumbling around in the dark, is an unforgettable challenge. Anyone in good health can make this climb. (See p. 205)

5. **Tobago: Trails of Little Tobago.** A pleasant, easy walk on the small cay of Little Tobago, a seabird sanctuary. The dramatic, sheer ocean cliffs where seabirds nest are reminiscent of the nesting colonies in the Galapagos Islands. Beautiful scenery and a chance to view up close species of seabirds on their nests in spring. The dramatic views are a pleasant shock. Easy walking except for the initial ten-minute ascent, which is somewhat steep. (See p. 336)

6. **Trinidad: Asa Wright Nature Centre.** Pleasant pathways cut through this huge, open-sky aviary. More hummingbirds at close range than you ever thought possible. Also, the opportunity to see rare oil birds. Very easy walking for the most part. (See p. 351)

7. **U.S. Virgin Islands: St. John.** The entire island. Two-thirds of it is a national park crisscrossed with 20 different hiking trails, most quite short. The Reef Bay Trail with the detour to the Petroglyph Pool and the Ram Head hike are my favorites. (See p. 367)

8. **Puerto Rico: El Yunque Peak.** For sheer spectacle, variety, and accessibility, the Caribbean National Forest is difficult to top. The hike to El Yunque Peak offers an overview of all the main tropical forest types on a single walk. Compared to many mountain walks, it's not that tough. (See p. 274)

9. **Grenada: Mt. Qua Qua Summit Trail.** A walk through tropical rain forest with excellent panoramic views on one of the Caribbean's lushest and friendliest islands. This is a moderately difficulty climb that is often slick in spots. A knowledgeable guide enhances the climb tremendously. (See p. 159)

10. **St. Kitts: Carib Petroglyphs.** A brief walk to a canyon containing about 100 petroglyph rubbings made by the Caribs before a thousand of the Indians were massacred in this narrow passageway in 1626 by combined British and French forces. The sense of history while standing among these ancient drawings is stunning. Some tricky rock walking and river crossing. (See p. 298)

Honorable mention: Virgin Gorda: The Baths. As much a Caribbean tourist attraction as Walt Disney World but understandably so. The astonishing pile of giant boulders on the beach creates a maze of passageways and pools fun to explore, almost in the shadow of the real Treasure Island.

Summary: This brief list of ten hikes should give you an idea of the tremendous variety waiting in the Caribbean. Experiences that would fill more than one lifetime are awaiting. One piece of advice before you strike out on your own:

Old West Indian Proverb: *"Long pass draw sweat, short pass draw blood."*

Translation: *"Short cuts usually get you into trouble."*

1 What Hiking and Walking in the Caribbean Are All About

Old West Indian Saying: "Flea have money, he buy his own dog."

Translation: "Money doesn't make a gentleman, but it can buy almost anything."

The Caribbean is made up of a variety of cultures, some as different from each other as they are from our own. How these people look at life—and at tourists—needs to be discussed in candid detail if you expect more than a superficial look at the countryside. By no means do I claim to be an expert on the Caribbean mind or culture. I can tell you only what I have observed after three decades of travel in the region and provide the information the local people have shared with me.

Wherever possible, I let them say it instead of me. That is why this guide is sprinkled with proverbs and sayings, little insights into how West Indians think and perceive the world. Sometimes the comments are humorous, other times bitter and harsh, but all are a view about a particular part of life. They frequently contain a wisdom and tolerance that would benefit everyone to adopt. Such as:

Old Jamaican Proverb: "How-de-do and thank you break no square."

Translation: "It is not only good manners to be polite, it does no harm."

So, How Do You Say Caribbean?

The islanders say "Car-i-BEE-an," and this is also the preferred pronunciation in most dictionaries. A second option is a British-fied "Car-RIB-ee-an." Common sense would seem to indicate there is only one proper pronunciation, but consider this remarkable statement from the novel *Caribbean* about why author James A. Michener and others embrace the second choice. Michener states: "A wag explained, 'The hoi polloi use the first, but intellectual snobs prefer the second.' And so do I."

My own philosophy differs. According to the dictionary, the term hoi polloi is a "contemptuous" term used to refer to "the common people, the masses"; in other words, the islanders themselves. I travel to the Caribbean to be with the locals, to interact with them, and have fun. Others apparently prefer not to be around the locals, an attitude that allows them to stay

Proper footwear is essential to avoid thorns on the trail

separate and play the self-admitted role of snob. The plantation owner/slave relationship is thus not entirely forgotten.

Almost all Caribbean hiking guides are locals. If you choose to use a guide, you will be spending six to eight hours a day walking and talking together. If you find the idea of being with islanders uncomfortable and would rather simply be around them, then the Caribbean may not be the place for you. I doubt it will come as a shock that I say "Car-i-BEE-an." I like it when people pronounce my own name correctly, just as you probably want people to pronounce yours the way you prefer, and without condescension.

THE PEOPLE

The racial and cultural mix is often very different from island to island. Trinidad, for instance, calls itself the Rainbow Island because its people are a blend of 40 different origins, including African, Chinese, and East Indian. On some islands, the white population makes up less than a full percentage point.

I find Caribbean islanders among the friendliest and most fun-loving people to be with. Many of them are poorly educated, but they have something far more important than wealth, technological advances, or book learning. They have discovered—or retained—what life is all about: to have fun, whatever you're doing.

Most West Indians have a natural joy in their manner and their style of living. It is the Caribbean's relaxed, laid-back, "No problem," "Don't worry, be happy" approach that still permeates so many islanders, particularly in the countryside, which makes me think of them as "the joy people." Watch how much the locals laugh, talk, joke, and interact with each other. On many islands tourists are readily embraced and treated the same way. On others, it takes time for locals to drop their reserve. Islanders are generally quite shy, and this can be mistaken for an unfriendly or indifferent attitude.

You may meet a few people who won't hide their dislike for outsiders. But how the situation resolves itself can be largely up to you.

SPEAKING PROTOCOL

One of the greatest cultural misunderstandings between tourists and locals is who should speak to whom first. Islanders normally are very polite people and expect to be treated with courtesy. They like to be spoken to when you pass them, even if it's just a nod. They expect visitors to initiate any conversation or the passing "hello." Considering that many visitors come from big cities where residents are afraid to make eye contact, this type of old-fashioned island politeness is a foreign way of behavior.

You may walk to a hotel desk and no one pays any attention to you. As the paying guest you feel frustrated. In your country, the customer always receives preferential treatment. Before long, you get so irritated that the first words popping out of your mouth tend to be less friendly than they could be. The desk clerk responds in the same less-than-friendly way that you greeted him or her. Words and conduct on both sides may escalate from there.

From the West Indian point of view, the visitor has been rude throughout: by not acknowledging the desk clerk and then by starting the conversation in a hostile manner. Hotels are training their staffs in the quirks of tourists—that strangers visiting the Caribbean expect islanders, whose home it is, to speak first—but it will be decades before our traits are fully understood.

The easiest approach on any island is to always speak first, as politely as you would converse with a colleague at work, and say it with a smile. It's almost always returned.

I had this who-should-speak-first pattern explained to me in Antigua. Once I discovered the proper protocol, I was amazed at how much friendlier the Caribbean suddenly became.

They hadn't changed. I had.

POVERTY

The chance of encountering someone who is hostile because of your skin color, whatever it may be, is remote in the British West Indies. If there's a problem, it's usually based on something else—poverty. Islanders see tourists on vacation wearing expensive clothes and living a lavish resort lifestyle most islanders can only dream of. After watching plane- and boatloads of tourists walk around for many years, some islanders feel resentful. The tourist industry aside, there are few jobs, except perhaps seasonal sugarcane cutting and banana picking. The unemployment rate on some islands is as high as 25 percent.

To compensate, a few have taken to panhandling, begging for a share, though in the West Indian culture such conduct is considered bad manners. Others have taken up selling carvings or shells, things you have no need for. It is the best their circumstances allow them to produce. If you refuse, they may resent it. You are their only source of livelihood. If the situation was reversed, how would you react?

So, instead of another T-shirt, why not buy a shell or a necklace? If this sounds like economic do-gooding, I guess it is. But it's also a way of avoiding other peddlers: Show the next salesperson what you've already bought, and they'll often leave you alone. As much as they would like you to also buy from them, whether it's spoken or not, there is an acknowledgment that you've already helped a brother. Helping one another is what island life is all about. Unemployment may be high, but usually no one starves or has to sleep in the streets. Family and friends take care of their own.

A healthy tourist trade is one of the most important economic bases an island can have. Some island governments are making their people aware that tourists in their sometimes irritating ways are good for everyone's economic health. On the island of Bonaire in the Dutch Antilles, the importance of making visitors welcome is a part of the school curriculum.

Old Jamaican Proverb: "*Beg water can't boil cow skin.*"

Translation: "*One cannot live off the proceeds of charity.*"

PHOTOGRAPHING PEOPLE

Photographing people in the Caribbean can be tricky. The guiding principle is to ask first. Islanders don't dress in colorful costumes and speak quaintly to impress tourists. This is their lifestyle.

If you're not carrying a camera, or if you have it slung over your shoulder so it's not about to be used, people are generally friendly and open. With a camera in hand, these same people may be reserved or hostile.

Some islanders don't like to be photographed unless they are dressed in their finest. Others have been hassled by tourists so often they resent posing. I asked a woman at the fish market in Grenada if I could photograph her. She turned her back to me and said, "I no monkey!" I was welcome to take pictures of her fish.

For a few islanders, having their photograph taken is considered a dangerous thing. Although Christianity is the avowed religion of most islands, what we call voodoo is still practiced. The most dangerous thing a believer in the dark arts can imagine is someone capturing their likeness. The photograph can then be used in spells against them to cause sickness and misfortune.

Some islanders expect to be paid for their likeness because they've seen their photos show up in magazines, so they know pictures are worth something. You're getting another souvenir by taking their photograph. What are they gaining, if you don't buy something?

If you are dealing with someone at a roadside stand or some other business, you may be amazed at the cooperation you may receive if you purchase an item first, even if it is only a trinket. That way it becomes a give-and-take situation with both parties gaining something.

Always ask permission and, if a person declines, respect his or her wishes.

CARIBBEAN TIME

You enter a strange time dimension when you land on a Caribbean island. It's not that time stands still in the Caribbean, or that it even runs backward. Things just don't happen as quickly or as precisely as you may be accustomed to. This characteristic varies enough from island to island that each seems to have its own unique set of clocks. It drives many visitors crazy for the first few days.

No doubt about it, "Caribbean time," or "island time," can be frustrating. After rushing to put things in order at work, dashing around to shop and then pack, and hurrying to the airport, many visitors arrive in the Caribbean in warp drive. Some quickly get upset when islanders don't share the same sense of time pressure. Others become infuriated that locals won't respond as promptly and as efficiently as employees or service personnel might back home.

There are two ways to deal with the situation—a situation no one is going to change. Either adapt to it, or fight it. Yes, your visit is on a time budget. You want to fit in as much as you can—but you also want to enjoy every activity as much as possible. It's the old quantity versus quality issue. The setting has just changed, that's all.

One way to decompress from Western-style living is to do nothing the day of your arrival except have something to drink, eat, look around a little, and go to sleep early. You should wake up in a more relaxed mood the next morning. If you arrive tired and stay tired— hiking is a vigorous activity—your vacation may turn into nothing but an ordeal.

Find out what the time flow is and go with it. Do things usually start ten minutes late? Or is the average closer to 20 or 30 minutes? Or maybe—and this actually does happen on quite a few islands—real time, as opposed to Caribbean time, is the norm.

The amazing thing is that if you don't fight the system, everything eventually gets done. Perhaps not in the way you expect, but it eventually happens. Visitors to Jamaica, after their first few days and after getting acclimated to the usual delays, quickly adopt the phrase "No problem, mon" as part of their vocabulary. "Soon come" is another popular island phrase when something doesn't appear at the appointed time.

Of course you can try and fight the system. That doesn't work much better in the Caribbean than it does back home. Islanders are used to impatient tourists. Anything you say to them won't be anything new. And, don't ever forget, they are in the position of power.

Explains Peter Bentley, one of the Caribbean's leading hiking guides and former president of the Jamaica Alternative Tourism, Camping and Hiking Association: "Here's how we work. Push, you don't get much. Take it easier, get much more." And have a happier time, too. Some visitors never do adapt to the concept of Caribbean time. They usually don't go back.

There is, however, a difference between poor, sloppy service and doing things at a different tempo. Definitely complain about poor, sloppy service.

STAYING HEALTHY IN THE TROPICS

Just because you are on vacation and taking a break from work doesn't mean you should take a break for keeping yourself healthy and safe. Of all the potential health problems, overexposure to the sun is the most common. The Caribbean sun is more intense than almost anywhere else in the world. It's at its worst between 10 a.m. and 3 p.m. Gradual exposure to it is mandatory to avoid that painful Larry the Lobster look.

Remember to wear sun block (SPF 20 and higher) and drink lots of nonalcoholic liquid to keep from being dehydrated. It may be necessary to wear sunblock even on your lips. Be particularly careful to cover ears, jaws, and the lower part of your neck. Sunglasses are essential. Bright sun reflected off the water is uncomfortable to the eye.

High Humidity and Dehydration: You'll lose a lot of liquid walking around, and not replacing it will make you feel lousy. It takes about two weeks to adjust to the Caribbean's high humidity, but you can keep your energy level up several ways, including:

1. **Air conditioning:** If you're accustomed to it at home, sleep with it on at night. You will feel far more rested than if you sleep with a ceiling fan and a natural breeze; you're making a lot of high-energy demands on your body during the day, so pamper it at night.

2. **Electrolytes (primarily sodium and potassium):** You need to increase your intake of water in the tropics, especially if you're out hiking and sweating. As you sweat, your body loses not only water, but also electrolytes such as sodium and potassium, which are vital for muscle function (including the heart). To replenish electrolytes, drink rehydration fluids such as Gatorade and eat well balanced meals. If you experience leg cramps, try eating a banana or two every morning to boost your potassium stores. If you still feel crampy or drained, and can't kick into gear, try supplements in moderation.

COMMON AND UNCOMMON HEALTH CONCERNS

Below are some more common health problems as well as some potentially harmful or dangerous animals and plants that you should learn to avoid.

Heatstroke/Sun Poisoning: Okay, so you didn't listen. Symptoms of oncoming heatstroke are dizziness, vertigo, fevers, blister, headache, nausea, sudden lack of sweat, and delusions. Get out of the heat immediately. Take a cool bath or shower. Drink fruit juices or Gatorade if available to replace lost electrolytes. If there's no improvement, see a doctor.

Intestinal Problems: These are usually the result of a bacterial infection or from consuming strange foods and drink (beware those rum punches). Always carry your own water and avoid drinking from streams or falls, no matter how clean they look or how much the locals reassure you. In some remote regions, tap water may be unsafe during the rainy season. Diarrhea and dehydration are the most serious problems: Drink plenty of fluids except alcohol and milk, which seem to prolong diarrhea. A bland diet of tea and toast seems to help some people. Although diarrhea usually clears up on its own after a couple of days, the problem can really interfere with your hiking. Medication can control attacks almost immediately. Use loperamide (brand name Imodium) or atropine (Lomotil).

If you have fever and severe abdominal pains, pass blood in your stools, and generally feel weak, you may have been unlucky enough to contract either amoebic or bacillary dysentery. If in doubt, see a doctor immediately, and see a physician once you return home to minimize long-term health effects.

Colds and Allergies: It's possible to get a cold in the Caribbean, but it's more likely you will suffer an allergic reaction to a plant you may have never encountered before. With hundreds of species of trees, flowers, and orchids, something is always in bloom and always dropping pollen. Bring nondrowsy antihistamines to plug the sniffles and stop tear-streamy eyes during the day. At night, don't worry about something that may knock you out. Take whatever works best and get some sleep.

Bilharzia (also called schistosomiasis): This parasite is very common in lakes or slow-moving streams infested with snails. It can enter the body through an open cut or by drinking the water. This disease has been around a long time, as the mummies of ancient Egyptian pharaohs have revealed. Islands where this has been a problem are few: Martinique, Guadeloupe, and St. Lucia. Bilharzia can be fatal. If you are concerned that you have been exposed, a blood test a month or so after your visit can confirm this.

Hookworms: Besides comfort, here's a good reason for always wearing shoes: Hookworms are picked up by walking around barefoot.

Prickly Heat: When the humidity is high, it's easy to develop a rash. Avoid it by powdering yourself in the morning and evening with talcum powder or powder containing zinc, such as Gold Bond. Never hike in tight jeans or clothes that bind.

Malaria: Currently found only in Haiti, the Dominican Republic, and occasionally Trinidad. Antimalaria treatment, available under a doctor's care, begins before departure and continues afterward. Most tourists are content with insect repellent and do quite well.

AIDS: It is becoming increasingly present but nowhere near the levels of the United States. Primary means of transmission is through heterosexual contact. Condoms are not always available. Women as well as men who intend to seek a new sexual partner should carry their own condoms. Warning: A lot of rum combined with a lot of sun and a lot of hiking in an exotic locale, capped off with a relaxed moonlit swim/walk on the beach, can produce surprising libido stimulation.

Finding a Doctor: The likelihood of requiring medical attention is remote. To be best prepared in case of an accident, contact the International Association for Medical Assistance to Travelers, 745 5th Avenue, New York, NY 10022; (716) 754-4883; www.sentex.net; or Intermedic, 777 3rd Avenue, New York 10017; (212) 486-8974. They have the names and locations of well trained, English-speaking physicians all over the world. Remember to check your insurance card to see if your policy covers overseas travel; otherwise, consider temporary medical/accident insurance. Carry your insurance card.

Basic Health Supplies
- Polarized sunglasses
- Waterproof sunblock
- Insect repellent, including coils to burn in your room/tent
- Band-Aids for blisters

- Water-sterilizing tablets or portable water purifier
- Dusting powder for groin and feet
- Antidiarrhea medicine
- Anticonstipation medicine (we all react differently)
- Aspirin
- Antacid tablets
- Ankle support device in case of sprain
- Commercial rehydrating salts
- Motion sickness medicine, if so prone
- Antihistamines
- First-aid cream and first-aid kit with tweezers

PAINFUL THINGS TO AVOID

I had lots of surprises hiking around the Caribbean, but the biggest revelation was the scarcity of biting insects. I went prepared with repellent and even a repellent-treated mesh jacket. I get bitten more often at home in Florida than I ever do in the islands.

Still, insect repellent is a good item always to have close at hand. Avon's Skin So Soft is not only effective, it doesn't have the industrial chemical odor of most strong commercial repellents. Use Skin So Soft in a pump aerosol, and liberally spray your ankles and waist to repel ticks and mites. Also spray your clothes. Otherwise, rely on chemical preparations containing DEET. Avoid sweet-smelling soaps, perfumes, and colognes, which usually attract insects better than they do the opposite sex.

Always be very familiar with your medical condition and prepared to meet your medical needs in an emergency. If you have severe allergic responses to any insect or plant, be sure to include injectable epinephrine in your first-aid kit and know how to use it.

Mosquitoes: Generally not found at higher altitudes. Found most often in the lowlands and the beaches, especially in the rainy season. To my amazement I never encountered mosquitoes in the rain forests. On St. Lucia I was told the reason mosquitoes are rarely a problem is the lack of standing, stagnant water for them to breed in. The only things in the rain forest that holds water for more than a few seconds are plants like the heliconia, which has sheaths shaped like lobster claws where water can gather. Mosquitoes are much more apt to be a problem in your hotel room or campsite than while hiking.

Bites: Baking soda solutions help relieve itching. Or use papaya, the same ingredient in Adolph's meat tenderizer, which grows fresh in the islands. It's a good painkiller for nonpoisonous stings; the papaya enzyme breaks down the insect venom so it no longer stings. Antihistamine tablets also help reduce swelling and itching; antihistamine in cream form may cause skin allergies. Cortisone cream also helps stop itching, rashes. One way to reduce bites: Always wear socks.

No-see-ums: Also called midges and sand flies, they are so tiny as to be invisible—but what there is must be all teeth. Usually on beaches around sunrise and sunset. In Spanish, they are known as mi-mis (pronounced "me-mees," as in "a case of the screaming mee-mees!") Long pants and shoes/socks are the best protection.

Ants: All over the place in many rain forests but they usually don't bite, except for the appropriately named fire ant, who seems to be all jaws. If you're allergic to ant bites, carry medication.

Scorpions: Found in drier regions, they have a nasty habit of crawling into hiking boots at night and making their presence known the next morning only after you try to put your boot on. They are easier to avoid than treat. Shake out your boots or keep them wrapped in a plastic bag (though the resulting smell may be worse than the bite). Scorpion stings hurt like the dickens but are rarely lethal. Treatment: heavy, sustained cursing during the first few minutes seems to alleviate some tension and divert attention from the painful wound. Also, pounding the offending scorpion to a bloody pulp with your boot is extremely satisfying. Now, if you have a scorpion sting kit, use it. See a doctor if conditions don't improve.

Centipedes: Remember *Dr. No,* the first James Bond movie set in Jamaica, and the graphic scene where Bond finds himself in bed with a tarantula crawling the length of his body? A spider was used in the movie for instant visual effect. However, in the Fleming novel (written in Jamaica, as were all the Bond books), 007 was confronted with something far deadlier: a centipede. Fortunately, poisonous centipedes are scarce, and you're not likely to encounter one. If you do, don't pick one up out of curiosity to examine it as some tourists have done.

Christmas-bush: Dark green, deeply toothed leaves and red berries make this bush look like Christmas holly. Growing to 20 feet tall, it should be treated like poison oak or poison ivy. Any contact with the plant or its leaves will result in a rash, though it may not appear for several hours. The toxin is particularly nasty, able to travel through the body and cause eruptions anywhere, not just at the point of contact. Also called poison ash, cock's spur, and chicharron.

Snakes: Let's hear it for the mongoose! This weasel-like animal was introduced into the Caribbean by Europeans to eliminate rodents and vipers, and the animal is credited with killing off all the poisonous snakes in most of the Caribbean. Their deeds may be overrated. As some scientists have pointed out, there are still poisonous snakes on some islands that have mongoose. Still, the mongoose is the Caribbean's St. Patrick and—as such—is above mere scientific debunking.

Aruba has a small rattlesnake that is rarely seen. Martinique, Trinidad, and St. Lucia are home to the deadly fer-de-lance, most often found in dry coastal areas. Supposedly it's easy to frighten away the fer-de-lance by making enough noise to let it know you're coming, but some people like to use walking sticks to poke ahead in the thick dry bush. Or they like to walk third or fourth in the hiking line. The bite of the fer-de-lance can be fatal if not properly treated, but attacks are rare. Locals know where the snakes hide; follow their warnings. Besides the fer-de-lance, Trinidad also has several other poisonous species. Carry a commercial snake bite kit if it will make you feel better. Hospitals stock snakebite serum, but they will need to know what kind of snake bit you.

You will hear stories of how plantation owners introduced the fer-de-lance from South America to keep slaves from running away into the mountains. This appears to be more legend than fact. First, the snakes are usually on the coast, not in the mountains. Second, the fer-de-lance appears to have reached only three islands—among the southernmost in the Caribbean—by riding across on uprooted trees following severe floods on the South American continent. This theory explains why the poisonous snakes are so geographically limited, not distributed farther north throughout the Caribbean. It appears there just never were that many poisonous snakes in the Caribbean to begin with, before or after the mongoose.

Fish Poisoning/Ciguatera: A deadly toxin can be found primarily in reef fishes, such as snapper, very large grouper, and barracuda. Symptoms include tingling, itching or numbness of the fingertips and lips, stomach cramps, nausea, and vomiting. In severe cases, seek medical help immediately. It can be fatal. Freshness of the fish or its handling has nothing to do with whether the fish is tainted. The toxin is carried up the food chain; you get it from something you ate which also ate something that ate . . .

Stick to ocean-roaming fish such as tuna, wahoo, mahi mahi (dolphin fish, not Flipper), and you should have no problem. I once dined with eight people where we all ate from the same fish and one person got a mild case of ciguatera (lip tingling). Why only him and not the rest of us? Some scientists theorize it may also be a matter of individual susceptibility.

Razor Grass: Just as sharp as its name implies, cuts from this long slender grass seem to take a long time to heal. Usually found in rain forest areas, razor grass is sharp enough to cut through light clothing. Ask someone to point it out to you before you make its acquaintance.

Manchineel Tree (also called the Manzanillo Tree): Look for and avoid this tall tree in the lowlands, particularly around coastal regions. It produces a small, green crab-apple fruit that is very poisonous, sometimes fatal, known on some islands as the apple of death. Apparently a lot of early Spanish explorers ate these things on landfall, only to die of severe throat constrictions. According to conventional wisdom, when it rains, the mere run-off from the manchineel tree's leaves and branches can cause a rash and the sap itself may blister you. Some people have far more severe skin reactions than others. Gel from an aloe plant will work wonders in healing the rash. Quite often these trees are marked with a warning sign in heavily trafficked areas. Have someone point out a specimen.

Marijuana Farming: Never, ever, go anywhere near where you suspect it's growing, much less pick a sample of the crop. It could get you killed. In certain remote mountain areas, marijuana (ganja) farming is an important way of life. If you are on your own, without the company of a local guide, you could be mistaken for a thief or a police spy. Most marijuana farmers are armed. In certain places, they set trap guns to blow away the unwary and the unwanted. Never assume an island is yours to roam freely, particularly on Jamaica and Trinidad. Marked trails like those described here generally are safe. Hiring a local guide is your best insurance policy. On an island, everyone tends to know everyone and what they do, and from who and from where to stay away.

CLOTHES TO WEAR AND TEAR

Unlike hiking in a lot of exotic places that require special clothing of almost an expeditionary nature, Caribbean wear is relatively simple and inexpensive.

Shoes: These are your single most important item. Many people will simply wear an old pair of sneakers, but if you're going to do some serious hiking, you need serious footwear. A lot of trails are rocky and unstable; high-top hiking boots offer more ankle support. They should be comfortable when wet, because your feet could be muddy and soaked most of the time. Most important, they should have nonskid soles. You will encounter lots of mud, but the real problems are the rain-slicked and moss-covered rocks. Flip-flops and the newer sport sandals are a disaster in the making—they provide little support, and most offer little protection from sharp rocks. Some local guides can hike the rain forest in bare feet, but that doesn't mean you should try. Not only have they been walking on this slippery and tricky terrain since their very first steps, their feet have calluses as thick as horse hooves. Try to go native in the foot department and you may have to be carried out. Use one pair of shoes for everyday walking, another specifically for hiking. The hiking pair will be too dirty and damp to wear for anything else.

Have someone point out a manchineel tree so you can avoid it

Slacks/Shorts: Loose, quick-drying running shorts are all you need on some islands. On others, because of razor grass or high altitude temperatures, you need full-length slacks. Take both and consult your guide before setting out; each trail is different. An ideal compromise are the Kenya convertibles sold by Cabelas and other outfitters. These pants are essentially shorts that have legs you can zip on and off, according to conditions.

Socks: Always wear them. They help prevent scratches and insect bites. They also should make walking a lot more comfortable. Be prepared to throw them away at the end of a trip. Some of the mud, especially in Dominica, is impossible to get out.

Shirts: Those with collars offer more protection against the sun. Long sleeves help prevent sunburn and can always be rolled up (or down) according to temperature.

Hats: Baseball caps help protect your nose but little else. Wide-brimmed hats protect your ears (which can burn easily) and your neck against sun. They also keep the rain off your face.

Windbreakers: Buy lightweight nylon that can be easily stuffed in a pack. You will need it for protection against rain and chilly winds.

Umbrellas: The small, collapsible kind that will fit in a day sack is best. When walking through open, exposed areas in direct sunlight for mile after mile, nothing keeps you cooler, offers better protection, or works better at keeping the rain off your face or out of your contact lenses than an umbrella (just don't get heat-absorbing black).

Plastic Garbage Bags: For wrapping clothes and cameras on rainy days and transporting your damp and filthy hiking shoes home in your suitcase. Makes a great instant poncho, too.

Sunglasses: Vital for the bright sunlight. The best are polarized and provide complete protection against UV rays, which have the potential to cause permanent eye damage.

Clothing Care: Plan on washing clothes in a sink at the end of every afternoon and letting them dry the next day. This way, you can get by with only three changes of hiking wear, regardless of how long you stay. Shampoo works almost as well as liquid soap for clothes.

Cameras: Carry one, though it will require some extra effort. On some of the more strenuous ascents you need both hands free to scramble up a hill or hug the side of a mountain trail. Be able to put the camera well out the way, in your knapsack or a special padded hip holster designed for just this purpose. If you're crossing difficult terrain and the camera is dangling around your neck, it could divert you, throw you off balance, or crash against something. Be prepared to waterproof it instantly in case of rain. You will also need a flash because of the low light in the rain and cloud forests, unless you are using incredibly fast film. Also, you will want to use a flash to bring out the color and details on many of the colorful plants.

Basic Hiking Checklist:
- Day pack
- Hip camera holster or waterproof plastic bags to protect camera
- Spare batteries for camera and flash
- Wide-brimmed hat
- Loose cotton clothing
- Nonskid hiking boots
- Fanny pack with two water bottles
- Windbreaker
- Sweater
- Small collapsible umbrella
- Flashlight with spare batteries
- Snacks
- Gray duct tape (always good for something on every trip)

ABOUT HIKING GUIDES

With this book you will be able to make most of the walks and hikes on your own, but I'd suggest using a local guide whenever you visit an island. Tropical forests are so diverse and every island so different local knowledge is mandatory to appreciate fully everything you're seeing. As complete as this guide has tried to be, it can't begin to provide the history, folklore, and botanical knowledge that a personal guide can.

Besides, a personal guide will know precisely where to take you to see rare St. Lucia parrots or something else you would never find on your own. Guide companies are listed in the general information section for each island. Prices for guides are for the most part very reasonable, from $30 to $75 per person per day depending on food and transport provided.

CAMPING

Camping in the Caribbean can be a problem. It is forbidden by law on many islands. Those laws are enforced, often at Customs: Your camping gear could be confiscated and held until your departure. Part of the reason for this restriction is to ensure that only a certain type of visitor (one with money) is permitted on the island. With a greater emphasis on promoting ecotourism and hikes into the bush, this attitude will probably change. Check with the individual tourist boards or guide services listed in each chapter for the latest changes.

THE WEATHER

Many people imagine walking/hiking in the Caribbean as a stroll through a hothouse or steam room, with every stitch of clothing sticking to them. How enjoyable can that be?

THE HEAT

Actually, the Caribbean has a tremendous range of temperatures. At sea level and in the lowland jungle, the middle of the day is just as blistering and miserable as you can imagine. You do have to be a mad dog or an Englishman to go out in the noonday sun without a hat and plenty of water.

Fortunately, the Caribbean's best hiking is in the mountains or cool rain forests. Much Caribbean hiking is above the 1,000-foot mark, more often at the 2,000- to 3,000-foot level, sometimes going as high as 10,000 feet. The temperatures are much lower at those levels, regardless of what the thermometer reads at the seashore. Factor in the constant tradewinds that often reach 20 mph and you may have more trouble staying warm than keeping cool if you go underdressed.

For instance, in Puerto Rico's Caribbean National Forest (El Yunque) they have worked out the following temperature chart (in fahrenheit):

Sea level: 80°

500–1,800 feet: 75°

1,800–2,400 feet: 70°

2,400–3,000 feet: 65°

3,000–3,500 feet: 60°

And so on. It drops about 5 degrees for each 500 to 600 feet, according to these statistics.

However, in Jamaica's Blue Mountains, they estimate a three degree drop for every 1,000 feet of altitude, quite a different reckoning. Whose figures are correct? Both temperature estimates may indeed be right. Then again, because hiking in the Caribbean is still in the formative stage, this may be one of many instances of contradictory and conflicting information.

Who is precisely correct is not important. The essential point is this: It can get downright chilly in the Caribbean. A windbreaker is a good idea anywhere above 2,000 feet, particularly in winter months. It also can get cold at even relatively low altitudes if it rains, which it often does, especially between June and October. Climb Pico Duarte in January and you may wake up with frost on the ground.

THE RAINY SEASON

It varies from island to island, but generally the rainy season begins in May and lasts until December. If you're not interested in photography, cloudy weather provides what is actually the most comfortable hiking. Don't avoid the Caribbean just because it's the rainy season. Elderly islanders have stopped trying to predict accurately what the weather will be at a particular time of year. They say the patterns are changing too much. So it may rain during the sunny season and be sunny during the rainy season. You have no guarantees.

The descent into Dominica's Valley of Desolation is the Caribbean's number one hike

Hurricanes

The season begins in June and ends in November with the greatest activity typically in August, September, and October. September is often the most active month, a time some islands almost shut down because tourism is so dead. If you and a hurricane are headed toward the same island destination, change your path: cancel or postpone. Heavy downpours always accompany these storms, which may create landslides. Severe hurricanes can disrupt island life for six months or longer because of the amount of destruction. Hiking trails are one of the last items governments worry about clearing.

Sahara Sands

This is a phenomenon that occurs annually from about mid-May to mid-summer. Sands blown from the Sahara Desert in Africa create hazy conditions in the Caribbean, so you lose those incredible long-distance vistas from the mountaintops. If you have dust allergies, you might want to learn more about the Sahara sands and whether they might impact you.

Prices

The cost of a Caribbean trip is strongly influenced by the weather. Hotel prices double or triple every December 15 and come down on April 15, when it's sunny at home. Visitors are willing to pay premium prices to flee the cold back home when the Caribbean is warm. If, however, you want to spend your funds on activities rather than hotels, consider the end of April through May, a period that typically offers prime hiking conditions with clear skies and sun. The weather may be as good as in February or March but prices are far lower.

2   HISTORICAL OVERVIEW

Old Caribbean saying: Time is longer than rope.
Translation: Time heals all wounds.

The islands of the Caribbean may be scattered, but their stories are basically the same, with only slight variations. Here, the historical perspective of the entire region is presented in condensed form rather than being detailed for every island.

THE FIRST INHABITANTS

The first settlers were an unknown race of Stone Age people who lived in the Caribbean about 4,000 years ago. Apparently without permanent settlements, they were hunter-gatherers. The only evidence of their existence were stone tools they left behind, which the next inhabitants, the Arawaks, found very useful. The Arawaks called this unknown race Ciboney, after the Arawak word *ciba* for stone. Modern archaeologists still have no idea where the Ciboney wandered in from or off to, but they were gone from the Caribbean almost 1,000 years before the Arawaks arrived.

Paddling their big dugout canoes over from South America, the Arawaks spread out into the Caribbean from the Orinoco region of Venezuela around 500 B.C. Thus, the Arawaks discovered the Caribbean more than 1,000 years before Columbus arrived.

The significant impact of the Arawaks on the modern world is not generally appreciated. They are credited with introducing Europeans not only to the hammock and its wonderfully restful properties but also to tobacco and syphilis.

For at least a millennium the Arawaks, a peaceful people, lived a Caribbean idyll similar to the South Sea Islanders of the Pacific. They wore almost no clothing, hunted and fished as they needed, and grew crops such as yams, and, most important, cassava, which was ground to make bread. The Arawak concept of beauty was interesting. The ultimate turn-on was a pointed head, so babies had their heads pressed between slats of wood to "enhance" their beauty. Not surprisingly, the Arawaks lived in conical-shaped shelters, made of thatch rather than pressed wood.

They liked to dance, play games similar to volleyball and badminton, and party under the influence of maize alcohol and a powdery drug ingested up their noses. Reportedly, the early Spanish explorers were frightened when they first saw Arawaks puffing on firebrands of tobacco, one of the earliest versions of cigarettes. Possessions apparently meant little to the

Islands were stripped of vegetation to make room for the planting of sugarcane, which changed the topography of the Caribbean

---

individual Arawak unless someone tried to steal them. Theft was considered a major crime, and thieves were slowly skewered to death with a pole.

When the early Spanish explorers showed up in 1492, the Arawaks were more than happy to share what they owned. Columbus himself noted the Arawaks were generous, gentle, and honest. The Arawaks should have skewered *him*.

Within 50 years, the Arawaks as a race were destroyed, forced by the Spanish into slave labor to work their gold mines. Though peaceful, the freedom-loving Arawaks were not the most cooperative of slaves. The Indians had a strong belief in an afterlife, in a place they called "Coyaba," where one feasted and danced all day long without the interference of hurricanes, sickness, or the Europeans. Rather than submit to a life of servitude, many Arawaks committed suicide with this afterlife in mind.

The Carib Indians, immortalized today through the names of the Caribbean region and island-brewed Carib beer, did not succumb so easily. Already established on many islands, the Caribs had come from the Orinoco region in Venezuela about 200 years before Columbus arrived. They were actually in the process of expanding throughout the Caribbean, conquering and absorbing the Arawaks, when the Europeans landed. The Caribs expanded as far north as Puerto Rico. They also refused to live as slaves, preferring to kill themselves by jumping off cliffs or by eating dirt until they died.

If the Europeans and Caribs had been evenly matched in weaponry and manpower, the history of the Caribbean probably would be quite different. The Caribs were known for the speed with which they could fire arrow after arrow at a target. It's said they could split a coin at 100 yards. It's no wonder the huge fort on the island of St. Vincent is famous for the direction that its cannons point—they're aimed inland. The British soldiers hiding inside were far more afraid of being attacked from land by the Caribs than by passing European warships. Unfortunately for the Caribs, the Europeans had guns, and so it wasn't long before most of the Caribs were overwhelmed.

The Caribs enjoyed dressing up, painting their skin red, and wearing parrot feathers and necklaces with the teeth of their victims in war; the Caribs were also cannibals. At least, that's what the Europeans claimed, even inventing the word *cannibal* based on a corruption of what the Spanish called the Caribs, "Caribales." In war, the Caribs rarely harmed women but took them as property. What they supposedly did to their male captives has become legendary: the male captives were flame-broiled on a spit for dinner after their legs and backs were split open and stuffed with herbs and pimento. The Caribs were not indiscriminate in their tastes. It's said they found the Spanish too stringy and revolting, preferring the French above all others for their tastiness (because of the French wine?). Next in preference were the English and Dutch. However, many believe that Europeans called the Caribs "man eaters" as part of a propaganda campaign to demonize the Caribs and help justify their extermination.

Christianity made little impact on the Caribs, who were never much concerned with any kind of organized religion anyway. They consented to be baptized for the gifts that went along with the ceremony.

Try as they might, the Europeans never succeeded in exterminating the Caribs. A Carib reservation, some 3,000 strong, still exists on the island of Dominica, where the British realized it made more sense to trade with the Caribs than fight them. Small numbers of Caribs can also be found today in Guyana, Honduras, and on St. Vincent, but nowhere else in the region. The last person known to have spoken the true Carib language died in the early 1900s.

In addition to the Arawaks and Caribs, there was a third group of people who lived north of Guadeloupe. These are the people Columbus encountered in Haiti/Dominican Republic. They called their island Bohio ("home") and themselves Taino, "men of the good," to distinguish their race from the more warlike Caribs. By all accounts, including those of Columbus, the Taino were a hard-working, peaceful, and extraordinarily generous people.

Estimates of the number of Taino living on Bohio in 1492 range from half a million to 7 million. Whatever the real figure, within 50 years, their culture, which had originated in the Orinoco region of South America 2,000 years earlier, was annihilated by Spanish disease, slavery, and brutality.

Yet traces of the Taino still remain. The Taino had turned the dry southwest into a bountiful agricultural region by bringing water to the fields from the mountains, a method still employed today. Their square homes made of palm wood with thatch roofs, also called bohios, are still the predominant form of rural housing in the Dominican Republic. For an excellent overview of the Taino Indian culture, consult *The Tainos, Rise and Decline of the People Who Greeted Columbus* by Irving Rouse (1992, Yale University Press).

COLUMBUS AND THE SPANISH

Even after four voyages to the New World, Columbus always was convinced he had landed somewhere in Asia or India, which is why he named the islands the West Indies and its natives Indians. Those inaccuracies were never changed by succeeding generations while there was still time to set the record straight.

Columbus landed in the New World either in the Turks & Caicos chain (probably the correct theory) or on the island of San Salvador in the Bahamas, which has several markers honoring his landing. According to artifacts uncovered on the North American continent, Columbus was not the first to discover the New World, but for centuries no one was anxious to change all those encyclopedias. It's always hard to replace myth with fact, except in Portugal where students were taught that Portuguese sailors found the Western lands about a dozen years earlier and returned with tales that motivated Columbus.

Columbus, born in Genoa, Italy, sailed under the Spanish flag for the Spanish king and queen, Ferdinand and Isabella. Following the tradewinds on a westerly course across the Atlantic, he and his three ships made landfall October 12, 1492. He returned to Spain triumphant in 1493, convinced that he had discovered Japan. He returned (1493–94) to found the first settlement on the island of Hispaniola, this time bringing 17 ships and volunteers. His third voyage (1498–1500) ended in disgrace. After Columbus was made governor of Santo Domingo, the people there rebelled against his harsh authority, and he was returned to Spain in chains in 1500. He was allowed to make a fourth voyage (1502–04) if he promised to stay away from Santo Domingo, which he did. He explored the coast of Central America and then shipwrecked in Jamaica.

Columbus was not universally admired, especially after he was thrown out of Santo Domingo. When he shipwrecked in Jamaica and two of the survivors paddled to Santo Domingo, they couldn't hire anyone to come and rescue the former governor. The Santo Domingans preferred to let Columbus rot in Jamaica for a year before his rescue. Columbus returned to Spain and died in 1506 at the age of 50. His daughter-in-law had his remains buried in Santo Domingo in 1544. There is a dispute over whether his body was removed after the Haitian invasion of 1796 and taken to the nearest Spanish soil, Cuba. Presumably it was, because remains identified as Columbus's were sent to Seville a century later. The body of Columbus (or whoever) was returned to Santo Domingo for the 500th anniversary of the discovery of the New World. Somehow, all this confusion about Columbus's remains seems bizarrely appropriate because he never knew where he was while alive.

DIVIDING UP THE NEW WORLD

Columbus not only sailed under the Spanish flag, he acted as an ambassador of God, and the Catholic Church in particular, in his discoveries. Consequently, the pope carved up the New World as he saw fit: Anything 100 leagues west of the Azores was Spanish territory, and trespassers would be shot on sight. Because this division overlooked the tip of Brazil, the Portuguese were allowed to settle there. The rest of the Caribbean became contested territory, as other European countries became aware of the gold being plundered from the Indians.

The British were especially interested, sending in privateers under contract to the government to steal what they could. These included such well known historical figures as Sir Francis Drake and Sir Walter Raleigh (who later had a cigarette and a city named after him). The French, too, sent in freelancers, some more interested in pillaging Spanish settlements than in exploring for their own gold. These raiders were called pirates.

However, the true buccaneers of the Spanish Main originated on Hispaniola. These pirates stole beef, cured it, and sold it to passing ships. They became known as buccaneers because the oven they used for smoking meat was called a boucan. The buccaneers gradually grew in number and spread out through the islands, looking primarily for Spanish ships to attack. Then they returned to ports like St. Thomas and Port Royal in Jamaica to sell their spoils.

Despite the bloodthirsty tales told by survivors of pirate raids, the buccaneers were actually a pretty good outfit to work for. Calling themselves Brethren of the Coast, they sometimes took remarkably good care of each other, supplying compensation for a lost limb or eye and caring for the wounded out of captured booty. One of the most notorious pirates was Henry Morgan, who headquartered in Jamaica's pirate stronghold of Port Royal. Operating in the late 1600s, this notorious cutthroat invented the tactic of attacking towns inland as well as along the coast. After becoming quite wealthy, he double-crossed many of his buccaneers, then switched to an even more dubious profession, politics. He became the lieutenant governor of Jamaica and helped rid that region of pirates.

Although the Spanish claimed possession of most of the Caribbean, they did not seriously attempt to settle most of the islands except for Hispaniola, Puerto Rico, and Cuba. They found far more profit in extracting gold from the Indians on the mainland of South America. Also, the Spanish preferred not to deal with the warring Caribs. Through default, the Spanish left many islands to the British, French, and Dutch, allowing them to fight out any claims among themselves. The British and French fought continually over their respective territories, sometimes swapping them back and forth as many as a dozen times. On some islands even today, the locals speak a blend of both English and French, a patois carryover from the continuous political turmoil.

SUGAR AND SLAVERY

Originally brought from the Canary Islands, sugar was first grown in this hemisphere in Brazil, then Barbados. Sugar plantations forever changed the environment and complexion of the Caribbean. Sugarcane and the enormous wealth it generated are what made the islands colonies worth fighting for.

For maximum profit, the islands were stripped of all native vegetation—except in the highlands, where the cane wouldn't grow well—and sugarcane planted in its place. The islands were deforested so dramatically, it's said that Dominica—rugged, mountainous, and inhospitable to farming—is the only island Columbus would still recognize.

To prosper, the plantations needed cheap labor and lots of it. It's recorded that even the smallest sugar plantation needed as many as 250 slaves. The slaves, mostly taken as prisoners of war or in night raids by other Africans, endured a cruel, 6- to 12-week ocean voyage to the West Indies that left an average of 12 percent of the "cargo" dead. Slaves were chained and forced to stand in the holds like telephone poles, without enough space to sit. Some died of disease; others preferred to jump overboard and drown in their chains. On arrival, the slaves were fattened, oiled, and taken to the auction block. The Spanish, relying on the Indians for slaves, imported relatively few Africans.

Before long, the slaves dominated the Caribbean, far outnumbering the white planters. To maintain control, planter discipline over the slaves was strict and violent. Any uprisings were quickly put down.

Ironically, it was an imported European concept—the right of the free individual as enunciated in the French Revolution of 1789—that led to the abolition of slavery and the downfall of the plantation system. As word of this radical idea from France spread, slave uprisings became more frequent. In 1804, a full-scale rebellion in Haiti led that country to declare its independence. In 1834, the British outlawed slavery in all of its colonies. In 1844, the Dominican Republic (which shares the island of Hispaniola with Haiti) declared its independence. Slavery ended in the French colonies in 1848 and the Danish West Indies in 1863.

Unfortunately, freedom did not automatically bring economic independence, or even a hint of the former prosperity of the sugarcane days. The former African slaves, now newly independent West Indians, found the era of colonialism in the late 1800s perhaps even more poverty-ridden. With nothing coming out of the islands, Britain certainly did not want to invest anything back into them. Most of the West Indies went into a severe economic decline.

The former slaves may have inherited the Caribbean, but there was little for them to enjoy but sunshine and warm weather. Land was parceled out and some survived by subsistence farming. Others continued to work at low wages on the few struggling sugarcane plantations. World War I brought an increase in the price of sugar and encouraged the islands to diversify into other crops, such as bananas, spices, cocoa, and coffee. Tourism became popular after World War II.

By the end of the twentieth century, most of the British West Indies chose independence, though the Cayman Islands decided to remain British. Guadeloupe, Martinique, and St. Martin, which pretend to be an extension of Europe, continued as French outposts in the Caribbean.

Since the end of the great plantation days, the tropical vegetation of the Caribbean slowly has been reclaiming the land. The original growth is gone in most places, replaced by what's called secondary growth, a mix of native trees and exotic (imported) plants, such as bamboo—altered, perhaps, but not necessarily any worse. The argument could be made that the forests have never been more beautiful or colorful. Indeed, it is almost impossible to distinguish between what is "imported" and what is "native" anymore.

Today is the best time since the 1600s to see the Caribbean at its most lush and green, to revel in the mountains and woodlands. The locals call it the bush, the same term used in Africa to designate the wilderness. For walkers and hikers, the Caribbean is better now than it has been for centuries. On many islands, these are the "good old days."

CARIBBEAN FLORA AND FAUNA: HOW IT EVOLVED

The Caribbean, which extends over a million square miles of seabed, has changed dramatically over the last few thousand years. Some present-day islands were peninsulas or plateaus during the last Ice Age, when the water was as much as 200 to 400 feet lower in the Caribbean. Cuba, for instance, may have been connected to Florida.

In addition, the Puerto Rican plateau consisting of Puerto Rico, the U.S. and British Virgin Islands, and other landfalls, may have been one large island. Jamaica may have been joined to Nicaragua. Trinidad, an exposed mountain peak of a sunken Andes range, was linked to South America only 8,000 years ago. Because Trinidad was linked to the mainland by a land bridge, it has more variety of plant and animal species than any other island in the Caribbean.

Except for Trinidad, all of the West Indies are classified as oceanic islands, formed from fiery volcanic upheavals and other cataclysmic events. They were born bare and accumulated their plant and animal populations in several ways. Some plants, such as mangroves, have seeds that float on the ocean currents for months, make landfall, and sprout. Other species spread by "rafting," where a seed or animal hitches a ride on a floating platform, a tangled pile of tree branches, or something as small as a leaf, and travels to an island.

Many plants and animals were rafted to the Caribbean during the seasonal flooding of the Orinoco River. The mats of vegetation included rafts of bamboo, whose hollow spaces provided secure places for frogs and small lizards. Tree roots offered good cover for snakes and burrowing reptiles. Hurricanes also made rafting a relatively easy and regular phenomenon, uprooting whole trees (if not entire sections of forests) to send scores of hitchhikers (snakes, lizards, frogs) floating out to sea. Storms, along with prevailing air currents, have also helped distribute birds and insects, which have been known to stay aloft for days, sometimes weeks, and still survive. This is how the common cattle egret, now distributed on so many islands, is believed to have come over from Africa—on the winds of a hurricane.

According to the rafting theory, mammals and amphibians (which require considerable fresh water to survive) should be scarce in the Caribbean because they could not raft successfully over long distances without water. Indeed, their presence is meager. The most common mammals are rodents and bats, and only about three dozen species of frogs and toads are found in the region. Consequently, most of the animal life you see when walking even the thickest and healthiest Caribbean rain forest will consist of birds, lizards, and insects. The real variety is the plant life.

TYPES OF TROPICAL FOREST

Because plants offer the primary scenery, it's essential to have a basic understanding of the different forest zones found in the Caribbean. These are determined primarily by altitude and rainfall.

All of the islands fall in the tropical zone, but West Indian vegetation technically is classified as neotropical, meaning it grows in the New World tropical zone. (Pantropical refers to species found in tropical zones throughout the world; paleotropical to species confined exclusively to the Old World.)

On most islands the growing conditions seem ideal. Temperatures in the Caribbean vary little, regardless of season. Surprisingly, it's often hotter in New York in summer than the Caribbean, where it rarely gets above 90 ° F. Like the temperature, days and nights are fairly constant, lacking the dramatic shift between short winter and long summer days. In the Caribbean, every day lasts about 12 hours.

Rainfall, however, can vary dramatically from season to season. It's not the amount of rain an area receives, but whether it falls consistently and in enough quantity over all 12 months that determines whether the vegetation is that of a true rain forest or that of a humid green forest or a dry forest.

The Humid Green and Dry Forests

Depending on mountain height and wind direction, it's possible to have both humid and arid regions on the same island. An area is designated humid when the rainfall exceeds the rate of evaporation.

On islands with alternate wet and dry seasons, such as the Virgin Islands, the trees shed their leaves in the dry season and resemble a bare winter scene. But when the water comes back on, everything is green again. This alternating pattern of grimness and greenness, which makes up a great deal of the Caribbean, is referred to as dry and green humid forests.

In the driest regions, where little rain falls at any time during the year, dry scrub vegetation is the major characteristic. The arid islands of Aruba, Bonaire, and Curaçao fit this category perfectly. Rainfall is so scarce that most of the water for human consumption is supplied from sea water through desalinization plants. The cactus in these dry regions come in many different varieties and shapes may be small or 20 to 30 feet high. Agaves, spiny opuntias, and thorny shrubs are also characteristic of this kind of rugged, tough terrain.

The Coastal Mangrove Jungle

Many coastal hiking trails skirt thick mangrove forests and their impenetrable interlocking root system. Found on the sheltered side of an island, the three different types of mangroves (red, white, and black) provide an important nursery for many species of crab, shrimp, and fish. They also seem to house great quantities of mosquitoes, most active early and late in the day. Mangrove leaves are thick and evergreen, and the trees vary tremendously in height from only several feet tall to 20 feet or more.

The Rain Forest

The windward sides of the islands, which receive the direct brunt of the tradewinds, tend to be the wettest. On these coasts, from the lowlands until about 3,300 feet, you find the famed evergreen tropical rain forest. This contains some of the world's lushest and most diverse vegetation, with perhaps several hundred different species fighting for the same space.

In this tropical rain forest the tree canopy can extend as high as 130 to 150 feet. Many species tend to be slender and well buttressed due to their shallow roots. The roots are shallow because most nutrients are in the upper soil levels. The rich tree crowns of the rain forest canopy absorb most of the light, leaving the ground in almost perpetual shade; only three percent of the daylight actually reaches the rain forest floor. The jungle, therefore, is in the thick canopy above, not on the ground. That makes rain forests good, tangle-free places for walking, although the slick, muddy soil found there provides its own frequent challenges.

Rain forests are where you sometimes find Tarzan-sized vines hanging from trees and colorful, flowershop-quality bromeliads and orchids. Ferns can be incredibly dense and rich: 500 species of fern grow on Jamaica alone. Moss and lichen flourish profusely, making rock-hopping a tricky maneuver.

The Caribbean Rain Forest (El Yunque) of Puerto Rico is a classic example of evergreen tropical rain forest. Between 3,300–6,500 feet the vegetation changes due to wind and increased rainfall to what's classified as mountain rain forest. The rule of thumb: The higher you go, the wetter it gets.

The Cloud Forest/Elfin Woodland

From 6,500 to over 10,000 feet, the vegetation becomes the most fantastic of all, in the cloud forest or elfin woodland. The trees grow thicker and farther apart than at lower levels. Due to the harsh conditions of cold and wind, they also grow much more slowly than in the lower rain forest (figure a 3 degree drop for every 1,000 feet). At this altitude, epiphytes still appear in great numbers, but many of the lowland creeping plants disappear.

The cloud forest, the highest level of the Caribbean, is almost always covered in clouds, mist, and haze. Its nickname of elfin woodland shows that early European naturalists who explored the high altitudes of the Caribbean had a sense of imagination and wonder. To them, the combination of twisted and stunted vegetation, moss, dense foggy atmosphere, clouds, and the eternal eastern tradewinds must have seemed a sinister, mysterious place . . . just the kind that the elves of German literature were said to inhabit.

Where the canopy of the lower rain forests may reach well over 100 feet, elfin forest trees rarely stretch above 15 to 20 feet. Only about 40 species of trees and shrubs have adapted to the harsh weather and high humidity at the Caribbean's highest points, a far lower diversity than the hundreds of species found in the lowland rain forest.

Puerto Rican botanist Vicente Quevedo reported that a combination of elements accounted for the stunted nature of the trees in the Caribbean National Forest, which would also generally apply elsewhere. These factors include decreased oxygen, poor clay soils that are saturated by heavy rainfall, the resulting poor transport of nutrients from the roots to the branches, and a low transpiration rate (casting off of waste products) due to the constantly high relative humidity. In addition, damage from high winds, the low amount of direct sunlight and its corresponding reduced rate of photosynthesis, lower temperatures, and other decreased biochemical processes also appear to play a part in dwarfing the trees.

Animals don't fare well in such extreme conditions. In the cloud/elfin forest, you normally find only birds and lizards.

TREES AND VINES OF THE CARIBBEAN (BUSH MEDICINE 101)

Because many trees in this climate grow constantly, their timber is not marked with clearly defined growth rings, resulting in a fine-grained wood prized for furniture making and construction. Mahogany is a classic example of a rain forest wood, so sought-after that plantations of it have been cultivated on West Indian islands; the tree, however, is not native to the region. Today, it's hard to find an island without mahogany of some sort growing on it.

Most of the other trees aren't as familiar as mahogany, but they all have their uses. Some have remarkable curative properties, what's come to be known as "bush medicine."

Common Trees and their Uses
- *African Tulip Tree (Spathodea campanulata):* Also called flame of the forest, this fiery red tree's unopened buds squirt water when pinched. A popular ornamental from Africa.
- *Almond Tree (Terminalia catappa):* Recognized by its spreading horizontal branches, this tree grows to 30 feet. It has large, leathery leaves that turn red before falling. Its popular fruit is edible.
- *Autograph Tree (Clusia rosea):* A West Indian evergreen whose large, thick leaves were used for playing cards and writing paper by early Spanish explorers. The wood is used in construction, and its leaves, bark, and fruit have medicinal qualities.
- *Banyan Tree (Ficus benghalensis):* Named for Hindu traders named Banyan, these huge evergreens have aerial roots that help support the branches.
- *Bay Rum (Amomis caryophyllata):* The leaves are used for bay rum.
- *Black Mangrove (Avicennia nitida):* The heartwood contains lapachol (anti-tumor agent).
- *Black Sage (Cordia cylindrostachya):* The leaves are steeped to treat coughs and colds.
- *Bois Bande* (both *Parinari campestris* and *Roupala montana*): The bark has aphrodisiac qualities; known in Grenada as "man's best friend."
- *Calabash (Crescentia cujete):* The fruit is made into ornaments.

- *Candle Tree (Parmentiera cereifera):* From Panama, this tree has one- to three-inch fruits that have a waxy texture and look like handmade candles. They also have an apple-like aroma.
- *Cannonball Tree (Couroupita guianensis):* This is a strange-looking ornamental, kind of like Medusa of Greek lore, with long dangling branches holding six- to eight-inch hard-shelled, cannonball-like fruit. The fruit pulp has an unpleasant odor. These fruit start as flowers that are pushed out of the tree bark.
- *Cassia (Cassia grandis):* There are several different types of this widely spread ornamental, but the coral shower or pink cassia tree is the first one to bloom in the spring.
- *Casuarina (Casuarina equisetifolia):* Also called the Australian pine, this coastal tree has long green needles year-round and grows to 100 feet. It's a popular windbreak, but a line of them on a beach will also prevent turtles from reaching their nesting sites.
- *Cherry Guava (Eugenia floribunda):* The fruit is made into preserves.
- *Coffee Tree (Coffea arabica):* A small evergreen 12–15 inches tall, its berries ripen in the fall, about 1,000 to a pound. It was introduced into the Caribbean in the early 1800s.
- *Cordia (Cordia sebestena):* Also the geranium and geiger tree, this salt-resistant evergreen thrives where there is little water. A popular ornamental on the drier islands.
- *Crappo (Carapa guianensis):* The seeds are a medicinal oil.
- *Divi-Divi Tree (Caesalpinia coriaria):* This wind-blown tree is almost a national symbol on Aruba, Bonaire, and Curaçao. An evergreen capable of growing to 30 feet, it normally grows with a wind-swept look. Its pods, containing tannin, were once exported.
- *Flamboyant (Delonix regia):* Also called the flame tree, royal poinciana, and flame of the forest. The national flower of Puerto Rico, the red blossoms begin in spring and last through summer. Its long, brown pods have been used for necklaces.
- *Fustic (Chlorophora tinctoria):* The wood is used for khaki dye.
- *Ginger Thomas (Tecoma stans):* Also called yellow elder, yellow trumpet, and yellow cedar. The official flower of the U.S. Virgin Islands, this evergreen can flower twice a year.
- *Hog Plum (Spondees monsoon):* The fruit is made into jellies and preserves, and the leaves can be made into a tea to stop diarrhea.
- *Incense (Portion guianense):* The bark exudate is burned for its smell.
- *Jumbie Bead (Erythrina spp.):* The dried seeds are made into necklaces.
- *Lignum Vitae (Guaiacum officinale):* Meaning "wood of life," this is the heaviest of all woods and sinks in water. A popular source of resin, it has blue flowers in the spring. A slow-growing tree, it can grow up to 30 feet.
- *Mahoe (Sterculia caribaea):* The bark is used as a rope substitute.
- *Mahogany (Swietenia mahogani):* Also called Dominican mahogany, this evergreen grows to 75 feet. It is a favorite lumber for furniture, ships, and cabinets.
- *Monkey Ear (Enterolobium cyclocarpum):* Also called elephant's ear, it is known for its three-inch, ear-shaped, brown seedpods. The seedpods are used for necklaces or food. The wood is used for building, the bark for soap, medicine, and tannin.
- *Quassia or Bitter Ash (Quassia amara):* The wood is made into medicine, the leaves are an insecticide.
- *Red Mangrove (Rhizophora spp.):* The bark is used for tanning material.
- *Rokoo Jab (Ryania speciosa):* The stem and branch have insecticidal properties.

- *Sandbox (Hura crepitans):* This large tree has a poisonous, milky sap that may cause blindness. The seed capsules, looking like three-inch pumpkins, explode when ripe. They were once used to hold sand for blotting ink, hence its name.
- *Seagrape (Coccoloba uvifera):* The fruit is edible and also used as an astringent.
- *Silk Cotton (Ceiba pentandra):* Also called the kapok tree, its seed floss is used for stuffing pillows; it is also used in baths to relieve fatigue and to counteract poisoning.
- *Tamarind (Tamarindus indica):* The brown, sour fruit pulp is used for candy, preserves, and drinks.
- *Tan-Tan (Leucaena glauca):* Also called wild tamarind, this is a common roadside tree whose leaves and long, brown pods are used to feed goats and cattle. However, horses and donkeys will lose their hair temporarily if they eat them.
- *Tirite (Ischnosiphon arouma):* The leaves and stem are used for handicrafts.
- *Tree Fern (Cyathea spp.):* Used today mostly as an ornamental, the Caribs used the trees to preserve and carry fire.
- *White Cedar (Tabebuia heteropyhlla):* For making posts and poles but also in shipbuilding.
- *Yellow Poui (Cybistax donnell-smithii):* Also called the sunshine or gold tree. Known for its strong, durable wood and beautiful flowers. The rains often come after the tree flowers.

Palm and Palm-like Trees
- *Anare (Geonoma vaga):* The stem is made into walking sticks.
- *Cabbage Palm (Roystonea oleracea):* The terminal bud is edible.
- *Camwell (Desmoncus major):* The stem is used for basket making.
- *Carat (Sabal mauritiiformis):* The leaves are used for thatch.
- *Coconut Palm (Cocos nucifera):* Growing to 80 feet or more, the fruits are large and round and covered with smooth thick husks. These palms formed the great copra plantations. The leaves are good for thatch.
- *Cocorite (Maximiliana caribaea):* The leaves are used for thatch, the kernels for edible palm oil.
- *Cycad (Cyas spp.):* Often mistaken for a palm because of its appearance, this tree has changed little in over 200 million years. Its crown of large fernlike leaves makes it a popular ornamental.
- *Gri-Gri (Bactris cuesa):* The fruit is edible.
- *Gru-Gru (Acrocomia aculsata):* The fruit, kernel, and leaf bud are all edible; the trunk is made into walking sticks.
- *Mamoo (Calamus rotang):* The leaves are made into handicrafts.
- *Manac (Euterpe oleracea):* The leaf bud is edible.
- *Roseau (Bactris major):* The stem is used for thatching.
- *Royal Palm (Roystonea regia):* Originating in Cuba but now widely distributed, these tall stately palms (60 to 100 feet) have leaves that grow to 15 feet in length.
- *Screw Palm (Pandanus utilis):* Also called a screw pine, it is not a palm or a tree but a shrub. It branches out at ground level, and the stems look like stilt roots. The leaves, about five feet in length, can be used for brushes, thatch, or basket weaving.
- *Timite (Manicaria saccifera):* The leaves are used for thatching.

- *Traveler's Palm (Ravenala madagascariensis):* More closely related to the banana than to palm trees, the tree is a popular ornamental because its leaves grow vertically to look like a single huge fan.

Vines, Shrubs, and Herbs

- *Bamboo (Bambusa vulgaris/Gramaineae):* Made into vases, baskets, waiters, tables, blinds, and trinket boxes.
- *Bow-String Hemp (Sansevieria thyrsiflora/Liliaceae):* The fiber is woven or plaited for ropes, hats, bags, and slippers.
- *Cachibou (Calathea discolor/Marantaceae):* Made into waterproof baskets.
- *Khus Khus (Vetiveria zizanoides/Gramineae):* Used to make floor and table mats, hats, bags, coasters, and blinds.
- *Sisal (Agave sisalana/Amaryllidaceae):* Fiber for ropes, twine, bags, mats, and hats.
- *Supple Jack (Paullinia pinnata/Sapindaceae):* Used for fish poison, baskets, chairs, and walking sticks.

COMMON FRUITS AND VEGETABLES (BUSH MEDICINE 102)

These are common sights on many Caribbean walks. However, some of the items can make you sick or possibly kill you if they're eaten at the wrong time of year or not prepared properly. No matter how appetizing something might look, always ask before you bite.

- *Ackee:* One of the national dishes of Jamaica (served with salt fish). Imported apparently from the South Seas, perhaps by Captain Bligh himself, who introduced other important foodstuffs. The tree produces leaves and greenish-white flowers, but the fruit is the real prize—but to be eaten only when it is red ripe and the fruit is split open. Ackee that is unripe (or overripe) can be poisonous, even lethal. Perhaps it's for this reason that ackee isn't eaten much outside of Jamaica.
- *Arrowroot:* Once utilized to help heal wounds from Carib arrows, hence its name. A very starchy plant, arrowroot has been used as a poison antidote, for starching clothes, in face powders, and in glues. It is also quite edible—one of the more digestible foods around—generally used to thicken soups and sauces.
- *Avocado:* Also grown in warmer regions of the United States, this native of Central America is used in salads, as an entrée, or even in a mousse. It is supposed to have blood sugar–regulating properties helpful to hypoglycemics. On some islands the leaves are used in a tea to treat high blood pressure. Either round and pear-shaped, an avocado has green skin that is thick and warty.
- *Banana:* Related to the fig, bananas originated in India and Malaysia. A large, herbaceous plant, banana trees can grow over 20 feet high. The dark purple flower that hangs from the stem is a remarkable sight. You'll often see bananas covered in plastic bags to prevent insects from discoloring the skins. The insects do not harm the fruit, but export crops have to be blemish-free. Bananas with brown spots are often left to rot.
- *Breadfruit:* Brought from the South Pacific into the Caribbean around 1793 by the infamous Captain Bligh, it was intended as food for slaves, who didn't like it. Now a Caribbean staple, breadfruit is loaded with carbohydrates and vitamins A, B, and C. The large, green,

spherical fruit has a kind of pimply skin. It can be made into pie, bread, or puddings or served boiled like potatoes as a side dish.

- *Cashews:* The fruit looks like a small, red, oblong apple. It's used for stewing, fermented into wine, or consumed as a vegetable. The more famous (and expensive) nut grows at the end of the apple. However, it is the kernel inside the nut you want: The shell oozes a liquid that can cause skin irritation and even death.

- *Cassava:* The root has been an important staple since the days of the Amerindians. However, it is also another of those items that must be cooked properly to remove prussic acid or it, too, can be lethal. Carib Indians supposedly ate cassava raw to avoid slavery. Its most important use is in the making of cassareep to create pepperpot, a kind of stew whose stock can be used for years.

- *Christophene:* A gourd imported from Mexico, it's eaten raw or cooked, typically to accompany a main dish. It is very watery.

- *Cocoa:* Responsible for the dread addiction among those known as chocoholics. Originally grown by Indians in South and Central America, the ten-inch pods turn from green to reddish brown when ripe. The pods have to be broken open and the cocoa beans extracted and dried. When not sprinkled with sugar, the beans taste surprisingly bitter.

- *Coconut Palm:* Used to supply drinking water (chop off the top of a green coconut nut with a machete and enjoy the milk, actually a sweet water). Dried coconut is, of course, used in cooking and in making soap. Coconut oil is sometimes called tropical oil or palm oil on food packages.

- *Custard or Sugar Apple:* This deliciously sweet fruit is a lumpy reddish brown, almost the shape of a blunt-ended pine cone.

- *Dasheen:* The underground roots are loaded with starch, like potatoes. They must be cooked/boiled to remove a bitter taste. The young green leaves of this plant are made into an excellent soup called callaloo. Do try this. Prepared properly, it can be exceptional.

- *Ginger:* From Southeast Asia, the root is ground and used in flavoring, particularly cakes, syrup, and drinks. A teaspoon of ginger (mix it with some liquid) helps prevent/reduce motion sickness, and it won't make you sleepy like some commercial seasick remedies.

- *Grapefruit:* A popular juice or eaten in half at breakfast, today's grapefruit appears to be a hybrid between the orange and something called a shaddock, a fruit brought into the Caribbean from the South Pacific by a sailing captain named Shaddock. No one liked the shaddocks because they were too bitter; however, they grew so well they spread throughout the islands. Somehow, probably through creating a hybrid, the fruit became a lot sweeter. Grapefruits with lumpy skins tend to be quite sour and may be part of the original shaddock strain.

- *Guava:* Apparently brought to the Caribbean by the Arawaks, the tree grows to more than 20 feet. The pear-shaped fruit is only about two inches long. It is eaten raw or used to make jellies; a tea from the tree bark is said to help with bouts of diarrhea.

- *Jackfruit:* Related to the breadfruit and somewhat resembling it, the jackfruit grows close to the tree on short stalks. A member of the fig family, jackfruit also grows big—as much as 40 pounds. Its many seeds can be eaten raw or roasted like chestnuts.

- *Mammee Apple:* The rough, oval, brown fruit grows on an evergreen that's believed to be native to the region. The small fruits are eaten raw (peeled first), stewed, or made into jams and preserves.

- *Mango:* One of the most common and favorite fruits throughout the Caribbean. The kidney-shaped fruit (pink or yellow when ripe) grows on tall trees that reach roof-top high. Usually eaten raw, it's also made into pie, ice cream, and mousse.
- *Naseberry* or *Sapodilla:* This oval fruit with a reddish-brown skin has a sweet-tasting pulp used for custards and ice cream. The tree sap produces chicle gum, used in making chewing gum.
- *Nutmeg:* The principal export of Grenada, the tree grows to a massive 40 feet. The flowers produce a fruit looking much like a peach with a nut inside. The skin of the nut provides the spice mace; the nut itself is the nutmeg. Nutmeg is either ground into powder or crushed into oil. It is sometimes used in small amounts as a medicine, said to help prevent strokes. However, taken in large quantities, too much nutmeg is said to be poisonous.
- *Okra/Lady's Finger/Bamee:* The six-inch pods, shaped like a woman's finger, are used as a vegetable and to prepare coo-coo, a sweet corn dish. Medicinally, it's good for the eyes and inflammations of the reproductive system. Often served in the United States in a can and referred to as "slimy okra."
- *Passion Fruit:* This sounds like an aphrodisiac, but the name seems to come from the fruit's purple color. Cut in half, the mushy, seed-filled pulp looks disgusting but tastes quite good. The pulp is used in making ice cream and passionfruit drinks. The skin is used in salads.
- *Papaya/pawpaw:* A melon that grows on a tree, well off the ground and close to the trunk. Often eaten with a bit of fresh lime squeezed over it, Columbus called this delicious fruit the "fruit of angels." Papaya is a prime ingredient in Adolph's meat tenderizer; wrapping meat in papaya leaves will achieve the same effect. Pawpaw is supposed to help relieve hypertension; the latex of the leaves, stem, and roots is used for treating boils, ringworm, and warts.
- *Pigeon Peas:* Brought from either Africa or India, pigeon peas mixed with rice (with or without curry) is a favorite in many parts of the Caribbean. The peas grow on a shrub that reaches up to nine feet high. The pods vary from light green to dark brown.
- *Pineapple:* Named for its resemblance to the pine cone, it is native to the Caribbean. Some pineapple species, particularly at altitude, produce only colorful flowers and no fruit.
- *Plantain:* A cousin to the sweeter, yellow banana, plantains don't ripen in the same manner and they taste starchier. When ripe, they are often cut in slices, fried, and sprinkled with sugar for a sweet dessert. It's sometimes used in casseroles.
- *Seagrape:* The plants are usually found most often near the coastline, seeming to enjoy a healthy dose of sea and salt. The green fruits do grow in grapelike clusters, eventually turning a ripe purple. Still very sour, seagrapes are most often mixed with sugar and made into jelly, sometimes even into a soup.
- *Soursop:* A fast-growing tree, the spiny green fruit is oval-shaped. The fruit is sizable, growing six to eight inches, and the inside has the thickness of a custard. It is most often made into ice cream or preserves. It's considered a sedative for children.
- *Star Apple:* The extremely tall trees (up to 50 feet) provide wonderful shade. The mildly sweet fruit is purplish and about the size of an apple. The name comes from the pattern revealed when the fruit is cut open: a starburst effect of seeds in gelatinous flesh.
- *Sugarcane:* At one time this member of the grass family was the most important crop of the Caribbean. The stems are crushed to produce the sugar. It can also be made into molasses

and rum. You may want to sample the raw cane and compare it to the refined sugar most of us use. The raw is far sweeter and tastier. Molasses (from sugarcane) is the main ingredient of rum, which differs remarkably from island to island.

- *Yams:* Growing on a vine sometimes up to six to eight feet high, the yam tuber is particularly starchy and may be served boiled, baked, or fried. A particular variety, called drug yams, are used in making oral contraceptives.

ORCHIDS

Orchids are sometimes referred to as the aristocrats of the plant kingdom. With more than 25,000 different species, the orchid may be the largest family of flowering plants. Perhaps as many as another 25,000 varieties have been developed by crossing wild with cultivated plants.

What makes orchids so popular are their intricately shaped flowers, the rainbow array of the colors, and their wonderful fragrances. In the Caribbean, most orchids are epiphytes, or tree dwellers. You may also see some clinging to rocks; these are called lithophytes. Orchids are not parasites but use a tree or rock for support while their roots absorb moisture from the air and nutrients from various sources, including bird droppings.

According to David Williams of the Forestry Division on the island of Dominica, all orchids are similar in structure, having three sepals and three petals. Another common feature is their fleshy, club-shaped column that is a fusion of the pistil and stamens, the reproductive organs. The most colorful part of the orchid is called a lip or labellum, usually large and elaborate in shape.

Some people tend to get quite carried away by orchids. Should you ever become entrapped by someone in the ecstasy of explanation, you can usually shorten their lecture by asking where the name "orchid" comes from. It derives from the Greek word *orchis,* meaning testicles. Evidently the first orchids ever categorized had two bulbs that resembled the testes of the human male.

INSECTS

If you wear repellent and socks—and watch where you sit and walk—insects are rarely a problem. Mosquitoes tend to be pesky only at lower altitudes around water.

Some tropical insects are familiar ones, others come with a new sting:

- *Tarantula:* Greatly feared because of its hairy looks and reputation, its bite usually is no worse than that of a bee sting. Tarantulas are often found near banana groves. Some forage at night, others during the day.
- *Orb Weavers:* Beautifully colored spiders that weave some of the larger webs, usually hanging between trees. This includes the famed black widow. The golden silk spider, which weaves webs as much as two to three feet across, is another example. The strength of their silk webs is so great that it's actually been used in the manufacture of fabrics.
- *Scorpions:* These feed on spiders and other insects, usually at night. Human contact usually occurs when the scorpion, sleeping in a boot or under some rotted wood, is disturbed.
- *Centipedes:* As distinguished from the harmless, wormlike millipede, the centipede legs are large with only one pair per segment. It is only the larger, foot-long centipede *(Scolopendra*

dromorpha) that give a truly mean bite. The jaws of all centipedes have poison to paralyze their prey.

- *Killer Bees:* Found only in Trinidad and Tobago, islands closest to the South American continent. Far from true killers, this species escaped from a laboratory in Brazil and is simply more aggressive and therefore more likely to sting than the domestic honey bee. Unless you are messing about with a bee's nest, you should have nothing to worry about.
- *Dragonflies:* Most common are the skimmers found near water. These are differentiated from damselflies according to how they hold their wings when at rest. Dragonflies hold their wings horizontal; damselflies do it vertically, to the rear.
- *Termites:* Most (but not all) Caribbean termites construct huge, spherical nests in trees or on stumps and do not live on the ground. Termites usually forage at night, so the chance of seeing them at work is slim.
- *Leaf-Cutting Parasol Ants:* You'll probably see lots of these. They're constant workers, cutting bits of small leaves and carrying them back to their nest like a parasol. The leaves are not eaten by the ants but chewed up as a food for a fungus that grows in the underground chambers, on which the ants feed.
- *Army Ants:* You can't mistake the mass of them streaming by. Just step out of the way and they won't bother you. One islander told me how army ants were kind enough to come and exterminate the bugs in his house almost annually. He says the ants suddenly show up and, starting from the roof down, kill or chase away every bug in his house. The fellow leaves his home for a couple of hours, lets the ants do their work, then returns to a clean, orderly house. The only problem: The cleaning schedule is erratic, and not always at the best of times, especially if he has company.
- *Spider Wasps:* If you see something running on the ground flicking its wings, don't bother it. It's probably a spider wasp out looking for another tarantula with which to adorn its nest. Spider wasps can grow quite large, with a wingspan of up to three inches.
- *Click Beetles:* Like fireflies, these bugs are bioluminescent, with two light-producing organs on the sides of their thorax. They are called click beetles because of the sound they make to turn themselves right side up when overturned. Click beetles have the remarkable ability to snap a fingerlike spine on their thorax, something other beetles cannot do. Once on its back, a click beetle will keep trying until it finally rights itself. The beetles are sometimes captured and used for decorations at parties.
- *Butterflies:* Beautiful ones, big ones, in pairs and flying alone, often surprise you on a rain forest path. Hundreds of different species of butterflies thrive throughout the Caribbean. Some are bright and colorful, others camouflaged. On a hike, they are always a joy to see. The butterflies you see will probably be darker and more vivid than what you are accustomed to at home.

3   Antigua & Barbuda

Antigua

Old Caribbean Saying: *Where horse is tied, is there he eats grass.*
Translation: *You must make the best of wherever you find yourself.*

Long a favorite cruise ship stop, Antigua is the largest of the British Leeward Islands, claiming 365 beaches, one for every day of the year. Antigua (pronounced An-TEE-ga) does have many beautiful beaches, but take its claim of a beach for every day of the year with more than a grain of sand. From a walker's point of view, Antigua has some of the Caribbean's most historical strolls as well as some of the flattest.

The contrast between old and new reveals that Antigua is a relatively poor island, as are much of the former English possessions whose prosperity once depended on sugarcane. Today, tourism, offshore banking, and agriculture—mainly cotton, vegetables, fruit, and cattle—provide most of its income. Antigua's poverty is most obvious in the countryside, where luxury tourist villas sit alongside small shacks.

Whether you arrive by plane or boat, you'll probably end up in St. John's. St. John's is primarily a shopping port, requiring only an hour or two to explore. Unfortunately, compared to so many of the other lively, pastel-colored port towns, you may not find the capital city of St. John's as visually appealing. It definitely needs a new coat of paint to cover many of the old, drab exteriors that make it appear almost slumlike. However, a few sections, such as Redcliffe Quay, have already been renovated to attract shoppers, so someone recognizes the potential to beautify St. John's.

Those with limited time budgets would do best to set right out to explore the countryside, as the more interesting sites lie outside the city. A taxi guide will be considerably less frustrating than renting your own car. Signs are almost nonexistent in the countryside, so venturing forth (even with a map) is an expedition into uncharted territory. You will eventually find everything you set out to look for—Antigua is only 108 square miles.

Regardless of mode of transportation, immediately make your way to English Harbour, home of Nelson's Dockyard, which is probably the Caribbean's finest historic re-creation. Nelson's Dockyard was a base for the British fleet protecting its sugar and spice colonies from the French, Spanish, and Dutch.

Another interesting site on Antigua is Shirley Heights, the principal fortification for British troops, stationed high over English Harbour. Besides housing a museum and old military

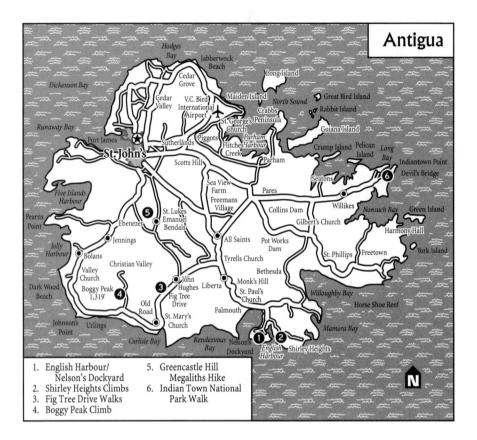

cemetery, on Sunday afternoons it hosts practically the entire population at a lively barbecue with excellent steel band music.

Antigua was settled as far back as 2400 B.C. by the little-known Ciboney (stone people). The rocky limestone island has no exotic, forested areas, and the highest elevation is only 1,330 feet. Antigua is considered an ideal island by those who like typical beachfront resort vacations, but from the hiker/walker's point of view, it is worth only a day or two at most. In a way this is regrettable, because the people are among the friendliest and most civil in the West Indies. Remember: They do expect to be spoken to first.

TRAVEL TIPS

Area: Antigua is 108 square miles; neighboring Barbuda is 62 square miles.

Language: English is the official language, but Creole is also spoken.

Population: 67,000, with about 30,000 residing around St. John's.

Time Zone: Atlantic Time, one hour ahead of Eastern Standard Time.

Rainy Season: The island receives only 45 inches of rainfall annually; this is a hot, dry place in summer. Showers are most frequent September through November.

Getting There: V. C. Bird International Airport is an important Caribbean hub. Every major airline serving the islands stops here. A few carriers even fly in directly from Europe. Antigua is such an important airport that it's possible to fly from here to 24 other island destinations and even South America. Carriers include American, Continental, BWIA, Air Canada, and British. LIAT connects from other islands. Flights to Barbuda all leave from Antigua's V. C. Bird airport.

Documents: A valid ongoing/return ticket is a must. American, Canadian, and British citizens need only supply proof of citizenship, such as a birth certificate with a raised seal and a photo ID. Everyone else needs a passport and perhaps even a visa.

Getting Around: Taxis are not metered; therefore all fares should be settled in advance. Make sure fares are being quoted in EC (Eastern Caribbean Currency) or U.S. dollars. Taxis are easily identified by the "H" on their license plates. A list of government-approved taxi rates is usually listed in tourist booklets available at the airport and hotels. Auto rentals are easily available if you pay US$12 for a local, temporary driving license. Look out for potholes and pay close attention while driving the narrow country roads. Many streets in St. John's are one-way, so observe signs and the traffic flow; avoid driving after dark because conditions can be dangerous. Fuel is expensive, more than US$2 per gallon. The island averages 11 miles across at most point, so if you stray from the main road you can't go too far. In Barbuda, taxis and rental cars are available at Codrington Airport; there is no public transportation.

Where to Stay: Antigua can be very expensive. The top resorts include the 300-acre offshore island of Jumby Bay, (800) 223-7636; the St. James' Club at Mamora Bay, (800) 345-0271; and Curtain Bluff, considered the island's premier resort, (888) 289-9898. At Nelson's Dockyard is the Copper and Lumber Store Hotel, (268) 460-1058; the Admiral's Inn at English Harbour, (800) 223-5695; and the Inn at English Harbour, (268) 460-1014; fax (268) 460-1603; www.theinn.ag). The Catamaran Hotel & Marina at Falmouth is a popular but inexpensive property, (800) 223-6510. Some hotels close in September and October.

Camping: Illegal and the law is strictly enforced. The island likes to project an upscale image, and campers don't fill the bill. Furthermore, officials have been known to refuse entry to travelers who don't look like they have sufficient funds to cover their stay.

Currency: The Eastern Caribbean dollar, worth about US$2.70. U.S. dollars are good anywhere. Most prices are quoted in EC. Banks are open 8 a.m. to 1 p.m. and from 3 p.m. to 5 p.m. Monday through Thursday; from 8 a.m. to noon and 3 p.m. to 5 p.m. on Friday.

Taxes & Tipping: An 8.5% government hotel tax and a 10% service charge. Taxi drivers expect 10–15% and porters EC$1 per bag. The departure tax is US$12.

Electrical Current: 220 volts in most places, though 110 is provided in some hotels. Transformers are usually available.

Safety/Health Warnings: Not dangerous but highly annoying are the tiny insects called no-see-ums, a nuisance on the beaches around sunrise and sunset. Carry repellent.

Snakes & Other Venomous Creatures: None.

Hiking & Walking Services: Hiking is still in its formative stages. However, a walk through tropical forest to the top of the hills at Antigua's southern end are offered twice daily by **Tropikelly Tours,** located in St. John's. The trail passes Wallings Dam, an important water source before desalinization was introduced. The end of the climb offers a good view of the island and, on a clear day, a look at Montserrat, Guadeloupe, and Nevis. The climb is short, between 40 and 50 minutes. Cost of the hike is $35 per person, including transfers to and from your hotel. The departure times for the hikes are 8 a.m. and 3 p.m. For information, call (268) 461-0383 or fax (268) 462-5464; www. tropikellytrails.com; email tropikelly@jalypso.com.

Additional Information: In the United States, Antigua and Barbuda Dept. of Tourism, 610 Fifth Avenue, Suite 311, New York, NY 10020; toll-free (888) 268-4227. In Canada, 60 St. Clair Avenue East, Suite 304, Toronto, Ontario M4T IN5; phone (416) 961-3085. In the United Kingdom, Antigua House, 15 Thayer Street, London W1M 5LD; phone (071) 486-7073/5, fax (071) 486-9970; www.interknowledge.com/antigua-barbuda.

St. John's Afoot!

Time: 1-2 hours. | **Difficulty:** 1. | **Trailhead:** Court house/museum.

Unless you stop to shop, you should cover St. John's easily in an hour. Frankly, there isn't much to see outside the boutiques. St. John's started out as just one of many towns built haphazardly on virtually every sheltered harbor, large or small, on Antigua. Eventually, six towns were recognized as official trading centers (places where goods could be sold legally) in an attempt to discourage smuggling and to better organize military protection.

St. John's became preeminent as far back as 1681, but it has since suffered greatly. Two major fires (1769 and 1861) and two major earthquakes (1690 and 1843) destroyed the earliest structures, all made of wood. Yet much of the existing town is quite old by Caribbean standards, with a large number of buildings dating back to the 1840s. Not always well maintained, they also give parts of the city a slightly ramshackle appearance.

Until the 1980s, one of those rundown sections was Redcliffe Quay, where old wooden "barracoons" once held slaves awaiting auction or shipment to other islands. Like Nelson's Dockyard, Redcliffe Quay has been restored, turned into one of Antigua's best shopping districts.

A description of St. John's published in 1844 says the main area along "a well made broadstreet being inhabited principally by Scotsmen is known by the appropriate name 'Scotch Row.' You may, in truth, buy anything and everything in these 'Scotch Shops,' from three farthings' worth of tape to the most costly articles. Dresses of all kinds; ribbons, laces, flowers and bonnets; coasts, vests, pantaloons, umbrellas and shoes. The streets of the capital all have their proper appellations, although no painted board announces such a fact to the traveller." Apparently the tradition of not supplying street signs to direct travelers is a long and honored one!

Fortunately for travelers today, St. John's is laid out in a simple grid pattern, so once you determine which street you're on, finding your way is not difficult.

St. John's is far tamer today than it was back in the 1700s. Back then it was noted for having more than its fair share of grog shops and houses of ill repute. Drinking, wenching, cock-fighting, and gambling were the favorite recreational pastimes of this sailor's city. Today, a Saturday morning in the lively fruit and vegetable market on aptly named Market Street is considered a hot ticket. See the map on page 42 for the following sites.

1. **Court House/Museum of Antigua and Barbuda:** Originally built as the courthouse in 1747, this stone building suffered considerably during the earthquakes of 1843 and 1974. During its heyday, it hosted bazaars, charity sales, and official dinners. The restored building now houses the island's main museum and archives. The exhibits of pre-Columbian and colonial artifacts are well worth a look.

2. **Heritage/Redcliffe Quays:** Built in 1988 as a lure for cruise ship visitors, this very modern duty-free complex lacks the charm and color of nearby Redcliffe Quay, where brightly painted wooden buildings make it my preferred shopping area. However, Heritage Quay does boast a casino with big-screen TV.

3. **The Market:** A lively and colorful place on Saturday mornings between 8 a.m. and noon.

4. **Anglican Cathedral of St. John the Divine:** Usually referred to simply as St. John's Cathedral, this huge building dominates the town. Its baroque spires can be clearly seen from the waterfront. The original cathedral was a wooden one built in 1683. It was replaced in 1722 by a newer and bigger church, which was in turn destroyed in the great earthquake of 1843. Reconstruction began in 1845; the building was consecrated in 1848. The interior is encased in wood to protect it from both earthquake and hurricane damage, one reason it survived the earthquake of 1974. The figures at the southern entrance represent St. John the Baptist and St. John the Divine.

5. **Government House:** The residence of the Governor General is not open to the public, but you can admire the architecture. It was originally two houses standing side by side with a street between them. The original buildings are of wood in seventeenth-century colonial style, but extensions have been added in concrete.

6. **Fort James:** Used for defending the harbor entrance, it was originally built in 1675, though most of the buildings seen today date from 1749. Ten cannons, each weighing 212 tons, are still in the fort. It is said the cannons required 12 men each to fire.

ELSEWHERE ON ANTIGUA

1. ENGLISH HARBOUR/NELSON'S DOCKYARD

Time: 1-2 hours. | **Difficulty:** 1. | **Trailhead:** From St. John's, drive 11 miles southeast on the island's main road. Open daily 8 a.m.–6 p.m.

Fifteen-square-mile Nelson's Dockyard National Park is a small nautical version of Colonial Williamsburg, Virginia. This restored eighteenth-century garrison originally was established by England's Royal Navy to protect ships anchored in English Harbour with cargoes of sugar, which was once as valuable as gold or silver.

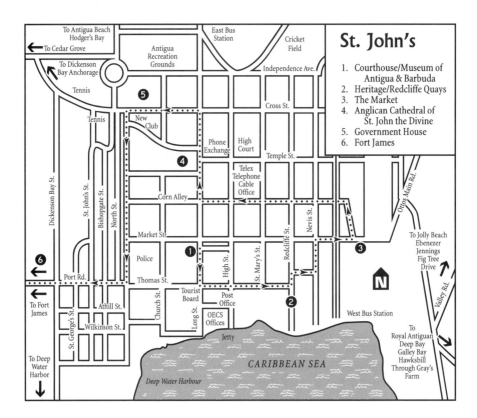

To Antigua Beach
Hodger's Bay
← To Cedar Grove

To Dickenson
Bay Anchorage

Tennis

Tennis

Dickenson Bay St.

St. John's St.

Bishopgate St.

North St.

New Club

Corn Alley

Market St.

Police

Port Rd.

Thomas St.

6
←
To Fort
James

Athill St.

St. George's St.

Wilkinson St.

To Deep
Water
Harbor
↓

Church St.

Long St.

Tourist Board

OECS Offices

Jetty

Antigua Recreation Grounds

5

4

Phone Exchange

High Court

Telex Telephone Cable Office

1

High St.

St. Mary's St.

Post Office

Deep Water Harbour

East Bus Station

Cross St.

Temple St.

Redcliffe St.

Nevis St.

3

2

West Bus Station

Cricket Field

Independence Ave.

Ottos Main Rd.

To Jolly Beach
Ebenezer
Jennings
Fig Tree
Drive

Valley Rd.

To
Royal Antiguan
Deep Bay
Galley Bay
Hawksbill
Through Gray's
Farm

N

CARIBBEAN SEA

St. John's

1. Courthouse/Museum of Antigua & Barbuda
2. Heritage/Redcliffe Quays
3. The Market
4. Anglican Cathedral of St. John the Divine
5. Government House
6. Fort James

The garrison's namesake, Horatio Nelson, arrived in 1784 at age 26. Legend has it he gained command of Antigua after his predecessor put out his own eye while chasing a cockroach with a fork. (No reports are given of how much grog was consumed during the cockroach chase.)

Initially, this site was known simply as the Dockyard; Nelson was dead 150 years before it adopted his name, something he might have found amusing because he and Antigua didn't suit each other very well. Nelson was extremely unpopular with both the locals and English merchants of Antigua because he insisted on enforcing the Navigation Act, which opened English Harbour only to English ships. Before Nelson's arrival, ships from the newly independent United States had been carrying on a lively trade in Antigua with the approval of well-bribed on-site officials.

English Harbour was important for its excellent anchorage: Ships could ride out hurricanes there, and repairs could be made under strong military protection. Damaged ships from other islands often traveled to the American colonies for repair because of dangerous conditions created by marauding French and Spanish. Except for the sugar trade, little has changed in the makeup of Nelson's Dockyard since it went into use in the 1720s.

The Dockyard was shut down in 1889 and reopened in 1961 as a historical monument and as a well-equipped center for cruising yachtsmen. The main social center is the Admiral's Inn. Like most of the Dockyard's buildings, the Inn is built of local stone and brick imported for ballast. Its 14 small rooms are furnished as they would have been a century ago, but the outdoor patio attracts most of the attention as the area's favorite watering hole.

What once was the Dockyard's old copper and lumber store is now a restaurant and inn, imaginatively called the Copper and Lumber Store Hotel. It, too, has just 14 rooms. The building that Nelson lived in has been turned into the Dockyard Museum, containing charts, furniture, and nautical memorabilia from the eighteenth and nineteenth centuries.

From the Dockyard, it's an easy walk to **Fort Berkeley,** situated on a thin spit of land overlooking the narrow entrance to English Harbour. Fort Berkeley defended the harbor not only with cannons but a chain-and-timber boom that would be drawn across to block the channel during sieges. Nature trails lasting from 30 minutes to 5 hours criss-cross the area, including the **Lookout Trail** that leads to the following site, Shirley Heights, which overlooks English Harbour.

2. SHIRLEY HEIGHTS CLIMBS

Time: 1 hour at the site, 2 or 3 more if you climb from and return to the base of the hill. | **Difficulty:** 3 for the long walk.

Overlooking English Harbour is another restored garrison called Shirley Heights, where residents and visitors alike congregate on Sundays for the liveliest party in Antigua. This installation was named after General Sir Thomas Shirley, a former governor. One of the main buildings, known as the Block House, was put up as a stronghold in 1787 in case of a siege.

Shirley Heights commands a strategic and spectacular view of English Harbour with a view of Montserrat and Guadeloupe. The impressive fortification was built to provide added security to the Dockyard, but on Sunday afternoons it is the site of the island's biggest cookout and steel band concert. It's not necessary to sample the barbecue to be welcome here; many people come to enjoy the music.

If you are really in the mood for a strenuous walk, park at Clarence House and hike to Shirley Heights. Clarence House was built for the duke of Clarence, the future King William IV, who served under Nelson as a captain. Or climb to Shirley Heights via the **Lookout Trail,** a nature trail through the forest that originates at English Harbour. After your climb to the ridge of hills overlooking English Harbour, you'll understand why the fortification was never in much danger of being taken. You can also walk several side roads and area paths.

3. FIG TREE DRIVE WALKS

Length: 20 miles. | **Time:** 40 minutes for the woodlands walk. | **Difficulty:** 1. | **Trailhead:** At the town of Liberta, north of Falmouth.

Hardly a soul walks this 20-mile circular drive through the mountains, but you'll want to stop at many places to get out, walk, and view the lush rain forest or the small thatched fishing villages. Don't expect to find real fig trees, though—*fig* is the local name for bananas. At the small Antigua Cultural Center between the villages of Swetes and Old Road, stop and ask directions for the trail to **Wallings Dam.** The woodlands walk takes about 40 minutes.

4. BOGGY PEAK CLIMB

Time: 30–60 minutes round-trip. | **Difficulty:** 1–2. | **Trailhead:** On Fig Tree Drive roughly halfway between the villages of Urlins and Old Road. Look for the dirt road that turns inland.

At 1,358 feet, Boggy Peak is the highest point on Antigua. Leave your car at the parking lot to hike the road leading to the peak, less than a mile away. Like the peaks of many Caribbean mountains, Boggy Peak is cluttered with communications facilities, which you'll soon forget once you start enjoying the superb view of the coast and even distant St. John's.

5. GREENCASTLE HILL MEGALITHS HIKE

Time: 1–2 hours round-trip. | **Difficulty:** 1–2. | **Trailhead:** Going south from St. John's on the main highway toward Jennings, turn left to go to Emanuel. Go for about a mile after making the turn until you reach a brick factory. Park and hike to the hilltop on the dirt road nearby.

Is this the Caribbean version of Stonehenge, where ancient people aligned the big rocks for astronomical purposes or to worship the sun and moon gods? Geologists say no, these stones are natural formations known as volcanic rockfall. Regardless, you'll have a fine view of Jolly Harbour.

6. INDIAN TOWN NATIONAL PARK WALK

Time: 5–6 hours. | **Difficulty:** 1–2. | **Trailhead:** At the Island's eastern end. Drive through the towns of Pares and Willikies to Long Bay, west of Indian Town Point and a deep cove known as Indian Town Creek. The park fronts the Atlantic at Long Bay. Hiking trails lead to and along the coastline. Alternatively, you turn right before Long Bay to reach Indian Town Point.

This rocky, wind-swept shore is not often visited. A land mostly of acacia trees (locally called "cassie") and limestone formations, including some especially good blowholes when the wind is right. The most famous site is the Devil's Bridge, a limestone arch formed by endless wave action. Located at the mouth of Indian Town Creek, it's surrounded by a meadowy headland.

BARBUDA

Old Caribbean Saying: He's a person who would take milk
out of coffee.

Translation: He's a person who would do a dishonest act.

This tiny island, just 62 square miles, lies 30 miles north of Antigua. Daily flights on LIAT are the easiest connections, although an overnight boat charter is also available. Eight-mile-long Coca Beach is a spectacular strip of sand that so far has seen little development. It won't stay that way for long. The beach is gorgeous, the water clear. This is what Grand Cayman and other overdeveloped beachfronts must have looked like before the construction cranes arrived. There is no shade against the hot sun, and the beach seems to stretch on forever. If you're a true beachcomber, get here quickly, before it changes. Highland House, part of the once massive Codrington plantation, is at the highest point on the island: 124 feet. The 56-foot-high Martello castle and tower, once used to spot ships wrecking on the reefs, is on the south coast.

FRIGATE BIRD SANCTUARY WALK

Time: 5–6 hours | **Difficulty:** 1, after you get there. | **Trailhead:** In the island's northeast lagoon, accessible only by boat.

Barbuda is a birder's paradise. Best time to visit is in the fall during the courting period when the male frigates display their red throat pouch. About 5,000 *Fregata magnificens* live here. Also called man o' war birds, the frigates have wingspans of four to five feet. They share the sanctuary with another 170 species of birds.

4

BARBADOS

Old Caribbean Proverb: "*Don't drink bush for other people's fever.*"
Translation: "*Don't take on someone else's problems.*"

Situated 1,612 miles southeast of Miami and 575 miles southeast of Puerto Rico, Barbados is located in the region known as the deep Caribbean. Though this may be well off the beaten tourist path, approximately 360,000 visitors come by plane and even more by cruise ship each year. Canadians, especially, have a fondness for Barbados.

Barbados is the Caribbean's most densely populated island, so it understandably lacks the remote forest hikes of the more rugged, mountainous islands. Exploring is confined primarily to the Bridgetown area, various historical structures scattered throughout the countryside, and the almost-deserted Atlantic coast. This is almost tenderfoot-grade walking, some of the Caribbean's easiest.

If you don't mind crowds, you can join the Barbados National Trust's weekly hikes, which cover the natural, historical, and cultural aspects of the island.

More than most islands, Barbados developed as a genuine country while at the same time becoming a popular vacation playground. The Portuguese were the first Europeans to locate the island in 1536, calling it "Los Barbados" after the bearded fig trees growing on the beaches. However, the only impact the Portuguese had on the island was to leave behind some wild pigs, which thrived. Indians had been on Barbados for at least 1,000 years, but they were gone when the English arrived to colonize in 1627.

One of the strangest early European visitors was Ferdinando Paleologus, who claimed to be a descendent of Emperor Constantine the Great. Forced to flee Constantinople when the Turks invaded, Paleologus was buried in St. John's Church Yard in 1678 after a 20-year residence. He chose Barbados for his exile, though some say he was only a great impostor. In any case, the tale makes a good story, and the "royal" grave is interesting to visit.

In traveling around Barbados, you may be amazed to see mile after mile of sugarcane fields—much of the country remains agriculturally oriented. Barbados, in fact, was one of the first Caribbean countries where sugarcane was introduced, brought by Jewish immigrants from Brazil in the early 1620s. Following its success here and in Martinique, sugarcane became the dominant crop of the Caribbean and determined the social and economic climate even to this day.

Agriculturally, Barbados was far more blessed than many islands. Much of its limestone base had transformed into a rich, loamy soil. Even in recent years, as much as 80 percent of the land has been planted in sugarcane or sour grass, used as mulch and fodder for cattle. Although tourism is now more important, sugar proved a solid bedrock for centuries. It was on the old Bajan sugar plantations that a whole new industry developed that would affect the rest of the Western world—the development of world-famous Barbados rum. The Spanish first distilled a spirit from the molasses residue left in the refining process, but considered the product so low-grade, it was fit for only slaves and Indians.

In Barbados, however, "Rumbullion" became a popular export appreciated throughout the hemisphere. Although rum technically may not have been invented in Barbados, the name clearly did originate here, and Barbados was the first country to export it.

Travel Tips

Area: 21 miles long and 14 miles wide, with almost 800 miles of hard surface road.

Language: English; no other European culture ever gained a foothold here. The country has been referred to as "Little England."

Population: About 255,000 people, making it one of the most densely populated countries in the world.

Time Zone: Atlantic Time, 1 hour ahead of Eastern Standard Time.

Rainy Season: From June to November, though Barbados enjoys sunshine throughout the year: 3008 hours of it annually. Temperatures vary between 75 and 85°F, but winter nights with a brisk wind can be chilly.

Getting There: All flights arrive at Grantley Adams International Airport, located 10 miles east of Bridgetown. American Airlines offers frequent service, as does LIAT (800) 468-0482), BWIA, Air Jamaica, Air Canada, and British Airways. Note that any tickets you purchase for trips originating in Barbados have an added 20% tax levied on them.

Documents: U.S. and Canadian citizens coming directly from North America need a certified birth certificate and photo ID for stays under 3 months. A passport is required for longer stays. Technically, an ongoing ticket is also required for admittance.

Getting Around: With 800 miles of paved road and a new highway from the airport, driving is the recommended way to see the island. Motorcycles can be rented. A local driver's license (US$5) is necessary. Driving, of course, is on the left. You'll want to visit the rugged Atlantic coast, which is reminiscent of the British Isles. Taxis are identified by the letter *Z* on their license plates. They can be expensive, and drivers don't always go by the posted fares.

Where to Stay: Much of the Caribbean coast on the south and west sides is ringed with hotels, some of the Caribbean's best and most expensive. The Atlantic side, where the ocean is generally too rough for safe swimming and diving, has a few hotels for those who want to be far away from the crowds. The tourist board can also provide a list of guest houses, apartments, and villas. Hotel rates can be as much as 50% less in summer. An interesting option is the 22-suite Peach & Quiet located on 4 acres in the southern part of the island. It specializes in week-long walking tours during the winter months, (246) 428-5682; fax (246) 428-2467.

Camping: Not permitted.

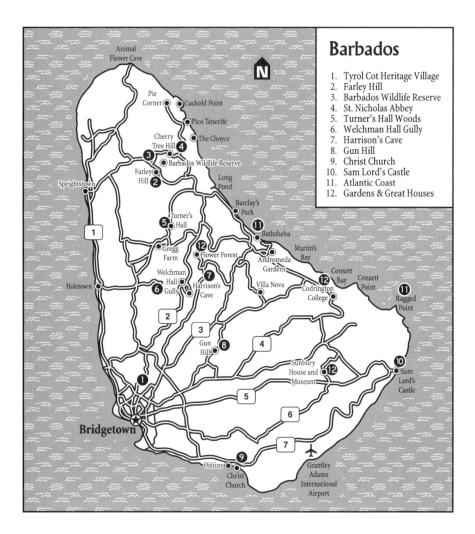

Barbados

1. Tyrol Cot Heritage Village
2. Farley Hill
3. Barbados Wildlife Reserve
4. St. Nicholas Abbey
5. Turner's Hall Woods
6. Welchman Hall Gully
7. Harrison's Cave
8. Gun Hill
9. Christ Church
10. Sam Lord's Castle
11. Atlantic Coast
12. Gardens & Great Houses

Currency: Although everything is quoted in dollars and cents, it's in Bajan currency. US$1 is worth $2 Bajan, so cut the posted prices by half to get the U.S. equivalent. Banks are open 9 a.m. to 3 p.m. Monday through Thursday; 9 a.m. to 1 p.m. and 3 to 5 p.m. on Friday.

Taxes & Tips: Barbados keeps getting more expensive. A 7.5% government tax and 10% service charge are added to hotel bills. In addition, a 15% VAT (value added tax) applies to all meals, plus the 10% service charge. Ouch! The departure tax is US $12.50.

Electrical Current: 110 volts but 50 cycles instead of 60. Some hotels have transformers or 220-volt outlets.

Safety/Health Warnings: If you're out after dark, stay away from Nelson Street and the poorer areas of Bridgetown. In general, this is a safe island, and the people are helpful and friendly.

Snakes & Other Venomous Creatures: None.

Hiking/Walking Services: Since 1986 the **Barbados National Trust** has organized free walks on Sunday for residents and visitors alike at 6 a.m. and 3:30 p.m. Called Hike Barbados, they've become so popular that at times as many as several hundred people may show up. About 100 different walks have been mapped out. They include everything from forest hikes to road walks through villages and past power plants. On the longer morning hikes you have a choice of groups based on your ability. The "Stop 'n' Stare" group strolls between 5–6 miles. The "Here and There" walkers do 8–10 miles. The brisk "Grin & Bear" cover 12–14 miles. Regardless of the distance, all hikes last about 3 hours. In the afternoon, the 3:30 walks are "Stop 'n' Stare" only. Moonlight walks (starting at 5:30 p.m.) can also be arranged; bring a flashlight. The hikes are listed in the local newspaper and on the Web at www.barbados.org/hikemain. For more information, contact the National Trust, (246) 426-2421; fax (246) 429-9055. Although the hikes are free, donations are welcome for both the National Trust and the Future Centre Trust, a co-sponsor helping Bajans work toward a sustainable, happy future.

The **Arbib Nature and Heritage Trail,** also sponsored by the National Trust, is walked on Wednesday, Thursday, and Saturday at 9 a.m. and 2 p.m. This hike includes local culture and history at Speightstown's old port and the adjacent countryside. You can choose the longer 3.5-mile walk or an easier 2-hour hike. The walks, which cost $7.50 per person for at least two people, must be booked by 3 p.m. the day before your hike. For information, contact the National Trust.

For a complete walking vacation, join a week-long **Walkers' World** trip during the winter. Operated by Teacher Travel of Canada, the hikes cost about $775 per person and includes accommodations, breakfast, and five dinners. Groups stay on the southeast coast but roam the whole island. For information, call (800) 268-7229 or visit www.walkersworld.com.

Local Source Book: Here's a plug for an excellent book that details 34 varied Barbados walks with maps, directions, and local lore about each hike. Priced at $14.25, *Walking Barbados* by David H. Weeks is available locally from the National Trust (the publisher) and Barbados bookstores.

Additional Information: Barbados Tourism Authority, 800 Second Ave., New York, NY 10017; toll-free (800) 221-9831. In Canada, 105 Adelaide St. West, Suite 1010, Toronto, Ontario M5H 1P9; phone (416) 214-9880. In the United Kingdom, 263 Tottenham Court Road, London, W1P 0lA; phone (0171) 636-9448; www.barbados.org.

BRIDGETOWN AFOOT!

Time: 1–2 hours. | **Difficulty:** 1. | **Trailhead:** Trafalgar Square.

Dating from 1628, this is an easy place to walk around, taking a couple of hours at most to explore. The sun is hot, so wear a good hat or sunblock. Almost half the island population lives here.

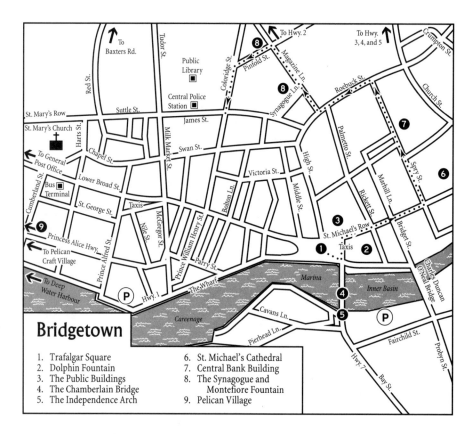

Bridgetown

1. Trafalgar Square
2. Dolphin Fountain
3. The Public Buildings
4. The Chamberlain Bridge
5. The Independence Arch
6. St. Michael's Cathedral
7. Central Bank Building
8. The Synagogue and
   Montefiore Fountain
9. Pelican Village

1. Trafalgar Square: One of Bridgetown's biggest surprises is a statue of Admiral Lord Nelson in a place called Trafalgar Square. However, Bridgetown's Lord Nelson is not an imitation of London's more famous statue. Native Bajans had a strong affection for Nelson. He visited Barbados, in command of the British fleet, just six months before his death at Trafalgar in 1805. Following the admiral's demise, an existing square was renamed Trafalgar and his statue erected in 1813, about 36 years ahead of England's more famous one.

2. Dolphin Fountain/: Bridgetown had piped-in water as early as 1861. A local newspaper suggested a proper fountain be erected in a central spot; the citizens donated money and the fountain, with its water-spewing dolphins was installed in 1865. Work on the gardens surrounding the fountain didn't begin until 1882. Note the curious cannonball tree here.

3. The Public Buildings: Barbados has the third-oldest parliamentary body in the English-speaking world, dating from 1639, second only to Britain and Bermuda. The earliest building was built in 1640 but burned in the Bridgetown fire of 1668. For the next 30 years, the officials had to meet in people's homes and—quite frequently—public taverns. The west wing of this building was completed in 1871, the east in 1874. Both the

Senate and House of Assembly meet here. Stained-glass windows in the east buildings show many statesmen dating back to the time of Queen Victoria, including Oliver Cromwell.

4. The Chamberlain Bridge: According to legend, the capital city of Bridgetown received its name from the Arawak Indian bridge the first settlers found spanning the inlet. First known simply as "The Bridge," it later was changed to Bridgetown. Today, the Chamberlain Bridge spans the inlet where the Indian bridge probably existed, at a spot known as the Careenage. The Careenage, a concentration of waterfront restaurants, colorful fishing boats and fishing charters, marks the place where the old sailing ships were tilted over—careened—so their bottoms could be scraped.

    Note the colorful wooden boats in this area. These are the flying fish boats, for taking that most popular of local foods. Bajans eat flying fish the way Americans eat hamburgers.

5. The Independence Arch: Built in 1987 to mark the island's 21st year of independence.

6. St. Michael's Cathedral: The present church was built in 1789 and became a cathedral in 1825. Its arched roof was at one time the widest in the world. Many famous Bajans are buried here.

7. Central Bank Building: At 11 stories, the tallest building on Barbados, it also contains a 500-seat modern concert hall. The entire structure cost $60 million.

8. The Synagogue and Montefiore Fountain: Claiming to be the oldest synagogue in the Western Hemisphere, the original building went up in 1654, came down in the hurricane of 1831, and was reconstructed in 1833. The adjoining Jewish Cemetery, still in use, has tombstones dating to the 1630s. The Jews who came to Barbados from Brazil in the 1620s introduced sugarcane to the Caribbean.

9. Pelican Village: Located near the Deep Water Harbour along Princess Alice Highway. This is the main arts-and-crafts center established by the government.

10. Queen's Park: (Not on map.) Farther east of the Bridgetown harbor. Originally this was the residence of the person commanding the British troops in the West Indies. Before the days of Queen Victoria it was known as the King's House. A baobab tree in the park with a 61.5-foot circumference is perhaps the largest tree in Barbados. The tree, a native of Africa, is an estimated 1,000 years old. That seed had to float a long way in the ocean currents. Imagine the odds of it landing and surviving here.

1. Tyrol Cot Heritage Village

Time: 1–2 hours. | **Difficulty:** 1. | **Trailhead:** Located 1.5 miles north of Bridgetown on Highway 2. | **Operating Hours:** Open 9 a.m. to 5 p.m. weekdays only. Call (246) 424-2074. Admission fee.

No one had ever heard of a "modular mobile home" when the Bajans built thousands of them in the 1800s and early 1900s, creating one of the Caribbean's most distinctive folk architecture designs. Locally called chattel houses, they are now considered models of Georgian symmetry and harmony.

They were built after Emancipation when landless slaves were allowed to rent property and build on plantations. Because the slaves could be evicted at anytime, their homes had to be chattel, or "movable possessions," that in a single day could be taken down quickly, placed on an ox cart, and reassembled; truly mobile homes.

Dimensions of the chattel houses were determined by the only available building material: precut, cheap pinewood of 12- to 20-foot lengths (even sizes only) imported from North America. Not surprisingly, most chattel houses were built with a front door in the middle and a window on each side.

Chattel houses often started as a single unit, then expanded to the rear one roof at a time whenever family circumstances dictated or money allowed. Eventually porches or verandahs and perhaps even a stone foundation if land could be purchased.

Every visitor to Barbados probably has stopped to photograph some of the most elegantly designed chattel homes, but few tourists have ever seen the inside of one. That opportunity is available at Tyrol Cot Heritage Village at Codrington Hill. The creation of the National Trust and the island's first ever heritage village, the Chattel House Museum contains seven replicas of classic designs, all outfitted with furniture and ornamental decoration from their respective time periods. Each house also has a traditional artist or craftsperson who fashions basketry, leather goods, candy, and clothing. Besides the chattel houses, the museum also includes a combination rum shop and restaurant, a working blacksmith shop, and a replica of an 1820s slave hut.

The Cockspur Rum Shop offers some truly old-time Bajan foods: sweet breads, fish cakes, and coconut cakes. For anyone needing a sugar fix, the ice cream shop in back of the Cockspur has locally made ice cream, jellies, jams, and chocolates.

The museum is located on the grounds of historic Tyrol Cot Mansion, often called the birthplace of Barbadian democracy. Open to the public, the fully restored home was built in 1854 of huge coral limestone blocks and ballast brick. It was eventually the home of Sir Grantley Adams, one of the country's best-known leaders. He was the first premier of Barbados and the only premier of the short-lived West Indies Federation; his son was the island's second premier. The home is furnished with locally crafted mahogany furniture collected by the Adams family over the past two centuries.

To commemorate the early 1930s when Grantley Adams and his new bride first occupied the house, the grounds are planted in roses, ferns, bougainvillaea, and other local plants, all of it in a natural "wild" style that was popular in the 1930s.

ELSEWHERE ON BARBADOS

2. FARLEY HILL

Time: 30–45 minutes. | **Difficulty:** 1. | **Trailhead:** From Speightstown take Highway 1 east for about 3 miles. Open during daylight hours.

Yet another opulent testament to the past glory of Bajan gentry is Farley Hill, built in 1861 for a visit by Prince Alfred, duke of Edinburgh. Once a beautiful mansion that was a regular stopover for visiting English royalty, including Prince George (later King George V). Farley Hill overlooks acres of cane fields; the grounds are well forested and lushly landscaped. It is picturesque enough to be a movie set—and was—for *Island in the Sun*. Fire gutted the

Bridgetown has many interesting, old buildings

interior in 1965 and only the shell remains, but the site is still worth visiting for the panoramic view and a taste of the greatness that once existed. Now it is a protected park, with picnic tables set out under the trees near the abandoned great house.

3. BARBADOS WILDLIFE RESERVE

Time: 1 hour. | **Difficulty:** 1. | **Trailhead:** Across the road from Farley Hill National Park. | **Operating Hours:** Daily 10 a.m. to 5 p.m. For information, call (246) 422-8826. Admission fee.

Created in 1985, this small, three-acre sanctuary protects and controls the green—or vervet—monkeys imported from West Africa. This is the same species found on St. Kitts and Nevis. Bounties were offered on these agricultural pests as early as 1680 because of the massive crop destruction they caused. The monkeys became a problem again during this century, and, instead of hunting them again, this wildlife reserve was created. It manages the population through trapping and sale of the animals for use in medical research. "Green" monkeys are actually brownish-gray with green flecks. They are allowed to roam free in a sizable stand of mahogany trees. Other animals on exhibit include rabbits, caimans, agoutis, and otters. A walk-in aviary is also featured.

4. ST. NICHOLAS ABBEY

Time: 45–60 minutes. | **Difficulty:** 1. | **Trailhead:** From Speightstown take Highway 1 east then head toward Cherry Tree Hill. | **Operating Hours:** Weekdays 10 a.m. to 3:30 p.m. For information call (246) 422-8725. Admission fee.

One of the oldest buildings in the English-speaking world, the surviving structure here demonstrates that early sugar plantation owners lived as sumptuously as English noblemen. Historically, the most important home in all Barbados, built just 25 years after the first settlement, the manor house is virtually in its original condition. Undoubtedly that is partly due to its construction of durable coral stone. The main quarters are probably as sound today as when they were built around 1650. One of the owners, a Sir John Yeamans, helped colonize South Carolina, becoming its third governor. Furnishings include antiques of European and Bajan origin.

5. TURNER'S HALL WOODS

Time: 1–2 hours. | **Difficulty:** 1. | **Trailhead:** Turner's Hall Woods is located on the Turner Hall Plantation, south of the famous Morgan Lewis Mill. Follow Highway 1 south, past the windmill.

Because Barbados is one of the most heavily developed and populated islands, and much of it stripped bare for the planting of sugarcane, remote woodland walks are rare. One of the best is Turner's Hall Woods, a 50-acre farm containing a remnant of a lush tropical forest, including the indigenous macaw palm, which covered Barbados until the introduction of sugarcane in the 1600s. At least 32 species of trees have been identified, including silk cotton, sandbox, bulletwood, trumpet tree, locust, fustic, and cabbage palm. The woods, with its fairly steep hiking trail of about half a mile, are a popular place for walking and hiking, a showcase of Barbados at its most natural. The higher you walk, the thicker the vegetation. This is not a true rain forest, despite the mullet-layered tree canopies and the presence of lianas and ferns. Only about 60 inches of rain falls here annually; a true rain forest receives 200 or more.

6. WELCHMAN HALL GULLY

Time: 1 hour. | **Difficulty:** 1. | **Trailhead:** On Highway 2 near Mount Hillaby, highest point on the island. | **Operating Hours:** Daily 9 a.m. to 5 p.m. Admission fee.

What do you call a cave after it loses its roof? In Barbados, it becomes a gully. In this instance Welchman Hall Gully, a wide, deep trench cutting through the limestone bedrock, which covers most of the island. The Barbados National Trust owns this 0.75-mile-long humid gully protected from high winds, allowing incredibly luxuriant plant life to grow out of the side walls. A gigantic pillar reveals the subterranean origin of this now-open gully more than four and a half feet in diameter, reputedly the world's largest example of a stalactite and stalagmite coming together to form a single column.

Once a barren subterranean chamber, Welchman Hall Gully has become a flourishing microcosm of the plant and animal life of Barbados. It's one of the most reliable places in the Caribbean to encounter free-roaming families of green monkeys darting among the thick, jungle-like canopy of palms and other tall trees that pack the gully.

"A touch of jungle" is precisely how the Barbados National Trust describes a walk through the ravine, which is thickly stuffed with some 200 species of tropical plants. It even feels a bit like the jungle in there, too, because the high cliffs bordering the gully block out the wind, making this one of the most humid places on the island, though not uncomfortably so.

Welchman Hall Gully was created after the roof of a series of immense caves collapsed and fell sometime in the distant past. The gully, in fact, is less than a mile from Harrison's Cave (see below), one of the largest caves in the Caribbean. The gully takes its unusual name from an early Welch settler who owned the sunken corridor. It's said to be the one place on the island that most closely resembles how Barbados appeared to the first settlers in 1627.

A walk through the gully begins from the car park located at the north end. The maze of growth here is almost bewildering, but the National Trust, which has operated the gully since 1963, untangles much of the confusion by providing a leaflet that identifies many of the plants and several of the most important natural features. The gully doesn't open until 9 a.m., a little late for the green monkeys to be moving, so a late afternoon walk around 4 p.m. is often the better time.

Green monkeys were brought to Barbados from West Africa about 350 years ago, apparently as pets. Today they're considered pests because of the damage they cause to fruits and vegetables. Even though there's been a bounty on the animals, somewhere between 5,000 and 8,000 of them still flourish, some of them in the reserve created especially for them. Their favorite haunts are the heavily forested sections, which is why they're a fairly dependable sight in Welchman Hall Gully. Look for them feeding on the ground and not just in the trees.

You may spot only a single monkey, or you could see a whole troop of about 15 animals scrambling through the tree canopy. If you do get a good view of a monkey through binoculars or a telephoto lens, pay particular attention to its face. Although only about 75 generations have passed since they were brought in, the Barbados green monkeys already have evolved some physical differences from their African cousins. The Barbados green monkey has more of a doglike face and less fur around the eyes; its vocalizations also are said to be different.

Because of the cliffs lining the gully and the thick tree canopy, much of the walk is in perpetual shade. The one exception occurs at midday when the sun passes almost directly overhead. Many of the trees and plants in Welchman Hall Gully naturally grow on Barbados, but quite a few introduced species have been added over the years. They include guava (from Central and South America), the golden apple (from the South Pacific), nutmeg (the Moluccas or Spice Islands), and avocado pear trees (from Mexico). Look for the marker on the bearded fig tree with its hanging, beard-like roots. In Portuguese it was known as "Los Barbados," the bearded ones, and it is from this once common tree that Barbados is thought to have gained its name.

Another unusual tree is the swizzle stick tree, which until recently was thought to be extinct on Barbados. Rum, after all, was perfected on Barbados, and cocktails or swizzles are said to be a Caribbean innovation, so swizzle sticks were something of a necessity. Wood from the swizzle stick tree was used to make the cocktail stirrers.

You'll also see orange trees here, too, but no grapefruit trees. It's not widely known, but the grapefruit evolved on Barbados as a hybrid between the shaddock and the orange. Originally called the "paradise fruit," it was one of the items that impressed George Washington when he visited Barbados in 1751.

Because the gully is fairly wide in parts, it's easy to overlook the towering limestone cliffs that flank this sunken jungle. Actually, sometimes it's just plain hard to distinguish the walls from their heavy mantle of ferns and tree roots. But in places where the cliffs do close in and where openings in the cliff are large enough to stand under, you're reminded just what an unusual environment this truly is. What's even more remarkable is that Welchman Hall Gully hasn't been allowed to be invaded by that most ubiquitous of Caribbean species, the craft vendor. In fact, you won't find a single one anywhere. Welchman Hall Gully is a jungle of the most natural kind.

7. HARRISON'S CAVE

Time: 1–2 hours. | **Difficulty:** 1. | **Trailhead:** On Highway 2 continuing south beyond Welchman Hall Gully. | **Operating Hours:** 8:45 a.m. to 4 p.m. daily. Admission fee. For information, call (246) 438-6640.

One of the island's greatest natural spectacles, Harrison's Cave is a huge natural underground system charted as far back as 1760 but somehow forgotten until heavy rains created an entrance just a few years ago. The government quickly recognized what a unique attraction this would make, so it quickly built the Caribbean's first subterranean tram ride. This is a very well-organized excursion.

After a slide presentation, you board a 36-passenger electric tram for an hour-long tour. Very effective use has been made of indirect lighting to magnify the eeriness and beauty of the caverns. Most memorable are the several cascading waterfalls and the great Rotunda Room, a 250-foot-long by 100-foot-high chamber glistening with creamy and white geologic formations. Tours are given every day on the hour, but because long lines can form, this is one place you do need advance reservations.

8. GUN HILL

Time: 30 minutes. | **Difficulty:** 1. | **Trailhead:** Take Highway 4 from Bridgetown toward St. George Church. Gun Hill will be on the left. | **Operating Hours:** Monday through Saturday, 9 a.m.–5 p.m. For information, call (246) 429-1358. Admission fee.

This is a seventeenth-century signal station as well as a garrison for soldiers. The white limestone, ten-foot-tall lion standing proud at Gun Hill commemorates British strength of centuries past. Its inscription translates, "He shall have dominion from sea to sea and from the rivers unto the end of the world." This commands a stunning view of the entire southern half of the island, best viewed in late afternoon. Soldiers were once sent here to convalesce.

9. CHRIST CHURCH

Time: 30–45 minutes. | **Difficulty:** 1. | **Trailhead:** On a hill overlooking Oistins, a fishing village, just east of Bridgetown on Highway 7.

By now you should realize I have a fondness for ghost stories and legends. The happenings at Christ Church in the 1800s are more than just an eerie tale. Rather, they are one of those true historical oddities yet to be fully explained. This is where the famous moving coffins of Barbados kept shifting around in the sealed Chase Vault. But first a note about the church: As this is written, the one standing is the fifth parish church. All the others were destroyed by hurricane, flood, or fire; not a tranquil place.

The well-documented unsolved mystery is as follows: in 1812 the vault was opened for burial of Col. Thomas Chase. To everyone's amazement, the heavy lead coffins were found scattered about the vault. The same situation was observed twice in 1816 and once in 1817. At the next opening, in 1819, the governor of Barbados was present when the vault was reopened. Once again the scattered coffins were put back in their proper place and the governor placed his royal seal in the vault as it was cemented closed. In 1820, the coffins were found again to be strewn about the vault. Practical joke? Unexplainable phenomenon? The matter was resolved when all the coffins were removed and buried separately in the churchyard, where they have happily stayed in one place to this day. Obviously, the family that lives together doesn't always want to spend eternity together.

10. SAM LORD'S CASTLE

Time: 30–60 minutes. | **Difficulty:** 1. | **Trailhead:** Just northeast of the airport.

Sam Lord's Castle is the administrative building for the huge resort of the same name; but the grounds and residence are open to the public. Sam Lord was a Bajan planter, reputedly the local version of Blackbeard the pirate, though of a more refined ilk. Instead of attacking merchant ships at sea, Lord lured them onto the reefs near his home. He supposedly built his castle in 1820 from the spoils taken off the wrecks. The castle looks more like a theme park exhibit than the real thing, but take a look at the furniture, paintings, plaster ceilings, and beautiful mahogany columns inside. You definitely will be convinced of Sam Lord's wealth, then. The windy beach with its big stands of coconut palms is also worth a look.

11. ATLANTIC COAST

Time: Varies from 1.5 to 4 hours each way. | **Difficulty:** 1–3 depending on hike. | **Trailhead:** Take Highway 3 from Bridgetown toward Bathsheba, one of the largest settlements on the Atlantic coast.

With its stone fences and sloping green hillsides, the Scotland District coast indeed recalls the British Isles. The rugged Atlantic coast offers excellent coastal walks, many of them passing through small fishing villages. One of the best places for walking is between Bathsheba and Long Point, where the road parallels the coast. It's one of the easiest places for walking, and hikers can either follow the beach or the road. Yet you'd be surprised how few tourists ever stop to enjoy this area. The giant boulders scattered along the coastline near Bathsheba are an awesome sight, especially on a rough day. Andromeda Botanic Gardens, a scenic overlook and tiny garden, is just beyond Bathsheba. (Open daily 9 a.m. to 5 p.m.; call (246) 433-9384.)

If you prefer to walk through the fishing villages, the 16-mile-long stretch from the lighthouse at Ragged Point to Bathsheba and Pico Tenerife is a good option. It can be walked as a single stretch, though many people prefer to break it into short segments. From Ragged Point to the fishing village of Consett Bay is about four miles and a two-hour walk one-way. Consett Bay to Martin's Bay, another small fishing village, is three miles (two hours). From Martin's Bay to Bathsheba is also three miles (90 minutes); and from Bathsheba to the Choyce and Pico Tenerife is four miles (about four hours). Pico Tenerife is a 300-foot-high hill that overlooks the rugged Atlantic coast, providing some splendid views—a great end to your trek.

12. GARDENS AND GREAT HOUSES

Time: Varies. | **Difficulty:** 1

The *Flower Forest* at Richmond Plantation in St. Joseph parish is a 50-acre tropical garden on an old plantation. It offers many beautiful trees and shrubs and spectacular views. The plants are labeled for a self-guided walk. Admission fee. Open daily 9 a.m. to 5 p.m. Call (246) 433-8152.

Codrington College, which opened in 1745, is the oldest seminary in the Western Hemisphere. It has scenic grounds ideal for strolling. The entranceway is famous for its royal palms. No fee. On Highway 4 near Conset Bay.

The *Sunbury House and Museum* have one of the island's finest collections of antique furniture, antique tools and vehicles. Over 300 years old, this is the island's only plantation house with all rooms open to the public. Located on Cross Road in St. Philip. Admission fee. Open daily 10 a.m. to 5 p.m. Call (246)423-6270.

5   BRITISH VIRGIN ISLANDS

Old West Indian Proverb: Good luck is better than witchcraft.

Sixty miles east of Puerto Rico lie the British Virgin islands, a place so colorful it's difficult to separate fact from fable. For instance, it was on Dead Man's Chest Island (one of 50 islands, rocks, and cays that make up the British Virgins) that Blackbeard marooned 15 of his buccaneers with only a bottle of rum and a cutlass. It's not known how many survived, but we still commemorate their ordeal whenever "Yo-Ho-Ho and a Bottle of Rum" is sung.

This is also the land of Long John Silver and Treasure Island. Robert Louis Stevenson visited the British Virgin Islands shortly before writing his classic novel, though what he called Treasure Island is actually known as Norman Island, named for the pirate whose treasure is believed to be still buried there.

The British Virgin Islands, adjacent to the U.S. Virgin Islands, are an extremely picturesque group. Most are mountainous and—during the early summer rainy season—lushly green. When it's dry, the landscape turns deep brown and more desertlike, but palms, mangoes, cactus, loblolly, frangipani, hibiscus, and bougainvillaea all manage to thrive here.

The British Virgins are the kind of islands most people dream of retreating to. Temperatures are almost perfect: 77 to 85 ° F in winter, 80 to 90 ° F in summer, with temperatures dropping about 10 ° each evening.

Traditionally, the British Virgin Islands are a totally water-oriented community, with little in the way of nightlife or other social opportunities. All after-dark activities, other than night dives underwater, are confined to the hotels or the private boats. Just as for the pirates of old, the British Virgins are still a place for total escape.

Most of the BVIs border the Sir Francis Drake Channel, a historic sea highway. Over the centuries an estimated 150 ships have sunk on the reefs and cays near the channel.

Tortola is the largest and most populated landfall. Road Town, the capital city, is located there. Other large islands are Virgin Gorda, Jost Van Dyke, Anegada, and Peter Island. All of them, with the exception of Anegada, are hilly. The highest point, Sage Mountain on Tortola, is only 1,780 feet, so the hiking is hardly strenuous.

TRAVEL TIPS

Area: 59 square miles of land mass.

Language: English.

Population: 15,000, of which 2,300 live in the capital city of Road Town, Tortola.

The giant boulders of The Baths on Virgin Gorda are one of the Caribbean's best known landmarks

Time Zone: Atlantic Time, one hour ahead of Eastern Standard Time.

Rainy Season: From June through November.

Getting There: Because there are no direct flights from North America, you will need to fly from another island. American Eagle (phone (800) 433-7300) flies several times daily from San Juan into Beef Island, just a few minutes' drive from Road Town in Tortola. You also can fly into St. Thomas, then reach the main island of Tortola by inter-island ferry from Charlotte Amalie, just a 45-minute trip through Drake's Channel. Boats include Native Son, (284) 495-4617, and Smith's Ferry Service, (284) 495-4495. Ferryboats from Tortola make daily trips to Virgin Gorda, the only other major island in the British Virgin Island chain. Peter Island, a privately owned resort, has its own ferry.

Documents: U.S. and Canadian citizens need a government-issued photo ID and an authenticated birth certificate. Passports are required for everyone else.

Getting Around: Rental cars are readily available, about US$35 per day. You'll need a temporary driver's permit: US$10, available from the rental agency.

Where to Stay: Most hotels are clustered at Tortola and Virgin Gorda. To visit as many landfalls as possible, you may wish to charter a sailboat with crew or captain your own boat (but you must have the necessary experience). Approximately 1,000 sailboat rentals are available from several different companies. Most boats carry four to six persons.

Camping: Forbidden except in three designated areas, and the prohibition is strictly enforced. Probably due to its strong sailing tradition, the British Virgin Islands have managed to convince tourists to do their camping on the water, anchored on an expensive charter sailboat, instead of staying in a cheap canvas/nylon shelter on land. The strict no-camping enforcement helps keep the beaches clean for everyone.

Brewer's Bay Campground on Tortola offers prepared sites that include a 10' x 14' floored tent with beds, linen, stove, and all cooking implements. It offers a few open spots for people who bring their own tents. Contact Brewer's Bay Campground, Box 185, Road Town, Tortola; call (284) 494-3463. Rates are $35 for a prepared site, $10 for a primitive one.

On Jost Van Dyke, located northwest of Tortola, **White Bay Campground** overlooks gorgeous White Bay Beach. Tented sites ($35) that accommodate two include bed, electric lamp, and ice chest. Primitive, bare sites ($15) face the beach. Call (284) 495-9312.

Anegada, the most northerly of the British Virgins, situated 30 miles east of Tortola, has two campgrounds. **Mac's Place Camping** provides showers, toilets, grills, and a dining area. Tents are $35 per night and prepared sites are $15–35. Call (284) 495-8020. **Neptune's Treasure** overlooks a beach; tents are staked under palm trees. Showers are located outside, bathrooms inside the restaurant. Tents with foam mattresses, pillows, and linens are $15–25 per night, or $90–150 per week. Bare tent sites are $7 per night. Call (284) 495-9439.

Currency: The U.S. dollar is the official currency (even though this is a British territory). Major credit cards are accepted in many places, but personal checks are not. Banks are open 9 a.m.–3 p.m. Monday through Thursday and 9 a.m.–5 p.m. on Friday.

Taxes & Tips: A 7% hotel tax and 10% service charge. The departure tax is US$10 by air, US$5 by sea.

Electrical Current: Deferring to its largely American clientele, the electrical current is 110 volts, 60 cycles, not the expected 220 volts.

Safety/Health Warnings: None. This is one of the Caribbean's safest regions.

Snakes & Other Venomous Creatures: None.

Hiking/Walking Services: Not really needed in the British Virgin Islands because hikes are short and everything is so well marked. If you want a local guide, contact The National Park Trust, Administration Building., Road Town, Tortola. BVI; call (284) 494-3904. They do not offer tours themselves but should be able to recommend someone.

Additional Information: In the United States, contact the British Virgin Islands Tourist Board, 370 Lexington Ave., Suite 313, New York, NY 10017; phone (212) 696-0400. In Canada, British Virgin Island Information Office, 801 York Mill Road, Suite 201 Don Mills, Ontario M3B 1X7; phone (416) 443-1859. In the United Kingdom, BVI Information Office, 110 St. Martin's Lane, London WC2N 4DY; phone (0171) 240-4259; www.bviwelcome.com.

BEACH WALKS

Every island in the British Virgins has a potential beach walk. The problem is that most islands—though open to the public—are inaccessible unless you have your own boat. Only Tortola, Jost Van Dyke, and Virgin Gorda have regular ferry service; small planes fly into Anegada. Beyond that, you have to charter a boat or throw yourselves on the mercy of other sailors who might be bound for a landfall that interests you.

Tortola: On the north coast is *Brewer's Bay,* the location of one of three campgrounds in the British Virgin Islands. An exceptional walk. *Long Bay* is a mile of white sand beach with relatively little commercial development as yet. *Cane Garden Bay* has perhaps the best beach in all of the British Virgin Islands: 1.5 miles of white sand, but largely developed. Cane Garden Village is home of the small *Calwood Rum Distillery,* after 200 years, the oldest—in fact the only—one still bottling anywhere in the British Virgins.

Tortola's *Apple Bay* is worth visiting the night of the full moon when a wild party is thrown at Bomba's Shack. Bomba's monthly mind-blower is staggering … as in, barely walking. It's an important local ritual to observe even if you don't participate. Bomba's is a real shack, too; you must see it by daylight to appreciate its true shackiness. Picturesque is only skin-deep, but shacky goes to the bone.

Peter Island: This private resort island has its own ferry service several times daily. The beaches and roads are easy to follow from the marina landing. You can see most of the island in three to four hours. **Jost Van Dyke** and **Anegada** also offer good hiking possibilities.

ANEGADA

Little-known Anegada is the second largest of the British Virgin Islands, a mass of 15 square miles with a maximum elevation only 30 feet above sea level. Not a volcanic upstart like other impetuous land masses we could name, Anegada is a large coral midden that grew gradually

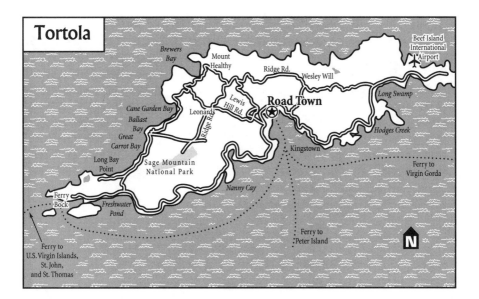

Tortola

Brewers Bay
Mount Healthy
Ridge Rd.
Wesley Will
Beef Island International Airport
Long Swamp
Cane Garden Bay
Leonards
Lewis Hill Rd.
Ridge Rd.
Road Town
Ballast Bay
Great Carrot Bay
Hodges Creek
Long Bay Point
Sage Mountain National Park
Kingstown
Ferry to Virgin Gorda
Nanny Cay
Ferry Dock
Freshwater Pond
Ferry to Peter Island
Ferry to U.S. Virgin Islands, St. John, and St. Thomas
N

from the ocean floor. The north coast offers almost 20 miles of white-sand beaches, one of the longest unbroken beach walks in the Caribbean. But without any shade or water, you need to come to this part of Anegada properly prepared.

TORTOLA

ROAD TOWN AFOOT!

Time: 30 minutes to an hour | **Difficulty:** 1.

If you don't stop to look at sailboats or shop, you can easily walk from one end to the other of Tortola's capital city in less than 30 minutes. To see Road Town at its liveliest (and even at its peak, that's not saying much), avoid a Sunday visit, when all the stores will be locked up tight … unless a cruise ship happens to be in.

1. **The Moorings:** Located at Wickham's Cay 2, this is where you get nautical. The Moorings is the main charter dock of the British Virgin Islands, the place to arrange day sails/boat rentals.

2. **Botanic Gardens:** Located on Main Street several blocks inland from the waterfront, this often overlooked site is one of the prettiest spots on Tortola. It is only four acres, but the botanical display features colorful tropical flowers and herbs, a palm garden, fern house, bamboo and grass exhibits, as well as a pond and waterfall.

3. **Main Street:** *The* shopping street of tiny Road Town, it is located one block off Waterfront Drive. None of the shops are large or fancy, but almost all are interesting. You can

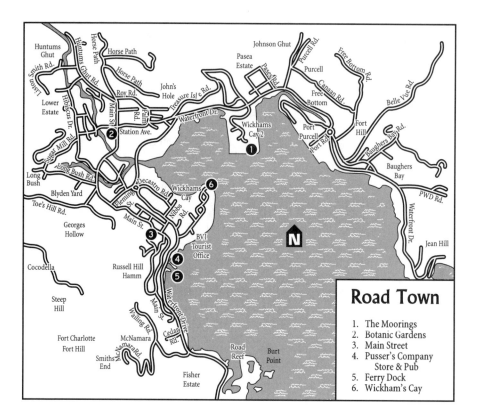

Road Town

1. The Moorings
2. Botanic Gardens
3. Main Street
4. Pusser's Company
   Store & Pub
5. Ferry Dock
6. Wickham's Cay

buy spices, honey, spiced rums, Cuban cigars, model sailboats, and hand-painted fabrics.

4. Pusser's Company Store and Pub: Located on Waterfront Drive, The Company Store is a nautical version of Banana Republic, with a complete and well-done fashion line. Pusser's Rum not only tastes good, it's a good gift. The pub lunches are superb; try the shepherd's pie. This all may seem pretty touristy, but a lot of locals hang out here.

5. Ferry Dock: For the ferryboats to Virgin Gorda or the U.S. Virgin Islands. Located diagonally across from Pusser's.

6. Wickham's Cay: This is the original Wickham's Cay, site of many of the best restaurants and shops.

SAGE MOUNTAIN NATIONAL PARK

It's not often you can hike an entire national park in a leisurely two hours, but that is part of the charm of the 92-acre Sage Mountain National Park on Tortola. Consisting of three short trails, the park has relatively few visitors, even though it offers one of the most scenic views in

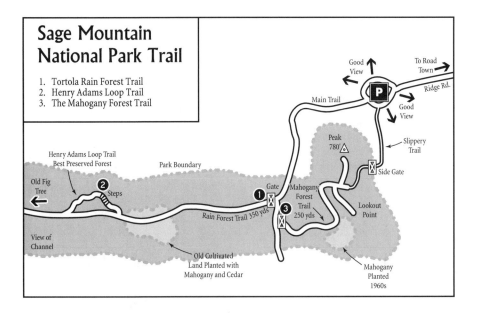

Sage Mountain National Park Trail

1. Tortola Rain Forest Trail
2. Henry Adams Loop Trail
3. The Mahogany Forest Trail

Good View

To Road Town

Main Trail

Ridge Rd.

Good View

Peak 780'

Slippery Trail

Henry Adams Loop Trail
Best Preserved Forest

Park Boundary

Side Gate

Old Fig Tree

Steps

Gate

Mahogany Forest Trail

Rain Forest Trail 350 yds

250 yds

Lookout Point

View of Channel

Old Cultivated Land Planted with Mahogany and Cedar

Mahogany Planted 1960s

---

all the islands. The park area was donated to the British Virgin Island government in the 1960s by Laurance Rockefeller. A concerted effort has been made to reforest the area. No signs point the way to Sage Mountain from Road Town, but the park is easy to find. From Road Town, drive up Joe's Hill Road to the top of the hill, turn right, and keep climbing until the next intersection. A sign points left to Sage Mountain. Turn left and follow the road to its end. Part of the road is quite steep and unpaved, a challenge in rainy weather, but don't give up. You'll know you've arrived when you see a small dirt parking lot on the right and the magnificent view of Jost Van Dyke in the distance.

A single path leads to all three Sage Mountain Park trails, which interconnect. The access trail is gravel-covered and at first skirts the edge of Sage Mountain. At 1,780 feet, this is the highest point in either the British or U.S. Virgin Islands.

At the outset, don't concentrate entirely on the panoramic view of Jost Van Dyke. Bovine droppings lumped among the gravel call for vigilance. That hazard is left behind at the swinging wooden gate leading into the longest path, the Rain Forest Trail, and the short side excursion, the Henry Adams Loop Trail. The gate is kept latched (but not locked) to keep the poop off the loop. It's 10–15 minutes from the parking lot to this first gate.

1. Tortola Rain Forest Trail

Length: About 0.75 miles. | **Time:** 20 minutes, one way. | **Difficulty:** 1. | **Trailhead:** Sage Mountain parking lot.

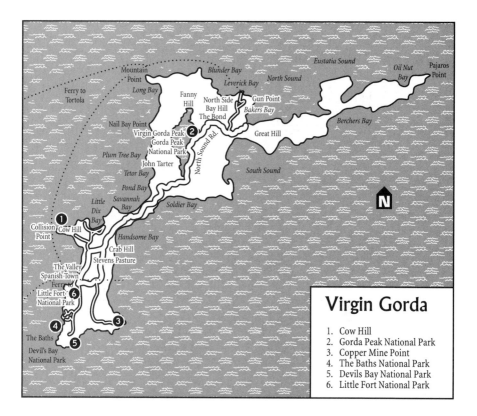

Virgin Gorda

1. Cow Hill
2. Gorda Peak National Park
3. Copper Mine Point
4. The Baths National Park
5. Devils Bay National Park
6. Little Fort National Park

The entire trail is graveled and easy to walk. It alternates between thick, lush foliage and open spaces where the trees are more stunted. Signs identify the wide variety of native trees in this area where some replanting has been done.

Most notable of all the rain forest trees is the white cedar, the national tree of the British Virgin Islands. The trail is also thick with mountain guava, which is quite colorful when blooming. Rose apple and redwood myrtle, Spanish oak, and West Indian mahogany all border the route. Big elephant ear plants are prolific. One of the more unusual trees is called the "stinking fish."

At one point you'll encounter two small, unmarked paths. They lead to a toilet facility off to the right. There's also a marked side path that leads up to a look-out/rain shelter, its purpose depending on whether this rain forest is living up to its name.

After passing the shelter, the trail descends and the forest grows quite thick. This is the first time you're likely to hear birds. Mountain dove, Caribbean martin, pearl-eyed thresher, and American kestrel all live in the forest, but it's not always easy to spot them.

The trail officially ends at a large fig tree, although a pathway continues to the right. The brush thickens quickly and several logs across the path hint that you've run out of trail and that it's time to turn back.

2. HENRY ADAMS LOOP TRAIL

Time: 1-2 hours. | **Difficulty:** 1. | **Trailhead:** Tortola Rain Forest Trail.

The loop trail displays the best-preserved part of the forest. This short, marked trail is a steep hike to the top and could be slippery. The massive bulletwood tree grows here, reaching a height of 100 feet and a girth of 4 feet. Bromeliads and ferns grow in profusion. This loop returns to the main Rain Forest Trail a few yards from where it cuts off.

3. THE MAHOGANY FOREST TRAIL

Time: 30 minutes from the entry gate back to the parking lot. | **Difficulty:** 2. | **Trailhead:** Atop Sage Mountain.

When you return to the main gate after hiking the Rain Forest Trail, turn right to the clearly visible Mahogany Forest Trail sign. The trail begins behind another cow-blocking gate. Because the path is not graveled, it's slick during heavy rain. It does not contain tree/plant identification signs, but red-arrowed signs prevent most wrong turns.

This trail leads to the highest point in any of the Virgin Islands, so it's steady climbing for the first ten minutes through the former plantation grounds where mahogany and white cedar were planted in the 1960s. In many sections, the ground is dense with a layer of ferns, though the forest alternates between thick and sparse growth. A side trail off to the right leads to a viewing point at 1,710 feet.

Returning to the main path, take the exit sign to the right, which leads to a barbed-wire fence and gate. On the other side, turn left and proceed down the rocky trail to the parking lot. This path, which can be slippery when wet, goes across open land and past a cluster of tree ferns, something unusual in the British Virgin Islands.

VIRGIN GORDA

This very mountainous island—called the "fat virgin" by Christopher Columbus because of the bulge in her middle—is far less developed than Tortola. Reach it by ferry from Road Town, going over early in the morning and returning the same afternoon. The ferry docks near the Virgin Gorda Yacht Harbour in Spanish Town, also called The Valley. The easiest way to get around spread-out Virgin Gorda is by taxi. The drivers will either wait while you climb or come back at an appointed time. The drivers at Mahogany Car Rental are very tolerant of hikers and their quirks.

1. Cow Hill

Time: 30 minutes, one way. | **Difficulty:** 2. | **Trailhead:** Parking lot of the Little Dix Bay Resort.

This triangular-shaped mountain with the rounded top is just to the left of the ferry dock, the most prominent feature on the horizon. The marked trail up Cow Hill begins at the parking lot of the Little Dix Bay Resort. It is a steady but not especially difficult climb all the way to the top. This is usually an open, hot hike, so it's best done early in the morning or late in the afternoon. In the dry season, the cactus scrub and dry woodland on the hillside can look almost dead. These drought-resistant plants are alive, though they will sometimes lose their leaves and become dormant during dry spells. On a clear day, the summit offers a spectacular view of nearby islands.

2. GORDA PEAK NATIONAL PARK

Length: 800 yards for the shorter trail; about 1,600 yards for the second. | **Time:** The main trail—20 minutes, one-way to the summit; the longer route—35 minutes. | **Difficulty:** 2. | **Trailhead:** Located off North Sound Road, about four miles from the ferry dock.

Technically, everything above the 1,000-foot level is national park on Virgin Gorda, an area totaling 265 acres. The park was established in 1974 to protect both the tropical forest and the watershed.

The main trail to the 1,359-foot summit is prominently marked with a sign on the left side of the road. Stone steps begin the hike but quickly give way to dirt, rocks, and tree roots. Be alert: The summit trail makes a sharp right just a few yards from the road, splitting from another pathway that goes straight ahead. Red paint on the stones and trees blaze an easy trail.

It's a leisurely 15-minute walk through the grove of small cedars before reaching the level clearing with three picnic tables and a portable potty. It's another eight to ten minutes to the large wooden observation tower, painted gray to blend in with the granite boulders at the summit. The trees obstruct the view to the east toward Great Hill and Grassy Ground. You can actually see better from the North Sound Road. Looking north, Fanny Hill lies below the national park, but it's hard to spy her rump for all the thick bush.

Returning to the picnic area, you can retrace your steps or take a clearly defined but unmarked trail, which begins a 25-minute walk to a grassy carpark a considerable distance below the beginning of the summit trail on North Sound Road. The trail ascends for the first few minutes, reaching a large, red, lichen-covered granite boulder worthy of close inspection. In fact, the huge stones along this particular route are the most interesting sights. They tend to be lichen- or moss-covered or have fig roots wrapped around them from the trees growing high above.

You may hear rustling sounds in the leaves along the path—perhaps one of the many lizards and geckos found here, but more likely a large hermit crab, which often position themselves right in the middle of the trail. Pick one up and look at it. Be careful not to drop it when it suddenly thrusts out its tiny claws to urge you away.

Arrange for a taxi to pick you up at the car park or hike up North Sound Road to reach your rental car back at the summit trailhead.

3. COPPER MINE POINT

Time: 10–30 minutes. | **Difficulty:** 1–2, depending on route | **Trailhead:** About two miles south of the Yacht Harbour at the stone ruins of a copper mining operation.

The copper mine was first worked by the Carib Indians. They mined extracted copper for trade, which was alloyed with gold to make the gold more durable.

The Spanish came by way of Puerto Rico after 1528 to mine for gold here, but found only copper. The mine was unused until the 1850s, when tin miners from Cornwall, England, worked the mine. A 160-foot-deep shaft runs under the ruins, which are fenced to keep visitors a safe distance away. It's still possible to get a good look at the block building and stone smokestack.

Below the copper mine, the Atlantic waves make a powerful display as they crash onto the point, surge high, then wash back down the gray-colored promontory. You can climb down the hill for a closer look, or simply take telephoto pictures from the top. But if you want to feel the raw power of the Atlantic, make the descent.

4. THE BATHS NATIONAL PARK

Length: 300 yards. | **Time:** 8 minutes, one way. | **Difficulty:** 1. | **Trailhead:** Take the main road south to the parking area overlooking The Baths. The road also crosses the Spring Bay Trail, which offers a short descent to a beach far less spectacular than The Baths.

This boulder-strewn beach is the most famous landmark in the British Virgins and one of the Caribbean's most renowned. The Baths take their name from the massive round granite boulders that form caves, pools, and grottoes. There is nothing else like this huge boulder pile anywhere in the Caribbean or in this hemisphere. It was formed during the creation of the islands 70 to 100 million years ago, when volcanoes thrust up from the seabed. It's been an up-and-down existence for the islands ever since. Today, all we see are peaks of a drowned mountain range that were once connected by land to Puerto Rico and the nearby U.S. Virgin Islands. They became isolated after the last Ice Age ended about 15,000 years ago, and melting glaciers raised sea level another 200 to 400 feet.

Geologists say the granite boulders are the product of molten rock that seeped up into the existing volcanic rock but never reached the surface. Instead, the molten rock cooled slowly, thus forming a hard, crystalline rock layer. Eventually, the softer volcanic covering eroded, exposing the granite blocks. Weathering rounded the gigantic stones into the huge pebbles we see today.

At times The Baths are overrun with people because it is a popular playground for hikers and swimmers. Early in the morning—before the day sails from Tortola make anchor—is the least crowded time. That's also the best time for shore photography; in the afternoon, the best place to shoot is from a boat.

A narrow passageway leads to the heart of The Baths, a stone-canopied pool almost perpetually shaded, which rises and falls with the tide.

5. DEVIL'S BAY NATIONAL PARK

Length: 600 yards from the road. | **Time:** 15 minutes, one way. | **Difficulty:** 1. | **Trailhead:** The trail is to the left of the pathway leading to The Baths. It might be a good idea to walk this one first, so you can get a cold drink later at The Baths' oceanside restaurant/bar.

This open, ever-descending trail leads to a secluded coral sand beach that sees far fewer people than its more famous neighbor, The Baths. The topography is also remarkably different. The open trail passes some of the same granite boulders, then goes through an enormous cactus garden. Organpipe cactus grow to 22 feet. Barrel cactus with flowering red tops, and jumping cactus (named because the ground stems break off into segments carried off by people and animals) are everywhere. Ground doves, crested hummingbirds, and sparrow hawks (locally called killi-killi) may also be seen, along with small harmless ground snakes, geckos, and lizards.

6. LITTLE FORT NATIONAL PARK

Time: 20 minutes. | **Difficulty:** 1. | **Trailhead:** On main road south of Spanish Town.

Mentioned on all the maps, the old trails are mostly overgrown. If you proceed carefully over the boulders, you should find the remains of an old fort. Not really worth it, compared to other sites, but since the maps mention it, so should we.

BIRAS CREEK TRAILS

Time: 1 hour. | **Difficulty:** 2. | **Trailhead:** Located in the Biras Creek Hotel Resort on North Sound. These trails can only be reached by boat. If you're not a guest, getting permission from the resort first is a fine idea.

The trails go through scrub that gradually grows thicker as you ascend. It is mostly steady climbing and constant sun, so take water. All the while you have an excellent view of North Sound, one of the finest boat anchorages in the British Virgin Islands. From the top, on the Atlantic side, search for land. If you see anything, you have darn good eyesight. The nearest landfall is Africa.

6   Cayman Islands

Old Caribbean Proverb: Don't drive fleas from another man's cow.
Translation: Don't interfere with other peoples' business.

Grand Cayman, Little Cayman, and Cayman Brac form the tiny Cayman Islands chain, located 480 miles south of Miami and just west of Cuba. In terms of size, they are little more than specks in the ocean. All three islands are actually the jutting peaks of a huge undersea mountain. Not surprisingly, all three are very popular diving destinations.

The largest and most commercially developed is Grand Cayman, which houses about 94 percent of the Cayman population. It also has one of the Caribbean's best self-guided town walking tours, beautiful Seven-Mile Beach, plus a few rather unusual attractions—watching marine turtles breed or literally going to Hell, at a small patch of bizarrely shaped rock. It also has the Mastic Trail, a genuine hike in the woods, and an extensive botanical garden that takes at least half a day to explore.

Grand Cayman is one of the most prosperous islands in the Caribbean. A melting pot of British colonists, Canadians, Americans, and Caribbean islanders, it is ranked as one of the world's three major international banking centers, on a par with Switzerland and Liechtenstein. It has a staggering total of more than 500 registered banks and 300 insurance companies. But they are discreetly hidden; they don't stick out on every corner like 7-Elevens.

What is very obvious is the wealth these financial institutions have brought to the island. Like many places, Grand Cayman has been experiencing a condominium boom. Shopping malls are popping up all over, and the island now boasts more restaurants per capita than any other Caribbean island. George Town, Cayman's main city and the country's capital, is a clean, pleasant community that many find reminiscent of Florida's Sanibel Island.

For many years, scuba divers were the only tourists. The diving is so good that Grand Cayman is often called the "Superbowl" of scuba.

Grand Cayman's biggest celebration occurs every October during Pirate's Week, a festival recalling buccaneer days. Locals dress in festive pirate costumes (tourists are encouraged to do so as well) and, in general, everyone tries to see how much grog they can drink.

Little Cayman is at the opposite extreme. With fewer than 50 permanent residents, Little Cayman is like Grand Cayman was many decades ago. Little Cayman's airport is still nothing but a grass airstrip, and only a handful of guesthouses and small hotels have been built to provide visitor accommodations.

Little Cayman's nearby neighbor of Cayman Brac is in a transitional stage between Grand and Little Cayman. Still mostly rural, tourist development so far has been limited to several small hotels and condos on one tip, which are often filled with anglers, divers, and nature lovers ready to explore the largely unspoiled island.

Considering the diversity of the three islands, it's unfortunate that most visitors never get beyond Grand Cayman to Little Cayman or the Brac (as Cayman Brac is called). But it's also quite understandable, too, because Grand Cayman has the best airline connections, the biggest hotels, and the best beaches.

Regardless of the island you visit, you'll find the Cayman locals to be genuinely likable people who also like us. That makes it especially easy to relax and see the sights.

TRAVEL TIPS

Area: Grand Cayman, located 180 miles northwest of Jamaica and 480 miles south of Miami, is 22 miles long, 4 miles wide. Cayman Brac, situated 89 miles northeast of Grand Cayman, is 12 miles long and slightly more than 1 mile wide. Little Cayman, 5 miles west of Cayman Brac, is 10 miles long and just over 1 mile wide.

Language: English, the queen's kind, spoken better than by many Americans.

Population: 32,000, 94% of which reside on Grand Cayman.

Time Zone: Eastern Standard Time all year long.

Rainy Season: June through November

Getting There: About 1.5 million people (mostly Americans) visit annually, and almost 75% arrive by cruise ship and spend only a single day on the island. Direct flights are available from Canada, England, Cuba, and Jamaica as well as the United States, and fly into Owen Roberts International Airport (just east of George Town) on Grand Cayman. There are more than 100 commercial flights a week into the islands, about 70% coming from Miami. American, Delta, USAirways, Northwest, and British Airways are the major carriers into Grand Cayman. The neighboring island of Cayman Brac is served only by Cayman Airways and Island Air, (345) 949-5152; and Little Cayman by Island Air only.

Documents: A birth certificate or voter's registration card and photo ID will suffice for U.S. and Canadian citizens. All others require passports.

Getting Around: Motor scooters are popular and rental cars are easily available, and several companies offer island tours via motorcoach. Driving is on the left.

Where to Stay: Grand Cayman can be a very expensive island and has sometimes been referred to by shocked tourists as "Grand-a-Day Cayman." However, the hotels are some of the Caribbean's most varied. They can be broken down into three main categories:

Luxury Hotels: These include the Hyatt Regency Grand Cayman ($200–550 per double, daily), Westin Casuarina Resort ($200–500 per double, daily), the Marriott ($170–500 per double, daily), and Indies Suites ($180–350 per suite, daily). In mid-2002, the Ritz-Carlton is scheduled to open on Seven Mile Beach.

Condominiums and Villas: This is a popular family choice because the kitchen facilities can save considerable money. These are also a favorite for people who want privacy

Welcome to Hell, a large and oddly-shaped rock formation

and don't like having to go out for every meal. There is a wide choice to select from, both on and off the beach, and in all price ranges. Check out www.caymanislands.ky for descriptions and contact information.

Inexpensive Hotels/Guest Houses: These are among the least expensive choices, realizing that nothing in Grand Cayman is truly cheap. A good choice is the 121-room Sleep Inn (phone (345) 949-9111), not far from Seven Mile Beach.

Camping: Not permitted anywhere.

Currency: The Caymans have their own dollar (CI), but everyone takes U.S. currency. The U.S. dollar is worth only 80 cents CI. That exchange rate is another factor making the Caymans so expensive.

Taxes & Tips: Government room tax of 10% and a 10–15% service charge is usually added automatically to all bills. There's also a departure tax of $12.50.

Electrical Current: Even though this is a former British colony, most of the buildings are of such recent vintage that they have standard 110 volt, 60 cycle.

Safety/Health Warnings: Because so much of the area is lowland and not far from mangroves, carry insect repellent any time you're in the bush. Beware the maidenplum, a bush that resembles the North American sumac. It can cause painful skin blisters if the sap touches your skin.

Snakes & Other Venomous Creatures: None.

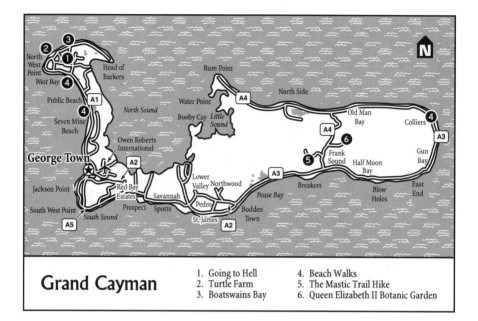

Grand Cayman

1. Going to Hell
2. Turtle Farm
3. Boatswains Bay
4. Beach Walks
5. The Mastic Trail Hike
6. Queen Elizabeth II Botanic Garden

Hiking/Walking Services: The National Trust for the Cayman Islands will provide a guide for the Mastic Trail, which the trust owns. Trail reservations are made at (345) 949-1996; email ntrust@candw.ky. You can hike this trail without a guide because it is open to the public during daylight. Elsewhere, you're on your own, but it's easy to find your way around on any of the islands.

Additional Information: There is an anti-litter ordinance with a possible fine of up to CI$500 for the slightest offense on either public or private property. For more information contact the Cayman Islands Department of Tourism, 6100 Blue Lagoon Drive, Suite 150, Miami, FL 33126; phone (305) 266-2300. In Canada, Travel Marketing Consultants, 234 Eglinton Avenue East, Suite 306, Toronto, Ontario M4P IK5; (416) 485-1550. In the United Kingdom, Cayman Islands, 100 Brompton Road, London SW3 1EX; (071) 581-9418 or fax (071) 581-9960; www.caymanislands.ky.

GRAND CAYMAN

GEORGE TOWN AFOOT!

Length: 1 mile. | **Time:** About 1.5 hours. | **Difficulty:** 1. | **Trailhead:** Park in the small paved lot left of the Atlantis submarine office, located on the waterfront in the center of town. Start walking to the right, toward the cruise dock.

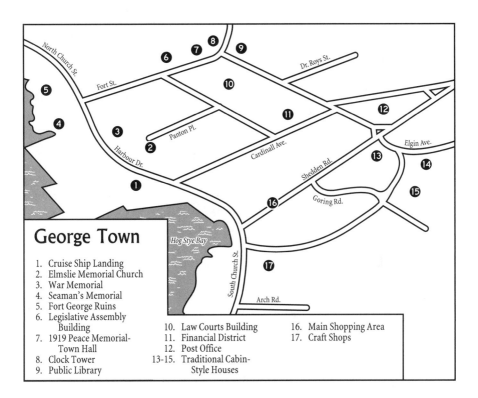

George Town

1. Cruise Ship Landing
2. Elmslie Memorial Church
3. War Memorial
4. Seaman's Memorial
5. Fort George Ruins
6. Legislative Assembly
    Building
7. 1919 Peace Memorial-
    Town Hall
8. Clock Tower
9. Public Library
10. Law Courts Building
11. Financial District
12. Post Office
13-15. Traditional Cabin-
    Style Houses
16. Main Shopping Area
17. Craft Shops

Grand Cayman's original capital was not George Town but a place called Bodden Town. At the time, George Town was known as The Hogstyes, apparently a reference not to the citizenry but to edible animals kept penned at the site. Cruise ships land at what is still called Hogstye Bay.

1. Cruise Ship Landing: Where tenders usually unload cruise ship passengers.

2. Elmslie Memorial Church: Located across the street and to the left of the cruise ship landing, this church was named for the first Presbyterian missionary to serve in Cayman; the church was constructed between 1920 and 1922 but is on the site of a church built in 1846. Until modern times, the tolling of the church bell signified a death on the island. The old grave markers, moved from one side to allow building of the carpark, date back to the 1800s.

    The church was the first concrete structure ever made in Cayman. The builder, a Captain Rayal, was obviously more familiar with building ships than churches. He bought the molds to make the concrete blocks, but no one on the island knew how to mix the concrete properly. He wrote to the Portland Cement Company for instructions, then went to Jamaica to learn how to work with cement. The church's timber ceiling, largely salvaged from a shipwreck, is said to be Rayal's unique signature: timbers that resemble the upturned hulls of the schooners he built.

The pews were fashioned by another shipbuilder who had the mahogany imported from Belize. They cost £5 English pounds each, and members were asked to pay for them. Parishioners did, thereby obtaining informal family pews.

3. **War Memorial:** Located in the churchyard, this is a memorial to Caymanian sailors lost at sea in World War II. Although not subject to conscription, about 200 Caymanians served in the British Merchant Navy, and hundreds more served in the Royal Navy to defend Britain itself. In World War II, 800 Caymanians joined the Trinidad Royal Navy Volunteer Reserve; roll call must have been confusing because 40 of these volunteers were named Ebanks, one of the island's most prolific families.

4. **Seaman's Memorial:** The names of the 153 Caymanians known to have been lost at sea are inscribed on tablets around the base of the George Town Harbour navigation light, which is powered by solar cells. The beacon's eternal message, as stated at the dedication, is "Come home safely, as we would have liked you to do."

5. **Fort George Ruins:** A fort built around 1790 by islanders to defend against Spanish attack from neighboring Cuba, it commanded control of the harbor entrance. It seems to have had nothing but bad luck. Never known to have actually seen battle, one local tale about the fort says that invaders landed and the Caymanians discovered to their horror they were out of cannon balls. They loaded the cannon with nails and fired, which caused the invaders to flee.

Ignominious in battle, the fort was demolished in 1972 following a small war between the Port Authority and a developer who used a backhoe to push down the walls. A few outraged residents placed themselves against the remaining walls and heavy equipment. The fort was deeded to the protection of the National Trust in 1987.

Subsequent archaeological digs revealed that treasure hunters had already excavated to at least seven feet below the road level. The site was so disturbed it was impossible even to find the foundations on the southern side. The outline today is based on old drawings and photographs. The oval-shaped fort was made of coral rock four and a half feet high. Wall thickness varied from five feet on the seaside to two feet landward.

6. **Legislative Assembly Building:** Looking like a misplaced Mayan pyramid, the design was the first-place winner of an international architectural competition. The controversial structure, built between 1971 and 1972, was the first poured-concrete building in the Caymans. Even 50 years after Elmslie Memorial was built, the locals hadn't quite gotten the hang of how to mix concrete, so it had to be poured pail by pail in a bucket brigade. It is fitting that the cornerstone was laid in 1971 by the same Captain Rayal who traveled to Jamaica in the early 1920s to study the marvel of concrete blocks so he could build Elmslie Memorial Church.

When the assembly is in session, visitors (no bathing suits) are allowed in the Visitors' Gallery to watch the proceedings. The first floor is decorated with old photos of George Town.

7. **1919 Peace Memorial–Town Hall:** Located next to the assembly building, the town hall was Captain Rayal's second civic structure, built in 1923, immediately after Elmslie Church. For many years this was the hub of Caymanian life because the building served also as the Court House and Assembly Room as well as the Town Hall. That the 1919 memorial commemorating World War I was called a Peace Memorial instead of a War Memorial discloses a key aspect of the Caymanian nature.

8. Clock Tower: Built in 1937 for a princely sum of £140, it commemorates the reign of King George V, grandfather of Queen Elizabeth II.

9. Public Library: More of Captain Rayal's handiwork, the library dates from 1939. The distinctive ceiling is decorated with the shields of Britain's most distinguished places of higher learning. The area behind the library was a U.S. Navy base in World War II.

10. Law Courts Building: Built and designed by the same individual who built the Mayan-looking Legislative Assembly Building. Wigged barristers still argue before elaborately robed judges, as in England. Tourists are permitted to observe from the back of the courtrooms, located on the second floor.

11. Financial District: Edward Street, once a residential section, is an important part of the Cayman financial district. Look at the listings at the building entrances and you'll see that scores of banks from around the world are registered here.

12. Post Office: Considered Captain Rayal's second-best edifice after the Elmslie Church. Built in 1939, its original wooden doors follow the curved building facade. The vaulted ceiling may be Rayal's best timber work of all.

Stamp collectors will want to pay special attention to the post office. Grand Cayman has long been known as a philatelist's center because of the island's beautiful and exotic stamps. The Philatelic Bureau usually has many on hand as First Day Covers.

13–15. Traditional Cabin-Style Houses: These were fashioned from woven strips of wood that were spread with a lime plaster made by burning coral rocks in a kiln. The houses are on raised posts known as ironwood because of its hardness and longevity; ironwood posts are good for at least a century. The kitchen or "cook rooms" are separated from the houses not only to avoid the heat but also because the cooking was done in a wooden box filled with sand. The boxes occasionally caught fire—better to lose the kitchen than the whole house.

16. Main Shopping Area: Most of the larger clothing, perfume and jewelry stores are located here. Besides black coral torn from the coral reefs (a destructive practice to the living reefs), the jewelry stores specialize in a mineral known as caymanite. It is a stone comprised of different metals and fossils created millions of years ago. It is found only in the Cayman Islands, and so far scientists cannot explain its uniqueness. Caymanite is made into rings, pendants, and sculptures.

17. Craft Shops: Several small shops here are known for their handicrafts, including black coral jewelry.

ELSEWHERE ON GRAND CAYMAN

1. GOING TO HELL

Time: 15–20 minutes. | **Difficulty:** 1, as long as you don't try walking on the rocks. | **Trailhead:** From George Town, go north on main highway to town of Hell.

Hell is a small formation of jagged ironshore some say resembles the fires of hell (although how they know that has not been determined). Ironshore, which looks very much like volcanic rock, is limestone estimated to be 1.5 million years old. Initially a white color, the black surface is a coating of algae that secretes acid and creates the unusual shapes.

Hell even has its own post office for sending home postcards with the Hell postmark. A gift shops sells T-shirts with the name. This patch of ironshore is probably notable only because it's located away from the water. Ironshore is found all along the coastline south of George Town.

2. Turtle Farm

Time: 30–45 minutes. | **Difficulty:** 1. | **Trailhead:** From George Town, go north on main highway.

Like a freak show at the fair, there is something irresistible and voyeuristic about watching turtles mate at the Cayman Turtle Farm, the world's only farm devoted to raising endangered green turtles.

Several thousand marine turtles, ranging from newborns to mature adults, live at the Turtle Farm, which furnishes all of the island's fresh turtle steaks. The farm shows how the turtles are reared and bred. Turtling was an important livelihood for islanders for many years; a peg-legged turtle is even the island's symbol. Although the Turtle Farm releases many thousands of creatures in the wild each year, none of its products can be imported into the United States due to a ban on turtle products. Several thousand mature greens never make it beyond the restaurant kitchens, appearing as turtle burgers and turtle steak on menus. Don't hesitate to try them because on Grand Cayman the turtles were pen-raised for this purpose. It does not deplete the species.

3. Boatswains Bay

Length: 1 mile, one-way. | **Time:** 45–60 minutes. | **Difficulty:** 1. | **Trailhead:** From George Town, go north on the main highway just beyond the Turtle Farm to Boatswains Bay Road. Park wherever you can.

This mile-long coastal walk will take you past an old cemetery and old school house. The rocky ironshore extends to Spanish Bay Road and provides dramatic views of big waves rolling in during winter storms. In this section, there is no offshore reef to blunt the powerful waves before they reach shore.

4. Beach Walks (Grand Cayman)

Time: 3–4 hours to circuit Seven Mile Beach, 45–60 minutes for most of the others. | **Difficulty:** 1. | **Trailhead:** Various locations along the main coastal highway.

Grand Cayman's finest land feature is the beautiful strip of sand called Seven Mile Beach, which is actually 5.5 miles long. That exaggeration could have come from one of the early real estate developers, as Seven Mile Beach clearly is hotel row.

Seven Mile Beach is Grand Cayman's main water sports center with lots of sailboats and jet skis. Thankfully, it is one of the few people-packed Caribbean beaches where peddlers are rare. Sunbathers are allowed to doze, readers are permitted to read, and people-watchers are allowed to stare without any confrontations with bead and coral salesmen.

Less crowded but equally fine is West Bay Beach, just a bit north of Seven Mile Beach. For something a little more adventurous, go to the eastern end of the island. The area between Tortuga Club and Spotter's Bay is virtually undeveloped, a walk that includes both beaches and ironshore.

5. THE MASTIC TRAIL HIKE

Length: 2 miles. | **Time:** 2–3 hours. | **Difficulty:** 2. | **Trailhead:** This is the most difficult part because the turnoffs are not well marked. Take the shore road toward East End. Before arriving at East End, turn left onto Frank Sound Road, which leads to the North Side. The remains of a fishing boat mark the left turn. You'll soon pass a fire station with a tall radio mast located on the left. A little farther—and also on the left—is the Mastic Road, a dirt road that looks like it leads to a farm. Take the road for about three-quarters of a mile to the parking lot of the southern trailhead, on the right.

The two-mile Mastic Trail penetrates the heart of Grand Cayman's most pristine, interior woodlands. This nature walk is named after the mastic tree, a prized hardwood that has almost vanished. However, a splendid example of this impressive tree is located about mid-way along the trail in one of the densest, least disturbed forest sections. It's a rare glimpse of Cayman the way it used to be.

The Mastic Trail offers a walk through a Grand Cayman that no one living today has ever seen. Back when Francis Drake's fleet of ships sailed through the Cayman Islands in 1586, the Caymans were still densely forested with mahogany, West Indian cedar, and other giant hardwoods. "So full of woods as it can grow," reads one of the ship's logs, a remarkable description considering how treeless the islands are today.

On Grand Cayman, all of the woodlands were removed from the island's western half by the beginning of the twentieth century. Settlers scalped the landscape to build homes and ships, then sold the excess lumber for export.

Fortunately, Grand Cayman's eastern half proved more difficult to clear. There, it was necessary to drag out a tree for a mile or more over a sharp limestone and dolomite terrain putting even the craggy spires of Hell to shame. The logging that did occur was done on a more selective basis. Ironically, it is a centuries-old logging path that has now become a part of the Mastic Trail.

The Mastic area, also called the Mountain, covers about 1,000 acres. It is the largest contiguous area of old-growth woodland in the Caymans and one of the few remaining tracts of dry, tropical, low-elevation woodlands in the Caribbean. To date, the Cayman National Trust has been able to purchase and protect about 260 acres of the Mastic region; it hopes to acquire the rest.

The Mastic Trail is well laid out and easy to follow in most places. Besides hardwood forest, the trek also highlights thick mangrove swamp, agricultural land, and, depending on the time of year, the opportunity to see both Cayman and Cuban parrots, West Indian woodpeckers, the Caribbean dove (which is seen only in undisturbed areas), butterflies, frogs, and lizards.

Because the trail is open to the public during daylight hours, you can make the walk on your own. Carry water bottles because this can be a hot walk, especially in afternoon. (It's also sometimes wet; Cayman's wettest period is June through November.) However, the best way to appreciate the hike is on a guided walk. Guided walks are conducted at 8 a.m. and 3 p.m. daily except Sunday. Reservations must be made in advance through the National Trust for the Cayman Islands; Call Monday through Friday between 10 a.m. and 3 p.m.; (345) 949-1996; email ntrust@candw.ky. The fee is US$30.

During my walk, I went with National Trust guide Albert Hines and learned facts I would have been unaware of had I gone alone. For instance, I'd never heard of the "duppy bush" until Albert showed one to me. The shrub and its small green leaves didn't seem very noteworthy, but I knew that "duppy" was the Caymanian term for "ghost." So what was a duppy bush? A place where ghosts hung out together after dark?

"No," Albert laughed. "It's named that because it glows in the dark when there's a full moon."

If the duppy bush isn't unusual enough, Albert described a section of the hike where all the trees are rooted in a fine, red soil called "red mold." This mold, Albert explained, is not a red clay but a complex chemical mixture dominated by iron and aluminum oxides. Scientists determined that the soil had been created by a fine dust blown across the Atlantic from the Sahara Desert of Africa; just another of many informative tidbits I learned because Albert was there to explain.

Albert and I began our hike shortly after 8 a.m. An illustrated sign at the trailhead noted the major landmarks we would pass. Initially, the trail passed over open, flat land that's still being grazed by cattle. After a few minutes, we entered a dense swamp of black mangroves where the water was at least knee-deep in places.

The old Mastic Bridge provided us a high, dry footpath through the swamp. Like the original bridge built over a century ago, this version uses mahogany logs anchored in a fixed pathway by large rocks. Coral rubble brought from the beach was placed on top of the slippery logs for better footing. Today, the beginning of the bridge is re-created with some of the original mahogany logs.

The black mangroves in the Mastic swamp reminded me of South Florida, where the same unmistakable fingerlike pneumatophores (which are solid wood) protrude above the water and, like straws, transport air down to the roots. The leaves on several of the mangroves look like they'd been doused by a salt shaker: black mangroves eliminate the excess salt they absorb from the water through their leaves, which is how they're able to survive in such an inhospitable environment.

Leaving the swamp, we entered a drier woodland containing mahogany, bitter plum, and huge royal palms. Royal palms in remote locations are one of the best places for spotting woodpeckers, which like to drill holes and build their nests in old royal palms. Cayman parrots also favor the older palms and nest at their very top, in the hollow created after the crown of a tree rots off.

Albert told me an estimated 1,600 Cayman parrots are found on the island—a lot more than I would have guessed—but that nest-robbing sometimes is still a problem. A number of royal palms here have been cut down by nest-robbers, so Albert is always on patrol during the height of the parrot nesting season in May and June.

I didn't see or hear a woodpecker anywhere on the walk, but I did spot several parrots and heard others squawking in the distance. "To see lots of birds, you must start early," Albert advised. "I begin the special walks for birders at 6 a.m."

Beyond the royal palm hammock the trail enters an orchard of wild mangoes and tamarinds. No fruit was in season, but Albert reassured me I wasn't missing anything. Wild mangoes tend to be stringier than the ones I'd buy in a market, though the wonderfully delicious taste is often the same.

After we passed the fruit trees and another stand of royal palms, the trail sloped uphill a few feet as we entered the heart of the Mastic Reserve, where rocks and boulders perform the function of soil and hardwoods actually are rooted in stone. The trees can succeed here only because they can reach the ground water stored in the cracks and fissures of the rocks.

Anyone who has seen Grand Cayman's Hell rock formation would have to admit the attraction is second-rate compared to the incredibly rocky terrain of the ancient Mastic heartland, laid down as an underwater limestone sediment some 11 to 16 million years ago. Over time, the limestone turned into dolomite, a much harder rock.

Geologists say this particular rocky section has remained above sea level for at least the last 2 million years, and over that period some 100 species of trees and 550 species of plants have evolved. They grew by chance, the seeds carried here by wind, birds, and ocean.

In addition to rocks, this section is the richest place in all the islands for both plants and animals. The most obvious animals are the legions of hermit crabs that continually scuttle and crawl on the ground and up the rocks. Because many of the crab shells grow the same green lichen that thrives on the rocks, they look like a large moving army of pebbles. If a crab doesn't move, it blends perfectly into the rocky landscape.

It's also in this heartland that the huge mastic tree thrives, on the right-hand side of the trail, impossible to miss. The tree is so thick that four or five people are needed to join hands around its girth. I can't picture what the Caymans must have been like when they were forested by hundreds or thousands of such trees.

The thick forest canopy created by this single huge mastic and other tall trees is so dense that my sunlit morning seemed more like twilight. I used a flash to take any pictures. I never expected to see so much shade on sunny Grand Cayman, but it's just another of the many surprises along the Mastic Trail.

6. QUEEN ELIZABETH II BOTANIC GARDEN

Length: There is a 1-mile walking trail through a 40-acre woodland preserve. | **Time:** 3–6 hours. | **Difficulty:** 1. | **Trailhead:** Take the road to the East End. After the Breakers village, turn left onto Frank Sound Road, which leads to the North Side. This turnoff is beyond Bodden Town and marked with the remains of an old fishing boat; this is the same turnoff that leads to the Mastic Trail. The botanic park will be on your right after a couple of miles. | **Hours:** Daily from 9 a.m. to 6:30 p.m. with the last admittance at 5:30 p.m. Admission fee required.

This 65-acre botanic garden is probably the Caribbean's best planned and most comprehensive park. Expect a leisurely half-day to fully explore its various sections. During the rainy season (June through November) large sections may be flooded by as much as four feet of water. For information, call (345) 947-9462.

It's estimated that 40 percent of the island's native flora grows in this preserve: mahogany forest, cactus/agave thickets, native palms, orchids, bromeliads, ferns, and buttonwood. The one-mile Woodland Trail passes most of them. The trail also passes several rare blue iguanas (*Cyclura nubila lewisi*) that are displayed in an open-air pen. There is no screen or wire to interfere with photography. The iguanas often are most visible in early morning.

In addition, the botanic park has a Heritage Garden that features the re-creation of a traditional Cayman homesite with early twentieth-century original furnishings; a 2.5-acre Floral Colour Garden that highlights plants in strikingly different colors, including red, orange, yellow, white, blue, purple, and lavender. A two-acre lake here has become an important nesting site for native birds, including the rare West Indian Whistling Duck.

CAYMAN BRAC

1. BLUFF CLIMB AND LIGHTHOUSE

Length: About 2.5 miles. | **Time:** 2–3 hours. | **Difficulty:** 2–3. | **Trailhead:** On the northeastern end of the island at the village of Spot Bay.

Eighty-nine miles northeast of Grand Cayman and a world away is Cayman Brac, which so far has been spared the traffic and overbuilding that has occurred on Grand Cayman. The word *brac* is Gaelic for bluff, and the one that tops out at 130 feet makes up virtually one end of Cayman Brac.

Until the Mastic Trail opened in 1995, the bluff walk was the most famous hike in all the Caymans, and it's obvious why. The bluff trail at Spot Bay used to follow a rugged farmer's path to the top, but most of this has been replaced by a wood stairway. You'll pass caves and other interesting photo stops on the way. At the top, you'll overlook the village of Spot Bay and have a magnificent view of the Atlantic.

From the end of the ascent path, it's about a two-mile walk to the lighthouse. Take plenty of liquids, as it gets hot up here. Little Cayman Brac is the large rock off the island's northeast tip. This point offers excellent bird-watching, including peregrine falcons and other migratory species. Long-tailed tropic birds nest in the bluff in spring.

2. BLUFF ROAD HIKE

Length: 6.8 miles. | **Time:** 4 hours round-trip. | **Difficulty:** 1–2. | **Trailhead:** Park at the beginning of the Bluff Road, which is reached by driving east and taking the cross road leading to Tibbetts Turn. The Bluff Road is about midway to Tibbetts Turn.

It's also possible to reach the lighthouse by walking east on the straight, flat Bluff Road cutting through the center of the island. The 3.4-mile road is tarmac, easy walking. Along the

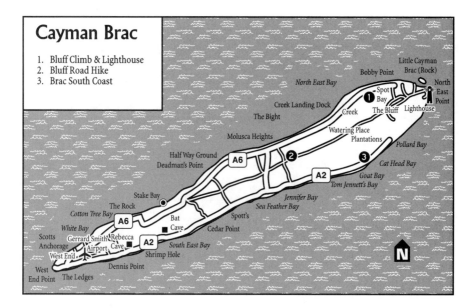

Cayman Brac

1. Bluff Climb & Lighthouse
2. Bluff Road Hike
3. Brac South Coast

way you'll pass a heavily wooded sanctuary for the endangered Cayman parrot, a subspecies of the Cuban parrot. However, you'll have more luck spotting parrots in the fruit trees across from the museum at Stake Bay, particularly in May.

The services of a local guide can be arranged through any of the hotels. It is a wise idea because locals know the parrot nesting areas, often on private land. A very important unwritten rule in the Caymans is never leave open gates or fences, even when passing through land that may appear long unused. Please keep that in mind when hiking on your own.

3. BRAC SOUTH COAST

Time: 45 minutes. | **Difficulty:** 2–3, depending on how far you go. The ironshore gets tricky | **Trailhead:** Take the south coast road (A2) until it ends in a cul de sac.

After parking, you can take a rugged walk along the ironshore and head toward the northeast tip of the island. This is a strikingly beautiful place to watch the morning sun turn the bluff a deep yellow-brown. This is also the area where Caymanite is found. If you look closely at the rocks you'll see a number of places where local jewelers extracted portions of the stone.

LITTLE CAYMAN

Located 80 miles northeast of Grand Cayman (and about 5 miles from Cayman Brac), Little Cayman is the kind of deserted island some vacationers dream of running away to. There are about 50 full-time Caymanian residents on this nine-mile-long and single-mile-wide island,

Snipe Point

Mary's Channel
Callabash Spot
East Point

Sand Bay Channel
Mary's Bay
The Bluff

Big Channel
Crawl Bay

Lower Spots
Jackson's Point
Cork Landing
A8
Rosetta Flats
Sandy Point

Charles Bight

Bloody Bay Point
A8
Tarpon Lake
Wearis Bay

Southern Cross Club
The Bight
Salt Rocks
South Hole Sound
Edward Bodders
Airstrip
Owen Island
West End Point
South Town
Pirate's Point
Lighthouse

N

Little Cayman

as well as several hundred hotel/condo guests and staff. Most visitors to Little Cayman are scuba divers or hard-core anglers who enjoy some of the finest bonefishing and small tarpon angling anywhere.

For walkers, Little Cayman offers excellent bird-watching, especially at the Governor Gore Bird Sanctuary and its Booby Bay Pond. An estimated 5,000 pairs of red-footed boobies reside here; they're believed to the largest nesting colony in the Western Hemisphere. Wild iguanas are commonly seen in the bush.

SOUTH SHORE WALK

Time: 5–6 hours to walk half of the island and return. It's not possible to make a complete island circuit yet. But, as they like to say here, soon come. | **Difficulty:** 3. Carry lots of liquid. | **Trailhead:** The airport.

A pleasant walk is from the airport and along the south coast road, passing South Hole Sound and Tarpon Lake (lots of small landlocked tarpon that are terrific fun on fly rod or light spinning). A good ending spot is Point of Sand, a beautiful swimming area.

7 THE COMMONWEALTH OF DOMINICA

Old Caribbean Proverb: *"When bull is old, you need tie him only with plantain thrash."*

Translation: *"Too often humiliation comes with old age."*

If you make only one hike in the Caribbean, make it in Dominica (Dom-in-EEK-a). The demanding, roller-coaster assault into the island's interior will take you to sites as wondrous as their names: the Valley of Desolation and the Boiling Lake.

Dominica, located between the two French islands of Martinique and Guadeloupe, is a ruggedly beautiful island whose landscape has changed little since the arrival of the first European explorers. It's said that when Columbus was asked to describe Dominica to his fellow Europeans, the explorer simply crumpled up a piece of paper and placed it on a table. Supposedly he explained to his audience, "This represents Dominica, a small island with jagged peaks rising sharply out of the sea."

As noted in the introductory chapter, early planters scalped most Caribbean landfalls of their vegetation and replaced the forests and flowers with fields of lucrative sugarcane. Dominica is the exception: Its towering mountains, thick rain forests, cascading waterfalls, and crisscrossing rivers were too tough to conquer. Dominica is probably the least spoiled island in the Caribbean. It has an estimated 365 different water sources (rivers, streams, etc.) and until recently was referred to as the Water Island. It now rightly calls itself the Nature Island of the Caribbean.

Approximately two-thirds of the island is still forest natural vegetation, mostly due to the inaccessibility of the interior. It's not that no one has tried to harvest Dominica's forests. From 1962 to 1967 a foreign logging company decided to take its best whack at the undisturbed rain forest, but gave up because of the rugged terrain and wet, inhospitable climate.

However, the failed logging operation was enough to alert islanders to the need for protective measures, because other companies were bound to try later. So, in 1975 Dominica established its Morne Trois Pitons National Park in the southern part of the island, named for the three-peaked, 4,550-foot high mountain. Just two years later it added the 22,000-acre Northern Forest Reserve, with its fine examples of primary and secondary rain forest, montane forest, and elfin woodland—the entire gamut of the tropical forest spectrum. The Cabrits National Park on the northwest point of the island joined the park system in 1986. In 1998, Morne Trois Pitons National Park was recognized by UNESCO as a World Heritage Site and became the first enlisted Natural Site in the Eastern Caribbean.

Commonwealth of Dominica

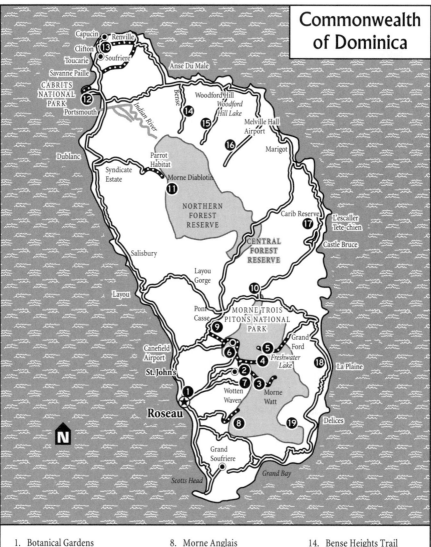

1. Botanical Gardens
2. Trafalgar Falls
3. The Valley of Desolation and the Boiling Lake
4. Freshwater Lake Trail
5. Boeri Lake
6. Middleham Falls Trails
7. Wotten Waven Hot Springs
8. Morne Anglais
9. Morne Trois Pitons Trail
10. Emerald Pool
11. Morne Diablotin Peak/ Syndicate Parrot Preserve Trails
12. Cabrits National Park
13. North Coast Trail
14. Bense Heights Trail
15. Simpa Heights Trail
16. Palmiste Ridge Trail
17. The Carib Reserve
18. Sari Sari Falls
19. Victoria Falls

The 8,242-acre Morne Diablotin National Park was created in 2000 to protect old-growth rain forest in the northwest section of the island. Named after the island's tallest mountain, it has the highest diversity of plant and animal species anywhere in Dominica and some of the Caribbean's least disturbed rain forest. It has an average of 60 different tree species per acre. Fifty-three species of birds have been recorded here, including the endemic sisserou parrot, Dominica's national bird. Most of the rugged parkland is above 2,000 feet. A deep ravine, Picard Gorge, runs through the park's northwest area. Portions of the watersheds of 12 major rivers are contained in Morne Diablotin National Park.

Dominica is the last stronghold of the fierce Carib Indians, whose dreams of expansion and domination of the region were checked by the better-organized expansionists from Spain and England. The Carib Reserve on the northeast coast is home to about 3,000 of their descendants. The last true Carib-speaking Indian died around 1900. Today's Caribs are mostly farmers who grow bananas, although they still practice traditional basketry and canoe-building skills.

Dominica received its name because Columbus happened to be sailing by on a Sunday in 1493; the island just as easily could have been named Thursday or Friday. Columbus was obviously not feeling inspired that day. The Caribs had called it Waitikubuli, meaning "tall is her body." Today, its formal name is Commonwealth of Dominica to distinguish it from the Dominican Republic.

Both the English and French fought over Dominica, deciding finally in 1748 that maybe it would be better if no one owned it, and the island was simply left to its original owners, the Caribs—an innovative concept, but not honored for very long. In 1763 the English received ownership of Dominica through the Treaty of Paris. In 1795, the French evidently had a change of heart, because they tried to take the island back by force. Conflict between the English and French continued until 1805. The French finally were bought off with a ransom of 8,000 English pounds after they burned down the main city of Roseau.

Dominica remained a British colony until 1967. In 1978, it became the fully independent Commonwealth of Dominica. The French influence still strongly survives through many of the place and family names and the Creole language that is widely spoken.

Travel Tips

Area: Covers an area of 289.5 square miles; 29 miles long and 16 miles wide.

Language: English is the official language. A Creole and French patois are widely spoken, especially in the outlying areas.

Population: About 71,000, of which 20,000 live around the capital city of Roseau (pronounced "Ro-zo"). About 3,000 Caribs live in their 3,700-acre territory in the northeastern part.

Time Zone: Atlantic Time, one hour ahead of Eastern Standard Time.

Rainy Season: Rainfall varies considerably, from 50 inches on the coast to over 300 inches in the interior. The wettest months are July to October. The driest period is from January through April.

Getting There: Tiny Dominica is not yet on many air routes. From the United States, American Eagle,(800) 433-7300, flies direct to Melville Hall from San Juan. American Airlines also flies via San Juan into Antigua. From Antigua, Barbados, and St. Lucia, LIAT, (800) 468-0482, connects to both Melville Hall and Canefield airports. Melville Hall is 38 miles from Roseau, and Canefield is just 3 miles from the city.

In addition, L'Express Des Iles, a high-speed catamaran, connects Dominica to Guadeloupe, Martinique and St. Lucia.

Documents: U.S. and Canadian citizens need only proof of citizenship; passports are required of everyone else. All arrivals are expected to have an ongoing or return ticket.

Getting Around: Rental cars are readily available in Roseau but not at Melville Hall airport itself. It's US$16 by taxi from the airport to Roseau's rental car companies. Traveling the roads on your own is normally not difficult. However, there are few road signs, so a good map is essential. It's also necessary to buy a local driving permit (US$11.10). Driving is technically on the left, although the locals seem to prefer driving fast and straight down the middle of the road. Traveling off the main roads without a local guide can be almost impossible. Minibuses run from Roseau to different parts of the island. The Old Market is the terminus for traveling south; the West Bridge for traveling north.

Where to Stay: The Fort Young Hotel in Roseau is the island's largest facility; the food and service are good. Most of the other places to overnight in Roseau are guesthouses of varying quality. The Anchorage Hotel, located on the Caribbean, has large rooms, good food, and reliable service.

Camping: Not permitted in the national parks and generally not allowed anywhere.

Currency: The Eastern Caribbean Dollar, which is worth about US$2.70. Banks are open 8 a.m. to 3 p.m. Monday through Thursday and until 5 p.m. on Friday.

Taxes & Tips: A standard 10% service charge, plus a 5% government tax at hotels and a 3% government sales tax for food, drinks, and merchandise. There is a US$14 departure tax.

Electrical Current: 220/240 volts, 50 cycle.

Safety/Health Warnings: The walk around Freshwater Lake recently seems to be attracting muggers and thieves who break into rental cars to steal valuables. It's suggested you never visit this area alone, but with several other people.

Snakes & Other Venomous Creatures: The native boa (called the clouded-face boa) grows up to six feet long, but it eats rodents and is harmless to humans. There are no poisonous snakes.

Hiking/Walking Services: Dominica's best-known guide service is **Ken's Hinterland Adventure Tours & Taxi Service** (KHATTS) Ltd., (767) 448 4850; www.khatts.dm). It offers all of the major hikes as well as scenic coastal drives with very knowledgeable locals. **Ras Tours** operates from Cocoa Cottage located at Trafalgar, (767) 448-0412. This bed-and-breakfast in the Roseau Valley is close to many of the most popular trailheads. Motor coach tours to some of the most popular sites are the specialty of Raffoul Luxury Tours, (767) 448-2443; fax (767) 448-7490; www.raffoultours.com). A guided hike to the Valley of Desolation and the Boiling Lake costs about $80 per person. You can cut costs by taking a chance and picking your own guide in the village of Laudat near the beginning of the trailhead. You're bound to meet locals who will offer to guide you, and some will do a good job for far less money. However, you probably won't have any references or other credentials on which to base your selection. In this case, your adventure begins as soon as you start looking for a guide. You can always contact the tourist office to see if they can recommend anyone.

Additional Information: In North America, the Caribbean Tourism Association, 20 E. 46th St., New York, NY 10017; phone (212) 682-0435. In the United Kingdom, the Dominica Tourist Office, 1 Collingham Gardens, Earls Court, London SW5 OHW; phone (071) 373-8751; fax (071) 373-8743. The most complete information is on island at the Dominica Tourist Board, Box 73, Roseau, Commonwealth of Dominica (always include this formal title or your mail could go to the Dominican Republic), W.I.; call (767) 448-2186/2351. Mail is incredibly slow. On the web, visit www.dominica.dm/basics.

1. BOTANICAL GARDENS

Located in Roseau, these were reputed to be some of the most beautiful grounds in the Caribbean until 1979's Hurricane David, which did considerable damage here. Situated below the Morne Bruce Hill, the 40-acre tract is the largest semi-open space in the capital city of Roseau; it served as a popular cricket ground in the 1960s and 1970s.

Although just 68 feet above sea level, the gardens receive more than 85 inches of rain annually, making them an ideal site for growing a wide variety of tropical plants. Originally a sugarcane field, the ornamental planting began in 1890 and was beautifully landscaped with a fountain, iron gates, ponds, and 500 species of exotic and indigenous shrubs and trees.

The most interesting site displays the remains of a large yellow bus crushed beneath a massive baobab tree, an ever-present reminder of Hurricane David's devastation. The Forestry and Wildlife Division here offers *A Guide to Selected Trees and Shrubs* to help identify plants. An aviary contains two species of parrots, the imperial and the red-necked. The aviary is part of a captive breeding program to increase the number of parrots in the wild.

Jack's Walk, which leaves from the gardens near the east gate, will take you up Morne Bruce for a panoramic view of Roseau.

2. TRAFALGAR FALLS

Time: 15–30 minutes . | **Difficulty:** 1–2. | **Trailhead:** About 6 miles east from Roseau. Take the Valley Road from Roseau to Laudat, but well before Laudat you'll turn right above the village of Fond Cani and go through the village of Trafalgar. Go for another mile to the hydroelectric plant next to the Papillote Guest House.

Trafalgar is actually the site of two falls (the "father" and the "mother") between 180 and 200 feet high that converge in rocky pools. The falls, particularly the taller father one, was impacted by a rockslide in 1995. An unusual feature is the hot water springs coming from the base of the taller falls. Anyone not in good physical shape is advised to stay at the platform because the boulders are large and slippery. A guide is also a good idea for locating the easiest route to the hot water springs.

It's a 15-minute walk to the observation platform near the base of the falls and another 10- to 15-minute scramble over the slick boulders to reach the pool at the base, where you can swim. Because of the easy access, this is a popular outing for cruise ship passengers.

Morne Trois Pitons National Park

Located in the south central part of Dominica, this 16,980-acre park of primordial rain forest offers spectacular hikes. Morne Trois Pitons refers to the "mountain of three peaks" that rises to 4,672 feet. The legendary Valley of Desolation and Boiling Lake hike is located within this park.

You won't see any large mammals in the park, but Dominica does possess a wide range of insects, birds, crustaceans, and a few reptiles. There are four species of snakes, all of which are nonpoisonous.

A surprising characteristic here, as on most islands, is the lack of bird calls in heavy forested areas at upper elevations. Although 54 species of birds nest on the island, the only one you're likely to hear on a steep climb is the siffleur montagne, a mountain bird heard only in Dominica and whose song has a striking clarity and sweetness. Dominica is also home for two endangered parrots, the sisserou *(Amazona imperialis)* and the jacquot *(Amazona arausiaca).* You're much more likely to see the Antillean crested hummingbird and the purple-throated hummingbird.

At sunset or when it rains, the little (two-centimeter) tree frogs known as the gounouge are responsible for the chorus of piping sounds. A remarkable example of adaptation to its environment, these amphibians are born as perfect frogs without an aquatic, tadpole stage. They don't have the luxury of a prolonged adolescence in still, safe water because the rivers are so swift, the streams contain little food, and the water flow is highly seasonal. To survive, the gounouge must be born "standing up and talking back."

The crapaud, or mountain chicken, is a bulky, solid frog hunted for food and occasionally offered on hotel menus. Mountain chickens, which grow up to 15 to 20 centimeters, have been seriously depleted through overhunting. As one who visited when they were not legally available, I can't comment on their taste, but they are considered a great delicacy.

3. The Valley of Desolation and the Boiling Lake

Length: 5–6 miles. | **Time:** 7–8 hours round-trip, depending on weather. Always start early, by 8 a.m., to allow enough daylight. | **Difficulty:** 5. This is crucial: All gear should be kept in a backpack so your hands are free at all times to scramble up and down the mountain. Take snacks and something to drink. You will require a recharge for the return when you're tired. A guide is strongly recommended. | **Trailhead:** The path starts at the bottom of the village of Laudat.

The seven- to eight-hour round-trip walk to the Valley of Desolation and the Boiling Lake surpasses any other Caribbean hike I've made. It's a rigorous walk because of constant ascents and descents both coming and going. There is very little flat ground to offer a rest. In addition, the trail is often slick from rain, which requires a bit of tricky scrambling over sections of vertical ground. This is a tough hike, yet one that people in decent physical condition

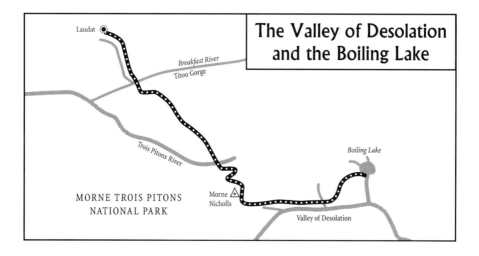

The Valley of Desolation
and the Boiling Lake

Laudat

Breakfast River
Titou Gorge

Trois Pitons River

Boiling Lake

MORNE TROIS PITONS
NATIONAL PARK

Morne
Nicholls

Valley of Desolation

should be able to complete. However, the length and difficulty also make it potentially dangerous if you don't have a guide or don't make a very early start. At least one tourist has died on this trail. Please take very seriously the warnings and precautions accompanying the detailed description of this hike. If this walk sounds too demanding, you'll find Dominica has many others that are far easier (though less spectacular).

At one time it was possible to reach the Boiling Lake on a relatively short hike without going through the Valley of Desolation. No more; the former trail is gone. Now, it's all or nothing. In real time, the Boiling Lake is only about another 30 minutes beyond the Valley of Desolation. In hiking time, it seems hours longer because of the wear and tear reaching the valley.

There are so many horror stories about how difficult this hike is that many locals have never attempted it and swear they never will. What to expect? You will get wet. You will get muddy, perhaps coated with grime. And you will get tired . . . probably *very* tired.

This hike is awesome and deserves to be described in detail. As the Caribbean's best hike, it deserves such recognition . . . and respect. The hike can be divided into three distinct phases. The first hour is deceptively easy, starting with a moderate 25-minute ascent, followed by some ups and downs until you reach the Breakfast River at the end of about 60 minutes of steady walking. The river apparently was named by travelers crossing the island who would stop here for their morning meal.

Phase II is a 45-minute walk up the side of Morne Nicholls, a steep and sometimes very slippery climb. Phase III is the slow, 45–60-minute scrambling descent into the Valley of Desolation (which itself takes only 5 to 10 minutes to cross) then another 30–45 minutes to reach the Boiling Lake.

On my hike, I hooked up with Henry, a local guide, and several other intrepid adventurers. From Laudat we followed the path beside some large pipes to Breakfast River and the Titou Gorge, a deep, narrow volcanic fault. I found the first phase of the walk fairly easy. Morne

Nicholls, however, is a deceptive trickster. In many places it seems as if you're about to reach the summit, but it always turns out to be just another bend in the path. There are always many more yards to climb.

About halfway up the mountain we were enveloped in cloud, and the valley on our left was completely covered in mist. The scene was like an Oriental painting showing a shadow world with only the outlines of trees and shrubs depicted in different shades of gray; it's also the type of scene frequently encountered in black-and-white creature-feature movies of the 1930s, just at sunset when the vampire or the werewolf is about to show up.

Actually, we were passing through montane forest and one of the best stands of Wezinye Montany, Dominica's only native conifer. Nearer the top we entered the fantastically shaped elfin woodland, trees stunted by strong winds whose branches and trunks are nearly encased in mosses and lichens.

When we finally reached the 3,000-foot summit of Morne Nicholls, Henry turned and asked if it had "gotten hellish yet." This was about the halfway point, and though the mountain climb had been strenuous and constant, it wasn't as bad as I expected. He smiled; I tried very hard to decipher that smile. Was the worst behind us, or yet to come?

It was extremely windy at the top of Morne Nicholls. The gusts literally were strong enough to push me off balance, precisely what happened several years earlier to a woman crossing a narrow path at the top—she either misstepped or the wind literally shoved her off the mountain. The fall killed her, the trail's one known fatality. As we went on, I found this amazing—I'd certainly have expected more heart attacks.

We were fogged in, but I was told that on a clear day there's a panoramic view of Morne Macaque to the north and the sharp cone of Morne Watt to the south. Looking west is Roseau, Laudat, and Morne Prosper.

The next part of the path was designed by someone with a sick sense of humor. A long series of steps lead down from the summit, but they are placed so far apart it is impossible to simply walk down them. Only a person eight or nine feet tall could make it from step to step. These were also slick from the constant wet wind; we did a lot of sliding here. Steps are harder to walk than a natural slope, but they were placed to keep the trail from washing away, not to help hikers. We passed a shelter just past the summit. Five minutes later, it started raining.

Then came the hard part: a slow, very tricky descent into the Valley of Desolation on a slippery mountain-goat trail of rock and mud. It's very easy to misstep here. Chivalry emerged for the first time as the men helped the women (their shorter legs were the problem) reach some of the small stepping stones that jut out just a few inches out of the mountain. In some places it was easier to slide on your butt or turn and step down, like descending a ladder.

This was perhaps a half-hour of tedious work. Descending, we got our first evidence of volcanic activity. We could see steam rising around a bend in a distant valley—at last, the Valley of Desolation.

But first we had to work our way down a small waterflow, too small to be called a stream or creek. The rocks were rusty red, and the water was cold. We inched our way down a steep mini-waterfall next to a rock wall. At least it was a chance to wash off some of the mud.

Up until this point, we had followed an obvious path. Now, entering the Valley of Desolation, the path disappeared. The valley floor was bare of vegetation but craggy and uneven. Coated in sulfur, the earth was colored red, silver, and black. Some rocks were also covered with yellow sulfur crystal. Brightly colored hot springs were scattered over the valley floor,

Steam issues from the ground in the Valley of Desolation

their blue, white, black, and orange colors the results of minerals deposited by the water. It would have been no surprise if a lumbering *Tyrannosaurus rex* suddenly appeared.

The Valley of Desolation, located on the flanks of Morne Watt, stretches about a quarter of a mile across: At the edge we could see several big steam vents, hear water bubbling, and spot a few mud pots here and there. A small stream contained water that was oil-black in color, spilling over the rocks to create a white foaming bottom, an incredible contrast. The water here was quite warm.

When first discovered around 1870, the region was still thickly forested. It was discovered by two Englishmen working in Dominica, Mr. Watt and Mr. Nicholls, who now have two mountains named after them. A volcanic eruption of ash in 1880, originating either from the Boiling Lake or this valley, may have been responsible for the increase in the size of the fumarole area. Scientists predict that the Valley of Desolation will remain an active fumarole region for decades to come. With more than 50 fumaroles and hot springs in the valley, the main danger here is stepping through a thin crust of earth hiding a hot fumarole. We followed Henry closely.

Though once lushly forested, the valley floor now has only a dense mat of moss and lichen interspersed with yellow- and white-flowered "thyme sauvage" and grasses able to survive the harsh sulfur fumes. These fumes are credited with wiping out the forest. Surprisingly, wildlife does still exist: lizards, stoneflies, mayflies, ants, and of course the planet's hardiest survivor, the ubiquitous, indestructible cockroach.

At the far end is a huge steam vent that Henry invited us "to come stand in for your complexion." After crossing the valley diagonally through the middle, we were back in thick forest, where we walked for another 20 minutes before coming out at the stream where the rocks were coated white with sulfur. Henry drew an arrow for those lagging behind to take photos. Someone else drew a Carib-like petroglyph of a smiling face on one of the stones; we all avoided stepping on the rock to keep from defacing the finger painting.

More climbing, as we cut diagonally across another valley, then started scrambling over large boulders. This was some of the hardest climbing of all. We all wanted to stop, rest, eat, and recharge. There was still not the slightest sign of the Boiling Lake. How much longer could this go on? Could we go on? And why had I assumed the Valley of Desolation would be above the Boiling Lake, not below it?

We turned a corner and there it was, a big bowl of steaming white milk virtually obscured by the thick steam. We waited for the winds to shift and push enough of it away to catch a momentary glimpse of the actual part of the lake that bubbles and churns. That's a relatively small area of only about 20 to 30 yards. The entire lake measures about 70 yards across. Ironically, Boiling Lake is Dominica's smallest lake, but it is the world's largest boiling lake (the only other rivaling it is in New Zealand).

Its first recorded sighting was in 1870. Even though it seems to be the ends of the earth, it is actually only five miles east of the town of Roseau. The Boiling Lake is believed to be a flooded fumarole, a crack through which gases escape from the molten lava below. The natural basin of the lake collects the rainfall from the surrounding hills, which then seeps through the porous lake bottom, where it is trapped and heated by the hot lava. Tests conducted in 1875 found the water temperature at the lake edge to be between 180° to 197° F; the water temperature at the center, where the lake actually boils, could not be measured. The depth was recorded at more than 195 feet.

The Boiling Lake keeps changing over time. After 1875, the water level decreased and a geyser developed that spewed water and mud 60 feet or higher in the center. A photograph from 1895 shows the Boiling Lake dry, with a prominent pumice cone from the geyser in the middle. In April 1988, Boiling Lake stopped boiling and its level dropped to 29 feet before returning back to normal.

Today, no one knows for certain how deep the lake is. The cauldron's sides, which rise 60 to 100 feet high, are a mixture of pumice, clay and small stones. The water is usually described as a grayish-blue, but I still think it looks more like milk.

However, the water color was not a topic of conversation in my hiking group. We were too busy eating fresh pineapple and sandwiches, resting, and (with a good deal of dread) thinking about the walk out. We were all pretty tired.

Going back was worse than coming in. As we reached the mountain we had slid down butt-first, it began to rain. The mountain turned into a mass of slick clay that we tried not to fall from. Even worse were the giant steps that led back to the summit of Morne Nicholls. Coming down was a snap compared to the climb back up them. Scaling this stone ladder really stretched the leg muscles .

In one hour, we were back at the summit. Thank God! We rested briefly, wondering what the steep other side of the mountain would be like, now that it's rained. The answer was obvious: slick, slippery, and muddy. Anyone who had managed to stay relatively clean until now quickly underwent radical changes. So did our attitudes. Where we had walked diligently around any muddy spots on the way in, we were so tired and the ground was so sloppy that it didn't make any difference anymore what we did. We were muddy and getting muddier.

One hiker abandoned the path and tried walking the narrow ridge above it to see if she could make better time that way. She slips, and—instead of falling to her left, and plummeting down the mountain—she ended up straddling the ridge. She caught her breath and rejoined us on the trench-like trail.

We washed off when we get down to Breakfast River. Some water bottles we left here to chill earlier were quickly drained. Even the hikers in their early twenties are slowing down. One was sitting and cleaning his shoes off in the water, his legs visibly shaking from fatigue. My own were numb.

The first phase, so easy when the hike began, looked strange and unfamiliar. How many days ago was it that we passed this way? Didn't I experience something similar to this in a previous life: the Bataan Death March?

Near the end we had a look at another amazing Dominican phenomenon, the Titou Gorge, which we'd ignored in our anticipation to climb. The sides of this narrow, deep gorge undulate, indicating that it was not cut by the river that now washes through it. Instead, as the molten lava was cooling, it split and pulled apart, almost as a drying mud puddle splits and cracks. I found these facts difficult to appreciate until we were back at our vehicles and I was able at last to sit, knowing I did not need to move again that day unless I wanted to.

It was three days before my legs stopped hurting. Everyone on the hike reported a similar condition. Some local guides make the walk two or three times a week in season. Would I ever do it again? Maybe . . .

4. FRESHWATER LAKE TRAIL

Length: 2.5 miles one-way. | **Time:** 2 hours round-trip. | **Difficulty:** 1. The hike is a flat grade and runs along a hydro pipeline. The trail goes west to east along the southern flank of Morne Macaque. | **Trailhead:** A former carriage road from a small shrine in Laudat leads to Freshwater Lake. It is possible to drive this unpaved road to a parking lot at the northwest end of Freshwater Lake where you pick up the trail to Boeri Lake (the hike described after Freshwater Lake). *Warning:* Robberies and hassles are being reported in increasing numbers in this area. Don't come here with fewer than three other people. Only singles and couples have been bothered.

Located two miles northeast of Laudat, this nine-acre lake is the largest of Dominica's five freshwater crater lakes. More important, several hiking trails into other parts of the Morne Trois Pitons National Park start from here. The spring-fed lake is used as part of a hydropower project to provide more electricity island-wide. The lake has been dammed and the water level raised 20 feet. A snaking trail of creosote-treated wood pipes transports water from the lake to the power station at Laudat, a sight as lovely as an appendectomy scar.

Situated at 2,500 feet, Freshwater Lake is surrounded mostly by montane forest, characterized by its short, thin trees and open canopy. High winds and shallow soil prevent the type of thick growth characteristic of the rain forest. However, the montane forest is loaded with

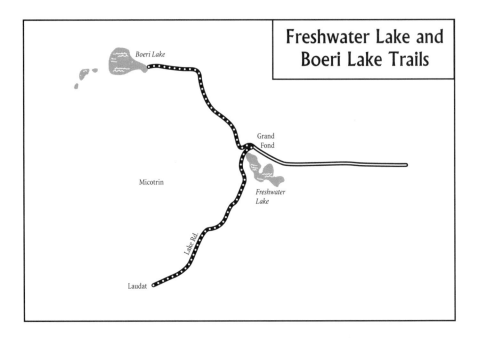

Freshwater Lake and Boeri Lake Trails

Boeri Lake

Grand
Fond

Micotrin

*Freshwater
Lake*

Lake Rd.

Laudat

epiphytes, plants that use others for their physical support. They are so thick in some places it's almost impossible to see the trees on which they grow. This is a great place to view delicate, almost transparent ferns, large-leafed anthuriums, and large, showy bromeliads.

At the highest level is the elfin woodland, also called mossy, cloud, and dwarf forest on other islands. The dominant species here is the gnarled kaklen, whose spreading branches and roots make parts of the forest almost impenetrable. Note how small and leathery the leaves are here, and how from a distance the forest looks like a well-trimmed hedge. The leaves are leathery to prevent being torn by the fierce winds.

Birds are the most obvious wildlife. Both the purple-throated Carib hummingbird and the Antillean crested hummingbird are common. The rare blue-headed hummingbird has also been spotted here. An unforgettable sound is the beautiful song of the mountain whistler (sifle montany).

Take the path past the interpretive signs and wooden shelter to the gully overlooking the lake where the trail splits in two. One is the mountain trail (Chemin d'Etang), a historic four-mile trail that descends into the Rosalie Valley to end at the village of Grand Fond. The walk takes about two and a half hours. Before roads linked the small agricultural community of Grand Fond with the rest of the island, judges, doctors, and even magistrates would ride this trail on horseback because it was the only access to the village.

The other fork in the trail goes up steps to the ridgetop east of the Freshwater Lake, part of a rim of an old volcano. The ridge offers a splendid panoramic view, one of Dominica's best. It also helps you appreciate the volcanic origins of the island: Morne Micotrine to the west is a young volcanic cone separating Freshwater from Boeri Lake, which also formed on the same crater floor. You'll also spot many peaks and ridges created by several volcanic eruptions.

5. BOERI LAKE

Length: 1.25 miles. | **Time:** 45 minutes, one-way. | **Difficulty:** 2. *Warning:* During the dry season, the huge boulders surrounding the shoreline of Boeri Lake are exposed, a real temptation for rock hopping. These boulders are extremely slippery—always—and are renowned as ankle-twisters and leg-breakers. Admire them from a distance.. | **Trailhead:** Access is from the Freshwater Lake Trail. You can either hike to the trailhead or drive to Freshwater Lake and begin hiking there.

The trail to Boeri Lake is actually an extension of the Freshwater Lake trail. The walk takes you past hot and cold-water springs gushing from the side of Morne Macaque, past clear streams, and through both montane and elfin forest. There are some abandoned gardens the local wildlife has claimed as their own vegetable market.

Boeri Lake, one of Dominica's largest, is located at 2,800 feet in the crater of an old volcano. Almost perfectly circular, with a surface of 4.5 acres, Boeri may be as much as 135 feet deep. Fed by rain water and runoff, which accounts for its dramatic variations, it may fall as much as 25 feet during a dry spell. The lake is usually at its highest level between October and December.

The montane forest here is dominated by cabbage palms, maho kochon, and gombo moutayn, a relative of the hibiscus. Ferns, including tree ferns, are luxuriant along parts of the trail. The red and yellow heliconia, with their lobster claw–shaped flowers, add a considerable amount of color. The elfin forest, as all other forests on Dominica, is an open canopy, with tree stems and branches dripping with mats of mosses and liverworts.

The small tree lizards (zandoli) take on a different color pattern than those found at lower altitudes. This is another good place to hear the song of the mountain whistler, view migratory waterfowl, and look for the siwik, or river crab, which lives in the boulders marking the shoreline.

The walk up the ridge to Boeri Lake offers some excellent panoramic views of Grand Fond and Morne Jaune to the east. Utility lines and poles are also quite evident. To the south is Freshwater Lake. Morne Nicholls, the climb that marks the beginning of the second and difficult phase of the journey to the Valley of Desolation, is also quite visible.

6. MIDDLEHAM FALLS TRAILS

Length: 1.8 miles (Sylvania Trail); 2.3 miles (Cochrane Trail). | **Time:** 7 hours (Sylvania Trail); 6 hours (Cochrane Trail). | **Difficulty:** 2 to 3 for both routes. | **Trailhead:** The Middleham Trails have three entrances: at the villages of Sylvania, Providence, and Cochrane. The most popular trail (and the following description) begins at the village of Providence. To reach Providence from Roseau, take the Valley Road to Laudat. When you see the second sign for Symes Zee's Villa, proceed for about 0.75 miles where a track on the left descends sharply. Follow the track to the small parking area. A sign points to the trailhead.

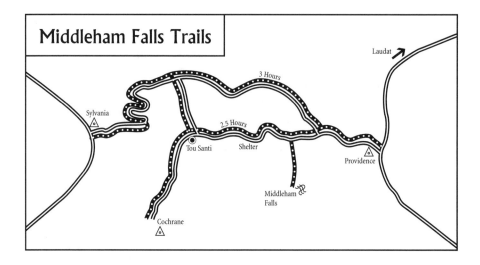

Middleham Falls Trails

These trails in the northwest portion of the national park wind through a 950-acre tract of primary rain forest that is among the most beautiful and best preserved on all Dominica. The land was donated by a U.S. citizen, John D. Archbold, to the Dominican government through the Nature Conservancy. There are two major sets of trails plus one offshoot.

The trail to Cochrane and Sylvania is fairly easy though during rainy periods the rocks are slick at the stream crossings. It first passes through banana and citrus trees before reaching the rain forest. After about an hour the trail splits. The right trail goes to the former coffee plantation of Sylvania, recognizable by the crumbling foundations. Sylvania is about 2 to 2.5 hours away from this point. The left trail goes to Cochrane, about 1.5 to 2 hours away.

Taking the Cochrane Trail: You'll soon reach the turnoff for the 15-minute walk to the 275-foot-high Middleham Falls, among Dominica's highest. You're welcome to swim in the large rock basin beneath the falls. Located in an area known as Narodney, the Middleham Falls and several other streams join to form the Boeri River, more commonly known as the Canefield River.

Returning to the main trail to Cochrane, the walk passes the Tou Santi (Stinking Hole) just to the right of the path. This is a collapsed lava tube that emits hot air and the squeaking sounds and odor of numerous fruit bats *(Brachyphylla cavernarum)*. The bats seem to squeak almost any time of day. You can see them flying around the entrance at dusk. On the Cochrane route, you'll have to cross perhaps a half dozen small streams, making this a moderately difficult hike in the rainy season.

Taking the Sylvania Trail: Like the Cochrane Trail, this path goes through a fine section of rain forest. A chief characteristic of the forest here is the comparatively open forest floor. Because only about 10 percent of the sunlight is able to penetrate the thick forest canopy, hardly anything is able to grow on the ground, which makes for easy walking. This rain forest is dominated by two tree species—gommye *(Dacryodes excelsa)* and chatannye *(Sloanea spp.)*—but there is also incredible diversity in some places. As many as 60 different species of trees have been recorded in one ten-acre plot. In wet areas where the drainage is poor, one of the most common species is the mang blan *(Symphonia globulifera)* with an elaborate system of prop roots providing support on the thin soil.

The trail ends at the crumbling ruins of the old Sylvania coffee plantation.

7. WOTTEN WAVEN

Time: 15 minutes, one-way. | **Difficulty:** 1. | **Trailhead:** From Roseau take the road skirting the north side of the Botanical Garden. Cross a bridge near the corner of the Gardens, continuing through Bath Estate, Louisville, Copthall, and reaching Wotten Waven. Opposite the school is the trail leading down to the hot springs.

A sign in Wotten Waven tells you where to park and where to start the hike. This is an easy spot to find. The village is home to the boiling gray mud pots that dramatize Dominica's volcanic history. The major mud pot here is notable for its constant noise and wave action. Its steam has a definite sulfuric smell.

8. MORNE ANGLAIS

Length: 4.5 miles round-trip. | **Time:** 2 hours each way. | **Difficulty:** 3–4, depending on conditions. It's easy at the beginning but becomes steeper. | **Trailhead:** From Roseau go south toward Loubière. Turn left at the entrance to Citronier and drive up to the village of Giraudel. The trail starts at the top of the village, beside a small stone reservoir.

From Morne Anglais, which rises to 3,683 feet, you'll have good view of the surrounding countryside and the south coast. The walk to the summit takes you through both an orchid-filled montane forest and an almost perennially cloud-covered elfin woodland that receives as much as 300 inches of rain a year. The last 100 feet to the summit are the steepest part, but the view is well worth the effort.

9. MORNE TROIS PITONS TRAIL

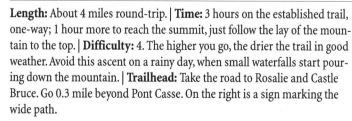

Length: About 4 miles round-trip. | **Time:** 3 hours on the established trail, one-way; 1 hour more to reach the summit, just follow the lay of the mountain to the top. | **Difficulty:** 4. The higher you go, the drier the trail in good weather. Avoid this ascent on a rainy day, when small waterfalls start pouring down the mountain. | **Trailhead:** Take the road to Rosalie and Castle Bruce. Go 0.3 mile beyond Pont Casse. On the right is a sign marking the wide path.

This is the largest mountain in Morne Trois Pitons National Park and, at 4,550 feet, the second highest on the island. The established park trail does not lead all the way to the top; that takes another hour of walking. Most hikers don't bother because the last part involves a lot of climbing over vegetation. At the summit the vegetation is much thinner due to thinner soil.

This is a steeper, tougher climb than Morne Anglais, so you need to be in good shape. However, if you can survive the hike to the Boiling Lake, you can make it to the top of Morne Trois Pitons. True, it's a four-hour trudge to the top, but at least the walk out is downhill. (What makes the trek to the Boiling Lake so tough is that you're always climbing up and down, never long in just one direction.) As on Morne Anglais, you will pass from montane to elfin forest.

10. EMERALD POOL

Length: 0.9 mile. | **Time:** 20 minutes. | **Difficulty:** 1–2, some climbing. This is a favorite stop on the way from Roseau to the Carib Territory. | **Trailhead:** Located 3.5 miles northeast of Pont Casse on the road to Rosalie and Castle Bruce. Take the left fork that goes to Castle Bruce. The small parking lot is half a mile on the left.

Reached by a half-mile loop trail, the Emerald Pool is by far the most accessible spot in the entire Morne Trois Pitons National Park. Emerald Pool is actually a waterfall-fed pool that appears bright green in the tree-filtered sunlight.

The forest here technically falls into what is known as a transition zone, not true rain forest or montane forest. The majority of plants are young trees—not shrubs—that create a massively thick canopy, prompting many vines to grow upward from ground level; others, established in the tree tops, send down their roots. Epiphytes are especially fond of the filtered sunlight, and the trees are covered with them. Both the agouti, a guinea pig–like rodent, and the nocturnal manicou, a small opossum, live here, but you are far more likely to spot birds, particularly hummingbirds, and hear the song of the mountain warbler.

It's possible to swim in Emerald Pool; in fact, on a hot day you'll probably want to. If you do, go stand behind the 20-foot-high waterfall; there's plenty of room in the eroded stone behind it. But be careful: The rocks are slippery.

The short trail has three lookout points, illustrating how heavily forested and natural Dominica remains. The first lookout is of Morne Trois Pitons. The second looks across Belle Fille Valley and Morne Negres Marrons (2,248 feet). Part of the trail past the second viewpoint is paved for a short distance. This is part of the old track used as a main road by the Carib Indians from perhaps 800 years ago to as late as the 1960s. The third outlook shows the Atlantic Coast at Castle Bruce and Anse Quanery. If you happen to be here near twilight, enjoy the chorus of tree frogs and crickets. Bats, too, will appear, devouring the island's insects.

THE NORTHERN END

MORNE DIABLOTIN NATIONAL PARK

This is Dominica's newest national park. The land is so rugged that it was favored by runaways slaves, called maroons. Six maroon camps—Pharcel, Clemence, Cicero, Quashie, Juba, and Robin, all named after their leaders—were located within the park. However, the exact locations of the camps still are unknown.

The first recorded ascent of 4,747-foot Morne Diablotin was made by Scottish physician, Dr. John Imray, in 1867. There is a section of the mountain known today as Imray's view. Two princes, Albert and George, climbed the peak in 1880.

11. Morne Diablotin Peak/Syndicate Parrot Preserve Trails

Length: The Syndicate Trail is an 0.8-mile loop. | **Time:** It is a 20 to 30-minute walk from the car park to the beginning of the Syndicate Trail. From this point, it is about 3 hours to the summit of Morne Diablotin and another 2 hours back. | **Difficulty:** For the Syndicate Trail, 1–2; to the summit, 3–4. Steepness is what makes the summit hike moderately difficult. Also, in the last 45 minutes to the top you may have to do some tricky scrambling.. | **Trailhead:** Take the main coastal road to Portsmouth on the northwest coast. Before Portsmouth, and just north of the village of Dublanc is a signposted turn to the right. It's a 30-minute drive from the signpost to a small hut on the left-hand side of the road in the Syndicate Estate. This marks the crossroads for several trails. Take the left fork for both the Syndicate and summit trails.

Making the walk more than worthwhile is the 0.8-mile loop trail within the Syndicate Parrot Preserve, an annex of the park. There is a short side trail to the Parrot Lookout, where you may be fortunate enough to see Dominica's two endangered parrots. The path follows the Picard River gorge and has three overlooks for sighting the two birds: The imperial parrot (or sisserou), the largest Amazon parrot in the world, and the more abundant red-necked parrot (or jaco). The best times for parrot watching are sunrise and sunset. Distinguishing the two from a distance is not difficult. The imperial parrot, the larger bird, has a modulated call that rises and falls, and the red-necked parrot emits a high-pitched squawk.

After the parrot walk, there is the matter of the Morne Diablotin trail that continues on to the summit from the turnoff to the parrot preserve. At 4,747 feet, Morne Diablotin is Dominica's highest peak and the second highest in the Lesser Antilles. The path starts gradually and then becomes steep, remaining that way to the summit. You'll have spectacular views as you climb from rain forest through montane forest into elfin woodland. This superb montane forest is home to many bird species: tremblers, red-necked pigeons, forest thrush, and blue-headed hummingbirds. Also keep an eye out for agouti and wild pig. If it's a clear day, at the summit you'll see the mountains of Trois Pitons, the town of Portsmouth, Rupert Bay, and the Cabrits peninsula. Guadeloupe (to the north) and Martinique (south) may also be visible.

12. Cabrits National Park

Time: 2 hours. | **Difficulty:** 1–2. | **Trailhead:** The northwest coast just beyond the village of Portsmouth.

Established in 1986 at Portsmouth, the island's second most important town, Cabrits Park is 1,313 acres, but much of it (1,053 acres) is underwater. Two forested hillsides contain the scattered buildings of the once-huge Fort Shirley complex, on which restoration began in

1982. Clearly marked paths meander the hillsides past the Commander's Quarters, Douglas Battery, and other sites. Only the main buildings have been cleared; ficus roots still hold most of the rest hostage. A small museum is housed in a former powder magazine.

The highest point on the Cabrits headland is only 600 feet in elevation, so the trails are not difficult, though inclines in some spots may be steep for short stretches. Besides scenic coastal vistas, you're likely to see more of Dominica's lizards and hummingbirds. The plant life is particularly interesting if you have the booklet *Cabrits Plants and Their Uses* available from the Forestry Division office located in the Botanical Gardens in Roseau.

13. NORTH COAST TRAIL

Length: 12 miles. | **Time:** 6 hours. | **Difficulty:** 2–3. | **Trailhead:** Go north from Portsmouth for 6 twisting miles to where the road ends at Bellevue just north of the village of Capucin.

You're not likely to see any other visitors in this remote part of Dominica. The trail goes through tall, dry forest as it follows the north coast around to Carib Point before turning inland at the Delaford Estate. It crosses several shallow river valleys, then joins a driveable road at Delaford Estate. The road connects the village of Pennville and Guilet. Perhaps the most unique part of the walk is climbing Bellevue Mountain and reaching the place Cold Soufrière. Cold Soufrière is a volcanic crater that often attracts numerous boa constrictors, which come to bask on the warm ground crust.

14. BENSE HEIGHTS TRAIL

Length: 2 miles to Ti Branches. | **Time:** 1 hour, unless you decide to continue another 3–4 hours up to Morne Turner. | **Difficulty:** 1–2 to Ti Branches; 3–4 to Morne Turner. | **Trailhead:** In northeast Dominica, just beyond the village of Anse de Mai, take the road off to the right to the village of Bense

The hike is the next two miles of rough road after Bense, which follows the ridge south to Ti Branches. Not only does this walk offer an excellent chance to see red-necked parrots, the views across the rain forest are among the island's best. The mature rain forest is the pristine covering of Morne Diablotin, Dominica's highest peak. About halfway a short track to the left leads to the Hampstead River with deep rock pools for swimming.

At Ti Branches, a path just over the crest of the hill follows the Hampstead Ridge to Morne Turner (2,341 feet). A guide is advised if you want to tackle this 3 to 4-hour route. It starts out easy but becomes tough, and it's not always well marked.

15. SIMPA HEIGHTS TRAIL

Length: 5 miles. | **Time:** 5–6 hours. | **Difficulty:** 2–3. | **Trailhead:** Go inland to the village of Woodford Hill, just north of the Melville Hall Airport. Follow the feeder road for 3.5 miles through coconut and banana plantations to the edge of the Forest Reserve. Just before the track reaches the crest of a hill, take the right fork into the Forest Reserve and a small parking area.

This walk moves through a closed canopy of mature rain forest on the flanks of Morne Diablotin. The ridge dips and rises except in a few steep places as you pass huge gommye, chatannye, and baw dyab. The higher you go, the better your chance to see or hear both the imperial and red-necked parrots. After about two and a half hours you'll come to a rare opening in the canopy with views of the Hampstead Valley. From this point the trail becomes difficult to follow; unless you have a guide, it's time to turn back.

16. Palmiste Ridge Trail

Time: 4 hours round-trip. | **Difficulty:** 2–3. | **Trailhead:** Go north of the Melville Hall airfield and turn left onto a small feeder road that is just beyond a wet pasture. The road skirts the edge of the airfield and about 1.75 miles later forks to the left; go straight. After another half mile you may have to stop and park because the road becomes so rough. Otherwise, continue for another mile (hopefully in a four-wheel-drive vehicle) to the small hut that marks the beginning of the trail up Fire Flint Ravine to Palmiste Ridge.

The first 500 feet are steep up a narrow ridge. Then the path flattens out as you enter mature rain forest that becomes ever taller and denser. After about a mile the forest growth becomes dramatically reduced, which allows good views of Melville Hall River to Morne Concorde and Mang Peak.

Another hour or two of walking will take you well into the Forest Reserve and high up on the slopes of Mosquito Mountain (3,500 feet), but the trail is not well defined because it is seldom used. Turn back whenever the path seems to disappear, so you don't, too.

17. The Carib Reserve

Time: 2 hours to drive through the reserve, stop, and see the sights. | **Difficulty:** 1. | **Trailhead:** From Melville Hall Airport, take coastal road south to Castle Bruce

The East Coast

This 3,700-acre reserve on the northeast coast has a population density of less than one person per acre. The Caribs grow bananas and fish from dugout canoes using hand lines, as their ancestors did. No historical pageant, museum, or any sort of tourist attraction has been established, although several good stands offer Carib-made artifacts, including hand-woven baskets and carved turtles.

In addition to trading with and observing how Caribs of today look and live, there are two short stops of interest. One is L'Escalier Tête Chien, which translates from the Creole patois as "the trail of the snake staircase." Tête chien ("dog's head") is the local name for a boa constrictor whose head is shaped like a dog's. The snake's staircase is a hardened lava flow that juts into the sea from the headland. The surface of each staircase "step" in the flow is patterned with a circle or mark, just like a snakeskin. This natural formation is important in Carib history, although explanations for the importance differ. One legend has it that the formation is that of a petrified snake that once came ashore to grab a virgin. Another version says that the Caribs used to follow the staircase up to its head in the mountains to obtain special powers. The stone snake is a 15-minute walk from the village of Sineku.

A more interesting stop is the Catholic church, an A-frame "mouina" called St. Marie of the Caribs. The altar is of special note: It is a canoe similar to the ones that brought the Caribs from the Orinoco region. Those original canoes were much larger, according to legend, able to hold as many as 50 occupants. Murals on the church walls inside and out depict Carib history. The Church of the Immaculate Conception at Salybia also has a canoe altar.

18. SARI SARI FALLS

Length: About 2 miles round-trip.. | **Time:** 80 minutes. | **Difficulty:** 2–3, unless it rains. Then, look out—and get out because the area is prone to flash floods. | **Trailhead:** On the east coast high in the valley behind the village of La Plaine. The path to the 180-foot falls is at the end of the village.

The falls are at the end of a canyon outside the national park. The trail starts easily in open fields, then becomes tougher as it borders the river and passes through secondary rain forest. The last 15 minutes offer a moderately tough rock scramble up the White River to the falls. This dry riverbed and the canyon are subject to flash floods in the rainy season, so this hike should not be undertaken without local assistance. Absolutely avoid this spot during the rainy season.

19. VICTORIA FALLS

Time: 90 minutes round-trip. | **Difficulty:** 2–3 in the dry season. | **Trailhead:** The village of La Roche on the east coast.

Victoria Falls is among the island's most photogenic waterfalls. To reach it, you'll hike another dry riverbed through another steep-sided canyon. This is another hike not recommended during the rainy season because flash flooding is potentially even greater here than at Sari Sari. Remember, it can be dry on the coast while torrential rains pelt the interior. Use a guide to find the easiest route over the big boulders.

8   DOMINICAN REPUBLIC

Local Saying: "It is better to have a stubborn donkey than a jealous wife."

A frequent complaint about Caribbean hiking is that most trails are short, only day trips at best. Welcome to the Dominican Republic, where week-long hikes through high mountains are a routine activity, not an unusual adventure.

The Dominican Republic occupies two-thirds of Hispaniola; Haiti owns the other third. The Caribbean's second-largest island, Hispaniola is very mountainous and houses the Caribbean's highest hill, Pico Duarte, 10,700 feet high. Climbing it can be tough, which may explain why the first recorded ascent wasn't until 1944, to mark the 100th anniversary of independence from Haiti.

Besides having the tallest mountain, the Dominican Republic has the most varied terrain of all the Caribbean islands. There are tropical rain forests, fertile valleys, cascading waterfalls, rushing rivers, inviting ocean beaches, giant sand dunes, mangrove jungles, ancient Taino ceremonial sites, plenty of caves, picturesque villages and cities. . . . and the Caribbean's most historic city walk, the old city of Santo Domingo. It features historic buildings dating back to the earliest European settlement of the New World.

The Dominican Republic was one of the islands visited by Christopher Columbus on his first voyage. After landing in the Bahamas and then at Cuba, Columbus arrived here on December 5, 1492. The island's mountainous terrain reminded him of Spain, so he called it La Isla Espanola, the Spanish island. Corruption of the term changed it to Hispaniola.

Columbus wrecked the *Santa Maria* trying to find the gold a Taino chief told him was on an island called Cibao located farther east. The morning after the ship went aground, Tainos helped the sailors salvage whatever was left. The ship's planking was used to build a fort, La Navidad, to commemorate the fact that it was Christmas Day.

Shortly after, Columbus sailed back to Spain, where he was treated as a hero. He returned to Hispaniola in 1493 with a fleet of 17 ships and landed at Fort Navidad on November 23, 1493. Columbus had left 39 men behind at the fort; on his return he found the fort burned and his men dead. A local Taino chief had ordered them killed after they kidnapped and raped a number of local women.

Columbus decided to leave the area and establish a colony, La Isabela, farther to the east. In its first 18 months, fire destroyed two-thirds of La Isabela, his men were plagued by sickness, and a hurricane sank several ships. Yet the Spaniards managed to build a chain of fortresses from the north coast to the south coast, many of which would grow into towns and cities (such as Santiago, Concepcion de la Vega, and Bonao). In 1496, Columbus left Hispaniola.

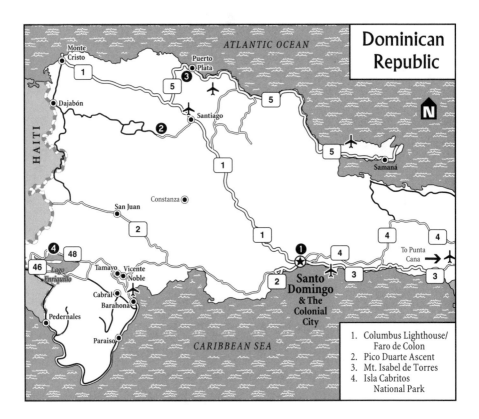

Dominican
Republic

ATLANTIC OCEAN

Monte Cristo
Puerto Plata
Dajabón
Santiago
Samaná
HAITI
Constanza
San Juan
Tamayo Vicente Noble
Lago Enriquillo
Cabral
Barahona
Pedernales
Paraiso
CARIBBEAN SEA
Santo Domingo & The Colonial City
To Punta Cana →

1. Columbus Lighthouse/
   Faro de Colon
2. Pico Duarte Ascent
3. Mt. Isabel de Torres
4. Isla Cabritos
   National Park

Before departing, he made his brother, Bartolome, governor of the island and ordered that another city be attempted, this time on the south coast. Nueva Isabela was a success but not by its original name—residents preferred to call it Santo Domingo to avoid the bad luck of La Isabela.

Despite the island's long history, the Dominican Republic remains a landfall still unknown to the majority of Americans, even those who frequently travel to the Caribbean. Yet Canadian and European charter flights bring hundreds of thousands of tourists annually to pack the many modern resorts located on some of the hemisphere's most beautiful beaches. These travelers have discovered that the Dominican people are some of the warmest, friendliest, and most generous people anywhere.

The Dominican Republic seems out of favor with Americans for several reasons. For one, the name is odd compared to most islands and not very appealing. Yet the name has an important origin. It is a tribute to the Dominican friars who fought to better conditions for Indians on the island almost 300 years before the French Revolution. However, the term *republic* may only emphasize the country's past political troubles.

Ironically, the well-known Dominican passion for baseball is the result of U.S. troop occupation from 1916 to 1924, the first of two U.S. troop deployments due to political unrest.

From 1930 until his death in 1961, the infamous dictator Rafael Trujillo dominated the country. After his death the country fell into turmoil, which in 1965 prompted an invasion of 20,000 U.S. troops to restore order. Once things settled down, Dominican politics became known for corruption and powerful strongmen. Democracy and stability didn't take firm root until the 1990s. That political past isn't very encouraging to Americans, who are notoriously timid tourists, avoiding any possible trouble spots.

Bottom line: What probably makes many Americans most uncomfortable is who shares Hispaniola with the Dominican Republic—Haiti. Haiti is the Caribbean's poorest and most unstable country. Most of all, Haiti is a land ravaged by AIDS.

So, American tourists go to what seem like safer places, particularly to islands where the people speak their language. For the Dominican Republic, this is unfair guilt by association. The Dominican Republic is one of the hemisphere's most violence-free countries, and it doesn't have a serious AIDS problem. As for the language difference, it's not a serious inconvenience. Sign language, gestures, and a smile achieve successful communication almost every time.

I wasn't particularly interested in visiting the Dominican Republic myself, until I went in 1999, and then only because of a magazine assignment. Within nine months of my first visit, I'd returned twice. I like the Dominican Republic that much, especially its people, who may be as poor as church mice but they're cheerful and friendly and they'll do anything to help you. I'm completely sold on the place. A lot of other Americans would be, too, if only they would visit. In addition to the tallest peak, the Dominican Republic also has the region's lowest spot (Lago Enriquillo, 130 feet below sea level). The beaches truly are outstanding, among the Caribbean's best.

Compared to many other islands, vacationers will find Dominican prices a real bargain. You should take a look. If you enjoy hiking, how can you not?

TRAVEL TIPS

Area: The eastern two-thirds of Hispaniola, an area of 18,712 square miles.

Language: Predominantly Spanish. English is most likely to be spoken in resort areas. German is spoken widely along the north coast. Hand signals work well anywhere.

Population: About 8 million; 2.5 million live in Santo Domingo, the capital city.

Time Zone: The island has a twice-yearly time change to stay on the same schedule as New York and Miami.

Rainy Season: December and May are usually the rainy months in the central mountain range (Cordillera Central), which includes Pico Duarte. Of course, it can rain at anytime of year and does quite frequently.

Getting There: Who *doesn't* fly here? The Dominican Republic receives far more tourists than any other Caribbean country. It has 7 international airports. More than 60 chartered airlines (mostly from Europe and Canada) fly into the Santo Domingo, Puerto Plata, and Punta Cana airports. Carriers from the United States include American, Continental, and Northwest.

Documents: U.S. and Canadians citizens do not need passports; an original birth certificate with photo ID will suffice. A US$10 tourist card is required for entry. Tourist cards are available for purchase in the Dominican Republic's international airports before you proceed through Immigration and Customs. Keep the tourist permit safely tucked away with your passport because you will need to surrender it at departure.

Getting Around: Rental cars are readily available at all the international airports. In Santo Domingo, most cars more than five years old look like they've been attacked with ball peen hammers; it's from all the collisions. Driving in the Dominican Republic is like finding yourself in the middle of a video game with you as the target. Compounding the problem are the swarms of motorcycles that serve as taxis. Their owners, who may never have passed a driving test, are as pesky and annoying as a mosquito swarm.

If you spend too much time in the capital city, you may find yourself driving just as crazily as the residents. In the country, beware the tour buses. They hog the road and have no regard for automobiles. They do kill quite a few people each year, as I saw first-hand. Never take your eyes off the road in front because you never know what will suddenly confront you.

Taxis and public buses may be the best alternative if you're going to stay only in Santo Domingo.

Where to Stay: Where there are good beaches (and that's just about the entire coastline) there are all-inclusive resorts. For a description of the Casa Marina and Amhsa properties, look at www.amhsamarina.com. For the Allegro resorts, call (800) 858-2258; www.allegroresorts.com. However, the many small hotels throughout the country are a good bargain. If you're going to climb Pico Duarte, you should spend a night or two at Rancho Baiguate in Jarabacoa in the Cordillera Central, where it's wonderfully cool in the evening, (809) 696-0318; www.ranchobaiguate.com.do.

Camping: Permitted in Armando Bermudez and Jose del Carmen Ramirez National Parks, located in the Dominican Alps.

Currency: The Dominican peso, although American dollars are accepted everywhere. The rate of exchange varies but is around US$1 = RD$15. Banks are open weekdays from 9 a.m. to 4 p.m. You might find some banks open on Saturday mornings. The Casas de Cambio offer the same exchange rate as banks and have expanded hours, staying open form 8 a.m. to 6 p.m. weekdays and until 2 p.m. or 4 p.m. on Saturdays.

Travelers' checks are often difficult to cash, but international debit cards work all the time. ATMs that honor Plus or Cirrus International are located in all big cities around the country. The first menu choice asks whether you want to make the translation in Spanish or English, so they are easy to operate. Avoid the "quick-change artist" on the streets who wave wads of bills in your face, trying to tempt you with high exchange rates.

Taxes & Tips: Hotels charge a total of 23% in taxes: 5% room tax, 8% sales tax, and 10% service charge. A 10% tip is standard in restaurants and bars. The departure tax is US$10.

Electricity: 110 volts, 60 cycles, same as the United States.

Safety/Health Warnings: Avoid the tap water everywhere. Drink only bottled water. Raw vegetables and ice can also be serious problems. The local beer, El Presidente, is excellent. Malaria is present, so always wear insect repellent in the wilderness. You may want to take medication if you're going to spend a few months on the island.

The Dominican Republic is one of the most crime-free and violence-free nations in Latin America. However, in Santo Domingo the police sometimes stop motorists and demand money. I had one get in my car, show me his ID and his gun, and demand US$100. He left empty-handed, disgusted and shaking his head when the woman with me laughed at his request. Her laughter seemed to deflate his macho pride. We didn't have that much cash on us, anyway.

Snakes and Other Venomous Creatures: No poisonous snakes but look out for tarantulas, whose bite is painful but rarely fatal. Beware of scorpions in the lowlands if you've left your boots outside overnight; shake them out before putting them on.

Hiking/Walking Services: Two outfitters make the trek up Pico Duarte and they're both good. **Iguana Mama** is located in the wind-surfing capital of the Caribbean, at Cabarete on the Dominican Republic's north coast, (800) 849-4720 or (809) 571-0908; www.iguanamama.com. The owner is American, and the staff (many from the States or Canada) is fluent in English. Mountain biking is the real specialty, but hiking is a close second. Fully guided trips up Pico Duarte (including transportation from Cabarete on the north coast close to Puerto Plata), guides, food, mules, and most equipment are $350 per person for 3 days, 2 nights; $425 per person for 4 days, 3 nights. Iguana Mama begins the climb at La Cienaga, the most popular route.

Rancho Baiguate in the Dominican Alps at Jarabacoa offers trips to Pico Duarte as well as rafting, canyoneering, paragliding, and mountain biking; (809) 696-0318; www.ranchobaiguate.com.do. Most trips include a first night at the ranch, transportation to the ranger station at La Cienaga, mules, guides, and camping equipment. Three trekking programs are offered. The Pico Express of 3 days and 2 nights is US$450 for one person, which drops to $270 each for 4 or more. The slower-paced Pico Relax is 3 nights and 4 days at $755 for 1 person, $322 each for 4 or more. Pico Duarte with a side trip to Valle del Tetero is $930 for 1, $450 each for 4 or more.

For walking tours of the Colonial City, the Columbus Lighthouse, and other interesting places in Santo Domingo, contact **Student and Researcher Services**; (809) 221-6471; www.bravo2000.com/educationalservices. Lynne Guitar and her staff offer tours in English, Spanish, and French.

Additional Information: If you plan to hike Pico Duarte, you'll need quite a few items, including warm clothing. It can drop to 18° F at the summit in winter and it's chilly any time of year. Examine the Pico Duarte Check List in this chapter before you depart. You'll need everything on it.

For more information, call (800) 752-1151 in the United States. Or visit any of the following websites: Ministry of Tourism, www.dominicana.com; National Hotel and Restaurant Association at www.drhotels.com; or www.hispaniola.com. In Canada, call (888) 494-5050. In the United Kingdom, (44) 171-242-7778; www.domrep.touristboard@virgin.net. In Germany, call (4969) 9139-7878; www.domtur@aol.com.

SANTO DOMINGO-THE COLONIAL CITY AFOOT!

Time: 2–3 hours, longer if you go in some of the museums. | **Difficulty:** 1. | **Trailhead:** There are many possible ways to stroll the Old City. This route starts at the fortress of Diego Columbus, son of Christopher, located in the Plaza de Espana across from the Las Atarazanas Street.

As the first European city in the Western Hemisphere, the City of Santo Domingo de Guzman is a UNESCO World Heritage Site. The old Colonial City is home of the first cathedral, first hospital, first monastery, first university, and first court of law in this hemisphere, all of which survive in some restored form. Situated beside the Ozama River, the Colonial City with its cobblestone streets, medieval fortresses, and palaces is a walker's dream.

But this is not a dead city. In the evening, after the tour groups depart, shuttered buildings turn into sidewalk cafés that breathe a whole new life into the streets and plazas. Across the Ozama, looking like the flames of a departing rocket ship, is the huge Columbus Lighthouse, containing the purported remains of the explorer. The monument definitely is worth visiting after dark. The Old City can be enjoyed day or night.

1. **Museo Alcazar de Colon:** This former fort now turned museum was built by Columbus's son, Diego, during the early 1500s to be the seat of the viceroy court (*colon* is the Spanish word for Columbus). Diego and his wife, Maria de Toledo, lived here until 1523, when he was recalled to Spain. Other relatives lived here for decades afterward. The building was abandoned in 1770 and turned into a garbage dump. Cave-ins in 1809 and 1835 left the building in ruins. Skilled stonecutters first restored it in 1957, with added refinements made during several later restorations. Serious attempts were made to remain faithful to the original construction and decor. The fortress is now a museum with furnishings that were provided by Spain—twice. The first set of furnishing and decorations were mostly destroyed by American gunfire and bombing during the 1965 invasion, requiring their replacement by the Spanish government.

2. **Plaza de Espana:** This large, open-air plaza in front of the Alcazar de Colon fronts numerous small restaurants and outdoor cafés that are quite popular in late afternoon. The street bordering the plaza is closed to traffic. In the past it was the Plaza de Armas, where soldiers paraded. Before that it was the *conuco* (cultivated fields) of the native Tainos.

3. **Puerto de San Diego:** Built in 1571, for a time this was the city's main gate. The wall was intended to defend against any attack from the river. Some of the original wall remains.

4. **Museo de las Casas Reales:** The Museum of the Royal Houses is considered one of the Dominican Republic's best. Each of its rooms, displaying artifacts from the sixteenth to eighteenth centuries, including salvaged treasure, has been richly restored. The great anchor outside the museum belonged to the *Nuestra Senora de Guadalupe* that sank in 1724 during a storm in the Bay of Samana, located far to the northeast. Open 9 a.m. to 5 p.m. Tuesday through Saturday and 10 a.m. to 1:30 p.m. on Sunday.

5. **Reloj de Sol:** The sun dial was built in 1753 and situated so that the nobility could easily tell the time from their windows.

6. **Pantheon Nacional:** Constructed in 1747 as a Jesuit church, this impressive building and its neoclassical facade are built of limestone blocks. It later became a tobacco warehouse and theater until Rafael Trujillo turned it into the National Mausoleum in 1958. Many of the country's top leaders are sealed in the two marble walls. A soldier is always stationed at the entrance. Open to the public, but no shorts or tank tops allowed.

7. **Hostal Nicolas de Ovanado:** This large building with a Gothic facade dates to 1509. It was the home of Governor Nicolas de Ovanado who ordered the city rebuilt in its present

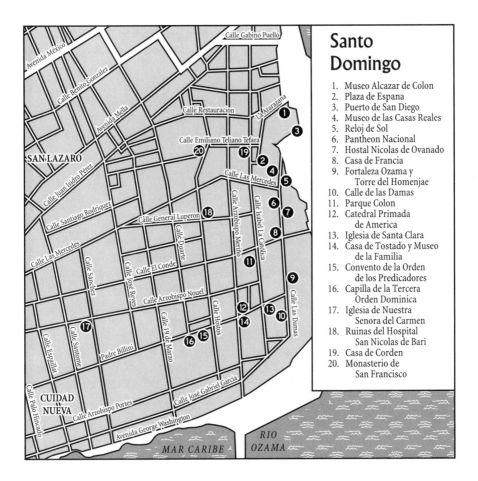

Santo Domingo

1. Museo Alcazar de Colon
2. Plaza de Espana
3. Puerto de San Diego
4. Museo de las Casas Reales
5. Reloj de Sol
6. Pantheon Nacional
7. Hostal Nicolas de Ovanado
8. Casa de Francia
9. Fortaleza Ozama y
   Torre del Homenjae
10. Calle de las Damas
11. Parque Colon
12. Catedral Primada
    de America
13. Iglesia de Santa Clara
14. Casa de Tostado y Museo
    de la Familia
15. Convento de la Orden
    de los Predicadores
16. Capilla de la Tercera
    Orden Dominica
17. Iglesia de Nuestra
    Senora del Carmen
18. Ruinas del Hospital
    San Nicolas de Bari
19. Casa de Corden
20. Monasterio de
    San Francisco

location after the settlement on the east bank was destroyed by a hurricane. This building and the attached buildings along the entire block will eventually be a 300-room five-star hotel.

8. Casa de Francia: Built in the early 1500s, this was the house of Hernán Cortés, who planned the conquest of Mexico. It was later turned into a series of government offices, a bank, and court offices. Today, the House of France is home to the French embassy. This building apparently had the same architects as the Museo de las Casas Reales (see p. 110). Similarities include double bays in the lower and upper stories and the repeating pattern of windows and doors on both levels.

9. Fortaleza Ozama y Torre del Homenjae: Built in 1505, this oldest fort in the Americas was amazingly well constructed. Until the 1960s it served as a prison and military garrison. From the main gate you'll see the Torre del Homenjae whose two-meter-thick walls are rampant with rifle holes. Its tower offers an excellent view of the city. A statue of the famous historian Gonzalo Fernandez de Oviedo is on the esplanade. Tour guides normally station themselves at the main gate. If you take one, agree on a price beforehand. The fort is open daily 9 a.m. to 5 p.m.

10. **Calle de las Damas:** Running north and south in front of Ozama Fort, this is the hemisphere's oldest European paved street. It was paved to provide Dona Maria and her ladies of the court palace to take their afternoon stroll. Paved streets were nothing new in the Americas when the Spanish arrived. The Incas had them hundreds of years earlier.

11. **Parque Colon:** The shaded park, with a large statue of Columbus, is a regular meeting place for residents. You'll also find a small horde of taxi drivers and persistent tourist guides. A cigar factory and one of the country's two Amber Museums border the park. (The other Amber Museum is in Puerto Plata.) This one is open daily 9 a.m. to 5 p.m.

12. **Catedral Primada de America:** The Cathedral of Our Lady of Santa Maria of the Incarnation is the Colonial City's most famous landmark. It is the oldest working church in the New World. Diego Columbus laid the first stone in 1514, but it wasn't until 1521, when a new bishop arrived, that serious construction began. Building continued until 1540 under different architects who emphasized different styles. That's why the high vaulted ceiling is Gothic, the arches Romanesque, and the ornamentation baroque.

   The cathedral has 14 small chapels, a main chapel, and 2 altars. Instead of a cross vault, it has three naves. The interior underwent massive changes when Drake and his pirates used it as their base when they attacked the city in 1586. Anything that could be carried away left with Drake. The cathedral was restored in 1998. Open daily 9 a.m. to 4 p.m. *Note:* No one wearing shorts or tank tops is permitted inside the old cathedral. On a hot day, you might want to visit it first, then change into shorts.

13. **Iglesia de Santa Clara:** The hemisphere's first nunnery, built in 1552 and thoroughly sacked by Drake in the 1580s, was restored with funds from the Spanish monarchy. The Renaissance-style portal has a bust of St. Claire. Closed except during Sunday mass.

14. **Casa de Tostado y Museo de la Familia:** Formerly the home of Francisco Tostado, this sixteenth-century building with its combination of Moorish and Gothic ornamentation is now a museum containing nineteenth-century furniture and artifacts. Open daily 9 a.m. to 2 p.m.; closed Wednesday. Tostado and his family made their fortune as owners of sugarcane plantations.

15. **Convento de la Orden de los Predicadores:** Built in 1510, this is the New World's oldest still-standing church. The chapel vault is notable for its astrological and mythological depictions carved in stone. This is the first convent of the Dominican order in the Americas and where the chronicler of the Spanish atrocities against the Tainos, Father Bartolome de las Casas, penned his accounts.

16. **Capilla de la Tercera Orden Dominica:** Built in 1529, the Chapel of the Third Dominican Order is the only building to survive the centuries without needing extensive renovation. Today it is a church office.

17. **Iglesia de Nuestra Senora del Carmen:** Built during the mid-1500s, the church initially was constructed of stone, then of brick. Drake set it on fire in 1586. After being rebuilt, it served as a hospital, a church, a jail, and an inn. Today the church is known for the mahogany figure of Jesus, venerated on Wednesday during Holy Week.

18. Ruinas del Hospital San Nicolas de Bari: Until much of it was knocked down as part of a 1911 public works project, the New World's first hospital survived everything humans and nature had thrown at it. It was ordered built in 1503 by Governor Ovando, with the floor plan in the shape of a cross. This building and the Franciscan monastery are the two major monuments the Commission of Monuments has decided to maintain in stable condition without renovation.

19. Casa de Corden: The Cord House, with a central courtyard and brick arcade, is the first Spanish-style residence in the Americas. Built by Francisco de Garay, the gate is trimmed with a cord similar to that of the San Franciscan monks.

20. Monasterio de San Francisco: Built on a hilltop overlooking the city in 1508, this first monastery in the Americas initially had three connecting chapels. Like many other buildings, it was set on fire by Drake in 1586. It was rebuilt and destroyed by earthquakes in 1673 and 1751. From 1881 to the 1930s it served as an insane asylum. A hurricane demolished much of the building, which is now open to the sky. Some of the chains once used to restrain asylum inmates remain.

1. COLUMBUS LIGHTHOUSE/FARO DE COLON

Time: 2 hours. You should visit the site both during the day and at night to appreciate the differences in appearance. | **Difficulty:** 1. | **Trailhead:** From the Colonial City drive east to the Columbus Lighthouse located across the Ozama River. On Avenue Espana in the Sans Souci district.

This is a strange-looking monument, created in the form of a cross with the base stretching for a very long block. It is 688 feet high (taller than the Washington Monument) and 131 feet wide. It was built between 1986 and 1992 at a cost of US$200 million to celebrate the 500th anniversary of the discovery of the New World. The interior has numerous exhibits related to Christopher Columbus and the early colonial days. Most of the items are reproductions, and few of the accompanying explanations are in English. An ornate tomb is supposed to contain the remains of Columbus, but that's unlikely because both Spain and Cuba claim to have them, too. Naturally, the lighthouse is most impressive at night. When the clouds hang low, the 149 xenon searchlights on the roof create a brilliant white cross; on other nights the lights simply shoot skyward. The exhibits are open 10 a.m. to 5 p.m. Tuesday through Sunday.

PICO DUARTE

2. PICO DUARTE ASCENT

Length: Varies according to route. | **Time:** At least a full day, preferably 2. | **Difficulty:** Varies according to route and whether or not you ride a mule.

There's an old Caribbean saying: "Canoes without good bottoms shouldn't go to sea." People without good bottoms shouldn't try ascending Pico Duarte, either. I spent far more time riding a mule up the Caribbean's highest mountain than I ever expected. A lot of hikers do. But the bruises to my pride were nothing compared to those on my hindquarters, which only thick layers of moleskin were able to soothe.

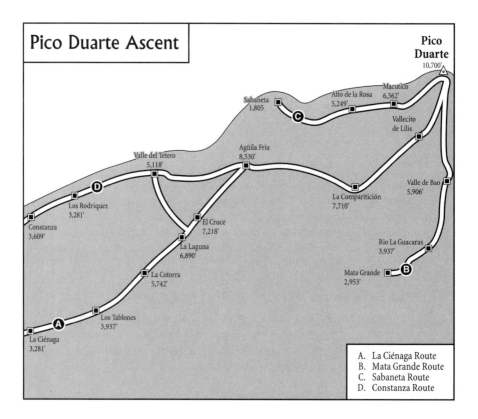

Pico Duarte Ascent

Pico
Duarte
10,700'

Macutico 6,562'
Alto de la Rosa 5,249'
Sabaneta 1,805
Vallecito de Lilis
Agüila Fria 8,530'
Valle del Tetero 5,118'
La Comparitición 7,710'
Valle de Bao 5,906'
Los Rodriquez 3,281'
El Cruce 7,218'
Constanza 3,609'
La Laguna 6,890'
Rio La Guacaras 3,937'
La Cotorra 5,742'
Mata Grande 2,953'
Los Tablones 3,937'
La Ciénaga 3,281'

A. La Ciénaga Route
B. Mata Grande Route
C. Sabaneta Route
D. Constanza Route

Mules are commonly taken on summit attempts. They're used to haul up equipment and hikers having trouble with the altitude. However, you need specifically to rent mules for riding; you can't plop on just any mule. If you do rent a riding mule (US$10 to 20 per day) make sure it has a mane. The mane is what you'll be gripping much of the time, especially on the way down. If the mane is shaved off, you'll have nothing to hold onto. Also be sure to get a saddle with a saddle horn, too. Have the cinches checked regularly—particularly on the descent, when the animals may have to do some gully jumping—or your saddle and you could fall off. I saw that happen. The rider was knocked unconscious briefly and bruised, but amazingly suffered no broken bones.

Pico Duarte rises 10,700 feet; regardless of how athletic your hiking companions are, the climb is arduous, especially if you're not accustomed to altitude. You can't reach the actual summit by mule. You have to hoof it yourself over the last stretch, an effort beyond a lot of people who can't handle the thin air. According to park officials, of the many thousands who attempt to summit Pico Duarte every year, only about 1,000 succeed. Two hundred of these are tourists, the rest Dominicans.

When I started my own climb I realized that I was in bad company after I met my fellow hikers: a young, amazingly fit couple who are members of the Norwegian armed forces and a marathon cyclist from the Virgin Islands. Being burdened with a few more decades of living than they, I suspected I would be rear guard.

We registered at the park office at La Cienaga and arranged for a park guide and pack mules. Then we made the first leg of the hike, a one-hour, very gradual 2.5-mile walk to Los Tablones, one of two shelters on the trail. The second shelter is considerably farther along, 8.7 miles from the first and just 3.1 miles from the summit of Pico Duarte. So, the first day's hike is a breeze, the second a real grind if you're spending only two nights on the trail, as we were.

Near sunset, as we sat in the smoke of our campfire to avoid the thick clouds of mosquitoes and prepared to eat, the pack mules of a much larger group started pouring into our tiny camp. We rushed back to the cabin to claim the best sleeping quarters, a sort of bedroom. At least it had a door that closed. The 16 strangers had to pile together in the dining room. The next day, we departed early to claim the prime spot at the next shelter. As we began the marathon walk, I noticed a boy about 11 years old slowly trailing me on a mule. It turned out the mule was for me when I pooped out. Why should anyone expect that? I'd had no trouble the day before. But the summit is almost 12 miles away and 6,000 feet higher than Los Tablones. Our schedule called for making the summit in late afternoon, then descending another 2.5 miles to stay overnight at the second shelter. Definitely a demanding hike, but I intended to walk most of the way with only an occasional time-out on a mule.

However, the youngsters who were my climbing companions wanted to see if they could climb Pico Duarte in record time. Their cheetah-like lope made it impossible for me to keep up if I stopped and photographed the extraordinarily beautiful flowers and ferns, which I did. My picture taking, compounded by the burden of a longer (but fruitful) life, caused me to fall farther behind. I gave up and began riding the mule long before I'd dreamed I would. But at least I could pause to take photos without feeling like I'd never reach the summit.

The weather was picture-perfect until after lunch, when we made the final assault on Pico Duarte. In minutes we were covered in clouds. The sharp, clean smell of the mountain fog arrived just ahead of the sound of distant thunder. As the rain started and thunder surrounded us, I came across two unexpected, grisly scenes. One was the seven-month-old skeleton of a mule, the other a carcass of a horse. No one was sure what happened to the mule, but the horse had apparently died from lung problems just the day before. Altitude sickness? Well, no one talked about it much, but people also die, usually of heart attacks, while attempting this climb.

The thunder subsided, but it was drizzling at the summit, which is marked by a statue and flapping, wind-tattered Dominican flags. A metal pole beside the flags hummed with the sound of enough electricity to power a small village. Lightning obviously was still present, and this was not a place to stay for long, especially because the clouds obscured almost everything.

Returning to the shelter, we found that the other hiking group had just arrived. They were drenched long before reaching the shelter, and many were exhausted. Although it was only 6 p.m., several were already sacked out in their sleeping bags. They didn't plan to seek the summit until morning, when the peak is often sunny and cloudless. After making the peak, they would go only part way back, spending three nights on the trail instead of just two. Many of these hikers were close to my age, and I envied them. They had the opportunity to stay afoot and hike at their own pace.

My younger companions made fun of the other group's slow progress. Then the marathon cyclist realized he never noticed the two dead animals near the summit. He was amazed that he was so immersed in himself that he could have overlooked something so out of the ordinary. I found that a little scary. Slow and mule-driven I may have been, but at least I always knew and appreciated where I was. It was worth my mightily sore butt.

PICO DUARTE CHECK LIST

Most Caribbean hikes are walks of only a few hours. You have few chances to undertake a major expedition anywhere, which makes the Pico Duarte climb very special. The hike is a major undertaking that requires careful planning and coordination. You can't just put on some sandals and head out.

Following is a list of the items you'll need. How much you have to gather and pack depends on whether you're hiking on your own or joining a guided hike, where the outfitter takes care of the major essentials.

Food: You'll need to bring everything with you because there are no grocery stores in the small villages marking the various trailheads.

Water: Carry at least two water bottles on each day's walk. Water is available in some places, but always use a filter.

Hiking Boots: Not tennis shoes but the real thing. You'll need good ankle support and traction on this often muddy trail.

Camp Shoes/Slippers: Get out of your hiking boots and walk around camp in something comfortable.

Rain Gear: Come prepared, because the odds are you'll get wet at some point.

Sunscreen, Lip Block, and Sunglasses: You need these anywhere in Caribbean but particularly at high altitude.

Hat: To keep the sun and rain off your face.

Day Pack: With insect repellent, camera and film, toilet paper, and snacks. Your rain gear and water bottles should be stored in the day pack or add a fanny pack to carry some of the items.

Flashlight

Short & Long Pants; Short and Long Sleeve Shirts: Enough clothing, including underwear and socks to last the trip.

Sleepwear: Especially if you plan on staying in the cabins, because there will be lots of other people around.

Sleeping Bag: Some outfitters rent them.

Swimsuit, Small Towel

Toiletries

Duct (gray) Tape: Indispensable and always good for something.

Sweater or Jacket: It's chilly at La Comparticion, the Caribbean's highest campsite. In winter, the temperature has dropped as low as 18°F. Frost is common in December and January.

Garbage Bags: To pack clothes in so they don't get wet. On a guided hike, you won't have access to your gear from the time you break camp and until it's set up again.

A. La Cienaga Route

Length: 14.3 miles. | **Time:** 3–4 days. | **Difficulty:** 5, vertical ascent of 7,464 feet. | **Trailhead:** The most popular route is to leave from near La Cienaga. You must register with the ranger in the Armando Bermudez National Park before setting out. The park office is 2.5 miles from La Cienaga. The trail description is broken up into sections below

The path gradually rises and follows the Los Tablones River, which has several homes along it. You'll see mostly dense, tropical broadleaf forest and sections of wild cane.

Section 1: La Cienaga Ranger Office (3,281 feet) to Los Tablones (3,937 feet). **Length:** 2.5 miles.

There are only two cabins on the trail. One is at Los Tablones. Some hikers, as we did, set out in the afternoon and spend their first night here. It's a tough 9.3 miles to the next cabin at La Comparticion, only 2.5 miles from the peak. You can camp in specified areas if you have a tent, but most travelers use the cabins.

If you're in excellent shape, you can hike from Los Tablones, ascend the peak, and then come back to use the shelter at La Comparticion, all in a single day. That's a total of 14.3 miles, most of it uphill. On the third day, it's a 11.8-mile trip downhill to the park office. In some ways, it's as difficult as the ascent.

Another option, no less grueling, is to hike the entire day to reach La Comparticion, spend the night there, and then leave at 4:30 a.m. for the peak to watch the sunrise before returning to La Cienaga. However, you're not as likely to be rained on at the summit if you make the ascent in the morning.

If you're in average shape, break the hike up over three nights, not just two. You'll enjoy it more. Whatever plan you decide, it's still 7,464 feet of vertical ascent.

Section 2: Los Tablones (3,937 feet) to La Cotorra (5,742 feet). **Length:** 2.5 miles.

You'll follow the river for 0.3 mile and then turn to start a rapid ascent. This climb is a good indication of the steep incline you'll encounter elsewhere. Along the way you'll have a good view of the La Cienaga Valley. The vegetation changes to a mixed broadleaf and pine forest, including almonds and sierra palms, which are important foods for the wild boar that roam here. Note the air plants (epiphytes) in the trees and the many ground ferns bordering the trail. La Cotorra is a good place to spot the Hispaniola parrot.

Section 3: La Cotorra (5,742 feet) to La Laguna (6,890 feet). **Length:** 1.5 miles.

This section offers lots of scenic views as you follow the ridge line. Broadleaf and pine forest still prevail. Water is available at the La Laguna rest area, but you'll need a filter.

🌴 SECTION 4: LA LAGUNA (6,890 FEET) TO EL CRUCE (7,218 FEET) TO AGUITA FRIA (8,530 FEET).

Length: 3.4 miles.

After a steep climb to El Cruce, you pass a junction to Valle Tetero. If you want to extend the ascent by an extra day, take the trail and overnight at the Valle Tetero campground (see below). Otherwise, continue on the ridge line through pine forest. Just before reaching the Aguita Fria rest area, you'll pass a large, wet bog that's the source of two rivers, the Yaque del Norte and the Yaque del Sur. *Adding an extra day:* El Cruce (7,218 feet) to Valle Tetero (5,118 feet) to Aguita Fria (8,530 feet). Distance: 9.3 miles. From El Cruce you'll descend to a large, grassy valley with terrific views of the surrounding mountains. A large boulder in the valley has a Taino petroglyph, the only one on the trail. After overnighting in the Valle Tetero, it's a rugged 5-mile climb to rejoin the main trail at Aquita Fria, only 4.6 miles from the peak.

🌴 SECTION 5: AQUITA FRIA (8,530 FEET) TO LA COMPARTICION (7,710 FEET).
Length: 2.2 miles.

Some downhill at last! Of course, you'll make up for it later. You'll enjoy some great views of the surrounding mountains during the descent to the cabin at La Comparticion. Because this is the main way station on the way to the peak, expect it to be crowded. The campsite may not have running water or indoor plumbing, but it does have a satellite telephone. It may be tempting to try to order a pizza, but the telephone is for emergencies.

🌴 SECTION 6: LA COMPARTICION (7.710 FEET) TO PICO DUARTE (10,700 FEET).
Length: 2.5 miles.

From this point it's a short distance to the summit, almost 900 vertical feet higher. This last leg does some major culling. The majority of hikers (Dominicans) can't handle the altitude and don't make it to the top. Only several hundred tourists reach Pico Duarte each year.

You'll have a steady climb through pine forest before reaching the open meadow at Vallecito de Lilis. With luck you should have a good view of both Pico Duarte and La Pelona, another high peak. If the clouds have moved in, you'll be lucky to see anything at all. To reach the peak, you'll climb through a sparse pine forest before reaching the boulders that mark the summit. The Dominican flag and a bust of Juan Pablo Duarte mark the crest. If there is lightning in the vicinity, be careful about approaching the summit. Now, it's time to return the way you came.

B. MATA GRANDE ROUTE

Length: 43.5 miles. | **Time:** 6 days. | **Difficulty:** 5; vertical ascent of 12,474 feet. | **Trailhead:** At the small community of Mata Grande just outside the park. It is reached from San Jose de la Matas.

This is the longest, most scenic route with the advantage that you won't retrace your steps on the descent. It's also one of the toughest routes. You will need to arrange transportation because your starting and ending points are far apart. The hike is described in four stages below.

 **SECTION 1: MATA GRANDE (2,953 FEET) TO RIO LA GUACARAS (3,937 FEET).
Length: 12.5 miles.**

The last leg of the day's climb is known as Loma del Cono, the Hill of Cursing. 'Nuff said. The problem is the trail sharply ascends and descends continually until you reach the campground at Rio La Guacaras where there is a small shelter and plenty of camping space. The river can be used for bathing.

 **SECTION 2: RIO LA GUACARAS (3,937 FEET) TO VALLE DE BAO (5,906 FEET).
Length: 6.8 miles.**

This short hike is probably the easiest of all because there are no difficult mountains. Valle de Bao is one of the country's most beautiful high mountain valleys. This can become a crowded camping area, so pitch your tent early. You'll need all the rest you can get for the next day's trek.

**SECTION: 3: VALLE DE BAO (5,906 FEET) TO PICO DUARTE (10,700 FEET)
TO LA COMPARTICION (7,710 FEET). Length: 11.2 miles.**

Start out early because today could be long and grueling. Before you can set foot on Pico Duarte, you have to scale the country's second highest mountain, Pico La Pelona (10,123 feet). It's a steady ascent up La Pelona, followed by a slight drop into Vallecito de Lilis, the Caribbean's highest mountain valley. From here it's only a short walk up to Pico Duarte, then a 2.5-mile descent to the shelter and campground at La Comparticion. Expect La Comparticion to be crowded. Also expect chilly weather at night.

**SECTION: 4. LA COMPARTICION (7,710 FEET) TO LA CIENAGA (3,281 FEET).
Length: 11.8 miles.**

After a brief climb to the resting spot known at Aquita Fria, it's downhill all the way to the ranger station at La Cienaga. This descent is described in detail in the first Pico Duarte hike.

C. THE SABANETA ROUTE

Length: 30 miles each way. | **Time:** 5 days. | **Difficulty:** 5+; vertical ascent: 12,474 feet. This is the toughest route thanks to all the hills and valleys. It also means you should find fewer hikers at the campgrounds. | **Trailhead:** This small community on the southwest side of the park is reached from San Juan de la Maguana. To make thing confusing, another community on the north side of the park also is named Sabaneta. That's the wrong starting point. The hike is described in stages below.

SECTION 1: SABANETA (1,805 FEET) TO ALTO DE LA ROSA (5,249 FEET).
Length: 8.1 miles.

The first 6.2 miles of this walk are easy enough until you reach Arroyo Limon. Then you have to turn into a mountain goat and climb almost straight up from 1,969 feet to 4,593 feet in less than a mile to reach the rest stop at Los Mineros. Thankfully, it's only a short distance and a much less steep walk to the cabin and campground at Alto de la Rosa.

 SECTION 2: ALTO DE LA ROSA (5,249 FEET) TO MACUTICO (6,562 FEET).
Length: 13.7 miles.

No rest for the weary. Today is mostly a continuous up and down with only one relatively flat section. You'll climb almost to 8,200 feet before gradually descending to the cabin and campground at Macutico.

 SECTION 3: MACUTICO (6,562 FEET TO PICO DUARTE (10,700 FEET)
TO LA COMPARTICION (7,710 FEET).
Length: 9.9 miles. Or return to Macutico this same day, a distance of 14.9 miles.

By now you fully comprehend why this is not a very popular route. You still have before you 7.5 miles of tough climbing, first tackling Pico Barraco and then Pico La Pelona, the region's second-highest peak. At Pico La Pelona you'll join the Mata Grande-Pico Duarte trail (see p. 118).

Once atop Pico Duarte, you have a choice of routes: spend the night at La Comparticion just 2.5 miles more and then pack out to La Cienaga the following day or return to Macutico and spend the following night still on the trail at Alto de la Rosa.

D. THE CONSTANZA ROUTE

Length: 36.5 miles. | **Time:** 5–8 days, depending on your exit route. It's 3–4 nights just to Pico Duarte, depending on your pace. | **Difficulty:** 5; vertical ascent: about 6,562 feet. | **Trailhead:** Constanza is a city, not a village, and is reached from La Vega, Bonao, and the Duarte Highway turnoff.

This is the longest route by far though not necessarily the most scenic because you pass through a lot of farmland at the outset. It is described in stages below.

 SECTION 1: CONSTANZA (3,609 FEET) TO LOS RODRIQUEZ (3,281 FEET).
Length: 14.9 miles.

This is a long first day that you can cut almost in half by stopping at the Los Cayetanos campground. But if you do, you'll add another day to the hike. The ascent is gradual until you reach Los Cayetanos at about 4,593 feet high and 7.5 miles from the trailhead. Then the trail descends before rising slightly. It's over 6.2 miles to Los Rodriquez from the Los Cayetanos campground.

SECTION 2: LOS RODRIGUEZ (3,281 FEET) TO VALLE DEL TETERO (5,118 FEET).
Length: 11.8 miles.

Don't let the moderate altitude of your next camp lull you. Today involves some steep climbing up Pico Alto Valle (6,890 feet) before the path drops sharply to the Valle de Tetero and its natural grass meadows. You have a choice of the cabin or the campground. A large rock here has a Taino petroglyph.

 SECTION 3: VALLE DEL TETERO (5,118 FEET) TO LA COMPARTICION (7,710 FEET).
Length: 7.2 miles.

After ascending for a fairly strenuous 5 miles, you'll join the main La Cienaga–Pico Duarte trail at Aguita Fria. From this point it's only 2.2 miles to the La Comparticion campground. There should be plenty of time left to climb to Pico Duarte, just 2.5 miles away and return. Or, wait until 4:30 in the morning and set out for the peak to watch the sunrise.

SECTION 4: LA COMPARTICION (7,710 FEET) TO LA CIENAGA (3,280 FEET) OR
LA COMPARTICION (7,710 FEET) BACK TO CONSTANZA (3,608 FEET).
Length: 11.8 miles (first option) or 34.4 miles (second option)

Which route you take depends on how soon you want to end your trip. You can walk down to La Cienaga by the afternoon. If you retrace your route, you'll have two more nights on the trail.

ELSEWHERE ON THE DOMINICAN REPUBLIC

 ### 3. MT. ISABEL DE TORRES

Time: 3–4 hours steady walking. | **Difficulty:** 2–3. | **Trailhead:** Just outside the western edge of the city of Puerto Plata, near the old cable car facility.

For many years the cable car trip up the mountain was one of Puerto Plata's most popular attractions, but the cable car no longer operates. The only way to get to the summit of 2,700-foot-high Mt. Isabel is to walk.

You could probably easily do this on you own, but you'll find the experience more enjoyable if you join the daily early morning eco-walk with a guide from Iguana Mama, (800) 849-4720 or 571-0908. Besides, they bring breakfast and lunch; their hike lasts from 8 a.m. to 4:30 p.m.

Mt. Isabel, which has five indigenous bird species, is one of four protected scientific reserves in the country. At the summit you'll not only enjoy a terrific view of Puerto Plata and its harbor, you'll find the Caribbean's highest manicured garden. The garden, almost the size of a football field, was a crowded attraction when the cable car was running. Hikers are the only ones who see it today.

4. Isla Cabritos National Park

Length: 1.6-mile walk across the island. | **Time:** 1 hour round-trip. | **Difficulty:** 3–4. It gets unbelievably hot early in the morning. Don't even think about the afternoon. Carry lots of water. | **Trailhead:** The island is located in Lago Enriquillo, the lowest point in the Caribbean, in the southwest part of the country near the Haitian border. The only way to reach the island is by a park boat. The park is 3.1 miles east of the town of la Descubierta. Hours: 8 a.m.–4:30 p.m. daily. *Warning:* The island has a sizable scorpion population. Wear shoes, not sandals.

Lago Enriquillo is a remarkable body of water. Besides being the Caribbean's lowest spot (130 feet below sea level), it is a saltwater lake, covering about 77 square miles. It is part of the channel that once connected a bay on the southeast near Barahona with Port-au-Prince to the west. An upward movement of the continental plate closed off the channel to create the lake.

The lake is also notable for its American crocodiles, once almost exterminated but which are making a comeback. In the 1980s, only seven crocodiles survived in Lago Enriquillo. Farmers had killed the rest. In 1997, the last time a crocodile census was conducted, 480 of them were living in the 13-mile-long saltwater lake. Several more hatching seasons have passed since then, so the crocodile count should be higher. The crocodile population was established by the government in the 1930s in an attempt to attract visitors to this very out of the way region. Many decades later, it looks like the crocodiles are finally becoming a major tourist attraction, as originally planned.

The Dominicans are quite serious about protecting the crocodiles. As my guide, Juan-Luis, told me, "We say that you're better off if the police find you with a dead man in your car than a crocodile. At least with a dead man you can claim self-defense."

Lake Enriquillo is bordered by two mountain ranges on the north and south. The lake is named after the famed Taino leader Enriquillo (Guarocuya), who led the first insurrection against the Spanish (1520–1533). The lake and its three islands, a two-hour drive from the nearest hotels located in the city of Barahona, are a protected national park. The largest island, five-mile long Isla Cabritos (Goat Island), is the best place to see crocodiles now. The island is also home to two endangered species of large iguanas, Ricord's and an endemic species of rhinoceros iguana.

As the lowest point in the Caribbean, daytime temperatures on Goat Island sometimes climb to 110°F. Neither humans nor beasts like that kind of heat. The best time to see crocs is early, when they're sprawled on the beach. Later, they'll slip into the water.

As anyone who's seen *Peter Pan* or *Crocodile Dundee* knows, crocodiles are regarded as fearsome creatures that will dine on people as readily as a dog or any other animal. So when Jean-Luis and I stepped into the small boat that will carry us to Isla Cabritos, I was amazed to watch our boatman walk into the dark brown water and push us out chest-deep so he can lower the outboard motor. Didn't he see *Crocodile Dundee?*

"The crocodiles are very shy," Juan-Luis explained. "They are scared of humans." Being hunted almost to extinction might do that. Still, I wondered how many years it will be before Enriquillo's crocodiles realize they have nothing to be afraid of.

The 20-minute ride to the island gave me the opportunity to appreciate how much the lake represents just one of the region's many micro-climates. The lake has its own separate weather system; at that moment a line of puffy clouds was hanging over the lake well below mountain level. The cloud band, with the dark mountains behind it, reminded me of an approaching storm front.

Goat Island, like much of the Barahona region, consists mostly of acacia trees and tall cactus. It's hard to believe there once was a cattle ranch in this desolate, dry spot, though the location would certainly keep rustlers away.

The ranger told us that the crocodiles had moved to the other side of the island, a distance of 1.6 miles. We walked quickly across the island but found the beach deserted. A single crocodile floated on the surface a few yards from shore. One look at us and the creature became a submarine. We never saw it again.

Newly hatched baby crocodiles still practicing their swimming technique floated everywhere in the shallows. The ranger splashed into the water to retrieve one. I waited for Mama to come charging to the rescue, but it's every crocodile for itself. The ranger opened the baby croc's mouth to display its teeth, a nasty bunch of sharp needles. This baby croc was lucky to be alive. After the ranger released it, he uncovered two nests loaded with eggs. However, all the eggs were destroyed, apparently by a recent rain; I was told that the eggs won't hatch properly unless they stay completely dry.

If crocs were scarce, the big iguanas were not. They grow up to three feet long, a very good eating size, but they also are protected. It's possible to get quite close to many of them. The rhinoceros iguana, with a small hooked point on its snout, is appropriately named.

On the walk back to the boat, I discovered how brutal life on Goat Island can be. Temperatures felt like they had reached 100°F, and I'd already slurped down my only water. I reached the boat so drained that I considered joining the boatman for a swim when he waded out to retrieve our anchor. But in the dark water I feared a crocodile might regard my white skin as a neon "Dine Here." I was content to let the spray of the waves cool me off on the way back.

9 THE DUTCH ABCs

Antillean Saying: *"To take advantage of a situation, you usually select the easiest victim."*

You don't need a new vocabulary to learn the Dutch ABCs: Aruba, Bonaire, and Curaçao simply spell perpetually warm sunny weather, myriad activities, and friendly people. That all goes well in any language.

These picturesque Dutch lands off the coast of Venezuela are true isles of perpetual summer, with nary a cloud to mar the days, except from September to November, when most of the precipitation (only 20 inches annually) falls. But the excellent climate is only part of their allure. The islanders themselves account for the rest. They are people descended from the Dutch and intermixed with other European stock to create their own unique culture, including a special language called Papiamento, a blend of English, Spanish, Dutch, and Portuguese. But not to worry: most everyone speaks several languages, including excellent English.

The shallowness between Aruba and Venezuela has made some scientists theorize that Aruba was once part of the South American continent. However, most believe the ABCs were broken from a formation somewhere in the mid-Atlantic and simply drifted down the continental shelf toward South America.

The ABCs escaped the often brutal patterns of colonization seen elsewhere in the Caribbean. The dry climate did not favor the crop that changed the face of the Caribbean—sugarcane. As a result, the ABCs were one of the few areas where the natives were not slaughtered by European colonists. On Aruba and Bonaire, the Arawaks not only were left alone but also were allowed to maintain contact with other Indians on the mainland and permitted to raise cattle, sheep, horses, and goats. On Curaçao, however, the Arawaks were forcibly removed to Hispaniola as slave labor.

Because the islands apparently lacked gold, the Spaniards labeled them "useless islands" and never spent much time on them. The Dutch, looking for wood to build their ships, salt to preserve their foods, and a military foothold in this hemisphere, took up forceful occupation in the ABCs between 1634 and 1636. The Dutch invasion of Bonaire in 1636 is reported to have found only six Arawaks and a few cattle on the island.

The vividness of today's bright, white-washed buildings with colorful orange roofs are a remarkable contrast to the desertlike terrain of each island: Large cactus and scrub are the ABCs only natural vegetation. According to legend, early explorers cut down all the trees for ship building.

Goats have kept new forests from growing. Goats were introduced by the Spaniards in the sixteenth century because they were one of the highest-grade sources of protein on these barren islands. By the seventeenth century Aruba was known as a "goat island." The hardy breed that evolved here causes real problems in dry years because the animals will graze on every green leaf they spot. About once every ten years conditions will be so dry the goats even devour the evergreen lignum vitae, which they normally overlook.

The goats which roam free over the islands often appear to have no owner, but just hit one with your car and you'll be amazed how quickly a grieving claimant will pop out of the cacti. As much as a lot of locals would like to declare the goats a public nuisance and hunt them virtually to extinction, the goats all belong to someone, usually the poorer people. So, for the most part, they have to be tolerated. As the saying goes, "Every goat is still a vote!" so politicians aren't as active as they might be in eliminating these harmful pests from the national parks and other protected areas.

TRAVEL TIPS

Area: Aruba is 70.9 square miles, 19.6 miles long and 6 miles at the widest point. Bonaire is 122 square miles, 24 miles long and from 3–7 miles wide. Curaçao is 180 square miles, 38 miles long and from 2 to almost 8 miles wide.

Language: Officially Dutch, but Papiamento, Spanish, and English are widely spoken.

Population: Aruba, 67,000; Bonaire, 11,000; Curaçao, 140,000.

Time Zone: Atlantic Time, 1 hour ahead of Eastern Standard Time.

Rainy Season: None of the islands receives as much as 30 inches of rain annually. Most showers occur from September to December. They usually are short, quickly pushed away by the tradewinds.

Getting There: The major gateways to the ABCs are from Miami, Orlando, Atlanta, and New York. American Airlines flies to Aruba and Curaçao. Venezuela's Aeropostal has direct flights to Aruba from Atlanta and Orlando. Continental flies to Aruba. ALM Antillean Airlines flies to all three islands. Unfortunately, ALM is notoriously inefficient. Air Aruba (www.interknowledge.com/air-aruba) may or may not be still in business. Air Canada flies from Toronto and Quebec to Miami, a main hub for the other carriers.

Documents: Americans and Canadians need only valid proof of citizenship. All others need passports. A return or ongoing ticket and proof of sufficient funds may also be required.

Getting Around: Rental cars are easily available on all the islands and most of the large name companies (Avis, Budget, Hertz) are represented. Cost is reasonable, around $200 per week for a small car. Driving is on the right.

Where to Stay: Aruba is mostly large resorts and hotels, with prices averaging US $125–174 a day; however, the tourism authority has a list of guest houses and apartments as low as US $30 per day.

On Bonaire, if you're diving as well as walking, try **Captain Don's Habitat,** one of Bonaire's best resorts, (800) 327-6709. Captain Don Stewart started taking divers on tours in 1962, long before diving was even available in much of the Caribbean. Colorful Stewart is also one of Bonaire's greatest natural attractions. Most other Bonaire resorts

Goats eat any new vegetation, leaving the Dutch ABCs a land of cacti and thorns

are also dive-related. The tourist board here should also have a list of small guest houses. Curaçao has a wide selection of hotels, resorts, and guest houses that also are available from the tourist board.

Camping: Not available.

Currency: Aruba has its own currency, called the Arubian florin. The Netherlands Antillean guilder (abbreviated NAFL) is used on Curaçao and Bonaire. Regardless of island, every American dollar is worth 1.77 florin. Prices are often quoted in both currencies. Dollars are readily accepted everywhere, and the Antilleans are usually scrupulously honest at working out the exchange rate. Bank hours vary on all islands but generally are open from 8:30 a.m. to noon and 1:30 p.m. to 3:45 p.m.

Taxes & Tips: On Aruba, a 6% government tax and a 15–20% service charge on rooms and food are standard. The departure tax is US$20. Some hotels also charge an extra US$3–5 a day energy surcharge. On Bonaire, the room tax is US$5.50 per person daily and a US$10 departure tax; a 10–15% service charge is standard. On Curaçao, the room tax is 7% plus a 12% room service charge. The departure tax is US$12.50. Porters expect about US$1 for each bag.

Electrical Current: It, too, is different on every island. On Aruba, it's the same as in the United States, 110 volts, 60 cycles. On Bonaire, it is 110–130 volts, 50 cycles, or 220 volts, 50 cycles, which causes problems for appliances that normally run on 60 cycles, such as hair dryers. Curaçao is also 110–130 volts and 50 cycles instead of 60. In Bonaire and Curaçao, hair dryers and curling irons are likely to overheat. Definitely use a surge protector for computers or any sensitive electronic device. Borrow a transformer from your hotel.

Safety/Health Warnings: Because of the constant cooling tradewinds, many people do not realize just how hot the sun is in the Dutch Antilles. They are among the southernmost islands in the Caribbean, and precautions are necessary the first few days to avoid burning to the color of a robust rose wine. The tap water on all three islands is some of the purest anywhere. Locals claim the water is why Curaçao-made Amstel beer tastes so good. Wear long pants, socks, and good shoes for protection against the elements, specifically, cactus.

Snakes & Other Venomous Creatures: You'll rarely find reference to rattlesnakes in the ABCs, but Aruba is home to a venomous rattlesnake, the colebra *(Crotalus durissus)*, though they are seldom seen. They normally inhabit the most sparsely populated areas of Aruba between Jamanota, Fontein, and San Nicolas. All other snakes are harmless. Locals say that possession of a snake rattle is good luck, perhaps because they are so rare.

Hiking & Walking Services: Check with the national park offices on each island for the latest information on any tours they might provide. On Bonaire, **Discover Bonaire** offers nature tours every Friday from 8 a.m. to 3 p.m. Led by a local naturalist, the tours explore the 13,500-acre Washington-Slagbaii National Park. The cost is $40 per person plus a 10% service charge and 5% sales tax. The tour includes transfer to the park at the northern end of the island. For information, call 011 (599) 717-5433 or fax 011 (599) 717-5151; email info@discoverbonaire.com.

Additional Information: Contact the Aruba Tourism Authority, 1000 Harbor Blvd., Weehawken, NJ 07087; phone (201) 330-0800. In Canada, 86 Bloor Street West, Suite 204, Toronto, Ontario, M5S 1M5; phone (416) 975-1950; www.aruba.com.

The Bonaire Government Tourist Office at Adams Unlimited, 10 Rockefeller Plaza, Suite 900, New York, NY 10020; phone (800) U-BONAIR; www.bonaire.org.

Curaçao Tourist Board, 475 Park Ave. South, Suite 2000, New York, NY 10016; phone (800) 270-3350; www.curacao-tourism.com.

Also check out www.netherlandsantilles.com.

ARUBA

Antillean Saying: "There are more days than weeks, so don't rush time."

The westernmost island, situated just 15 miles from the Venezuelan coast, Aruba is no longer part of the Netherlands Antilles group but a separate entity within the Kingdom of the Netherlands. It is best known for two things: beautiful palm-lined beaches and shopping. The beaches are some of the cleanest and brightest in the Caribbean. They seem to stretch on forever, making them ideal for early morning and late evening walks.

Though the beaches and shopping district of Oranjestad are the main hubs, there's a great deal more to see on the tiny island. Driving is easy because the roads are good, but navigating is hard because many are unmarked. You will have to consult the local road maps frequently. Or, you can take your bearings from the ever-present divi-divi trees. The divi-divis (locals say the trees grow sideways instead of up) are all bent eternally in the direction of the easterly tradewinds, which means they all point southwest.

You'll also spot plenty of curious man-made objects as well: Ayo features Indian petroglyphs. Slightly more modern but in a similar spirit are the ornate carvings of flowers and strange symbols bordering the doorways and windows of many old cottages. Formed in cement, these are hex signs, made to ward off evil spirits.

Aruba's most famous landmark is the De Olde Molen, the old mill, a full-sized windmill brought over from Holland. It's still in operation, not as an energy source but as a very popular and unusual restaurant. This is also near the Palm Beach area, a hot bed of windsurfing activity. With a 16-mile-per-hour tradewind, this is a superior place to put in some board time or learn how to windsurf.

Not many people realize it, but gold mining was an important industry on Aruba. It was one resource the Spanish managed to overlook. Gold was discovered in 1825, and more than 3 million pounds were mined before operations shut down in 1916.

A huge oil refinery, at one time the world's largest, was built near San Nicolas. Now tourism is the number-one industry. However, Aruba lacks the extensive hiking trail system found on Bonaire and Curaçao. It's more a matter of locating the most interesting sites and then walking around.

Bird-watchers will want to obtain the color booklet entitled "Stinapa 26, Discover Aruba's Wildlife," available locally in bookstores or from the Aruba Foundation for Nature and Parks, Seroe Colorado P.O. Box 706, Aruba, Netherlands Antilles.

1. BUBALI POND

Time: 30 minutes. | **Difficulty:** 1. | **Trailhead:** Located on the north side of Eagle Beach and south of De Olde Molen, the famous windmill restaurant.

This pond is one of the best places, as well as most accessible, to see bird life on Aruba. Originally a salt pond used to make salt from sea water, it is now kept wet year-round by serving as an overflow from the sewage plant. This is not as yucky as it might sound, because the nutrient-filled waters are rich in fish life, which in turn attracts a host of birds. This puts Aruba in the vanguard of an exciting new wetlands technology now being explored in many major U.S. cities.

Brown pelicans are particularly fond of this spot, and small squadrons of them can sometimes be spotted in perfect formation, scooping the water surface for dinner. Other birds common at this site include black-crowned night herons *(Nycticorax)*, the common egret *(Egretta alba)*, little green herons *(Butorides virescent)*, and the beautiful snowy egret *(Egretta thula)*, sometimes called "the lady with the golden slippers" because of its yellow feet and black legs. As at most birding locations, best viewing is near dawn and dusk.

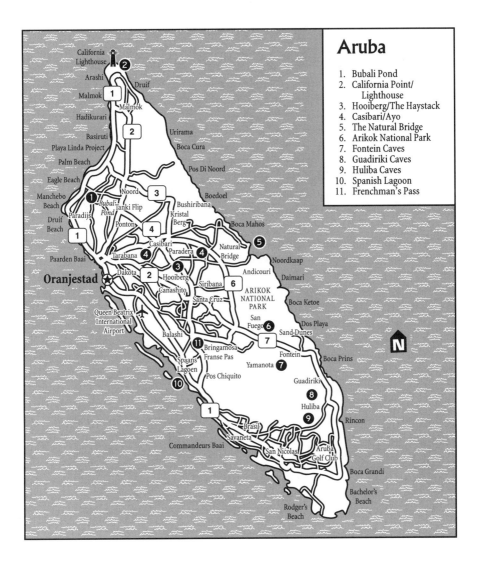

Aruba

1. Bubali Pond
2. California Point/
   Lighthouse
3. Hooiberg/The Haystack
4. Casibari/Ayo
5. The Natural Bridge
6. Arikok National Park
7. Fontein Caves
8. Guadiriki Caves
9. Huliba Caves
10. Spanish Lagoon
11. Frenchman's Pass

2. CALIFORNIA POINT/LIGHTHOUSE

Time: 1 hour. | **Difficulty:** 1. | **Trailhead:** Located on a hill at the northern end of Aruba, the lighthouse is named for the 1891 wreck of the *California*, offshore in only 15–30 feet of water.

California Point has an extensive area of sand dunes. It also is an important nesting area for brown pelicans. The lighthouse is encircled with huge boulders that make the landscape almost moonlike. On the drive here you may be fortunate enough to spot Aruba's large iguana, which grows as long as three feet. A vegetarian with a special fondness for blossoming hibiscus, the iguana is highly prized as a food delicacy. It's not just their dorsal crests and dinosaurian looks that make them so sought-after as a table centerpiece: It's also the tastiness of the meat and the fact that the males—like all lizards—have two penes, which give the dish a reputation as an aphrodisiac. Iguana meat is so highly prized it's usually offered to tourists sparingly, in a delicious soup.

3. HOOIBERG/THE HAYSTACK

Time: 45–60 minutes. | **Difficulty:** 3. | **Trailhead:** Located almost in the center of Aruba, and can be seen from virtually anywhere on the island.

This 541-foot-high volcanic formation is usually called the Haystack, though its official name is the Hooiberg. Its vegetation is mostly yellow poui and the typical cacti found everywhere. You may even see the real divi-divi tree or watapana *(Caesalpina coriara),* as opposed to some other plants often mistaken for it. The true divi-divi has inconspicuous but fragrant blossoms and thick, curled pods rich in tannin. At one time the pods were exported to Germany for use in the leather industry. You can still use them for shining the dust off your shoes.

But wait until after you've climbed the several hundred steps that lead almost to the top of the Haystack. You can easily make the summit, although the 580 steps you climb do not yet reach to the top; a maintained trail is planned for the future. Like the high points on most islands, TV antennas and other communications equipment occupy part of the summit. On a clear day, you can see Venezuela and view yellow orioles and several species of doves.

4. CASIBARI/AYO

Time: 45 minutes to 1 hour each. | **Difficulty:** 1. | **Trailhead:** On the road from Oranjestad to Boca Mahos, at the village of Paradera turn east to reach Casibari. Ayo is located several miles away, to the northeast.

These two spots are littered with huge boulders weathered into fanciful animal shapes by the eternal tradewinds. At Casibari, you can climb the rock steps to the top for surveying the island or viewing the Haystack. The more developed of the two spots, Casibari has a souvenir and drink stand. It is ranked the second most popular tourist spot after the Natural Bridge.

Ayo, just to the northeast of Hooiberg and usually less crowded, has been called the Stonehenge of Aruba. No steps have been cut into any of the rocks, so you have to do all the scrambling yourself.

If you're lucky, at dusk or dawn you may spot a burrowing owl or one of the rare mammals found here before European contact. Spanish explorers recorded a small species of mouse, several kinds of bats, and a cottontail rabbit. Similar to their North American cousins, Aruba and Curaçao cottontails bear a distinctive black patch on their necks. It's believed the rabbits were probably imported in pre-Colombian times by the Indians, because the cottontails around the Maracaibo region of Venezuela also have the same distinctive neck markings.

5. THE NATURAL BRIDGE

Time: 1 hour to explore thoroughly. | **Difficulty:** 1.
| **Trailhead:** On the north coast, about midway down the island.

Probably the most visited tourist site, Aruba's Natural Bridge is considered the Caribbean's finest. It rises 25 feet above the sea and extends for about 100 feet. Seen from the water line, people walking across the rock span are the size of toy soldiers. Tours here come by the bus load, particularly in the middle of the day, but later in the afternoon it is often quieter and the light is best for photography. A small café and souvenir stand are open throughout the day. A small, sandy cove frames the pounding surf hurling itself against the Natural Bridge. However, the bridge may not have been formed by this violent wave action. A popular theory is that the bridge was formed inside-out, that rainwater coming from the land side washed away weak spots of the coral barrier. An interesting theory, but it doesn't rain that much here, at least not recently.

6. ARIKOK NATIONAL PARK

Time: 45 minutes to 1 hour. | **Difficulty:** 1. | **Trailhead:** Located on a triangle of land between Boca Prins and San Fuego.

Arikok National Park, which contains 18 percent of the island, has a few easy trails that are well laid out and easy to follow. Petroglyphs are still evident on some of the rocks. The island's highest points, Mount Arikok (577 feet) and Mount Jamanota (617 feet), are inside the park. A small garden at the foot of the mountain (a hill, really) displays most of the trees and shrubs common to Aruba.

The park also contains several animals endemic to Aruba: the Aruba island rattlesnake, Aruba cat-eyed snake, Aruban whiptail lizard, Aruban burrowing owl, and the Aruban parakeet.

7, 8, AND 9: CAVES

Time: 1 hour each. | **Difficulty:** 1. | **Trailhead:** The caves are located on the eastern side of Arikok National Park. Consult the map for locations.

These caves are easy walking if you have a light and stay on the main path. Go wandering off into the darkness and you could step into a pothole and twist your ankle. Flashlights are often provided by guides or vendors at the cave mouths. Admission to the caves is free.

The *Fontein Cave*, near Boca Prins, is the largest of Aruba's caves. It contains a big chamber with natural pillars at the entrance, leading to a tunnel with Indian paintings. Rumor has it that these paintings may not be authentic, but were painted by a film company.

Nearby are the *Guadiriki Caves*, which contain two large chambers lit by sunlight coming through an opening. The chambers are connected by a tunnel that may require a light

This windmill was brought from Holland and turned into a popular restaurant

because the passageway often turns into a shadow world. Bats live in this cave system, but none on the island are infected with rabies.

Also in the vicinity is the *Huliba Cave,* also known as the Tunnel of Love. It is about a 30-minute walk with a 10-minute return to the entry point on the surface. The cave contains stalagmites and stalactites.

10. Spanish Lagoon

Time: 1 hour. | **Difficulty:** 1. | **Trailhead:** On the south coast road to San Nicolas, about 3 miles east of Oranjestad.

A desalinization plant and the Aruba Nautical Club are at the mouth of this old pirate hangout. Go to the other end for some of the best bird-watching on Aruba: egrets, herons, frigates, and brown pelicans. This is where large green and yellow parakeets—about twice the size of those usually seen in pet stores—nest in the steep cliffs along the roadway. Sunset is the best time to see them. All three types of mangroves—red, black, and white—are represented. Insect repellent may be required when you're out of the wind.

11. Frenchman's Pass

Time: 1 hour. | **Difficulty:** 1. | **Trailhead:** Situated northeast of Spanish Lagoon.

Frenchman's Pass is a scenic walk/drive through a pass where branches canopy the roadway. The French are supposed to have fought for control of the island with both pirates and Indians in the seventeenth century. The road veering to the right leads to the Bushiribana gold mine ruins from 1898. The cement ruins are a favorite hangout for parakeets early in the day. Going east, you can walk/drive to the top of Mount Jamanota, which at 617 feet is the highest point of land.

BONAIRE

Antillean Saying: *"No matter how strange, ugly, evil, or crazy someone is, there will always be admirers."*

Although Bonaire is considerably larger than Aruba, it's far less developed. It also lacks Aruba's beaches and shopping opportunities. Bonaire has been described as a desert island surrounded by an oasis of coral reefs, some of the lushest and most colorful in all the Caribbean. Not surprisingly, most visitors are scuba divers. You don't need to be a scuba diver to explore Bonaire's underwater treasures. Snorkeling is also excellent.

Island touring on Bonaire is divided into two distinct segments, south and north. Taking up almost all of Bonaire's southern tip is the solar salt works, where salt water is let into shallow flats called pans; over a period of time, the water evaporates to leave only salt crystals. The salt is scooped up by steam shovels and loaded into trucks, then washed and piled to dry before being shipped to the United States and elsewhere. If it wasn't for the warm sunshine, it would be easy to mistake the huge salt piles for glistening mountains of ice.

On Bonaire's northern end is Washington-Slagbaai National Park. Living here, as well as in the solar salt pans, is a large population of flamingoes. Flamingoes, in fact, have traditionally outnumbered people on Bonaire. The park is also home to many migratory birds and herds of free-roaming goats; they roam all over the island.

On the way to the national park you'll descend into an area known as Goto Meer just before the town of Rincon. Easily Bonaire's most scenic inland region, you can be sure of finding several hundred flamingoes strolling this inland lake. Many are usually close to the road, but they will start walking away as soon as you open the car door. This is a good place to watch the daily flight of flamingoes to Venezuela at sunset.

Lac Bay, a favorite surfing spot, is a beautiful cove on Bonaire's east coast. The water is shallow with a sand bottom, perfect for shelling or swimming. Fishermen's huts line the shore. The piles of empty conch shells are free for the taking.

KRALENDIJK AFOOT!

Time: 1 hour. | **Difficulty:** 1.

Pronounced "Crawl-in-dike" and meaning "coral dike," Kralendijk is Bonaire's main city. Situated on a natural harbor on the lee side with the additional protection of neighboring Klein Bonaire, Kralendijk is a relatively new city, begun about 1810. Fort Oranje, designed to stave off any invaders, was built just shortly before the end of the eighteenth century.

With about 1,700 residents, Kralendijk is still quite small, though it's been undergoing a massive face-lift since the end of the 1980s to compete for more cruise ship business. The main street, Kaya Grandi, parallels the coastline and runs north–south. It takes only about ten minutes to walk through the island's main business district.

Mirroring the yellow and orange structures of Aruba and Curaçao, Kralendijk offers a pleasant, safe walk, day or night. The more interesting stops are the Governor's House, built in 1837 and restored in 1973. The waterfront, Roman-style fish market, usually selling vegetables rather than seafood, dates from 1935. The center of town is the newly renovated and quite picturesque Wilhelmina Square. The small Protestant church in the middle of the square is from 1857.

The prettiest time to walk Kralendijk is in the afternoon. As the sun sets in the west the colorful buildings lining the harborfront reflect the beautiful yellow glow as the sun dips toward the horizon. As you watch the sun set over the water, look for the rare and famous green flash, which—if it is going to appear—will happen immediately after sunset.

ELSEWHERE ON BONAIRE

1. SOLAR SALT PANS/SLAVE HUTS

Time: 45 minutes to several hours, depending on how much territory you wish to explore. | **Difficulty:** 1, but the sun can be a scorcher. | **Trailhead:** Take the coastal road south from the airport. The glistening white mounds of salt will be on the left, the slave huts on the right. Pull off and park.

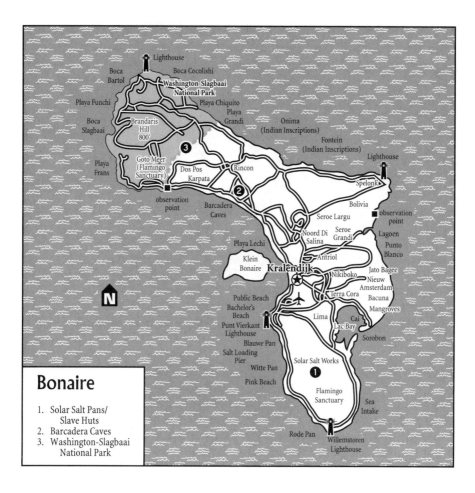

Bonaire

1. Solar Salt Pans/
   Slave Huts
2. Barcadera Caves
3. Washington-Slagbaai
   National Park

Salt was valuable to the Dutch as a means of preserving herring, an important livelihood. With salt, the herring could be preserved indefinitely; without, the fish would rot in just a few days. Until the Eighty Years' War (1568–1648) between the Netherlands and Spain, the Dutch had obtained their salt from Spain. These hostilities made them look elsewhere for salt. Venezuela and the Caribbean turned out to be the best sources.

Salt is always present in a dissolved form in sea water. The flat southern end of Bonaire was ideal for creating large, flat pans in which the sea water would evaporate, leaving behind salt in its crystalline form. The salt was then scooped up and sent to the Netherlands.

This was labor-intensive work, however, requiring the importation of slaves. The small huts you see—so small you have to stoop to enter—were once used to house these slaves, who slept four to a hut during the week. On Saturdays, however, they were given the opportunity to walk the seven hours to their homes in the village of Rincon in the northern hills; on Monday, they came walking back.

Slave huts near Bonaire's salt flats

Salt pan work was considered some of the toughest possible not only because of the work involved but because the constant bright glare from the crystals was hard on the eyes. After emancipation in 1863, the pans were abandoned until the 1960s. Using the latest in modern equipment, the Antilles International Salt Company resumed work in 1966, and it has continued ever since. Most of the salt is exported to the United States for industrial use, including water softening and sprinkling on snow-covered roads.

Approaching the solar salt works, the first thing you'll see are the crystallizers where the sea water is evaporating. During the process, which takes about a year, the water turns into shocking pink and purple crystals. The crystals are scooped up by trucks, slurried with brine, and cascaded over grates to remove impurities. The salt goes aboard ship by conveyor belt.

The tall stone obelisks near some of the huts have no religious significance. Instead, the four stone markers were vital to ship captains for their bearings; much of the lee island is protected by shallow reef, and it would not be difficult to pile up a ship on shore. They were each painted a bright color for easy visibility at sea: red, white, blue, and orange. An appropriately colored flag would be hoisted to let the approaching captain know which pan to approach. The orange obelisk has since been destroyed. You can spend the night in one of these huts. Bring your own bedding and any other comforts.

THE FLAMINGOES

At one time, the number of flamingoes on Bonaire was estimated at about 1,500. Today the population is believed to be more than ten times that size. Bonaire's solar salt works provides one of the world's few nesting places for the pink flamingo.

A sanctuary has been set aside where the flamingoes can lay their eggs in 12- to 15-inch-high conical nests, undisturbed by human contact. However, the flamingoes only go to the sanctuary during the spring nesting season. The rest of the year they can be seen close to the road in the crystallizers or other places around the salt pans, or in Washington Park on the north tip of the island. A good pair of binoculars is necessary to observe the shy birds, who will move away as soon as you attempt to approach them. Flamingoes make a high, nasal honking sound like geese: "chogogo," also the Bonairean name for the birds.

Some Bonaire flamingo trivia: They were reported nesting on the island as early as 1681. Only three other places in the world have nesting colonies of pink flamingoes: the Bahamas, Mexico's Yucatán peninsula, and the Galápagos Islands off Ecuador. Out of a world population of 60,000 flamingoes, 20,000 live in the southern Caribbean.

New World flamingoes, the ones you see on Bonaire, are technically known as red flamingoes; those of the Old World are the true "pink" flamingoes, though Bonaireans obviously don't care about this distinction because they paint everything pink after the birds. Flamingoes are born a fluffy gray. The carotene in their natural food supply of brine shrimp, algae, brine fly pupae, lagoon snails, and tiny clams gives these birds their bright color. They live eight to nine years. When food is scarce on Bonaire, the flamingoes will fly two to three hours to feed in Venezuela.

The trick question is how can humans distinguish male from female flamingoes, since they both have the same plumage? Well, during the mating season, the birds often walk in rows with their necks extended straight up. The birds with the longest necks are the males. That's a fact!

2. Barcadera Caves

Time: 1 hour. | **Difficulty:** 1–2. | **Trailhead:** Take the coastal road to Washington Park and make a sharp turn uphill to the Caribbean Club hotel and bar; immediately on your right you'll see a stone pyramid, which marks the entrance to the caves. Flashlights are essential.

The current owners of the Caribbean Club are incredibly friendly, and a member of the family will sometimes take you on a free caving tour of about a half hour if you'll buy some drinks and snacks as a kind of trade-off. Better yet, negotiate for a full three-hour tour of the caves; the low price may surprise you. These caves are something most Bonaire visitors are unaware of, yet they are one of the island's best natural attractions. To contact the very reasonably priced 40-room Caribbean Club, fax 599-7-7900; the telephone number is 599-7-7901.

WASHINGTON-SLAGBAAI NATIONAL PARK

3. WASHINGTON-SLAGBAAI NATIONAL PARK (DRIVING TOUR)

Length: The green route is 15 miles. The yellow route is 22 miles. There is considerable overlap of the two. | **Time:** 3–5 hours. | **Difficulty:** 1. | **Trailhead:** North of Rincon, the oldest settlement. | **Operating Hours:** The park opens daily except holidays at 8 a.m. and closes at 5 p.m.; however, no admittance is allowed after 3:30 p.m.

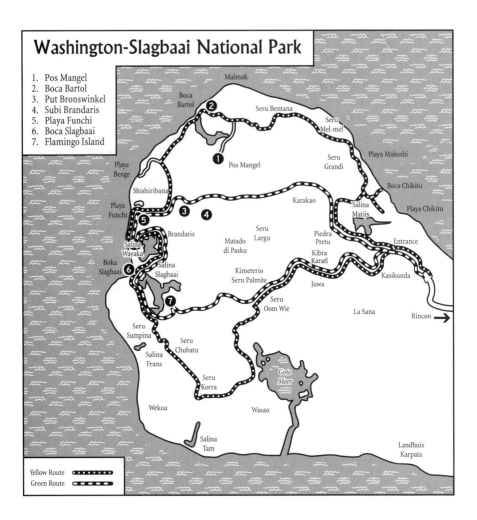

Washington-Slagbaai National Park

1. Pos Mangel
2. Boca Bartol
3. Put Bronswinkel
4. Subi Brandaris
5. Playa Funchi
6. Boca Slagbaai
7. Flamingo Island

Malmok

Boca Bartol

Seru Bentana

Seru Mel-mel

Playa Makoshi

Pos Mangel

Seru Grandi

Playa Benge

Shishiribana

Boca Chikitu

Playa Funchi

Karakao

Salina Matijs

Playa Chikitu

Brandaris

Seru Largu

Piedra Pretu

Entrance

Matado di Pasku

Salina Wayaka

Salina Slagbaai

Kibra Karatl

Boka Slagbaai

Kimeterio Seru Palmite

Juwa

Kasikunda

Seru Oom Wie

La Sana

Rincon →

Seru Sumpina

Seru Chubatu

Salina Frans

Goto Meer

Seru Korra

Wekua

Wasao

Salina Tam

Landhuis Karpata

Yellow Route •••••••
Green Route ▪▪▪▪▪

This 13,500-acre park is a preserve for bird life. Formerly, it produced divi-divi, aloe, charcoal, and goats. It was sold to the government at the end of the 1960s. This is a driving tour with frequent stops for walking. You have a choice of two routes, normally driven counterclockwise, that have some overlap. The longer yellow route drives along the northeast coast and loops through the park's southern section. The green route goes through the middle of the park. The two overlap at the beginning and end of the drive and on the coast near Boca Slagbaai.

Two kinds of cactus dominate the scenery. Kadushi cactus, looking almost treelike, grow more than 30 feet. The straight-standing and roseate-bristled yatu cactus *(Lemaireocereus)* is still used to construct fences and other enclosures on Bonaire. Stick a cut-off piece of yatu in the ground and it starts growing again; cactus fences hardly ever need to be replaced, and they certainly never need painting.

Places of special note in the park:

1. Pos Mangel (yellow), or "sweet well," is one of the few places in the park where fresh water is always available. As such, it is one of the best spots on the island for bird-watching; creep up slowly in order not to scare them away. Species common here include the yellow-winged parakeet, yellow warbler, ground dove, common bananaquits, tropical mockingbirds, and many more. Other parakeets may also be present, but they have a tough time surviving the droughts on Bonaire, which occur every five or six years. Besides facing starvation during droughts, the birds have to feed in the village fruit gardens, where the parakeets are often caught and caged for show.

2. Boca Bartol (yellow) is another prime bird-watching spot. Yellow-crowned night herons are almost always present halfway up the terrace or near the water. Snowy egrets, brown pelicans, and cormorants are all frequent visitors.

3. Put Bronswinkel (green) is another freshwater well that is superb for bird-watching. This is the place to see some of the island's rarest birds, but to do so you must sit quietly for a long time. If you're feeling too restless, pass up this spot out of consideration of the serious birders who will go from ecstatic to murderous if you noisily blunder into their sanctuary. The trees may appear full of nests, but these are actually epiphytes (air plants).

4. Subi Brandaris (green) is a by-road that ends at a parking lot where you can begin the 1.5-hour climb (Difficulty Level 3) to the top of Brandaris, which at almost 800 feet high is Bonaire's highest point. The hike starts with a footpath that soon gives way to a ridge; the ridge route is marked with yellow circles painted on the boulders. From the top you'll have a great view of the entire island, perhaps to as far south as the salt pans. Mountains in Venezuela or Mount Christoffel, Curaçao's highest peak, may also be visible.

5. Playa Funchi (green/yellow) is home to a subspecies of lizard found only on Bonaire, the harmless *Cnemidophorus murinus ruthveni*. They are quite tame at this spot, well acquainted with bread crumbs, and will even eat out of your hand if you're still enough. Females and juveniles are brown, and the brightly colored male has a blue head and greenish-blue hind feet and tail-root. You may also see a flock of flamingoes in the salina here. Playa Funchi was the harbor for Washington plantation, as the pier remnants show. Today it is a very popular place for snorkeling, swimming, and sunbathing. There is no current inside the bay, making this a safe place to swim.

6. Boca Slagbaai (green/yellow) is one of the finest snorkeling and swimming beaches on the island. Dive boats come all the way here from the Kralendijk area, as much as a 45-minute run away. Historically always an important harbor, it gains its name from the Dutch word *Slagten,* meaning "slaughter." This is where the cattle on the northern part of the island were processed and turned into steaks before export. Salt was also exported from here for a time. Besides being one of the finest swimming spots, this is another excellent bird-watching site: Snowy egrets and flamingoes are almost always in the salina here.

7. Flamingo Island (green), a peninsula in salina Slagbaai that allows you to see flamingoes at the closest point yet. The square island in the middle of the salina always

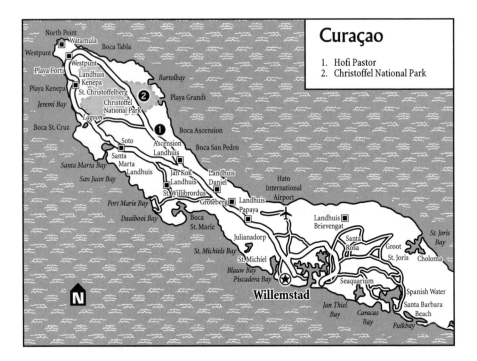

contains a few birds, some of which breed there. Slagbaai is an important feeding area for the flamingoes, which skim the water for brine shrimp or graze (dive) to a depth of about three feet for their forage.

CURAÇAO

Antillean Saying: "I need to be paid for my services. Saying thank you is not enough."

Curaçao is not only the largest of the Dutch ABCs, it is the busiest island. Of all Dutch ports, Curaçao's Willemstad Harbor was for decades second only to Rotterdam in importance, primarily because of the large oil complex developed here.

Taking your first look at Willemstad, you may experience a case of déjà-vu, and no wonder. It seems whenever magazines or advertisers want to depict the cheerful Old World architecture found in some Caribbean cities, they often choose Willemstad's striking yellow and orange waterfront. Understandably so, as these stores and homes, many dating back several hundred years, create a welcoming atmosphere modern neon and plastic can never match.

However, Curaçao's Dutch influence could reduce you to the stilted pronunciation of the recently literate when it comes to the local tongue-twisting names, like Grebbelinieweg or Goeroeboeroeweg. When it comes to writing directions here, a single scrap of paper may not be enough, as some of the street names have more than 30 letters!

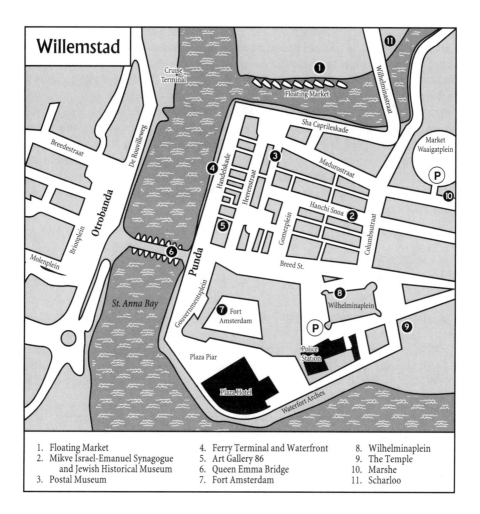

Willemstad

1. Floating Market
2. Mikve Israel-Emanuel Synagogue
   and Jewish Historical Museum
3. Postal Museum
4. Ferry Terminal and Waterfront
5. Art Gallery 86
6. Queen Emma Bridge
7. Fort Amsterdam
8. Wilhelminaplein
9. The Temple
10. Marshe
11. Scharloo

Curaçao's cosmopolitan population (more than 70 different nationalities) is best reflected in its tremendous choice of dining establishments. The local specialty is the *rijsttafel* (rice-TAH-fel). It's a kind of transplanted Indonesian smorgasbord containing from 15 to 40 different dishes, including pork, shrimp, chicken, beef, vegetables, and fish that are broiled, stewed, or fried. Peanuts and a relish of chopped peppers can be added to spice things up even more.

1. Willemstad Afoot!

Time: 2 hours. | **Difficulty:** 1. | **Trailhead:** Floating Market. Don't leave your car in the parking lot there; it's for market shoppers only. Park on one of the nearby side streets.

Willemstad is divided into two almost separate entities by the main channel that makes this such a valuable port. A pontoon bridge known as Queen Emma conveys pedestrian traffic across to the other side of the channel. When Queen Emma is retracted to allow a ship to pass through (or when it's put out of commission because a tanker has collided with it), a ferry boat transports you across instead.

The two sides of Willemstad are known as Punda and Otrobanda. Punda, meaning "point," sits on the east bank. It is the older settlement, dating back to 1634. In Otrobanda, which means "the other side," development began in 1707. The Punda side is the more visitor-oriented; this is where the walking tour below takes you. Not only does it contain most of the old restaurants and stores in storybook colors, it is one of the great shopping malls of the Caribbean. With offerings as varied and sophisticated as anything in New York, London, or Paris, it far surpasses even Aruba.

1. **Floating Market:** One of the city's most famous and colorful sights. Venezuelan produce is regularly brought over by boat. This is the freshest produce on the island, and it's quite safe to eat. The Venezuelans, who stay for weeks at a time, live aboard their boats. The market is open from 5 a.m. to 6:30 p.m. Monday through Friday, until noon on Saturday, and is closed Sunday.

2. **Mikve Israel-Emanuel Synagogue and Jewish Historical Museum:** Dedicated in 1732, this is the oldest continuously operating synagogue in the Western Hemisphere. Its floor is loose sand. The museum contains many artifacts from the congregation's history, including replicas of seventeenth-century gravestones, Hanukkah lamps, and Torah scrolls. Open Monday through Friday 9 a.m. to 11:45 a.m. and 2:30 p.m. to 4:45 p.m. Also open Sundays when large cruise ships are in port.

3. **Postal Museum:** Located in an elegantly restored wood and stone structure, this is the oldest standing building in Punda (1693). The museum contains permanent exhibits of Netherlands Antilles stamps and related materials, such as old post boxes. Open Monday through Friday 9 a.m. to 5 p.m., on Saturday 10 a.m. to 3 p.m. Admission charge.

4. **Ferry Terminal and Waterfront:** This is the famous view of old merchant houses. This is also the place to catch the free ferry to Otrobanda when the Queen Emma bridge is open. Probably the most famous building here is Penha, at the corner of Breedestraat and Handelskade. It is a notable example of eighteenth-century Dutch colonial architecture with curlicue gables and galleries that wrap around the second floor.

5. **Art Gallery 86:** It may be the island's largest art gallery, but it's still small. It showcases work by both local and Dutch artists. Open Monday through Friday 9:30 a.m. to noon and 3 p.m. to 5:30 p.m.; on Saturday from 10:30 a.m. to noon.

6. **Queen Emma Bridge:** Affectionately known as the "swinging old lady," the first floating pontoon bridge, Emmaburg, was built in the 1880s. The bridge allows easy pedestrian access across the channel. On busy days, the bridge is moved out of the way to allow cruise ships and huge oil tankers to pass through. It's quite a humbling sight to be at the waterfront when one of these behemoths comes through. The bridge is sometimes lit at night with numerous lights but always at Christmas.

7. **Fort Amsterdam:** Another large yellow building and seat of government for the Netherlands Antilles. In front of the Fort is the Horn of Plenty Monument given by Holland for

loyal assistance during World War II. You'll enter the fort courtyard through a covered alleyway. The bright yellow building with white columns is the Cabinet of Ministers. The lighter yellow building with the cupola is the old Fort Church, home to Curaçao's first Dutch Protestant congregation. In back of it is the Fort Church Museum. Besides congregational relics, the museum contains some of the Curaçao's oldest maps. The museum is open Monday through Friday 9 a.m. to noon and 2 p.m. to 5 p.m.

8. **Wilhelminaplein (Wilhelmina Plaza):** This pleasant plaza and adjacent park is dedicated to Queen Wilhelmina, who ruled the Netherlands for half a century, from 1898 to 1948. The plaza, which is well shaded, has benches, a small bandstand, and a children's playground. Cultural events are sometimes held here.

9. **The Temple:** Many tourists mistake this worn-looking synagogue built in the late nineteenth century as the oldest in the Western Hemisphere because it looks like it should be. It's not, and there is constant talk of renovating it that never seems to go anywhere.

10. **Marshe (The Old Market):** It's noisy, but the best places to sample local food are at these independently owned food stands. Seating is first come, first served at the long counters and small tables. Portions are generous, the prices the best in town, and it's all safe to eat. But be here between 11 a.m. and 2 p.m. only, Monday through Friday.

11. **Scharloo:** Cross the Wilhelmina Bridge and begin a wonderful one- to two-hour walking tour of nineteenth-century mansions in Scharlooweg, a once thriving Jewish community. The buildings were built with a neoclassical style, brighter colors, and far more intricate detail than those of the Dutch. They set the standards that plantation houses all over the island would copy. Their intricate and elaborate details, windows, gables, various colored roofs, stairways, and courtyards show more variety in these few blocks than you'll see on the rest of the ABCs combined. Amazingly, this area was almost in ruins until the late 1980s, but now that it's an important business district many buildings have been renovated.

Except for the public buildings open to everyone, you'll have to admire the rest from the outside. One of Curaçao's most famous buildings is here, the green and white National Archives. It's appropriately nicknamed the "wedding cake" because the front of the building looks like it's covered in elaborate white frosting. Although it's Scharloo's best-known building, it's also one of the youngest, built in 1916. Regrettably, on some structures still awaiting renovation you'll see what locals fittingly call "wall cancer," the peeling away of the plaster facade by the salts in the sea stones and sand used in constructing the buildings.

Elsewhere on Curaçao

1. Hofi Pastor

Time: 45–60 minutes for each trail. | **Difficulty:** 1. | **Trailhead:** Located in the village of Barber, beside a large church, in the western part of the island. Admission fee. Open sunrise to sunset. Benches and picnic areas provided.

Hofi Pastor (Priest's Orchard) covers 30 acres and is operated by Friends of the Earth. It offers two different hiking trails. Both start at a magnificent 300-year-old kapok tree with huge plank roots. The Yellow Trail passes through a forest of mahogany and calabash trees and the arid countryside, ending at the top of a hill with an excellent panoramic view of the surrounding area. The Orange Trail goes through some of the island's largest trees. Of particular note is the surun di mundi tree with its large, light-green leaves; it is almost extinct on Curaçao. This shaded trail also ends at the top of a hill with a panoramic view.

Most of Curaçao's hofis (orchards) have been neglected over the years and no longer yield fruit. This hofi was sold to a catholic priest Father Nieuwindt in the early 1800s. He became a thorn in the side of local landowners when he started holding weekly masses in the corn barn of a friendly neighbor. Over 500 slaves attended each service, and locals were afraid they would rebel. After the governor stopped the weekly sessions in 1829, Father Nieuwindt received permission to build Barber Church, adjacent to the hofi. In the late 1800s the hofi became known as St. Josefsdal, but people today still call it Hofi Pastor.

2. Christoffel National Park

Located on the northwest part of the island, on the road to Westpunt. The park is open Monday–Saturday at 8 a.m. Admission to the mountain side is closed at 3 p.m., to the ocean side at 4 p.m. On Sundays, the park is open from 6 a.m. to 3 p.m. Guided tours are possible; special walks at dawn and dusk occasionally offered. Call 640363 for full information.

Opened to the public in 1978, Christoffel park consists of three former plantations: Savonet, Zorgvlied, and Zevenbergen. Savonet starts at the park entrance. Walk this route first to become oriented to the park plant life. The route goes along the north coast and includes a look at caves with Indian drawings. This is a land of cactus that grows to 10 feet tall and 236 bird species. The following descriptions are of trails, often driven but easily walked.

A. Savonet Route

Length: Almost 6 miles. | **Time:** 3 hours of walking. | **Difficulty:** 3 if you choose to walk in the open sun. Take drinks and snacks. | **Trailhead:** The route begins on the left just inside the park, at the Savonet country house.

Savonet Plantation, one of Curaçao's largest, was established sometime before 1662. Dairy products, sheep wool, and cattle raising provided what one 1861 planter called a "moderate and relatively decent living" in this fairly harsh land.

The medium-sized country house of Savonet, rebuilt after a surprise English attack in 1806, is considered typical eighteenth-century architecture. It is oriented east–west as was typical, is surrounded by a parapet, and has no interior corridors.

Starting at the plantation, follow the blazes marked in a very obvious shade of blue. Continuing, you will pass mesquite *(Prosopis juiliflora)* widely used for making charcoal because of its rapid growth; and the divi-divi trees, whose pods were in great demand for their high tannin content (60 percent). Savonet exported about 40 tons of pods annually in the late 1800s, until chrome alum replaced tannin as the favored tanning agent.

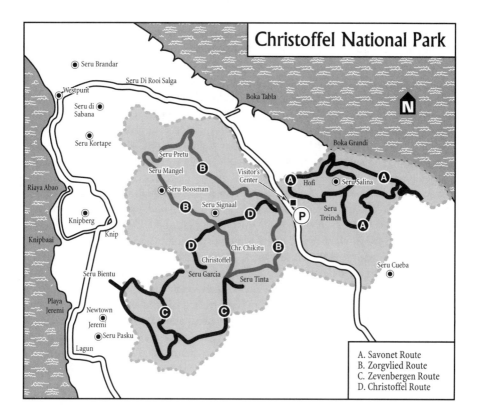

Christoffel National Park

Seru Brandar

Seru Di Rooi Salga

Westpunt

Boka Tabla

Seru di Sabana

N

Seru Kortape

Boka Grandi

Seru Pretu

Seru Mangel **B**

Visitor's Center

A Hofi **A** Seru Salina **A**

Riaya Abao

Seru Boosman

B Seru Signaal

B

D

P Seru Treinch

A

Knipberg

Knip

Knipbaai

D

Chr. Chikitu **B**

Seru Cueba

Christoffel

Seru Bientu

Seru Garcia

Seru Tinta

Playa Jeremi

Newtown

Jeremi

C

C

Seru Pasku

Lagun

A. Savonet Route
B. Zorgvlied Route
C. Zevenbergen Route
D. Christoffel Route

The large fields of prickly pear cactus you see have been flourishing since the mid-1950s. Prickly pears were able to establish themselves quickly because the discs readily snap off, to be transported by animals or humans. The discs then fall to ground and take root. It's possible to use prickly pears for animal forage, but you have to eliminate the thorns first. One way the farmers attempted—this is true, not a joke—was with flame throwers. They worked well but were too expensive.

Lignum vitae, which often has black tears of resin on its spotted trunk, was an important wood for shipbuilding. Because of the high resin content, the wood formed a watertight seal around propeller shafts. Always green, its blossoms are blue flowers that produce a heart-shaped orange fruit.

Resembling the lignum vitae but with a much rougher trunk is the "mata piska" or fish killer *(Jacquinia barbasco),* which exudes a penetrating sweet smell when in bloom. If you throw berries, leaves, or bruised branches into still (nonflowing) water, dead fish soon start floating on the surface. Fish have been caught this way for centuries by South American Indians. The toxin is not harmful to humans.

As the road bears right, you'll pass dyewood trees, another important export crop for Savonet. Rasping the wood produces a red color suitable for dyeing cloth. The trees are easy to distinguish because their trunks are unusually grooved.

At the crossroads, go straight and descend into a "rooi," from the Spanish word *arroyo,* a dry bed that holds running water only after a heavy shower. Growing in the rooi and along the sides of the road is a shrub you don't want to touch called locally "bringamosa" (fighting young lady). The stinging hairs on the leaves and branches contain a substance that causes itching, scratching, and, for very allergic people, a high fever. Also growing in the same area is a natural antidote called flaira *(Jatrophya gossypifolia).* It looks just like the fighting young lady but has red flowers and lacks the stinging hairs.

Next you emerge onto a plateau and a sign that indicates a good view of the north coast. Boka Grandi is a rough, wave-swept beach on one side of the viewpoint; Savonet house and Christoffel Hill are on the other.

Look carefully among the melocaccti if they are in bloom. Whiptail lizards love dining on the pink flowers and fruits, as do several species of hummingbirds, including the ruby-topaz *(Chrysolampis mosquitus)* and blue-tailed emerald hummingbird *(Chlorostilbon mellisugus).* The limestone soil is full of ribbed milky-white shells that look like wicker beehives. These land snails are endemic to the Dutch islands. The fact that no South American snail species are present cuts a hole in the theory that the ABCs were once connected to South America.

The road next makes a steep descent onto a shallow salt flat (or *salina*) where you may see herons and American oyster catchers. Soon you'll reach a parking lot near Indian drawings and caves. The reddish-colored Indian drawings, looking almost as if they had been done in crayon, are fenced to protect them from being defaced. Similar drawings have been found on the South American continent. Based on the pottery shards found here, it appears that the artists originated in Venezuela. The Indians did not live in the caves hereabouts but in oval houses made of wood and intertwined branches. Figures drawn in the caves, estimated between 500 and 2,000 years old, are considered abstracts that may have had some religious significance. The figures are drawn in white and black as well as terra cotta.

The most interesting cave is the second one, but the bottleneck at the entrance requires that you scuttle inside on all fours. You'll need a light to go farther, but the cave soon opens so you can stand upright again. The cave extends for a distance of about 410 feet. Its ground is covered with grayish-brown guano from the four species of bats that reside here. You'll make a sharp right to enter a white chamber whose walls are made of soft marl. Drops of water over thousands of years have formed the stalactites and stalagmites. Don't worry about any fearsome-looking cave spiders you see. Although relatives of the whip scorpion, the spiders lack poison glands. Finally you'll enter the well-lit sanctuary of the "cathedral" hall where barn owls sometimes are seen. The return road also offers fine coastal views with the opportunity to scale a couple of large boulders.

B. Zorgvlied Route

Length: An option of 4.7 miles or 7.5 miles. | **Time:** 3–5 hours, depending on the route taken. | **Difficulty:** 1. | **Trailhead:** On the southwest side of Christoffel Park, across from the Savonet plantation house and Visitor Center. Park there or at the several designated spots along the trail.

The green-blazed route explores the Zorgvlied plantation, which was merged with Savonet in 1830, making it one of the largest and most important on all Curaçao in the 1800s. The trail leads to Mount Christoffel.

Like Savonet, the *Zorgvlied* Route is a botanical, geological, and historical tour. The Dutch name Zorgvlied means a place "where worry flees." No one has worried about the country house since 1832, when this plantation merged with Savonet, and it shows. Only the walls are still standing, though the porch is in decent shape.

Starting out, you pass one of those exotic-import ideas that went badly astray: the rubber vine, *Cryptostegia grandiflora,* brought from Madagascar during World War I to produce latex, which is made into rubber. The plant actually bleeds latex when pinched. Unfortunately, the rubber vine and its whiplike runners thrived too well and soon overgrew the local vegetation. Officially considered a pest, it is too difficult to eradicate because the roots must be dug up to prevent the plant from sprouting anew.

Leaving the estate ruins, the road steeply descends to provide a good view of Mount Christoffel. If you go left at the T-junction, it will take you immediately to the foot of Christoffel, where you can take the Christoffel trail to the summit. Ahead of you is a once-fertile valley were millet was grown. If you're tired of the scenic tour and ready to really hike, go left to Christoffel.

Going straight ahead, the road descends into two more roois (overflow areas), then slopes steeply with two Z-bends and leads to a hilltop overlooking an area known as Rancho Grande. The geology of the hill covers an incredible time span. The lower terrace facing the sea is an estimated 125,000 years old; low inland hills comprising the middle terrace are 510,000 years old. Rocks on these hills are an estimated 100 million years old, part of the Curaçao Lava Formation. The geology of the ABCs, obviously long and complicated, is well explained in the park guide for sale at the entrance.

The trail then goes along a ridge that is the most scenic part of the Zorgvlied Route. After a final steep descent, the route takes you to the foot of Mount Christoffel.

C. Zevenbergen Route

Length: Almost 7 miles. | **Time:** 2–3 hours. | **Difficulty:** 3, due to the sun and occasional climbing. | **Trailhead:** On the Mount Christoffel side. Park in the designated area near Seru Tinta.

Marked in yellow, this undulating road passes through the Curaçao Lava Formation and ends up at the base of Mount Christoffel. Start by making about a ten-minute climb of Seru Tinta. Besides excellent panoramic views and the chance to view more of the island's geology, the real reason for the climb is Piedra di Monton—what looks like a large heap of stones deposited by several dump trucks.

Instead, they represent the dreams of escape of eighteenth- and nineteenth-century slaves. The legend handed down is this: Salt is crucial in the tropics because without it, you lose your own body salts by sweating. Slaves apparently believed that if they didn't eat salt, they would be able to fly (probably because of the feeling of light-headedness symptomatic of salt deprivation). It was believed that slaves who had not eaten salt could place a stone at the foot of Mount Christoffel and sing a song that would enable them to fly back to Africa. In the twentieth century, the stone piles (Piedra di Monton) were appropriated to help maintain the park roads. Although it may be tempting, it is forbidden to collect anything, even stones, in the park.

Taking the main yellow route, climb about 623 feet for an excellent view of Santa Martha Bay to the south. In this spot are the only two species of orchids that occur on the island. The prettiest is the purple orchid, which blooms in July and August. White orchids peak in December and January but are present anytime there's sufficient rain.

Continuing along the main road, you'll come to the Seru Bientu trail, a ten-minute path to the top of a hill whose name literally means "wind" *(bientu)*. The climb is not steep, but the wind can be strong enough literally to stop you in your tracks. The trail begins among dye-wood trees and shrubby kamalia, although lichens and bare rock soon become characteristic on the right side. In the valley below on the left is a manganese mine that closed in 1881.

At the summit, the leaves of the sabal palms are a soothing but dynamic sound in the ever-present wind. Another walk of ten minutes on the trail along the northern slope will reward you with impressive views of the Knip and Lagun regions.

The final stop is the Zevenbergen mansion, unusual for its time because it was two stories instead of the typical single level. The name *Zevenbergen* means "seven mountains," and you have a view of them all from here. Unfortunately, when this plantation merged with Knip plantation in 1864, the owner lived at Knip. These buildings were allowed to be almost leveled by wind and time.

The food storehouse *(magnasina)* on this plantation played an important role in the slave uprising of 1795. The Dutch did use slaves, but local historians like to look kindly on their treatment in the ABCs compared to elsewhere. Still, slaves on Curaçao rebelled twice, and their leaders were put to death. So, things weren't necessarily all that different.

In 1795, about 1,000 slaves from all over the island took possession of several food storehouses in the Christoffel area, including this one. Bolstered by these supplies, the slaves could have withstood a siege indefinitely. Fierce fighting here broke the revolt when the slaves were forced to surrender. This rebellion, like many in the Caribbean at this time, was prompted by the spreading news of the French Revolution in 1789. Slavery was abolished here in 1863.

D. Christoffel Route

Time: 1 hour from the base to the top. | **Difficulty:** 2–3. Christoffel is about 1,230 feet high. | **Trailhead:** The parking lot at the base of the mountain, opposite the Visitor Center.

Begin early because of the constant sun/heat. The pathway—blazed in red—is on the lee side of the hill, out of the wind, so you don't have the benefit of the tradewinds to keep you cool.

The trail follows a large rooi (overflow) bordered by numerous rubber vines and manchineel trees. In the rooi, bird-watching may be quite good: sparrows, bananaquits, and warblers. You're more likely to hear than see the shy St. Christoffel pigeon, which lives in the tree-tops. Its easily identifiable call is "roo-coo-coo."

Gradually climbing becomes more difficult. Keep a lookout for the green juvenile iguanas and the better camouflaged adults. As on Aruba, these are widely hunted with pellet guns or slingshots for their meat. You may also spot whiptail lizards *(Cnemidophorus murinus murinus);* when the males run at full speed, they raise their tails and the front part of their bodies, looking like dinosaurs on the move. You're also likely to see light brown lizards with a gray lateral stripe *(Anolis lineatus)* on tree trunks or twigs.

If you start the climb early, you could spot tiny, very shy white-tailed deer *(Odocoileus virginianus curassavicus)*. They aren't much larger than a goat. Curaçao is the only Caribbean island where deer were present before the arrival of Christopher Columbus.

As you climb, the gradual transition to a more humid micro-climate becomes evident, with beard moss and other lichens and a definite predominance of large-leafed, thornless trees. A couple of fern species will also be evident in the rocks off to the left.

The hike ends with a scramble to the top, where the blessed tradewinds will cool you off. The view from here, the top of Curaçao, is exceptional. On clear days you can spot Aruba to the west, Bonaire and the distant mountain ranges of Venezuela to the east. Sit, relax and enjoy the view.

10   GRENADA

Old Grenadian Proverb: "If you have patience, you will see ant's belly."
Translation: "If you wait long enough, you will get what you want"

Grenada is one of the Caribbean's lushest landfalls, rich in rain forest, waterfalls, and agriculture. It so reminded early Spanish sailors of the beloved green hillsides above their homeport, that they named it Granada. However, the French and British later corrupted the name to a different spelling and pronunciation. The Spanish city of Granada is called "Grah-NAH-dah," whereas the deep Caribbean island of Grenada is known as "Greh-NAY-dah."

Located 158 miles southwest of Barbados and 100 miles north of Venezuela, Grenada is only 12 miles wide and 21 miles long, yet its mountainous interior provides some of the Caribbean's most scenic—as well as most accessible—hiking. Grenada began protecting its natural resources well before the concept of eco-tourism was invented, so the landscape is wonderfully unspoiled.

Called the spice basket of the Caribbean, Grenada produces 12 different spices, including cloves, nutmeg, ginger, cinnamon, and mace. Sailors claim they can smell their sweet fragrance as far out as 20 miles out at sea. Grenada's most important spice is nutmeg, supposedly introduced to the island in 1843 as a surprise addition to the rum punch at a local bash. Since then, no one in Grenada would consider drinking rum punch without it.

Maybe it's because the nutmeg is so fresh, but I swear the best rum punches *are* in Grenada. Nutmeg is also used locally to aid against colds and is even an ingredient in the Vicks VapoRub cold remedy. Grenada is the world's second-largest nutmeg producer after Indonesia.

Grenada received worldwide publicity in October 1983 when the United States invaded the country, an action the grateful Grenadians refer to as "the intervention" because it brought them a democratic government. American troops were warmly welcomed when they came ashore, and Americans are still held in high regard by most locals. Of course, President Ronald Reagan's $57.2 million commitment to stabilizing the Grenadian economy, which transformed the pitiful road and telephone systems into some of the Caribbean's best, didn't hurt.

The main port city of St. George's, a horseshoe-shaped harbor known as the Carenage, is very photogenic. Its Saturday morning market is incredibly lively and colorful, perhaps the best open-air market in all the Caribbean. The best place to photograph it is from a balcony, overlooking all the activity.

Grenada's high mountains receive more than 160 inches of rain a year, creating a verdant forest with 450 species of flowering plants and 85 different types of trees. Most of the island's 150 types of birds, especially the rufous-breasted hummingbird, live in the main sanctuary, the Grand Etang National Park. Grenada has no poisonous snakes and few biting insects; Grand Etang is too high for mosquitoes to be much of a bother.

TRAVEL TIPS

Area: Grenada is 340 square miles or about 21 miles long by 12 miles wide.

Language: English and Creole.

Population: About 100,000.

Time Zone: Atlantic Time, 1 hour ahead of Eastern Standard Time.

Rainy Season: The rainy season lasts from June through November. Although the sun is frequently out in coastal areas during this period, you can almost count on the mountains being socked in. Rain may last for several days at a time in summer.

Getting There: Carriers include American Airlines offering flights from New York and Miami. BWIA flies from New York. LIAT, (800) 468-0482, flies to Grenada from Barbados. British Airways flies from London's Gatwick Airport. Grenada's Point Salines Airport is just a few minutes from 2-mile-long Grand Anse Beach, where the major hotels are located.

Documents: A passport is necessary for all but U.S. citizens, who will need two documents, one with a photograph, proving citizenship.

Getting Around: Cars rent for an average US$40 per day. A local driving permit (US$12) is required. Driving is on the left. Taxis are plentiful and the tourist board sets fares. A water shuttle runs regularly to Grand Anse Beach from the Nutmeg Restaurant in St. George's.

Where to Stay: The Rex Grenadian at Point Salines with 212 rooms is the island's largest hotel, (800) 255 5859 or (305) 471 6170; email grenrex@caribsurf.com. La Source, 100 units on Pink Gin Beach, is an upscale, all-inclusive property that even offers spa treatments along with scuba diving and other sports, (800) 544-2883 or (473) 444-2556; fax (473) 444-2561; www.lasource.com.gd. Some of the better beachfront small hotels include Spice Island Inn, (800) 742-4276; Secret Harbour, (800) 437-7880, (473) 444-4548, www.secretharbour.com; and the La Sagesse Nature Center at St. David's, www.lasagesse.com.

Camping: Available in the Grand Etang National Park.

Currency: The East Caribbean Dollar is the local currency. The exchange rate is US$1= EC$2.70. U.S. currency is freely exchanged in stores, but the exchange rate there is much lower than at the banks. Banks are open 8 a.m. to 1:30 or 2 p.m. Monday to Thursday and to 5 p.m. on Friday.

Taxes & Tips: There's an 8% room tax and a US$14 departure tax. A 10% tip is added in most restaurants and to most hotel bills.

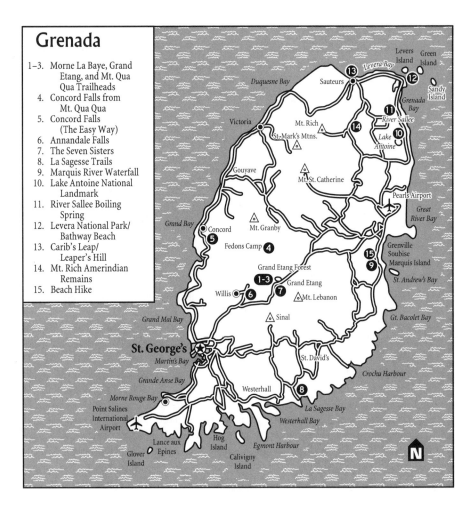

Grenada

1–3. Morne La Baye, Grand
   Etang, and Mt. Qua
   Qua Trailheads
4. Concord Falls from
   Mt. Qua Qua
5. Concord Falls
   (The Easy Way)
6. Annandale Falls
7. The Seven Sisters
8. La Sagesse Trails
9. Marquis River Waterfall
10. Lake Antoine National
   Landmark
11. River Sallee Boiling
   Spring
12. Levera National Park/
   Bathway Beach
13. Carib's Leap/
   Leaper's Hill
14. Mt. Rich Amerindian
   Remains
15. Beach Hike

Electrical Current: Voltage is 220, 50 cycles. A transformer is needed for all U.S. appliances. Hotels generally have transformers but sometimes not enough to meet the demand. Some hotels also provide one or two 110-volt outlets in their main offices.

Safety/Health Warnings: Although Grenadians are among the Caribbean's friendliest people, street crime is increasing. Be careful in isolated areas. And everywhere, after dark. Passports are a favorite target for theft. Report its loss immediately to police and local U.S. consulate.

Snakes & Other Venomous Creatures: None.

Hiking Guides: You have the services of two of the Caribbean's best, Denis Henry of Henry's Tours, (473) 444-5313, and Telfor Bedeau, (473) 442-6200. I highly recommend either one. Telfor Bedeau is based at his home in Soubise, about a mile south of Grenville, and presently all his organized hikes begin and return there. The reason: Telfor doesn't have a car yet to transport people to other parts of the island. Should you have a car and engage Telfor for a day, the entire island is at your disposal. He will arrange a rendezvous point or come to meet you. Denis Henry, who has a small fleet of air-conditioned vans, makes many of the same hikes.

Additional Information: Grenada Tourist Office, 800 2nd Avenue, Suite 400-K, New York, NY 10017; call (800) 927-9554. In Canada, the Grenada Board of Tourism, Suite 820, 439 University Avenue, Toronto, Ontario M5G 1Y8; call (416) 595-1339. In the United Kingdom, Grenada Board of Tourism, 1 Collington Gardens, London SW5 0HW; call (0171) 370-5164; www.grenada.org.

Dress Code: Visitors are requested not to wear bathing suits or mini-shorts in the streets or stores.

ST. GEORGE'S AFOOT!

Length: 1 mile. | **Time:** 2 hours. | **Difficulty:** 1–2. | **Trailhead:** At the Bianca C Statue, near the midpoint of the semicircular harbor front.

The harbor, which easily accommodates cruise ships, was once an inland lake and may be the crater of an extinct volcano. The town of St. George's, named after King George III, is one of the Caribbean's most attractive. The old homes are painted delicate shades of yellow, beige, and rose; their second stories flaunt ornate ironwork balconies.

The spine of a steep hill divides St. George's: The harbor side is the most picturesque. It's known as the Carenage, while the more drab Esplanade fronts the Caribbean. However, the small mountain cutting through St. George's is quite steep, so this is not the easiest walk. During the annual carnival, steel band platforms have to be winched up and down the main roads because motorized vehicles have great difficulty hauling heavy loads on the dramatic inclines.

1. **"Bianca C" Statue:** Commemorates the gallantry of the Grenadian people in saving passengers aboard the 600-foot Italian luxury liner which caught fire in St. George's Harbour in 1961. Three crewmen were killed in the boiler explosion. The "Bianca C" now rests in 160 feet of water offshore, the second largest Caribbean wreck accessible to scuba divers.

2. **St. George's Anglican Church:** This beautiful stone and pink stucco building was completed in 1825. It contains many plaques commemorating British victims of Fedon's Rebellion, a slave uprising of 1795.

3. **National Library:** A former brick warehouse is where the library has been located since 1892; the library itself was established in 1846.

4. **Tile-roofed Warehouses:** Examine the red tiles on these eighteenth- and nineteenth-century stone and brick warehouses. They are fish-scale tiles originally used as ballast.

5. **Fort George:** Built by the French in 1705 to overlook the harbor mouth, this is now the city's main police station. The imposing fort supposedly still contains a system of underground tunnels once linked to other fortifications. This is where Maurice Bishop and his colleagues were killed in 1983, prompting U.S. intervention.

HIKING PHILOSOPHY

Telfor Bedeau is one of the Caribbean's original hiking guides, in business since 1962. He explains his background and philosophy: "I started with some young-sters—but we were all young at the time—not even thinking I would be hiking 40 years later. So far I have covered over 350 hikes and walked a total distance of over 6,000 miles. So these legs of mine have done a wonderful job and I don't know how long they will continue, but I plan to keep hiking as long as I am fit. I have hopes of getting younger folks (Grenadians) interested, so that instead of doing all sorts of nonsense and mischief, they will go hiking, learn about their country and make themselves better citizens."

Telfor is known for his "marathon hikes" that might climb five or six mountains peaks and cover as much as 30 miles. However, he won't take anyone on such a hike until he has "broken them in" on what he calls a "medium hike."

He explains, "Sometimes a visitor will come saying, 'I am fit!' and 'I do this exercise and that exercise.' But the hiking terrain in Grenada is a totally different thing, and when you think you are fit, you have not begun to be fit."

6. Traffic Police Control Station: Watch the policeman control traffic as he stands safely above the motorized vehicles in a special box. Considering the steep inclines, this is the only way drivers from all directions can see his traffic signals.

7. Antilles Hotel: One of St. George's oldest buildings, it has served as French barracks, a British prison, a hotel, and a warehouse. Now the Grenadian National Museum, it houses a small collection of artifacts and old newspapers dramatizing the island's history and culture. Included are Arawak petroglyphs, the marble bathtub of Empress Josephine (who grew up on Martinique) and a rum still.

8. Sendall Tunnel: Named after the governor when this technological wonder was completed in 1895. Still used today, the 340-foot-long tunnel is a shortcut through the hill to link the Carenage with the Esplanade.

9. St. Andrew's Presbyterian Kirk: Better known as Scot's Kirk and located on Church Street, it was built in 1831 with assistance from the Freemasons.

10. Esplanade: The commercial waterfront area of St. George's, including the fish market, most active at the end of the day when the catch is brought in, or almost anytime on Saturday.

11. Marketplace: Site of the unbelievably colorful fruit and vegetable display on Saturdays, where women sell small bags of spices (cloves, cinnamon, and nutmeg) to tourists as useful and fragrant reminders of Grenada. The spices sold are pretty much the same; it is the colorful packaging (cloth sack, straw box, or reed box) that should determine whom you buy from. Take time to shop and compare; the spice ladies won't go anywhere, I

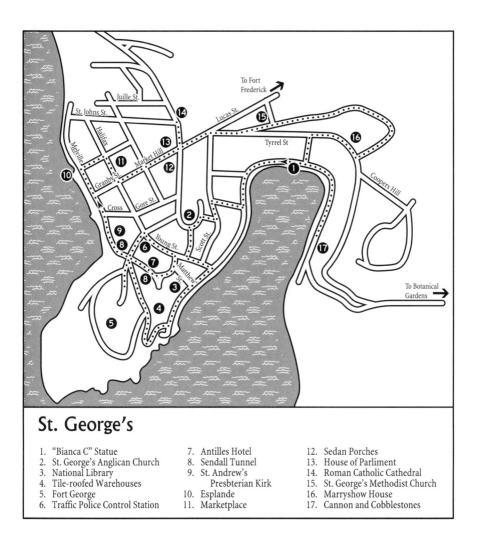

St. George's

1. "Bianca C" Statue
2. St. George's Anglican Church
3. National Library
4. Tile-roofed Warehouses
5. Fort George
6. Traffic Police Control Station
7. Antilles Hotel
8. Sendall Tunnel
9. St. Andrew's
   Presbterian Kirk
10. Esplande
11. Marketplace
12. Sedan Porches
13. House of Parliment
14. Roman Catholic Cathedral
15. St. George's Methodist Church
16. Marryshow House
17. Cannon and Cobblestones

assure you. The market square also is the rallying place for political speeches, parades, and religious activities.

12. Sedan Porches: These porches are open at both ends so wealthy planters in sedan chairs could travel under the row of roofs and avoid the rain.

13. House of Parliament: Both the Senate and House of Representatives of Grenada meet here.

14. Roman Catholic Cathedral: The tower from 1818 is the oldest part; the rest of the cathedral is much later, built in 1884 on the site of an 1804 church.

15. St. George's Methodist Church: Built in 1820, it is the oldest original church building in St. George's.

16. **Marryshow House:** This fine building was the home of T. A. Marryshow, the Grenadian leader who attempted to turn the entire West Indies into one nation. Today, it is the local center for the University of the West Indies.

17. **Cannon and Cobblestones:** This is an excellent example of St. George's many cobblestone streets and illustrates a practical use for all the old cannon removed from Grenada's various forts. The cannon are used as bollards to tie up ships and to protect corners of masonry walls from cars and trucks.

HIKING GRAND ETANG NATIONAL PARK

Situated high in true tropical rain forest where the mountain peaks are frequently obscured by clouds, Grand Etang Park is a wonderful conservation example to governments around the world. Grand Etang, headquarters for Grenada's National Park System, is supported by the British Development Division, the U.N. Development Program, The Organization of American States, the U.S. Peace Corps, the U.S. Agency for International Development, and the government of Grenada. That's quite an impressive array of backers, and it makes one wish this sort of international cooperation was a common practice, not something to point out as unusual.

Grenada's best hiking is here in the Grand Etang National Park. Only eight miles from the center of St. George's, the park is more than 2,000 feet above sea level, high enough to cause decompression sickness (the bends) in anyone foolish enough to scuba dive and then go hiking the same day. Grand Etang ("large pond" in French) is named after a small lake at 1,740 feet, actually an old volcanic crater.

The park vegetation is extremely diverse, including cloud forests, montane thickets, palm brakes, and elfin woodland as well as rain forest. A modest interpretive center called the Park Centre has a receptionist and guide who, if contacted in advance, may personally escort you. Displays feature the island's wildlife, forestry, and natural history, including more than 20 different wood samples. Several small food stands located near the Park Centre sell cold drinks.

Most hiking trails are well marked and require little assistance, although it's always more enjoyable to have a guide who can share the local folklore. With 160 inches of rain falling annually, the trails can be quite muddy and slick. Long pants are not essential if you stay on the trail path and avoid encounters with razor grass, a climbing grass with extremely sharp edges. I find it takes a long time for even minor razor grass cuts to heal.

Grand Etang is most noted for its tall mahogany and gommier trees, ferns, and other plants. Animals include the mona monkey, armadillo, broad-winged hawk (locally called "gree-gree"), Antillean crested hummingbird (the "little doctor bird"), and the Antillean tanager (called "the soursop").

1. MORNE LaBAYE TRAIL

Length: Less than 1 mile. | **Time:** 15 minutes. | **Difficulty:** 1. | **Trailhead:** Behind the park headquarters.

This short interpretive trail has excellent examples of Grenada's rich foliage, and it's a good introduction to the park. One of the first plants you'll see is the indigenous Grand Etang fern, found in this area of Grenada and nowhere else in the world. The fern has a distinctive spore pattern under the fronds. The mountain palms, whose fruit and fronds Grenadians use in many different ways, are also characteristic of this part of montane forest.

You'll observe an interesting symbiotic relationship between the slender bois canot tree *(Cereropia)* and the ants living in its hollow trunk. In return for shelter, the ants repel opossums and other animals trying to climb the tree to graze on tender new shoots. What botanists call a pioneer species, bois canot is one of the first to reappear after severe hurricane winds destroy a forest.

Another pioneer species is the colorful heliconia (or balisier, pronounced "bah-lee-zyay"), a member of the banana family. You've probably seen the blooms, shaped like a long row of lobster claws, made into decorative bouquets in hotel rooms. These yellow, orange, or red ornamentals have flowerlike bracts that are almost scimitar-shaped. Mosquitoes thrive in the water pockets of these bracts, which sometimes provide the only stagnant water for breeding.

Looking skyward you'll see the tall marouba tree, with its spreading branches and small leaves. The marouba takes its nourishment from the sun above the high canopy, instead of from the forest soil. Locals say marouba bark can drug or stun fish, making them easy to catch.

Besides bamboo, the Morne LaBaye Trail contains lots of elephant grass, which resembles sugarcane but is distinguished by its jointed stem. This elephant grass was originally planted decades ago to provide a convenient refueling stop for horse and donkey-drawn wagons crossing the island. It is still used for fodder when meadows on the farms wither away in the dry season.

At the morne ("small hill" in French) itself is a small weather station to monitor the complex and frequently changing conditions of Grand Etang. At the River Turning Crater you'll find lingering evidence of Hurricane Janet's destruction in 1955: a stand of huge, dead gommier (gum) trees, now serving as display posts for countless air plants.

The gommier *(Dacryodes excelsa)* is the most common large tree of the rain forest. Its bark contains a gum that can be used to light fires. Only, some of the gommier trees have no bark. Their trunks withstood the hurricane's 150-mph winds, but their branches and leaves were stripped away. Unable to photosynthesize energy from the sunlight, they died.

2. GRAND ETANG SHORELINE TRAIL

Length: 2–3 miles. | **Time:** 1.5 hours, round-trip. | **Difficulty:** 2. |
Trailhead: This relatively easy walk begins on the Morne LaBaye Trail and encircles the lake shoreline at the edge of the Palm Break.

Grand Etang, in the caldera of an extinct volcano, has five different subclimatic plant communities. This is one of the Caribbean's few hikes as high as 2,000 feet: Be prepared for a chilly wind.

Before reaching the lake, you'll cross a small pond. Look closely into this runoff from the lake, and you may be able to spot both crayfish and ling (a small-scale freshwater lobster).

Moving along the lake shore, you'll walk through a palm brake dominated by fern trees and mountain palm *(Euterpe* palm). Above the palm break is a colorful forest of mahogany trees with orange, scarlet, and yellow hibiscus growing on them. The mahogany was brought in

St. George's Harbour is one of the Caribbean's most colorful harbors

from Jamaica after Hurricane Janet in 1955. Besides helping reforest Grenada, the timber has a remarkable blue-green grain that makes outstanding furniture and handicrafts; it's also used in fencing.

If you didn't see any mona monkeys hanging out at the food stands near the Park Centre, you're almost certain to spot some around the lake. Most active at sunrise and sunset, as they swing through the forest canopy, Mona monkeys were brought from northern Africa during the early days of slavery. If you don't see them, listen for their deep "buff-buff" grunt as they call out to one another. Mona monkeys (and opossums) like to hang out in the clusters of giant bamboo, which grow as high as 60 feet.

Incidentally, Grenadians don't anthropomorphize their animals (they did not grow up watching Bambi and Thumper or other cuddly Disney characters) but make full use of their wildlife. So you'll not only see monkeys as pets, you sometimes will find monkey—and opossum and armadillo—on the menu at some restaurants in St. George's. The monkey and armadillo are tasty; pass on the opossum.

As you search the landscape for mona monkeys, take time to appreciate the staghorn ferns, wild orchids, and epiphytes that grow on the sides of many trees. You may also spot nests of the red-necked pigeon in high trees; those small birds darting through the foliage are probably the Antillean crested hummingbird (males have a blue-green head crest) or the rufous-breasted (rust-colored) hermit hummingbird.

Along the shoreline are cattle egrets, which migrated over from Africa and first appeared in Grenada around 1950; hooded tanagers (iridescent plumage with a black cap); and little blue herons. The symbol of Grenada's national park system is the broad-winged hawk (brown and white with a banded tail), which likes to soar high over the water. The lake itself is slowly filling with reeds and may one day become merely a grassy marsh.

3. Mt. Qua Qua Summit Trail

Length: 3 miles. | **Time:** 2.5–3 hours, round-trip. | **Difficulty:** 3–4, depending on slipperiness. | **Trailhead:** From the park headquarters, walk for a few hundred yards on the paved road leading to St. George's. A sign on the right marks the start.

The hike to Mt. Qua Qua passes through true rain forest territory that is apt to live up to its name suddenly, so bring a windbreaker for showers and the cool tradewinds. Also take water and snacks for a break at the summit.

This is a challenging hike leading to the rocky summit of Mt. Qua Qua and its famous view of the northeast coast. At various points there are also some good panoramas of distant Grand Etang. This is an excellent hike for photography, but keep your camera in a backpack or holster; you'll need both hands for scrambling up and grabbing tree roots.

You'll experience little gradient until you pass a junction sign leading to the Grand Etang Trail, which goes off to the right (Hike #2, p. 157). From this point the trail to Mt. Qua Qua keeps going up and down, sometimes quite steeply, and the red clay soil along the crater rim is icy-slick when wet. In some places, the slippery trail is only a few feet wide: Dramatic drop-offs on either side demand caution. As troublesome as this wet clay may be, early settlers found it ideal for chinking their wood and bamboo dwellings.

As you start to climb, the plants and trees on the lake slope take on the characteristics of elfin woodland, forest that's been stunted and sculpted by the ever-constant tradewinds. In fact, on windward slopes all throughout Grenada you'll see similar formations where the winds have dwarfed, twisted, and folded back the vegetation. It's more pronounced the higher you go.

Interpretive "Q" signs mark several places. *Q1* is a vantage point to appreciate how the foliage overlooking the lakes have been sculpted and stunted by constant high winds to form the fairy-like elfin woodland. *Q2* is a large bui tree *(Micropholis chrysophyuoides)* blown over in 1955 by Hurricane Janet; its huge roots make good shelter from the rain. *Q3* identifies many mosses overhanging the trail. Forest workers use the moss, which is almost always damp, to wrap around newly grafted tree branches to speed healing.

Q4: This is razor grass, which you want to avoid. It's sharp enough to cut through light clothing. If you feel compelled to test its edge but want to avoid drawing blood, use a blade of it to shave some hair off the back of your arm. *Q5* is a mountain almond *(Bandizabocu)* that has a distinctive mottled bark; it produces a large, inedible fruit in the fall.

Q6 is a bois gris or bagui tree, an excellent hardwood that becomes even stronger in water, making it a preferred material for docks and sea jetties. *Q7* is a possible landslide area, so be careful near the edge. It offers a good view of Grand Anse beach and the southern end of the island. Many of the trees descending to the valley below (an important watershed region) are bois jab or tree ferns.

Proceeding, you'll see a clearing on the left, which is a firebreak not worth following. Instead, keep bearing to the right, where purple orchids drape over the different bushes.

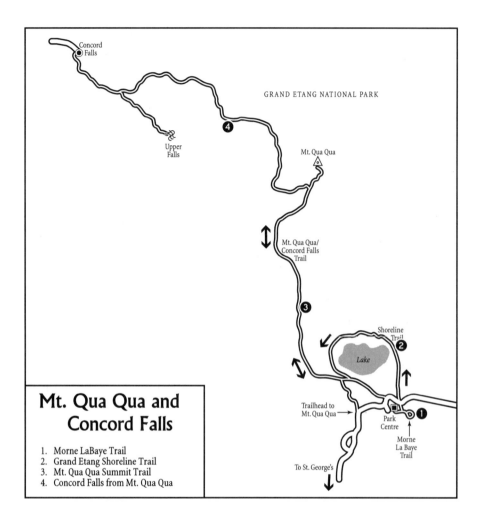

GRAND ETANG NATIONAL PARK

Concord
Falls

Upper
Falls

Mt. Qua Qua

Mt. Qua Qua/
Concord Falls
Trail

Shoreline
Trail

Lake

Trailhead to
Mt. Qua Qua

Park
Centre

Morne
La Baye
Trail

To St. George's

Mt. Qua Qua and Concord Falls

1. Morne LaBaye Trail
2. Grand Etang Shoreline Trail
3. Mt. Qua Qua Summit Trail
4. Concord Falls from Mt. Qua Qua

Q8 marks the boundary into true elfin forest, which looks like it's kept cut back and miniaturized by Japanese bonsai artists; yet it's all wind effect.

After *Q8*, which is about one hour on the Mt. Qua Qua Trail and close to the summit, you'll come to a pass leading off to the left. That's the start of the Concord Falls Trail (Hike #4, p. 161).

As long as you grab tree roots and trunks where necessary to combat the mud, you should have no real problem making it to the top of Mt. Qua Qua, 2,372 feet above sea level. Near the summit you won't even be walking on clay but a thick mat of tree roots. You'll know when you've begun walking on air because your ground support will suddenly feel spongy, almost like a trampoline. The situation lasts for only a few yards—quite memorable ones they are, too, as the real ground is a couple of hundred feet below.

At the summit is a tall boulder on the right and a wonderful view of the eastern mountains, the windward coast, and the Point Salines airport.

Walk around the high boulder to a pathway between it and another large rock. Step to the edge and—after the hot, humid climb—greet what feels like all the winds of the world. Amazingly, its only the full, unblunted force of the 22-mph trades that blow constantly across the peak, the same northeast-north breezes that brought Columbus and the other early explorers across the Atlantic. If the breeze is too much (it will be around 12° colder than at sea level), backtrack and shelter in the boulder's lee side. If you're up for some rock climbing, it's possible to scale the summit boulder for an even more elevated look around.

On the return trip are wonderful views of Grand Etang you'll have missed unless you kept looking over your shoulder on the way up. To me, the descent is far more picturesque than the climb up.

Even though the Mt. Qua Qua trail is marked clearly enough that no guide is necessary, I met several people who'd turned back, claiming the trail was too slippery and impassable. We made the summit with no difficulty. If you feel you might need a little extra moral support, don't hesitate to contact professional guides Denis Henry or Telfor Bedeau (contact information is in Travel Tips, above), who are always good company. The view from Mt. Qua Qua (in clear weather) is well worth any effort.

4. CONCORD FALLS FROM MT. QUA QUA (INCLUDING FEDON'S CAMP)

Length: About 10 miles. | **Time:** 4.5 hours, one way, including 1 hour on the Mt. Qua Qua Trail. There is no need to make the return to Grand Etang Park. | **Difficulty:** 3–4, depending on how wet the conditions. A walking stick is advisable. | **Trailhead:** A marked turnoff from the Mt. Qua Qua Trail after passing information sign *Q8* (see p. 160). It takes about 1 hour to reach this turnoff, near the Mt. Qua Qua summit.

You have several ways to visit the falls, one easy (so easy you don't even have to get out of your vehicle) and one quite challenging. Because one of the reasons you're in Grenada is to walk, let's look at the more difficult option first. It involves taking the first hour of the Mt. Qua Qua trail, then branching off left, to the falls, for the climb down.

The Concord Falls Trail wanders under rain forest canopy, over hilltop vistas, and across clear streams in the heart of Grenada's countryside, where you are apt to see most of the 85 different species of Grenada's trees. In many places you will see trailing vines, including the familiar philodendron, hanging from many large trees. These vines could prove useful if you run short of liquid: Local hunters cut them to obtain clean drinking water.

Hunters have a particular use for the damarin tree, which is of less value to hikers. They grind part of the root, then blow it into their dogs' faces to make them sneeze violently. This cleans the dog's sinus passages and readies the animal to follow a new scent, kind of like clearing your palate with sorbet between courses of a gourmet meal. If there's someone hiking with you that you really want to annoy ...

The Concord Falls Trail has a limited number of interpretive markers. Branching off from the Mt. Qua Qua path and going down, *C1* indicates numerous trees at the beginning of the descent, mostly handsome small-leafed santai *(Slonea caribea)*. Despite its appearance, the wood is not durable and so not widely used. *C2* marks the bois rouge tree *(Guavea macrophylloides)*, known for its attractive red grain, popular in furniture making.

Grisly as it might sound, if you fall off the mountain you'll probably be shipped home in a relative of *C3*. The bois lait tree *(Neoxythece pallida)* is used primarily in making coffin boards, because the white timber is very tolerant of wet ground. The tree produces tiny red blossoms in September.

Symbolically, opposite the coffin board marker and off to the right is a steep, 30-minute climb to Fedon's Camp, a site associated with some of Grenada's greatest bloodletting. Julien Fedon was a Grenadian hero, a mulatto planter who led the slave uprising of 1795. The flag motto of "Liberté, Egalité ou la Mort" (liberty, equality, or death) was closely adhered to: It was death for almost everyone involved. With supplies brought in from Guadeloupe, Fedon and the slaves overran Grenada, slaughtering many British settlers and suspected collaborators. Fedon had such control of Grenada he was able to take the British governor and 50 other hostages to his mountain stronghold, where he murdered them. The British spent almost a year retaking the island and capturing the revolt's ringleaders, who were executed or exiled to Honduras. Fedon himself was never taken and is believed to have escaped—perhaps to Cuba—or drowned while attempting to reach Trinidad. Fedon's insurrection left Grenada in a shambles. Slavery was abolished in Grenada in 1838.

Fedon's former estate at Belvedere, from which he masterminded the revolt, is below the peak known as Fedon's Camp. The Fedon's Camp lookout has a superb view.

The hike to Fedon's Camp can be rigorous, as these incidents from guide Telfor Bedeau illustrate: "Going down the west side on a very steep hill, we were also young and everyone wanted to have a competition to see who could walk the most. We were running down the steep hill and I was in front of some of the other guys when I reached a sudden step down— of maybe about five feet. I had just gotten down there when I heard someone call out behind and I looked: a guy had been coming with so much speed that both of his feet left the earth, he passed above me and fell on the ground a few feet in front of me. He sank in mud up to his waist. Fortunately, nothing harmful happened to him."

Continuing down the Concord Falls Trail, *C4* designates the broad-leaf seegum plant used for cattle fodder. It must be good stuff, because locals warn against feeding too much of it or the cattle may get "too fat to breed." *C5* is the sturdy mauricif *(Byrsonima martincensus)* used to build scaffolding. The mauricif is typical of many rain forest trees that have buttress roots to hold the trees upright in the shallow soil. Frequent rainfall leaches the soil of nutrients, which is replenished only by decomposing leaves and animal bodies. Because of the poor soil, 80 percent of the nutrients in a rain forest are hoarded in the plants themselves, with only 20 percent in the soil—exactly opposite of a temperate forest, where soil is richer.

The tight-grained hard fibers of the penny piece *(C6)* is burned to make cooking charcoal. It also provides a yellow, edible, plumlike fruit in May and June. *C7* is the maruba tree *(Simarouba amara)*, which resists warping and splitting, making it highly prized for construction.

After passing the sneeze-producing damarin tree at *C8,* descend the slope to the river carefully. The official trail terminates across the river on the right, but you'll have a choice whether to travel another ten minutes on a very obvious pathway to either the lower or upper Concord Falls.

Because lower Concord Falls is a very popular tourist attraction, especially with cruise ships visitors, you may find the gaggle of tourists annoying after the solitude of the mountains. I recommend postponing culture shock and reentry into civilization; take the left trail to the more secluded upper falls for a plunge in the large natural pool. After almost five hours on the trail, you'll probably be ready for a dip.

The lower falls is normally a crowded place, so you may be able to get a taxi to get back to your hotel. If not, walk downhill another 30 minutes to Concord Village and flag down a St. George's–bound minibus, which run until 5 p.m. Monday through Saturday.

Concord Falls the Hard Way: Make the ascent up from Concord Falls, climbing to Grand Etang. That takes about six hours, a 4–5 on the difficulty scale

5. Concord Falls the Easy Way

Time: 1–2 hours. | **Difficulty:** 2–3, slipper rocks. | **Trailhead:** Drive to the Concord Valley and Concord River from the west coast.

This is the drive-in approach, the one most visitors take. However, the majority of people see only the first waterfall, look, and leave; only a few take the extra 20 minutes to walk to the upper falls.

At the lower or first falls you can buy drinks as well as paddle around in the basin at the foot of the 35-foot-high falls. Headed toward the upper falls, you'll pass through a nutmeg plantation. The nutmeg trees, always green, grow to 60 feet tall. Their fruit looks like a small yellow apple and is popular for making jams and preserves. When ripe, the fruit splits open and falls to the ground, revealing a brown shell covering the brown nut inside with a red, waxy netting over it. The red waxy stuff is the source of the spice known as mace. The brown nut is processed into nutmeg. If you want to see how the whole process is carried out, visit the Grenada Nutmeg Cooperative Association in Gouyave.

At the upper falls, also called Fountainbleau Falls, the water streams down about 65 feet into another fresh water pool that's good for swimming.

Elsewhere on Grenada

6. Annandale Falls

Time: 30 minutes, round-trip unless you picnic, swim, whatever. | **Difficulty:** 1. | **Trailhead:** Within the Beausejour River Valley on the outskirts of Willis, about 15 minutes from St. George's.

At the other extreme of the marathon mountain hike is this easy—though hilly—walk to a mountain stream just a 15-minute drive from St. George's. Tourists and Grenadians alike regularly visit this popular spot where two different falls drop about 30 feet into a beautiful tropical pool surrounded by elephant ears and lianas. You're allowed to swim and picnic. Different plants are marked with their names, but you need a guide to appreciate that the foliage is more than just ornamental. For instance, the leaves of the huge bocano tree near the parking lot are used to make a tea for treating blood pressure and "for cleaning the blood." This was bush medicine I'd never have known without guide Denis Henry.

7. The Seven Sisters

Time: 1–3 hours each way, depending on guide. | **Difficulty:** 2.

The Seven Sisters is a series of cascading waterfalls with deep pools, located about a mile below Grand Etang National Park. They are far more remote than Concord Falls. The walk to the falls is on a rugged road of stones that requires careful footing. At the falls are two large pools for swimming. From the bottom, the most you can see is two sets of waterfalls, known as St. Margaret's Falls.

8. La Sagesse Trails

Time: 2–3 hours. | **Difficulty:** 1–2. | **Trailhead:** On the southwestern coast, 10 miles east from the Point Salines Airport.

Several diverse ecosystems occur at the estuary of the Las Sagesse River within La Sagesse Bay. They include a mangrove estuary, a salt pond, three beaches, littoral woodland, and thorn scrub cactus woodland. The coral reefs offer excellent snorkeling.

Hiking trails to the beaches begin at the La Sagesse Nature Center, a small inn.

9. Marquis River Waterfall

Time: 1 hour, round-trip. | **Difficulty:** 1–2. | **Trailhead:** The Marquis River from the southern main road, just south of the town of Marquis in St. David's parish.

This 30-minute walk up the river to the waterfall is scenic. There are lots of fruit trees and agriculture along the way, very little of the original dry forest. However, the vegetation near the falls is mature because of the constant mist that waters it.

The town of Marquis itself is also worth a visit. It is the island's traditional handicraft center, where villagers use straw to make tablemats, slippers, baskets, hats, and more. Most of the men are farmers or fishermen, but it is their job to collect the wild pine, the main material used by the women and children for weaving the various items.

10. Lake Antoine National Landmark

Time: 1 hour. | **Difficulty:** 1–2. | **Trailhead:** On the eastern side about 6 miles north of the town of Grenville. Go north on the road to Tivoli. Turn east to La Poterie, then north across River Antoine. A narrow road will take you to Lake Antoine, a crater lake formed by the collapsed cone of a volcano.

From the top of a hill you'll have a fine overview of this perfectly shaped crater. Take the track down to walk the perimeter of the shallow crater lake, which covers 16 acres. The water level in Lake Antoine usually is no more than 20 feet above sea level and is 20 feet at its deepest. Although this is in a relatively dry, hot region of the island, it's a good spot for birders. Snail kites, fulvous whistling-ducks, limpkins, and gray kingbirds are commonly seen.

11. RIVER SALLEE BOILING SPRING

Time: 30–45 minutes. | **Difficulty:** 2. | **Trailhead:** In the northeast section, 1.5 miles north of Lake Antoine and south of Levera National Park.

Located in the River Sallee area where the surface is composed of soft porous volcanic sediments, six boiling springs can be found, each with a water temperature reaching 35°C. The largest hole, which contains muddy brown water, is five meters in circumference and about two meters deep. The other, smaller holes are filled with clear but highly salty water, more than a mile from the sea. Orange-yellow sulfur deposits occur in the runoff channels.

These boiling springs have special religious significance for local Baptists, who perform baptisms and other rituals here. Other visitors toss in coins and make a wish.

12. LEVERA NATIONAL PARK/BATHWAY BEACH

Length: 1.5–2 miles. | **Time:** 2–3 hours. | **Difficulty:** 1–2. | **Trailhead:** Located at the northeastern tip of Grenada. From Lake Antoine, go north to the roundabout at River Sallee. Turn right to enter the park.

The mangrove swamp, one of the country's largest, is the northern most extension of the scarlet ibis and the only place it roosts in Grenada. The park includes two conical-shaped hills. The one on the mainland is Levera Hill; the other forms an island called both Sugar Loaf and Levera Island. Twenty-three acres of sea water are collected between the two depressions in Levera Pond, surrounded by red and white mangroves. Coconut palms, cactus, and woody scrub grow in the upland regions next to the pond. The coastal sand beaches are important turtle nesting sites.

You can walk the road for about 1.5 miles to the beach and its facilities. On your right will be Sandy, Sugar Loaf, and Green Islands. It's also possible to walk around the mangrove area.

13. CARIB'S LEAP/LEAPER'S HILL

Length: Several hundred yards, round-trip. | **Time:** 30 minutes. | **Difficulty:** 1. | **Trailhead:** Directly north of the town of Sauteurs on the promontory where St. Patrick's Roman Catholic Church, School, and Cemetery are located. Drive up the hill past the school to the cemetery gate. Walk through the cemetery gate to the steep cliff face that drops over 100 feet to the sea. This is where the Carib inhabitants are said to have jumped to their deaths rather than be enslaved.

It wasn't until 1626, over 100 years after Columbus discovered the island, that both the English and French became interested in settling Grenada. Until then, the native Carib population had been mostly ignored. The French tried settling in 1638, but the Caribs drove them off. In 1650 a successful French colony was established on land bought for some knives and hatchets, lots of glass beads, and two bottles of brandy. A year later the Caribs started hostilities again. The French reinforced their colony and decided to obliterate the natives.

The Indians were driven to this promontory on the northern part of the island. Although they fought fiercely, they were defeated. An estimated 40 Caribs, the only survivors, threw themselves from the cliff rather than surrender. In their memory the French named the spot "le morne de Sauteurs," or leaper's hill.

While here, examine some of the headstones in the cemetery. On the basis of the dates of birth and death carved on the markers, the average life span of Grenadians was quite long before the advent of modern medicine.

14. MT. RICH AMERINDIAN REMAINS

Time: 1 hour round-trip. | **Difficulty:** 2–3. | **Trailhead:** Located in the St. Patrick's river valley near the village of Mt. Rich in the parish of St. Patrick. Take the main road from Sateurs to Mount Rich village. The access path is on the left. It may or not be marked. If not, you'll need a guide.

You'll scramble over some rocks in the riverbed to reach a large stone. Look at the top and sides for six carvings. It's been established these petroglyphs were left by the Caribs and may be over 300 years old. The displays of pottery, tools, spears, and headpieces are all representations of the Carib's daily lifestyle. This area has the most extensive petroglyphs on the island. Other smaller rocks here also bear carvings, but many are faded and others are indistinct due to the algae growing on the stones.

15. BEACH HIKE

Time: Leisurely, 8 hours. Can also be made at a faster pace of 5–6 hours. | **Difficulty:** 3 | **Trailhead:** The village of Soubise on the southern main road.

Telfor Bedeau's most popular easy hike is from his home in Soubise to Carobet Beach. In Telfor's own words: "We leave Soubise at seven and we walk down southward to Marquis, the next village and the straw capital of Grenada. They use the wild pine to make hats and bags and mats and so on. Close to Marquis is one of the most spectacular waterfalls in Grenada, the Mt. Carmel Falls, what some people also call Shoto.

"From Marquis we enter another village, which we call La Poterie, a little way inland from the main road. From La Poterie, we head into beautiful, isolated areas. At each beach we reach we take a dip, so we walk with our trunks on. Some of the hikers, while crossing the stream, might pretend to fall just to pretend to take a dip. At the end, we sometimes roast breadfruit or have smoked herring or some type of thing. We bathe or relax or sometimes we play cricket on the beach. Around two or three o'clock in the evening we set out for home again. That's what we call a small hike."

11   GUADELOUPE

French West Indies Proverb: *"It's you who should direct your life, and not let your life direct you."*

Often described as an island shaped like a pair of butterfly wings, Guadeloupe's two halves couldn't be more different. The half that looks like it flew too close to the fire, Grand-Terre, is the flatter part of the island. It has several sandy coasts, and is home to the capital city of Pointe-à-Pitre, which houses most of the industry and the majority of resorts.

Basse-Terre, on the other hand, is a land of tall-forested mountains, with a huge, smoldering volcano that caused a massive evacuation from this part of the island as recently as 1976. A walk up the steam-vented sides of this restless volcano, La Soufrière, is one of the Caribbean's best hikes. I rate it as the second best of all Caribbean hikes.

Comparatively speaking, an ascent up La Soufrière is not as difficult or as dangerous as it might first sound: Local schoolchildren regularly make field trips to the volcano top (4,813 feet/1,444 m) of what they fondly term the "Old Lady."

Basse-Terre is also home to the 74,100-acre Parc Naturel, which is not only one of the Caribbean's most visually lush parks but unique in that it has no gates, no admission fees, and no opening and closing hours. That means you can walk its 180 miles of hiking trails whenever you wish, taking days if you like.

In all, about 40 percent of Basse-Terre is still a tropical forest of gommier and mahogany trees, climbing vines, and orchids. On the warmer coastal levels, bananas, sugarcane, coffee, and vanilla plants account for most of the land usage.

Incidentally, the names Basse-Terre and Grand-Terre appear to have been mixed up by a cartographer somewhere along the way. Grand-Terre is actually the smaller part, and Basse-Terre enjoys the higher ground.

Guadeloupe is often characterized as the least sophisticated of the French West Indies, as if the snobbish veneer of Martinique is a matter for pride. People are far friendlier than on Martinique, perhaps because there is more of a pro-independence feeling. Guadeloupe—like Martinique—is officially part of France. Its road system is remarkably good and well marked, allowing easy travel around the island.

The Caribs called Guadeloupe "Karukera," island of beautiful waters, and considering the hot water springs and tall tumbling falls, it was aptly named. Christopher Columbus, who never showed much poetic inspiration except in naming the Virgin Islands, gave Karukera another of his mundane, saintly names, this one after the monastery of Santa Maria de

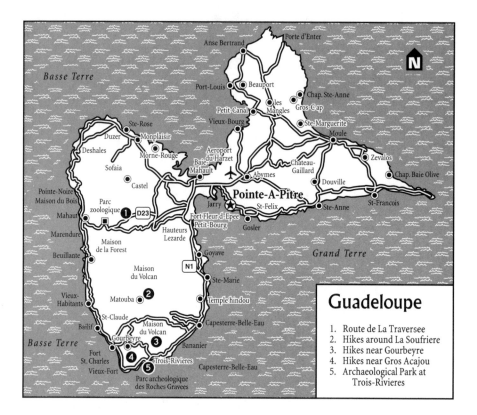

Guadeloupe

1. Route de La Traversee
2. Hikes around La Soufriere
3. Hikes near Gourbeyre
4. Hikes near Gros Acajou
5. Archaeological Park at
   Trois-Rivieres

Guadeloupe in Extremadura, Spain. The Spanish never settled here; the French, who arrived in 1635 with their sugar plantations and slave labor, never bothered to change the name.

Conditions in Guadeloupe were too unsettled for prosperity on the same scale as in other parts of the French West Indies. Four chartered companies tried in vain to colonize the island, which was finally turned over to the French crown, to become a dependency of Martinique.

The British coveted the island so openly that a threatened Louis XV bribed them away with Canada and other goodies through the Treaty of Paris in 1763. The French Revolution's message of human equality sparked slave revolts, causing some plantation owners to be guillotined, others to flee. Slavery was abolished, but later reintroduced in 1802.

When slavery was abolished for good in 1848, the plantations went into decline because of the lack of cheap labor. Even indentured workers brought in from India could not take up the slack.

Today, sugar, rum, and molasses are still important exports, as are bananas.

TRAVEL TIPS

Area: The two islands cover 1,510 square kilometers; Basse-Terre, the larger, is 777 square kilometers.

Population: About 430,000, most in the Grand-Terre region.

Language: French and Creole; English is spoken only in larger hotels and tourist areas.

Time Zone: Atlantic Time, one hour ahead of Eastern Standard Time.

Rainy Season: July to November are the wettest months, with most of the rain falling between September and November. January to April is the official dry season.

Getting There: American Eagle, (800) 433-7300, from San Juan has good connections with American Airline flights from the States. Air Canada flies directly from Montreal. Inter-island service is available on LIAT, (800) 468-0482, if you're hopping over from a neighboring island. Air France also flies direct from Paris, with other flights by way of Miami. The airport is on the Grand Terre side at Pointe-à-Pitre, which is only a few minutes' drive from Basse-Terre. A 3.5-hour ferry trip between Martinique and Guadeloupe runs once or twice a day, costing US$60–90 round-trip. Call Expres des Iles, (0590) 83-12-45.

Documents: American and Canadian citizens staying less than 90 days do not need a passport, only an official birth certificate copy, driver's license photo ID and an ongoing ticket. A valid passport is needed for stays over 90 days. All others need passports; residents of some countries require visas.

Getting Around: The Raizet airport has the best stock of rental cars on the island, including those of international agencies, such as Avis and Hertz. No need to purchase a temporary local driver's license. Driving is on the right. You can get to almost anywhere by bus from Pointe-à-Pitre, but you should know French to use the system efficiently.

Where to Stay: The Tourist Board has an office at the Raizet Airport; they can be very helpful in locating hotels, inns, or campgrounds. Most of the major resorts are on Grand-Terre, which is not a convenient location if you plan to do extensive hiking and exploring. The **Relais Creoles** are small (from 6 to 40 rooms) private hotels located in the countryside, usually with their own excellent Creole restaurants. Close to La Soufrière is **Hotel St-Georges** in St-Claude; phone (0590) 80-10-10, or visit their website at www.pro-wandadoo.fr/hotel.st.georges. Guadeloupe's small hotels are represented in the United States by **International Tours and Resorts** at (800) 223-9815. Another alternative are the rooms and kitchenettes called *gites,* popular with many budget-minded French travelers. Some of these also are quite isolated, but because you'll need a car to get around anyway, just select one in good hiking country. A list of these are available from the tourist offices in Basse-Terre or Grand-Terre, or through the **Syndicat d'Initative de Deshaies;** phone (0590) 28-49-70. The Syndicat charges a 5% commission/rental fee.

Camping: Not only can you camp, you can arrange overnight treks of four to five days along the trails of the **Parc Naturel** with one of the forest service personnel. Their English isn't always the best, but the guides try their hardest to explain the amazing variety of terrain you'll pass through. Campsites are available (as are small bungalows) off the beach at **Sable d'Or** near Deshaies in Basse-Terre; call (0590) 28-44-60; **Camping Traversee** near Mahaut on Basse-Terre; and the **Guadeloupe Hotel** at Saint-Francois, also offering complete camping facilities. Fully equipped campers sleeping up to six can be rented from **Vert'Bleu** in Deshaies, Basse-Terre; call (0590) 28-51-25. Or check with the local park service office or police about other sites that might look interesting to you. Be aware that commercial campgrounds sometimes are so crowded tents are up against each other.

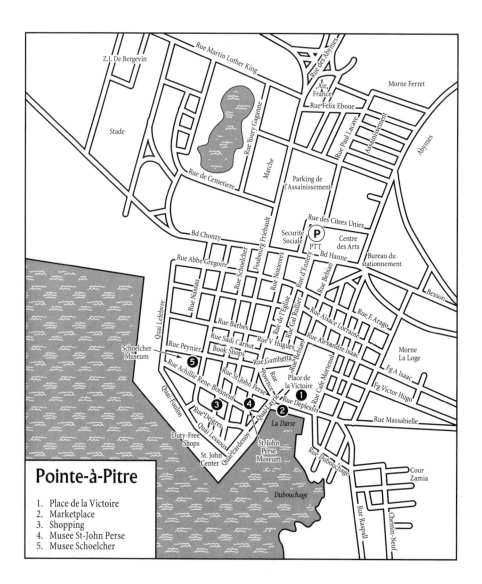

Pointe-à-Pitre

1. Place de la Victoire
2. Marketplace
3. Shopping
4. Musee St-John Perse
5. Musee Schoelcher

Currency: The French franc (F) is the coin of the realm. The rate of exchange varies considerably, around US$1 = FF5.90. Banks and exchange houses have the best exchange rates, although they may also charge a 1% commission and a 4% filing fee. Money exchange is handled only in the morning. Bank hours are 8 a.m. to noon and 2 p.m. to 4 p.m. Monday through Friday.

Taxes & Tips: Checks will often come marked "service compris," in which case no tip is necessary. Otherwise 10–15% is standard. Taxes are included in hotel room rates and airfares.

Electrical Current: 220 volts, 50 cycles. U.S. and Canadian appliances need both a French plug converter and a transformer.

Hiking/Walking Services: This is one island where you can walks for days, specifically from Vieux Fort on Basse-Terre's south coast to Pointe Allegre near Ste.-Rose on the north. Contact the **Organisation des Guides de Montagne le la Caraibe,** Maison Forestiere, 97120 Matouba; phone (0590) 94-29-11. They are familiar with all the best hikes inside the national park. Through them, you can arrange day hikes or treks of a week or more. Having a helpful guide describe the terrain and vegetation on the La Soufrière climb made all the difference between knowing and guessing about what I was seeing.

Health & Safety Warnings: The manchineel tree and its caustic sap is always a danger. The trees are called "le manceniller" and are usually marked in red paint. Come prepared for rain. The higher slopes receive 250 inches annually. Drink bottled water.

Snakes & Other Venomous Creatures: None.

For Complete Information: French Government Tourist Office, 444 Madison Ave., New York, NY 10022; call (202) 659-7779. The Guadeloupe Tourist Office, 161 Washington Valley Rd., Suite 205, Warren NJ 07059; call (732) 302-1223; www.frenchcaribbean.com. In Canada, French Government Tourist Office, 1981 Avenue MacGill College, Suite 490, Montreal, H3A 2W9; call (514) 288-4264.

POINTE-À-PITRE AFOOT!

Time: 2 hours. | **Difficulty:** 1. | **Trailhead:** Best to catch a cab or public transportation into town; parking is almost impossible.

The real beauty of Guadeloupe is in the countryside, as the big-city, congested streets of Pointe-à-Pitre quickly demonstrate. Finding a parking place anywhere in Pointe-à-Pitre is a challenge unless you're there early in the morning, and even then you may need to walk a good distance to the center of town. Talk about a place that needs high-rise garages, this is it!

If this seems out of character for the Caribbean, then so is the stifled feeling created by the intense traffic. The city is so crowded compared to the open spaces of Basse-Terre's countryside that it feels almost claustrophobic.

Nature has been mean to Pointe-à-Pitre. It was hit hard by hurricanes in 1979, 1980, and 1989. The 1989 winds of hurricane Hugo were so strong they virtually destroyed almost all the coconut palms on the island.

So why visit Pointe-à-Pitre? For its historic and shopping qualities, which are considerable.

1. **Place de la Victoire:** Named in honor of Victor Hugues's victory over the British in 1794, this shady park is where Hugues put the guillotine to work, lopping off the heads of selected landowners at the end of the eighteenth century. The streets surrounding the park contain the oldest buildings, though few of the truly old colonial structures survived the earthquake of 1845.

2. **Marketplace:** A daily, not just a once-a-week event, where island women in colorful costumes sell and haggle over the breadfruit, tomatoes, bananas, and other assorted items. You can also buy hats and local spices; in fact, some of the sellers can be quite insistent about it.

3. **Shopping:** The main streets are rues Noizieres, Frebault, and Schoelcher. In addition, a shopping arcade is open near the waterfront, targeted specifically at cruise ship passengers and other visitors.

4. **Musee St-John Perse:** Few outsiders know that a Guadeloupan won the 1960 Nobel Prize for Literature. The museum contains the complete poetry collection, personal effects, documents, and photographs of St-John, poet and diplomat. Open Monday through Saturday, 9 a.m. to 12:30 p.m. and 2 p.m. to 6 p.m.

5. **Musee Schoelcher:** This museum illustrates the life of Victor Schoelcher, who helped abolish slavery in the French West Indies. The ornate museum building alone is worth seeing, even if you never go inside. Open weekdays, 9 a.m. to noon, 2:30 p.m. to 5:30 p.m.

ELSEWHERE ON GUADELOUPE

THE PARC NATUREL

1. ROUTE DE LA TRAVERSEE

Time: Half a day. | **Difficulty:** 2–3. | **Trailhead:** Take N.2 from Pointe-à-Pitre, then join N.1 and head south. At Versailles, turn right onto D.23.

This route, the Transcoastal Highway, effectively divides Basse-Terre into northern and southern halves. Although the best hiking trails are farther south, this scenic roadway (about 16 miles) borders the Parc Naturel, providing an excellent introduction to the plants and wildlife of Guadeloupe.

Route de la Traversee offers several very interesting stops and climbs you easily can do on your own without the services of a guide. Starting at the village of Vernou, go north for about three miles until you reach the carpark near the Cascade aux Ecrevisse, or "Crayfish Waterfall." It's only a short walk to the picturesque waterfall plummeting into the Corossol River. Feel free to swim, but beware the very slippery rocks.

The Parc Tropical de Bras-David is just two miles farther on. Its small network of hiking trails takes about an hour to explore if you walk leisurely and take time to investigate the plant life. A small forest house has displays (in French) explaining much of the area ecology. Picnic tables make this a good place for a lengthy, restful stop.

Go another 2.5 miles to Guadeloupe's famous twin peaks, Les Mamelles, meaning "breasts." If the thought of climbing contoured hills clearly shaped like and named after women's breasts is disturbing, you will not want to visit any of the beaches where toplessness is a casual, accepted way of life. Mamelle de Petit-Bourg reaches 2,350 feet, and Mamelle de Pigeon peaks out at 2,600 feet. Hiking trails vary from easy to challenging. A lookout at almost 2,000 feet up Mamelle de Pigeon is spectacular, as is the scenery in the valley running between the twin peaks.

The stone steps to the Zoological Park and Botanical Gardens require almost no effort to view turtles, iguanas and cockatoos. Titi the Raccoon is the mascot of the Parc Naturel. These animals, however, are relatively rare in the wild, so this will be one of your few chances to see one close-up. The park is open daily from 9 a.m. to 5 p.m.; admission fee.

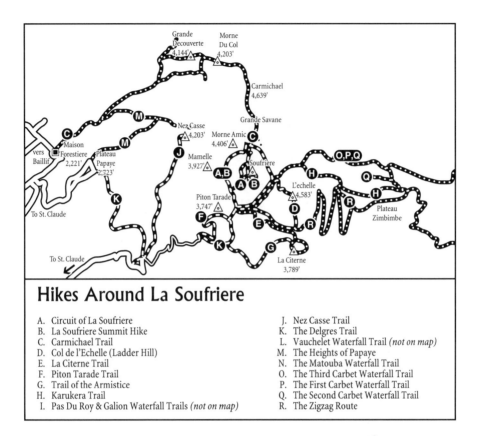

Hikes Around La Soufriere

LA SOUFRIÈRE

2. HIKES AROUND LA SOUFRIERE

It's not often you can walk the slopes of an active volcano (last eruption, 1976), look into its sulfur-spewing craters, and experience the heat still radiating from deep in the earth. That's why I find the climb up Guadeloupe's 4,813-foot high La Soufrière fascinating. I rank it No. 2 of all the walks on all the islands of the West Indies.

The La Soufrière climb is mild compared to the one hike in the Caribbean that I believe surpasses this one: Dominica's hike to the Valley of Desolation and the Boiling Lake, a round-trip ordeal of seven to eight hours. Instead, La Soufrière is a pleasant half-day jaunt. Besides the summit ascent, numerous other trails criss-cross the region, many of them looping back to the same parking lot.

The region of La Soufrière is typically hidden in cloud and mist, which only emphasizes the primordial atmosphere. Come prepared for drizzle and rain and brisk winds on the summit. School kids make this climb as a class outing, so it is none too hard. Should the day be clear, be prepared for a lot of company on the trail. Clear weather lures people to the mountain like sugar attracts ants. Most of the trails depart from or near the parking lot of Savane a Mulets, which translates as savannah of mules. To reach it, take N.1 south, then turn west at Capestre-Belle-Eau toward Routhiers. The road is well marked.

Note ahead of time that many different trails branch off from the main trail (Hike A) circling La Soufrière, including Hikes B, C, and D. Plan ahead of time how much walking you intend to do so you can join the trails accordingly and provision properly. Take a flashlight in case you end up on the trail longer than you anticipate. There is so much to distract your attention it's easy to lose track of time. This mountain is not time, or reality, as we normally know it.

A. Circuit of La Soufrière

Time: 1.5 hours for the circle walk around the volcano. | **Difficulty:** 3. | **Trailhead:** Depart from Savane a Mulets parking lot, altitude 3,746 feet (1,142 m).

This trail goes around the volcano, ascending on the west via the Chemin de Dames (Road of the Ladies), marked in yellow. For the descent, the trail passes by Col de l'Echelle (Ladder Hill), an impressive area littered with boulders from the 1976 eruptions.

An information board (if you read French) gives the history of this volcano, which is a relatively young one. During the last 1,000 years, La Soufrière has shown considerable activity, marking the Basse-Terre region with lava lahars (flows). The longest major eruption was in 1976. Others occurred in 1797 and 1560.

The hiking trail begins with a few hairpin turns, then conforms to the gentle slope of the mountain. The path is interrupted by two flows and all along the trail is a thick bed of dried sludge, which destroyed the vegetation in this part of the cone in 1976. Plants are making a comeback, which becomes more evident farther along.

Approaching the west and northwest slopes, you'll border a zone that did not suffer the destructive effects of the last eruption;— the flora here is intact. As you reach L'Eboulement (the landslide) Faujas after less than a half hour of walking, you'll see peat-mosses, lichens, and mountain pineapples hanging on the fault.

The panoramic view is exceptional: the southwest of Basse-Terre, the Caribbean Sea, and closer by summits like Nez Casse ("Broken Nose") and Carmichael. Looking toward La Soufrière, the volcano shows its teeth—an amalgam of precariously balanced rocks.

A few minutes later you will arrive at the north-south Great Fault, also called the "North Crevice." Its sheer walls, 60 meters high, are barren of vegetation.

Here the trail divides. To the right is the summit hike, taking about an hour to explore thoroughly (described in Hike B, p. 175). If you're going to make the climb, now is the time to do it. Refer to Hike B and begin.

The left path, however, continues circling the volcano. About 100 meters beyond, after some hairpin turns, the trail joins a swampy plateau called the Great Savane, and a bit farther on you arrive at a second crossroads. If you continue straight ahead to the north, you'll reach Matouba by the Carmichael Trail (the starting point for Hike C). About 100 meters from the crossroad are the Collardeau Fumaroles; these 10 vents are periodically used for gas samples.

At the crossroads, bear right toward Ladder Hill. Vegetation is sparse, mostly gray or orange lichens and mountain pineapples that, from 800 meters to the summit, decorate La Soufrière with big, red-spiked flowers.

If you're fortunate to have clear weather, you'll see above, on the right, the Northeast Fault. Beyond the fault is Sanner Trail, a more strenuous path to reach the dome. Moving lower and to your left, the fumaroles of Carbet manifest themselves, through a strong odor of sulfur.

About 20 minutes after leaving the crossroads to the Matouba and Carmichael trails, you'll enter a craggy stone landscape. At the edge of this is yet another marked crossroads. The left trail joins the Chutes de Carbet Trail (Hikes O, P, and Q). However, for the volcano circuit, stay right and follow the trail blazed in blue leading down to Ladder Hill.

This region was one of the places most affected by the 1976 eruption: it is here that on July 8 the most important explosion occurred, which reopened and reactivated the large southern fault crossing the entire flank of the volcano.

However, the view is beautiful over the Windward Coast, the Capesterre region, and Grande-Terre; when visibility is good you can even see the island of Marie-Galante.

At Ladder Hill you'll pass an enormous rock fractured into two pieces. You can stand in the fracture and pose like Superman, splitting the boulder with super strength. On the left are the fumaroles of Ladder Hill: sulfurous vapors of 96°C escape from a hole where you can spot a sizable deposit of sulfur crystals. Still to the left and a little higher is the geophysical shelter, severely damaged by the last 1976 eruptions.

Leave Ladder Hill and descend across the debris. The trail, still marked with blue blazes, goes along the Matylis Ravine, which in 1976 was site of the main flows. While descending, you can observe to the right, on La Soufrière's southeast flank, the so-called mouths of explosion, which hurled out the surrounding rocks now covered with a thick coating of lichens.

Zig-zag ahead for ten more minutes to reach La Citerne volcano, which is used as a TV relay. Bear right and within five minutes you should be back at Savane a Mulets, your departure point.

B. La Soufrière Summit Hike

Length: Time: 2.5 hours. | **Difficulty:** 3–4. Blazed trail, but can be very slippery. | **Trailhead:** Depart and arrive at Savane a Mulets. For access, use Hike A (p. 174).

Arriving at the Great Fault on the north face, go right along the trail that has some very slippery rocks. It's a short climb—only ten minutes to the summit. Proceed with extreme caution and watch your steps carefully. I took my worst fall in the Caribbean on the slippery summit rocks; or, as they say on some islands, "I bust my ass."

Don't expect to find a single immense crater, as you may have imagined. La Soufrière possesses clustered, numerous eruptive mouths called pits or craters, which are arranged in a string along the fracture zones.

Once on the plateau, you'll follow the length of the Great Fault, likely to be hazed over by escaping sulfurous vapors. Your route, marked with green posts, highlights the most obvious formations. Feel free to leave the official trail to explore on your own. Now is when a guide would be most useful. Although it's safe to wander around on your own, you may not find some of the formations without local help.

At the end of the Great Fault, take the rocky trail to the right, which climbs past a small concrete refuge and leads to La Decouverte, at 1,467 meters, the highest point of La Soufrière. When the weather permits, the view is exceptional.

Continue south until you are above Dupuy Pit on your left. Then skirt the fracture of the Faujas Landslide and bear right. About 100 meters after La Decouverte is a trail bearing right to reach Piton Saussure or Piton du Nord at 1,464 meters. The view of the leeward coast is grand.

Returning to the primary trail, you'll enter a vast lunar landscape, the result of an intense downpour of stone and sludge projectiles in the 1976 eruption; even the hardest rock formations were softened, rounded by this hellish brown sheet. Vegetation totally disappeared and is only now slowly coming back.

At your feet will be a pool established after the last eruption, not far from the former "Devil's Pool," which disappeared at the same time. Before you, bordering the cone to the southwest, is the piton (peak) of the South or Piton Dolomieu. That ascent is extremely dangerous and ill-advised.

Follow the green trail to la Porte de l'Enfer (Hell's Gate) on your left. To some, this rock resembles a tall silhouette of the devil. Others call it "la guenon" ("she-monkey" or "ugly woman").

Beyond is another vast basin of earth and stones. Before 1976 it was so rich in plants it was called L'Herminier Garden, named after a doctor and man of science living in Guadeloupe during the 1800s. The once-beautiful garden is now only a wasteland.

Some ten meters after Hell's Gate is a natural bridge crossing the great north-south fault you followed at the beginning of the ascent. On your left, Dupuy Pit is filled with water and sludge from the last eruption. On your right is Tarissan Pit, which is so deep no one is certain what's at the bottom. Tarissan Pit will bathe you in sulfur fumes some days.

After the natural bridge, turn right and follow the looping trail to the south. On your left is Piton Napoleon, with many fumaroles. The side of this peak is also covered with a thick coat of sludge.

After climbing a little hill and bearing left, you'll approach the south crater at the extreme edge of the plateau. This cauldron bubbling with thick vapors may be invisible in foggy weather, but the odor is unmistakable and you're bound to feel its radiating heat.

Descending toward the southeast along the edge of the cone you'll have an excellent view over Ladder Hill (Col de l'Echelle), 200 meters below, and over la Citerne, the volcano with the well-known classic cone.

For the return, you can either retrace your steps to reach the fork near the natural bridge, or reach the same destination by continuing toward the north, keeping Napoleon Crater on your right.

At the fork, keep the Tarissan and Dupuy Pits on your left and continue in a northerly direction along the Great Fault. On the right you will notice a little lake of dried mud surrounded by pathetic shrubs burned by the gas. A little farther, still on the right, vegetation is mostly mountain pineapples. You'll also find the Sanner Trail, which tumbles down toward the springs of Carbet. Continue retracing your ascent to rejoin the trail near the North Fault.

C. CARMICHAEL TRAIL

Time: 4.5 hours, one way. | **Difficulty:** 3 down, 4 to return. | **Trailhead:** Depart from La Savane a Mulets, altitude 3,746 feet (1,142 m). You will follow the first half of Hike A, turning left at the crossroads toward Matouba. This trail is marked in both directions. Be sure to take water.

If you join this trail while making the volcano circuit (Hike A), you'll already have completed about an hour of walking. The Carmichael Trail is well marked. The vegetation on this great marshy plateau (the Great Savane) is primarily mountain mangroves, whose leaves resemble those of rubber plants. You'll spot a few mountain palms and mountain aralie.

On the left, about ten yards away, are isolated fumaroles called Colardeau Fumaroles. A little farther, on the right, is a little-used path to Ladder Hill (Col de L'Echelle).

About 40 minutes from the crossroads, the trail, which can be very muddy during the rainy season, takes you to the summit of Mt. Carmichael, a height of 4,639 feet (1,414 m). After Carmichael, the trail descends, bends toward the west, and reaches Morne du Col at 4,203 feet (1,281 m). From both summits the view in good weather is magnificent.

After a bend toward the southwest, the trail leads to a landslide area overlooking a valley with a large cabin, the dilapidated shelter of the Montagnards, a mountain climbing club.

Go around the landslide and descend the straight ridge on the right, which divides the sloping basins of the River Class to the right and the Red River to the left. At the hill, bear to the left toward the south. (The path straight ahead climbs the slopes of the Grande Decouverte and joins the Victor Hugues Trail.)

The trail descends rapidly, then reaches a flat and wet portion, where it splits in two again. To the left is a Montagnard shelter. Continue on the main trail and descend in a southwesterly direction. The trail is wide, the vegetation grows thicker, becoming the typical tropical forest. Numerous raspberry bushes line the trail's edge.

About 20 minutes after the last crossroads, the Carmichael Trail joins the Victor Hugues Trail. About 30 minutes later, you'll pass another fork. Continue ahead, ignoring the marked trail on your left that leads to the Hot Baths of Matouba (Hike N) and permits a return to Savane a Mulets by the Delgres Trail (Hike K).

From this last crossroads it will take you less than 30 minutes to find the cultivated fields of Frezias and the reforested parcels planted with laurel trees. Next is the Forestry House of Matouba, your destination.

D. COL DE L'ECHELLE (LADDER HILL)

Time: 2 hours. | **Difficulty:** 3. Trail is not blazed.. | **Trailhead:** Depart from La Savane a Mulets, altitude 3,746 feet (1,142 m).

This hike acquaints you with the vegetation of high-altitude savannahs and provides beautiful panoramic views.

From Savane a Mulets, take the road leading to La Citerne. You will pass a trail on your left—this is where you'll come out at the end of the hike. It's also the end of the La Soufrière circuit (Hike A). After about 15 minutes you'll see the branch trail that ascends the southern face of l'Echelle on your left. Take it.

Numerous switchbacks will get you to the summit of L'Echelle in 30 to 40 minutes. During the climb, you'll have a good look at La Citerne (Cistern) volcano with its circular crater partially filled with water. The low altitude vegetation here is often filled with blooms in October and November: fuchsias with garnet "bells," the yellow flowers of mountain daisies, gracious and delicate orchids with their sweet perfume, mountain pineapples with their red or yellow flowers, and the lycopods, which resemble tiny Christmas trees.

At the 1,397-meter summit, you can see La Soufrière just to the northwest. Notice the different "mouths" of explosion from 1976.

Begin the rather steep descent in a northwesterly direction. The trail passes beside a large rock, the "Devil's Footstool," and arrives at the hill of Morne Mitan, where you'll find an electric post. Bear right toward the north, in the direction of the geophysical shelter, which you see below. At Col de l'Echelle, turn left between the fractured rock and the fumarole, then follow the blue trail into the mass of debris above the Ravine Matylis. You'll soon arrive at the road. Turn to the right; Savane a Mulets is about 1,300 feet (400 m) away.

From L'Echelle you can also make the circuit of the volcano using Hike A in reverse.

E. LA CITERNE TRAIL (CISTERN)

Length: Time: 1 hour. | **Difficulty:** 2–3. Trail not marked but simple to follow. | **Trailhead:** Depart from La Savane a Mulets, altitude 3,746 feet (1,142 m).

La Citerne is an ancient volcano, perhaps merely dormant, whose crater, about 650 feet (200 m) wide and around 164 feet (50 m) deep, is occupied by the small Camille Flammarion Lake.

From Savane a Mulets, take the road leading to La Citerne, marked by the antenna of the television relay (which you may not see if the clouds are low). After passing the impressive debris of Col de l'Echelle, the odor of sulfur is everywhere. Note the scattered fumaroles with yellowish surfaces, mainly sulfur crystals.

Soon after the first fumaroles, on the right you'll see others scattered on the denuded and whitish slope of Morne Mitan. The fleshless trunks and tree branches bear witness again to the damage done in 1976, the result of asphyxiating vapors.

After Morne Mitan you'll see the trail on your left that climbs the southern flank of L'Echelle, described in Hike D (p. 177).

The Cistern Trail now takes a sharp right turn and arrives at the hill separating L'Echelle and La Citerne. Ignore the left trail: it's only about 3,280 feet (1,000 m) long.

To this point you've been sheltered from the breeze. Now, the wind may feel as piercing as a harpoon, as you experience the true meaning of windward and leeward coasts.

Arriving at La Citerne, you'll find the classic-shaped crater is dense with vegetation. You can quickly circle the outer rim. Following the trail, you will reach a television relay, the first relay transmitter erected on Guadeloupe. Near the relay is a trail to the left that's barely visible. It descends by way of the Plateau de la Grande Chasse to rejoin the Etang de l'As de Pique (Pond of the Ace of Spades). Not maintained, the trail is difficult to follow.

In the east, along the Plateau de la Grande Chasse, you should be able to spot Grand Etang (Big Pond), then the Windward Coast with Capesterre and its vast banana plantation. Farther in the distance is the island of Marie-Galante; to the northeast is Grande-Terre.

Looking south, Madeleine tops out at 3,185 feet (971 m) at Piton l'Herminier, and to its right is Morne Gros Fougas with its almost perfectly circular crater; at your feet are the banana warehouses of Moscou. With good visibility, you can see Dominica.

On the summit of La Citerne, the vegetation is essentially mountain pineapple, upland lilies, mountain thyme, mosses, and orchids. About 800 feet (250 m) after the TV relay, a trail goes off to the left and leads to Galion Falls, the river whose upper valley you now overlook.

Now that you've circled La Citerne, rejoin the blazed trail for the 15-minute trip back to Savane a Mulets.

F. Piton Tarade Trail (Tarade Peak)

Time: 20 minutes. | **Difficulty:** 2–3. Trail not marked but simple. | **Trailhead:** The departure point is indicated by a blaze at the northwestern corner of the Savane a Mulets parking area.

Piton Tarade is a shoulder on the southeast slope of La Soufrière. A mere 10-minute walk on the small trail leads you to its 3,936-foot (1,200-m) summit, through a forest zone devastated by the 1976 eruption. After crossing a rocky area, the trail starts climbing via a service path overgrown with grass. A bit higher, the trail becomes clearer and arrives at the summit, where you can appreciate the ambience of a small, high-altitude botanical garden. Notice the small purple flowers of mountain thyme, very common in this region above 3,280 feet (1,000 m).

The small windmill here turned by the tradewinds helps generate electricity for the seismograph that you may have seen on the edge of the road before Savane a Mulets. This seismograph is part of a surveillance network detecting an average of 150 tremors here each year.

G. Trail of the Armistice

Time: 2 hours. | **Difficulty:** 3. | **Trailhead:** Depart from the Savane a Mulets parking lot. The eastern end of the Armistice Trail starts at La Citerne (Hike E) and goes to Galion Falls (Hike I), which allows you to make a circuit.

Once at La Citerne, continue left and go around the crater to find the trailhead. The crater ruin has plant growth characteristic of moist ridges, including the red pineapple, but it has an elegant orange flower, different from the common red pineapple. Turn left.

The descent toward the Galion Valley leads you across the stunted high-altitude forest of mountain mangroves, orchids, and yellow lilies. The trail bends to the southwest, permitting a glimpse of Basse-Terre, before you enter a sparse rain forest of cabbage palms and marble wood.

The trail now arrives at a flat place bordered by a cliff, overlooking Galion Falls. The trail continues to the left, then ends with a very abrupt drop before reaching the riverbed. The descent is slippery and difficult—possibly dangerous—after a rain. Take your time and hold onto roots.

At the Galion, continue right to reach the falls. Descend left some ten yards, then cross the river. On the other side, continue on the trail described in Hike I, in reverse order, which will take you to Savane a Mulets by way of Pas du Roy (Steps of the King).

H. Karukera Trail

Time: 2 hours, one way. | **Difficulty:** 3–4. Not marked. Advisable to take water. Always use caution during foggy weather, notably around Col de l'Echelle. | **Trailhead:** Depart from Savane a Mulets parking lot. Walk the road toward La Citerne for about 0.25 mile and go left onto the tail end of the La Soufrière circuit (Hike A, p. 174).

The path will shortly take you to Col de l'Echelle. After descending the hill, the trail bears to the right and follows orange blazes which mark the beginning of the Chutes du Carbet trails. After going between two ravines and scaling the ravine on the right, the trail is dominated by a vertical wall. In the flat portion that follows is the departure point of the Karukera Trail.

Begin this rather steep ascent by the first path to the left—the other trails are cul-de-sacs. In the next 30 minutes, you'll cross three small ravines in thick mangrove forest where the humidity oozes, climb for several meters holding onto mangrove roots, and after about 40 minutes, finally arrive at a clearing where the panorama is superb.

From the plateau, the trail veers left immediately, toward the east. Descending, listen as a dull roar grows louder: it's the second Carbet waterfall, which you'll soon see off to your left. About ten minutes later, you'll reach the waterfall's picnic area (1,968 feet/600 m) by an old forest road passing among white gum trees, characterized by a slender, light gray trunk and a high, dense tuft.

I. Pas Du Roy and Galion Waterfall Trails

Time: 1.5 hours. It takes 20 minutes to get to Pas du Roy (Steps of the King). | **Difficulty:** 2–3. Marked only at the trailhead, this is an easy trail. | **Trailhead:** Depart from the Bains Jaunes (Yellow Baths) parking area, located southwest of Savane a Mulets in the direction of Saint-Claude.

At the Bains Jaunes parking area, near the abandoned refuge, a stele (a carved or inscribed stone slab) marks the entrance to the Pas du Roy Trail, opened in 1887 by the colonials. At the beginning, you'll go along the basin of the Bains Jaunes, dry except in the rainy season.

About 984 feet (300 m) from the start is a fork to the right leading to Galion Falls, the goal of your walk. To the left, you can continue the Pas du Roy, which ends at the tar road, then either go back down to the Bains Jaunes (Yellow Baths) parking area or to the parking area at Savane a Mulets.

Along Le Pas Du Roy: For about ten minutes the rocky trail has steps. In a dramatic turn to the left, a break in the greenery permits you to see the mountain mass of L'Echelle and, below, at the bottom of the Galion Valley, an entire mountainside that was carried away in the 1976 slide.

Several minutes later, the trail continues climbing and comes out to a little cleared plateau for a panoramic view of Belvedere. To descend, choose the short walk to Savane a Mulets or retrace your steps back to Bains Jaunes.

To Galion Falls: At the crossroads, continue right. The wide trail descends in a gentle slope across relatively low and sparse growth, mainly mountain mangroves, tree ferns, and marble wood. The marble wood here is stunted due to the altitude.

After 15 minutes, the view on your right reveals Basse-Terre and its surroundings. To the southeast, surrounded by the banana warehouses of Moscou, is Morne Gros Fougas, a classic volcano form.

The trail then plunges into a ravine and, after a few zigzags, runs beside the Galion River. It should have taken you about 35 minutes to come this far. Access to the falls is either by the trail going straight ahead or by climbing back up the riverbed to reach the foot of the 40-meter falls.

To the right of the falls is the very steep departure point for the Armistice Trail leading to the summit of La Citerne. By walking five or six minutes on this trail, you'll reach a superb viewing point, but it's slippery and risky. On the left bank, another trail will lead you across a maze of enormous rocks to the cascade of the Ty, just before it meets the Galion.

Retrace your steps to your departure point, a trip of 45 minutes.

J. NEZ CASSE TRAIL

Time: 5 hours. | **Difficulty:** 4. Not blazed, this trail's easy beginning is followed by a difficult ascent. Take water and snacks.. | **Trailhead:** Depart and return on the Soufrière Road, at the Beausoleil picnic area, located just beyond the Bains Jaunes parking lot, headed toward Saint-Claude.

Ascending Nez Casse will take you into the forest of Bains Jaunes, 1,640 to 3,280 feet (500 to 1,000 m) high. This forest shows the diverse stages of old-growth and secondary-growth forest.

From the picnic area, walk the right bank of the canal for about 20 minutes to the small dam on the Riviere Noire (Black River). When the water is high, you'll have to sidetrack to keep from getting wet. The vegetation around you is lush. Besides the classic plants and trees of the rain forest such as the small-leafed chestnut, you'll find clumps of bamboo; heliconias with red, yellow, or variegated leaves; all sorts of epiphytes; and the chestnut canes that carpet the bottom of certain ravines. The harmless-looking chestnut cane is very caustic. Also called burning cane, it smells incredibly bad when the stem is broken.

Walk the dam to reach the other side of the Black River. The trail then continues along the riverbank following the current. Rather than cross at the dam, you could cross the river several meters downstream.

Now the ascent of Nez Casse really begins. The first 15 minutes demand effort and sweat, up a steep rise. Afterward, the slope is less steep and more regular, but the ridge is narrow. Don't wander to the right.

Water cascading over rocks at the First Carbet Waterfalll

Your final 20 minutes will be dedicated to a rather acrobatic ascent through the tangled foliage of mountain mangroves. Eventually you'll reach the summit ridge of Nez Casse, thin as a knife-blade between dizzying peaks of more than 200 meters.

With just a little more effort—but only if you're not subject to vertigo—scale this last rock, the true summit of Nez Casse, at 4,203 feet (1,281 m). In good weather the panorama is exceptional: nearby, toward the east, La Soufrière and Morne Amic; to the north, Carmichael (4,639 feet/1,414 m) and La Grand Decouverte (4,144 feet/1,263 m), which, with Nez Casse, form a beautiful mountainous ring where the Riviere Rouge (Red River) is born. At your feet are the Hot Baths of Matouba.

Your return by the same trail will seem much quicker than the ascent.

K. The Delgres Trail

Time: 1 hour. | **Difficulty:** 2–3. The trail, not marked, is relatively easy except for one steep rise. | **Trailhead:** Depart on the Soufrière Road at the Beausoleil picnic area, altitude 2,460 feet (750 m). Arrive at Plateau Papaye, altitude 2,821 feet (860 m).

This hike climbs through dense rain forest, where you'll see large trees, heliconias, epiphytes, and perhaps a few birds. Near the trailhead is a tree with large drooping leaves and blooms of little yellow or pink bells.

The Beausoleil picnic area goes along the right bank of a canal, but you abandon it about 30 meters before the basin, to go left on another well-cleared trail. Some ten minutes later, after crossing several ravines, you'll reach a group of three spectacular vine-covered trees with powerful and slender aerial roots.

The trail bends slightly left for the first ten minutes, then sharply veers to the left, passes over tree roots and descends along the escarped flanks of the Black River Valley. Arriving at the river itself, you're halfway along the trail to Plateau Papaye.

Catch your breath now, because a steep climb awaits you—a good 15 minutes of continuous effort. Eventually the slope becomes gentler and some ravines are even terraced. In this forested zone, you may hear the hammering or the raucous, crow-like cry of birds living in the tall tree tops.

The forest cover lightens gradually and opens onto fields from which you can see the leeward coast. This is the Plateau de Papaye with its prairies and its cattle.

Soon the trail enters the road near the Clinique des Eaux-Vives (Clinic of the Living Waters), 200 meters off to your right. To the left, the road descends toward Matouba. About 100 meters down is a magnificent view of the Caraibes mountains.

L. Vauchelet Waterfall Trail

Time: 45 minutes round-trip. | **Difficulty:** 2. This trail is marked only at the beginning. | **Trailhead:** Depart from and return to the Saint-Claude police station across from the prefect's residence.

After parking near the police station, stay on the concrete road that ends at a house. Go around the house by walking to the left, below a small wall. The trail, narrow at the beginning and sometimes overgrown with tall grass, becomes wide and shaded.

The hike takes about 20 minutes, giving you time to notice several interesting plants: the chestnut, with large leaves and fat prickly burrs; and also the resolute tree *(Chimarrhis cymosa)*, with its clusters of white flowers. Its yellowish-orange wood—very hard and insect-resistant—is used in construction.

Along the path's edge, you'll also see sang dragon (or swamp bloodwood, a large tree with enormous buttress roots and blood-red latex in the sap), heliconias, cannon wood, numerous tree ferns, and the rose apple, whose fruits are delicious and fragrant.

The trail overlooks the River Noire, bends right, then descends and becomes narrower, bringing you opposite the tumbling waters of the Riviere Noire. The cascade, or waterfall, is located about 500 meters northeast of Saint-Claude and was formed by a rupture in the river bank. The cascade has a 20- to 30-meter drop. Cross the bridge (flanked on the right by an enormous chestnut tree) to reach the waterfall basin. To the left and a little before the pool are the remains of a shelter built by the Montagnards. Return by the same route.

M. THE HEIGHTS OF PAPAYE

Time: 2 hours; Bains Chauds (Hot Baths), 1.5 hours, round-trip. | **Difficulty:** 2–3. A blazed trail, rather easy. | **Trailhead:** Depart from the Clinique des Eaux-Vives of Papaye altitude 2,821 feet (860 m). Arrive at the Forest House of Matouba, altitude 2,188 feet (667 m).

At the foot of the northern slope of Nez Casse are 104° F sulfur springs whose therapeutic properties are used by the Clinique des Eaux-Vives on the Papaye Plateau above Matouba. This "Clinic of Living Waters" draws the wealthiest people of Guadeloupe. It is also the starting point for your hike. Park in the lot.

The first 200 to 300 meters follow the road in a northeasterly direction, then pass vegetable gardens and fields of grazing cattle. After crossing a muddy section, the trail becomes wide and rather gentle, following roughly the curves of the northwest side of Nez Casse.

About 1,500 meters after leaving the fields, the trail curves left to the Chaude Ravine, a green opening composed of giant trees, tree ferns, heliconias, and raspberries.

The trail leads you 300 meters farther to a fork. The path to the right, which will take you to the hot baths, meanders through a stunted forest, a growth pattern that precedes the high-altitude savannahs.

After visiting the hot baths, you can either return to your departure point by returning along the path described above, or continuing on the well-maintained trail for another hour to the ranger station of Matouba. From there, you can get back to the Plateau Papaye parking area by following the road going through Matouba village, with its pretty wooden houses and colorful gardens.

The first half of the Matouba Waterfall Trail follows along the same path as the Carmichael Trail (Hike C, p. 177). The trail starts just to the right after the banana seasoning shed. Follow the rocky path until it curves to the left. Follow a sign there to an alley bordered by sang dragon (swamp bloodwoods).

N. The Matouba Waterfall Trail

Time: 45 minutes. | **Difficulty:** 2. A blazed and easy trail. The small, 5-meter-high Matouba Waterfall is not well known. | **Trailhead:** The Josephine Residence in Matouba. To reach the Josephine Residence, drive the Matouba Road from Saint-Claude. After the bridges crossing the Riviere Noire and the Ravine des Ecrevisses (Crayfish), get off N.3 by turning left at the curve not far from a stele erected in memory of Delgres (former head of the Basse-Terre district). After about 270 yards (250 m), first going in a straight line and then curving right, the road makes an abrupt turnoff to your right: a sign visible at the last minute indicates your destination. You'll drive through a vast banana plantation, then encounter a straight road bordered by red mahoganies, Gabon tulip trees with big orange flowers, American palms, and—finally—the Josephine Residence. Only the foundations of the main house and a few outbuildings remain. Park near the oak tree, a rare species for Guadeloupe.

After a beautiful view of La Soufrière and the Plateau Papaye, you'll head into the forest, and in just five minutes more you'll reach the bed of the Saint-Louis River and the Matouba Waterfall, a small waterfall that spurts out of a volcanic gully into a deep basin.

What appears to be a refreshing paradise in the tropical heat may be dangerous to swimmers. Locals say a whirlpool at the foot of the falls has already caused some accidents.

O. The Third Carbet Waterfall Trail

Time: 1.5 hours, round-trip to visit the third waterfall; 2.5 hours to both visit the third waterfall and reach the Carbet Falls picnic area. The third waterfall, seldom visited, is 20 meters high. | **Difficulty:** 2–3. A blazed trail: provisioning is a good idea. The truly strenuous path: Climbing up the Carbet, you also have the option to visit the first and second waterfalls using Hikes P and Q, and to visit La Soufrière. All this is a pretty strenuous route (Difficulty: 4–5) of about 6 hours. | **Trailhead:** The Carbet falls picnic area. Drive to Capesterre. At the entrance to the city coming from the south, leave N.1 and turn left onto D.3 toward Routhiers. D.3 passes in front of the Marquisat factory; at the first crossroads turn right; at the second, after a long straightaway, take the left. Then about 100 yards (100 m) farther, turn right again. You are in Routhiers. The road turns into a macadam road going through a mahogany forest mingled with banana plantings. The road stops at our departure point, 1.9 miles (3 km) farther on.

Park at the end of the road and take the wide path (which can be muddy) across the edge of a sparse forest containing mahogany, giant philodendrons, and tree ferns.

After 20 minutes, cross an enclosed ravine by angling to the left. Several minutes later you'll encounter a marked crossroads: to the right are the first and second waterfalls, Hikes P and Q; opposite is the third waterfall, which you are going to visit.

Use special precautions as you descend an uneven area of about 50 meters ravaged by landslides. Halfway down you'll see the waterfall; continuing the descent into the river bed shouldn't pose any difficulty. Reaching the river takes about ten minutes.

Returning to the crossroads, you can either take the 30-minute trek back to your vehicle, or, by going left, continue your hike toward the first or second falls. The second falls are closer; about 1.5 hours away.

If you decide to proceed, the trail goes along the Carbet River for about 15 minutes, then crosses its tributary, the Dauriac. Some five minutes later, the trail crosses another tributary, then continues along a small ridge. Afterward, you'll cross a relatively flat zone where the forest is essentially gommier and chestnut trees, and an occasional mangrove with its famous aerial roots.

Fifteen minutes after crossing the Dauriac River, you'll arrive at the edge of the Carbet and the foot of a very steep climb. During the first 600 m of walking, you will ascend 558 feet (170 m). The trail follows the line of the largest slope, then descends and climbs again; 40 minutes later, you're at another marked crossroads. To the right, the trail continues toward the first Carbet waterfall, 1.5 hours away, then moves on to La Soufrière.

To the left, a ten-minute walk brings you to yet another marked crossroads. From this point, you can be back at the picnic and parking area within 15 minutes by turning left and following the zigzag trail after the bridge. Or, you can reach the second—and most spectacular—Carbet waterfall in even less time by taking the right fork.

On this hike you'll see about 20 species of lianas, vines which are large enough even for Tarzan to swing on, one of the most impressive aspects of this tropical forest.

P. The First Carbet Waterfall Trail

Time: 4 hours, one way. | **Difficulty:** 4–5. A blazed trail, take water and snacks. | **Trailhead:** Depart from the Carbet falls picnic area (see Hike O for directions). Arrive at Savane a Mulets parking lot at the base of La Soufrière.

To reach the first waterfall, start from the Carbet Falls picnic area. At the end of Habituee Road, a break in the brush lets you see the first two Carbet falls. The farthest away is also the highest: It plummets more than 125 meters in two stages. Its summit is 1,005 meters. The other waterfall, actually closer, measures about 110 meters. Hike Q (p. 187) will take you there.

Immediately on your left is the zigzag track that goes around the flanks of L'Echelle (Hike R, p.187). After going into the forest about 200 meters, another maintained trail leads to the left: the Karukera Trail, which leads directly to L'Echelle (see Hike D, p. 177).

Follow the trail to the first falls where you'll snake downward toward the river. Along the way you'll spot the white gum, a very tall tree easily identified by its straight and slender trunk, the source of an amber-colored resin. The trunk of this tree, hollow and wide, was once used to build long, narrow unstable boats, called gommiers. Gum-tree boats are no longer used in Guadeloupe, but can frequently be seen on neighboring islands.

You'll cross the Carbet by a footbridge. Several meters farther is your first crossroads; the left path leads to the second waterfall (see Hike Q, p. 187). Instead, follow the trail climbing regularly in a westerly direction, through a luxuriantly forested hillside. About a kilometer after the crossroads, veer left and walk the steep incline into the Longueteau Ravine, tributary of the Carbet. After crossing to the other side, on the spur formed by the two valleys, is another fork. The right trail continues toward La Soufrière.

Stay left and in about 15 minutes reach the Carbet River bed and the first waterfall. There are really two successive falls here: The first, from a height of 115 meters, falls onto a little platform, then becomes a second fall about 10 meters high. Returning to the crossroads, you have the option of walking toward L'Echelle to reach the north cliff, where the waterfall originates, and eventually come out at Savane a Mulets. Most people simply retrace their steps.

Q. The Second Carbet Waterfall Trail

Time: 1 hour, round-trip. | **Difficulty:** 2–3. Trail marked and simple. | **Trailhead:** Depart and arrive at the waterfall picnic area.

The grand second Carbet Waterfall is the most frequently visited. Leave your vehicle at the Carbet falls picnic area. From there, through a break in the vegetation and when the clouds are high enough, you can see the first two waterfalls. Your goal—the second—is nearest.

Follow the road described in Hike O (just follow the signs). The road joins the zigzag trail on L'Echelle, then the Karukera Trail (see Hike H, p.180).

From the first crossroads, the trail makes a rapid descent toward the riverbed. You will notice some interesting trees: resolute wood, with large, light-green leaves; white gum, the resin of which is used for lighting fires; and sturdy chestnuts. The latter are the most abundant species in this dense forest, and are frequently decked out with impressive, elongated roots up to ten meters high. Numerous epiphytes grow on the different trees.

In about ten minutes you'll cross the Carbet River on a footbridge rebuilt in 1978, after the original was carried away by a five-meter-high volcanic flow. This flow, courtesy of L'Echelle, also severely damaged the site of the second waterfall. A few meters past the footbridge is a crossroads: To the right is the access to the first and third falls; straight ahead is your trail.

About 200 meters farther, bear to the right via the maintained trail that soon takes you to the river, which you'll cross again. You can't help but see the impressive waterfall in front of you now. To get closer, the trail on the right bank continues to a rocky terrace where you can delicately make your way to the foot of the waterfall. The rocks here are always wet (you soon will be, too) due to the spray.

R. The Zigzag Route

Time: 2 hours. | **Difficulty:** 5, and possibly dangerous. The trail is not marked; carry water. | **Trailhead:** Depart from the Carbet Waterfall picnic area. Arrive at Savane a Mulets, altitude 3,746 feet (1,142 m). To avoid the most difficult parts, climb the Karukera Trail (Hike H, p. 180), then take up this route.

An attempt was once made to connect the trail leading to La Citerne to the one ending at the Carbet Falls picnic area. The aborted project did create some switchbacks in the flank of

L'Echelle, which provide a pretty hike. But if you want to endure some of Guadeloupe's toughest walking, depart from the Carbet Falls picnic area and take the marked trail that goes off to the left immediately after the last shelter.

The trail climbs through the dense forest, made more difficult by the tall razor grass. Avoid touching the grass—it's so sharp it can cut you deeply, even slice through your clothing. Look at it this way: the narrow trail permits closer contact with nature.

After going about 500 meters, the trail crosses two ravines (the second is much deeper than the first). A little farther, the path goes along another ravine running on the left 20 meters below. In about another ten minutes, you arrive at a clearing on the edge of the ravine you've been following.

This opening permits you to reach the streambed and to climb up about 50 meters beyond. There, on the left, you'll find the point where the digging for the Zigzag Trail was abandoned.

The regular trail continues straight ahead and your path continues climbing through the forest. It comes out in the middle of a thicket of tall grasses to join the Zigzag Trail, about a 100 meters below a hairpin curve (a difficult and relatively dangerous section).

It should take you about an hour to reach this point. At this stage, you may have had enough and want to retrace your way back to the Carbet Falls picnic area. Or, you can also continue to climb the trail up the eastern flank of L'Echelle with its views of the Windward Coast.

Walk ahead, and 200–300 meters before another hairpin curve, you'll find a concrete road that, after a kilometer on the flank of L'Echelle, rejoins the La Citerne route. From there, La Savane a Mulets is a 20-minute walk by following the route on the right. You could also do the circuit of la Citerne with Hike E (p. 178), or the ascent of L'Echelle with Hike D (p. 177).

THE TRAIL OF THE PONDS

Time: 2 hours each way. | **Difficulty:** This trail is marked. Warning: Fog and night come on quickly in the forest. | **Trailhead:** Depart from the Grand Etang parking area on Carbet Falls Road. Arrive at Moscou, altitude 700 m, 5 km northeast of Gourbeyre.

When hiking the Soufrière range you'll see several bodies of water in the southeast that maps designate as "etangs," freshwater pools or ponds comparable to a mountain lake. They form when depressions in the ground are enclosed by volcanic gullies that retain water. This is how a former volcanic flow came to rest on Morne Boudoute to create the 748-meter Etang As de Pique (Ace of Spades Pool). Its overflow runs to the east and feeds, 350 meters below, Grand Etang (see Hike A, p. 189).

Two other nearby ponds, Roche and Madere, are wedged between the southern flank of Morne Boudoute and the Madeleine range. Often dry, they may look like vast grassy expanses, a rare sight in a dense forest.

Another small pond, Etang Zombi, at 410 m, is several hundred meters northeast of Grand Etang. Fed by the waters of the Tonnelle Ravine, it is bordered by a network of raised roots that makes the approach difficult.

Starting from the trailhead at Grand Etang, in about ten minutes abandon the Grand Etang circle and go right on a trail that climbs fairly steadily, then makes switchbacks to a blazed fork where you have two possibilities: To the right, the main trail leads to Ace of Spades and

Moscou. To the left are the pools of Madere and Roche. It should take 15 minutes to explore around Roche and Madere, a little longer for Moscou.

3. Hikes Near Gourbeyre

A. The Grand Etang Circle

Time: 1 hour. | **Difficulty:** 2–3. The trail is marked. | **Trailhead:** Located at the Grand Etang parking area on the extension of Route D4, about 1.3 miles (2 km) west of the Grande Chasse Residence.

The circle of Grand Etang not only permits you to see the lake from different perspectives but is also noteworthy for the plants and crayfish that live in its waters.

Park, and take the concrete road to the edge of the pond (about 300 meters), where a sign directs you to begin the circle to the right. The wide trail ventures into a dense forest characterized by tall trees with powerful roots and many epiphytes.

On the first part of the hike, the pond is scarcely visible. However, you will see great clumps of bamboo, which make an eerie creaking when the wind blows the reeds together. Abundant all around the pond, bamboo was introduced from Asia centuries ago on sites like this one, then transplanted just about everywhere in Guadeloupe. After about ten minutes, you'll reach a marked fork in the trail. The path to the right allows you to get back to Moscou and the Gourbeyre via the switchbacks of the etangs trail described on page 188.

Continuing straight ahead, the lake appears on the left, its edges overgrown with aquatic plants. As you progress, a rustling sound becomes clearer: the stream feeding Etang As de Pique, whose divided bed you cross in three stages. Soon after, it rises several meters above the level of the pond. Little by little, through scattered vegetation, you begin to really discover Grand Etang and the grasses and mosses circling it.

You may see a thrush or a kingfisher at the lake edge. Grand Etang used to have a reputation as a bird-watcher's paradise, but the area has been overhunted. At the southeast corner of the pond, you'll discover an enormous isolated rock in the water, decorated with plants and shrubs. Next, the trail passes above the subterranean flow of the pond, which is audible.

B. La Madeleine Trail

Time: 5 hours. | **Difficulty:** 4–5. Not marked; take food and water. | **Trailhead:** Coming from Basse-Terre , the departure for this hike is located at the crushing station to the southeast of La Madeleine, on N.1 past Gourbeyre and La Regrettee. You can park nearby.

La Madeleine is one of Guadeloupe's most important volcanoes. The trail is for experienced hikers skilled at finding their way. The trail—not blazed—is sometimes confusing, especially after the climb to Petit Carbet, where it meanders into mostly marshland.

After parking and reaching the end of the crushing station, take the concrete service road through the banana plantation, a severe and difficult incline. Fortunately, it levels out.

Three hundred meters farther—and here you have to pay attention—the trail bears right from where the hibiscus branches form a vault. Stay on this trail; a concrete stretch will eventually appear. You are now in a dense forest populated with redwood and white mahogany, a slender tree of moderate size, with smooth, light bark. The trail now climbs steadily and makes a sharp left turn, followed shortly by another turn to the right. At the end of the path you'll have to step over a tree trunk. A few minutes after this obstacle, leave the main trail that continues straight and turn right to follow a narrow trail bending left for a good 100 meters on level ground. This then descends rapidly to Petit Carbet, whose source is on the southeast flank of La Citerne, at the bottom of a difficult ravine.

The trail crosses a calm river where you might see some large crayfish, armed with pincers. Beyond, the trail continues into flat and marshy terrain. It is sometimes difficult to follow the trail beyond this point. About 300 meters after the junction, cross a ravine that comes from the mountain on your right at a perpendicular angle. About ten meters farther, turn right and climb back up to the ravine, which is shallower and wider at this point.

The trail then bears to the east, going near the steep wall of la Madeleine. Now you begin the ascent. This will be long and arduous—about 1.5 hours—and you will no doubt need several recovery stops to catch your breath. *Warning:* Be careful not to grab hold of tree ferns. They can spike you with thorns that are difficult to extract.

After about 40 minutes of ascent, you should have on your right an almost vertical rocky wall covered with vegetation. After scaling a steep passage, the trail flattens out as it approaches a ravine.

Continue parallel to the ravine, until you can cross it on some large rocks. There remains the ultimate ascent, that of Piton l'Herminier, at 971 m the highest point of the Madeleine range. Thirty minutes of acrobatic weaving through the jungle of mountain mangroves is necessary to reach the summit. Appreciate the mountain lilies or orchids as you climb.

The summit plateau of La Madeleine is more far-reaching than that of La Soufrière, with its mere 1,500-meter diameter and its deep longitudinal depression dominated by several peaks. If the sky is clear, nearly all of Guadeloupe spreads out before you. At the summit, you will also find a cylinder with volcano monitoring instruments. The return trip is by the same trail and should be a bit faster than the 2.75-hour ascent to the top of Piton l'Herminier.

A Quicker Trail: It is possible to make this ascent by leaving from Moscou in Gourbeyre. This reduces the approach walk, starting nearly 300 meters higher. But be careful not to wander into the middle of the banana fields and the drainage canals, where you could get lost.

C. THE BASSIN BLEU AND THE PARABOLE

Time: 2.5 hours. | **Difficulty:** 2–4. Parts of this hike require wading in water, scrambling up walls, and some rock climbing. Not marked; the trail is easy to Bassin Bleu, difficult after that. | **Trailhead:** Depart and arrive on the Moscou Road, 4 km northeast of Gourbeyre. To get there from town, take the Plateau du Palmiste Road (next to town hall) by following the signs for the Park-Trace des Etangs (Trail of the Ponds). A second sign is located 3 km from the town hall; take the road to the left. You will pass two roads going off to the left. Park at the bottom of the hill after the second road, at a crossroads area on the left. From the crossroads, go about 10 meters to a break in the hedge on the left, the starting point for your hike. This hedge break can be hard to spot when the grass is high.

The Galion River is born at the foot of La Soufrière, and tumbles down a series of cascades, entering the Caribbean near Fort Saint-Charles. If the large Galion Waterfall (Hike I, p. 180) is well known, the same certainly is not true of other cascades like Bassin Bleu and La Parabole, which are rarely visited.

This trail was created to facilitate construction of a water intake in Bassin Bleu. After a ten-minute walk, this wet and humid trail crosses a banana grove, then climbs a ravine and goes into a forest. Shortly, you'll come out into the main bed of the Galion River, across from the Bassin Bleu. It takes only 20 minutes to reach this small body of water, wedged between 2 rock walls and fed by a vigorous stream spurting from a volcanic gully 6 meters above.

Continue toward La Parabole, scaling the small rise on the right. A rope may be there; otherwise, grab some roots to help you up. Follow the culvert past the concrete structure, to where it crosses the river to collect the cold water of the misnamed Ravine Chaude (*chaude* means "warm"). From this confluence, you have only the river to guide you.

To reach La Parabole, it's necessary to look for a trail on the bank, wade in the water, leap from rock to rock, climb the wall of a small cascade . . . an adventure of sorts, if you're up to it. Otherwise, it's best to turn back. In deciding whether to go on, remember, too, heavy rains occur suddenly at this altitude; real gully-washers that make the rivers swell dangerously, especially in the gorges.

If you do proceed, about 15 minutes later you should reach another tributary on the right bank, the Ravine Madame Toussaint. It descends in small cascades and joins the Galion. If the current is weak, you can continue by the river; scaling two small cascades with a two-meter drop. The first cascade is after the confluence where the Galion makes a bend. The second is about 15 minutes farther on, but it can be skirted thanks to a pathway on the left bank.

There is an alternative to wading if the current is strong; you can climb the rocky wall on the left, just after the confluence of Madame Toussaint Ravine and a little before the small basin after the cascade. After passing through a tiny ravine, you will go into the forest on the trail farthest to the right. In about 15 minutes you'll come out a little upstream from the second cascade, on an overhang.

Cross the river and follow the trail on the left bank. After a five-minute walk through some beautiful trees, you'll see the Galion again near a cascade that is more impressive than the previous ones. At the bottom of this cascade (four meters high) the water pours into a slit after being slowed by two bathtub-like wells, then plunges six meters into a large basin. This narrow gorge and fine green moss covering certain rocks makes a splendid photograph.

Pass on either side of the cascade, proceeding along the river bed. Take the trail on the right to reach La Parabole, a beautiful waterfall of about ten meters, which tumbles into an arena with walls tinted ocher, red, and black. If you haven't taken a plunge (involuntary) into the water, you might want to do it now. Return by the same route.

D. Le Houelmont

Time: 2.5 hours, one way, to visit the summit of Houelmont. | **Difficulty:** 3–4. Trail not marked, but not too tough; take water. | **Trailhead:** On the old national road linking the city of Basse-Terre and Gourbeyre, turn right after Blanchet toward Bisdary. About 400 meters farther on, at the end of the tarred road, veer left, then quickly to the right. Park on the first service road wherever you find space.

The trailhead at the foot of le Houelmont gives a wonderful view of the green pastures of Bisdary, one of the great dairy-farming areas of Basse-Terre. Follow the service road that climbs a small valley crossed by the Ravine Blanche. Lots of interesting flora beautifies the beginning of this hike; notably, the Saint-Jean liana, a vine with clusters of violet stars, and the savonnette wood with its mauve flowers in July.

Fifteen minutes after departure, you will reach a fork. Go right and cross the Ravine Blanche. The trail will climb steadily and soon reach an area planted in bananas, a few scattered royal palms, breadfruit trees, and rose apples, whose fruits are delicious.

At the next crossroads, continue right. You are now at an altitude of about 1,000 feet (300 m). A bit farther, through the mahoganies bordering the trail, you will see a part of the city of Basse-Terre and above, Saint-Claude. You'll reach the hill in about 40 minutes.

On the right, a spur trail goes to the summit of Le Houelmont (1,400 feet/428 m), which takes about 20 minutes . Along the way you'll notice on the left a small steep path; this is only a cul-de-sac that ends at a pool. Your trail, bordered in spots by small ferns, now cuts through a mahogany forest, creating a pleasant and shady setting.

To return to Bisdary without retracing your steps, continue on the same path almost to its end, where a trail forks off at a right angle. All in switchbacks, this new trail veers to the right; in about ten minutes, it descends to become even with a fig tree with lots of branches. The trail continues into the rocks of a very steep ravine. This route is rather strenuous.

The trail then takes a 90° turn to the right, and 100 meters farther on, makes another 90° turn, this time to the left. This turnoff is barely visible. Ten minutes later, you leave the new trail on your left, then come into a clearing near the farmlands. Finally coming out onto a service road, take a right to return to your departure point.

4. Hikes Near Gros Acajou

The extreme southern end of Basse-Terre is formed by a well-defined mountain range, the Caraibes Mountains, separate from the rest of the island chain. Its volcanic activity independent of the Madeleine-Soufrière group to the northeast, the Caraibes arise from an older and more western fracture, going from Saint-Rose to Vieux-Fort and passing by Piton de Bouillante.

The departure point for hikes in the Caraibes Mountains is at Champfleury, in the town of Gourbeyre, situated about a kilometer south of Dos d'Ane on N.1. From there, after an hour's walk on a common section, the two hikes separate.

A. CHAMPFLEURY TO GROS ACAJOU TRAIL

Time: 1 hour, each way. | **Difficulty:** 2. | **Trailhead:** At the end of the Champfleury Road.

At the end of the Champfleury Road, leave your vehicle and take the path that extends from it to the south. Still paved for a good distance, it has concrete sections to assist up the steepest slopes. The trail is sometimes blazed with white arrows and red dots. After the first 15 minutes, it rises steadily across a diffuse landscape and wastelands scattered with cannon wood. Turning around, notice the beautiful view of the Dole banana plantations and Trois-Rivieres, overlooked in the north by La Soufrière.

At a mostly paved platform, the trail bears right. The slope becomes steeper, giving way to a narrow path bordered by ferns and heliconias. A bit farther, and you'll be in the forest, where you will easily recognize clumps of bamboo. After about an hour, you'll reach Gros Acajou Hill. This is where Hikes B (below) and C (p. 194) separate. *Note:* It is possible to do a loop, connecting the two hikes by walking between Marina de Riviere Sens and Vieux Fort, but it will take you eight or nine hours of walking. That is most suited for seasoned hikers.

B. COL DU GROS ACAJOU TO MARINA DE RIVIERE SENS

Time: 4 hours, one way. | **Difficulty:** 3–4. The trail is marked in part; take water. | **Trailhead:** Gros Acajou. From Gros Acajou, take the trail to the right, where you will continue your ascent along a ridge line in the midst of a rain forest, ending finally on the coast

About 20 minutes from the start, a sign will invite you to make a circle around the cleared summit of Morne Cadet, from which you can enjoy a beautiful view of Basse-Terre. This circle trail, leading off to the right, takes about 20 minutes to complete. On this side trail, you may surprise a partridge, or you may hear its call, seeming to well up from the mountainside itself.

Back on the main trail, in just 200 meters you reach the highest point of the Caraibes, Morne Vent Souffle. The 2,250-foot (686-m) altitude, though modest, affords an exceptional 360˚ panorama almost defying description.

You quickly descend Morne Vent Souffle, first by a ridge leading to the south, then 15 minutes later, by a second ridge to the right. Several meters lower on the trail, a break in the undergrowth allows you to see the Vieux-Fort lighthouse on the left.

On the right, the trail again leaves the ridge to steeply descend in zigzags. It veers left and meets another ridge taking you to the two summits of Morne Grand Voute. After scaling a small section where you will find handholds— which rain can make slippery—a trail on the right allows you to reach the first and nearest summit, 1,778 feet (542 m). After about 700 feet (200 m) farther, the trail passes over the second summit, which peaks at 1,824 feet (556 m).

On the slopes of le Vent Souffle, you'll note the changes in the vegetation surrounding you: the strange "tails" hanging from the branches, the dryer plant carpet, the diminished size of the trees. You'll see more and more rare epiphytes. This is an intermediate stage between rain forest and dry forest, called mesophilic forest.

On the slopes of le Vent Souffle, and to a lesser degree on the slopes of Gros Acajou, this mesophile forest is well conserved and striking. Lower down, it has been largely stripped to create banana plantations, market gardens, cocoa and coffee plantations. Here is where the majority of forestry planting is done, especially the large-leafed mahogany.

From the second summit of Morne Grand Voute, the trail turns swiftly to the northwest. It ends at the Marina de Sens Riviere, which you can reach in 90 minutes. The descent, long and steep, traverses increasingly dryer vegetation. Two-thirds of the way down, on the western flank of Morne Griselle, the trail comes out suddenly onto a wide service road that you'll take to the right, in the general direction of the climb.

You'll then see the quarries of the Riviere Sens. Amateur vulcanologists can see these quarries by taking the route along the sea leading to Vieux-Fort. They are magnificent geological cuts.

Follow the trail for 30 minutes and you'll reach a parking area for factory equipment, on the level of the marina and the shore. From the marina, go to Vieux-Fort by the seaside trail, leaving it a little before the crossroads access to the lighthouse and Anse Dupuy. To the left is the trail to Vieux-Fort, which you would take to connect to the end of Hike B (p. 193).

C. Gros Acajou to Vieux-Fort

Time: 2 hours, one way from Gros Acajou. | **Difficulty:** 4–5. Blazed in part; take water. | **Trailhead:** Gros Acajou.

After 15 minutes into this forest setting of bamboo and heliconias, the trail offers a view of the distant islands, the Isles de Saintes. At your feet is the eastern flank of the range which you are about to cross, overlooked by two summits that jut into the sky. In front of you and slightly to the right is 1,879-foot (573 m) Bout Morne, and a little below and to the left, Morne La Voute with its 1,325-foot (404 m) peak. A little to the rear and on your right is the highest summit of the Caraibes Mountains, Morne Vent Souffle (2,250 feet/686 m).

Now that you've enjoyed the view, it's time to pay for it—your next 15 minutes are dedicated to the perilous descent of a very steep slope, first by switchbacks, then across rocks of a small, dried-up ravine, to reach Ravine Dejeuner (Lunch Ravine). Along the trail, swamp bloodwoods accompany you practically to the end of the hike.

After a brief climb, the trail divides into two branches that rejoin 250 meters ahead. The left pathway goes near a hut and looks out over the Ravine Grand Fond, wider and even more cultivated than the preceding ones. Its bottom is punctuated by numerous royal palms.

A little later, you'll reach the rocks of the Ravine Grand Fond, shaded by the mango trees and coconut palms growing there. Do not take the steep trail to the left. Instead, bear to the right to climb the flanks of Morne la Voute. In only 20 minutes you'll arrive at the high point, which permits you to appreciate the route you've been taking for the past hour.

A little farther, bypass the trail on the left going toward Beausoleil. Take the one on the right, marked with red paint. It cuts through a dry forest, or xerophile, characteristic of the southern zones of the island. It lasts until the end of the trail.

A second trail veers left toward the coast, about 600 m farther, but don't take it. Rather, follow the trail climbing slightly and turning right.

You'll cross another ravine on the left soon after entering a cultivated section. After descending 200 meters through woods, you'll rejoin the road to Vieux-Fort. To the right it crosses a small bridge and leads to the road to Basse-Terre; to the left, it goes back to town.

The hike back to your starting point at Champfleury, including the common trail, is about three hours.

5. Archaeological Park at Trois-Rivieres

Time: 1 hour. | **Difficulty:** 1. | **Trailhead:** Easily found on any map showing Basse-Terre's south coast.

The park contains petroglyphs dating from A.D. 300–400, and the walk passes through a garden/boardwalk setting that meanders by huge boulders with presumably Arawak

This rock carving in the Archaeological Park at Trois-Rivieres may be 1,800 years old

petroglyphs. Some drawings are quite worn and faded; a brochure provided after you pay a modest admission fee locates and deciphers some of the sites and also explains the island foliage. The most important carving is the head of a chief who may be buried inside the cave the drawing marks. This is a very pleasant walk requiring little exertion compared to most walking on Guadeloupe. It's a nice place to relax after your La Soufrière climb.

12

Jamaica

Old Jamaican Proverb: "*Bottle without cap belong to cockroach.*"
Translation: "*Unprotected possessions may become anyone's property.*"

I consider the ascent up Blue Mountain Peak, described in more detail later, to be one the Caribbean's best hikes ... No. 4, to be precise. Blue Mountain peak reaches 7,402 feet, making it a Matterhorn among islands where the land rarely rises above 5,000 feet.

The classic way to the top is to start walking at a chilly 2 a.m., go 7 miles in total darkness, and arrive at the 7,402-foot summit in time for a glorious sunrise. A fairly strenuous hike, scrambling up the mountain in the dark is a fun challenge. The views from the top and coming back down are magnificent.

The Arawaks, Jamaica's earliest known inhabitants, named their land well: Xaymaca, "land of woods and streams." They left out the mountains, however. Jamaica is very hilly and between 40 and 50 percent is still forested. It has tremendous geographic variety: desert, high mountains, beaches ... almost everything but snow (though it may get below freezing on Blue Mountain Peak in winter). Jamaica also houses more indigenous birds, ferns, reptiles, and orchids than any other island.

Yet some people feel uneasy about visiting Jamaica. For one, they don't want to witness the poverty for which the island is well known. So they stay away. No doubt about it, Jamaica is a poor country. The small shacks some people call home are disturbing to see. Yet if one is genuinely concerned about a county's economy, the most effective thing to do is visit and spend money. That's what creates jobs and keeps people employed.

There also is the accompanying problem of drugs and crime. Jamaica's major tourist areas, like towns everywhere, do have parts that shouldn't be visited after dark. As most hotels have their own security staff, room break-ins tend to be rarer than crime on the street.

How safe is it to walk/hike around Jamaica? Probably as safe as anywhere else if you show reasonable care. As one who was almost killed here in 1977 when I blundered into a drug pickup, I do not say this lightly. (I was in the wrong place at the wrong time, and no one knew what to do with me: to live or let die.) That happened in the 1970s, when foreigners generally were disliked and the government was leaning to the left. Ten years passed before I went back to Jamaica.

Now I'm there at least once or twice a year. I feel safe and welcome—but whenever I go off into the bush, it's with a reliable Jamaican.

In hiking around, no one should be foolish enough to hire a "guide" who approaches you. You may get shaken down instead of shown the sights. Would you entrust your safety to the first stranger who approached you in London, New York, or Miami and offered to show you around, especially to take you off the beaten path?

In Jamaica, be prepared for the open sale of illegal drugs, particularly the local herb, ganja (marijuana). Pot is not only one of the major cash crops, in the countryside it's sometimes consumed the way Americans drink beer at a Sunday picnic. Expect to be offered a sociable smoke and decide in advance how you want to handle it. If you don't care to take a few puffs, that's agreeable with the locals. They never push it, only offer.

The great contradiction to all this: There are harsh penalties for drug use. An estimated 50 foreign tourists may be in Jamaican jails at any one time for breaking the drug laws. No one in his or her wildest, most drug-stoned dreams should ever consider taking any drugs out of the country.

With all its problems, Jamaica is a rose with very obvious thorns. The best description on how Jamaica works comes from Peter Bentley, Jamaica's original hiking expert and past president of the Jamaica Alternative Tourism, Camping and Hiking Association (JATCHA). This is how Peter describes Jamaica and its people:

> *Push, you don't get much. Take it easier, get much more. When we speak, expect to be baffled! Our patois sounds like a foreign language. Sometimes it might sound like you are being scolded, but we love you. We argue hard, but at the same time we will happily share a rum or a smoke with you. We can be mighty inquisitive, or extremely shy. We are a poor country. Hustling is almost a way of life, a necessity—meet the hustler with humor and compassion, and continue with your mission.*
>
> *We like to be acknowledged even if it is only slightly raising the index finger as a greeting or saying one word, "Irie" [pronounced "Eye-ree" and meaning "everything's going wonderful" or "just great"—a greeting also to describe a person or the day or "good morning" or "good night," i.e., meaning "good evening."]*

It is disconcerting the first time a Jamaican greets you in the evening and his first words are "good night." No, he's not leaving or dismissing you. After all, it *is* night. Saying "good evening" (when the evening is the briefest part of the night) doesn't make much sense. The Jamaican perspective about time is a very logical one.

There is a saying: "The Jamaica you find depends on the company you meet." How true. On that basis I've become very prejudiced about all things Jamaican, including the people, the music, the food and the countryside—I like them all. A lot.

Blue Mountain Coffee

Potent and strong and considered some of the world's finest, Jamaica's coffee industry can be traced back to 1728 when the first trees were imported from Ethiopia. You will have many opportunities to buy, but the best prices are in the Blue Mountains from the farmers themselves. The best coffee comes from the higher altitudes. Japanese investors own many of the best Blue Mountain coffee plantations, and most of the coffee (about 90 percent) is exported to Japan, which accounts for its exorbitant price.

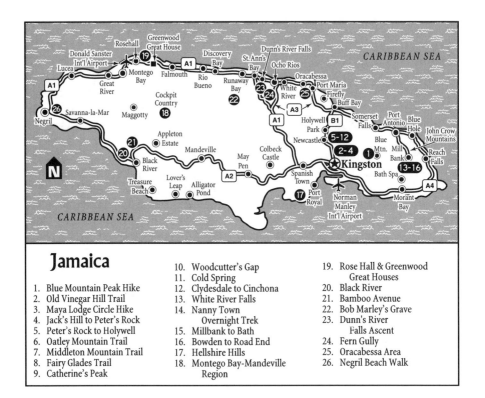

Jamaica

1. Blue Mountain Peak Hike
2. Old Vinegar Hill Trail
3. Maya Lodge Circle Hike
4. Jack's Hill to Peter's Rock
5. Peter's Rock to Holywell
6. Oatley Mountain Trail
7. Middleton Mountain Trail
8. Fairy Glades Trail
9. Catherine's Peak
10. Woodcutter's Gap
11. Cold Spring
12. Clydesdale to Cinchona
13. White River Falls
14. Nanny Town
    Overnight Trek
15. Millbank to Bath
16. Bowden to Road End
17. Hellshire Hills
18. Montego Bay-Mandeville
    Region
19. Rose Hall & Greenwood
    Great Houses
20. Black River
21. Bamboo Avenue
22. Bob Marley's Grave
23. Dunn's River
    Falls Ascent
24. Fern Gully
25. Oracabessa Area
26. Negril Beach Walk

Jerk Food Stands

The Jamaican version of fast food, *jerk* is a terribly misleading name for the best barbecue you will ever eat in the islands. Jerk is a slow cooking process of highly seasoned meat over green pimento wood (allspice). Jerk pork is the classic, but jerk chicken is equally tasty. Every small village has jerk stands, many of them using old oil drums transformed into a huge cooker. Jerk food often tastes best when accompanied by the good local beer, Red Stripe. Ask for Red Stripe cold; some Jamaicans like to drink it at room temperature.

Rastafarians

Although a minority of the Jamaican population, they are the obvious standout. Their dreadlocks, almost like a lion's mane, are a symbol of their faith, which in essence is a peaceful protest against their oppression, particularly by whites. Basically a nonviolent movement, members believe in the divinity of Ras Tafari Makonnen, who assumed the throne of Ethiopia as Haile Selassie I, King of Kings, Lord of Lords, Conquering Lion of the Tribe of Judah, Elect of God, and Emperor of Ethiopia.

Rastas, as they call themselves, base their belief on one quotation of Haile Selassie's in particular: "Until the philosophy that considers any one race superior to another is finally and absolutely challenged and discarded, until there are no longer first-class and second-class human beings, the dream of a lasting peace will remain an illusion."

Rastas believe they are a people in exile, that one day their God, Jah, will lead them back to Ethiopia, their promised land, also called Zion. Jamaican hero Marcus Garvey, who prophesied the ascendance of Haile Selassie, is considered the religion's major prophet. Garvey, who is recognized internationally as an early leader in creating black awareness and unity, suggested the formation of a black homeland in Africa as early as 1916. In 1929, Garvey predicted: "Look to Africa where a king would be crowned, for the day of deliverance is near."

Poor Jamaicans, who had given up on whites and Christianity, were ready to welcome Rastafarianism. So When Haile Selassie I was named emperor of Ethiopia in 1930, that was divine sign enough to embrace the Rasta religion, which was defined by Jamaican educator George Beckford as "originating in Africa but distilled in Jamaica."

Haile Selassie, viewed by Rastafarians as the manifestation of god, took note of the Jamaican religious movement. In 1955, 500 acres of his personal land in Shashemene, 170 miles south of Addis Ababa, the capital, were offered to "black people of the West" to settle on. The first arrived in 1971.

Ironically, Haile Selassie was overthrown in 1974 after a series of strikes and demonstrations that prompted the armed forces to depose him. Although he had played an important role in international affairs, he'd ignored such urgent domestic problems as government corruption, inequality in the distribution of wealth, rural underdevelopment, rampant inflation, and more. In 1975, the monarchy was abolished, and Ethiopia became a republic. Haile Selassie died that same year, still in the custody of the military junta that had overthrown him.

Genuine Rastafarians do not eat meat but are vegetarians. Ganja is their sacred herb. References justifying its use are referenced in the Bible, such as Genesis 1:12: "And the earth brought forth grass and herb yielding seed after this kind, and tree yielding fruit whose seed was itself, after his kind and God saw that it was good."

Rastas see the world, which they call Babylon, destroying itself because of its inequality and materialism and they attempt to stay self-sufficient, apart from it. Recognizing that tourists (particularly women) are intrigued by the Rasta look, some Jamaican men wear fake dreadlocks.

Reggae

Reggae is the protest music of the Rasta religion, with Bob Marley as its high priest. Reggae is the most important development in Caribbean music since the steel band. Unlike calypso, which sings about yellow birds and other idyllic things, reggae is an honest, often harsh look at the world through the eyes of black islanders. Anything but sentimental, reggae is primarily message music about poverty, social injustice, and worshiping Jah. Bob Marley (the museum to him in Kingston is holy ground to reggae lovers) is credited with developing the form. As a prophet, he sang the praises of Jah. However, as with every music form, there is good reggae and there is junk. It is not all "sacred music."

TRAVEL TIPS

Area: The third largest Caribbean island, 146 miles long and varying between 22 and 51 miles wide. Quite mountainous, almost half of the land area is above 1,000 feet.

Language: English and a Jamaican patois.

Population: 2.5 million, mostly located around Kingston. Other population centers, in order, are Montego Bay, Mandeville, Port Antonio Ocho Rios, and Negril.

Time Zone: Jamaica is on Eastern Standard Time year-round.

Rainy Season: The rainy season varies in the different regions. In the center and the west, it's usually summertime. On the eastern side, it's October–November and a small rainy season in May–June. For the island overall, the rainy season is considered to be October into December and May through June.

Different regions of the island receive dramatically different amounts of rainfall. For instance, the capital city of Kingston gets only about 35 inches. Jack's Hill, the first of the Blue Mountains, receives about 75 inches. Farther up in the Blue Mountains at sites called Holywell and the Fairy Glades Trail, it's now 125 inches. At the highest peaks, we're talking from 150 to 200 inches and more. The worst place is the John Crow Mountains. This region receives an estimated 300 inches of rain a year. Understandably, not many people hike there.

For hiking, the weather usually doesn't make much difference. Clouds also provide the coolest, most enjoyable walking conditions. Go prepared for rain, and it won't be as much of a bother as you might think

Getting There: Jamaica is an easy island to reach. U.S. carriers include Air Jamaica, American Airlines, USAirways, and Northwest. Air Canada flies from Toronto and British Airways from London-Gatwick. Most carriers land at Montego Bay, but if you're going to hike the Blue Mountains, opt for a flight that continues on to Kingston. Otherwise you'll have to fly Tropical Airlines to Kingston; call (876) 979-3565.

Documents: An original birth certificate and government-issued ID (driver's license) are acceptable for U.S. and Canadian citizens. A passport always is preferable. All others need passports.

Getting Around: Rental cars are some of the Caribbean's most expensive, costing as much as $100 per day in winter. The reason: In addition to the rental charge, there's a collision-damage waiver ($15 per day) that's sometimes mandatory, plus a 15% government tax. Hiking tour operators sometimes arrange for hotel pickups. Should you choose to drive in Jamaica, stay alert because driving requires your full, close attention. Roads are narrow, and big trucks come barreling around the curves with no warning. In general, Jamaicans tend to drive like the devil is chasing them and closing fast.

Where to Stay: Just outside Kingston is the **Ivor Guest House** on Skyline Drive; call (876) 927-1460. This old nineteenth-century villa has just three guestrooms but also full dining room service. Ivor enjoys a good overlook of Kingston, a spectacular sight at night. Cost is about US$65 for a double.

Also in the Blue Mountains near Gordon Town and Content Gap are the **Pine Grove Mountain Chalets,** a 90-acre coffee farm with restaurant and bar; call (876) 977-8009 or fax (876) 977-8001. The views are magnificent, ranging a full 360 degrees. Rates are about US$40 for a double. When hiking Blue Mountain peak, many people stay at venerable **Whitfield Hall Hostel,** a dorm-like facility with bunk beds. Rates are US$20–70; call (876) 927-0986 or (876) 926-6612. Younger hikers seem to like the less

The Jamaica you find depends on the people you meet

regimented tone and slightly cheaper rates of nearby **Wildflower Lodge.** Accommodations in the two-story house are similar to Whitfield Hall; call (876) 929-5394. Unfortunately, due to recent security problems, Maya Mountain Lodge is no longer a recommended place to stay.

Camping: The Jamaican Forestry Department offers cabins and dormitories in the Blue Mountains, but permits must be paid for and picked up in advance at the Kingston office. You cannot simply show up at the site and pay. No linens, blankets, or kitchen utensils are at any of the forest camps.

Camping and cabin reservations for all but Whitfield Hall can be made by calling the forestry department at (876) 924-2667 or (876) 924-2668. **Holywell National Recreation Park** offers tent camping and several cabins with fireplace, small kitchen, and full bathroom. **Clydesdale** is an old coffee plantation/pine nursery at 3,700 feet with a bunk bed dormitory that can sleep 30 and more; facilities include flush toilets, showers, and a fire pit for cooking. The walk from Clydesdale to the public **Cinchona Botanical Gardens,** where tent camping is available, takes about an hour. On the hike up Blue Mountain Peak, most people overnight at the privately owned **Whitfield Hall Hostel,** which may also permit you to tent camp; call (876) 927-0986. About one to one and a half hours beyond Whitfield Hall on the way to the peak is the **Portland Gap Forestry Hut** at 5,200 feet. The hut is rustic and you sleep on the floor. It also has running water, an outhouse, and space for about 30 tents. At **Blue Mountain Peak** itself is a rough, graffiti-covered forest hut often used by partying groups from Kingston on weekends. Water may not be readily available, and it gets quite cold at the peak from December through February. Tent camping is permitted.

Currency: Prices are usually posted in Jamaican dollars, but check to make sure. The recent exchange rate was roughly US$1 = J$45. When prices are given without any indication whether the are US$ or J$, the price usually is in U.S. currency. Always keep currency exchange slips if you intend to convert back before departing. In Montego Bay there is a bank in the departure lounge, but it usually has long lines and if you're running late, you may not have time to take care of business. Banks are open 9 a.m.–5 p.m. Monday through Friday.

Taxes & Tips: A government tax of 12% on all hotel rooms, 15% on all rental cars, and 15% on overseas phone calls. Tipping is 10–15% although a service charge of this amount is usually added to all bills. The airport departure tax is J$1,000 (US$22), payable in either currency.

Electrical Current: Most hotels have 110 volts, 60 cycles, as in the United States. Older properties may run on 220 volts, requiring an adapter and transformer.

Safety & Health Warning: Be very careful where you walk after dark, particularly around downtown Kingston. Crime is an increasing problem, mainly pick-pocketing. However, despite the occasional bad publicity, Jamaica's crime rate is lower than most North American cities. Don't leave any valuables unattended anywhere; use hotel safes. Police use surprise roadblocks to catch those carrying drugs. Use the obvious care you would traveling anywhere and you should be fine; don't get caught off guard by too relaxed an attitude.

Snakes and Other Venomous Creatures: None.

Hiking and Walking Services: The number of hiking operations has mushroomed in the last decade. Ten years ago there was only one real guide service, Maya Mountain Lodge at Jack's Hill, Kingston. The guide service arm of Maya is known as **Destinations,** (876) 960-5705. Guides are US$28 per day, up to US$100 for specialists in ornithology or entomology. Maya Lodge is the starting point for many hikes that you can make with or without a guide. The trails (locally called "tracks") lead three hours to the top of Jack's Hill (2,050 feet) or Peter's Rock (2,900 feet); return the same route. It's seven hours either to Mount Horeb (5,000 feet) via Holywell or Mount Roseana (4,100 feet), also circular hikes. A tough walk is the 11-hour trek and return to the Cinchona Botanical Gardens (5,200 feet).

    Sun Venture, 30 Balmoral Ave., Kingston, (876) 960-6685 or fax (876) 929-7512), will take you up Blue Mountain Peak by day or night. If you go by day, you can camp the night, meet the sunrise, and then tackle neighboring East Peak before returning. Sun Venture also offers a wide variety of hikes, including three-day hikes. Costs vary, from US$35 for group of three or more to US$50 for a single hiker.

    Blue Mountain Adventure Tours: Located in the remote village of Section. Local guides charge US$20–50 per day depending on their knowledge and expertise; phone (876) 997-8044.

    Touring Society of Jamaica: Located at Strawberry Hill, this group offers custom Blue Mountain tours for bird-watchers and botanists at US$250 per day for 1 to 4 persons. They also offer walks to waterfalls and other sites. Call (876) 954-2383.

    Veterans Hiking Group: A Jamaican club that makes weekend hikes into the Blue and John Crow Mountains; visitors welcome. Expect to split some of the costs. Call (876) 924-2667.

    Valley Hikes: This group specializes in hikes near Port Antonio and the Rio Grande Valley. Valley Hikes has established a number of trails that range from easy to rugged. They include hikes deep into the Rio Grande Valley, to ruins of old banana plantations, waterfalls, and caves. Special tours are offered into the Land of Look Behind, Maroon Country, which was settled by runaway slaves. All guides are from the Rio Grande Valley and knowledgeable about bush medicine, plants, and bird life. Multiday package tours include meals, lodging, transportation, and guides. Guided hikes of 3 to 4 hours average US$35 per person; 4–6-hour hikes are US$35–50. In Jamaica, contact Valley Hikes at (876) 993-3881 (tel. and fax). Valley Hikes is represented in the United States by Unique Destinations. Phone and fax (401) 934-3398; www.portantoniojamaica.com.

    Cockpit Country Adventure Tours takes visitors into the Trelawny area, the Cockpit Country located between Montego Bay and Mandeville. Hikes include the Burnt Hill Road natural history tour, a 3.5-hour trip between historic Albert Town and Barbeque Bottom with an emphasis on nature viewing, herbal cures, and local folklore. The four-hour Rock Spring Cave and River Adventure is an exploration of the 1.5-mile-long cave, which is riddled with chambers and formations. You'll get wet and dirty in the cave because you have to cross underground rivers; helmets and lanterns are provided. The Quashie River Sink, Cave and Bush Tour is a demanding five-hour trek that starts with a

The Blue Mountains grow the Caribbean's best coffee

hike up Congo Hill and a natural history lesson along the way. Following a bush-cook of traditional foods at Quashie River Sink, it's down into the cave via steep ladders and rope handrails, ending in a huge cathedral room and a rope-assisted waterfall descent. Unusual cave formations and fossil remains are among the many high points. Cost for the trips are between US$20 and US$40 per person. To contact Cockpit Country Adventure Tours, call (876) 610-0818; fax (876) 610-0819.

Countrystyle Limited, located in the Astra hotel in Mandeville, can make hiking arrangements and customize special interest trips. For more information, contact them at (876) 962-3725; fax (876) 962-1461.

For tours in the St. Elizabeth region, contact **St. Elizabeth Safaris:** (876) 965-2374. Located ten miles south of Ocho Rios at Goshen, St. Ann, is the **Wilderness Adventure Outpost.** Short hikes are just one of its specialties, which include fishing, horseback riding and guided ATV tours.

Additional Information: In the United States, call (800) JAMAICA; www.jamaicatravel.com; email jamaicatrav@aol.com. In London, 1–2 Prince Consort Rd., London, England SW7 2BZ; call (441) 71 224 0505; fax (41) 71 224 0551; email jtb_uk@compuserve.com.

Special Hiking Note: Jamaica may be considered a tropical island, but most of the organized hiking in the Blue Mountains near Kingston is done at altitude. The rule of thumb for the Blue Mountains is a temperature drop of 3° F for every 1,000 feet. Atop Blue Mountain Peak after a winter cold front it may drop below freezing. The lowest recorded temperature is around 25 degrees F. Definitely not sandals and T-shirt weather, especially if the wind blows, as it usually does.

All hiking times given, assume you *don't* stop to take a few puffs of the local herbs and commune with nature. It may take as much as 50% longer (perhaps more) to hike stoned unless you are a regular connoisseur of cannabis. Jamaica's ganja is known for its wallop. Of course, it is also illegal.

Afoot in the Blue and John Crow Mountains National Park

The famed Blue Mountains are part of the 194,000-acre Blue and John Crow Mountains National Park, which represents 6 percent of Jamaica's total land mass. The country's largest national park, it includes Blue Mountain Peak, the Clydesdale Forest Reserve, and Holywell Recreational Park. It's also the watershed for more than a million people, raining as much as 300 inches a year in parts of the John Crows, sometimes as much as a foot in a single night.

The Blue Mountains, higher than any in the eastern United States, are so tall that they serve as beacons for some migratory birds. Both the Blue and John Crow Mountains also contain much of the Caribbean's last migratory habitat. One of the world's most diverse tropical rain forests, the park also is the habitat of more than 800 plants found nowhere else on earth and home to the hemisphere's second largest butterfly, the giant swallowtail.

Without its park status, the Blue Mountains would likely turn into the "Brown Mountains." As much as 3 percent of the country's forests were lost annually for charcoal making, vegetable growing, and ganja farming. Many squatters have moved in and started raising vegetables on small farms even though they don't own the land. Their produce is certainly needed to help feed the Kingston area, but at the same time the farming is doing irreparable damage.

1. Blue Mountain Peak Hike

Length: 14 miles round-trip from Whitfield Hall Hostel; starting at Mavis Bank adds 7 additional miles one-way. | **Time:** 2 full days. The first afternoon trek to Whitfield Hall Hostel takes 3–5 hours. The trip to the peak takes 3–4 hours. The return to Whitfield Hall averages 2–3 hours. | **Difficulty:** 3–5 depending on the part of the track. | **Trailhead:** Mavis Bank or Whitfield Hall.

Much of the forest that remains includes many introduced species (particularly from Australia), such as eucalyptus, which can tower as much as 150 feet high.

Without doubt, one of the Caribbean's best hikes. If you make no other walk in Jamaica, this is the one to take. The peak has one of the remaining remnants of montane mist forest, a name derived from the mist that often hovers on the peaks between 10 a.m. and 4 p.m. Elfin woodland begins at about 5,500 feet, gradually fading into windswept scrub at the summit.

Trees at the peak are gnarled, short, and twisted. They often wear a greenish-gray moss, ferns, lichens, epiphytes, and sometimes host a dwarf species of orchid. Flowers hardy enough to grow in the chilly climate include honeysuckle, rhododendron, ginger lilies, and the so-called Jamaica rose.

EXPECT THE UNEXPECTED

Hiking trips don't always run smoothly. One of the most memorable parts of my Blue Mountain Peak hike is where many things went wrong after the climb was over. A car was supposed to come to Mavis Bank for me and my guide, Buckey. The car never showed up, so Buckey and I tried to board the bus to Kingston, an hour's drive away. Pulling up, the bus driver announced his vehicle was broken and there was no telling when a replacement would arrive. Then he walked off.

About 40 of us stood at the bus stop. We all needed to get back to Kingston that night. But how? Rescue came in the form of a driver with a huge flatbed truck with tall sides. The driver would take us to Kingston, for a price. When Buckey and I finally climbed aboard, the truck was full of people jammed together standing like telephone poles.

As the truck pulled away, the driver began shouting crazily, and we all suddenly realized just how drunk he was. He barreled down the mountain with a great grinding and shifting of heavy gears, stopping at every little shop to replenish his empty rum bottle. We yelled at the shops not to sell him any more drink. Thankfully (or I might not be writing this) all the shops owners responded to our

The full hike up Blue Mountain Peak typically begins at Mavis Bank, situated at about 2,500 feet, where you'll immediately descend 1,000 feet to cross the Clyde and Green Rivers. Although this descent is well shaded, you face an open, continuous climb from Green River to the community of Penlyne Castle before reaching Whitfield Hall Hostel. This climb is usually made in the afternoon, the warmest part of the day. Because there is no forest canopy to shade you, expect to work up quite a sweat getting to Penlyne Castle. Some consider this leg the toughest part of the entire summit hike. A small collapsible umbrella keeps off the sun.

You should arrive at Whitfield Hall Hostel, a 200-year-old coffee plantation home surrounded by eucalyptus trees, in late afternoon. Whitfield Hall, located at 4,200 feet, is the farthest you can drive up Blue Mountain Peak. The majority of hikers motor here, then lace up their boots for the hike. If you've walked up from Mavis Bank, judge not harshly those who didn't. Yes, they are only 3,000 feet to the peak from Whitfield Hall, and you've just climbed 2,700 feet just to reach the hostel, but try not to call them wimps, at least to their fresh, clean faces.

Whitfield Hall, made mostly of cedar, sleeps between 30 to 40 people in bunk and double beds; it also has a full bathroom, including a shower. A huge fireplace cuts the chill in the large communal dining area. Kitchen facilities are available, but you must bring your own food. If you're hiking on your own, make advance reservations to ensure a place to sleep, (876) 927-0986. Sometimes the caretaker will check the sky around 10 p.m. to predict whether the peak will be cloudy or clear the next morning. The forecast is usually accurate.

After dinner is a good time to read comments in the guest book penned by previous hikers. Using a kerosene lamp (the only illumination available) you will find such thoughtful compleas. Each time the driver was refused more rum he returned to the truck, cursing and grumbling, and threatened to make us all get off. Then we would lurch down the hill again.

The truck's great horn blared at every curve but we rarely slowed down. As I gripped the side of the truck and continually ducked tree branches I wondered if we would successfully navigate the next corner. Was my Caribbean hiking odyssey going to suddenly end in the back of a truck with all these laughing and yelling Jamaicans? Before long, I found myself yelling and laughing along with them. What a roller-coaster ride it was! This situation was out of my control. Either I would survive this, or I would not. My fingers were cramped for 30 minutes after we arrived in Kingston.

I had been up since 2 a.m. for the Blue Mountain Peak climb, but my day was not yet over. Around midnight, several locals and I climbed the water tank overlooking Kingston. What an unforgettable view ... and climb down.

Obviously, none of the evening's events were planned or supposed to happen, yet they are some of my best memories.

ments as "Never again!" or my favorite by Rosalie Alexander of Kingston: "I was an ass to return after all these years, to endure the torture and pain, and the rain, the miserable ass-holes that came along. Next time I'll stay at Whitfield Hall." Based on these comments, visitors seem to enjoy the hike more than Jamaicans do.

Most people don't hike up strange mountains in the dark, but you should start the second leg of the climb at 2 a.m. if you want to reach the summit in time to greet the sunrise. Before setting out, eat something and gulp some strong Blue Mountain coffee; the energy will be needed. Good flashlights are essential because there are some sharp drop-offs and you don't want to put your foot in the wrong place. Even Jamaicans have gotten lost in the dark, not finding their way back for several days. In daylight, the track to the peak from Whitfield Hall is clearly defined, and it's also pretty obvious during a full moon.

During the nighttime ascent, you'll have a wonderful, unpolluted view of the stars and the coastal town of Kingston, which looks as brightly lit as Los Angeles. The first hour is the toughest, encountering a stretch called Jacob's Ladder, which you blunder into almost immediately while you're still partially asleep. After about ten minutes you may begin to wonder whatever possessed you to go stumbling around in the wilderness at an hour so ungodly that even the marijuana growers are still asleep.

About 2.5 miles from Whitfield Hall, you'll reach the campground at Portland Gap, 5,200 feet, which has a water tap and room for up to 30 people. (To stay here, make reservations through the Forest Department in Kingston; call (876) 924-2667.) Once you arrive at Portland Gap, it's only 3.5 miles more to the summit.

Past Portland Gap, you'll climb through a series of switchbacks. You'll know you're close to the top when you reach "Lazy Man's Peak," a steep slope where the trail appears to turn inland. The agonizing sight of the track disappearing farther uphill convinces many to stop and declare this the finish line. However, it's only another five to seven minutes from here to the actual top. The peak appears suddenly, as you turn a corner, and it's one of the sweetest sights on earth. This is the true peak, the place to sit down and honestly say, "I've done it!"

What other emotions you feel will depend on the weather. You may not see anything except the inside of a cloud, which covers the peak much of the time. If you have a clear morning, as I did, you'll enjoy a great overview of the Blue Mountains.

If you still have more stamina and a good guide, you can continue another hour to the nearby summit of East Peak, but it's not recommended that you try for East Peak without expert help.

Coming back down, the trail looks very different in daylight. Some hikers swear that if they'd seen in advance the route they would be forced to climb, they never would have attempted it, fearing the track too difficult. So there are some advantages to climbing in the dark. You'll be back down the mountain and at Whitfield Hall between 9 a.m. and 11 a.m., depending on how long you tarry at the top.

If all this sounds like too much work, it is possible to arrange for horses or mules to carry you from Whitfield Hall, even in the dark. Given a choice, take a mule over a horse. Not only are mules more sure-footed and less likely to spook, they won't rub your backside as raw as the gait of a horse may.

Hikers with a good sense of direction should be able to make the climb on their own. However, a guide usually makes the trek more enjoyable. A good guide contributes to at least half of the experience. And he does all the cooking.

Hikes in the Jack's Hill Area

2. Old Vinegar Hill Trail

Length: 25 miles one-way. | **Time:** 2–3 days. | **Difficulty:** 3. Not as steep at Blue Mountain Peak. | **Trailhead:** Maya Mountain Lodge, at Juba Springs on Jack's Hill.

This hike is a beauty because it takes you through the wilderness along a historic route that dates to the 1600s, when people would go by mule, donkey, horse, or foot. Once the only regular trading route between Port Antonio on the North Coast and Kingston, it is little used now. Today the track is used by only a handful of people (local farmers) each month. Farmers on the north side of the mountain grow yams and root crops, and those on south produce spices, herbs, and vegetables. You will need to hire a guide to follow this little-used trail.

The track goes up to Holywell, along an especially striking stretch called the Fairy Glades Trail, through Silver Hill Gap, and over Morris Gap (5,700 feet) on the Grand Ridge of the Blue Mountains. Old Vinegar Hill is the only trail that goes over the Grand Ridge.

On the north side, you're in genuine wilderness. You'll also pass through a pristine montane forest, some of Jamaica's last. Because it is largely untouched, it surpasses the vegetation of Blue Mountain Peak.

You'll pass through Vinegar Hill at about 3,000 feet, then come down to about 2,000 feet where you can be picked up and taken to Crystal Springs, a 200-acre property with cottages about a half hour away. Crystal Springs has the largest orchid collection in Jamaica, about 25,000 plants, located right beside the Spanish River.

You may want to take a side trip off the Vinegar Hill Trail to visit My Best Falls. This ten-mile round trip takes about five to eight hours. The exact height of the falls isn't known, but they're estimated at 700–900 feet, which would make them among Jamaica's highest. The water cascades over in a single drop, with a ledge partway down.

3. MAYA LODGE CIRCLE HIKE

Length: 12 miles. | **Time:** 6–9 hours round trip. | **Difficulty:** 2–3. |
Trailhead: Maya Lodge in Jack's Hill, on Peters Rock Road, (876) 702-0314.

You could make a loop or do it a little easier with a pickup at Gordon Town. Passing through coffee plantations and montane forest, you come back down along waterfalls, a river valley and through a couple of villages. The steepest part is the Fairy Glades Trail, which requires a couple of scrambles. Maya Lodge offers lodging and guides to the area.

4. JACK'S HILL TO PETER'S ROCK

Time: 2 hours, one way. | **Difficulty:** 3. | **Trailhead:** The Adventist Church at Jack's Hill.

Head down Jack's Hill Road, cross a small bridge and turn right. After passing a vegetable garden, turn left (uphill) and walk until you reach an old road. Turn right and follow the road up the ridge and to the left.

After about 20 minutes you'll reach a section of tall grass, but the trail should be plainly visible. It's going to get steep fast, so you may consider a couple of rest stops. An hour later you'll make a strenuous hike up a ledge to Peter's Rock, elevation 2,894 feet. The rock is distinctive for its pyramid frame and stone foundation.

From the rock you should be able to see the village of Woodford, where you can arrange to be picked up. If not, begin the return walk or continue on to Holywell recreation area (see hike below).

5. PETER'S ROCK TO HOLYWELL

Time: 2 hours, one way. | **Difficulty:** 3. | **Trailhead:** Peter's Rock (above), reached after a 2-hour trek from Jack's Hill.

If you decide to walk all the way from Jack's Hill to the 300-acre Holywell Recreational Park, you'll probably want to stay in the park so you can explore the many area trails. Camping is US$5 per person. You can rent one of the three cabins, but they must be booked in advance, (876) 924-2667. The cabins cost only about US$20 per night. Understandably, many people come up from Kingston on weekends to take advantage of the always-cool climate.

To reach Holywell from Peter's Rock, go south to pick up the paved road that will take you uphill to the village of Woodford. Go past the post office. Near the last refreshment stand on the right, turn left and go uphill via a dirt road. A little over 30 minutes later you'll encounter a T intersection in the road. Turn left. You'll walk another hour before arriving at the concrete posts and metal gate that mark the Holywell Recreational Area. Enter the park and in a few minutes you'll reach the picnic tables and shelters and the cabins for overnighting. A large information board outlines the area's many trails.

If you plan to spend any time here, make sure you have rain gear. About 100 inches of liquid sunshine fall annually.

HIKES IN THE NEWCASTLE AND HOLYWELL AREA

The town of Newcastle, located two miles below Holywell, is the common trailhead for several well-known hikes. To reach Newcastle, take the B1, the principal access road for Blue Mountain hiking.

Newcastle has an interesting history. The British established it in 1841 because troops manning the lowland forts were dying of yellow fever in alarming numbers. The buttercups that grew in great numbers following the rains were blamed for exuding some sort of effluvium that caused the deadly sickness. The troops were stationed high in the forest at Newcastle so they would be far enough away from the buttercup fields to be affected. It was much later before someone made the connection between yellow fever and the hearty, thriving mosquito population that—along with the buttercups—also mushroomed with the rains.

Black slaves were much less susceptible to yellow fever than their British owners. Slaves named the buttercups after the white people (or "backras"), calling them "kill-backras." The saying also developed that "if backra wants to live long, he must ask nayga leave," because it appeared the less sickly slaves knew the secret to good health and long life.

Almost all of the area's hikes, such as the Fern Walk Trail, start at the Old Stables Inn.

6. OATLEY MOUNTAIN TRAIL

Time: 45–60 minutes. | **Difficulty:** 1–2. | **Trailhead:** Near the ranger station at Holywell Recreational Park.

Oatley Mountain is the forest behind the ranger station where this loop trail goes through the tunnel-like jungle of the small mountain. Platforms and towers offer many good views. You can continue on the **Waterfall Trail** (1.5 miles), which follows a riverbed to the Cascade Waterfall near the Green Hills Guesthouse. It's about a mile's walk back to Holywell from the guesthouse. A third Holywell Park Trail, the **Shelter Trail,** also departs near the ranger station. This 30- to 45-minute hike leads to a picnic shelter that offers a fine view.

7. MIDDLETON MOUNTAIN TRAIL

Length: 3 miles. | **Time:** 4–5 hours. | **Difficulty:** 3–4. | **Trailhead:** Cascade Waterfall near the Green Hills Guesthouse, a mile past Holywell on the B1.

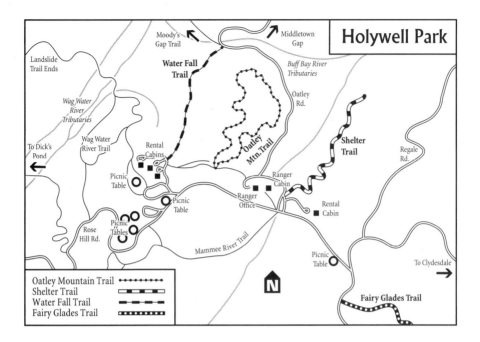

Oatley Mountain Trail ●●●●●●●●
Shelter Trail ▬■▬■▬■
Water Fall Trail ▬ ■ ▬ ■ ▬
Fairy Glades Trail ◆◆◆◆◆◆◆◆

Holywell Park

This uphill trek in the bush parallels the B1 road. You'll enjoy some good mountain views, ford a shallow river in two places, and end at the Wakefield district, also on the B1.

8. FAIRY GLADES TRAIL

Time: 2.5 hours to hike over Mt. Horeb, which will bring you to a road; another 30 minutes to take the road back to Newcastle. | **Difficulty:** 2–3. | **Trailhead:** Depart from the Old Stables Inn in Newcastle

The Fairy Glades Trail can be hiked separately or used as a connecting link with other tracks. One of the prettiest spots in all the Blue Mountains, hundreds of varieties of ferns and orchids grow in this misty, humid place. You will walk through several different forest systems, including montane and elfin woodland. Not a particularly difficult trail, it may require a few scrambles at the outset; the rocks can be slippery and expect a few steep sections. On top of Mt. Horeb, you'll be at 4,894 feet, not high by Jamaican standards but still one the Caribbean's loftier peaks. After Mt. Horeb, you emerge onto the concrete road that will take you back to the B1 and to Newcastle. Or, turn left and head up to Catherine's Peak (see below).

9. CATHERINE'S PEAK

Time: 1.5 hours round-trip from Newcastle. | **Difficulty:** 2–3. | **Trailhead:** Turn left at the end of the Fairy Glades Trail (above) or start at the Old Stables Inn, first taking the B1 and then hiking up the concrete road that branches off just north of Newcastle.

This hike was named for Catherine Long, who climbed the 5,060-foot peak in 1760; she was the first woman known to have scaled it. She had a much tougher time of it back then; she didn't have the concrete road available to modern-day hikers.

From the end of Fairy Glades Trail, follow the trail up a steep grade, with lots of tree ferns and rose apple trees along the road. It's often misty here but you'll enjoy a good view of Kingston if it clears.

10. WOODCUTTER'S GAP

Time: 2–3 hours. | **Difficulty:** 2–3. | **Trailhead:** Off the Catherine's Peak Road (see above).

Before reaching the top of Catherine's Peak, look on the left for the sign marking the trailhead to Woodcutter's Gap. The trail leads down into the valley known as Woodcutter's Gap. The hard part is where the trail rises to meet up with the Kingston-Buff Bay Road (B1), not far from Holywell.

However, you also have the chance to join two other trails at Woodcutter's Gap. If you go left you will be on the **Green Hills Trail** and exit on the Kingston-Buff Bay Road near the village called Section, famed for its Blue Mountain coffee. If you turn right at Woodcutter's Gap, you will join the **Silver Hill Gap Trail** that comes out at Silver Hill village just west of the B1. At this point you have a couple of options. From here you are only several miles from the forest camp of Clydesdale. You can also follow the road farther south through Content Gap and to Guava Ridge. At Guava Ridge you pick up the road leading back to Kingston.

11. COLD SPRING

Length: 4.5 miles. | **Time:** 6 hours. | **Difficulty:** 3. | **Trailhead:** The starting point is about 0.5 mile north of St. Peters on the same road that runs from Silver Hill to Content Gap.

Leave the road behind and follow trail as it winds north, eventually joining the two-mile Clifton Mountain Trail, which also begins in St. Peters. Both the Cold Spring and Clifton Mountain Trails run parallel before ending at Newcastle, about a half-mile farther on. You should have some good views of Kingston on a clear day.

12. CLYDESDALE TO CINCHONA

Time: 2 hours. | **Difficulty:** 2–3. | **Trailhead:** The town camp at Clydesdale near St. Peters.

Clydesdale is the name of both a town and one of the several forestry camps welcoming hikers to set up tents. Located on the River Clyde, about 1.5 miles up a bumpy road near St. Peters, the forestry camp (a former coffee plantation) rents a two-bedroom house. No bedding or other essentials are supplied. Advance reservations must be made through the forestry department in Kingston, (876) 924-2667.

The Cinchona Botanical Gardens was originally established in 1868 to cultivate Assam tea and the cinchona, a tree native to the high Andes whose bark supplies quinine for the treatment of malaria. The project was profitable only for a short time because large-scale production in India undercut the market. The operation was then turned into a botanical garden, one of three on the island that collected and studied exotic trees and plants from other continents. Many trees are from Australia, including the Caribbean's largest collection of eucalyptus trees, some over 150 feet high. Orchids, lilies, azaleas, and many other flowers make this a distinctive garden set at 5,000 feet. For information, call (876) 927-1257.

The walk to Cinchona is fairly easy, along a sometimes steep road that connects Clydesdale with the gardens. At the town of Clydesdale follow the descending road on the right that passes the old wooden coffee mill house. About 100 yards later the road divides. Go right and travel up to the junction at Top Mountain where the road becomes fit only for four-wheel-drive. Follow the left track to Cinchona Gardens. This last section is the steepest. You'll ascend 1,000 feet in less than two miles, but the trek is worth it because of the panoramic view in all directions. The John Crow and St. John's Peak are to the north, Kingston to the south and the main ridge of the Blue Mountains off to the east.

A half-dozen other hiking trails also end up here, making this a popular destination. From Cinchona you can hike to Westphalia, across the Green River to Penlyne Castle and to venerable Whitfield Hall, starting point for Blue Mountain Peak hikes.

HIKES IN THE JOHN CROW MOUNTAINS

The wettest part of Jamaica is the John Crow Mountains, which absorb the full brunt of the moisture-laden air coming off the Caribbean. This region reportedly receives as much as 300 inches of rain annually. The name John Crow is the local term for the turkey vulture (buzzard), the bald, red-headed scavengers that often make their nests in cliff hollows and on ledges.

The John Crows are considered almost inaccessible because of the great amount of rainfall, which eats away the limestone crust. The terrain is also steep in places and the rain forest is impassable following a downpour. It's said the last time anyone went through the heart of the John Crows was over a century ago, in 1890, a major expedition that lasted 12 days. In the lower altitudes of 1,000 to 2,000 feet, the explorers reported Amazon-like rain forest with 100- to 150-foot-tall trees. Today, no trails go through the John Crows, only along the edge and a short way into them.

Many trails begin or end at the town of Millbank, five miles south of Moore Town. Little-visited (the road stops at Moore Town), and fairly basic, this is the heart of Maroon country. Moore Town is, in fact, the capital of the Windward Maroons.

The Maroons are descendants of slaves who ran away from their Spanish and English masters in the 1600s. The Spanish called them *cimarron,* meaning "wild" or "untamed." To avoid capture, the Maroons retreated into the northern slopes of the Blue Mountains and into the trackless Cockpit Country. The Maroons were experts in guerrilla warfare who disguised themselves with leaves and tree branches from head to foot. They would "bush ambush" by surprise attacks with machetes and by stationing sharpshooters in the rocks. The Maroons were notorious for their ability to vanish without a trace, often into caves concealed behind waterfalls.

The First Maroon War ended only after the British sent in more troops along with Indians from the Mosquito Coast, tracker dogs, and freed slaves. Finally, they were able to destroy Nanny Town, the stronghold of Queen Nanny of the Windward Maroons who lived high in the Blue Mountains. The town, never rebuilt, is said to be haunted by Maroons killed in the battle. But they were not the first Maroons to surrender. The other contingent of Maroons who lived in the Cockpit Country surrendered in 1739 when their supplies were nearly depleted. The Blue Mountain's Windward Maroons followed a year later. Thus ended the First Maroon War.

The second began in 1795, and for five months 300 Maroons waged battle against 1,500 European troops and 3,000 local militia. The Maroons totally disrupted Jamaican life. One writer at the time said the island "seemed more like a garrison . . . than a country of commerce and culture." The Maroons surrendered only after 100 bloodhounds used for hunting runaway slaves were imported from Cuba.

Although the Maroons lost this second war, they continued to live apart and to develop their own culture. The Maroons still act like an independent nation with their own government subdivisions headed by colonels. Moore Town is home to the Maroon colonel who will find you a guide.

To reach Moore Town from Port Antonio, take the road to the town of Fellowship, then proceed through Newington and Windsor. Turn left at Seaman's Valley. The rocky road leads to Moore Town.

The oldest of the Maroon colonels is Col. Harris, who lives in the cement house next to the post office. Col. Stirling, the official leader, lives a little farther on. The monument across from the school, Bump Grave, marks the grave of legendary Nanny, founder of the town and now an official national hero.

To reach Millbank, trailhead for most hikes, turn right at Seaman's Valley instead of left. Millbank has no real accommodations. The closest is the Ambassabeth Cabins and Campsite, (876) 938-5036, at Bowden. The cabins have no electricity or running water. Bowden is an hour's walk south of Millbank. The reason to walk instead of drive is the rope-and-board suspension bridge that crosses the Rio Grande River, the only dry crossing to Bowden.

13. WHITE RIVER FALLS

Length: 4 miles. | **Time:** 7 hours. | **Difficulty:** 3–4. A guide is recommended. | **Trailhead:** Millbank

It's a fairly tough climb through pristine rain forest as you trace the White River to reach its seven different cascades. Most hikers stop after seeing the first one or two. You'll have to scramble up a slippery trail to reach the first fall, but your reward will be to thoroughly chill yourself in the cold water.

14. NANNY TOWN OVERNIGHT TREK

Length: Estimates vary from 10–15 miles. | **Time:** 1 day each way. | **Difficulty:** 4–5. | **Trailhead:** Millbank

From a distance, this looks like a trapezoid bump on the ridge of the Blue Mountains. Nanny Town was destroyed by the British and their allies during the First Maroon War. Nanny was the "skilled chieftaness" of the Windward Maroons, and Nanny Town was her stronghold. Ghosts of Maroons killed at Nanny Town are said to haunt the site. As for Nanny, she has been declared a national hero and goes by the charming title of "The Right Excellent Nanny."

This is not an easy hike. You should have a strong desire to see remote historical sites and/or to wander among spectacular forest to make the trek. Either reason is good enough if you have the endurance. Ask to see Nanny's Pot, a deep basin at the foot of Chatter Falls. "The Right Excellent Nanny" is said to have thrown British soldiers into a steaming cauldron there.

15. MILLBANK TO BATH

Length: 10–14 miles, one way. | **Time:** 6–7 hours. | **Difficulty:** 4–5. | **Trailhead:** Millbank

You have a choice of paths from Millbank. Both end at the Bath mineral springs north of Morant Bay. The tougher and longer route is to cross 2,250-foot high Corn Puss Gap (you have to love the name). This route passes through some of Jamaica's last true, virgin rain forest where the only residents are birds and butterflies. You may also have to ford streams that may be as much as waist deep.

The alternative trail is easier, mostly downhill through a shady forest skirting the dense growth (but at least you get a good look at it from a distance). This track runs from Millbank to Cuna-Cuna Pass (at 2,750 feet) to Hayfield before reaching Bath village.

16. BOWDEN TO ROAD END

Length: 2 miles. | **Time:** 2 hours. | **Difficulty:** 1–2. | **Trailhead:** Past the Ambassabeth Campground at the village of Bowden, south of Millbank.

You'll be hiking the wide road built in the 1970s by former British servicemen given large tracts of land. They planned to build a very prosperous community, and this road was supposed to lead to Bath village. It was completed less than a third of the way. The prospective settlers departed after finding the conditions too harsh and primitive.

The grassy road with its tree ferns takes you past Three Finger Jack spring, Quako River, waterfalls, and swimming holes before finding the road's end at the Rio Grande River. That's enough scenic places to make you may wonder whether the project was abandoned too soon.

ELSEWHERE ON JAMAICA

17. HELLSHIRE HILLS

Located very close to Kingston, this dry tropical forest gets only 30–40 inches of rain each year. The tree canopy here is a low 50 feet. Lots of cactus and what is known as macca bush, with prickles and thorns, grow here. The seven- to eight-foot-long Jamaican iguana, which until recently was thought to be extinct is here.

Rain makes the exposed limestone rock very sharp. Some local hikers half-jokingly suggest that if you hike along the coast here, you will need a new pair of shoes because of all the sharp rock. This wilderness would take a couple of days to hike through completely, but most people are content to go in and come back out the same day. Only one trail actually goes through the Hellshires, the other follows the coast.

THE COCKPIT COUNTRY

18. MONTEGO BAY-MANDEVILLE REGION

A tough hiking terrain similar to the John Crow Mountains, the Cockpit Country is a high plateau southeast of Montego Bay in the remote center of the island. It was a Maroon refuge in the 1600s, and their descendants reside here. The region is considered impassable except on foot. Not even four-wheel-drive vehicles attempt the Cockpits, which is largely uncharted.

It takes about a day to cross the Cockpit Country. You need to backpack overnight or have someone pick you up at the other end. This can be quite warm walking, very humid with jungly rain forest. Take lots of water; there is none available outside of the villages. A bromeliad called wine pine contains as much as a pint of water if you run seriously short. Ask a local to show you one.

The most comfortable time for walking is in the winter months, also the driest part of the year for a region with an annual rainfall of 100–150 inches. Mist often rolls in early and late. Ants and mosquitoes can be a bother; do be careful of your footing, not to break through the limestone crust.

The Cockpit Country is surrounded by mountains and limestone hills shaped like cones, some rugged but mostly round. Known technically as karst formations (a relatively rare phenomenon in the Caribbean) the landscape appears like the bottom of an egg carton, all steep ups and downs

This topography results when the limestone surface dissolves from rainfall while at the same time underground water forms caverns and caves. Because only a thin layer of limestone covers many of the deep caverns formed by such erosion, a single misstep could send you falling into some underground pit with serious consequences. A guide is a must. It's easy to get hurt in the Cockpits.

This strange-looking land of caves and ravines and thick, thorny vegetation also has typical lowland rain forest with a canopy of 80–100 feet. Broadleaf, mahogany, silk cotton, and mahoe trees all grow here. You may see hawks, parrots, and red-crested woodpeckers in the trees. Avoid the green plant with serrated leaves called a scratchbush; it will leave you itching for days. The Cockpit Country is a good area for long pants.

One of the best places from which to explore the area is Accompong, located just north of Maggotty. To reach Accompong, take the main (A2) road and turn north at Lacovia to Maggotty. Just beyond Maggotty you should begin seeing signs to Accompong, located to the north.

If you're traveling independently, call ahead to Mr. and Mrs. Harris Cawley (phone (876) 909-9222), the former Maroon colonel at Accompong who will arrange for a guide. Try to give him several days notice. If you plan to camp, you may need porters to carry food and equipment. The cost for a guide is modest, about US$20 per day.

In addition to several day trips, two trails about eight miles long cross the Cockpits and reach elevations of 3,000 feet. These tracks are not regularly used and they can be quite overgrown, requiring some machete work. Progress is about a mile per hour because of all the up and down walking—no possibility of going straight as the crow flies. The trails go from Quickstep to Deeside and from Windsor Cave to Crown's Land and onto Troy.

MONTEGO BAY AREA

19. ROSE HALL AND GREENWOOD GREAT HOUSES

For a change of pace, here are a couple of easy walks at two restored plantation houses—Rose Hall and Greenwood. Both are just east of Montego Bay on the road to Ocho Rios.

In the 1700s, Rose Hall may have been the finest great house in the entire West Indies. The great house had fallen into disrepair before it was restored. Rose Hall boasts one of Jamaica's best legends: A young Irish woman named Annie married Rose Hall owner John Porter. Three years later, John Porter mysteriously died, apparently by Annie's hand. She killed two more husbands before a fourth managed to escape. During a slave uprising, Annie herself was killed, leaving her spirit to haunt the house. Rose Hall is open daily 9:30 a.m. to 6 p.m.

Domestic conditions were less volatile at the lesser-known Greenwood Great House, which provides a good look at what life was like on one of the old sugar plantations. A highlight of the tour is the rare book library with copies dating back to 1697. Open daily 9 a.m. to 6 p.m.

Surprisingly, the countryside here is a virtually unknown region and seldom seen by tourists. However, guided walks are expected to become a major attraction in years to come. The river valley has some excellent hiking, but it's difficult to know where the trails start. They're unmarked, so you definitely need a guide to set off on the proper foot. This is low-level hiking between 500 and 1,000 feet, among streams and rivers with interesting views but no forest. The trail system is excellent, link adding to link so you can cover quite a distance. In fact you can walk all over Jamaica this way; it's a matter of knowing where the trails link up.

ST. ELIZABETH AREA

20. BLACK RIVER

The Black River, Jamaica's longest river, begins underground in the Cockpit Country to the north, then emerges north of Siloah. This is a very special walk with 29 waterfalls in two and a half miles. No giant cascades; the tallest is about 40 feet, the smallest around 10. South Coast Safaris offers tours through the Lower Morass of the Black River and treks to YS Falls. Call (876) 965-2513; fax (876) 965-2086.

Jamaica is a land of hidden streams and waterfalls

21. BAMBOO AVENUE

One of the most photographed spots in Jamaica, this huge tunnel is made up of bamboo up to 40 feet tall. Somewhat thinned by hurricane damage, this still is one of the nicest and certainly the longest bamboo avenue around. Creating bamboo walks like this was once a common practice in Jamaica's mountainous areas. The bamboo was planted, one young shoot at a time, to form a canopy that helps preserve dirt roads from erosion.

NINE MILE VILLAGE

22. BOB MARLEY'S GRAVE

Bob Marley, the high priest of reggae, is buried near where he was born, in the tiny village of Nine Mile, south of Runaway Bay between Claremont and Alexandria. It's a small place and not on all maps. The stained glass windows of the small chapel containing the crypt are in the rasta colors of gold, green, and red. Ganja has been known to grow in the church garden. Marley's birthday is February 6; on that night his fans gather to play his music, usually until dawn.

THE OCHO RIOS AREA

23. DUNN'S RIVER FALLS ASCENT

Just two miles from Ocho Rios going to Mo Bay Dunn's River Falls is the most famous cascade in Jamaica, if not the entire Caribbean. This scenic spot is used more than any other place to advertise and symbolize Jamaica. Open daily 8 a.m.–5 p.m.

The name Ocho Rios may not derive from the Spanish term "eight rivers" as is popularly supposed but instead is a very bad corruption of the word *chorreras,* a Spanish term that describes the many streams and rivers that plunge down the limestone rocks. Dunn's River is just one of them.

Dunn's River has 650 beautiful feet of waterfalls that can be climbed either on your own or with the assistance of a paid river guide (they're everywhere, don't worry about finding one). Either way, you will pay an admission fee to enter the lushly landscaped park. The rocks are slick, and some routes definitely work better than others. Watch where the guides go. However, one advantage of having a guide is that he can carry your camera and take pictures of you while you splash in the pools and the falls. Some river guides walk with so many cameras draped around them they look like they're photojournalists covering the arrival of the queen.

Considering that this is cold mountain water, it's most comfortably climbed when the sun and temperatures are at their highest, in the middle of the day. In afternoon, the main falls are fairly shaded. However, this also tends to be the least crowded period, a good time to walk up the rocks and enjoy the solitude.

24. FERN GULLY

Often crowded with auto traffic, there is talk of closing it to vehicles and turning it into a park. You will find several places to turn off and look around. The gully is on the road connecting Ocho Rios and Kingston that passes through Spanish Town.

Jamaica has more than 500 species of ferns, and you can see at least 300 of them in this dark, shaded gorge that's almost three miles in length. Until an earthquake around 1907, the gorge was one of the eight flowing rivers of the Ocho Rios area. The river disappeared during the earthquake, and the river bed was turned into a paved road. The dense fern growth appears to have been growing in place since the beginning of time, despite such a recent start.

25. ORACABESSA AREA

Spymaster Ian Fleming (James Bond) and playwright Sir Noël Coward wouldn't seem to have much in common, but they both did much of their writing on their respective estates near Oracabessa, about 20 miles from Ocho Rios on the way to Port Antonio. Open daily, 8:30 a.m. to 5 p.m. Call (876) 997-7201 for information.

Coward's estate Firefly, which sits 1,000 feet above the coast, is well marked and easier to find. The view from the estate, now a government-sponsored museum dedicated to the English author, is magnificent. The land originally belonged to the pirate Henry Morgan. Coward lived here from the 1950s until his death in 1973. You'll have four acres of grounds and gardens to walk at the top of the hill—no need to climb up the access road from the coast unless you want to. Fireflies are supposed to gather regularly atop the hill at night, supplying the inspiration for the name. Fleming's Goldeneye estate is closed to the public.

NEGRIL

26. NEGRIL BEACH WALK

No true hiking to speak of, only walking along the 5.5-mile beach (not 7 miles, as the brochures say).

Lots of interesting guest houses and hotels, large and small, so this is more of a resort walk than a genuine beach walk. However, you'll probably be hustled and hassled like nowhere else in Jamaica, offered everything under the sun, including sex, ganja, and possibly cocaine, which is imported into the island.

Fronting the westernmost tip of Jamaica, you'd expect Negril to witness many spectacular sunsets and it does. Rick's Cafe is the favorite overlook, a tamer Caribbean version of Key West's famous sunset celebration. The music is loud, the beer is cold, and the women worth watching (veteran travelers agree that Jamaica is home to some of the world's most beautiful women). On the road just beyond Rick's is an old lighthouse noticeable from the seaside bar. If the caretaker will let you in, you'll have a wonderful view from the 100-foot-high lighthouse. He can also show you where to climb down to the sea.

13   MARTINIQUE

Local Saying: "Life is a goat's behind hung up in smoke."

Martinique is a lovely island with some very scenic trails. However, it has a major problem that may make some people think twice about visiting here when there are so many other islands with equally good hiking and far friendlier folk.

Martinique is a little island with a big ego. Too often the attitude is: If you don't speak French, you don't belong here. Even residents who speak English well may refuse to speak to you or acknowledge you if you cannot speak French. For an island whose economy is partially based on tourism, this is a strange attitude. This is a culture where rudeness is considered an art form. I was not at all unhappy when it was time to leave Martinique. If you speak French, you will probably have a different experience.

One reason for this remarkable behavior is that Martinique is more attached to Europe than any other island in the Caribbean. Martiniquans have always had a strong affiliation with France, and in 1974, the island was officially made a region of France. In terms of its economic development, its telephone and road systems, Martinique is certainly on a par with Europe. France has invested a lot of money in Martinique, and it shows. France contributes to almost 70 percent of Martinique's gross national product. The people on Martinique have every right to be proud of their prosperous circumstances. Even so, Martinique's unemployment is among the Caribbean's highest, at about 25 percent. The majority of those who do work are in service jobs, often connected to tourism.

When Christopher Columbus discovered Martinique, its only inhabitants were the Caribs, who by that time had killed off the rival Arawaks. Called "Madinina," or island of flowers by the Caribs, Columbus renamed the island "Martinica" in honor of St. Martin. He said it was "the best, richest, sweetest country in the whole world."

Because of constant battles with the Caribs, Spain gave Martinique up in favor of richer pickings elsewhere. The French planters and accompanying African slaves arrived in 1635. The Caribs wanted nothing to do with any settlers and fought bitterly until 1660, when it was agreed by treaty the Caribs would live only on the Atlantic side. The treaty didn't mean much; soon all the Indians were annihilated.

The English took Martinique in 1762, but traded it back to France in exchange for Tobago, St. Vincent, the Grenadines, Senegal, and a sizable chunk of property called Canada; because of its sugar plantations, Martinique was at the time far richer than the other territories combined.

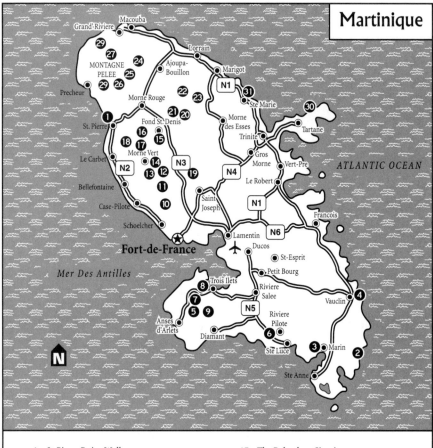

Martinique

The 1789 French Revolution's message of "liberty, equality, and fraternity" was heard in Martinique but disregarded in regard to the slaves. Anxious plantation owners, not wanting to risk the same slave revolts occurring elsewhere, asked the British to return and keep the peace, which they did from 1794 to 1802. England and France stopped fighting over the island in 1815, when it was returned to France. The French abolished slavery in 1848.

Martinique still has a very active volcano, which completely destroyed the former capital city of St-Pierre in 1902. The city of Fort-de-France, built around Fort St. Louis in the seventeenth century, was named the new capital. Located well away from Mount Pelee and its destructive force, Fort-de-France holds most of the island's population. The rubble of St-Pierre is now one of the island's main tourist attractions. Mount Pelee, quiet since 1902, contains many popular hiking trails.

TRAVEL TIPS

Area: 425 square miles; 50 miles long and 22 miles wide. Dominica is 15.5 miles to the north, St. Lucia 23 miles to the south.

Language: French and Creole. English is spoken only in larger tourist hotels. You may be viewed as uneducated if you do not speak French.

Population: 392,000, of which about 200,000 live in Fort-de-France.

Time Zone: Atlantic Time, one hour ahead of Eastern Standard Time.

Rainy Season: Considerably more rain falls here than on many other islands because of the high mountain contours. Wettest period is from June to November; rain can be heavy and sudden. Always be prepared.

Getting There: American Eagle, (800) 433-7300, flies here from San Juan. LIAT, (800) 468-0482, and Air Martinique fly in from neighboring islands. Air France flies directly from Europe and through Miami. Most of those flying in are French. However, most of the visitors from cruise ships are North Americans.

Documents: This is Europe, remember. You'll need a passport. And a return or ongoing ticket. Visas are required of some nationalities, but not U.S. or Canadian citizens.

Getting Around: Rental cars are available at the airport, though you want to avoid driving in the incredibly congested downtown of Fort-de-France, where parking is legal only if you have a season pass. For the best rates, make reservations while in the United States and rent only from one of the U.S. big three: Avis, Hertz, or Budget because of billing/mechanical complaints about local rental companies. There is a 9.5% VAT added to the rental total. Mopeds and bicycles are also easily available. Buses and taxis are other options for getting out into the countryside. Taxis are unmetered, so agree on price in advance; a 40% surcharge is in effect from 7 p.m. to 6 a.m. The roads are well marked and well maintained. Driving is on the right.

Where to Stay: Prices are high, almost equal to what you would pay in Europe. Best values are the family-run "auberges" in the more remote and scenic northern parts of the island, where you'll also find the best hiking. One of the most convenient is **Auberge de la Montagne Pelee,** located at the foot of the volcano at Morne Rouge. It offers eight rooms and several bungalows with hot water, a real necessity at this high, cool altitude.

Reservations should be made well before arrival; call (596) 52-32-09. Another good bargain are the 200 "gites," furnished apartments, studios and rooms in private homes specifically designed for vacationers. Contact **Gites de France,** (596) 73-67-92.

Camping: Martinique is one of the relatively few islands where this activity is popular in the forests and on the beaches especially between June and September. For details contact the **Office National des Forests,** (596) 71-34-50 or fax (596) 68-47-43). Close to Fort-de-France at Anse a l'Ane is **Le Nid Tropical** campsite, (596) 68-31-30 or fax (596) 68-47-43), which even rents tents, though you're welcome to bring your own. On the south coast is **Vivre et Camper**, (596) 76-95-52 or fax (596) 76-97-82, on the Pointe Marin beach in Ste-Anne. Also **Tropicamp** in Sainte-Luce, phone and fax (596) 62-59-00.

Currency: The local currency is the French franc (F) valued at about US$1 = 6.85F. Some stores give a 20% discount on goods purchased with a credit card or foreign traveler's checks. If you attempt to exchange your traveler's checks for francs, you will pay a commission to the bank or exchange houses, then pay full price for any items you purchase. Banks are open weekdays from 7:30 a.m. to noon and 2:30 p.m. to 4 p.m.

Taxes & Tips: A 10% service charge may be added to your hotel room, 15% in restaurants. A resort tax ranges up to US$1.50 per day per person. Porters expect 1F per bag. Surprisingly, it's not necessary to tip cab drivers.

Electrical Current: 220 volts, 50 cycles, requiring a French plug adapter and transformer.

Safety and Health Warning: The beautiful rivers naturally entice the weary walker to swim. Be very careful. Many rivers in Martinique are infested with parasites, especially the well-known bilharzia, which causes very serious problems. This is due to the insufficient sanitation control in rural areas. People pour waste buckets each night into the rivers. This perpetuates a condition already threatening to the population. Drink bottled or purified water.

Snakes & Other Venomous Creatures: The deadly fer-de-lance resides in Martinique. However, it likes the warm coasts and you'll probably be spending most of your time in the cooler mountains, so not to worry.

Hiking & Walking Services: An excellent city walking tour is offered from the Savanne in Fort-de-France by an outfit called **Azimut.** The walks last about an hour and a half, and the friendly, multilingual guides show you many aspects of Fort-de-France you would probably miss on your own. One of their stops is at a small cafe for a glass of cane juice; talk about sugar overload! Call Azimut at (596) 70-07-00.

Hiking should be arranged through the national park office, **Parc Naturel Regional** in Fort-de-France; phone (596) 64-42-59 or (596) 73-19-30. These tours are well organized, visit most of the popular sites, and cost only about US$12 per person. Most people speak French, which is no problem because you have a competent guide to get you where you need to go.

Several tour operators also offer guided hikes. **Caribtours,** (596) 50-93-52, in Lamentin does half-day tours of the rain forest and volcano; **Basalt** in Bellefontaine, (596) 52-57-82, and **Madinina Tours,** (596) 70-65-25, in Fort-de-France provide similar trips. The **Village des Z'Amandines** in St-Marie, (596) 69-89-49, has weeklong packages that include four days of hiking.

If you speak French and want a private hike, you can usually arrange for a guide to climb Mount Pelee at Morne Rouge.

Additional Information: French Government Tourist Office, 444 Madison Ave., New York, NY 10022; call (800) 391-4909. In Canada, Martinique Tourist Office, 2159 rue Mackay, Montreal, Quebec, H3G 2J2; call (800) 361-9099; www.martinique.org.

FORT-DE-FRANCE AFOOT!

Time: 1.5–2 hours.. | **Difficulty:** 1 for walking; 5 for dealing with many of the locals. | **Trailhead:** The closest parking spot you can find near Fort St-Louis.

You'll get the most out of this is you can arrange for a walking tour at the Savanne from the friendly, earnest guides of Azimut. However, because the city is laid out in a grid, it is quite easy to find your way around on your own.

1. **Fort St-Louis:** In 1637, two years after the first French settlement, a wooden fort was built on the south of La Savanne on a small peninsula. It was enlarged in 1640 to become Fort St-Louis. A French naval post today, it can be visited Monday through Saturday from 9 a.m. to 3 p.m. It is said that the low ceiling arches inside were intended to disrupt the advances of any invading British, who generally were taller than the average Frenchman.

2. **La Savanne:** A beautiful park and one of the best places to buy the local handicrafts, though local vendors can be extremely abrasive. Better to pay attention to the palms, tamarinds, and other tropical trees or an impromptu soccer match. Or check out the two historic statues. The one statue most visitors will relate to immediately is the white Carrara marble statue of Marie Josephe Rose Tascher de la Pagerie, born on Trois-Ilets across the bay in 1763 and later the Empress Josephine, first wife of Napoleon Bonaparte. The other memorial is of Pierre Belain d'Esnambuc, who established the first French settlement on Martinique in 1635.

3. **Bibliotheque Schoelcher:** Across the street from La Savanne, this impressive building was constructed in Paris in 1889 for the Paris Exposition by the architect of the Eiffel Tower, Henri Pick. The building, described as Byzantine-Egyptian-Romanesque, was disassembled in 1890 and shipped here to house the extensive book collection of Victor Schoelcher, who was responsible for abolishing slavery in the French West Indies. Still functioning as a library and open to the public, the interior is a must-see. The outside architecture is also one of the highlights of Fort-de-France, best photographed in the morning.

4. **Musee Departemental de Martinique:** Pottery, beads, and other items that belonged to the Arawaks and Caribs, including a partial skeleton excavated in 1972. There are exhibits illustrating colonial costumes, slave life, and planter's furnishings. Open weekdays 8 a.m. to noon and 3 p.m. to 5 p.m.; Saturday, 8 a.m. to noon. Located at #9 Rue de la Liberte.

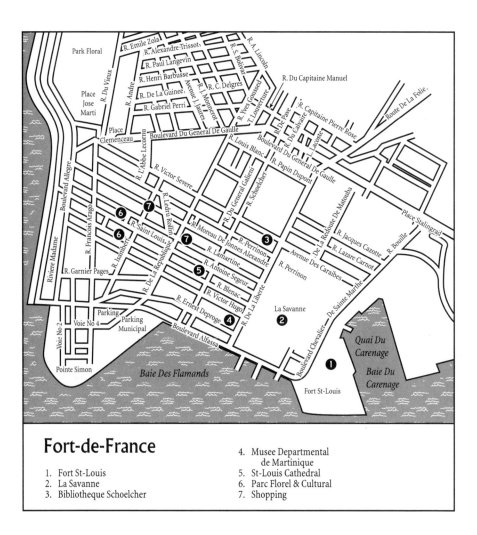

Fort-de-France

1. Fort St-Louis
2. La Savanne
3. Bibliotheque Schoelcher
4. Musee Departmental de Martinique
5. St-Louis Cathedral
6. Parc Florel & Cultural
7. Shopping

5. St-Louis Cathedral: The 200-foot steeple of this baroque church noted for its iron framework and decorated transepts, also the design work of Henri Pick, towers over the city skyline. Stained glass depicts the life of St. Louis. A number of Martinique's former governors are buried here. Over the centuries the church was built and rebuilt seven different times, the last in 1895.

6. Parc Floral et Culturel: A shady park with two exhibits, one featuring the geology of the island, the other, the magnificent vegetation. Fruit and vegetable markets near the park are open from 5 a.m. to sunset. You can also purchase flowers, coconut water, and exotic candies. The fish market is by the Madame River.

7. Shopping: Rue Lamartine and Rue Isambert have most of the jewelry shops, crystal, china, and silverware. Clothing is at the two galleries or malls on Victor Hugo. Remember to ask for the customary 20% discount for using credit cards and traveler's checks.

1. ST. PIERRE RUINS WALK

Designated a Ville d'Art et d'Histoire in 1960, the old city is located on the east coast about an hour's drive from Fort-de-France.

The new village of St-Pierre is growing up around it. Called the "Petit Paris" of the West Indies, St-Pierre was once the economic, cultural, and political capital of Martinique. St-Pierre was quickly transformed from the Petit Paris to the Petit Pompeii of the Caribbean on May 8, 1902, when Mount Pelee erupted. In three minutes a cloud of ash erupted from the volcano and covered the city, calcifying the occupants and destroying the buildings. Of the estimated 30,000 inhabitants, only 1 survived the explosion, a prisoner protected by the thick walls of his cell. Once released, the prisoner, whose name is variously reported as Cylbaris or Syparis, spent several years traveling in the sideshow of Barnum & Bailey Circus. His cell is behind the once-famed theater of St-Pierre. In front of the theater is a haunting statue of a woman who looks like she was calcified during the eruption. Crying out in pain, she symbolizes the agony of St-Pierre. Not to be missed is the Volcanological Museum, open daily 9 a.m. to 12:30 p.m. and 3 p.m. to 5 p.m. It contains many heat-deformed and charred objects, photographs of the disaster and distorted clocks stopped at 8 a.m. The ruins, which cover two terraces, and the museum take about 1.5 hours to explore thoroughly.

HIKES IN SOUTH MARTINIQUE

2. THE MACABOU/SALINES CIRCUIT BEACH WALKS

Time: 8 hours. | **Difficulty:** 2–3. Open sun the entire time. Avoid venturing into the mangroves, where the mud is often deep. Bring water and snacks. | **Trailhead:** Grande-Anse du Macabou. From Vauclin, drive 3 miles (5 km) south on N1, turning left on the road marked "Ranch Macabou." Past the gate of the ranch, follow the concrete road leading to Pointe la Voute, which separates Petite and Grande-Anse du Macabou.

This route skirts one of the most beautiful coastlines in Martinique. If you're not inclined to walk for ten hours, even with swimming breaks from time to time, you can choose any of the four sections. All are accessible by car.

 SECTION 1: MACABOU TO CUL-DE-SAC FERRE
      Time: 2 hours

Beginning at Pointe la Voute, descend toward Grande Anse du Macabou by a narrow path found at the south of the Pointe. Grande Macabou Beach, bordered with coconut palms, extends to Pointe Marie-Catherine, which takes about 30 minutes. Notice the contrast between the point, where nothing can grow in the wind, and the lush growth along the beach, mainly coconut palm and seagrape.

The Caribs once used tree ferns like these for torches

From the top of Pointe Marie-Catherine, go back down to Anse Grosse-Roche, whose name comes from the huge rocks on the beach to the south. (The rocks themselves are obscured by vegetation.)

Arriving at Point Macrem, you'll discover Four a Chaux Beach and Baleine Beach. Behind these beaches is an undergrowth of seagrape (the fruit is poisonous) and the manchineel tree (the sap may burn the skin). On many beaches manchineels are marked with red paint on the trunk as a warning.

After two hours you'll arrive at the magnificent Cul-de-Sac Ferre, an almost enclosed bay bordered by mangroves and gently sloping hills covered with pale green vegetation.

SECTIONS 2 AND 3: CUL-DE-SAC FERRE TO CAP CHEVALIER AND CAP CHEVALIER-TRABAUD

Time: 1.5 hours each section

After passing Trou Cadia and Pointe la Rose, which enclose Cul-de-Sac Ferre with impressive, sea-carved cliffs, follow the beach of Grande Anse du Cap Ferre to the cape proper. From there, you can take in the entire coastline, from Pointe Macre to Chevalier Island.

Next, walk along Anse la Balle and its beautiful stand of coconut palms. Past Pointe des Ebichets (where you may see frigate birds in flight), you'll walk along the shore of Anse Noire, divided by a small cliff. On Anse Esprit or Anse au Bois you may see several long, narrow fishing boats made of gum trees. The next section of Cap Chevalier is a popular spot where a number of locals have vacation homes. The path turns inland to avoid both the private homes and the mangroves bordering the coast. You'll rejoin the water at Baie des Anglais, which has some of Martinique's most beautiful mangroves. (Opposite the bay is the summit of Pointe Jaham. It would take about 1.5 hours to reach because of the deep mangrove forest growing well inland.)

Remaining on the beach, when you're in sight of "les Anglais des Grottes," you'll need to cross a small bridge to the west bank. In the rainy season, this can be tricky. Next, you'll pass beneath Baie des Anglais and the western flank of Morne a Vache before descending to Anse Trabaud, one of Martinique's most beautiful beaches.

SECTION 4: ANSE TRABAUD TO GRANDE ANSE DES SALINES
Time: 1.5 hours

Walking the length of Anse Trabaud, you'll enter the Savane des Petrifications, a former petrified forest. Unfortunately, almost all the fossilized wood has been removed. Next is a very dry savannah, bordered by dramatic cliffs perpetually beaten by the waves of the Canal of Sainte-Lucie, where sea birds nest.

After Pointe d'Enfer, Anse Baham, and Anse de l'Ecluse, you'll see the "Devil's Table" and the little island of Cabrits, the southernmost point of the island. A lighthouse and weather station occupy the summit.

Next, you'll walk along L'Etang des Salines to the south and reach Pointe des Salines, where you'll find one of the most popular tourist spots on the island: Salines Beach, planted with coconut palms, seagrapes, manchineels, and pear trees, recognizable by their pink flowers.

3. LE PITON DE CREVE-COEUR

Time: 1 hour. | **Difficulty:** 2–3. | **Trailhead:** From Marin take D9 toward Sainte-Anne. About 1.6 miles (2.5 km) outside of Marin, take a left at Poirier toward Cap Cabaret/Cap Chevalier. At the first fork, 1,000 meters farther, take the road to the *right*. After 1.2 miles (2 km), go straight ahead onto a wide dirt road, once the paved road has veered off to the left. After about 1,500 meters, the road will turn left to arrive at the foot of the peak, a vast grassy expanse with ruins of an old sugar factory. Leave your vehicle in the shade of a calabash tree.

Peaking at 656 feet (200 m), the Piton de Creve-Coeur overlooks the entire peninsula of Sainte-Anne and offers a remarkable panorama. Its volcanic formation has two heads in profile, a notable landmark for the southern part of the island.

After visiting the sugar mill ruins, now taken over by magnificent gum trees, locate the summit trail to the right of the parking area, behind a hedge. The path goes around the peak from the north. First, you'll see the ruins of the old house. Above the house, a shelter maintained by the Office Nationale des Forets (ONF) permits a last rest before the ascent. The slope now becomes steeper, but steps to a ramp have been installed to help you up.

At 606 feet (185 m), you'll arrive at a flat area that offers a superb view of the southern part of the peninsula. Climbing to 656 feet (200 m) and standing among the agave plants, you'll enjoy an even better 360° panorama.

The same road takes you back to your point of departure.

4. VAUCLIN MOUNTAIN

Time: 1.5 hours round-trip. | **Difficulty:** 2. In the rainy season the trail is slippery in places. | **Trailhead:** From Vauclin, take D5 toward Saint-Esprit. About 1.6 miles (2.5 km) after leaving the town, take a right and follow the sign Coulee d'Or. Continue 2.2 miles (3.5 km) to the beginning of the trail. Using a crossroads still frequently traveled by religious pilgrims visiting a small chapel, this path will eventually take you to 1,653 feet (504 m), the highest point of on the southern part of the island.

The first part of the trail ascends past gardens of Chinese cabbage, yams, and onions, all growing in the shade of mango, apricot, and breadfruit trees. This slope is relatively steep; be careful when the soil is slippery. The climb is paced by the Stations of the Cross, symbolically marking the path of the crucifixion, where candles burn continuously.

Gradually you'll enter a more lush, thick area featuring sweet peas (not the climbing flower, but a shrub of the mimosa family), big-leafed manjack, and swamp dogwood. After a 30-minute walk, you'll reach the chapel, the end of the Stations of the Cross.

Across several breaks in the leafy vegetation you should be able to see a great part of the southeastern coast, from the Caravelle Peninsula to the southern tip of Sainte-Anne, from bays to points and headlands. Particularly outstanding is the Bay of Simon to the south of Francois, where you might see a plume of smoke from one of the remaining distilleries. You'll also have grand views of the point of Vauclin overlooking the town of Vauclin; the bay and point of Massy-Massy; and the islets of Francois to the north, surrounded by foaming coral reefs.

Return the way you came, or make the climb down by the eastern flank to the La Montagne district, a hike of about an hour.

5. MORNE CHAMPAGNE

Time: 45–60 minutes. | **Difficulty:** 1. | **Trailhead:** Take D7 through Trois-Islets to reach the beginning of this trail at the southern extremity of Grand Anse d'Arlet Beach between two houses. Park along the road. After taking the path behind the last houses on the beach, follow a gently sloping path on the flank of Morne Champagne.

This is a short and pleasant walk to a splendid view. All along this road you'll see blocks of black rock, a form of lava carved by erosion. In about ten minutes you'll arrive at a savannah surrounded in the north, east, and west by a fairly steep cliff. You are now standing in the crater of a volcano that has eroded over the past several million years. You'll have a tremendous view of Grande Anse, its beach, and the crystal-clear water where many sailboats are usually moored.

The path then leads to a small house. Not far from here you'll see a small pond bordered by calabash trees and large pear trees. This tranquil site is ideal for a picnic. Return by the same route.

6. Morne Larcher Trail

Time: 2.5 hours, one way. | **Difficulty:** 3. Constant sun and continual slope upward. | **Trailhead:** The trail ends are reached either by the Diamond (le Diamant) in the Anse Caffard district, which goes along celebrated Diamond Beach; or by Anse d'Arlet in the "Petite Anse" district. Plan on a 45-minute drive from Fort-de-France.

This walk will show you the entire southern coast of Martinique from the top of Morne Larcher (Larcher Hill) 1,312 feet (400 m) high. Leaving from the L'Anse Caffard end, the marked trail enters a dry, thickly wooded area with interspersed goat or sheep pastures. The foliage becomes denser as you climb.

After an hour's walk you'll reach a small savannah, scattered with mango and guava trees. This is also the highest point on the trail. From this point you'll see Diamond Beach in the foreground and the succession of points and bays named Marigot, Pimentee, and Philippeaux, which make up the Diamond Coast of Sainte-Luce.

After crossing the savannah around the summit of Morne Larcher, go down onto Petite Anse. The greenery is more moist, with many large trees, lianas and epiphytes.

After about 30 minutes' descent, you'll cross a relatively flat area. Another 20 minutes from here is the district of Petite Anse and its beach.

7. Montravail (Saint-Luce Community)

Time: 1 hour. | **Difficulty:** 1. | **Trailhead:** Arrive here via D8, between Riviere-Salee and Sainte-Luce. Signs indicate the direction to Montravail. At the entrance to the forest, a concrete road leads to a maintained parking lot next to a picnic area.

A network of trails diverge from the road toward the undergrowth. A woodland trail, 4.1 miles (2.5 km) long, is for runners. A sign with a detailed map provides directional details.

8. La Vatable (Trois-Ilets Community)

Time: 1 hour. | **Difficulty:** 1. | **Trailhead:** Arrive here by D7 leading to Riviere-Salee at Trois-Ilets. A sign indicates the entrance past the ruins of the former distillery.

Follow the central dirt road to a pathway entering a forest of mahoganies, Caribbean pines, and many other species, leading to the sea. Picnic shelters are at the beginning of the trail and seaside, which provides a glorious view of the Bay of Fort-de-France and its islets. A loop allows a return along the sea.

9. GALOCHA TO PAGERIE

Time: 2.5 hours one way. | **Difficulty:** 2–3. | **Trailhead:** Taking D7, drive across Trois-Ilets to Galocha. Just after a riding stable, facing the school, the trail begins on the concrete road leading toward the antennas of the TDF. The trail is actually driveable at first. After about 2.5 miles (1.5 km) you'll join a second route that also leads to Morne Bigot. Take the one going straight ahead. After an alley of coconut palms, you'll arrive at a path along a fence. The slope is relatively steep. Climb to the crossing and take a left, as going right leads to Anses d'Arlet. Continue your ascent and enjoy the variety of plant life in this humid area: bamboo, breadfruit, cocoa, and tamarind trees and rose apples.

You'll pass by the remains of a building formerly used by hunters. Twenty meters farther, you'll see a second camp in worse shape than the first. Here the slope is less steep. You'll arrive near a TV relay surrounded by enormous rocks. From here you can see Morne Larcher, Morne Gentil, and the coastline of neighboring St. Lucia. It's about 45 minutes to the summit of Morne Bigot, where the main antenna stands. This magnificent panorama encompasses the Salty River (Riviere Salee); the Pottery Works of Trois-Ilets; Lamentin and part of its industrial zone; Fort-de-France and its harbor, overlooked by the peaks of Carbet and Mandoline Island.

You'll now come out onto a road, turn right, walk some 20 to 30 meters before taking a path on the right. (The road itself leads to Anses d'Arlet.) After 1.5 hours you'll reach a small clearing where two beautiful calabash trees are standing—a good place for a rest and a drink of water. Continuing your descent, the trail goes around Morne Bigot and through a forest of India wood, seagrape, pimento, logwood, and sweet pea. Note how the vegetation differs on the two slopes of Morne Bigot: this one is much dryer.

When you arrive at another crossroad, take the right. Look—don't touch—these mangos, especially if it is mango season. The proprietors do not permit free samples. After two hours, the path becomes a wide and uncompleted road. A half-hour later you'll see "Croc-Souris" River, the end of the trail.

HIKES OF THE CARBET MOUNTAINS

10. LA DEMARCHE-MORNE ROUGE

Time: 6 hours round-trip. | **Difficulty:** 3. | **Trailhead:** From Fort-de-France take N2 north through the fishing village of Fond-Lahaye. Take the first road to the right after Fond-Lahaye Hill and follow it to La Demarche.

This is a fairly easy trail that leads to beautiful views of the harbor of Fort-de-France and Case-Pilote. The last section of the trail is forested.

The first hour passes by the savannahs along the heights of Schoelcher, in fields of thyme, onion and other home-grown vegetables. You'll already be able to see a good part of the harbor of Fort-de-France while going over this wide ridge. Next, you'll enter the forest and reach the first slopes of Morne Bois d'Inde. At first, the forest is shaded by large-leafed manjack trees and sweet pea. Then, after passing through a more humid forest of breadfruit trees, a hour's walk takes you to the Concorde Plateau and its mahogany groves.

A few minutes later, you'll arrive at the fork leading to Morne Chapeau Negre (Black Hat Hill) and the Pitons de Carbet. Take a left toward Piton Belly, still in the forest. Before reaching Morne Rose, an hour later, you'll go through young groves of Caribbean pines and mahoganies. Either arrange a shuttle to pick you up, or return the way you came.

11. ABSALON-VERRIER

Time: 4 hours, one way. | **Difficulty:** 3–4. The climb up Morne Chapeau Negre (at 3,000 feet) is difficult in some places due to erosion. | **Trailhead:** Take N3 (Route de la Trace) from Fort-De-France. After about 6.2 miles (10 km) take the fork to the left continue to the Station Thermale d'Absalon. This hike allows you to discover Martinique's gorgeous forest with views of Fort-de-France and Lamentin.

Departing Absalon, the trail begins with a steep incline under a canopy of white gum trees, riviera wood, cannon wood, and mahogany. In about 20 minutes you'll arrive at a crossroads. If you go left, you'll descend toward the Duclos River, which is full of the tiny crustaceans found in Martinique's streams. To stay on the trail, follow the blue and yellow blazes straight ahead into the mahogany forests planted by the Office of National Forests and across the Concorde Plateau and the Saint-Cyr Savannah.

The climb up Morne Chapeau Negre begins in a forest of breadfruit trees and cannon wood. After about 1.5 hours, the flora becomes the stunted trees of high altitudes, the elfin woodland, and its ferns and mosses. The last part of the climb goes up a narrow ridge where, if it's one of those rare clear days, you can look out over part of the northern Caribbean coast, the harbor of Fort-de-France, the plain of Lamentin, and the forests of La Donis, Morne Bois d'Inde, and Morne Rose. On clear days, you can see part of the Atlantic coast and the Caravelle Peninsula to the south.

The gradual descent through forest reaches Verrier after about an hour.

12. THE ABSALON CIRCUIT

Time: 3 hours. | **Difficulty:** 2. | **Trailhead:** Take N3 (Route de la Trace) from Fort-De-France. After about 6.2 miles (10 km) take the fork to the left continue to the Station Thermale d'Absalon.

One of the rare heavily forested trails close to Fort-de-France, this path offers a fairly easy walk. The path climbs for 20 minutes along a steep slope to a crossroad. The Absalon-Verrier trail heads off to the right, so go left and follow the marked path on the wooded ridge overlooking the Duclos River Valley. After a pleasant 45-minute walk on the ridgeline, you'll descend for 15 minutes and cross two streams to reach the parallel trail on the right, which leads back to within 33 feet (10 m) of your Absalon departure point.

13. THE PITONS DU CARBET CIRCUITS

Time: 6 hours round trip. | **Difficulty:** 5. Take water. Nearly constant exposure to the sun. | **Trailhead:** From Fort-de-France, take N3 (Route de la Trace) to the marked trailhead at Boucher Plateau. Or you may choose the southern trailhead at Colson Hospital, just outside the village of Colson, also off N3, which offers an easier walk.

This is a tough hike, best left to those who want a physically challenging climb. However, the multiple summits offer the most spectacular views in all of Martinique. When rain makes the path slick, climbs are like skating rinks, the descents become toboggan runs.

Leaving from Boucher Plateau, you face the longest climb of the trail. In about an hour you'll ascend some 1,300 feet (400 m) along a very steep slope. If it's slippery, look for the stakes hammered into the most critical spots to help you ascend. The flora will become more stunted as the great trees of the Boucher Plateau rain forest gradually give way to high-altitude shrubs like cabbage palms, orchids, mosses, ferns, and mountain pineapple (no edible fruit), all interspersed with small trees twisted into fantastic shapes by the wind.

The sloping trail between the summit of Piton Boucher and the ridge of Morne Piquet is scattered with many hollows. The crest of Morne Piquet is an hour and several spectacular views of the coastline away. From the peak of Morne Piquet, the view extends to the south as far as Diamond Rock and even to the neighboring island of St. Lucia. You can make out the city and the roads of Fort-de-France, the Sacre Coeur of Balata, replica of Sacre Coeur de Montmartre, and the agricultural plain of Lamentin.

On the summit of Piton Piquet you'll turn to the left to begin the one-hour ascent of Piton Lacroix (3,922 feet [1,196 m]). The trail going straight ahead leads to Morne Chapeau Negre (Hike 12, p. 233); going right will take you to Montjoly (Hike 13, below).

The descent from Piton Lacroix may be tricky—it's a muddy and slippery slope. At one point you'll need to cross a very narrow ridge only about eight inches wide. There's no shame in scrambling across on all fours or sliding across on your rear.

It will take about an hour to descend to a crossroad, where both paths join Route de la Trace. Although both take about two hours, the two routes are not equal. The right trail is a steep descent down Piton Dumauze that leads to Colson Hospital. Going left by way of Alma Peak is only for the most fit and experienced. It requires a steep ascent followed by a 50-foot descent that requires the use of ropes. This trail ends at the village of Colson.

14. THE PITONS BY WAY OF MORNE-VERT FROM MONTJOLY TO CAPLET

Time: 5 hours, one way. | **Difficulty:** 5, truly rough, perhaps Martinique's toughest. Take a guide to play it safe. | **Trailhead:** Take N2 to Bellefontaine, then go right onto route D20. Just before reaching the village of Morne-Vert, take the road indicated as Canton Suisse. After a kilometer (or just over half a mile), take the fork to the left at a small metal shelter. The trailhead is located 1.3 miles (2 km) from this crossroads.

This hike is one of Martinique's most demanding. The gradients are very serious: it's 2,362 feet (720 m) just to ascend Piton Lacroix. The slopes are steep: 40% is average for Lacroix; more than 50 percent for Morne Piquet; in other places, you'll even encounter slopes of 100 percent (90°). The entire path has places that require some climbing. Pay extra attention to the terrain, which can be very slippery.

From Montjoly, the trail first crosses several produce gardens. The slope becomes steeper, crosses a pasture, and enters the rain forest to begin the ascent of Morne Tranchette, 2,482 feet (757 m) high. The rain forest consists of breadfruit trees, heliconias, and—in less steep areas—trumpet wood. The summit takes about 45 minutes. The easy part is over.

After descending for a few minutes, you'll begin the 1.5 to 2-hour ascent of Piton Lacroix. This difficult climb takes place almost entirely in the forest; yet on the opposite slope, unsheltered from the prevailing winds, the vegetation thins out at around 2296 feet (700 m). The slope up Piton Lacroix is so steep, you'll need to scale several vertical sections.

The small plateau at the summit is 3,922 feet (1,196 m) high, so catch your breath while admiring some beautiful countryside. You'll feel a new respect for the wind during the 30-minute descent of Piton Lacroix's northern slope. Its high-country vegetation includes lycopods, mountain pineapples, ferns, and stunted shrubs. From the ridge joining Lacroix to Morne Piquet, off to the west you'll see the verdant district of Morne-Vert and its fields and hedges, a landscape some say resembles Normandy or the foothills of the Alps.

Toward the east you'll spot the interior of the peaks, the sources of Riviere Blanche (White River), the almost vertical slopes of Alma and Dumauze peaks, a landscape both languid and harsh.

From Piton Lacroix, it will take you 90 minutes to arrive at the summit of Morne Piquet (3,804 feet [1,160 m]), overlooking the region of Fond Saint-Denis. Then it's time to descend to Caplet, where you'll encounter the steepest slopes of the trail: muddy toboggan runs of 32 feet (10 meters) or so, best dealt with by sliding down on the seat of your pants. The ridge is sometimes only a foot wide. Fortunately, the vegetation becomes gradually denser, giving you more to hold on to. But watch out for razor grass; it can cut you badly.

An hour later you'll arrive at the foot of Morne Modeste, where your path crosses the trail between Morne-Vert and Fond Saint-Denis (Hike 16, below). If you go left it will take another 30 minutes to reach Caplet's rich grasslands not far from Morne-Vert.

15. HIKE FROM MORNE-VERT TO FOND SAINT-DENIS

Time: 3 hours each way. | **Difficulty:** 2–3, a steep part near Fond Saint-Denis. | **Trailhead:** Take N2 past Bellefontaine and turn right onto D19, which leads to Morne-Vert. Turn right at the church to Fond Caplet, taking the first right after crossing the river. Drive up the valley and park at the last house.

This rates as one of the island's most interesting hikes. It's easy, too, one of those rare family walks in the forest. Starting out, you'll climb for 45 minutes along the hillside in the midst of savannahs and food crops. You'll come to the edge of a mahogany forest on the hill between Morne Modeste and Morne Piquet. The view of the valley is splendid.

Going through the forest you'll reach a clearing at the foot of a beautiful and impressive waterfall surrounded by rain forest. You can refresh yourself in the stream—but don't drink the water—then follow the trail up the steep slope leading through the forest to a small plateau offering one of this walk's most beautiful views. Proceeding, you'll cross a forest of Caribbean pines to a second stream, just as nice as the first.

One more small climb and another forest (a section that may be filled with raspberries), then you begin the descent to Fond Saint-Denis, the last third of the hike.

During the last hour, the path twists first along a ridge of alternating savannahs and groves, then crosses a field of Chinese cabbage. The descent becomes steeper. You'll reach the bottom of the Carbet River Valley by going through some produce fields overlooking Fond Saint-Denis.

On the bridge, stop for a moment to admire the rapids. This is the end of your hike. It remains only to climb up to the highway, D1, in Fond Saint-Denis.

16. COLSON-PITON DUMAUZE AND PITON DE L'ALMA

Time: 3.5 hours. | **Difficulty:** 5. | **Trailhead:** Pick up the trail at the Colson Hospital parking lot, located off N3 (Route de la Trace) near the village of Colson.

This classic itinerary for attacking the Carbet Peaks has the advantage of being a circular route. Although tiring and difficult, your efforts are rewarded with diverse, beautiful country-side. Bring water and food for this long walk. Also, keep in mind that the sun can be intense if the day is clear. And if not clear, bring rain gear. The biggest drawbacks are the forest mud and a rather perilous passage near the summit of Alma Peak. You are strongly advised against undertaking this hike in bad weather.

The trail plunges immediately into the dark rain forest at the feet of the Carbet Peaks. A half-hour later you'll arrive at the Dumauze River. A tree with humongous aerial roots merits a 50-meter detour downstream. A path permits easy access.

Next begins the arduous, 90-minute ascent of Dumauze Peak. Once across the river, the path quickly becomes uneven. Gradually the trees become smaller, giving way to the high-altitude forest with its stunted shrubs and its countless lycopods and ferns.

Presently, you'll descend to the small plateau about 320 feet (100 m) below, which separates this peak from Alma Peak; a 30-minute walk. After a perilous passage at the very begin-ning—a cliff of about 32 feet (10 m), which you can scale down only with the help of a rope—the path follows a long line of ridges which dominate the Medaille district and the White River Valley. Then you enter a forest that is less dense than the first. You should plan on a good hour from here to Dans les Nuages, your point of arrival 656 feet (200 m) from the Colson Hospital parking lot.

17. THE RABUCHON CIRCUIT

Time: 3 hours. | **Difficulty:** 2–3. This is a nice stroll in the forest with a view of the White River. | **Trailhead:** Take N3 north. Turn right at a forest road, Foret de Riviere Blanche (White River). Follow the forest road to Coeur Bouliki, where you'll find plenty of parking and a picnic shelter.

The trail departs from the water collecting station, a bit beyond the White River forest road. First you must walk along the rocky river, then cross it at the top of a tributary. Your trail begins on the right bank, about 65 feet (20 m) upstream. It momentarily seems to retrace its steps before climbing straight up toward the line of ridges overlooking the valley. During the course of this rather steep 45-minute climb, you'll enjoy a beautiful view of the river, winding below into a green sea of forest and mahogany groves.

At the summit, you'll be under a compact canopy of trees. Follow the ridge toward the Bois du Parc, a pleasant 45-minute stroll with a magnificent panorama of Fort-de-France, its harbor, and the districts at the foot of Morne Cesaire.

Then you'll descend steeply sloping savannahs for 30 minutes to reach a spot about 820 feet (250 m) from where you set out.

18. BEAUREGARD CANAL OR CANAL DES ENCLAVES

Time: 1 hour each way. | **Difficulty:** 3. Not recommended for people with vertigo | **Trailhead:** Take N3, then D1 toward Fond Saint-Denis. Take the concrete road on the right just before leaving Fond Saint-Denis, descend to the canal and park.

Built in 1760, the canal served three distilleries in Carbet; it's still used and maintained today to irrigate several properties. It's not advisable to walk in or to drink the water. Pure or not, a species of freshwater crab with a bright yellow shell flourishes there. On this walk, the path beside the canal sometimes climbs so that you're almost level with the kapok and gommier trees. Not a good place for an attack of vertigo.

The Carbet Valley, at first hidden in the forest, opens into savannahs and small fields, as well as magnificent stands of bamboo. The canal goes through small plots of cultivated anthuriums, Chinese cabbage, yams, and a few fruit trees. After several tree-covered sections, the canal plunges into the forest on the slopes of Morne des Cadets. At the summit is the meteorological and vulcanological observatory. After an hour's walk you'll reach the irrigation station that marks the end of the trail.

19. THE MORNE CESAIRE TRAIL

Time: 2 hours. | **Difficulty:** 3 | **Trailhead:** Drive to the nursery of the ONF on N3 (Route de la Trace)just after Balata, going to Morne Rouge. The trail departs from the La Donis arboretum, near the picnic shelter at the upper entrance.

As interesting as it is pleasant, this short walk around the environs of Fort-de-France is noted for its walk through the arboretum as well as the superb views of Morne Cesaire's summit at the trail's start. The path climbs rapidly in a series of hairpin turns to a large savannah planted with anthuriums and other crops.

For the first 30 minutes you'll make a moderate climb, passing signs that name many of Martinique's trees. In addition, the view over the Pitons de Carbet, spread out behind the nursery's great royal palms, is particularly beautiful.

The trail enters an abandoned mahogany grove, and after another 30-minute walk you'll reach the summit of Morne Cesaire, your balcony several meters above and overlooking Fort-de-France and the coastline.

20. THE SAINT-CECILE CIRCUIT

Time: 4–5 hours. | **Difficulty:** 5. Take water. | **Trailhead:** The two hikes connect on the summit of Morne Jacob. For the Carabin-Morne Jacob trailhead, take N3 to N1; just after passing the village of Le Lorrain, turn right onto D22 to Carabin, a small village where the trailhead is marked. For the Saint-Cecile Circuit trailhead, take N3 toward Morne Rouge, Just before Morne Rouge, turn right on the road leading to the pineapple canning factory and Saint-Cecile. The trailhead is clearly marked.

One of the oldest volcanoes on the island, Morne Jacob is also one of the highest mountains in Martinique. From its summit, a cone of 2,768 feet (884 m), you'll enjoy a vast panorama of the entire northern part of the Atlantic coast, Mount Pelee, and the Carbet Peaks. However, the path is long and sometimes perilous.

The Sainte-Cecile circuit is less interesting and there is a very difficult section at the end. Therefore, hikers drawn by Morne Jacob should depart from Carabin.

The first hour of the hike climbs Morne Quatre-Vingts, where you'll traverse a largely unexploited rain forest and view the beautiful Lorrain River Valley and Piton Laroche on the other bank.

The hour-long ascent up Petit Jacob (1,931 feet [589 m]) is even more steep, but the view is even more beautiful. The route continues as it rises and falls for 1.5 hours, going from one summit to the next in the midst of vegetation shaped and molded by the altitude and exposure to the tradewinds.

After ascending for 2.5 hours, you arrive at the small plateau that forms the summit of Morne Jacob. The view resembles that of Petit Jacob, but with a beautiful glimpse of the Morne Rouge plain and the Carbet Peaks. It takes around two hours to descend by the same route.

If you prefer to continue on taking the Sainte-Cecile circuit, take the path to the right coming from the summit, and go toward Morne la Piquonne. Do not go all the way to the mountain; Look first for a crossroads that joins the Sainte-Cecile trail for a much quicker and more pleasant descent via that route.

21. COURNAN RIDGE TRAIL

Time: 3 hours, one way. | **Difficulty:** 3–4. Steep at both ends. | **Trailhead:** Follow N3 toward Morne Rouge, stopping at the Champflore Hospital on N3 (Route de la Trace). The trailhead is marked.

Long in time and short on views, this hike joins the Mount Pelee trail and others but avoids any roads. Departing from Champflore Hospital, it is possible (with an all-terrain vehicle) to drive to the foot of Morne la Piquonne and skip a good hour of walking. The trail then enters a rain forest and quickly reaches Morne la Piquonne after 30 minutes of particularly steep climbing.

At the summit, a trail joins Morne Jacob on the right; ignore this one and go left. Your trail follows the ridge of Cournan for 1.5 hours. The view is limited to a few glimpses of the banana groves at the foot of Morne-Rouge and on Mount Pelee. You'll then begin a 30-minute descent as steep as the climb and then join a wider trail through a succession of savannahs where guava and lime trees grow.

Just before its end, the trail crosses a little branch of the Capot River, with many overhanging bamboos.

22. THE TRAIL OF THE JESUITS

Time: 3 hours, one way. | **Difficulty:** 3. Hard to ford the Lorrain River; hard to hike without wetting your feet during the rainy season. Certain passages are muddy after a big rain. | **Trailhead:** Departs from N3 (Route de la Trace) about 0.6 mile (1 km) after the Deux-Choux tunnel, going toward Morne-Rouge. The trail comes out on the Deux-Choux/Morne-Rouge road (D1) about 1.8 miles (3 km) from the trailhead.

The Trail of the Jesuits is one of the best-known hikes on Martinique, and one of the most interesting in the National Forest. It offers the chance to visit one of the best primeval forests in Martinique, one with a reputation for being an "ecological trail" of superior quality. A parallel trail exists that allows you to return without taking the same route or the road, but it is not well kept.

The first 2,952 feet (300 m) of Jesuits' Trail snakes along a ridge overlooking Route de la Trace. View magnificent tree ferns, a panoramic view of Mount Pelee, the plain of Champflore, and the mahogany forest of Proprete. Then the descent toward the Lorrain River begins, plunging into a pristine rain forest of silence, moistness, and beauty. You'll see white gums; breadfruits; riviera-wood, with their powerful aerial roots; and magnolias, with their gracious and fragrant blossoms. All are draped with epiphytes, ferns, mosses, and lianas.

After about an hour's walk you'll see the Lorrain River, the trail's principal attraction. This is, in fact, a nice recreation area in the midst of splendid overhanging bamboo branches. Walk another hour up the other side of the Lorrain Valley to the Deux-Choux/Gros-Morne Road. You'll have beautiful views over the mountains to Morne Jacob and the Carbet Peaks, some 100 meters from your arrival point.

Once you arrive at route D1, go to the lookout point maintained by the ONF. A little farther toward the Deux-Choux crossroads, you'll be able to look over the magnificent forest you've just hiked, as well as the entire northern part of the island.

23. MORNE BELLEVUE TO RECULEE

Time: 4 hours, one way | **Difficulty:** 3–4. Constant ascents and descents. | **Trailhead:** Take N3 north to D1 and drive toward Gros-Morne. About 4 miles before Gros-Morne, turn onto a steep road on the left. Signs marking the trailhead will be on the right, not far from the D1 turnoff.

Almost a third of this trail, accessible to any skill level, surveys one of the island's most beautiful panoramas. The first 45 minutes, or about a third of the walk's distance, climbs Morne Bellevue and a magnificent rain forest that includes gommier trees. During the second third of the trail, you'll follow a succession of tiring switchbacks along a ridge overlooking the entire Lorrain River Valley, topped by the cone of Morne Jacob. On the right are mahoganies planted by the ONF.

After about 2.5 hours, you'll leave the forest for a splendid view of Sainte-Marie and Caravelle. The gradually dropping trail continues along the ridge for 45 minutes, ending in another mahogany forest, near Reculee.

HIKES OF MOUNT PELEE

24. GORGES OF LA FALAISE HIKE

Time: 3 hours. | **Difficulty:** 3–4. Plan on some swimming. | **Trailhead:** Reach the trail by following N3 from Morne-Rouge toward Ajoupa-Bouillon; 4.8 miles (8 km) after Morne-Rouge you'll find a concrete path on the left, indicated by a sign. About 320 feet (100 m) farther, a second sign marks the beginning of the trail.

This hike takes you to the impressive gorges of the Falaise River, one of Martinique's most remarkable geological formations. The narrowness of the gorge—less than two meters in places—forces you to walk the streambed itself. You may even have to swim several meters if the water level is high.

The trail goes through a field scattered with bamboos. Then you begin a descent toward the Falaise River, a 15-minute walk. Once at the riverbank, go up the stream bed about 650 feet (200 m) to find the main gorge. Always in shadow, and disturbed occasionally by the flight of blackbirds and by the thundering of the water, the gorge entrance has a slightly oppressive air.

But this feeling fades quickly when you wade into the river, walking or swimming from basin to cascade to arrive, 20 minutes later, at the principal fall. About 32 feet (10 m) high, these tumbling waters fill a circular room where you can bathe in a 16-foot-deep (5-m)pool at its base.

25. MOUNT PELEE BY WAY OF L'AILERON

Time: 5 hours. | **Difficulty:** 4–5. Steepest but shortest climb up Mount Pelee, which last erupted in 1902. Possibly dangerous holes covered by moss. | **Trailhead:** Leave N3 just after the northern exit from Morne Rouge. Take the road that goes up to the l'Aileron parking lot; a sign indicates the entrance. The trail departs from the TV relay tower.

Characterized by a beautiful view over the entire Atlantic coast, this walk permits the fastest ascent to Mount Pelee's summit which—at 4,575 feet (1,397m)—dominates all of the island. A guide is highly recommended for this trail, which is rarely explored, even during the dry season.

From the L'Aileron parking lot, go around the TV relay tower, then immediately begin one of the steepest climbs of the trail. After about 45 minutes, before reaching L'Aileron, the trail crosses several different pumice ravines that can be slippery. It then continues into narrow passages where it's necessary to hoist yourself from rock to rock.

From Aileron, you'll discover a splendid view of the entire Bay of Saint-Pierre and the Carbet Peaks, sometimes seeing even as far as neighboring St. Lucia. From here the ascent takes 30 to 45 minutes to reach the rim, an easy climb along a ridge path.

Once at the rim, follow a ridge beside it for 15 minutes, then arrive at a shelter situated on a plateau overlooking the deep crater, which is entirely covered by mosses, ferns, lycopods, and mountain pineapple. But it's another 820 feet (250 m) higher up to Mount Pelee's 4,575-foot summit.

After passing another cone, at nearly the same altitude as the preceding one, you'll have another 30 minutes of ascent up the marked La Chinos Trail, which can be perilous because of the many holes and crevices hidden by moss. From the summit, the panorama covers all of Martinique and the neighboring islands.

26. FROM GRANDE SAVANE TO THE SECOND SHELTER

Time: 4.5 hours, round-trip. | **Difficulty:** 4–5. Open sun, tricky walking over pumice. Numerous, moss-covered holes at the crater. | **Trailhead:** On route D10, at the southern entrance to Le Precheur, is a sign for the well-maintained road to your departure point. Another sign indicates the entrance to the trail itself. You'll find enough parking for several vehicles.

This trail, on the driest side of Mount Pelee, is noted for beautiful lookout points. It provides an ascent to the crater with less likelihood of rain.

During the first 45 minutes, the trail is mostly a wide road, suitable for an all-terrain vehicle. This is an important agricultural area, the Grande Savane, where the fertile earth produces abundant tomato plants, carrots, cabbage, and onions. Trees are scarce.

During the climb, you'll discover a magnificent view of Le Precheur and all the northern part of the island not obscured by Piton Marcel. After about an hour, you'll walk along a ridge overlooking two deep gorges with remarkable tree ferns.

From there, you'll have a superb view of the coast and the village of Saint-Pierre. Also from this point you'll encounter the high-altitude vegetation of Mount Pelee.

Now comes the last part of your ascent. The slope turns steeper, and in 30 minutes you'll reach the crossroads to the second shelter beside the crater. It's possible to ascend to the summit (La Chinos Trail) to the second shelter.

After a 30-minute climb, you'll overlook the picturesque crater of Mount Pelee, with its vegetation of moss, ferns, lycopods, and mountain pineapples. Also note the presence of orchids and a few raspberry bushes. The second shelter will appear soon, on the plateau at the foot of a rocky spur surmounted by a cross. Plan on about 1.5 hours for the return.

27. PELEE BY THE NORTH FACE

Time: 5 hours each way. | **Difficulty:** 5. Fog may make the ascent treacherous. There is one dangerous passage before Morne Macouba. Also be aware of a barbed-wire fence along the trail between the chapel and the savannah. | **Trailhead:** Take N3 to N1 and head toward the village of Macouba. After N1 ends in Macouba, pick up D10 and follow it for about 5 miles to the marked trailhead on the left.

Without doubt this is the least known and least used of the three routes to Mount Pelee's summit because of its length. Trail markings are satisfactory but take care not to leave the pathway while crossing the savannah, from the forest to the beginning of the ridge. It's easy to stray and lose a good hour finding the trail again, especially in foggy weather.

At the start, the trail traverses a banana grove, then takes a wooded path overlooking the Grand-Riviere Valley. After about a 1.5-hour walk, you'll arrive at a chapel, where the real hike begins. You'll first walk beneath beautiful foliage in a planted mahogany forest, then continue to climb in a rain forest of numerous mountain mangroves, breadfruits, and cabbage palms.

After 30 minutes more, you arrive at a large savannah, where shrub-like vegetation barely pushes through numerous crevices and ravines. The incline turns steeper and the savannah becomes a ridge after another 30 minutes. Then you begin your ascent of Morne Macouba, a 30-minute climb with splendid views of banana groves and pineapple fields in Basse-Pointe and Macouba. In the distance, you'll see the neighboring island of Dominica.

Once at the summit of Morne Macouba, you'll reach the Mount Pelee's second shelter following a 15-minute hike along a ridge that's actually the edge of the ancient crater.

28. THE HOT SPRINGS TRAIL (SOURCES CHAUDES)

Time: 4.5 hours. | **Difficulty:** 3–4. Open sun; take water. | **Trailhead:** Take D10 from Saint-Pierre north for 1.8 miles (3 km). The beginning of the trail is marked by a sign on the right.

Situated in the southwest foothills of Mount Pelee, this simple walk provides the only look at current volcanic activity, the sulfur springs. Because the lower part is regularly used by the army for target practice, the trail is closed to the public Tuesdays, Wednesdays, and Fridays (check for change of schedule).

The first part of the trail takes a shrub-covered savannah, a dried-out forest. After passing the gate by a zigzag trench, the rocky path rises in a regular slope toward the flanks of Mount Pelee. You will encounter several trees, including guava and crotons. After 1.5 hours in the direct sun, you will find yourself in line with Morne Penet or Morne Leonard, which rises about 500 feet (150 m) to the east of the trail.

The dry vegetation gives way to a dense forest of ferns and a few stunted shrubs. The trail almost disappears in places under this tufted cover. Be alert: You might see or hear a mongoose scampering away.

After another 30 minutes of walking, you reach the escarped bank of the Riviere Chaude (Hot River), which downstream becomes the Claire River. Feel for yourself how warm the water is (about 40°C or 104°F).

In about 15 more minutes you'll be at the hot springs themselves. Don't hesitate to walk in the riverbed. The water isn't cold, and it's safer than venturing on the steep banks of the gorge with its crumbly rocks. Green algae is common in this warm water. So is a yellow ocher on the rocks created by sulfur deposits.

Your hike terminates at a cone of debris about 65 feet (20 m) high and some 1,968 feet (600 m) from the summit of Mount Pelee. If you feel compelled to attempt the summit, watch for cave-ins and landslides. A rope is indispensable. This last section should be scaled only by experienced mountain climbers (as opposed to enthusiastic hikers).

29. Le Precheur to Grand-Riviere Hike

Length: 12.5 miles (20 km). | **Time:** 6 hours, one way | **Difficulty:** 5. Length, constant and strenuous ascents and descents, possible wet crossings after rain. | **Trailhead:** Take N2 to Saint-Pierre, then turn onto D10. Go through Le Precheur to the marked trailhead in a parking lot near Anse Couleuvre.

Your return is something to consider before you even depart. It is unlikely that after a six-hour walk you'll want to return to your car on foot. If you would like to have a look at the coastline from the water instead of the land, and if the sea is calm enough, you may be able to negotiate your return on one of the fishing boats of Grand-Riviere. Arrange this beforehand through the tourist board in Fort-de-France.

If you do decide to go entirely by foot, here's a word of advice: Night falls quickly between 6 p.m. and 7 p.m. in Martinique. It is therefore imperative to start the hike early. Take flashlights, water, and snacks. Interestingly, you will walk five or six hours without seeing a single house, exceptional in Martinique.

Although the region you'll travel is not inhabited, in places it does retain traces of past human occupation, such as an old sugar factory and rum distillery. The trail itself is an old road to the village of Grand-Riviere. But you'll also pass through the only section of Martinique where the rain forest landscape remains untouched at such a low altitude.

The diverse topography along the route has created a great variety of microclimates. You'll encounter dry forest (Anse Couleuvre/Cap St.-Marin) populated by swamp dogwood and kapoks, as opposed to the rain forest areas between the river at Trois Bras and Fond Moulin.

You might see a rare iguana or wading bird, both formerly found in many places on the island. You may also see the famous "matoutous," large, colored spiders with a dangerous bite.

30. The Caravelle Point Trail

Time: 3 hours. | **Difficulty:** 2–3. | **Trailhead:** Take N1 through Le Robert. Before reaching Trinite, take D2 through the village of Tartane and continue to Chateau Dubuc.

The trail departs from Chateau Dubuc, a seventeenth-century plantation now in ruins whose history is told in the little museum at the entrance. This walk goes through a natural reserve of 517 hectares composed of both mangroves and dry forest.

Follow the botanical path and turn to the right at station No. 15 to descend toward the mangroves of Tresor Bay. These mangroves shelter oysters and mangrove mussels, crabs, blue herons, saltpan plovers, and yellow-footed sandpipers.

Follow the coastline past a succession of calm bays and jagged capes beaten by the waves. From the meteorological station, climb to the 149-m-high lighthouse, built in 1861. From there, you can see Vauclin Mountain in the south, Mount Pelee in the north, and the Carbet Peaks in the west.

From the lighthouse, the return trail will take you into a forest of large-leafed grape trees, up to 40 centimeters in diameter; pear trees with mauve flowers, and gommier trees.

31. La Phillipe "Pointe Tenos" (Community of Sainte-Marie)

Time: 1 hour. | **Difficulty:** 1. | **Trailhead:** Go by N1 leading to Sainte-Marie in Marigot. 0.6 mile (1 km) after Fond Saint-Jacques, a sign on the right marks the entrance.

The ONF has developed several recreation areas with shelters, benches, and walking paths. Though not true hikes, they are the easiest way to see the forests of Martinique. A map outlines two itineraries. Two shelters are situated along the route, with a view of the Bay of Sainte-Marie. A trail leads to a cliff overlooking the usually rough sea. Groves of mahogany, pear trees, and Caribbean pines provide cool shade. Going toward Marigot by N1, you'll spot on the right the Pain de Sucre (Sugar Loaf) of Anse Charpentier, accessible only by a hiking path.

14

NEVIS

Old Caribbean Proverb: "*If you want good, your nose has to run.*"
Translation: "*Nothing good comes easily.*"

Nevis is decades behind the rest of the Caribbean, a rare gemstone in a sea of costume jewelry. Just 36 square miles in size, Nevis (pronounced nee-vis) didn't seriously become interested in tourism until around 1980, so most of its natural environment remains undeveloped.

The island's hallmark is brooding Nevis Peak, a lush, green, square-shaped volcanic mountain emerging from the water in an almost perfect cone shape. A sombrero of ever-present clouds usually obscures the 3,232-foot summit. Seen from the water, Nevis Peak's white puffy shroud has a very primeval aspect, the kind of place where you wouldn't be too surprised to find a living species of dinosaur or even King Kong himself.

The clouds that cover the Nevis Peak rain forest are typically so dense that from a distance they could be mistaken for snow. In fact, such a spectacle prompted Christopher Columbus in 1493 to christen the landfall "Nuestra Senora de las Nieves," Our Lady of the Snows, because it reminded him of the snow-covered Spanish Pyrenees.

That Nevis can appear moody, even threatening, from a distance is more than just a fanciful impression. Nevis has experienced several memorable earthquakes, including one as recently as 1950 that caused considerable damage. But that one was insignificant compared to the earthquake and tidal wave that destroyed the capital, Jamestown, in 1660.

Although it covers only a tiny area, Nevis is unusually well endowed with several spectacular beaches. The best is Pinney's Beach, truly the archetypal tropical beach—a wide ribbon of smooth, soft sand skirted by a thick coconut palm forest. Pinney's is considered one of the Caribbean's most beautiful beaches thanks to its combination of soft powdery sand, tall swaying palms, and the striking view of mountainous St. Kitts sprawling on the horizon just two miles distant.

Human habitation of the island goes back at least 4,000 years. Among the artifacts uncovered here are finely made stone implements and flint cutting tools made from non-native materials and beautifully colored pottery unearthed from burial mounds. The Caribs, the last Native Americans to "own" Nevis, called it "Oualie—Land of Beautiful Waters."

Nevis has a long and rich history and is inhabited by people with strong ties to the land. Legendary names like Alexander Hamilton and Admiral Lord Horatio Nelson (who married a local Nevisian) pop up as naturally in conversation as the usually idyllic weather does.

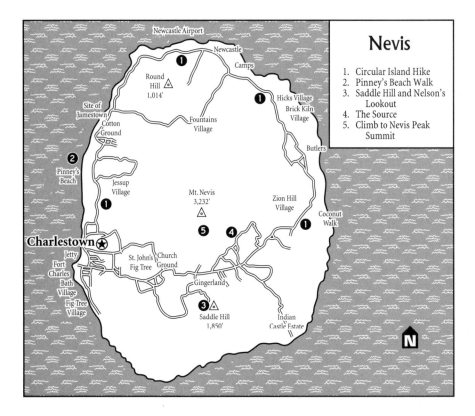

Nevis

1. Circular Island Hike
2. Pinney's Beach Walk
3. Saddle Hill and Nelson's Lookout
4. The Source
5. Climb to Nevis Peak Summit

Nevis first drew public attention in 1607, when Captain John Smith visited on his way to establish the first permanent English colony in North America. Jamestown turned out to be a swampy, mosquito-ridden site, so miserable a place, that 20 years later, Smith still fondly remembered his short but enjoyable six-day layover in Nevis. He recorded in his diary, "In the little isle of Nevis more than twenty years ago, I have remained a good time together to wood and water, to refresh my men and replenish stocks. Also hang two mutineers on the spot now called Gallows Bay." The bay off Charlestown is still known as Gallows Bay, probably not a name that would be selected today by land developers.

The British colonized Nevis in 1628. Until the 1640s, ginger, indigo, cotton, and provision crops for ships were the staple crops of Nevis. The introduction of sugarcane changed the island from a peasant agricultural base to a system of great sugar plantations in the sixteenth and seventeenth centuries. Many great houses were built (some now converted to inns), and an aristocratic planter class lived in splendid style. By 1778, the warm mineral springs of Nevis had made the island famous all over Europe, where it was called the Spa of the Caribbean. You'll have little trouble spotting the oldest buildings, with their ornate woodwork designed to create shade and collect the breezes.

Pinney's Beach, with St. Kitts in the background

TRAVEL TIPS

Area: About 7 miles in diameter, covering 36 square miles.

Language: English.

Population: About 10,000, mostly concentrated around Charlestown.

Time Zone: Atlantic Time, one hour ahead of Eastern Standard Time.

Rainy Season: September is the rainy month, although showers can occur any time of year in the highlands.

Getting There: St. Kitts still has the only runway for large jets. LIAT, (800) 468-0482, flies into Nevis from San Juan, St. Kitts, Antigua, and St. Maarten. Ferry service from St. Kitts aboard the 150-passenger *M.V. Caribe Queen* is possible for only US$4 each way, but the boat runs only in early morning and late afternoon. It does not run on Thursdays (maintenance day) or Sundays. An alternative is the 110-passenger *M.V. Spirit of Mount Nevis* that sails on Thursdays and Sundays for US$6 each way. Call (869) 469-9373 for more information.

Documents: Everyone needs a passport except for U.S. citizens, who need either a voter's registration card or birth certificate and a photo ID, such as a driver's license.

Getting Around: Because Nevis is all of 36-square miles in size, it is possible to make a grand tour in a single (long) day. Skeete's Car Rental, (869) 469-9458 is the main rental

247

car choice. A local driver's license is US$18.50. The one disadvantage in driving yourself around Nevis is that many of the mountain roads consist of just two narrow ribbons of concrete. Capacity: one car at a time. It's easy to stray from the straight and narrow and scrape the undercarriage as you veer onto the low shoulders.

Where to Stay: Nevis has many good hotels, some quite expensive. In the moderate price range is **Hurricane Cove Bungalows** situated on a hillside. They contain complete kitchens; call (869) 469-9462 or email hcove@caribsurf.com. Also consider the 34-unit **Oualie Beach Hotel** located on Oualie Beach; phone (869) 469-9735 or visit www.oualie@oualie.com. The unpretentious restaurant serves excellent local seafood dishes.

In contrast, the luxurious **Four Seasons** (the bathrooms alone are the size of a studio apartment) on Pinney's Beach is the island's best. With its own 18-hole golf course, rooms are over US$600 per day in winter; call (800) 332-3442. The **Mount Nevis Hotel,** which has a wonderful view of St. Kitts across the channel, is located near the airport. Its restaurant is renowned. Call (800) 756-3847 or (869) 469-9373; www.mountnevishotel. com. Keep in mind that it's warmer and more humid at the beach hotels. The mountain retreats, though cooler, tend to get more rain.

Camping: In keeping with the upscale tone of the island, you won't find any designated camping facilities, although there is a field near the base of Mount Nevis where climbers can overnight when accompanied by a local guide.

Currency: Based on the Eastern Caribbean dollar, with the rate of exchange pegged at US$1 = EC$2.70. American currency is accepted everywhere. Not all hotels take credit cards but—and this tells you how genteel the island's traditional clientele has been—many will take personal checks. Banks are open Monday through Saturday from 8 a.m. to noon and on Friday from 3 p.m. to 5 p.m.

Taxes & Tips: A 7% room tax plus a 10% service charge. Tipping in restaurants is 10–15%. The departure tax is US$10.

Electrical Current: Nevis is a mix with some hotels at 230 volts, 60 cycles; others are at 110 V, 60 cycles.

Safety & Health Warnings: None.

Snakes and Other Venomous Creatures: None.

Hiking and walking Guides: Eco-Tours Nevis with David Rollinson; call (869) 469-2091 or e-mail droll@caribsurf.com. **Top to Bottom** with Jim Johnson (cal (869) 469-2501) specializes in the island's birds and plants. **Michael Herbert** (phone (869) 469-2501) has a special 30-minute hike with many of the same views as Nevis Peak but without all the effort. Also check out **Sunrise Tours.** (869) 469-2758. Check with the Nevis tourist board in Charlestown for other possible guides; you can call the tourist board at (869) 469-1042.

Additional Information: Contact the St. Kitts–Nevis Tourist Board at 414 E. 75th St., New York, NY 10021; call (800) 582-6208 or (212) 535-1234. In Canada, 365 Bay St., Suite 806, Toronto ON M5H 2V1; call (416) 376-6707. In the United Kingdom, c/o the High

Commission for Eastern Caribbean States, 10 Kensington Ct., London W8 5DL; phone (0171) 376-0881; www.stkitts-nevis.com.

CHARLESTOWN AFOOT!

Time: 2 hours. | **Difficulty:** 1. | **Trailhead:** The Alexander Hamilton House.

Eighty planters from neighboring St. Kitts, who came over to make their fortunes in tobacco, founded Charlestown around 1660. Unfortunately, the Nevis soil was far rockier than St. Kitts's, so plans to create a major tobacco export center never materialized. The town itself, however, is one of the best-preserved old port cities in the Caribbean, including cobblestone streets.

Charlestown is a relatively small place, ideal for a leisurely two-hour walkabout. Exploring, you'll soon appreciate how Nevis's aristocratic past still influences the islanders: Nevisians retain a genuine, friendly civility. Nevis is a good place to walk, but be aware that some people don't like cameras much. Ask permission before taking anyone's picture downtown. Generally, you'll find that the description of poet Don Hecox generally accurate: "There are no strangers, only those friends you have not yet met."

1. **Alexander Hamilton House Birthplace and Museum of Nevis History** marks the birthplace of this illegitimate son of a Scotsman and a Creole. Migrating to America, Hamilton became a famed American statesman, serving as the first secretary of the Treasury under George Washington. He was later killed in the famous duel with his political rival, Aaron Burr. His likeness is immortalized today on the front of the US$10 bill.

    Both 1755 and 1757 (preferred) are given as Hamilton's dates of birth. The original Georgian-style home was built in 1680, but destroyed by an earthquake during the 1840s. Now rebuilt, the stone-block building contains Hamilton memorabilia, historical documents, and photos of Nevis, and antique furniture on the first floor. The Nevis House of Assembly sits on the second floor. Just a short distance from Charlestown is the Hamilton Estate, one of the last remaining sugar factories on Nevis, with all its production machinery still intact.

2. **St. Paul's Anglican Church:** You'll find St. Paul's hidden behind a tall wall. Although the church was built as recently as 1830, grave markers in the church sanctuary floor and cemetery date back to 1702. John Huggins, founder of the great Bath House hotel, was buried here in 1821. Stylistically similar to other English parish churches, St. Paul's has a mix of Gothic and classic elements. It is still an active place of worship.

3. **The Rookery Nook:** Built between 1850–60 as a livery stable, the Rookery Nook has been a popular local tavern since 1940.

4. **Wesleyan Holiness Manse:** This is one of the oldest stone structures still standing in Charlestown, dating to 1812. Now privately occupied and used for church business, it was built by the Huggins family, founders of the great Bath Hotel (p. 251).

5. **Charlestown Methodist Church:** Built in 1844, this is considered the most significant and most ornate structure of old Charlestown. A government-sponsored junior school

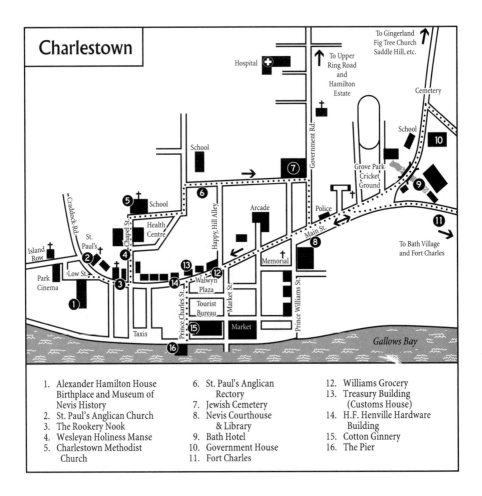

Charlestown

To Gingerland
Fig Tree Church
Saddle Hill, etc.

Hospital

To Upper
Ring Road
and
Hamilton
Estate

Cemetery

School

Government Rd.

School

10

Grove Park
Cricket
Ground

9

7

School

Craddock Rd.

5

School

6

Arcade

Police

11

Health
Centre

Happy, Hill Alley

Chapel St.

St.
Paul's

Main St.

8

To Bath Village
and Fort Charles

Island
Row

2

4

13

Memorial

Low St.

3

12

Park
Cinema

14

Walwyn
Plaza

Prince Williams St.

1

Prince Charles St.

Market St.

Tourist
Bureau

Taxis

15

Market

16

Gallows Bay

1. Alexander Hamilton House Birthplace and Museum of Nevis History	6. St. Paul's Anglican Rectory	12. Williams Grocery
2. St. Paul's Anglican Church	7. Jewish Cemetery	13. Treasury Building (Customs House)
3. The Rookery Nook	8. Nevis Courthouse & Library	14. H.F. Henville Hardware Building
4. Wesleyan Holiness Manse	9. Bath Hotel	15. Cotton Ginnery
5. Charlestown Methodist Church	10. Government House	16. The Pier
	11. Fort Charles	

uses the building's lower section. Amazingly, the yard and trees are little changed from the scene depicted in an 1802 print sometimes sold in the Hamilton Museum. The second floor of the adjacent Methodist Manse is considered the oldest wooden structure in Charleston, also dating at least to 1802. This may sound backward, but the ground floor is actually a much later addition, built in 1886. It was not uncommon in those days to lift the older, wooden first floors and build a more modern block structure under it. Considering the problem of wood rot in the tropics, the procedure makes a lot of sense.

6. St. Paul's Anglican Rectory: This is a typical cottage-style home of the 1870s, with a large entry and central living room. Now a private residence, it was the Government House of Nevis until 1890.

7. Jewish Cemetery: Although the Jewish community of Nevis is small, Jews were among the earliest pioneers. At one time Sephardic Jews from Brazil made up about 25% of the island's population. The cemetery, with tombstones in Hebrew, English, and Portuguese, contains graves dating from 1679 to 1768, with most burials taking place before 1710. Normally the cemetery is closed to the public, but you might be able to obtain entry through advance inquiry at the Tourist Office.

8. **Nevis Courthouse and Library:** The two-story stone structure you see today is a restoration, built in 1825, following the disastrous fire that swept Charlestown in 1873, destroying many valuable records. The first floor has always contained the law court, in which the death sentence was passed for at least one pirate and where Horatio Nelson is said to have been sued over a matter of £40,000. The public library now occupies the second floor. Thanks to its unique truss construction, it's considered one of the coolest places in town. The clock tower, dating from 1909–10, keeps accurate time.

9. **Bath Hotel:** What an incredible place this must have been during its heyday. Earthquakes have knocked down so many other apparently sturdy Charlestown structures, it's a marvel that the rickety Bath Hotel still stands. Its last guest checked out in the late nineteenth century; since then, the government has shored up parts of it as a tourist attraction, and the Spring House with its five hot thermal baths has been reopened. It costs only 50 cents for a plunge into the steamy, 108°F waters, a pittance compared to what it once cost upper-crust Brits. Designed to house only about 50 guests, the Bath Hotel was the ultimate getaway spa of its time and helped make Nevis's reputation as the "Queen of the Caribees" in the eighteenth century. John Huggins built the Bath Hotel in 1778 at an expense of £40,000. A novelty in its time, the Bath reputedly is the oldest hotel still standing in the Caribbean.

   The abolition of slavery in 1834 so disrupted the fortunes of the sugar planters, the hotel—like the rest of the island—went into decline. In the early 1900s, the Bath Hotel reopened as a health resort. Though its mineral waters supposedly help sooth rheumatism, gout, arthritis, and sap burns from the infamous manchineel tree, the attempt failed. So have all other attempts. You can explore the interior of the old hotel through an entrance at the back. Parts of it are in fairly good shape; others should obviously be avoided.

10. **Government House:** A relative newcomer to Charlestown, Government House was built in 1909. Closed to the public except by appointment, it is the residence of the deputy governor-general of St. Kitts–Nevis.

11. **Fort Charles:** This is more of a ruin than a monument. Originally called Pigeon Point, the fort was built on the site before the 1690s. Additions/renovations continued until 1783–90. Although as many as 23 cannons at a time faced the waterfront. If your time is limited, Fort Charles is a better place to read about than to actually visit.

12. **Williams Grocery:** This is more than a good place for a drink or snack, it's a good example of functional Caribbean architecture. The bottom floor is used for commerce, the upper for residence. The steeply pitched roof serves two purposes: the high-ceiling rooms underneath stay cool, and the larger roof surface provides a larger drain field for rainwater, which is stored in a cistern.

13. **Treasury Building (Customs House):** These government offices are typical of Caribbean buildings of the early nineteenth century. Built in 1837, these ministry offices are on the site of a much older structure; pipes and pipe stems dating back to 1650 have

been found in the rear garden.

14. **H. F. Henville Hardware Building:** Another good example of a Nevis commercial building from the 1840s.

15. **Cotton Ginnery:** Yes, indeed, one of the last true cotton gins still in use anywhere. It's open during the cotton picking season, but not to the public.

16. **The Pier:** This is where you catch the ferry to St. Kitts.

ELSEWHERE ON NEVIS

1. CIRCULAR ISLAND HIKE

Time: 1 full day. | **Difficulty:** 3–4 because of distance and the long walk in the open. | **Trailhead:** Charlestown.

There is much to see around the rest of the island, most of it near the coastline. Most people prefer to drive the 20-mile main road encircling Nevis, but a roundabout walk certainly is possible in a single day if you desire a really good stretch of the legs. It's also a good way to get in shape if you plan to tackle Nevis Peak, one of the Caribbean's toughest hikes.

Nevis's main road passes through the flatland of Charlestown, but it also runs through quite hilly regions, mostly in the south-southwest, where you'll find many of the historical sites. Going counterclockwise around the island from Charlestown, here are some places to look for:

Nevis played an important role in the life of famed British admiral, Lord Nelson. **St. John's Fig Tree Anglican Church,** an ancient stone building featuring a bell tower, proudly displays the faded marriage certificate that reads "Horatio Nelson, Esq., to Frances Nisbet, widow, on March 11, 1787." The Duke of Clarence, who became King William IV, stood up for Nelson.

Less than a mile from St. John's is the **Nelson Museum at Morning Star Plantation,** where Nelson's books, pictures and letters are on display. Admission is free. The poorly marked **Nelson's Spring** is where Nelson took on fresh water for his ships. It must have once been an impressive outflow of water, but today it's reduced to a small reflecting pond. It is considered historically important as the site where Nelson supposedly met Fanny Nisbet, his future wife.

Indian Castle Estate is a long detour to the south, down Hanley's Road to a government farm raising cattle and experimental crops. This was once a busy place, with ships loading sugar and its by-products for export to the United States, Canada, and England.

New River Plantation was the last sugar plantation on Nevis to go bust, surviving until the 1940s. It was built in the seventeenth century and "modernized" by converting to steam in the late 1800s. Government-owned and open to the public, you can still see the ruins of the great house and the big water cistern.

The **Eden Brown Estate,** built around 1740, is the island's haunted ruin. In 1822, it was occupied by Miss Julia Higgins, who was preparing to marry a gentleman named Maynard. On their wedding day, he and his best man had a falling out, and the two killed each other in a duel. One story says the distraught bride became a recluse and the mansion was closed down. Another version says that following the duel, she screamed until she died. Locals will tell you that whenever they're near the property, they feel the presence of someone . . . they're not sure if it Miss Higgins or Mr. Maynard, but it's definitely, someone. The government owns the property. This is one haunted house that doesn't welcome overnight guests, just day walkers.

The **Nisbet Plantation** beach is only a quarter of a mile long, but until Hurricane Hugo thinned out its palms, it was one of the most photographed ribbons of sand in the Caribbean. It's still worth a visit, if only to enjoy one of the fabulous burgers in the beach restaurant. The Nisbet Plantation is, of course, where Nelson's bride once lived. The great house is an excellent restaurant, with an eighteenth-century ambience, thanks to its fine dining room and mahogany bar.

The **Cades Bay Soufrière** is one of several active areas to remind you that Mount Nevis is not dead, only sleeping. Look for a burned-out gully or follow the unmistakable sulfur smell to its source. Steam sometimes shoots from the vents and the rocks are warm. This soufrière opened in 1951.

2. Pinney's Beach Walk

Length: The beach is 4 miles long. At the end it joins Oualie Beach. | **Time:** 1.5 hours one way. | **Difficulty:** 1. | **Trailhead:** Pinney's Beach Hotel at the north end of Charlestown.

Many islands boast of excellent beaches, but little-known Pinney's Beach definitely ranks among the best in the Caribbean. The beach begins at the comfortably old-fashioned Pinney's Beach Hotel, on the edge of Charlestown, and ends at Oualie Beach. It is, for the most part, an undeveloped, narrow strip of sand flanked by a thick forest of magnificent, towering palms. The beach sand takes its tawny color from quartz. Except for this and the beach at Newcastle, all other beaches are black volcanic sand. Pinney's was hit hard by Hurricane Hugo, as the stumps of many downed palms reveal. However, new palms sprouting through the sand promise that the beach will one day regain its full glory.

Just 15 minutes down the beach is the big Four Seasons Hotel, the beginning of a mass tourist influx that will—regrettably—propel Nevis well into the twenty-first century and forever change the completely unspoiled Pinney's Beach. Development was inevitable; fortunately a resort of the Four Seasons' caliber (with its 18-hole golf course) is in keeping with the island's long-established genteel character.

It's fitting and or ironic that such a classy resort is on the beach named after Azariah Pinney, one of the Caribbean's great rags-to-riches sagas. When he arrived in Charlestown in 1685, Pinney had only the clothes one his back, £15 in cash, a well-thumbed Bible, and the penance for being on the wrong side in the Monmouth Rebellion. Within 35 years, this astute businessman had developed an estate impressive enough to house the governor general. Other generations of Pinneys expanded the successful estate and were among the West Indies' wealthiest planters.

3. SADDLE HILL AND NELSON'S LOOKOUT

Length: About 1 mile. | **Time:** 1 hour. | **Difficulty:** 1–2. | **Trailhead:** Not as complicated as it sounds. Drive east from Charlestown and look for the sign proclaiming "St. George's Parish—the Food Basket of Nevis." Take the second right after the sign, then turn right again at the first opportunity. Follow this road until you see a concrete road going off to the left. Take the concrete road until you reach a dirt road going to the right, your hiking route.

Saddle Hill contains a small fort where Horatio Nelson, in charge of the British fleet for this part of the Caribbean, supposedly spent his free time looking for approaching enemy ships. The site is now marked by a radio tower and all the major artifacts have been removed. The hike is on an open dirt road, and the view of Nevis, Redonda, Montserrat, St. Kitts, and Saba is fine.

4. THE SOURCE

Length: 4 miles. | **Time:** 3 hours. | **Difficulty:** 3–4. | **Trailhead:** You have two possible starting points. One is at the Golden Rock Hotel, a magnificently preserved sugar estate with its own nature trail. That walk eventually leads to the Stonyhill Reservoir at Rawlins, where the Source Trail officially begins. Or you can simply begin at the reservoir. To reach the Golden Rock Hotel, go east from Charlestown and on the left look for the sign leading to the estate. Ask at the office for the map keyed to Golden Rock's nature trail.

Mount Nevis would seem to offer the opportunity for numerous hikes, but only two trails are used regularly. The Source hike, the most popular hike on Nevis, passes by a small stream, the main water source for Nevis and through semitropical to tropical rain forest. At several points you will pass by a centuries-old pipeline that brings water down from the stream to Stonyhill Reservoir, official starting point of the hike.

An easy trail to follow, because the path has been used for centuries; today it's maintained by the government. The hike is more rewarding with a guide to explain the scenery. The path is three to four feet wide in most places, up to six or seven feet across in others. Most of the area is unpopulated, although Nevisians apparently lived in the region until the 1950s and 1960s. My guide, Sylvester Pemberton, explained that one reason people have abandoned farming in the area is the continuing monkey menace.

How and why vervet monkeys ever got to Nevis is open to speculation. Evidently they were brought in as pets by the French. Sylvester warns these are not tiny creatures, but reportedly can grow to a height of three feet, their tails almost twice as long as their bodies. Traveling in packs of up to 40, they can take a big bite out of the local agriculture, which is why little farming is done in the high mountains today.

Starting out, you may be surprised to hear the continual pounding of the ocean surf, a good distance away. It is a pleasant sound that fades away about halfway up.

You'll pass by lemon trees, mangoes (ripe from April to August), and patches of what is known as "dung cane." Not to be confused with the sugarcane it resembles, dung cane can make your mouth swell up, a remarkably nasty side effect prized by plantation managers out to control pilfering. Sylvester said it originally was introduced to discourage thefts, especially after dark. Swollen mouths made suspects easy to identify.

The fruit trees eventually give way to rubber trees, figs, palms, and ferns. It may be difficult to believe that the metal water pipe you keep encountering was installed centuries ago, but the heavy moss coating testifies to its age. At about halfway, you'll reach a concrete water tank. Look for the massive rubber tree with a base like a giant cypress; it's a nice stop for a rest or a sheltered picnic, should it be raining.

During August and September, time of the greatest rain, you may find yourself wading almost knee-deep across streams that at other periods are almost dry.

From the water tank, the trail starts downhill. A deep ravine varying between 100 to 200 feet deep borders the right side. Locally, ravines like these are known as "ghauts" (pronounced guts). You'll come to two sets of steps (15 at the first, 32 at the second) just before the path curves to form a half-circle around a valley, actually part of a ghaut. After a fairly steep climb of about 15 minutes, you'll reach a water collector on the left. At some points you'll have to duck under the water pipe. Keep going until you reach the 70-foot-high ladder leading to the Source itself. You're welcome to make the climb and see where your drinking water comes from.

5. Climb to Nevis Peak Summit

Length: 4 miles. | **Time:** 4 hours. | **Difficulty:** 5. | **Trailhead:** The starting point, near Zetland Plantation, is difficult to locate. You definitely need a guide for this hike.

As difficult as the climb is, the hardest part may be coming down ... try to avoid descending all at once. Referred to locally simply as "The Trail," this is one of the Caribbean's tougher hikes, climbing to the 3,232-foot-high crater rim of Mount Nevis's dormant volcano. You can have a spectacular view, if the clouds are absent—but they rarely are. Therefore, this is a climb to be made for the sake of the climb itself, not for what you'll see once you reach the top. But you never know—you may be lucky.

The first 15 minutes are some of steepest and slipperiest as you stumble through big clumps of grass; if you find this too unpleasant, turn back. It only gets worse. After a few hundred feet, you join the Old Trail, which is narrow but not nearly as difficult. As the forest closes in, you'll see lots of ferns, almond trees, and an occasional mango. The smell is moist and earthy, a distinctive tropical smell. Only a few hundred feet more and the pathway opens to a breeze and a good view of Mount Nevis looming over you. Fifteen minutes from the outset, you arrive at a small plateau with a pond on the left. It is possible to camp in this field overnight, when accompanied by a local guide. Continuing, the trail is once more enclosed by the forest and gets steadily steeper. After about a mile, you can make progress only by scrambling and holding onto trees and roots. It's extremely tough when the ground is wet because of the moss and the mud; in some places the slope is a dizzying 60° to 70°, so this is almost mountain climbing. The summit is often obscured by a halo of clouds, so sight-seeing may be limited.

15

PUERTO RICO

Puerto Rican Saying: "*A shrimp that falls asleep will be taken by the current.*"
Translation: "*If you're slow, you'll be left behind.*"

Puerto Rico, often called "The Shining Star of the Caribbean," is located 1,000 miles southeast of Miami. A commonwealth of the United States, Puerto Rico is actually a combination Caribbean-American Island. By law, the U.S. and Puerto Rican flags must always fly side by side. Only 110 miles long by 35 miles wide, Puerto Rico is a land of great geographical contrasts. The north coast is wetter and greener than the southern tip, where cactus are common. In the northwest, caves, sinkholes, and haystack hills characterize the karst terrain. In the central mountain range, the altitude reaches an impressive 4,389 feet at Cerro la Punta.

These contrasts provide some very varied hiking, everything from dry forest to rain forest. The best-known hiking trails are those of the Caribbean National Forest, better known as El Yunque, located near San Juan. El Yunque receives so much attention that visitors usually aren't aware of the many other available hikes.

Scattered throughout Puerto Rico is a system of forest reserves that offer hiking from beaches to the highest mountain peaks. In addition, a stroll though old San Juan is easily the Caribbean's finest city walk. Two other cities, Ponce and San German on the southeast coast, also claim many historic buildings, all conveniently arranged around their main squares.

Puerto Rico definitely is a walker's dream.

TRAVEL TIPS

Area: 110 miles long, 35 miles wide; 3,515 square miles.

Language: Spanish; English is secondary.

Population: 3.8 million, principally in the San Juan area.

Time Zone: Atlantic Time, one hour ahead of Eastern Standard Time.

Rainy Season: July through November; August is usually the wettest month.

Getting There: Puerto Rico probably is the most accessible of all the Caribbean islands, thanks to the large number of airlines that fly there. American Airlines has made San Juan its hub for most of the Caribbean, bringing in more than three dozen flights daily from the United States. Other airlines providing service include Delta, USAirways, United, and Northwest. The flying time via a direct flight is short: two hours from Miami, three hours from New York, and four hours from Dallas or Chicago.

Puerto Rico

1. El Yunque Trails
2. Pinones Forest
3. Humacao Wildlife Reserve
4. Guanica Dry Forest Trails
5. Guajataca Forest Reserve
6. Carite Forest Reserve
7. Guilarte Forest Reserve
8. Toro Negro Forest Reserve
9. Rio Abajo Forest Reserve
10. Maricao Forest Reserve
11. Around Ponce
12. La Parguera Phosphorescent Bay
13. San German
14. Rio Camuy Cave Park
15. Arecibo Observatory
16. Caguanda Indian Ceremonial Park
17. Around Mayaguez

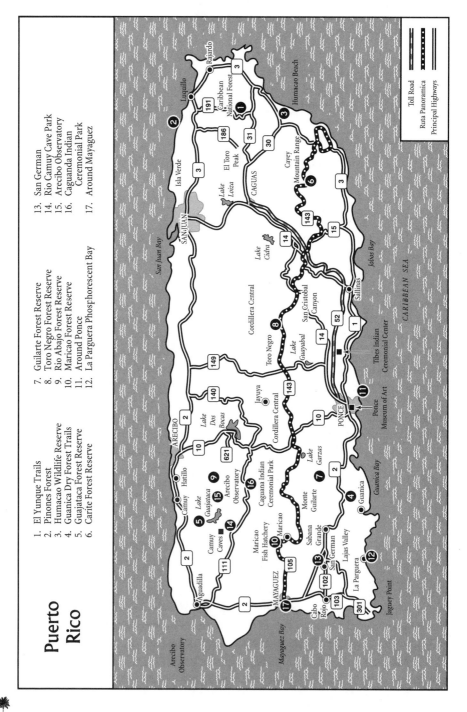

Toll Road

Ruta Panoramica

Principal Highways

CARIBBEAN SEA

The La Princesa Jail, built in 1837, now houses the Puerto Rico Tourism Company

Documents: U.S. citizens need a birth certificate or voter's registration card and photo ID. Citizens of other countries should carry a passport.

Getting Around: The easiest and least expensive way to travel is with a rental car. All the major agencies are represented at the San Juan airport. Be sure and get a road map because signs are sometimes scarce or downright confusing. Once you clear San Juan, driving to the national forests and preserves in the northwest is simple via a four-lane toll road. But once you start heading up into the mountains, be careful on the twisting and winding roads, which often have mud and other debris partially blocking them after heavy rains.

Where to Stay: El Convento—once a Carmelite nunnery—is the only major hotel in the heart of Old San Juan. The dining room is the former chapel. El Convento is well situated as a base for a walking tour of the old city, (800) 468-2779; www.elconvento.com. On the fringe of the Old City are the 22-unit **Gallery Inn** on Calle Norzagaray, (787) 722-1808, and the nine-story, 240-room **Wyndham Old San Juan Hotel and Casino** on Brumbaugh Street; call (800) 996-3426.

   Near El Yunque: Casa Cubuy Eco Lodge, ten rooms, a nonsmoking inn, Rates are $80–100 for a double with breakfast. Call (787) 874-6221. **Casa Flamboyant,** three rooms and a separate villa; heated pool. Rates range from $110–185 for the villa. Call (787) 874-6074. **Phillips Forest Cabins:** tent sites and economy cabins on a fruit farm.

Cabins start at $35, reduced for longer stays. A guide to the rain forest and nearby Taino petroglyphs is available; located on Route 191 above Naguabo. Call (787) 874-2138.

In the countryside, the least expensive places to stay are the **Paradores,** a chain of inns located in some of the most historic and scenic places, including the national forests. Sometimes not all the staff speaks English, but communication is always achieved somehow. The Paradores are operated by the Puerto Rico Tourism Company, charged with promoting the island. For information about Paradores and small inns, call (800) 866-STAR.

Camping: Unlike most Caribbean islands, camping is widely available, including in **El Yunque** and many of the **state forest reserves.** To camp in El Yunque, obtain a camping permit at the El Portal visitor center (see El Yunque hiking section for full details). To camp at the forest reserves it is necessary to obtain a camping permit in San Juan at the office next to the Club Nautico marina by the bridges. The fee is $4 per person, per night. It's possible to request an open reservation and travel at your own pace; otherwise you will need to establish a schedule and stick to it. For more information, phone (787) 724-3647, (787) 724-3724, or fax (787) 721-5984. You can also write the Dept. of Natural Resources, P.O. Box 9066600, Pta. De Tierra, San Juan, PR 00906-6600. This office also handles the permits for **Mona Island.** Because Puerto Rico is part of the United States, you can use priority mail at no extra charge.

On the island of **Culebra,** the government also operates a campground fronting scenic Flamenco Beach. Divided into 5 sections, it can accommodate up to 500 tents. The charge is $10 per night for up to 6 people with a 2-night minimum. Culebra is reached by a ferry from Fajardo. For reservations, call (787) 742-0700.

Currency: The U.S. dollar is the standard rate of exchange. Many U.S. banks have branches in San Juan. Credit cards are accepted in the larger cities, but be prepared to pay cash in the countryside. Keep lots of small bills for drinks, snacks, and so on. Banks are open weekdays from 9 a.m. to 2:30 p.m. weekdays. Canadian money is not always readily accepted.

Taxes & Tips: A 7% room tax in regular hotels, 10% if it has a casino. Tipping of 10–15% is standard and may automatically be added to your bill. The airport departure tax is included in the price of your ticket.

Electrical Current: Normally 110 volts, 60 cycles.

Safety & Health Warnings: San Juan is a large urban area with all the usual crime problems that implies. Cars should be kept locked and valuable possessions left in hotel safes. Drink bottled water rather than tap water. Avoid swimming in rivers because bilharzia could be present. There is a common flu-like illness called "la monga," which is not serious and disappears after few days.

Snakes and Other Venomous Creatures: Puerto Rico has four kinds of snakes, but none are venomous. Because El Yunque forest is near a major metropolitan city with a substantial crime rate, your greatest danger is from two-legged animals. Exercise reasonable caution and you should be fine, with or without a guide.

Hiking and Walking Services: Hiking is far more popular among visitors than locals, so the few operations that do exist cater to tourists. For a guide to El Yunque, contact **Robin Phillips** at Phillips Family Budget Cabins, (787) 874-2138; email phillips@east-net.com.

To find out about the annual hike from one end of the island to the other (a distance of 165 miles or 238.3 km) contact **Fondo de Mejoramiento,** P.O. Box 364746, San Juan, PR 00936-4746; phone (787) 759-8366.

Additional Information: The Puerto Rico Tourism Company sounds like a conglomerate, but that is the official government tourism branch. In the United States, write 666 Fifth Ave., 15th Floor, New York, NY 10103; or phone (800) 866-STAR. In Canada, 41–43 Colbourne St., Toronto, Ontario M5E 1E3; phone (416) 368-2680; www.prtourism.com. There are also branch offices at the San Juan international airport and in most of the larger towns. Be sure and pick up a copy of "Que Pasa," which lists all the major hotels, attractions, etc.

Dining Out: Puerto Rico has more restaurants than you can ever hope to sample in a lifetime. They range from gourmet to the simplest roadside eateries. However, the small restaurants in the countryside specializing in local cuisine offer full meals for as little as $7. It's easier and cheaper to dine in these small restaurants than it is to pack a picnic lunch; supermarket food is mostly imported.

OLD SAN JUAN AFOOT!

Time: 8–10 hours. | **Difficulty:** 1. | **Trailhead:** El Morro Fortress.

The crown jewel of Puerto Rico is Old San Juan, a seven-block area once completely enclosed by a city wall and guarded by one of the hemisphere's mightiest fortresses. Founded in the early 1500s as a military stronghold, Old San Juan by the nineteenth century had transformed into a picturesque residential and commercial district.

Today, this thriving community of narrow streets looks almost like a movie set, with its pastel-colored buildings flanked by wrought-iron, filigreed balconies. The town of Old San Juan takes at least a full day to thoroughly explore.

Old San Juan is not just a living historic monument but also a thriving, very lively place, particularly at night when the big department stores close down and the small cafes come to life. Strolling the streets after dark (you'll probably be surprised—and reassured—at the number of policemen you see), the shoppers and most of the motorized traffic now gone, it's possible to imagine what life may have been like here several hundred years ago. You may well stumble across a small eatery where no one speaks English, though the menu is likely to have English translations. Be adventurous and have some fun. How far wrong can you go in a land that bottles Coca-Cola and where soap operas are even more popular than in the United States?

Because traffic is often heavily congested and parking spaces almost impossible to find, the best way to explore Old San Juan is on foot. The place to start is the island's main landmark, the fortress San Felipe del Morro.

1. **El Morro Fortress:** Begun in 1540, the great fort rises 6 stories and 140 feet above the pounding sea. El Morro underwent many modifications until 1783, when it became the formidable structure standing today. Although impenetrable from attack by sea (Sir Francis Drake failed in 1595), it was taken by land attack by the Earl of Cumberland in 1598. He held the fortress only temporarily, leaving when the bottom fell out in a

Old San Juan

ATLANTIC OCEAN

To El Morro

City Wall

Calle Norzagaray · Calle Norzagaray

Calle Sol

Fort San Cristobal

Calle Luna

Calle O'Donnel

Avenida Munoz Rivera

Calle San Sebastian

Calle Sol

Calle San Francisco

Calle Cristo

Calle Luna

Avenida Ponce de Leon

City Wall

Calle San Jose

Calle Cruz

Calle San Justo

Calle San Francisco

Calle Fortaleza

Paseo de la Covadonga

Caleta las Menjas

San Juan Bay

Caleta San Juan

Calle Recinto Oeste

Calle Cristo

Calle San Francisco

Calle Fortaleza

Calle Tanca

Calle Tetuan

Calle Comercio

Calle Tetuan

Calle Recinto Sur

Parking Building

City Wall

Paseo de la Princesa

Post Office

Tourist Information Center

Calle Marina

Tourism Pier 3

La Puntilla

Tourism Pier 1

Catano Ferry Terminal

1. El Morro Fortress
2. San Juan Cemetery
3. San Juan Museum of Art and History
4. Plaza de San Jose
5. Pablo Casals Museum
6. San Jose Church
7. Quincentennial Square
8. Las Americas Museum
9. School of Fine Arts
10. Institute of Puerto Rican Culture
11. Plaza de Beneficia
12. Casa Blanca
13. Plazuela de la Rogativa
14. Children's Museum (Museo del Nino)
15. El Convento
16. San Juan Cathedral
17. Plaza de Armas
18. City Hall (Alcaldia)
19. San Juan Gate
20. La Fortaleza
21. Pigeon Park
22. Cristo Chapel
23. La Princesa Promenade
24. La Princesa Jail
25. Plaza Colon
26. Tapia Theater
27. El Castillo de San Cristobal
28. The Casino
29. The Capitol

dysentery epidemic. Both a World Heritage Site and a National Historic Site, El Morro is administered by the U.S. National Park Service. Orientation and slide programs are offered daily. With budget cutbacks, its opening times keep getting later; these days it's somewhere around 9 a.m., open daily until 6 p.m.; check by calling (787) 729-6536. El Morro makes a wonderful silhouette for sunset photographs with the sun behind one of the guard towers.

2. San Juan Cemetery: Adjacent to El Morro and visible from its ramparts. Besides being the burial place of many prominent Puerto Ricans, it is an impressive display of elaborate tombstones surrounding a circular neoclassic chapel dedicated (in 1963) to St.

Mary Magdalene. Near one of the poorer sections of the city, it is considered safe to visit only in groups. A view from a hill or El Morro is just as appealing.

The cemetery is flanked by a section of the massive city wall that completely surrounded Old San Juan in the 1630s. The city wall consisted of two separate 40-foot-high, parallel limestone-block walls with the space in between filled with sand. To discourage attackers, the exterior face was slanted, varying from 20 feet wide at the base to only 12 feet at the top. "Garitas," tiny rounded sentry posts that have become the symbol of Puerto Rico, still line the top. The wall was patrolled night and day, and every evening at sundown the six city gates were closed to completely cut off access to the city.

3. **San Juan Museum of Art and History:** On Norzagaray, corner of McArthur. Built in 1855 as a marketplace, it was used in the early twentieth century for government offices before being turned into a cultural center in 1979.

4. **Plaza de San Jose:** Flanked by some of the most impressive and important buildings in San Juan. The plaza itself seems bland until you realize the statue of Ponce de Leon, presiding over the plaza square, is made of captured British cannon, seized after the unsuccessful attack of Sir Ralph Abercromby in 1797.

5. **Pablo Casals Museum:** On Plaza de San Jose, the museum is dedicated to the cellist who came to Puerto Rico to live in 1957. The unimposing building contains manuscripts, photographs, and a library of videotapes of Festival Casals concerts that may be played on request. Open Tuesday through Saturday, 9:30 a.m. to 5:30 p.m.; call (787) 723-9185.

6. **San Jose Church:** Dominating the Plaza de San Jose and dating back to 1532, this is the second-oldest church in the Western Hemisphere. It has remarkable vaulted Gothic ceilings. The figure of Christ of the Cross on the church's left side is believed to date from the mid-sixteenth-century. The family of Ponce de Leon, the first governor, worshiped here. He was buried in the church from the sixteenth to the twentieth century. Open Monday through Saturday, 8:30 a.m. to 4 p.m. Mass at noon Sunday; call (787) 725-7501.

7. **Quincentennial Square:** Located on Old San Juan's highest hill, the square was built to celebrate the 500th anniversary of America's discovery by Christopher Columbus. A 40-foot-high, totem-like monument in black granite and ceramics rises from the square.

8. **Las Americas Museum:** The museum highlights folk art not only from Puerto Rico but all over the Americas. Open Tuesday through Friday from 10 a.m. to 4 p.m., weekends from 11 a.m. to 5 p.m.; call (787) 724-5052.

9. **School of Fine Arts:** Facing El Morro, this imposing building is not a tourist attraction but an institute of learning. Student shows are offered seasonally.

10. **Institute of Puerto Rican Culture:** Formerly the Hospital de Beneficia, this impressively restored building provides a good look at the island's culture and geology from prehistoric times. Open daily except Monday from 9 a.m. to 5 p.m.; call (787) 724-0700.

11. **Plaza de Beneficia:** Grab a bench and relax in this small park.

12. **Casa Blanca:** Built in 1521 as the home for Governor Ponce de Leon in gratitude for his achievements. However, he never personally occupied it. He died in Cuba before he could move in. Then Casa Blanca was destroyed by a hurricane. However, by 1523 his family was able to move in and make Casa Blanca the de Leon ancestral home for the next 250

years. After that, authorities decided that was gratitude enough, and the government turned the complex into the residence of Spanish military commanders. American army commanders followed the tradition, living here between 1898 and 1966. Today, Casa Blanca is a museum of island life, with a host of artifacts from colonial days; open daily 9 a.m. to noon and 1 p.m. to 4 p.m.; call (787) 724-4102.

13. **Plazuela de la Rogativa:** This statue of a bishop followed by three women holding torches refers to the 1797 British siege of Old San Juan. As legend goes, one night the British had second thoughts about attacking because they saw many torches moving along the wall. The British believed San Juan was being reinforced. Instead, it was a religious procession *(rogativa)* of women carrying torches and singing as they followed their bishop. The striking monument was erected in 1971 to mark the 450th anniversary of the event.

14. **Children's Museum (Museo del Nino):** Three floors of displays, many of them hands-on, including a mock dentist's office and a village of playhouses. Open Tuesday through Thursday from 9 a.m. to 3:30 p.m.; until 5 p.m. on Friday. Weekends, the hours are 12:30 p.m. to 5 p.m.

15. **El Convento:** Built in 1651, this was the New World's first Carmelite convent. Later it became a dance hall and Puerto Rico's most famous hotel. It was completely refurbished in 1997 at a cost of $275,000 per room. The first two floors, with restaurants and art galleries, are open to the public.

16. **San Juan Cathedral:** Begun in 1521 as a thatch-roofed structure, this magnificent Spanish colonial church is topped with three red and white cupolas. It is a rare and authentic example of medieval architecture in the Americas. The body of Ponce de Leon was moved from San Jose Church to a marble tomb here in 1913. Restoration of the entire church was completed in 1977.

17. **Plaza de Armas:** In the heart of the old city, this was the military parade ground, now an open piazza with fountains.

18. **City Hall (Alcaldia):** This replica of Madrid's city hall is notable for its double arcade flanked by two towers. Work on it started in 1609 but was not completed until 1789. More than a showpiece, it houses the city's main offices and a tourist information center. Open weekdays from 8 a.m. to 5 p.m.

19. **San Juan Gate:** The large wooden gate at the base of La Formalize was part of the city huge defense system. Upon arrival here, important dignitaries were escorted to San Juan Cathedral to celebrate a mass in thanks for a successful voyage.

20. **La Fortaleza:** Overlooking San Juan Bay from the top of the city walls, this governor's mansion was initially built as a fortress in 1532 against the fierce Carib Indians. The oldest executive mansion still in use in the Western Hemisphere, it is open to guided tours Monday to Friday 9 a.m. to 11 a.m. and 1 p.m. to 3 p.m. Tours in English on the hour, in Spanish on the half hour. This is a working government office; proper attire is required.

21. **Pigeon Park:** A nice quiet park for relaxing after walking the Old City. And, of course, it is filled with pigeons.

22. **Cristo Chapel:** According to legend, in 1753 a man lost control of his horse and would have plunged over the cliff at the street's end except that the horse suddenly stopped.

La Rogativa is one of Old San Juan's most famous statues

Considering this a miracle, and to give thanks, the rider built a chapel on the spot and dedicated it to the Christ of the Miracles. Originally it had only a tiny niche with a figure of Christ. Now it houses a silver altar. Open Tuesday, Wednesday, and Friday from 10:30 a.m. to 3:30 p.m.

23. **La Princesa Promenade:** This renovated street is a nineteenth-century boulevard paralleling the old city wall. Lined with palms and shade trees, it is one of the city's widest walkways.

24. **La Princesa Jail:** Dating to 1837, this distinctive gray and white building is now the home of the Puerto Rico Tourism Company. It probably never looked this good when used as a lock-up.

25. **Plaza Colon:** Named in honor of Columbus on the 400th anniversary of his discovery of Puerto Rico, bronze tablets at the foot of the Columbus statue record events of the explorer's life. The plaza was restored not long ago to further dramatize the statue. Some nice open-air cafés border the north side.

26. **Tapia Theater:** Where theater, dance, and other cultural activities are held. Construction on this theater began in 1832 and continued until the last quarter of the nineteenth century. It was financed by taxes on bread and imported liquor and by subscription.

27. **El Castillo de San Cristobal:** Another huge fort, rising 150 feet above the sea and covering 27 acres, San Cristobal is located just above the Plaza Colon. It was built in 1771 to defend the city from inland attacks after successful invaders like the Earl of Cum-berland made such a mess back in 1598. A rather belated response to the problem, San Cristobal is considered a strategic masterpiece. Attackers could storm the main fortress only after taking five structures connected by tunnels and a dry moat. Operated by the National Park Service, hours are daily from 9 a.m. to 6 p.m.; call (787) 729-6536.

28. **The Casino:** Looking like a French mansion of the Louis XIV style and now used by the State Department, the building was opened in 1917 as an aristocratic social club. Financial problems during World War I caused the Casino to back down on its plans to use marble on the floors and walls. Instead, everything was plastered and painted to look like marble. During recent restoration, real marble replaced the fake. The Casino's proper name is the Manuel Pavla Fernandez Government Reception Center. Open Monday through Friday, 8 a.m. to 4 p.m.; call (787) 724-5985.

29. **The Capitol:** Just to the east of the old city, this white-pillared building is the seat of the Puerto Rican legislature. Elaborate dome friezes depict island history. Open Monday through Friday, 8:30 a.m. to 5 p.m.; call (787) 721-7305 to arrange a guided tour by appointment.

THE CARIBBEAN NATIONAL FOREST (EL YUNQUE)

The most popular and most-visited place outside of San Juan is the 28,000-acre Caribbean National Forest, 25 miles (40 km) southeast and a 45-minute drive from San Juan. Better known simply as El Yunque, the nickname comes from the good Indian spirit Yuquiyu who ruled from the mighty forest peaks to protect the Taino Indians, the island's original inhabitants. It was set aside as a reserve by the Spanish in 1876, making it one of the hemisphere's oldest protected forests. It became part of the USDA Forest Service system in 1903 but wasn't named the Caribbean National Forest until 1935. It was declared a United Nations Biosphere Reserve in the 1970s.

El Yunque is the smallest forest and the only tropical rain forest in the U.S. National Forest System. In its highest and most inaccessible altitudes, the virgin forest remains much as it was 500 years ago. This is rare, because over the centuries Puerto Rico has been subject to such intensive agricultural development that only 1 percent of the land is considered virgin.

El Yunque consists of four distinct forest zones: rain forest, palo colorado forest, sierra palm forest, and dwarf forest. Located in the rugged Luquillo mountain range, El Yunque receives an incredible amount of rain. This is one rain forest that really lives up to its name. The higher peaks annually receive as much as 240 inches, and the forest overall averages 120 inches. That comes to about 160 billion gallons of water every 12 months, enough to provide water to San Juan for 2.5 years or the entire islands for 8 months. March is usually the driest month.

Although severely damaged in 1989 by Hurricane Hugo (the vegetation was stripped of its leaves so that the landscape resembled the dead of winter), the storm actually proved to be a benefit for visitors. New panoramic vistas opened that were previously blocked by a mantle of thick green vegetation. However, these lookout points eventually will be obscured by the new growth regenerating quickly in this warm, moist climate.

Hiking in El Yunque is quite easy: Most of the trails are surfaced with asphalt or concrete. In fact, you may be disappointed at how hard-surfaced most of the forest pathways are; the only exception are the few graveled pathways at high altitude where relatively few visitors go. There are two reasons for paving the trails. One is to combat erosion. Some sections of forest sidewalk have to be repaired and replaced almost every year because of the torrential runoffs.

The second reason for the hard-surfaced paths is wonderfully unique, even for the Caribbean. As one Puerto Rican tourism official explained to me, "We don't like to walk. We are a 'car' people and we like to drive everywhere. We would drive to the bathroom if we could. The idea of walking through the forest on dirt paths where you might get your shoes dirty does not truly appeal to a lot of us."

And so a mini-road system (the width of a typical bicycle path) travels through the El Yunque wilderness to make the forest as accessible and as alluring as the Puerto Rican culture will allow.

THE ANIMALS

The Coquis

El Yunque's best known and most vocal inhabitants are its millions of tiny tree frogs known as coquis (pronounced "CO-kee"). The coquis name applies to all 13 species of El Yunque's tree frogs, although only two of them (the forest and common coqui) actually produce the famous "co-kee" sound. (Eleven of the 13 species are found only in Puerto Rico.) Each of the other species has its own distinct call; some sound like "bobwhite" quail. With the variety of voices, you can expect an incredibly diverse sunset chorus.

The coquis sing loudest when it rains. Despite how often that occurs, the frogs seem to become deliriously happy with each new sprinkle. If you want to hear the coquis sing, expect to get wet; you probably will, anyway, as this a rain forest. But if it doesn't rain during your visit, hang around until sunset, when the coquis always sing. Forest Service biologists say the tree frogs call to defend their different territories used for shelter, feeding, and mating. As might be expected, the loudest calls are made by males defending their mating territory. Some scientists say that by calling out, the male coqui is trying to discourage other nearby males from attracting females.

Coquis are fascinating creatures. The coquis of El Yunque are only about an inch in length and vary in color from gray to brown to green to yellow. All species have pads or disks on their toe tips that enable them to cling to slippery surfaces. Arboreal or tree-living species have larger toe pads than those living on the ground. Most coquis found in the lowlands are arboreal, where in the high forest they are mostly ground-dwellers. Although the lowland species range high up into the mountains, the mountain residents rarely are found in the lowlands. Apparently, the mountain coquis know all about the heat lower down.

Sometimes, it's said that frogs literally fall out of the sky in the rain forest, and it's partially true. When the humidity is high, the coquis will climb as high as 100 feet in search of food, and predators like the tarantula are only too happy to greet them. The frogs that make it up high often jump off and drop to the forest floor rather than risk going back down the tree where predators are waiting. The frogs are so light they almost float to the ground. And that's how it rains frogs in the rain forest.

The Puerto Rican Parrot

Unfortunately, this colorful parrot is considered one of the rarest birds in the world. An estimated 1 million of them existed in Puerto Rico when the Spanish arrived. By 1971, only 16 parrots were known to exist in the wild; another 3 lived in captivity. Although they are making a comeback, their numbers are still small. You can identify the parrots by their call and their color. When they fly, they voice a loud, repetitive bugle-like call. Mostly green in color, the wing tips are a brilliant blue and easily visible in flight. About 12 inches in length, the parrot also has a vivid red forehead that you're most likely to see only at close range. Its tail is short and squared-off.

The Puerto Rican parrot essentially is a fruit eater but is known to eat seeds, flowers, and leaves. They mate for life and breed from February to June. However, if a mate dies, the surviving bird will usually find another partner by the next breeding season. This parrot doesn't build its own nest but uses cavities in palo colorado trees. A clutch of eggs numbers from 3 to 4, and the chicks hatch after 26 days. They are able to leave the nest at two months but remain with their parents until the next breeding season.

Although the Puerto Rican parrot is the most famous, about 50 other bird species are found in the Caribbean National Forest.

Lizards

The island has 12 native species, 8 of which are found in El Yunque. The largest is the Puerto Rican giant anole, whose body grows to five inches; the tail adds several more. All of the male lizards have a dewlap, or sac, on their throat that they inflate to defend their territory or to impress females. When their sac is inflated, the males will often erect a dorsal crest, bob their heads, wag their tails, do push ups, and/or stick out their tongues. Most of the lizards are able to change color, going from green to almost black or turning different shades of brown. The need to camouflage may be only one of the reasons for this. The color variations also appear to be related to changes in mood or temperature.

Freshwater Shrimp

Nine species of two different shrimp families live in the pools and streams of the forest. Most are nocturnal. At night you can find them on submerged tree branches, rocks, and roots. During the day look for them in pools and around rapids. Shrimp of the Atyidae family are filter feeders, consuming algae and decomposing materials. Shrimp in the Palaemonidae family are quite different, preferring to hunt and eat small fish, insects, and other shrimp.

THE FORESTS

The Rain (Tabonuco) Forest

More than 240 different species of trees, epiphytes, giant ferns, mosses and vines populate El Yunque; 26 of these are found nowhere else in the world. The most visually spectacular sections are not up high but on the slopes below 2,000 feet, the section considered true rain forest (also called the tabonuco forest).

Ironically, all this diversity causes some U.S. visitors a problem and they leave El Yunque frustrated and disappointed. As forestry technician Robert Rijos explained, "You can go to Sequoia National Forest and walk for miles and see the same tree and basically the same setting. The uniqueness in El Yunque is its diversity, that so many different species can share the same habitat. But the scenery may seem to lack any organization—it looks more like a jungle than a forest. Some people leave disappointed, unimpressed, because they came expecting to see only one or two different kinds of trees. Instead, they find all this."

Instead of disappointment, many first-time visitors probably feel overwhelmed. If you don't have a guide or a guidebook to explain what you are viewing, El Yunque is not only dazzling it is incomprehensible. Advance reading is mandatory unless you have a personal guide. Get all the information available at the Sierra Palm interpretive center before exploring. Otherwise, everything may blur into a maze of meaningless, moist, emerald objects.

Of course, the easiest way to gain understanding of the forest is through the Rent A Ranger Program. See El Yunque Fast Facts, (p. 270).

Palo Colorado Forest

This forest type grows between 1,987 and 2,950 feet, often in valleys and mountains, and is characterized by three species but dominated by the palo colorado *(Cyrilla racemiflora),* a crooked, reddish-colored tree that dominates this zone. This is the region where the endangered Puerto Rican parrot makes its nests, using openings in the palo colorado trunk made by other animals.

Sierra Palm Forest

The sierra palm forest is found in the highest points in the mountains of Luquillo and in ravines over 968 feet above sea level. Compared to the tremendous diversity of the rain forest, the palm forest is unique, a kind of monoculture consisting only of the sierra palm *(Presto montana).* Sierra palms have white flower spikes and erect prop roots. This is the most open of the four forest systems. The sierra palm fruit is a main food source for the rare Puerto Rican parrot.

The Dwarf (Elfin) Forest

Of El Yunque's four distinct forest zones, the smallest (only 3 percent) is the stunted and twisted vegetation of the dwarf forest. It grows only on the highest peaks and mountain ridges. Although referred to as dwarf forest in Puerto Rico, this same zone is more likely known on other islands as "elfin woodland" or sometimes even "cloud forest."

The weather is often harsh, and the adaptive, evolutionary process has created a vascular flora that is almost 40 percent endemic to Puerto Rico, found nowhere else in the world. As in most dwarf forests, animals are scarce. Amphibians include mainly tree frogs like the common coqui, the burrow coqui, the tree-hole coqui, and the warty coqui. Reptiles are limited to anoles, including the Puerto Rican giant anole, and only a total of 14 different bird species have ever been sighted in the dwarf forest. The elfin woods warbler was unknown to science until its discovery here in 1971. The best trails for exploring the dwarf forest are El Yunque and El Toro, which pass through all the various forest systems. The El Toro path peaks at the 3,523-foot Pico El Toro, highest point in the Caribbean National Forest.

EL YUNQUE FAST FACTS

Getting There: Reach El Yunque from San Juan by Route 3, connecting with Route 191, which leads directly into and through the forest.

Camping: There aren't any designated campsites, but you're allowed to camp in the forest. You must get a free camping permit from the El Portal visitor center on Route 191 before 3 p.m.

Rent-a-Ranger Program: Two-hour guided tours with a forest ranger to learn about the history, biodiversity and forest management of El Yunque. Tours are offered at 9:30 a.m. and 1:30 p.m. Monday through Saturday. There is no minimum size group; the maximum is 25. Reservations must be made two weeks in advance by calling (787) 888-1880 on weekdays. There is a fee, which must be paid at the time of reservation.

Forest Adventure Tours: No reservations are needed for these one-hour trail hikes with a naturalist guide. Fee required. For the latest information, call (787) 888-5646.

Safety Warning: Keep cars locked. Do not carry valuables. Women should not hike alone. Some residents consider this a high crime area.

Rain: Come prepared for it. Generally, the most concentrated rains fall in May, June, August, September and October. July tends to be drier, but no guarantees. Summer and early fall are when one tropical wave after another brings humidity and rain to the forest. March typically is the driest month.

Temperature & Clothing: El Yunque, so much cooler than the coastal areas, is like a refreshing water fountain in the mountains on even the hottest days. The Forest Service gauges the temperature range according to altitude.

If it is 80–85° F on the beaches, it may be:

75° F between 500–1800 feet;

70° F from 1,800–2,400 feet;

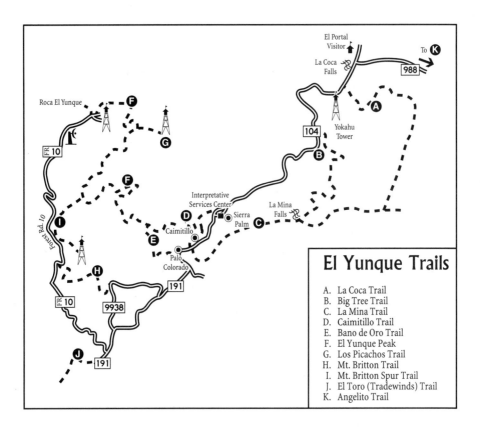

El Yunque Trails

A. La Coca Trail
B. Big Tree Trail
C. La Mina Trail
D. Caimitillo Trail
E. Bano de Oro Trail
F. El Yunque Peak
G. Los Picachos Trail
H. Mt. Britton Trail
I. Mt. Britton Spur Trail
J. El Toro (Tradewinds) Trail
K. Angelito Trail

65° F between 2,400–3,000 feet;

60° F from the 3,000-foot mark to the highest summit.

As it does get remarkably cool at the higher elevations, bring a jacket (with hood) for rain, a sweater for the wind. Good hiking shoes are essential. None of the trails should be attempted barefoot.

Picnic Sites: Located in the Sierra Palm, Caimitillo, and Palo Colorado picnic areas. They are all located between kilometer marker 11.6 through 12.1 on Route 191.

Waterproof Map: Rather than get this guide wet in the rain forest, you might consider the trails map published by National Geographic on recycled plastic paper. It sells at the Visitor Centers for about $10.

More El Yunque Information: The El Portal Tropical Forest Center is an air-conditioned, cathedral-like building at the foot of the forest. A video on the forest is shown in English and Spanish. Also a gift shop. The fee is $3 to enter El Portal but entrance to the forest is free. Access to the forest is available daily from 7:30 a.m. to 5 p.m. weekdays, until 6 p.m. on weekends. Contact USDA Forest Service, Caribbean National Forest, P.O. Box 490, Palmer, PR 00721; phone (787) 888-1810.

El Yunque Trails

Unless otherwise indicated, all trails begin on Route 191, which winds through much of the forest. Distances in Puerto Rico are measured in both miles and kilometers: 1 km equals 0.6 miles.

A. La Coca Trail

Length: 1.8 miles, one way. | **Time:** 2 hours. | **Difficulty:** 3. Slippery, steep at times. | **Trailhead:** Located on the left at km 8.6 on Route 191, just past La Coca Falls. If you reach the Yokahu observation tower, you've gone past it.

This gravel trail has a small parking area, so it's not heavily used. It's also steep and sometimes rocky. Remember, on the return it will be uphill most of the way. You'll cross two streams, not on a boardwalk but on rocks. Take the time to enjoy one of the quietest sections of the rain forest. The trail intersects with La Mina Trail.

B. Big Tree Trail

Length: 0.9 miles, one way. | **Time:** 50 minutes. | **Difficulty:** 1–2. | **Trailhead:** At km mark 10.4.

This is probably El Yunque's most popular walk. For one thing, it is the best walk through the tabonuco or true rain forest, offering more diversity in one small area than perhaps anywhere else. You can try counting and distinguishing the 160 different tree species here, not including ferns and vines (good luck!). This short walk also goes to La Mina Falls.

A distinctive species of the rain forest is the candle tree. The smooth gray bark oozes a pungent white resin (smells similar to pine pitch) that can be used to start fires. Even more remarkable is the laurel sabino that grows nowhere else in the world except in the Caribbean National Forest. The laurel sabino is draped with a dense community of vines and airplants that use the tree for support. They do not cause it any harm.

With luck, you may see some of El Yunque's eight different lizard species, most of which live in the rain forest zone. Each type has adapted to its particular niche so that none compete. For instance, some species live on the ground, others in trees; one in the sun, another in the shade ... a good example of peaceful coexistence.

Near twilight, you may see bats, an important resident in maintaining a tropical forest. By carrying and dropping fruit seeds or pollinating night-flowering plants, they help ensure the forest's regeneration.

Note also how many trees have wide buttressed roots. They require them because the soil is so saturated. Don't expect to see the usual, forest-type creatures in this or any other rain forest. They would need to float to survive here.

The trail ends at La Mina Falls, which has a 35-foot drop. You can stop here and swim, return to the trailhead or connect to the La Mina Trail (Hike C, below), which will take you to the parking lot at the Palo Colorado Recreation Center at km 11.9 on Hwy. 191. It's a mile-long walk from the center along Hwy. 191 back to the parking lot at Big Tree.

C. La Mina Trail

Length: 0.7 mile, one way. | **Time:** 50 minutes. | **Difficulty:** 2. It's a steep walk back. | **Trailhead:** Palo Colorado Recreation Center, km 11.9.

Leaving the trailhead, you'll cross over the La Mina River and pass a number of picnic shelters built in the 1930s by the Civilian Conservation Corps (CCC). It's amazing how far from the main road workers lugged in materials. The shelters with fireplaces were once used as honeymoon cottages. The CCC was also responsible for the trails' concrete steps that parallel the La Mina River and its series of cascades and pools.

After the picnic shelters the walk turns into a stroll through a garden of dense vegetation and Sierra Palms. You emerge above La Mina waterfall, then walk down in front of it. On hot days, especially weekends, there will be plenty of swimmers in the pool at the base of the falls. You may want to, too, before heading back.

If you thought it was a warm walk getting here, wait until you climb back up the steps. That's why the Big Tree trail, though slightly longer, is a more popular route to the falls. No steep return.

D. Caimitillo Trail

Length: 0.5 mile, one way. | **Time:** 40 minutes. | **Difficulty:** 1. | **Trailhead:** At km 11.7, across the street from the Sierra Palm Visitor Center.

This popular gravel and asphalt trail starts with a climb of 33 steps and passes the usually busy Caimitillo picnic area, then forms a short loop when it joins the El Yunque trail (see p. 274). You'll be walking through a lush palm forest, past wild impatiens (locally called miramelindas), bromeliads, and heliconias.

The trail ends just south of the Palo Colorado Visitor Center on Route 191. You can return the same way or on 191. There is a possible side trip for a look at the Bano Grande, the largest swimming pool built by the CCC. The pool is closed to the public.

E. Bano de Oro Trail

Length: 0.25 mile, one way. | **Time:** 30 minutes if you connect with the El Yunque Peak trail for a 1-mile walk that will loop you back to the Palo Colorado Visitor Center. | **Difficulty:** 1. | **Trailhead:** At km 12, just south of the Visitor Center parking lot.

Leaving the trailhead behind, you will almost immediately arrive at an old concrete swimming pool built in the 1930s by the CCC. It was named Bano de Oro, or "band of gold," apparently comes from the fact that a gold ring or something shiny was once found in the swimming pool, which has been closed for decades.

Continuing, you'll also see old stone tanks. They were once used in an attempt to introduce trout, a cold-water species, into the rain forest. It failed.

Despite all the man-made structures, this still is a scenic trail, with several stream crossings in the palm forest. When you reach El Yunque trail, go right to return to Route 191, then walk a short distance back to the parking lot. Go left at the intersection with the El Yunque trail and you're on the way to El Yunque peak.

F. EL YUNQUE PEAK

Length: 2.5 miles, one way. | **Time:** 2–3 hours. | **Difficulty:** 3. Often very slippery and even muddy in spots. | **Trailhead:** At km 11.9, the Palo Colorado Visitor Center.

This asphalt and gravel trail eventually leads to El Yunque Peak, 3,496 feet above sea level. It also connects with the Mt. Britton, Caimitillo, Los Picachos, and Bano de Oro Trails. All the trails are clearly marked, so there's no danger of ending up on the wrong one.

Palo colorado, or red trees, dominate the lower stretch. You'll also see giant ferns, bamboo, moss, and large vines. Look in the trees for nests of the rare Puerto Rican parrot. You're most likely to spot one near dawn or dusk. They like to fly across the mountain in this particular region. Artificial woodpecker nests, essentially man-made wooden boxes, have been set up in this area.

In several places you'll also begin to appreciate the massive problem of erosion the Forest Service personnel face here because of the tremendous runoff. In some spots, the asphalt trail is actually eight inches below ground level: That's how much the surrounding land has slowly built up over the years. When rain pours down the asphalt pathway, it flows like a stream. At times the Forest Service employs as many as ten people to continually cut back and dig out trails like this one.

On the trail, you'll also pass beautiful beds of pink-blossomed impatiens by the pathway. They grow wild all year. Farther along, you'll see both the sierra palm forest and the amazing dwarf forest.

Remember it's the dwarf forest that receives most of the rain, over 200 inches per year. It's always wet here as bands of fog clouds hang just above ground. Fortunately, the average temperature is a mild 65° F; even though there are several rain shelters along the trail, a windbreaker is advisable because of the strong breeze that is partly responsible for the small size of the trees. Epiphytes love these wet conditions, which is why they grow almost everywhere.

If it's clear at the top, the observation deck will give you a panoramic view of the forest, the Atlantic, and possibly even San Juan off in the distance. You'll be sharing the spot with a communications tower.

From El Yunque peak you can reach El Yunque Rock by taking Forest Road 10 to the south for a short distance. The trailhead to the rock will be on your right. It's a steep scramble to the top, worth it only if you have clear weather for more good views of the area.

G. Los Picachos Trail

Length: 0.2 mile, one way. | **Time:** 30–40 minutes each way. | **Difficulty:** 3. Steep and often muddy. | **Trailhead:** From the El Yunque trail.

Unpaved, the trail leads to another of the observation towers built by the CCC in the 1930s. You'll need to climb 45 steps to the observation tower, where on a clear day you can see the Virgin Islands.

H. Mt. Britton Trail

Length: 0.8 mile, one way. | **Time:** 60–90 minutes. You can also connect with the Mt. Britton Spur and El Yunque Trails to loop back to the Palo Colorado Visitor Center, about 4–4.5 miles total including an uphill walk back to your vehicle. | **Difficulty:** 2–3. Often wet and slippery. | **Trailhead:** Drive uphill on Route 191 almost to km 13 where the road is blocked. Turn right onto Route 9938; drive for 0.25 mile to the trailhead on your left.

This is not only a pretty walk, but on a clear day it offers a terrific view of the coast from the Mt. Britton observation tower. It's a continuous uphill trek through the palm forest, and you'll cross several streams before reaching Forest Road 10, which is closed to traffic. Continue on the road for about 500 feet and the trail will veer right and take you into the dwarf forest and to the Mt. Britton observation tower. Resembling a castle turret, this stone tower looks like it could house Robin Hood or the sheriff of Nottingham. Actually, this is one of the CCC projects from the 1930s.

I. Mt. Britton Spur Trail

Length: 0.85 mile, one way. | **Time:** 15–30 minutes for just the spur; considerably more time depending on how you access it. | **Difficulty:** 2. | **Trailhead:** From either the Mt. Britton or El Yunque Trails.

If you're on the Mt. Britton trail, retrace your steps from the observation tower to Forest Road 10. The Spur trail will be on your right. This short trail has some of the best dwarf forest anywhere in El Yunque. Bromeliads drape from the tree like hanging beards. If you're on the El Yunque Trail, you'll reach the Mt. Britton Spur trail turnoff shortly before El Yunque peak. You can return by the Mt. Britton Trail, which will put you above the Palo Colorado Visitor Center, allowing a complete downhill return to the parking lot there.

J. El Toro (Tradewinds) Trail

Length: 7.8 miles to peak and back; 6 miles one way to Route 186. | **Time:** 8 hours to peak and back. | **Difficulty** 3–4. It's likely to be overgrown in areas, so wear long pants and a long-sleeved shirt. Expect to get muddy. | **Trailhead:** On Route 191 about 0.25 mile below the locked gate. Park off the road near the gate.

If you want a remote part of the rain forest to yourself, this is the trail for you. Part of the National Scenic Recreational Trail system, the Tradewinds Trail is El Yunque's longest and probably most difficult walk. On it, you will pass through all four different forest systems to reach Pico El Toro at 3,523 feet, the highest point in the forest. This is the only maintained trail without gravel or hard surface; the soil is too unstable. In the rainy season, this route can be quite muddy.

From your car, walk up and past the gate. You will pass Forest Road 10 on your right, then shortly after that, the gravel trail to El Toro Peak begins. It's almost 4 miles to El Toro peak, another 2.2 miles to where the trail ends at km 10.8 on Route 186. This is not well maintained, and it can be very muddy. Still, the views of the forest, the south coast and the dwarf forest make it a memorable trek. Unless you arrange for a someone to meet you, you'll need to retrace your steps. That's not a good idea because that means a trek of at least 12 hours and, unless you left very early, a dangerous walk in the dark.

K. Angelito Trail

Length: 0.5 mile, one way. | **Time:** 10–15 minutes. | **Difficulty:** 1.
| **Trailhead:** This is one of the few trails that doesn't begin on Route 191. Instead, driving into the forest on Route 191, turn left, and take Route 988 toward Sabana for about 2 miles. The trailhead will be on your right about 0.25 mile past Puente Roto Bridge. There is no designated parking area.

This out-of-the-way walk will take you to the Mameyes River and one of its natural pools, Las Damas. This clay and gravel trail is an easy hike.

The State Forest Reserves

Puerto Rico has some of the Caribbean's lushest terrain, much of it protected through a system of forest reserves, many established by the Spanish government as far back as 1876. These are among the oldest forest reserves in the Western Hemisphere.

Also called commonwealth forest reserves, they are coordinated by the Natural Resources Department, P.O. Box 5887, San Juan, PR 00906; call (787) 724-3724. The normal office hours are from 8 a.m. to 4:30 p.m. weekdays. The forests open at 7 a.m.

2. Pinones Forest

Trailhead: Take Route 187 from Isla Verde to Boca de Cangrejos to Pinones Road; call (787) 724-3724. No camping allowed.

Directly east of San Juan, Pinones Forest contains Puerto Rico's largest mangrove forest as well as a rich variety of animal species that have adapted to living in an ever-increasing urban environment. Because it is so close to San Juan, Pinones Forest is heavily visited, used for snorkeling, fishing, and skiing as well as nature walks. Several small restaurants are located nearby. Along the way, you'll pass many small shops selling Loiza coconut masks used in an annual celebration featuring costumes, music, and dance that illustrates Puerto Rico's African heritage. For a guided tour of selected regions of this forest, contact **La Lamcha Paseadora** at (787) 791-0755.

The mangroves, which make up 70 percent of the forest, include all three species: red, white, and black. Visually striking because of their gnarled and intertwining root system, the mangroves serve as a vital nursery for many small marine creatures, including crabs and fish.

Pinones is home to about 46 species of birds, including various seagulls and pelicans. This reserve is one of the few remaining regions in Puerto Rico where gulls still regularly nest. Lakes Torrecilla and Pinones contain 38 different species of fish, including robalo, tilapia, and mojarra. Few places in the world can maintain organisms that are bioluminescent; Lake Pinones is one. Ghost crabs and lizards live in the sand dunes.

3. HUMACAO WILDLIFE RESERVE

Directions: Located in the southeast section of Puerto Rico, you reach this humid and subtropical reserve via Route 3 at km 74.3 in the area of Santa Teresa; call (787) 852-4440. Cabins and campsites are available; some campsites are on the beach. A permit is needed from the refuge office. It may be obtained only during normal hours (7:30 a.m.–3:30 p.m. daily) so officials can orient you to the facilities; phone (787) 852-6088.

Established in 1984, the refuge includes wetlands and lowlands and an estuarine system (mix of fresh and salt water) that is ranked as one of the most productive in the world. It receives 88 inches of rain annually, mostly from May to December.

About 90 species of both resident and migratory species live in the Humacao preserve, including ducks and gulls. The beach is a vital nesting place for two sea turtles species, the carey or hawksbill *(Eretmochelya imbricata)* and the tinglar or leatherback *(Dermochelys coriacea)*. Studies have been conducted on their reproductive cycles since 1986.

At the north part, between the Rivers Blanco and Anton Ruiz, is an interesting community of mangroves and "chicken trees" *(Pterocarpus officinalis)*.

GUANICA DRY FOREST

4. GUANICA DRY FOREST TRAILS

Trailhead: Located on the southwest coast about 90 minutes from San Juan. Take Highway 52, a toll road, to Ponce, then pick up Route 2. Several miles past the town of Yauco, turn left onto Route 116. Take Route 116 to Route 334 or Route 333. Route 334 goes into the heart of the forest, and Route 333 goes along the southern coastal edge. Camping is not permitted. The ranger station is on Route 334.

Bordering the Bay of Guanica, the dry forest is located in one of the sunniest, driest regions of Puerto Rico. Summer temps can reach up to 100° F and annual rainfall is only 30 inches, falling primarily around November. Guanica Dry Forest is one of the most important of the state reserves. It houses the largest number of bird species found anywhere on the entire island: at least 40 of the 111 resident species (including 14 indigenous and 9 endangered), plus numerous migratory visitors. Green turtles and leatherbacks nest on the beaches. However, hatchlings are sometimes picked off by mongoose.

Because it has been altered so little by human development, Guanica has the distinction of being perhaps the world's best preserved subtropical forest. It contains a great diversity of organisms and specimens unique to this one spot, including 700 tree and plant species. Like El Yunque, it has been recognized by UNESCO as an International Biosphere Reserve.

In addition to designated hiking trails, you can explore the forest by walking the dirt roads closed to traffic. Early and late in the day offers the best time spy the Puerto Rican bullfinch, the Puerto Rican emerald hummingbird, and others. The Puerto Rican nightjar, once thought to be extinct, has a colony of several hundred birds in this reserve.

The effects of the wind and salt from the ocean, and general lack of water limits the vegetation primarily to succulents, thorny bushes, and trees similar to many in arid climates. Most do not grow over five meters high. However, in moist ravines in the upper hills the trees grow taller and keep their leaves year-round. Of the 246 trees and bushes that grow in Guanica, about 48 are endangered species and 16 are endemic to this region only. Deciduous trees comprise as much as 61 percent of the forest, evergreens another 18.6 percent.

There are also several types of beach communities. Areas designated as unstable grow tiny plants with a little flower called dondiego *(Ipomea pres-caprae)*. The common seagrape *(Coccoloba uvifera)* helps stabilize other sandy stretches, and the rocky beaches grow what looks like a natural bonsai forest, trees stunted and twisted by the wind.

The coastal areas are also important nurseries for crabs and cave shrimps *(Thyphlatya monae)* that live only in this area and nowhere else on the island.

Where to stay: One of Puerto Rico's finest small hotels, Copamarina Beach Resort, fronts the Caribbean but backs up to the forest. This nicely casual, 18-acre hotel is an ideal base for hikers. Call (800) 468-4553. Web site: www.copamarina.com. The resort has a detailed guide to the dry forest for its guests.

Thirty-six miles of hiking trails and old roads help penetrate the 9,900 acres of the Guanica forest. These 12 trails (A–L) are in the eastern region.

A. BALEENA

Length: 1.2 miles (2 km), one way.| **Time:** 20 minutes. | **Difficulty:** 1–2. | **Trailhead:** On Route 333 near Punta Baleena.

This old road passes through a mahogany plantation near the forest office and ends up in dry limestone scrub with cactus. At 0.9 mile (1.5 km) a sign points to an interesting side trail into a cool, moist canyon where trees are able to keep their leaves all year. Some do quite well, as the 700-year old Guayacan tree and its six-foot girth demonstrate.

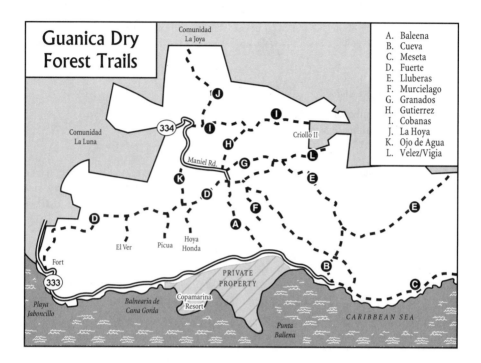

Guanica Dry Forest Trails

Comunidad La Joya

Comunidad La Luna

334

Maniel Rd.

Criollo II

A. Baleena
B. Cueva
C. Meseta
D. Fuerte
E. Lluberas
F. Murcielago
G. Granados
H. Gutierrez
I. Cobanas
J. La Hoya
K. Ojo de Agua
L. Velez/Vigia

J
I
H
G
K
D
A
F
E
L
E
B
C
D

El Ver   Picua   Hoya Honda

Fort

333

Playa Jaboncillo

Balnearia de Cana Gorda

Copamarina Resort

PRIVATE PROPERTY

Punta Ballena

CARIBBEAN SEA

B. Cueva

Length: 0.9 mile (1.5 km), one way. | **Time:** 20 minutes. | **Difficulty:** 1. | **Trailhead:** Drive to the parking lot at the end of Route 333. The trail is on the left.

Begin the hike in a coastal forest of seagrapes and tree-size milkweed with purple flowers and eventually reach agave and large prickly pear cactus. Butterflies are common along this trail. You may also hear the "troo-pial" call of the orange and black troupial bird. The hike ends where it meets the Lluberas Trail, one of the forest's longest.

C. Meseta

Length: 2.2 miles (3.5 km), one way. | **Time:** 45–60 minutes. | **Difficulty:** 1–2. | **Trailhead:** Go to the parking lot at the end of Route 333. Go through the gate and head east along the coast.

You'll have the chance to see how rugged the coast is here. With rocky headlands and sandy coves making up your route, you will end up in a remarkable "bonsai" forest of dwarf white mangroves, buttonwood, and cedar. Though small because of the pruning action of salt spray and wind, these trees many be over a century old. Look for brown pelicans, frigate birds, and the beautiful white tropicbirds. This walk bordering the Caribbean is one of the reserve's best.

D. FUERTE

Length: 3.4 miles (5.5 km), one way.| **Time:** 2 hours. | **Difficulty:** 2.
| **Trailhead:** Start at the forest headquarters on Route 33.

This sometimes rough road will take you to the site of an old fort that used as an observatory for the Spanish armada. As you would expect, the view of the forest, the Caribbean and Guanica town is perfect. The original fort was destroyed by U.S. troops when American troops invaded Guanica in 1898. Like everywhere else, the CCC was busy here in the 1930s and built a lookout tower on the ruins.

On the return, trip you may want to explore some of the three side trails, which are not factored into the length of this walk. Hoya Honda Trail goes into a valley with a shady mahogany grove and palms. Picua and El Ver Trails will also take you into ravines flourishing with evergreen vegetation and tree plantations such as the Guayacan tree, so heavy and dense that it sinks. It was heavily timbered for masts and prows by both the Spanish and Dutch.

E. LLUBERAS

Length: 5 miles (8 km), one way.| **Time:** 2 hours. | **Difficulty:** 2.
| **Trailhead:** Picnic area at the headquarters parking lot on Route 334.

This old road goes to the eastern boundary of the forest. It passes through all the major vegetation types including deciduous forest, which makes up about two-thirds of the reserve. In the dry season, about 40 percent of the trees will lose their leaves. As the rainy period nears, many trees will flower and fruit, attracting numerous birds. About mid-point in the trail it's possible to switch to the Cueva Trail, which will take you to the beach

F. MURCIELAGO

Length: 0.9 miles (1.5 km),one way.| **Time:** 25 minutes. | **Difficulty:** 2, on a hilly road. | **Trailhead:** At the picnic area at the headquarters parking lot on Route 334.

Start walking on the Lluberas Trail, and in about 600 feet (200 m), turn right onto the Murcielago Trail. Almost as soon as you turn you'll pass the Dinamita Trail that cuts off to the left. This is not a maintained trail, so it's difficult to follow in places. It's an exceptional walk if you can find your way, which will eventually take you to the Cueva Trail, which leads to the beach and Route 333.

Easier to follow and although much shorter, the Murcielago Trail is an eventful walk. First, you'll pass through a plantation of spindly mahogany trees that are actually a half-century-old and a dry deciduous forest, ending up in a moist ravine. The trail also cuts through limestone bedrock; listen for the sharp "meep" of the Puerto Rican todies, a small green bird that nests in the trees here.

G. Granados

Length: 0.6 mile (1 km), one way.| **Time:** 20 minutes. | **Difficulty:** 1–2.
Slightly hilly at the start.| **Trailhead:** Located 0.25 km north of the forest
headquarters on Route 334.

A short trail, but exceptionally good for bird-watching. Forty resident and migratory species
have been banded here. Lots of tall trees here, including guayacan, mesquite, and violet.
Rather than retracing your steps, you can return to forest headquarters on a section of the
Lluberas Trail.

H. Gutierrez

Length: 0.6 mile (1 km), one way.| **Time:** 20 minutes. | **Difficulty:** 1.
| **Trailhead:** About 0.3 mile (0.5 km) north of the forest headquarters
on Route 334.

In the 1950s this area supported plantations of mesquite, zarcilla and campeche. Part of it
was also cow pasture. Today, the forest is reclaiming it. This hike also connects with the
Cobanas Trail.

I. Cobanas

Length: 2.2 miles (3.5 km), one way.| **Time:** 30 minutes. | **Difficulty:** 1–2.
| **Trailhead:** Off Route 334, 1.2 miles (2 km) northwest of the forest
headquarters.

This old road follows a ridge through a deciduous forest. The last 0.3 mile (0.5 km) is an
abandoned plantation of campeche trees, once used to treat dysentery and to make black dye,
a truly strange combination. The road ends at the eastern forest boundary.

J. La Hoya

Length: 0.6 miles (2.5 km), one way.| **Time:** 45 minutes. | **Difficulty:** 2.
Sometimes hilly.| **Trailhead:** Off Route 334, 1.2 miles (2 km) northwest of
the forest headquarters.

Starts on the Cobanas Trail, then turn left 300 feet (about 100 m) onto La Hoya trail. You'll
enter a narrow ravine flourishing with uvilla, an evergreen that is kin to the coastal seagrape.
The uvilla is noted for the diverse size of its leaves. The ones near the canopy are about 1.5
inches long to minimize water loss; leaves growing lower down are 4 to 6 inches long. This
walk also has 15 to 30-foot high ucar trees, agave, and a good population of yellow, black,
purple, and brown butterflies.

K. Ojo de Agua

Length: 0.9 mile (1.5 km), one way.| **Time:** 25 minutes. | **Difficulty:** 2.
Hilly.| **Trailhead:** 1.2 km west of forest headquarters off the Fuerte Trail.

Yes, there are freshwater springs in this dry land, and this short trail goes into a well-nourished evergreen thicket with tea trees whose crushed leaves and flowers actually smell of lemon. This highly flammable tree was often used for torches.

L. VELEZ/VIGIA

Length: 0.6 mile (1 km), one way. | **Time:** 15 minutes. | **Difficulty:** 1.
| **Trailhead:** Picnic area at the headquarters parking lot on Route 334.

Follow the Lluberas Trail 0.6 mile (1 km) northeast of the forest headquarters until you see the Velez Trail going off to your left. A short trail, but it offers a lot. This tree-shaded walk takes you to Crillo 2, the highest point in the forest. It's also appropriately referred to as the vigia after the Spanish name for a ship's crows nest. In this case the crow's nest is actually the edge of a cliff that offers an excellent view of the northern sector of the forest, the Rio Loco Valley, and the different types of forest within the reserve. Turkey vultures like to fly on the thermals above the valley. You'll also enjoy a good view of the Cordillera Central and the town of Yauco.

5. GUAJATACA FOREST RESERVE

Directions: Located between Arecibo and Aquadilla and bisected by Route 446, south of Route 2; call (787) 872-1045. Camping allowed in the forest but not at the lake.

Guajataca Forest has more than 40 well-maintained hiking trails, covering 25 miles. This is the largest hiking trail system in the country. Try the ranger station for a map. One trail leads to an observation tower, another goes around a large depression framed by the haystack hills. Guajataca Forest is characterized by haystack-shaped hills and crater sinkholes, terrain that resembles an upside-down egg carton; in other words, karst country. This is the kind of classic, mystical Chinese landscape found around Guilin that Oriental artists have painted for centuries.

Karst is the result of millions of years of rain pounding on and dissolving the porous limestone terrain. The rain water flows along cracks underground, widening and deepening the cracks until they become underground caverns or stream channels. If water eats away enough ground close to the surface, the soil collapses, creating a sinkhole—one of the main features of karst country.

Like most karst terrain, there is little ground water here. More than a dozen man-made reservoirs make up the reserve. The most famous is three-mile-long Lake Guajataca, well known for its bass fishing. You'll need to bring your own tackle and boat.

6. CARITE FOREST RESERVE

Directions: This 6,000-acre forest is easily accessible off the Ponce Expressway near Cayey. It's on Route 184, south of Caguas. Camping is available at Charco Azul; call (787) 747-4545.

Bordering a lake of the same name, the Carite Reserve has a camping area shaded by eucalyptus and royal palms, a marked contrast to the sierra palms, which seem to outnumber all other species. This is another excellent bird-watching reserve: almost 50 varieties, including the Puerto Rican bullfinch and Puerto Rican tanager, both endemic species, and hummingbirds. Look for birds early and late at the several man-made lakes, including Lake Carite. The lakes are all reputed to be good fishing holes, but you must supply your own tackle and bait.

The main hiking trail, less than a mile in length, leads from the Charco Azul picnic site. It first passes a natural swimming hole, the Charco Azul, which is ten yards across and remarkably blue. The path then crisscrosses a stream that you must ford repeatedly. Eventually you will climb to Cerroa la Santa, the reserve's highest peak, at 2,730 feet high.

7. GUILARTE FOREST RESERVE

Directions: Just west of Adjuntas, south on Route 131 or Route 518; call (787) 829-5767. No camping. Rental cabins holding up to four people with cots and barbecue facilities but no electricity; $20 per night. Advance reservation required.

This 3,600-acre forest reserve offers what may be the most scenic hike in the Cordillera Central. Ask the ranger to find the beginning of the hike to Mt. Guilarte, which is near the intersections of Routes 131 and 518. The trailhead is unmarked. It's usually a slick, steep, 40-minute climb to the peak that passes through rain forest, sierra palms, and beautiful beds of pink impatiens, similar to El Yunque. Once at the summit, you have no radio or TV towers to spoil the view, as at the tops of El Yunque and Cerro de Punta. Seeing the countryside the way it was meant to be makes me wish for one of *Star Trek*'s Romulan cloaking devices to hide all utility poles, power lines, and media towers. What a beautiful place the world would be! The reserve has 105 species of trees and 26 bird species, 10 of which are endemic.

8. TORO NEGRO FOREST RESERVE

Directions: On Route 143 at km 31.8, east of Route 149; call (787) 867-3040. Camping permitted; at the country's highest elevation, expect the nights to be cool. A ranger station is located on Route 143 near the campground.

Straddling the Cordillera Central, this 7,000-acre reserve includes Puerto Rico's highest peak (4,390-foot high Cerro de Punta) and highest lake (bamboo-fringed Guineo Reservoir). When not cloud covered and rainy, the views of the Atlantic and Caribbean coasts can be stunning. Unfortunately you have to ignore the communications antennas sharing the top with you to appreciate it all.

Route 143 meets Route 149 to effectively divide Toro Negro into its eastern and western sections. Off Route 143 on the north side is a short but extremely steep road of several hundred yards that leads to the highest peak in Puerto Rico, Cerro de Punta. Although the road is paved, you may want to make the 20-minute walk up.

If you really want to struggle to rise to the mountaintop, you can make a three-hour hike from **Parador Hacienda Gripinas,** (787) 828-1717, in the town of Jayuya, off Route 527. This colorful 20-unit home-turned-into-an-inn is in the middle of an old coffee plantation.

To get to the peak of Cerro de Punta, you'll be following paved road, tire track paths, and eroded trails up the hillsides of still-producing coffee plantations. You'll need someone to point out where the trail starts. Naturally, it's not marked. As one forestry worker noted, why should it be "when everyone can drive to the top?"

Some impressive waterfalls and streams come out of Toro Negro, including the cascading Inabon, which heads south out of the reserve. Rock-hopping on this or any other river is always a real temptation, but conditions may be different than what you're accustomed to back home. Beware the slick and moss-covered rocks: anything green or red or discolored is potentially slick. This is how you "bust yo ass," as they say on some islands.

This is a region known for its unkind weather: The lowest temperature ever recorded on the island was here, 40°F. It may be as much as 10° to 15°F cooler in the mountains than Old San Juan. If it's raining and the wind is blowing, the wind chill will make the discrepancy greater. So rain gear—and in winter, yes, even a sweater—are often required.

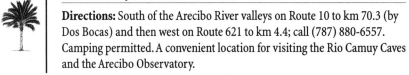

9. RIO ABAJO FOREST RESERVE

Directions: South of the Arecibo River valleys on Route 10 to km 70.3 (by Dos Bocas) and then west on Route 621 to km 4.4; call (787) 880-6557. Camping permitted. A convenient location for visiting the Rio Camuy Caves and the Arecibo Observatory.

This forest is part of a management program that has produced plantations of balsa, teak, and mahogany, all native species, as well as imports such as bamboo and Australian pines. You'll also find a wide variety of formations: caves, lakes, and spectacular views of karst country. Hiking is possible on some of the old lumber roads and footpaths. A mantle of vegetation conceals many of the terrain's karst features. Consequently, some people do not find the karst characteristics as starkly apparent as at other sites.

10. MARICAO FOREST RESERVE

Directions: North of Sabana Grande on Route 120; call (787) 724-3724. Camping permitted; also rental cabins with fireplace, $65 per night.

On the western slopes of the Cordillera Central near Mayaguez, the Maricao Forest Reserve hosts many bird species, particularly hawks, year-round. This is also one of the best-outfitted places for camping, offering two campsites and an attractive complex of cabins with a swimming pool. Also nearby is the **Parador Hacienda Juanita,** one of the chain of country inns operated by the Puerto Rico Tourism Company.

Maricao is home to more diverse tree species than any other reserve: 278 in all, of which 37 are indigenous to this particular reserve and another 133 are native only to Puerto Rico. Bird life is almost as prolific, with 44 species that include the Puerto Rican lizard-cuckoo, the Puerto Rican woodpecker, the sharp-shinned hawk, and even the rare elfin woods warbler at the highest levels.

Although the vegetation generally is more like that of karst country than the rain forest, this region receives a lot of rain. Ironically, the soil is of submarine volcanic origin, best suited to growing dry vegetation. The unusual soil accounts for the tremendous plant diversity.

The walking/sight-seeing here can be exceptional, if the weather cooperates. The sign lead-ing to Casa de Piedra, a stone mountain house, goes to a campsite with a fine view of the west.

You can also stop by the Maricao Fish Hatchery, Puerto Rico's only freshwater hatchery, which raises 25,000 bass, tilapia, and catfish annually for the island's man-made lakes and reservoirs. It is open daily 8 a.m. to noon and 1 p.m. to 4 p.m.; phone (787) 722-1726. A sel-dom-used trail will take you from the main ridge down to the hatchery, but the hike is seven hours each way and overgrown in sections. A compass, a machete, and a proclivity toward masochism help determine who makes this hike. A stone observation tower at the reserve's highest peak, the 2,625-foot-high Las Teta de Cerro Gordo, provides an excellent panorama of three coasts and distant Mona Island, 50 miles out to sea.

ELSEWHERE ON PUERTO RICO

11. AROUND PONCE

Directions: The Ponce Expressway, a modern highway running north to south, links San Juan with Puerto Rico's second largest city, Ponce (pro-nounced "Pon-tse").

The heart of Ponce is the old plaza central, **Plaza las Delicias** ("Plaza of Delights"). On one side, benches, pruned India-laurel fig trees, and statues surround the **Cathedral of Our Lady of Guadeloupe,** a seventeenth-century Spanish Creole church topped with rounded silver towers.

The **Casa Armstrong Poventud,** a restored turn-of-the-twentieth-century neoclassic mansion, faces the plaza and now serves as both a city museum and tourist information cen-ter. Ponce's most famous sight is its fire station, the **Parque de Bombas,** a red and black building built in 1883 for an architectural fair.

All the streets leading into the plaza are under restoration, including installation of replicas of the original gas lamps. Isabel Street is an example of how it will look. On Las Americas Avenue, across from Catholic University, is the **Ponce Museum of Art** containing more than 1,000 paintings (painters include Rubens and Gainsborough) and 400 sculptures. It is per-haps the best European art collection in the Caribbean. The building itself is something of an artwork, designed by Edward Durrell Stone, architect of New York's Modern Museum of Art. Open weekdays only 10 a.m. to noon and 1 p.m. to 4 p.m.; phone (787) 840-0505.

El Viega ("Lookout Hill") at the northern end of Ponce has a 100-foot-high concrete cross with an observation tower reached by elevator. The arms of monument, called the Virgin's Cross, extend 70 feet. It's quite a view.

A ten-minute drive on Route 503 from Ponce is a re-created Taino Indian village and a museum at the **Tibes Indian Ceremonial Center;** (787) 844-5575 or (787) 840-2255; open 9 a.m. to 4:30 p.m. daily except Monday. An Amerindian site discovered in 1974, it is the oldest burial ground yet uncovered in the Antilles. An audiovisual program in English describes the discoveries, which included 187 skeletons of the Igneri culture (A.D. 300). A museum houses ax heads, ceramic pots, and ceremonial idols. Seven ceremonial ball courts and two dance grounds date from A.D. 700. One may also be a pre-Columbian astronomical observatory. Stone points on one of the dance courts (which happens to be shaped like a rising sun) are said to line up with the sun during equinoxes and solstices.

On Route 10 at km 6.8 north of Ponce is the **Hacienda Buena Vista,** a restored nineteenth-century coffee plantation, farm, and grain mill. The original waterwheels, crushers, and turbines have been nicely restored, and the entire complex, amazingly, is driven by a network of waterways. Bilingual guided tours are offered of the two-story estate house, slave quarters, and mills. Open Friday afternoon, Saturday, and Sunday only; phone (787) 722-5882.

12. LA PARGUERA PHOSPHORESCENT BAY

Directions: Between Guanica and San German on the southwest coast. The easiest, though not most direct route, is to get off Highway 2 at the Guanica exit and take Route 116 directly here. | **Hours of Operation:** Boats depart nightly at 7:30 p.m. from the small marina and continue operating until there is no more demand. A dark moonless night is best.

About 45 minutes west of Ponce and 20 minutes from Guanica is the sleepy fishing village of La Parguera, which is also near the Guanica Forest Reserve. Phosphorescent Bay glows with the millions of microscopic organisms known as dinoflagellates that sparkle when disturbed. This phenomenon occurs only in the tropics, typically in mangrove-protected bays like this one. This is the best of the many different phosphorescent bays on the Puerto Rican mainland. (The best of all, however, is probably on the offshore island of Vieques.)

The tour boat travels to a small bay to the east of La Parguera. This is one time you might hope for a light rain. Then, the whole bay will light up, spectacularly glowing green, pink, and blue as the raindrops hit the water. When it really pours, the boats don't go out. To really stir things up and for maximum effect, visit the local dive shop and book a nighttime snorkel trip in the phosphorescent bay. Now, *that's* a trip!

You can stay overnight at 70-unit **Parador Villa Parguera,** which is a classic fishing inn known for its seafood; call (787) 899-3975. Nearby is the 40-unit **Parador Posada Porlamar;** phone (787) 899-4015. The rooms are plain but there's a dive shop on site. For considerably more luxury, the **Copamarina Beach Resort** at Guanica is less than 30 minutes away; phone (787) 821-0505.

13. SAN GERMAN

Directions: Directly off Highway 2, west of Guanica, on the southwest coast.

San German is the oldest town after San Juan. It still retains its distinctive colonial flavor with closely spaced old white homes, narrow balconies, and old-fashioned gas street lamps. You'll find two main plazas, each dominated by an architecturally important church. Off Calle

Doctor Veve is the **Porta Coeli Church,** primarily a religious art museum, which was built in 1606, a rare example of Spanish medieval architecture still surviving in the Caribbean. More ornate and at the other end of the plaza is the newer (nineteenth-century) **San German de Auxerre Church.** If it's possible, you might want to stay in the heart of San German in a converted 200-year-old family mansion. It is now the 34-room **Parador Oasis** with its own pool, restaurant, and weekend entertainment; call (787) 721-2884 or (787) 892-1175.

One of Puerto Rico's best-kept secrets is its extensive cave system, considered some of the most important in the Western Hemisphere. The Rio Camuy is the world's third-largest subterranean river. Yet it and the caves are relatively unknown because most visitors never venture this far into the countryside to discover them.

14. RIO CAMUY CAVE PARK

Directions: On the northwest side of the island. Coming from San Juan, take Highway 22 to Route 129 and the exit to Lares. Route 129 will take you directly to the caves, on the left, at km 20. | **Hours of Operation:** Wednesday through Sunday and most holidays from 8 a.m.–3:45 p.m. | **Information:** Call (787) 898-3100 or (787) 898-3136. | **Difficulty:** 2. The cave floor can be slick. It's 205 steps down to the Spiral Sinkhole, not really worth the effort because you can't go inside.

More than 220 caves have been discovered so far in Puerto Rico's karst country. Some are great, huge systems of passageways; others are only small openings in the earth. The biggest and best and most easily accessible system is the Rio Camuy Cave Park near Lares, which was discovered in 1958. Operated by the Administracion de Terrenos, the extensive system of passageways has been mapped for seven miles, but not all of it is open to the public yet. The capacity is 1,500 visitors per day.

The time to visit is in the morning, noon at the latest. Afternoon rains sometimes end the tours early because of concerns about rising water.

After taking a bilingual tram tour through a vegetation-filled sinkhole to the mouth of **Clara Cave,** you are guided past huge stalactites and stalagmites and into caves as much as 200 feet high (you can fit a 20-story building into this particular chamber). A walking side trip is also available to the 650-foot-wide **Tres Pueblos Sinkhole** that overlooks the Rio Camuy 400 feet below, seething through during flood periods. Across the street from Tres Pueblos is the **Spiral Sinkhole,** most notable for the scenic 205 steps down to it. The boardwalk stops at the cave mouth; you're not allowed inside. And the sinkhole interior is almost black, making it difficult to see anything. If you're running a tight schedule and need to get to nearby Arecibo (below), skip this and head to the observatory.

A separate excursion is rappelling and exploring in **Cathedral Cave.** The cost is $30 per person and requires advance reservations.

If this park is closed, the smaller and privately run Cueva de Camuy is nearby. Don't let the signs to Cueva de Camuy fool you into believing this is the government park. The privately owned cave is primarily an amusement park. You don't find pony rides or go-karts at the larger cave. Close to Rio Camuy is Arecibo, a place that will take you out of this world.

15. ARECIBO OBSERVATORY

Directions: On the northwest side of the island. Coming from San Juan, take Highway 22 to the Route10 exit to Utuado. After a few miles, turn left onto Route 652, which connects with Route 635 and Route 625, which will take you into Arecibo. Coming from Rio Camuy, take Route 129 to Route 134, continuing to the right on Route 635, then turning right again into Route 625 and Arecibo. | **Hours:** Wednesday through Friday from noon–4 p.m., weekends and most holidays from 9 a.m.–4 p.m. Admission fee. | **Information:** Phone (787) 878-2612 or visit www.naic.edu. | **Difficulty:** It's 500 steps to the visitor and educational facility. Bring an umbrella in case of rain.

An industrial center, Arecibo is most noted for 600-ton suspended platform of the Arecibo Observatory, the largest single-dish radar-radio telescope in the world. It discovered the first quasar, the star-like celestial objects that appear far from earth and that emit powerful radio waves. The Arecibo Observatory is actually a 20-acre dish fitted into a karst-created sinkhole 1,300 feet across. It is part of the National Astronomy and Ionosphere Center operated by Cornell University under an agreement with the National Science Foundation. The Angel Ramos Foundation Visitor Center and Educational Facility has 10,000 square feet of building and outdoor space. It contains 3,500 square feet of exhibits, an observation platform and an excellent view of the huge dish. The educational exhibits cover everything from basic astronomy to using the electromagnetic spectrum as an exploration tool that extends our direct sensory experience.

16. CAGUANDA INDIAN CEREMONIAL PARK

Directions: Near the central interior of the island. From Utuado, continue west on Route 111 to km 12.3. From Lares, go south on Route 129, east on Route 111 toward Utuado.

These 800-year-old stone playing fields located eight miles west of Utuado were built by the Tainos for ballgames and religious ceremonies. Covering 13 acres, it is a landscaped and shaded site with native trees, including royal palms and guava. Each of the ball courts was named for a different Taino chief, and several are bordered with stone monoliths. One ball court wall is famous for its petroglyphs. The Institute of Puerto Rican Culture operates the small museum open daily 8:30 a.m. to 4:30 p.m.; call (787) 894-7325. Admission is free.

17. AROUND MAYAGUEZ

Directions: Off Highway 2, 98 miles from San Juan at the western tip of the island.

Mayaguez is not a touristy town. Tuna packing is its major industry. This industrialized port city is Puerto Rico's third largest. The **traditional plaza** contains a stone walk, benches, bronze figures, and a statue of Columbus. The **Tropical Agricultural Research Station** attached to the University of Puerto Rico grows plants from all over the world. Cinnamon, citrus, and clove (smell the leaves!) are just some of the items neatly set out. On Route 65 north of the town, the Research Station is open weekdays from 7:30 a.m. to 4:30 p.m. at no charge; call (787) 834-2435. The **Mayaguez Zoo** contains exotic flora and animals from everywhere, including condors and tigers. It is open 9 a.m. to 4:30 p.m. daily except Monday; phone (787) 832-8110.

OFFSHORE ISLANDS

You may also consider visiting Culebra, Vieques, or Mona, small remote islands off the coast where a working knowledge of Spanish is recommended. For our purposes, Culebra is perhaps the most interesting because of its accessibility, the camping possibilities, and the chance to watch turtles lay their eggs in spring/early summer. Also, Culebra is a good choice if you feel the need for a snorkel break to get below sea level instead of staying hundreds of feet above it.

CULEBRA

Directions: Located 18 miles off east coat of Puerto Rico, 14 miles west of St. Thomas in the U.S.V.I. Regular ferry service from Fajardo for only about $5; call (787) 863-0707 for reservations and information. Air service from San Juan's Isla Grande Airport (not the international one) is available five times daily. The fare is $60 round-trip on Flamenco Airways; phone (787) 725-7707. Once on the island, transportation (except on foot) is limited.

Culebra, 7 miles long and 3.5 miles wide, covers an area of about 7,700 acres. It has some gorgeous white sand beaches. The population of about 2,000 took on the entire U.S. Navy to retain their island. For 40 years, the U.S. Navy used Culebra as a gunnery range day and night. Getting sick and tired of the noise (and probably grouchy from lack of sleep) the Culebrans finally protested by holding picnics in the target areas and exploding a few fireworks of their own (petrol bombs). In 1975, when the navy stopped making all its racket, Culebra again became a sleepy fishing village where not much happens. However, there is some excellent wildlife viewing here, both above and below the waterline.

The most popular regions are **Flamenco, Tamarindo, Resaca,** and **Larga beaches.** Culebra also has a **phosphorescent bay** and coral gardens ideal for snorkeling border much of its shoreline,

You'll find a tremendous variety of bird and marine life. The **Culebra National Wildlife Refuge** includes four land tracts on the island and 23 offshore islands. Known for its large nesting seabird population that includes terns and boobies, the refuge was established in 1909 by President Teddy Roosevelt. Besides four-foot-long iguanas, you'll find about 372 plant varieties, 33 that are rare and 3 that are indigenous to this island.

Perhaps the most interesting aspect of Culebra is the sea turtle nesting. Four species come here, nesting on the beaches at night between April and July. Join the Culebra Leatherback Project from April to June; (703) 450-0339). Or get a local guide. Finding a sea turtle laying eggs is a very hit-or-miss proposition; you may have to stay up all night. The proper procedure is to walk the beaches (best are Resaca and Brava) with a flashlight until you spy one of the creatures on the beach. You usually have to keep walking the same area, back and forth, several times before a turtle appears.

Until they actually begin laying their eggs, sea turtles may be very wary. You should not bother them with lights or noise or touch them, or they will retreat back to the water. However, once a turtle has dug out the sand with its back flippers and started depositing eggs, nothing can stop it. That is the time for photographing and stepping in close, but not before. This is a sight to be savored and planned for. Carry insect repellent.

You can camp at Flamenco Beach, with its own picnic and sanitary facilities. A portable refrigerator (this is tropical luxury!) is $2. You need a camping permit from the Conservation and Development Authority of Culebra; phone (787) 742-3880 or (787) 742-0700. You can buy all your foodstuffs on the island. Or stay at **Harbour View Villas** (call (800) 440-0700) or **Club Seaborne** (call (787) 742-3169).

VIEQUES

Directions: Pronounced "Byekess," Vieques is seven miles southeast Puerto Rico. Two ferry boats operate daily at 9:30 a.m. and 3 p.m. The ticket office opens at 8 a.m. On weekends, tickets ($4 adults, $2 children) sell out quickly for the morning ferry. For information call (787) 723-2260; reservations, (787) 863-0705. Flights to the island leave several times daily from Isla Grande Airport in San Juan (not the international airport). The fare is $45 each way. Contact Vieques Air Link (phone (787) 741-3266) or Isla Nena (phone (787) 741-6362).

Vieques has some of Puerto Rico's best beaches: 40 of them. The island is 25 miles long by 5 miles wide. Two-thirds of it still belongs to the U.S. Navy, which has held live bomb practices here. The 1983 Grenada invasion was dress-rehearsed on some of these beaches. Local protests against the Navy have resulted in a promise that the use of live bombs will end in a few years. When not playing war games, the Navy does open the beaches to the public.

Mosquito Bay is a phosphorescent bay considered more spectacular than La Parguera on the mainland. Don't come looking for the liquid flames: you have to create them yourself by paddling around in the water and stirring up the creatures responsible for the amazing phenomenon. If possible, use a mask to absorb the full splendor of the green and gold fires.

You can stay at the **Parador Casa del Francis** (phone (787) 741-3751) or Bananas (phone (787) 741-8700). Rental cars are available from Island Car Rental (phone (787) 741-1666) starting at $40 per day. Credit cards welcome.

MONA

Directions: Mona is 50 miles west of Puerto Rico and completely deserted. The only way to reach it is by plane or by boat. The Mona Passage is often rough, so be careful about the boat you choose. Camping tours are offered by **Encantos Ecotours,** including pickup at the San Juan airport and all land/sea transfers; call (787) 272-0005.

Often characterized as a mini-Galápagos, the island is home to endangered iguanas up to three feet long, red-footed boobies, and numerous other sea birds. The beach is also used as a nesting ground by three different species of sea turtles.

With cliffs that tower 200 feet high topped with dry forest, inland caves containing stalactites and stalagmites, and big iguanas, it's almost like no one was ever here. However, the Taino Indians visited, as did pirates, and for a time the caves were mined for bat guano.

The island is administered as a reserve by the Department of Natural Resources; (787) 724-3724 for the mainland office. They can tell you about the camping area at **Playa Sardinera.** You must bring all supplies, including water. Activities such as hiking and birding are coordinated by a resident biologist. To minimize impact, no more than 100 people are permitted on the island at one time.

The Annual Panoramic Hike:
Walk the Entire Length of Puerto Rico

The Panoramic Route is actually a country road that connects Mayaguez in the west with the town of Yabucoa in the southeast via Puerto Rico's mountainous backbone, the Cordillera Central. The vistas are spectacular. Although this network of roads extends for only 165 miles, it takes at least 2 to 3 days by car to cover this territory in a leisurely manner. One of the finest sights is the San Cristobal Canyon, a river ravine as much as 500 feet deep that is filled with tropical plants. However, there is a much better way to enjoy the Panoramic Route than by car.

Every spring the Fondo de Mejoramiento sponsors a hike of the full length of Puerto Rico, from Yabucoa in the southeast to Mayaguez in the west. Most people see the Panoramic Route only from behind a car windshield, staying on edge because of the series of spine-tingling, hairpin turns and the confusing lack of signs.

The panoramic hike shows a different Puerto Rico every weekend for two to three months, beginning in February or March. The richness of the country is evident as you walk through a knotted, twisting network of more than 40 roads that extend the full length of the Cordillera Central. The route includes tropical beauty as well as some strenuous climbing—these are some of the steepest parts of the island. All the hiking is done on the roadside of the twisted, winding Panoramic Route, none in the woods.

Ironically, although all the entire route is now paved, walking is the way it was intended to be seen by former governor Luis Munoz Marin, who first proposed the Panoramic Route around 1950. To open up the interior to tourism, Marin wanted to restore old highways and backways, leaving some sections open only to horses, people on foot, and four-wheel-drive vehicles. Today, hikers still enjoy the scenery as intended, but they walk the side of the paved roads instead of the center line .

Normally, the interior would not be the safest place for individual hikers, but the annual hiking group is accompanied by a police escort, a civil defense wagon to supply water, and a "broom bus" to pick up those who lag too far behind. The broom bus is easily identifiable— by a broom sticking out the front. Should first aid be needed, it is available in one of the small mountain towns.

The hike includes forests and farmland (coffee, bananas, citrus, vegetables). Four of the state forest reserves also cross the route. Expense is minimal, determined by each individual hiker. For the first several nights, hikers are close enough to return to San Juan in the evening; or you can stay in small hotels in the back country. The countryside hotels run about $30 to $40 per person for a double and include breakfast. Lunch and dinner are a separate expense.

Everyone starts the hike at the same time, and a day's walking covers an average of 10.5 miles (17 km). The sponsors stress that this is a recreational walk, not a competitive one; no one is in any rush to get there first. You'll find all types of people, mostly locals, from retired persons to those who took the day off from work just to make this walk.

On most days you will find small cafes typical of the back country of Puerto Rico, where you can get something to eat or take out food. Or bring your own provisions, if you wish. Trash bags are provided. For complete information, contact Fondo de Mejoramiento, Apdo. 4746, Correo Central, San Juan, PR 00936; call (787) 759-8366. There is no better way to see Puerto Rico or meet its people.

THE CHUPACABRA,
PUERTO RICO'S BIGFOOT

Pronounced "chew-pah-KAHB-rah" and meaning goat sucker, hysteria about this Puerto Rican version of Bigfoot comes and goes. The phenomenon is worth knowing about as the creature is said to hide/live in remote mountain caves and perhaps even in the forests of El Yunque.

The Chupacabra first came to life in 1994 when numerous goats and other livestock were found dead, drained of blood. The vampire-like killings started in Canovanas, where about 30 residents swore they saw the creature described variously as having red eyes, gray skin, fangs, a long darting tongue, powerful hind legs, and spinal quills. It's said to stand between four and five feet tall and weigh between 18 to 50 pounds. In other words, it resembled a small dinosaur from Jurassic Park.

Within weeks of the first deaths a flurry of reports of dead animals started coming in from all parts of the country—and then from Miami, New York, Los Angeles, Mexico, Costa Rica, the Dominican Republic, and even Russia. After an intensive two-year period of goat sucking, the creature seemed to disappear from Puerto Rico and everywhere else. Some believed that UFOs had captured the creature that wasn't meant to be here in the first place. Others claimed the military had finally gotten its genetic experiments back under lock and key.

Authorities in the various localities attributed the thousands of animal deaths to large stray dogs. The Chupacabra, they said, was also born of mass hysteria.

It turns out, according to anthropologists and Hispanic historians, that there are other legends of bloodsucking animals in several South and Latin American cultures and on some Caribbean islands—but only on the Spanish-speaking islands.

Goatsuckers actually do exist. Goatsucker is the name given to a family of nocturnal birds, such as night jars and whippoorwills, whose eyes reflect light at night. The birds are found in the Mediterranean where goats like to graze. Despite the name, animal blood is not part of the birds' diet. These goatsuckers feed almost exclusively on insects.

16

St. Kitts

Old West Indian Proverb: "It is not for want of tongue that cows don't talk."

St. Kitts was officially known as St. Christopher, named by Columbus for the patron saint of travelers. However, everyone called the place St. Kitts for short, so in 1988 St. Kitts became the new official name.

The tiny 68-square mile island was extremely important in establishing British domination throughout the rest of the Caribbean. Although discovered by Christopher Columbus, St. Kitts was the first English settlement in the Eastern Caribbean (1623), and from here settlers journeyed to Antigua, Tortola, Montserrat, and Nevis.

The French also used St. Kitts to launch colonists to Guadeloupe, Martinique, St. Martin, and St. Barts. Because St. Kitts was the staging area for the settlement of so many other islands, it became known as the "Mother Colony of the Caribbean."

The British didn't gain full control of St. Kitts until 1783, as a provision of the Treaty of Versailles. The capital city name of Basseterre (pronounced "bass-terr") reflects the long struggle between the English and French over ownership of St. Kitts.

Still, the French and British managed to live peacefully for about 60 years in the 1600s, agreeing by treaty not to battle each other even if their mother countries were at war. One of their first cooperative projects was to wipe out the Carib Indians, who initially befriended the original 16 British colonists when they landed in 1623. But after the French also established a colony, the Caribs became upset with the growing number of foreigners. They decided to rid the island of Europeans and called on Indians from adjacent islands to help.

The British and French learned of the plan and struck first, exterminating the St. Kitts Caribs and many of their allies. Although the Caribs were completely routed from St. Kitts, they did leave behind one of the most intriguing sites on the island: a ravine filled with petroglyphs that few tourists ever see.

For hikers, St. Kitts is a walking paradise. About 36 percent of the island (roughly 16,000 acres) is protected rain forest. It's been safeguarded since colonial times to retain the vital watershed.

The toughest walk of all is up the volcano, Mt. Liamuiga (pronounced lee-A-mwee-ga) which is 3,792 feet high. This hike is not recommended without a guide because the path is very unstable near the top. According to legend, the Caribs referred to it as Mt. Misery because of the devastating eruption just three years before the first European settlers arrived. Scientists say, however, that the last major eruption was 6,000 years ago, something of an

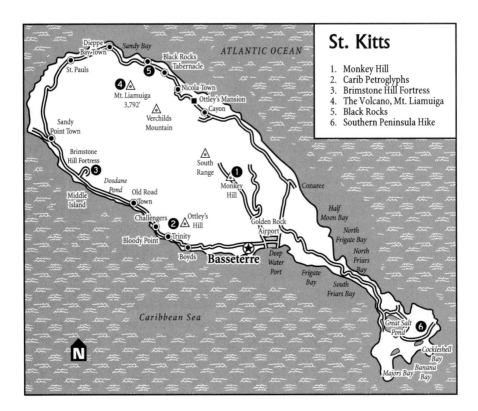

St. Kitts

1. Monkey Hill
2. Carib Petroglyphs
3. Brimstone Hill Fortress
4. The Volcano, Mt. Liamuiga
5. Black Rocks
6. Southern Peninsula Hike

obvious discrepancy. The name Mt. Misery endured until St. Kitts's independence from England in 1983 when it was changed to the less foreboding Mt. Liamuiga, Carib for "fertile isle."

The large fields of sugarcane still growing today attest to just how productive St. Kitts' soil is—acre after acre of flourishing fields. Many of the great plantation houses also remain, used for private residences and tourist hotels. St. Kitts has many abandoned windmills once used to help process the sugar, and you'll probably want to stop to take photos of quite a few.

The Main Road circles the perimeter of St. Kitts. The hikes described below start in Basseterre and follow the road clockwise around the island.

TRAVEL TIPS

Area: 23 miles long, 5 miles across at its widest.

Language: English.

Population: 35,000, living mostly around Basseterre.

Time Zone: Atlantic Time, one hour ahead of Eastern Standard Time.

Rainy Season: June through October, but some locals say the weather pattern seems to be changing and recommend May through early August as the best although this is part of the normal rainy period.

Getting There: American Eagle, (800) 433-7300, services St. Kitts's Golden Rock Airport from San Juan. Other airlines also serving St. Kitts include Winair, (869) 465-8010, from St. Maarten and LIAT, (800) 468-0482, from San Juan and Antigua. Air Canada flies from Toronto to Antigua; British Airways flies to Antigua from London.

Documents: A birth certificate with a raised seal and government-issued photo ID suffice for U.S. and Canadian citizens. All others need passports.

Getting Around: For a rental car, you must purchase a local driver's license, US$18.50; there's also a 5% tax. Driving is on the left.

Where to Stay: The Ocean Terrace Inn, usually referred to as the OTI, overlooks the Basseterre harbor with 53 air-conditioned rooms and a comfortable family-run feel. An older hotel, OTI can provide complete eco-packages. Call (869) 465-2754.

The **Bird Rock Beach Hotel** sits on a bluff across the harbor. Situated on the water, its guests can swim and snorkel just offshore; call (800) 621-1270; email birdrock@caribbeans.com.

For something truly upscale, try the 22-unit **Golden Lemon** at Dieppe Bay. The condos are luxuriously appointed. The resort was outfitted by the former decorating editor of *House & Garden* magazine; call (869) 465-7260. Also, the 17-unit **Ottley's Plantation Inn** is on 35 acres near a rain forest; call (800) 772-3039; www.ottleys.com. Also **Rawlins Plantation,** a former plantation also near Dieppe Bay. At 350 feet above sea level, it enjoys all the fine breezes; call (869) 465-6221; www.rawlinsplantation.com.

Camping: No campgrounds. Check with a hiking operator to see what they may be able to provide.

Currency: The Eastern Caribbean dollar is the standard. US$1 equals about EC$2.70. Most prices are quoted in EC$, but always check first. Banks are open 8 a.m. to noon Monday through Friday and from 3 p.m. to 5 p.m. on Friday. Shopping hours are 8 a.m. to noon, 1 p.m. to 4 p.m.

Taxes & Tips: There is a government room tax of 7% and most hotels add a service charge of 10%. Tipping is about 10%. The departure tax is US$10.

Electrical Current: A former British colony, the current typically is 230 volts, 60 cycles though some hotels have 110 V.

Safety & Health Warnings: Women should not go walking alone in deserted areas.

Snakes & Other Venomous Creatures: None.

Hiking & Walking Services: Greg's Safaris, c/o the OTI, P.O. Box 65, Basseterre, St. Kitts, WI; phone (869) 465-4121/5209; email g-safari@caribsurf.com. Greg Pereira and his staff offer a full-day volcano tour, a 5-hour rain forest tour, and a 6-hour plantation tour. Using four-wheel drive vehicles for the most remote areas, Greg has been conducting organized hikes around St. Kitts for years. He is a well-informed naturalist who believes in keeping his clients fueled with lots to eat and drink. A rest break after a hike tends to be more of an elaborate picnic than just a few snacks. Greg's Plantation Tour includes lunch at a private, 250-year old cut stone great house surrounded by exotic gardens. Also offering hikes is **Kriss Tours** at New Street, Basseterre, St. Kitts, WI; phone (869) 465-4042. Also try **Earl "The Duke of Earl" Vanlow** at (869) 465-1899.

Additional Information: In the United States, the Tourist Office at 414 E. 75th St., New York, NY 10021; call (800) 582-6208 or (212) 535-1234. In Canada, it's 11 Yorkville Ave., Suite 508, Toronto M4W IL3; call (416) 921-7717 or 924-0345; fax (416) 921-7997. In the United Kingdom, c/o The High Commission of the Eastern Caribbean States, 10 Kensington Court, London W8 5DL; phone (0171) 376-0881; fax (0171) 937-3611; www.stkitts-nevis.com.

BASSETERRE AFOOT!

Time: 1–2 hours. | **Difficulty:** 1. | **Trailhead:** The pier area.

An hour's easy walk will show you the highlights of Basseterre, the capital of St. Kitts with about 15,000 inhabitants. Basseterre is ideal for exploring on foot because everything is laid out in square blocks. Basseterre has been the British capital of St. Kitts since 1727, though it was part of the French sector when the two nations both held the island.

The name *Basseterre* in French means "low land," which most of the commercial district certainly is; it has been flooded several times.

Be sure to notice the colorful red and yellow wooden fishing boats near the pier with their nets drying in the sun; they make great photos.

1. **Pier Area:** Three different piers, including separate ones for cruise ships and the *Caribe Queen,* the island ferry that runs between St. Kitts and Charlestown, capital of Nevis. Friday and Saturday are particularly good times to be at the pier, when the colorful produce and vegetable market is in session. Ask first before taking photos of individuals, and don't be surprised if they say no or want you to buy something first in trade.

2. **Treasury Building:** One of the most architecturally interesting structures near the pier is the old Treasury Building with its big rotunda. Also the Customs house, this domed colonial building and its arches are a good reminder of just how rich sugar once made the island.

3. **The Circus:** In British lingo, a circus is not a good time under a big canvas tent but a circular open space at the intersection of several streets, as in London's Piccadilly Circus. The small roundabout is lined with good shopping, particularly at The Palms Arcade. Dominating the Circus is the large, green cast-iron Berkeley Memorial Clock. The ornate grandfather-style clock with four clock faces is a memorial to Thomas Berkeley, a former president of the Legislative Assembly.

4. **Independence Square:** Originally known as Pall Mall Square, it was built in 1790 for slave auctions and council meetings. It was renamed in 1983 to commemorate the independence of the island Federation of St. Kitts and Nevis from Great Britain. Nothing remains of its bleak origins. Instead, a large fountain decorates the center and the perimeters are bordered by old stone buildings and neat, aged, wooden structures painted in white and colorful pastels, all excellent examples of British colonial architecture.

5. **The Georgian House:** Bordering Independence Square, this restored brick home is now a gourmet restaurant.

6. **Court House and Library:** Directly opposite Independence (Pall Mall) square and adjacent to the Catholic church.

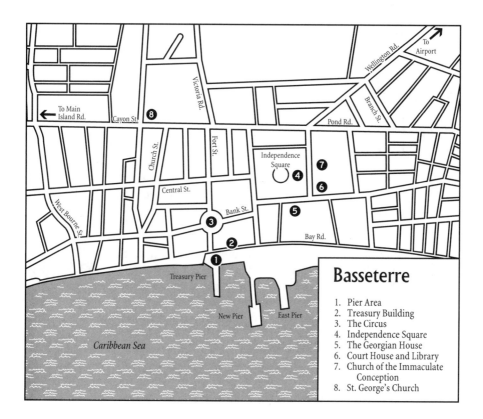

Basseterre

1. Pier Area
2. Treasury Building
3. The Circus
4. Independence Square
5. The Georgian House
6. Court House and Library
7. Church of the Immaculate Conception
8. St. George's Church

7. Church of the Immaculate Conception: This open, airy church is a reminder that during the French period, Catholicism was the predominant religion.

8. St. George's Church: A large brownstone church located on an interesting and fiery religious battle site. It's been destroyed so many times it's difficult to tell whose side God ended up on, the French or the British. Originally, the French built the church "Notre Dame" here in 1670, which the British burned down in 1706. The British rebuilt four years later, naming their new Anglican structure after the patron saint of England. However, a fire in 1763, an earthquake in 1843, a hurricane, then another fire in 1867 resulted in St. George's being destroyed and rebuilt three more times. What you see standing for the moment is the result of the last restoration, in 1869.

ELSEWHERE ON ST. KITTS

1. MONKEY HILL

Time: 1 hour. | **Difficulty:** 1–2, a relatively easy walk popular with locals and tourists. | **Trailhead:** Located just west of Basseterre.

`This area gained its name from the vervet monkeys often spotted here. The path climbing the hill, 1,319-feet high, goes by the ruins of "the Glen," a former great house. From the top you'll have excellent views of fertile Basseterre Valley and the Caribbean coast. However, the best place for a close-up look at monkeys is at the primate research station at Estridge Estate open to the public on Sundays.

2. CARIB PETROGLYPHS

Time: 1 hour. | **Difficulty:** 2–3. | **Trailhead:** At the village of Bloody Point, located on the island's main circular highway. Approaching Bloody Point from Basseterre, look on the right for a dirt road going uphill; this road is located almost directly opposite a large mahogany tree. Many locals know of the site and can point out the path.

When you arrive at Bloody Point, you'll be near one of the best petroglyph collections anywhere in the Caribbean, yet few tourists see the rock drawings. There are no markers or signs to indicate where they're located. These drawings are one of St. Kitts's best-kept secrets.

Walk up the road by the mahogany tree for five to ten minutes, until you reach a bridge. Don't make the mistake of crossing the bridge; instead, go beyond the bridge and look for a footpath that leads down to the river.

The path criss-crosses the river several times, and in places you will have to scramble up and around boulders in midstream, but your feet shouldn't get wet unless the river is high. Be sure to wear nonskid shoes for the rock hopping. About 15 minutes from the bridge—remember, you are going into the interior of the island, not toward the coast—you should reach a narrow canyon about 10 feet wide and 80 feet high.

The canyon is a time tunnel into the past. Carib drawings will be all around you on the canyon walls, beginning about five to seven feet up the cliffside. Some are difficult to discern because the rubbings are faded; others are unmistakable due to the way they've been outlined in red by a local artist. Hiking guide Greg Pereira of Greg's Safaris estimates there are perhaps as many as 100 drawings in the canyon. It is a remarkable sight and well worth the effort required to get here.

Most of what you see are human faces—the eyes, nose and mouth but no other parts of the body. Greg suggests they may be drawings of ritualistic importance or a register of events important to the Caribs. There are many theories, but no one knows for certain. However, you can make out other forms, too, including a bat, an owl, and a three-cornered hat, the kind the first settlers wore.

Many petroglyphs will be in the shade. To photograph them, use either fill-flash or come prepared with high-speed film. You could spend considerable time here, depending on how much you get caught up in the somber mood of the canyon.

It was in this canyon of petroglyphs that an estimated 1,000 Caribs were trapped and slaughtered by the combined British and French forces. The riverbed you're standing in literally ran red with Carib blood. It is easy to let your imagination roam freely when you realize this is where the Caribs made their final stand on St. Kitts, just three years after the first Europeans arrived. The town of Bloody Point is the spot where the Carib village once existed.

3. BRIMSTONE HILL FORTRESS

Time: 1 hour to explore the fort; 3–4 hours to walk up and down Brimstone Hill. | **Difficulty:** 1 inside the fort; 2–3 for the climb to it. | **Trailhead:** Brimstone Hill.

Brimstone Hill Fortress is one of the great forts of the Western Hemisphere and the most important historical site on St. Kitts. Brimstone Hill is named for the sulfur fumes frequently smelled at this end of the island, courtesy of nearby Mt. Liamuiga, St. Kitts' volcano. The thick walls of the Fort George citadel are made of black volcanic rock, once called brimstone.

Known as the Gibraltar of the West Indies, the 38-acre fortress had its first cannon hauled to the top of the steep cliff in 1690; by 1736 there were at least 49 cannon in place. Slave laborers needed almost 100 years to complete the massive 7- to 12-foot thick walls. Despite its impressive fortifications, a force of 8,000 French captured the fort from its 1,000 British defenders in 1782 by punching 40-foot holes in the fortress walls. The British garrison was allowed to leave as an undefeated force, in full uniform. The French had to give it back along with the rest of St. Kitts just a year later under the Treaty of Versailles. However, more soldiers died of yellow fever than from fighting during the fort's long history.

After severe damage from a hurricane in 1843, the fort was never fully rebuilt and abandoned in 1851. Since 1965 it has been a national park. Today, fully restored, Brimstone Hill Fortress affords one of the best island walks while offering excellent views of six neighboring islands.

The fortress is situated almost 800 feet above sea level, and if you want to experience colonial military life here, walk from the perimeter road. Walking may be safer than driving, actually. The road up is so narrow and twisting, it's always a challenge to meet another car without making contact.

Perhaps the most interesting feature is the architectural arrangement of the interior courtyard that can be reached only by crossing a moat. It's not by accident that the courtyard floor slopes toward a center drain: the drain creates a 13,000-gallon cistern with all excess water directed through a privy area. In effect, the drain helped create a huge flush toilet, the ingenious intentions of Brimstone Hill's designers who took excellent advantage of the clouds and rain that often obscure the fortress.

4. THE VOLCANO, MT. LIAMUIGA

Length: About 3.5 miles. | **Time:** 5 hours. | **Difficulty:** 3–4. | **Trailhead:** Hikes usually begin at the 1,500-foot level at the point where the road ends in Belmont Estates.

This is St. Kitts's toughest hike, requiring a minimum of a half day to reach the crater lip at 2,700 feet, as high as you can hike on the trail since Hurricane Hugo. The volcano is almost inactive, although it rumbles on occasion and belches sulfur. Once easily spoken of as Mt. Misery, Mt. Liamuiga's new name is the Carib term for "fertile isle." It's pronounced "lee-A-mwee-ga," most easily said if one has been drinking Carib beer.

Because of its circular route, the volcano hike takes you halfway around the island. In the rain forest here you'll see trees that tower 100 feet high, mostly virgin growth without any introduced species, such as bamboo. You'll find gommier and mastic trees, pigeon berry, and many varieties of ferns (over 120 species).

The hike is a steady 2.5 hours of moderate climbing. The first half of the hike, along a ridge, is gentle. On the second leg, which is much steeper, you have to make several ascents. Yet at its worst, the grade is little more than a 45° angle. You'll find plenty of roots to grab and pull yourself up with.

At about 2,500 feet, you enter the cloud forest and encounter vegetation that spends most of its life covered in white mist: mostly dwarf trees coated with orchids and mosses. A land of perpetual moisture, the trail here can be very slippery. However, it's over 1,000 feet higher to the summit, though you stop at the crater lip at 2,700-feet. At the peak of 3,792 feet, the growth is tropical alpine meadow.

At one time it was possible to descend to the crater floor, but Hurricane Hugo destroyed most of the trees that were essential handholds to keep from falling down the steep slope. Hugo's winds, with gusts clocked at over 200 mph, swirled into the crater and eliminated the trees on one side—the side the ascent trail happens to be on, which makes it relatively unsafe for climbing. Trees inside the crater on the opposite wall are still in prime condition, but no trail yet exists to climb that side.

5. BLACK ROCKS

Time: 15–20 minutes. | **Difficulty:** 1 on top of the cliff; 2–3 to descend and ascend the shoreline. | **Trailhead:** At the village of Belle Vue on the Atlantic coast.

A dramatic reminder of the island's volcanic past is the formation known as Black Rocks. In all of its millions of years, Mt. Misery has produced only one actual lava flow, and this is it. The continual pounding of the waves against the black lava cliffs has created this cluster of oddly shaped boulders.

6. SOUTHERN PENINSULA HIKE

Length: 10 miles. | **Time:** 5 hours. | **Difficulty:** 2–3. Take water. | **Trailhead:** Begin at Frigate Bay, once a favorite dueling ground but now a popular golf course. The pathway is obvious.

Until a new highway was completed in 1990, the only way to reach the narrow southern tip of St. Kitts was by boat or by walking. This stark, desert-like terrain is very different from the lush forests of the north. The main reason for taking this walk is the spectacular ocean views of the Atlantic pounding against the coastline and the possibility of seeing monkeys, wild donkeys, and deer. On early summer mornings it's also possible to find a sea turtle still in the process of laying her eggs.

The vegetation becomes scrubbier as the terrain flattens out the farther south you go. Wear a bathing suit to take advantage of the beautiful empty beaches. Also bring something to drink because this open walk can be quite hot, though a small restaurant at the southernmost tip serves drinks. The salt ponds near the end of the peninsula were the main salt source for many Kittians and Nevisians. In your wanderings, you may also pass the ruins of an old windmill tower.

THE MANSION SOURCE TRAIL

Length: 1.5–2 miles. | **Time:** 2 hours. | **Difficulty:** 2. | This is a private trail not accessible to the public. It is available only through Greg's Safaris; call (869) 465-4121.

The walk, located eight miles from Basseterre, provides an excellent and easy introduction to the St. Kitts rain forest. It starts at about 1,400 feet and goes along Verchild's Mountain, which has a freshwater pond on top. The perimeter of the rain forest is very lush, growing such diverse crops as mango, dasheen, yams, peppers, christopheen, bananas, and mountain cabbage palm.

In the rain forest live troops of African green monkeys (vervets) brought in by the French several centuries ago. These creatures, which grow to 18 pounds and gorge on fruit and leaves, cause so much damage to the farm crops the government offers a bounty of approximately EC$10 for every body brought in. Researchers interested in live specimens pay up to EC$100. Estimates of the St. Kitts monkey population run from 10,000 to 40,000.

Rain forest vegetation receives from 80 to 150 inches of rain annually, but the coastal regions where sugarcane is grown receive far less, only about 55 inches. Look for ferns, gum trees, philodendrons, elephant ears, and clumps of bamboo (which can grow three inches per day). The climb is moderate but sometimes slippery and muddy in parts.

17

ST. LUCIA

Old Caribbean Proverb: "All skin—teeth and laugh."
Translation: "Deception is often disguised by a smile."

Tiny St. Lucia (LOO-sha) is shaped like a teardrop, 24 miles long from north to south and 14 miles wide. Part of a relatively young chain of volcanic islands created by lava and ash from ocean-floor volcanoes, St. Lucia is just 21 miles south of Martinique and 26 miles north of St. Vincent. A land of many waterfalls, ridges, and valleys, St. Lucia is a walker's dream.

Its volcanic origins are most conspicuous in its two great spires—Gros Piton and Petit Piton, which jut a half mile high. They are among the Caribbean's most striking natural landmarks, formed by eruptions 30 to 40 million years ago. These pyramid-shaped cones capture every visitor's gaze, rendering insignificant all other features along St. Lucia's southern coast, even the coal-black sand beaches that rival Hawaii's.

St. Lucia is also home to what islanders call their "drive-in volcano": a small valley and ridge covering several acres that contain pots of boiling water and steam vents. It's only a 10- to 15-minute walk from the car park to the small smoking craters and bubbling sulfur pools. A major feat of exertion this hike is not.

Nearby are Diamond Falls and the Botanical Garden, which contain warm sulfur baths fed by underground springs from the volcano's sulfur pools. The St. Lucians take an annual dip in the baths, reputed to take off ten years and ten pounds. Apparently, you must be an islander to benefit from this miraculous transformation; it's never worked for me.

The mountainous countryside is often a bright kelly green and very similar to Dominica in that many of the plants and animals are of South or Central American origin. Only about 11 percent of St. Lucia is still true rain forest. Ironically, most of the cutting was done in recent years, not by early settlers. As late as the 1980s, about 3 percent of the rain forest was being cleared annually to grow bananas. Today, about 31,000 acres of rain forest remain, 19,000 of them under the jurisdiction of the Forestry and Lands Department. St. Lucians now understand that they possess something very special, fragile, and unique.

Including the coast and the interior, the entire island has less than 40 miles of designated hiking trails, though none of the walks are very long.

The best hiking is in the interior rain forest. There you'll see orchids and tree ferns and have the chance to glimpse the rare St. Lucian parrot. And, of course, there are the pitons to climb.

According to legend, Christopher Columbus sighted the island on St. Lucy's Day, December 13, 1502. However, it appears St. Lucia was discovered not by Columbus himself but by his mapmaker. Columbus's logbook shows he never saw the island and wasn't anywhere nearby on St. Lucy's Day. The Caribs called it "Iouanaloa," land of the iguana.

The Spanish ignored the island, and British settlement didn't take root until 1640. The French decided they also wanted St. Lucia and, during the next 200 years of intermittent warfare, the island changed hands back and forth 14 times, finally ending up with the British in 1814. In 1979, St. Lucia became independent.

Owned by the British for over 150 years, the French maintained significant influence on the island. Although English is the official language, a Creole patois is the common tongue. Further, the city and landmark names and most of the inhabitants' names are French. French cooking, with a strong Creole flair, predominates.

Although the main city of Castries is located in the north, St. Lucia's major hiking sites (the rain forest, the pitons, drive-in volcano, Diamond Waterfalls, and the Botanical Garden) are all well south, near the town of Soufrière, over an hour's drive away.

TRAVEL TIPS

Area: 238 square miles; 24 miles long, 14 miles wide.

Language: Officially, it's English but the locals favor a thick patois that is incomprehensible even to those who speak French.

Population: 150,000.

Time Zone: Atlantic Time, one hour ahead of Eastern Standard Time.

Rainy Season: From June through November. December through May is considered the dry period.

Getting There: Most international flights land at Hewanorra International Airport at the southern end, almost two hours from Castries. Those staying near Castries should use George Charles/Vigie Airport located just outside the city; American Eagle, (800) 433-7300, serves both airports. BWIA, Air Jamaica, Air Canada, and LIAT, (800) 468-0482, also serve St. Lucia.

Documents: Passport, or picture ID with a notarized birth certificate. Also a return or ongoing ticket.

Getting Around: For a rental car, drivers must be 25 years old and possess a St. Lucian driver's license (EC$30). Driving on some of the crater-pocked roads of St. Lucia is not unlike offroad driving over very bumpy terrain. Drive on the left.

Where to Stay: If you intend to hike daily, **Anse Chastanet** near the town of Soufrière is the most conveniently located hotel for the price. The 400-acre resort has been a leader in organizing walking and hiking tours for its guests with local, very knowledgeable guides. (From the beach, its main restaurant has 125 steps to the top, a nice vigorous climb before breakfast.) For information, call (800) 328-5285. The snorkeling on the reef out front is superb.

On the east coast, close to the Des Cartiers rain forest walk and the Fregate Islands Nature Reserve is the 12-bedroom **Fox Grove Inn** at Mon Repose. The Swiss/St. Lucian owners run a terrific restaurant here; try the garlic soup! Room rates are $55 for a single including breakfast, or $72 with dinner. A double is $65 including breakfast, $99 with

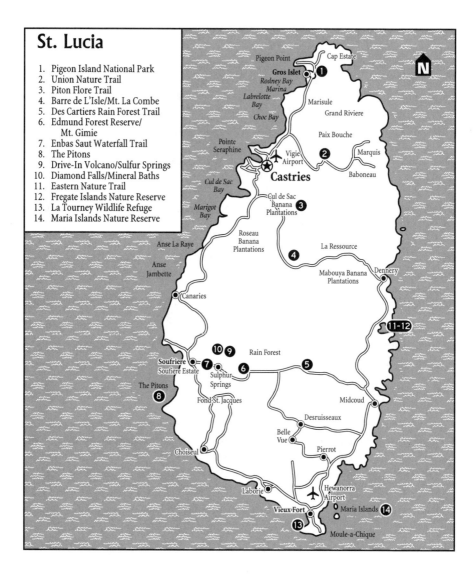

St. Lucia

1. Pigeon Island National Park
2. Union Nature Trail
3. Piton Flore Trail
4. Barre de L'Isle/Mt. La Combe
5. Des Cartiers Rain Forest Trail
6. Edmund Forest Reserve/
   Mt. Gimie
7. Enbas Saut Waterfall Trail
8. The Pitons
9. Drive-In Volcano/Sulfur Springs
10. Diamond Falls/Mineral Baths
11. Eastern Nature Trail
12. Fregate Islands Nature Reserve
13. La Tourney Wildlife Refuge
14. Maria Islands Nature Reserve

dinner added. Horseback riding is available on the beaches or hills. Call (758) 455-3271 or fax (758) 455-3800; www.foxgroveinn.com.

St. Lucia has many good all-inclusives. The famous couples-only **Sandals** chain, (888) SANDALS or visit www.sandals.com, has two operations here. Less well known but equally good is **Le Sport,** (800) 544-2883 or visit www.lesport.com.lc, which emphasizes outdoor activities, including early morning walks. Despite its Club Med–sounding name, Le Sport has no real French affiliation.

Camping: It's now available thanks to the National Trust, which in 1998 opened the **Environmental Education Centre** along a stretch of beach (Anse Liberte) in the fishing village of Canaries, 8 miles north of Soufrière and 25 miles south of Castries. Camping gear is available for rent. There are five miles of hiking trails. Staff gives tours explaining the emancipation history. Call (758) 452-5005 for information.

Currency: The Eastern Caribbean dollar, or EC$, worth about EC$2.70 for each US$1. US dollars can be spent anywhere but change is given in EC$. Banks are open 8 a.m. to 1 p.m. Monday through Thursday, on Friday from 8 a.m. to noon and 3 p.m. to 5 p.m.

Taxes & Tips: The government collects an 8% tax on hotel rooms and hotels add a 10% service charge to the bill, a combined total of 18%. There's a US$11 departure tax.

Electrical Current: 220 volts, 50 cycles.

Safety & Health Warnings: Unfortunately, the rivers aren't the cleanest. It's advised that you not swim in them, much less drink from them. St. Lucia is one of the few islands with bilharzia (also called schistosomiasis), a parasite that generally occurs in slow-moving, snail-infested water. It can enter the body by being consumed or through open wounds.

A guide and/or group is recommended when touring for the remote areas. Crime being what it is these days—prevalent—a few tourists have been robbed while walking on their own.

Snakes & Other Venomous Creatures: The fer-de-lance inhabits coastal areas. Be careful around piles of coconut shells in the lowlands.

Hiking & Walking Services: Rain forest hiking has become very popular, and that's both good and bad. The good part is it's now easier to find a guide. The bad part: hiking has become very commercialized and tour operators often take groups of 20 or more, certainly not the quietest company for enjoying the serenity of the rain forest. Castries tour operators include **Sunlink,** (758) 452-9678, and **Jungle Tours,** (758) 450-0434. Unless you have your own vehicle, you will probably be forced to join a tour group because there is no other economical way to reach the trailheads, most of them located far away from the local bus routes. Taxis are prohibitive.

Besides being commercialized, rain forest hiking is also highly structured. With the exception of the Enbas Saut trail near Soufrière, you're discouraged from simply showing up and taking a walk in the woods. Instead, you are supposed to call ahead to arrange for a guide as well as pay EC$25 for each trail you walk. Hiking, seemingly discouraged as a spontaneous activity, should be planned and organized days before.

Of course, the rain forest does house many rare and exotic plants, animals, and birds; strict control certainly helps ensure their well-being. But vacationers who like to do things on the spur of the moment may find the system stifling.

Two different branches of government are in charge of St. Lucia's hiking trails. The 19,000-acre St. Lucia Forest Reserve is maintained by the **Forestry and Lands Department** headquartered at Union in the northwest part of the island. It controls access to the island's most popular hikes: the Union Nature Trail, the Des Cartiers rain forest trail, the Barre de L'Isle trail, the Edmund Reserve and Mount Gimie, and the Enbas Saut trail. To arrange a forestry guide, call (758) 452-3231 or (758) 450-2078.

The **National Trust** owns and administers Pigeon Island National Park and the Fregate Island and Maria Islands Nature Reserves. The National Trust has become increasingly active in arranging and organizing hikes for studying plants in different parts of the islands, including walks up Gros Piton. For information or and to arrange for a guide to the reserves, call (758) 453-7656; fax (758) 453-2791; email natrust@candw.lc. No guide is needed for Pigeon Island.

The **St. Lucia Naturalists' Society** welcomes visitors to its monthly meetings at the Castries Public Library. Meetings are usually the first Wednesday of the month, starting at 6 p.m. It also conducts regular nature walks; check with the library for details.

In Soufrière, one of the most reliable and knowledgeable guides is Martial Simon, Bay Street, Soufrière, St. Lucia. Ask for him at Servil's Boutique or Anse Chastanet.

Additional Information: Contact the St. Lucia Tourist Board, 820 2nd Ave., 9th Floor, New York, NY 10017; phone (212) 867-2950; fax (212) 370-7867. In Canada, 151 Bloor St. West, Suite 425, Toronto, Ontario M5S 1S4; phone (416) 961-5606; fax (416) 961-4317. In the United Kingdom, 10 Kensington Court, London W8 5DL; phone (071) 937-1969; fax (071) 937-3611.

Special Doings: Every Friday is fete or party night at Gros Islet, a fishing village near Castries. The Mardi Gras–like street party features crowds, blaring reggae, rum carts, and coalpot barbecue cook stands.

Castries Afoot!

Time: 1 hour. | **Difficulty:** 1. | **Trailhead:** The waterfront market.

Unquestionably, the true allure of St. Lucia is the beauty of its countryside, not its cities. Castries, St. Lucia's bustling capital city, has few buildings of interest, despite its almost 200-year history. The city was destroyed by fire in 1927 and then again in 1948. Yet that doesn't quite explain its clapboard appearance, which many find unattractive.

The few buildings of historical importance are around **Columbus Square.** The cathedral is much more colorful inside than out: the walls and ceilings are decorated with frescoes. The covered **marketplace** is busiest on Saturdays. Basketware is the best local handicraft.

Increasingly, cruise ships call at Castries Harbour so visitors can make day excursions into the countryside. To take advantage of this traffic, a complex of duty-free shops are clustered at **Point Seraphine** in Castries. They are well stocked with jewelry, crystal, perfumes, and china. Bagshaw's, the noted producer of silk-screened and hand-printed designs, has a store at Point Seraphine as well as downtown Castries.

1. Pigeon Island National Park

Time: 2–3 hours to explore fully. | **Difficulty:** 1–3 depending on the walk you choose. | **Trailhead:** Located north of Castries between Gros Islet and Cap Estate.

This rugged 40-acre national park, connected to the mainland by a causeway and opened in 1979, is the most accessible and interesting walk in the Castries resort area. A small museum and restaurant are open, and the pathways through the woodlands are nicely shaded. Swimming is available. The most noticeable natural features are the two peaks joined by a saddle ridge. Climbing the path on these peaks to Fort Rodney takes about an hour and requires a little bit of stamina.

Pigeon Point's most important role was to serve as a strategic British observation post in the early 1780s. At the time, the French fleet at Martinique was planning to join the Spanish Armada off Haiti for a combined attack against Jamaica. The intent was to expel the British from the Caribbean once and for all. Martinique was so visible from the Pigeon Island lookout the that British were able to observe the French fleet build-up on a constant basis. Indeed, Admiral Rodney had a sailcloth awning made to shelter him in his patient vigil, waiting for the signal that the French fleet had set sail. When it did, with 10,000 men and 150 ships on April 8, Rodney and his fleet of 100 ships were in pursuit within two hours.

For three days the French avoided engaging battle. Rodney at last found himself in an ideal position to break through the French line and opened fire. Some of the ships under his command were carrying up to 74 cannon. The battle raged until the evening of April 12, when the French surrendered.

Pigeon Island would never again play such an important role in history. A hurricane in 1817 did severe damage to the buildings, which were only partly restored. Following an outbreak of yellow fever in 1834, only 35 soldiers remained garrisoned on the island. It was abandoned in 1861 and the guns sold. From 1909 to 1926 Pigeon Island was a whaling station.

The United States became interested in Pigeon Island before World War II. After the fall of France in June 1940 and the increased threat of German submarine traffic, the United States leased the island, establishing a base to help protect the Panama Canal and keep watch on Martinique. Pigeon Island was also a communications station, code-named "Peter Item." It was deactivated in 1947.

TRAILS IN THE RAIN FOREST

Hiking is of tremendous importance to St. Lucia's economy. After the Des Cartiers trail opened in 1996, it was credited with infusing US$750,000 into the local economy in its first four years. That's an impressive sum from one short hiking trail. It clearly demonstrates that hiking, a low-impact activity, should be encouraged on every island.

THE ANIMALS

Of all the animals inhabiting St. Lucia's amazingly varied terrain, one of the most startling is the green iguana, which grows up to six feet long. The tail, about two-thirds of that length, is a prized delicacy, which accounts for the animal's relative scarcity.

More common are the three species of anoles, tree lizards called "zandoli" on St. Lucia. Anoles are interesting because of the males' elaborate display, which involves a lot of head bobbing and push-ups, sort of like a boxer in training. A local myth says anyone touching an anole will get white blotches on the skin where they touched it. Not true. The worst anoles can do is give you a slight harmless nip.

The equally innocuous gecko also has a bad reputation. The gecko is easy to distinguish from an anole by its eyes, which are covered by a transparent membrane instead of eyelids, an adaptation for night vision. Geckos are also noted for jettisoning their tails, leaving them wriggling in the paws of a confounded enemy. The tails do grow back, but are not as long as the originals.

Caribs called geckos "Mabouia," evil spirits. According to legend, these fast-retreating animals would latch themselves so tightly to a person's skin that it required a hot iron to kill the animal and remove it. The myth apparently comes from the gecko's ability to cling to the smallest and smoothest object, even glass. It grips with the flap-like scales on the undersides of its toes.

The fer-de-lance *(Bothrops caribbaeus Garman)* is a pit viper of some importance (to avoid), so here's a few extra words about it. Any time a local talks about serpents, he's talking about fer-de-lances. Although other snakes live on the island, only the fer-de-lance is called a "serpent," with all the Old Testament connotations of evil. The snakes are nocturnal, so it's possible to see one on the road near twilight after a heavy rain.

The island's boa constrictor *(Constrictor constrictor orophias)* grows from seven to ten feet long. Its diet consists mainly of rats and birds. To keep down the rodent population, some St. Lucian farmers have even introduced them to their property.

Undoubtedly the most colorful creature is the St. Lucian parrot, the national bird, once hunted for both meat and the international pet market. The blue-green parrots are most active in morning and evening. Mating for life, the female lays only two eggs a year. They nest in the tops of the tall gommier trees and typically travel in family groups of twos and threes. Known locally as the "jacquot," there may have been as many as a million of the parrots when the first Europeans arrived. However, some suggest that seems like an awful lot of parrots on this one tiny island. In 1990, there were only about 200 birds in the wild. Today, that number has increased significantly but is still under a thousand.

2. Union Nature Trail

Length: 1 mile (0.6 km). | **Time:** 1 hour. | **Difficulty:** 1. | **Trailhead:** At the Forestry Department headquarters, at Union. About ten minutes north of Castries on the Castries-Gros Islet highway, turn inland on the Allan Bousquet Highway that leads to the village of Babonneau. After about 1.5 miles (2.5 km) you'll see a large fence on the right; turn right at the end of it to reach the forestry headquarters. The turnoff is easy to miss because of poor signage.

The small mini-zoo at the beginning of the trail offers guaranteed sightings of iguana, boa, and agouti. Behind the forestry buildings is a small medicinal garden devoted to herbal cures, or bush medicine. A free pamphlet describes some of the plants and their properties. For instance, islanders formerly used aloe and other, lesser-known plants until shampoos, medicines, and other products were imported. There is now a renewed interest in the properties of bush medicine, which bodes well for everyone: for the locals because it is cheaper and for tourists because it ensures protection of the forests.

The self-guiding nature trail takes about an hour and it's an easy path regularly used by young schoolchildren. A brochure explains the different kinds of trees and their uses:

Caribbean pine to make cabinets and the hearty gliricidia used for fence posts. You also may see a good variety of birds, including hummingbirds, thrashers, warblers, and mockingbirds.

3. PITON FLORE TRAIL

Time: 4–5 hours. | **Difficulty:** 2–3 depending on how slippery the conditions. | **Trailhead:** From Castries, drive east to the village of Forestière and follow the road to the end, where there is a forestry ranger station.

Much of the trail follows the 200-year old French road that connected Castries with Dennery. You'll see many impressive stumps of what were majestic Laurier canelle trees, felled for their durable wood. Fortunately, many other trees, some towering 100 feet and more, remain to shade the path.

Walk through the forest plantations for about 0.75 mile until you come to a blockhouse, where you turn right onto a small path. This is the route to the summit. A guide is not necessary but still a good idea. You'll have some fine views of the Cul-de-Sac Valley as you ascend higher.

4. BARRE DE L'ISLE/MT. LA COMBE

Length: The hiking trail is 1 mile. | **Time:** 1 hour for the trail, another hour to climb the mountain. | **Difficulty:** 2–3. | **Trailhead:** About a 25-minute drive east from on the road between Castries and the east coast village of Dennery. The trailhead is and midway between the two towns. Pay your EC$25 fee at the ranger's hut. This is an easy trail, but take a guide to identify the plants and trees.

There are two trails here. The mildly steep one leading up 1436-foot (438-m) Mount La Combe is located near the main trailhead on the side of the Castries-Dennery highway. The Barre de L'Isle trail follows the north-south ridge that runs down the center of the island and divides St. Lucia into its eastern and western halves. The hilly trail, which alternates between a thick tree canopy and open area, provides excellent views of the interior highlands. Cul-de-Sac Valley is to the west; Mt. Parasol, Grand Bois Forest, and the Caribbean are to the southwest.

On the northeast is La Sorcière Mountain, which has an interesting tale behind its name. It was named after the great sorceress who lives in the mountain range and was notorious for seducing men to leave all else and stay with her forever. A small cave near the summit looks down into the Mabouya Valley. Mabouya is an Amerindian name for calling up evil spirits, and this area has had a bad reputation for centuries. The tiny cave is said to be haunted. Many years ago a man was robbed and killed and his body dragged into the cave. His restless soul seeks revenge, so every full moon his ghost stalks the region, hoping to find a descendant of his killer so he can extract his own vengeance. As long as you have a guilt-free pedigree, the ghost will not harm you.

While we're telling ghost stories—and St. Lucia has many spirits said to roam the island after dark—I should warn you about La Jablesse, another one of those fatally attractive supernatural women. Unlike many spirits, La Jablesse prefers a matinee schedule, appearing only during the day, not at night. She is incredibly beautiful, with long black hair flowing to her waist. She has one obvious flaw: a cow's hoof that she conceals under her clothing. She generally dresses in either a long robe or in tight, figure-enhancing jeans (and how do you hide a hoof in those?).

La Jablesse is known for stealing men away from their wives and girlfriends; treating the hapless victims to a passionate, sex-drenched experience; and then stealing their spirits. It's said that such a man is never seen again. The sociological implications of this story are profound: La Jablesse is always described as either Indian or Caucasian, never black. At one time, men and boys in rural areas were taught never to entertain any beautiful strange woman who might accost them. She could be La Jablesse.

How do you tell if La Jablesse or just a mortal woman of extraordinary beauty is accosting you? The answer is easy if you have a cigarette or a dog. La Jablesse is afraid of smoke, and dogs will scare her away.

5. Des Cartiers Rain Forest Trail

Length: A 2.5-mile (4-km) loop trail. | **Time:** 1–2 hours. | **Difficulty:** 1–2. | **Trailhead:** Located in the southeastern interior, about 1.5 hours from Castries. The main road to the reserve is just north of the east coast village of Micoud. The turnoff into the interior is signposted and passes through the village of Anbre. It's 6 miles and a 30–45 minute drive to the trailhead from the main east coast road. At the first Y in the road, bear left. At the second Y, go left and follow the river. You'll cross a bridge, the road will climb, and you will encounter another Y; go left again. As you go uphill, there should be a sign to the trailhead indicating a right turn. Take another right at the next turn and the road takes you to the trailhead.

Located about 1,800 feet above sea level, this hike goes through moist tropical and montane forest. The area receives as much as 150 to 200 inches of rain annually; come prepared for it. This easy loop trail is one favored by commercial tour operators. Pay your EC$25 at the interpretive center near the trailhead. Note the number of red anthuriums growing along the path as you head into the high canopied forest. The trail follows roads carved out by the French in World War II. Several observation points deviate from the main trail. These are supposed to be good places for sighting the St. Lucian parrot, but the ones I spotted were on the main trail, not at the turnoffs.

At a northern part of the loop is a trail that links up with the Edmund Forest Reserve, a four-hour hike requiring a guide.

The trees bordering the Des Cartiers Trail path are tall and mature and some have Tarzan-sized vines hanging from their high branches. The gommier trees are big enough to fashion two or three canoes from. The chataigner is the emergent tree above the forest canopy, which soars to 120 feet in some places. Leaves on the trail are slick after a rain. The sounds here are marvelous. The wind in the trees sounds like rain, and swaying bamboo as it rubs together makes the creaking noises.

The banana plantation adjoining the trailhead is a reminder of the once rampant rain forest cutting. Acre for acre, it's doubtful that any banana plantation here generated as much income as this one modest hiking trail.

6. EDMUND FOREST RESERVE/MT. GIMIE

Length: 7 miles (10 km). | **Time:** 4 hours each way. | **Difficulty:** 3.
| **Trailhead:** It may seem like it takes as long to get to the trailhead as it does to make the hike. Coming in from the west coast, you need a four-wheel drive to make the five-mile (8-km) drive inland, which takes about an hour (depending on road conditions, it could be a 1.5-hour drive). From Soufrière on the east coast, take the inland road to Fond St. Jacques, passing through the village of Zenon. In Fond St. Jacques, turn left at the metal-roofed cement bus stop. In 20–30 minutes you'll eventually reach the ranger station.

Arrange for a guide at the ranger station, (758) 450-2231, because many side trails lead off the main path, and pay the requisite entry fee. One of the side trails leads to the highest point on the island, Mt. Gimie (3,117 feet). This is a tough trek and is not often made. If it's your intent to scale the mountain, let the forestry department know beforehand so they can arrange a guide familiar with the trek.

The Edmund Reserve's main trail goes through the Quilesse Forest Reserve and ends at the Des Cartiers Trail (the preceding hike). It is not a difficult trek despite the length. The trail is flat much of the way with convenient foot bridges for crossing the occasional stream. Walk for as long or as little as you like. If you do walk the complete length, you'll either need to retrace your steps or arrange transportation in advance at the other end.

This is the rain forest, so you should expect to get wet. Rainfall here is 100 to 150 inches annually, not much compared to some islands, but a deluge to the drier northern end of St. Lucia (40 to 50 inches). It is often cloudy here, but if you're lucky and the weather clears, you'll enjoy some wonderful vistas of Mt. Gimie and other peaks. Keep a lookout for the jacquot (the St. Lucian parrot) as well as hummingbirds.

7. ENBAS SAUT WATERFALL TRAIL

Length: 5 miles (8 km). | **Time:** 45–60 minutes. | **Difficulty:** 2–3 because of all the steps. | **Trailhead:** Six miles east of Soufrière. Take the road on the right-hand side of the Catholic Church, the same road that also leads to the Botanical Gardens and Diamond Falls. Follow the "To the Rain Forest" signs. Leaving the main road, you'll drive up a badly rutted track best suited to a four-wheel-drive, but a passenger car can make it if you're careful. Soon there is a ranger hut with a large sign on the left marking the trail.

Enbas saut means "below the falls," and this popular trail has two waterfalls and pools at the head of the Troumassee River. Located at the foot of Mt. Gimie, St. Lucia's tallest peak, the trail offers a mix of true rain forest and cloud forest. Birds common to the area include the St. Lucian parrot, the St. Lucia black finch, the blue-hooded euphonia, and mountain whistler.

You'll walk down on solid ground as well as scores of wooden steps before reaching the waterfall and natural pool that's a popular swimming spot. Lots of ferns and gommier, mahogany, and mahoe trees are along the trail and surrounding the falls. This is a self-guided trail and there may not be anyone to collect the usual EC$25 trail fee. But come prepared to pay it anyway.

AROUND SOUFRIÈRE

8. THE PITONS

Length: 2,619 feet, straight up. | **Time:** 3–6 hours to the top of Gros Piton; about 2 hours to the top of Petit Piton although hiking is discouraged there. | **Difficulty:** 3–4; the sides are sheer near the top. | **Trailhead:** You'll need a guide. Call the Soufrière Regional Development Council (phone (758) 459-5500). Cost: about US$40 per person.

Although the climb up Gros Piton is definitely a worthwhile effort, you'll probably appreciate the piton's beauty more from a distance than when you're actually walking on it. It is truly impressive to see the mountain from the sea as you approach it by boat. Because it is very possible to become disoriented while hiking up the steep half-mile to the top, a guide is recommended.

On the ascent, you first come to a Brigand camp, named for the slaves Robespierre freed in the new republic created after the French Revolution. The Brigands realized that when St. Lucia reverted back to English rule, their short-lived freedom would be ended. They banded together as "l'armée dans les bois" and instituted a reign of terror on the island.

About halfway to the top you'll notice significant changes in the vegetation. All four vegetation types, from dry coastal forest to elfin woodland or cloud forest, exist on Gros Piton, making it a wonderful natural laboratory. On top, you should be revived and exhilarated by the cool, damp atmosphere, where the clouds condense into droplets of water.

The natural hardwood forest at the top of Gros Piton is home to several species of rare birds, possibly including the Semper's warbler. The warbler hasn't been seen since the 1970s and may be extinct.

Petit Piton: No one is supposed to climb Petit Piton, which has become badly eroded from a 1987 fire. However, that doesn't necessarily stop the local guides from volunteering to take you up. It's your decision, but remember that several people have fallen off due to the unsta-

9. DRIVE-IN VOLCANO/SULFUR SPRINGS

Time: 45–60 minutes. | **Difficulty:** 1–2. The walk is short. You can see the active area from the car park. | **Trailhead:** Near Soufrière, off the road to View Fort.

ble soil conditions. In some places you have to scale sheer rock and entrust your safety to old ropes of dubious quality.

The sign near Soufrière advertising "the world's only drive-in volcano" marks the entrance to what is perhaps the most accessible sulfur fields anywhere in the Caribbean. The presence of sulfur is often strong enough to discolor silver jewelry. The rotten egg/onion odor is highly memorable. A kiosk at the entrance (small admission fee) will pair you with a guide, whether you need or want one.

This volcano, millions of years old, collapsed in on itself about 40,000 years ago. Theoretically it could erupt with hot ash and lava, not just gases. Mineral deposits have left the earth colored with orange, green, yellow, and purple streaks. The bubbling mud pots bordered by steam vents jetting as high as 50 feet are impressive. At one time it was possible to walk among this field in the remnant of a volcanic crater, but after a few hikers stepped through the earth crust and were almost seriously hurt, everyone was confined to a boardwalk. You can still get close enough to see everything clearly if you take binoculars and a telephoto lens. This is a hot, open place; far from what you would call beautiful, compared to the high surrounding vegetation, but nonetheless quite fascinating.

10. DIAMOND FALLS/MINERAL BATHS

Time: 1 hour. | **Difficulty:** 1. | **Trailhead:** A short distance from Soufrière. Follow the road on the right side of the Catholic church.

Louis XVI built the baths so his soldiers could take advantage of the strong mineral content of these curative waters. They were almost destroyed in the Brigand revolt during the French Revolution. They were reopened in 1976. Because they're out in the open, swimsuits are required. Underground pipes feed the baths, which are of differing temperatures, heated by an underground stream from the sulfur pools (above). An attendant on duty can explain the procedure to you.

Diamond Falls is also located here, as is a lush, well-landscaped garden. An admission fee is charged; this is one of the tourist hot spots.

THE NATURE RESERVES

11. EASTERN NATURE TRAIL

Length: 3.5 miles, one way. | **Time:** 2 hours. | **Difficulty:** 2. | **Trailhead:** On the East Coast at Maudele. A National Trust guide must be arranged. The fee is EC$10 per person plus the guide fee of EC$60. Call (758) 455-3099 or (758) 453-1495.

The Eastern Nature Trail, developed by the National Trust, is within the proposed Praslin Protected Landscape, 2,150 acres (871 hectares) located between Dennery village to the north and the Praslin community to the south. This 3.5-mile trail leads to the Fregate Islands Nature Reserve (see p. 314).

The winding trail runs parallel to the Atlantic through sparse vegetation and long grass which evolves to dense cactus and forest with shade. The first mile ends at Anse Galet.

Next, the trail dips to a stony beach and then back up a cliff to Trou Zombie, a place the Amerindians reportedly believed was inhabited by evil spirits. From this point only a mile remains. This is the most dramatic section, with caves and arches cut out by waves. The trail ends at the Fregate Islands Nature Reserve.

12. Fregate Islands Nature Reserve

Time: Half a day or more. | **Difficulty:** 1–2. | **Operating Period:** August through April, 9 a.m. to 5 p.m. daily. Available by tour only. Call the National Trust: (758) 453-7656 or (758) 455-3099. | **Trailhead:** On the east coast in the northeastern section of Praslin Bay.

These twin islands (huge lumps of rock, really) located just a few yards offshore are operated by the National Trust. Although spelled *fregate* instead of *frigate,* the cays were named after the frigate birds that nest here from May through July. Frigates are locally called "scisseau" (scissors) because of their distinctive forked tails. Frigates, also called great frigates or man-o-war birds, prefer bushes low to the ground for building their nests. The males are noted for bright red throat pouches that they inflate to attract mates. You are not allowed on the islands themselves but on the 1-mile (1.5-km) trail engineered across cliffs opposite the Fregate Islands. You return via a strip of fringing mangrove, then pass through a dry ravine and past a small waterfall. The ravine provides a shady canopy of tall bay trees and other dry forest species.

Other birds that can be observed include the trembler *(Cincloerthis ruficauda)* and the St. Lucian oriole *(Icterus laudabilis).* The ramier *(Columbia squamosa)* sometimes nests in this area. If you're lucky, you may also see a beautifully colored boa sleeping on the ground.

Since you are forced to look at everything from a distance, take binoculars and a good tele-photo lens. The inflated red throat of a nesting frigate, like that displayed by many lizards, is a sight you'll long remember.

13. La Tourney Wildlife Refuge

Time: 1 hour or all day, depending on how much you want to watch birds. | **Difficulty:** 1–2. | **Trailhead:** In the southern plains of Vieux-Fort.

If birds interest you, a trip to La Tourney will be very rewarding. This small marsh is incredibly rich in wildlife. It is well stocked with a species of fish known locally as "atkenson." This, the sedges, and water lilies provide ideal habitat for waterfowl.

The best month for bird-watching is November, when migrating species from North America come to St. Lucia. Some birds give up commuting and retire here permanently—as in the case of the little blue heron, the green heron, the blue-winged teal, and the sora rail.

14. Maria Islands Nature Reserve

Time: About half a day. | **Difficulty:** 1–2. | **Trailhead:** The interpretive center is located at Anse de Sables, near Vieux-Fort, the island's second-largest city. Closed to visitors from around May 15 to July 1, during the peak nesting season. For information and trip schedules, call (758) 452-5005.

The Maria islands are about 3,000 feet from the St. Lucia shore, separated by a shallow bay that sometimes turns quite rough. Visitors board small boats at the Interpretation Center at Pointe Sables for the crossing; call (758) 452-5005.

Located well south in the Vieux-Fort area, these offshore islands are tiny. Maria Major is only 25 acres, and Maria Minor encompasses only 4. Small they might be, but they contain plants and wildlife that are colorful, diverse, and not found anywhere else in the world.

The islands are unique because they have not been as badly disturbed as St. Lucia itself. Although man-made fires have swept over the islands and goats have been grazed on Maria Major, the Maria Islands still contain something close to 120 different plant types.

With a yearly rainfall of only about 40 inches, cactus and other desert species are common. So are the short grasses that are wind- and salt-resistant.

The rarest snake in the world, the kouwes *(Dromicus ornatus),* is found only on Maria Major, with an estimated population of fewer than 100 individuals. The snake once inhabited St. Lucia before the mongoose was introduced. It was thought to be extinct until 1973, when a kouwes was found and identified on Maria Major. Ten years later a new species or subspecies of butterfly was also found there.

Another endemic species is the large ground lizard, zandoli te. Numbering about 1,000 on Maria Major and 50 to 100 on Maria Minor, they are most active in late morning and late afternoon. The males grow to 14 inches long and have bright blue tails, yellow bellies, and dark blue backs. Females and juveniles, almost identical, are smaller, brown with dark stripes but no bright colors. The zandoli te was first discovered in 1958.

Other Maria Islands residents include geckos, terns (sooty, brown, and noddy), ground doves, Caribbean martins, and one of my favorites, the red-billed tropic bird. Sadly, pelicans and frigate birds were hunted heavily during colonial times. Their oil and grease was believed to have powerful healing properties, especially for gout. Brown pelicans have now almost disappeared.

Visitors on Maria Major follow a trail leading to an observation point in the woodland area. The lizards will normally stay close by if people are quiet.

Other scenic spots in the Vieux-Fort district: The Moule a Chique peninsula at the southernmost tip of the island, which provides a good view of all St. Lucia; on a clear day, you can see St. Vincent, 21 miles to the south. This is a dramatic spot because the peninsula reaches 800 feet and extends almost a mile offshore. You have to walk the last stretch to reach the lighthouse where the Caribbean and Atlantic meet, for the best panoramic views.

Also in the Vieux-Fort area are the Bellvue Historic Site, ruins of an eighteenth-century sugar mill, and Savannes Bay, with its thick mangroves and diverse bird life.

Coastal Walks

Time: 30 minutes to 3 hours, one way. | **Difficulty:** 2–3. | **Trailhead:** Various.

As the least accessible coast of St. Lucia, the northeast region is also one of the most interesting. Four marine turtle species—leatherbacks, loggerheads, hawksbills, and greens—come ashore to nest from February to October. You might be able to accompany a turtle watch with the Naturalists Society in Castries. Care should be taken around rock and coconut husk piles because this is fer-de-lance territory. Some of the better coastal walks in this and other areas include:

- Esperance to Pt. Hardie, 6 miles
- Ti Tance to Grand Anse, 3 miles
- Anse la Guadeloupe, 2.5 miles
- Mandele, 3 miles
- Vierge Point, 1.5 miles
- Anse Noir (Black Bay) to Laborie, 1.5 miles
- Choiseul to Anse L'Ivogrne, 3 miles
- Brigand Tunnel Canelles, 1 mile

Several additional areas are under consideration for National Trust protection. St. Lucia, fortunately, is taking all the steps in the right direction to preserve a good deal of its environment, while at the same time coping with the increased pressures brought about by growing tourism.

18 SINT MAARTEN/SAINT MARTIN

St. Maarten Saying: "*Their money melted like butter against the sun.*"
Translation: *Visit the duty-free shops in Philipsburg and find out.*

Talk about an island with a split personality! Sint Maarten (the Dutch side) shares this tiny spit of land with Saint Martin (the French side) in what is the world's smallest territory divided between two sovereign states. Located 144 miles east of Puerto Rico, Sint Maarten occupies about 17 square miles, Saint Martin a hoggish 20.

One reason the two groups have been able to live together so harmoniously is that they essentially have ignored each other as much as possible. A road connecting the two sides wasn't built until the 20th century.

St. Maarten/St. Martin (the short term) are well known for their beaches, especially the nude beaches on the French side. Most visitors are surprised to learn there's activity away from the water, but 25 miles of hiking trails are shared by both sides of the island. That's probably just about the right amount for a week's vacation.

At one time the trails crossing the valleys and mountains were the main thoroughfares for locals, but in recent years they became overgrown. Thanks to a few local hikers with machetes, the paths are now cleared again.

St. Maarten is a favorite cruise ship stop because of the extensive duty-free shopping in Philipsburg and the excellent beaches in both St. Maarten and St. Martin. The French town of Marigot also offers shopping but on a less frenzied scale. The cruise ship shoppers usually stay on the Dutch side, so the French and Italian boutiques in Marigot tend to be far less crowded. However, because English-speaking tourists make up the bulk of visitors to the island, you can get by in Marigot without speaking French far easier than you could in Guadeloupe or Martinique.

Except for its beaches, this island is not particularly scenic; the attractions are man-made, not natural. With a maximum elevation of only 1,500 feet, the vegetation leans more toward scrubby than luxuriant.

Whether Christopher Columbus ever saw this particular landfall is debatable. He did name an island St. Martin on his second voyage, but that may actually have been Nevis, which is not far away. In any case, the sailors who came afterward called the land St. Martin, and why not, because Columbus's names were boringly pious, not at all descriptive, and easily interchangeable. Correct or not, the St. Martin label has stuck ever since.

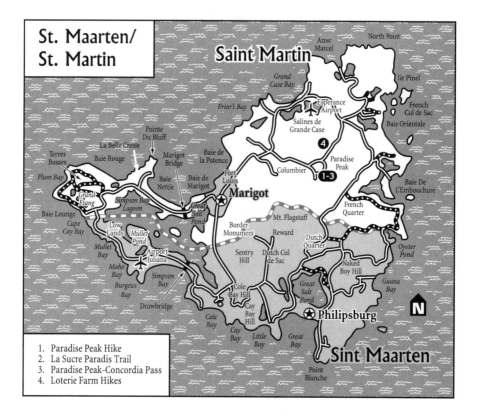

Saint Martin

Anse Marcel
North Point

Grand Case Bay

Friar's Bay

Pointe Du Bluff

La Belle Creole

Terres Basses

Baie Rouge

Marigot Bridge

Baie de la Potence

Fort Louis

Baie Nettie

Baie de Marigot

Marigot

Salines de Grande Case

Esperance Airport

Ile Pinel

French Cul de Sac

Baie Orientale

4

Columbier

Paradise Peak

1-3

Baie De L'Embouchure

French Quarter

Plum Bay

Grand Etang

Simpson Bay Lagoon

Baie Lounge

Cupe Coy Bay

Low Lands

Mullet Pond

Great Salt Pond

Border Monument

Mt. Flagstaff

Reward

Dutch Quarter

Oyster Pond

Mullet Bay

Airport Juliana

Sentry Hill

Dutch Cul de Sac

Naked Boy Hill

Maho Bay

Simpson Bay

Burgeux Bay

Cole Bay Hill

Great Salt Pond

Guana Bay

Drawbridge

Cole Bay

Cay Bay Hill

Cay Bay

Philipsburg

N

Cole Bay

Little Bay

Great Bay

Sint Maarten

Point Blanche

1. Paradise Peak Hike
2. La Sucre Paradis Trail
3. Paradise Peak-Concordia Pass
4. Loterie Farm Hikes

To the Indians, the island was known as Sualouiga, "land of salt," and indeed it was the salt pans that attracted the first serious European settlers. Because the island had no permanent water supply, the Arawaks and Caribs were left pretty much alone for the next 140 years after "discovery" except for occasional Spanish raids for slaves to work the gold mines. The French and Dutch began making plans for occupation around 1630, but the Spanish forcefully returned and built a fort at Great Bay.

In 1644, the Dutch West India Company commanded by one of its directors, Peter Stuyvesant, attacked to take the island back. The Dutch were victorious, although Stuyvesant lost a leg to a cannonball. It hardly put him out of commission—he later went to North America and became the governor of New York, then known as New Amsterdam. Four years later, the Dutch and French settlers of St. Maarten decided life for everyone would be easier if they did not war with one another even if their mother countries did. So they signed a treaty of eternal peace.

How did the French end up with more of the island than the Dutch? According to legend, a Dutchman and Frenchman starting at the same point walked around the coasts until they met, and their meeting spot established the new boundary. Both men were given a bottle to sustain them through the sweltering heat.

Naturally, the Frenchman selected a bottle of wine. The gin-drinking Dutchman supposedly was delayed for one or perhaps all three of the following reasons: the liquor slowed him down and/or he took a rest under a tree, and/or he was waylaid by a woman the devious Frenchman sent out to divert him from his appointed round.

Dutch St. Maarten prospered growing tobacco, cotton and sugar until emancipation. Then it went into a steady and swift decline until the 1960s when tourism began taking advantage of its many fine beaches and superb climate. Today, tourism is all-important, all-consuming for St. Maarten. The 20,000 residents of the Dutch side cater to 500,000 visitors annually, making it one of the Caribbean's busiest islands.

St. Martin and Marigot still have their French feel, most obvious not at the nude beaches but in the incredible array of fine restaurants. This is the first place I ever dined on ostrich, which was delicious; I'll try it again at the next chance. Such a meal obviously took major planning: after dinner I learned that the ostrich was imported all the way from South Africa.

TRAVEL TIPS

Area: Overall, 37 square miles: 20 are French, 17 Dutch.

Language: Dutch and French in their respective domains; English is widely spoken.

Population: Over 30,000, most on the Dutch side.

Time Zone: Atlantic Time, one hour ahead of Eastern Standard Time.

Rainy Season: This is a fairly arid place, with rainfall of only 45 inches a year. Rain falls mostly between September and December.

Getting There: St. Maarten's Queen Juliana airport is one of the Caribbean's most accessible, with major airlines flying in from North America and Europe. American Airlines' Puerto Rico hub is nearby, so passengers traveling through San Juan frequently arrive from New York, Miami, Orlando, Raleigh-Durham, Los Angeles and Dallas/Ft. Worth. KLM and Lufthansa fly weekly, Air France from Paris three times a week. Getting here from other Caribbean islands is easy because of the many interisland airlines that stop here. As mentioned, cruise ships make St. Maarten a regular stop because of its convenient location in the northern Caribbean near Puerto Rico and the Virgin Islands.

Documents: St. Maarten, the Dutch side where the international airport/customs/immigration are located, is normally all you have to worry about. U.S. and Canadian citizens need only birth certificates. All others need passports and perhaps visas. Cruise ship passengers or those in transit for a stay of less than 24 hours need some form of ID but not necessarily a passport. Air travelers need an ongoing ticket. St. Martin's entry requirements become important if you decide to take the 20-minute ferry ride from St. Martin to neighboring Anguilla; the ferryboats depart from and return to Marigot. U.S. and Canadian citizens need some sort of picture ID and birth certificate; a passport is required of everyone else. There are no formalities for traveling between St. Maarten and St. Martin. The border is unmanned, designated only by signs or markers. After a few days, you tend to forget you're crossing from one country into another.

Getting Around: Taxis are plentiful. Rental cars are reasonable and in good supply except during the peak season; arrange one when booking your hotel if you're traveling then. International and foreign drivers' licenses are accepted. All driving is on the right.

Where to Stay: Every type of resort imaginable, including gambling casinos, thrive on the Dutch side. Small hotels and guest houses are also available (get a list from the tourist board) but some will not accept young children or credit cards. The French side has far fewer rooms for visitors, though the number is increasing. Nudists should prefer the French side.

Camping: Not available.

Currency: The guilder, the French franc, and the euro are the official currencies, but dollars are accepted everywhere. You need never exchange them; in fact, you'll probably get a poor rate for the franc if you do. Banks are open 8:30 a.m. to 3 p.m. Monday through Friday.

Taxes & Tips: St. Maarten has a 5% room tax; a 15% service charge is common for both. When dining anywhere in St. Martin, look for "service compris" on your bill; that means the tip has already been included. There is a $20 departure tax.

Electrical Current: It differs on the Dutch and French sides: 120 V, 60 cycles on the Dutch, 220 V, 50 cycles on the French. Most hotels have transformers.

Safety/Health Warnings: Beaches are not the most secure places. Leave nothing valuable in your car, and leave nothing valuable on your beach blanket when you go for a swim. It might not be there when you get back. This is a very hot island; drink plenty of water, juice, and other nonalcoholic liquids.

Snakes & Other Venomous Creatures: None.

Hiking & Walking Services: Tri-Sport is the eco adventure outfitter on the St. Maarten side. They are located on Airport Road, Simpson Bay. Call 011 (599) 545-4384; fax 011 (599)545-4385; www.stmaartenstmartin.com/tri-sport. Many of the access points to the trails are marked and the trails blazed, each in different colors. You're advised not to leave the trails because the vegetation is thick and it's easy to get lost. Also, following several days of heavy rain, the trail and its markers may be nearly obscured by vegetation. Hike early. It can get very hot on these open trails.

Additional Information: St. Maarten and St. Martin share a website, found at www.stmaartenstmartin.com. It gives general information about both sides and leads to their respective websites.

PHILIPSBURG AFOOT!

Time: 1 hour; longer if you shop. | **Difficulty:** 1.

Philipsburg, the capital of St. Maarten, is second only to St. Thomas in its duty-free volume. It also happens to be an unusually easy city to walk around because it's located on a narrow strip of land between the ocean and a shallow lake. There's enough space for only two streets: Front and Back Streets. You can easily walk the length of the town in half an hour if you don't tarry to shop. Front Street has the major duty-free shops and essentially is a shopping/hotel/restaurant arcade. Back Street is more suited to Chinese restaurants and low-cost clothing.

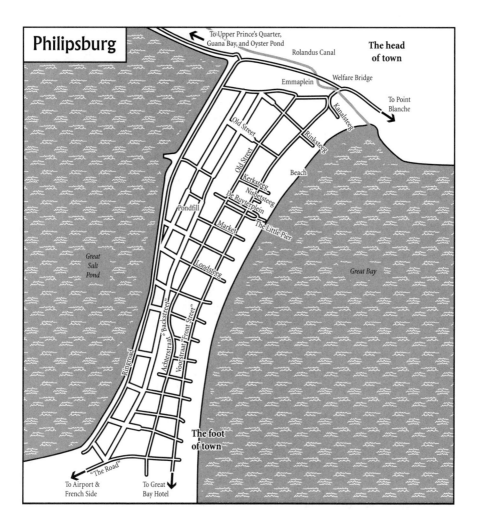

When the cruise ships are in, Philipsburg is crowded and congested. Every cruise ship day is like the day after Thanksgiving, traditionally the busiest shopping day of the year in the United States. As many of Philipsburg's stores are increasingly being staffed by Asians and East Indians, you'd never know you were in a Dutch nation. In St. Maarten, where you are is not important; what you buy is.

Stores are open 8 a.m. to noon and 2 p.m. to 6 p.m. Prices should be checked carefully to make sure you're getting a good deal; some items cost the same as back home. Some shoppers have recently complained of several devious practices: merchandise being switched when it is wrapped and being charged a sales tax when everything is not only duty-free but without any purchase or luxury tax. Sad to say, but success may be ruining St. Maarten. Let the buyer beware.

Philipsburg's most famous site is historic **Watley Square,** which faces the small pier near the middle of town. The old wooden courthouse and post office there date from 1793.

The **Old Street Mall** is a new shopping complex based on traditional Dutch architecture. Although the buildings are nothing but replicas, this still is one of the most picturesque spots in Philipsburg. If you stop in one of the bars, you may want to sample the guavaberry liqueur that has been made in local homes for over 200 years. Made from rum and guavaberries that ripen just before Christmas, it has a fruity/bitter/sweet/woody taste that is distinctive.

St. Maarten also has a carnival the end of April that is well worth seeing. It has all the revelry and competitions of a major carnival but on a more manageable scale. The costume parade is at a decent civilized hour, too, about 2 p.m. A terrific photo opportunity in gorgeous natural sunlight.

MARIGOT AFOOT!

Time: 1–2 hours. | **Difficulty:** 1.

Capital of the French side, this was a sleepy little town compared to Philipsburg until the opening of the **Port Royale Marina and Shopping Center** that brought malls to Marigot at the end of the 1980s. A lot of the city began sprucing itself afterward, so the town looks brighter and prettier.

Shopping and eating are the main pastimes. Because everything is imported and based on the French franc, full meals can be expensive. However, you can always retreat to a cafe or pastry shop. A small but lively **fruit and vegetable market** is held at the waterfront on Saturday. The people generally do not like their picture taken without permission. Overlooking the city is **Fort Marigot,** which you can reach by hiking uphill. Plan on one to two hours to explore Marigot thoroughly.

BEACH WALKS

Because the island has so many beautiful beaches, it's possible to make walks of a mile or more beside the surf. One of the most striking is **Cupecoy Bay** to **Long Beach,** the island's prettiest beach. A trek of over a mile, you'll pass sandstone cliff formations, which can provide interesting photography. **Rouge Beach** extends for almost two miles, ending at the coral formations at Pointe du Bluff. Mile-long **Orient Beach** is the official nude beach though sunning "au naturel" is sanctioned almost everywhere on St. Martin.

ELSEWHERE ON ST. MAARTEN/ST. MARTIN

1. PARADISE PEAK HIKE

Time: 50 minutes one way. | **Difficulty:** 2–3 considering the climb.
| **Trailhead:** The bottom of Route Pic Paradise. Just outside the town of St. Louis on St. Martin, follow the sign and turn inland to Paradise Peak, which at 1,492 feet is the highest point on the island. This track can also be driven, but if you're cramped and you need a good uphill walk, this is your best chance.

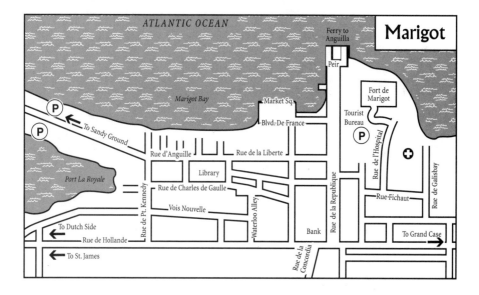

Begin the walk at the gate with two large urns on the right. As the highest point, this region receives the most rainfall, so the vegetation is lusher than anywhere else on the island. At the top you'll have to share the view with a radio tower, but ignore it and favor the excellent overlook of Philipsburg.

2. LA SUCRE PARADIS TRAIL

Time: 1 hour | **Difficulty:** 1–2. | **Trailhead:** At the end of the Paradise Peak Road.

This loop trail starts by the antennas at the southeast end of the road atop Paradise Peak. It leads to the old Paradis sugar mill built in 1779.

Starting out, the trail descends a heavily wooded slope and occasionally passes old retaining walls from 18th- and 19th-century agricultural terraces. Believe it or not, the gully paralleling the trail actually turns into a small stream in the rainy season.

It takes about 20 minutes to reach the overgrown walls of the sugar mill, which is still recognizable and shaded by a giant, ancient mango tree. Another five or ten minutes of walking brings you to a stone well and two huge vats built to boil sugarcane. Today, the vats are used as cattle troughs.

At this point, you'll join a marked blue and yellow trail that veers off to the left on the other side of the gully. The landscape now turns to dry forest. The markers will disappear as you reach the crest overlooking Colombier Valley. Follow the crest to your left as the winding trail cuts through tall Guinea grass alongside fencing walls. As long as you stick to the crest line between the two valleys it's hard to get lost even without markers.

It's about a 20-minute walk from the old well and the sugarcane vats to the Paradise Peak crest line trail, which is close to he clearly visible antennas that mark the end of the walk.

3. PARADISE PEAK–CONCORDIA PASS

Time: 3 hours one way. | **Difficulty:** 2–3. | **Trailhead:** The western end of the Paradise Peak Road in front of the French Telecom fence.

This walk will take you from the highest point on the island to Concordia Pass, above Marigot. This will offer some spectacular views on a clear day. Red and green blazes on tree trunks mark the way.

After a ten-minute walk along the crest line through old guava orchards you'll arrive at the foot of huge boulders. To your right, there will be occasional breaks in the 100-year-old orchards of mango and lemon trees that will give you a view of Marigot and the Colombier valley, with Anguilla in the background.

The trail will rise and fall as you traverse the spine of the peaks, and you'll receive a good lesson on the island's geography. On the east side of the island it's mostly dry forest thanks to the constant tradewinds. The west side, the lee side, is the lushest with tall gumbo, mango and kapok trees. Some locals refer to this as a rain forest, but it hardly receives enough precipitation to qualify.

You'll do a fairly steep rocky descent and reach a pass with an electric pylon about 45 minutes from the trailhead. The forest disappears as you cross a field planted with cabbage, cassava, yam, banana, papaya, hot pepper, tomato, chive, and thyme. This field may be in the middle of nowhere, but farmers who walk to it from the valley floor obviously tend it carefully.

The trail picks up again running northeast as it hugs a series of low retaining walls formerly used for agricultural terraces. After about 1.5 hours you'll come to a fork in the trail. One path leads up Mt. Flagstaff (390 meters). The one you want is marked Col de Concordia. You'll walk along a stone wall that marks the French-Dutch border.

About 20 minutes later, you'll reach a junction with the trail that leads from Colombier to South Reward near Philipsburg. Follow the green and red blazes leading through ficus, gum trees, cacti, and ferns. From here you have a good views of the Bay of Philipsburg and any cruise ships in port.

The trail continues to roll up and down. Shortly, you'll see Concordia Pass, both capitals and Simpson Bay Lagoon. The distant island is Saba.

You'll begin to descend along the crest line until you reach a dirt trail. On the right is a stone enclosure that made up the foundation of a traditional-style cabin. At Concordia Pass you'll join the dirt road that links Marigot with Philipsburg. Finally, you'll reach a stand selling Creole foods and cold drinks. And, hopefully, someone to pick you up.

4. LOTERIE FARM HIKES

Length: 4 miles maximum. | **Time:** Hikes vary from 45 minutes to 4 hours. | **Difficulty:** 1–2. | **Trailhead:** On the French side, at the base of Paradise Peak. Entrance is on the right about 500 meters after you turn onto Route Pic Paradis.

The 150 acres of farmland, tropical forest, and mountainous terrain is an eco-attraction that offers perhaps the island's most challenging hike, passing through the island's only remaining tropical forest system. All of the land on the right side of Route Pic Paradis belongs to Loterie Farm, an 18th-century sugarcane plantation whose ruins were only recently discovered.

To not change the environment too drastically, only a limited number of visitors are permitted each day. There is a basic admission charge to the farm itself. Other fees vary according to the activities you select.

The showcase walk is the 2.5-hour "eco challenge hike" that follows a previously hidden 18th-century supply route. The trail, just under four miles long, winds its way up to the top of the relatively cool, almost always windswept Paradise Peak (Pic Paradise). Along the way you will pass small waterfalls and pools for bathing.

The Source is a 45-minute guided walk following a fern-bordered dry riverbed. The walk enters the island's only tropical humid forest that also features mango trees, royal palms, and a good opportunity for birding. A sunset hike and campfire party are offered in the evening. A small, eclectic restaurant offers breakfast and lunch. For information, call 011 (590) 878616 or email loteriefarm@yahoo.com.

19

TOBAGO

Although joined politically with Trinidad in the Republic of Trinidad and Tobago, Tobago's geologic origins are still debated. Some scientists say only Trinidad was once a part of the South American mainland, as recently as 10,000 years ago. Others believe Tobago, located 22 miles off Trinidad's northeast tip, broke from the continent millions of years earlier.

Yet another theory claims Tobago was never part of South America at all. Scientists who support this view say that explains why Tobago does not harbor any poisonous snakes, compared to Trinidad's four poisonous types. Further, the variety of bird species differs considerably for two landfalls so close together. For instance, Tobago has about 20 birds that do not live in Trinidad.

Tobago has always endured second-rate status to oil-rich Trinidad. For example, electricity didn't arrive on Tobago until the 1950s. That's probably why Tobago still retains a rare old Caribbean feel and charm, much like the Caribbean in general was before World War II: slow living, friendly, and genuine. You don't yet find the huge shopping malls or high-rises as on Trinidad.

Bush medicine based on herbs and other natural ingredients is still popular. Including this particular arthritis remedy: "To relieve pain, go to the bee keeper and have some bees sting your joints." The treatment is guaranteed to lessen your arthritis pain; not because the bee stings hurt more but because the procedure really works. Just reapply bees periodically as needed.

For centuries, Tobago has always been considered one of the backwaters of the world, the perfect place for castaways. Daniel Defoe's *Robinson Crusoe* was set on Tobago. Walt Disney built a tree house in a huge Saman tree near the town of Goldsborough for filming *Swiss Family Robinson*. The treehouse, left as a tourist attraction, was destroyed by a hurricane. The Saman tree, now covered with bromeliads, still stands.

The island is sometimes compared to the shape of a turtle's back—a very long and thin turtle. Most people live on the edge of the shell, on the coast, and the steep center is largely unpopulated.

Christopher Columbus discovered Tobago in 1498 and called it "Bellaforma," one of his more original names. Tobago was left virtually alone until 1629, when the Swedes, British, French, and Dutch all attempted settlements. Following the transplant of 100 families from

Europe by the Duke of Courtland in 1654, Tobago became another island whose prosperity was based solely on sugarcane and cotton.

Today, Trinidad seems to overshadow Tobago in every way. After all, Trinidad's Asa Wright Nature Centre—a wonderful place to view birds—enjoys an international reputation. Still, I consider the 450-acre bird preserve at the offshore island of Little Tobago an equally good if not a far more dramatic walk because of the uncharacteristically rugged scenery. In addition, the chance to get as close as you could ever wish to nesting birds is truly unusual. Little Tobago may be little known, but it is one of my Top Ten Caribbean hikes (No. 5, one ahead of Asa Wright).

Scarborough, the main city, has good botanic gardens worth exploring but, quite honestly, little else to recommend it.

TRAVEL TIPS

(For information on currency, documents, taxes & tipping, and tourist board contacts, see the following chapter: Trinidad.)

Area: Located 22 miles from Trinidad, Tobago covers just 116 square miles. The island is cigar-shaped, 26 miles long and 9 miles wide.

Language: English.

Population: About 47,000.

Time Zone: Atlantic Time, one hour ahead of Eastern Standard Time.

Getting There: As the national airline of Trinidad and Tobago, BWIA offers the most frequent shuttle service from Trinidad; at least 12 flights daily, but weekends can be very crowded. LIAT also flies in from other islands. The airport runway has been extended so it can now accept direct international flights. Check other carriers, particularly American Airlines and American Eagle, (800) 433-7300, for the latest schedule.

A domestic ferry service also links Tobago with Trinidad. It carries not only people but vehicles and cargo. The 5.5-hour crossing costs TT$60 round-trip. The ferry offers dining and bars. Ticket sales close two hours before departure. Sailing times, Monday through Friday. Leave Port-of-Spain at 2 p.m., depart Scarborough at 11 p.m. On Sunday, the ferry leaves Trinidad at 11 a.m., returning from Tobago at 11 p.m. For information, in Trinidad call (868) 625-4906; in Tobago, (868) 639-2417. Tickets are valid for 90 days from date of purchase.

Getting Around: Driving is on the left. However, make sure the rental company's insurance is current. The police sometimes stop everyone checking for this. If the insurance is out of date, you lose your car—immediately. It happened to me. Stick with the larger companies.

Where to Stay: Most of the tourist hotels are near the southern coast by the airport and the capital city of Scarborough. However, Little Tobago and the Main Ridge Reserve, the two main hiking areas, are at the opposite end. The **Blue Waters Inn,** on Batteaux Bay, Speyside, is located directly opposite Little Tobago and tours depart here regularly; call (868) 660-4341; fax (868) 660-5195. In addition, it is also conveniently located to the Main Ridge hiking trails. The tourist board also has a list of guesthouses. The four-room

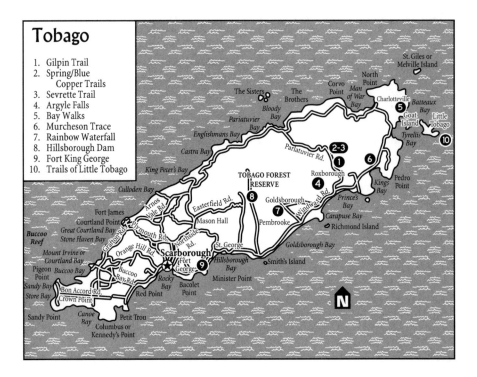

Tobago

1. Gilpin Trail
2. Spring/Blue
   Copper Trails
3. Sevrette Trail
4. Argyle Falls
5. Bay Walks
6. Murcheson Trace
7. Rainbow Waterfall
8. Hillsborough Dam
9. Fort King George
10. Trails of Little Tobago

Rainbow Nature Resort at Lure Estate, Goldsborough is a 25-acre nature reserve with trails and waterfalls. It has a full restaurant and bar. Call (868) 660-4755 or fax (868) 660-4755; email sharilee@tstt.net.tt. On the edge of the rain forest in Runnemede Valley is the ten-room **Cuffie River Eco-lodge and Nature Retreat**; Web site www.cuffie-river.com. In Plymouth on the Arnos Vale Road is the 12-acre **Adventure Farm and Nature Reserve**. It has air-conditioned villas with fully equipped kitchen, living room, and sun deck. Call (868) 639-2839; fax (868) 639-4157; email adventur@tstt.net.tt. **Footprints Eco Resort** has nine rooms, suites and two-bedroom villas thatched and perched on stilts like treehouses. Call (868) 660-0118; email contact-info@footprintseco-resort.com.

Snakes & Other Venomous Creatures: There are snakes, but none are poisonous.

Hiking/Walking Services: To fully appreciate Little Tobago or the Main Ridge rain forest, you need a guide, and Tobago has several excellent resident ones. **Walker's World,** an international outfitter with walking tours of Tuscany, Sicily, and other European regions also offers one-week walking tours of Tobago for about US$1,100; www. walkersworld.com. Personally, I highly recommend one of the forest service officers, **William Trim** at (868) 660-5529 in Goldsborough. Trim has tremendous enthusiasm for his subject. His friends nicknamed him "teacher" because of the incredible amount of information he is able to convey. His mother originally hoped he would become a teacher, but William couldn't stand the idea of being cooped up inside. As it turns out, Trim has become a teacher, holding his classes outdoors.

The overlook at Sea Bird I, Little Tobago

Perhaps Tobago's best-known guide service is **David Rooks Nature Tours,** which are personally guided by Rooks, who four times has been elected president of the Trinidad & Tobago Field Naturalist Club. He has two tours scheduled weekly. On Thursday it's Little Tobago, including boat trip and local lunch, $75 per person. On Saturday Rooks lead bird-watching and eco-tours into the rain forest, US$55 per person. There is a six person minimum for both tours. To contact Rooks on Trinidad: call (868) 622-8826; email rooks@pariasprings.com. In Tobago, call (868) 639-4276; email rookstobago@ trinidad.net.

Other guides to try: Jeb McEachnie for hiking and birding at **Nature's Touch;** call (868) 660-6464 or email jeb@natures-touch.net. **Newton George's** specialty is birds; call him at (868) 660-5463. **Renson Jack's** specialty is plants; call (868) 660-5175.

Main Ridge Reserve Hiking Trails

The Main Ridge recreation center, located about six miles beyond the village of Roxborough, argues that it is the oldest forest reserve in the Western Hemisphere, although Dominica and St. Lucia also make similar claims. The Main Ridge covers almost two-thirds of the island, running like a spine on a northeast-southwest angle. In 1765, the French perceived the importance of the forest as a major watershed and mandated it as a reserve.

Tobago's Heritage Festival

Tobago's two-week-long Heritage Festival offers one of the Caribbean's few authentic glimpses of traditional culture. Beginning in the middle of each July, the island celebrates its strongly held heritage through drama, oral traditions, and song and dance.

First celebrated in 1987, the Heritage Festival is intended to ensure the continuity of the island's varied cultural traditions shaped by African, Amerindian, and European influences. Tourists are more than welcome to attend the series of themed productions.

More so than on most islands, Tobago's heritage remains deeply rooted thanks to the island's relative isolation and its tight-knit sense of community. Its strong village orientation is best reflected by how the Heritage Festival is staged: events are held in a different village every day.

The festival covers everything from cradle to the grave. For instance, the Heritage Village of Bethel presents the Rites of Passage that looks at the traditions associated with birth while the village of Whim usually bases its production on the Wake and Bongo, the wakes held at the home of a dead one.

Not all the presentations are as serious. Patience Hill features a Festival of Dance with colorful costumes, and Golden Lane village showcases the courting approaches used many years ago in which the suitor had to prove his manhood by chopping a huge section of tree trunk into firewood. At Les Coteaux the village typically explores the myths and folk tales of Tobago. One year's production was about a woman who used unnatural powers to keep her husband under her bed.

Due to a technicality—the rampage of Mother Nature—Tobago definitely cannot claim to have the oldest protected plot of trees. Hurricane Flora destroyed most of her namesake on Tobago in 1963. The lush, thick rain forest you see flourishing today is relatively young with few old trees; incredible testimony to the awesome, destructive force of hurricane winds and the restorative powers of vegetation.

One tree that survived Flora's fury, a tree called a fiddlewood tree, is also one of the largest —its girth is an enormous 18 feet. The tree is hollow so you can actually crawl inside it near the base and stand erect. The fiddlewood is only 45 to 50 feet high; it's top was broken off.

The Main Ridge Reserve is totally user-friendly. On Sundays, many locals use the barbecue pits for picnics. Camping is not only permitted but encouraged. In fact, youngsters from all over the Caribbean sometimes come here on holidays and during summer. Weekdays, the park is practically deserted.

One of the most popular reenactments is the Old Time Wedding at Moriah village where more than a hundred participants dress in eighteenth- and nineteenth-century finery to re-create the weddings of a century ago. The men wear black stovepipe hats, black and white three-piece suits, bow ties, and white gloves and carry an umbrella to shade their female partners. The women are just as gussied up in bustle dresses, wide-brimmed hats with flowers, and as much jewelry as they can wear. This event is designed to show the European influences on the islanders.

It's a light-hearted event as the bride and groom are heckled throughout the ceremony, some times by a pregnant ex-girlfriend and sometimes by the jilted girl's whole family. Despite the interruptions the couple always gets wedded and afterward everyone files out of the church to "walk in de wedding" by dancing the "Brush Back" in the streets to the sounds of fiddles and tambrins. Food, speeches, dancing, and cultural entertainment at the wedding reception round out the afternoon. Spectators and their cameras are welcome everywhere. In fact, it wouldn't be considered much of a party unless they showed up, as hundreds of them always do.

As every festival should, this one ends with a bang. The Ole Time Carnival pulsates with sounds of pan (steel bands) and tamboo bamboo as revelers dance until dawn while masquerading as sailors, robbers, devils, and more. Everyone is invited to participate in J'ouvert.

For complete information about this year's Heritage Festival schedule and where the events will be held, contact Trinidad and Tobago tourism at (888) 595-4TNT or visit the official website: www.visittnt.com.

1. GILPIN TRAIL

Length: 2.2 miles (3.5 km). | **Time:** 2–3 hours. | **Difficulty:** 2–3 for the first 1.5 miles (2.5 km). The continual steep ascent of the last section rates a 3–4. | **Trailhead:** The trailhead is at mile marker 1.25 on the road to Bloody Bay, the Parlatuvier Road.

This is the park's main hike, named after an old road that islanders used to walk to Bloody Bay. The true road eventually veers off after the first couple of miles; the remaining trail is newly cut and leads uphill to the main Visitor Center/picnic area. From the Visitor Center back to the starting point, the last leg is along open road. The distance covered in the forest itself is about 2 miles (3.2 km). Tobago has the odd tendency to measure road distances in miles, hiking distances in kilometers. There's talk of adopting a uniform system.

Most people do not complete the full circuit but walk only to the first or second waterfall, then retrace their steps, which round trip takes about an hour.

In addition to a sign, the trail beginning is marked by a collection of a dozen or more walking sticks angling out of the ground like a patch of denuded forest. These sturdy sticks are provided because the trail is often slippery. The foresters themselves often wear rubber boots on this stretch; it's that muddy. Curiously, the mud here comes in enough different colors that Carnival's Mas players frequently visit the forest to get pigment for their costumes.

Orange-winged parrots, red-rumped woodpeckers, cockey crows, and many different kinds of hummingbirds occupy the reserve. One of the rarest is the white-tailed saberwing hummingbird, which one forester has seen only seven times in six years. He says that each occasion "was a privilege and honor to see it."

Agouti, armadillo, opossum, and a several harmless snakes, including the counterfeit coral snake, live in the thick foliage. Cicadas call loudest at two times, just before the rainy season begins and ends. Another signal that the rainy season is on the way is the yellow poui tree, which flowers just before the regular showers begin.

An underground stream also appears at the start of the Gilpin Trail. Appearing like a tiny brook initially, after the first kilometer it's carved a gully over 100 feet deep. You must cross on a large, reinforced log.

The trail is described according to how people usually divide up the walk:

Trailhead to the first waterfall: This short 0.9-mile (1.4-km) walk is the one most people make and never venture farther. You'll see at least 30 different species of ferns, including small tree ferns, as well as lots of bamboo.

Termites and ants furnish several unusual stopping points on this short segment. There are between 11 and 13 different kinds of termites, and each species exudes a kind of repellant to keep away predators. The system works: some of the Little Tobago mounds are huge.

Even more impressive is the six-foot-tall nest of leaf-cutter ants at the base of a tapana tree. The leaf cutters are the ones who carry small bits of green leaves in a wide line, so it sometimes seems the forest floor moves along like an escalator. A large ant trail on the right looks like it was created by a person sliding down the bank. According to folklore, ants are handy for first aid if you happen to cut yourself: the theory is to use the ants to bind your wounds. You let them bite you, then pinch their bodies off and leave the heads there. Tough on the ants, though.

At 0.9 mile (1.4 km) you will reach a small, unnamed waterfall that is part the Gold-Silver River. The river gained its unusual name partly from the color of water, which has a shiny silvery color. However, the background material the water flows over is gold in color, created by oxides deposited by the river. Hence the name Gold-Silver River. It takes about 30 to 45 minutes to walk to this point.

From the first to the second waterfall: One mile from the trailhead (1.6 km) and about 15 minutes beyond the first waterfall, is a second and smaller waterfall. It's apparent how few people walk this far from the change in the pathway. Until the Gold-Silver River, the trail is worn and muddy from frequent use. But because the heavy travel ends there, a layer of vegetation covers the path. The second waterfall, though small, is striking because of the water falling on the dark green ferns. The stream is so small here you can literally step across it.

From the second to third waterfall: About 2.5 km from the start is another small waterfall with a narrow stream that can be stepped across.

From the third waterfall to the interpretive center: The toughest part of the hike is from 2.5 to 3.2 km because of the occasional steep grade. The first third is uphill. The middle section undulates up and down. The toughest climbing has been saved for last. Good physical condition and a walking stick are essential. This last section of trail contains the hollow fiddlewood tree you can stand inside. You'll also see another small waterfall. The recreation center is at 3.5 km, a trek of 2.5 to 3 hours from the outset.

2. SPRING/BLUE COPPER TRAILS

Length: 1.9 miles (3 km) for both trails. | **Time:** 1 hour. | **Difficulty:** 2. | **Trailhead:** Located about 4.5 miles from the village of Roxborough on the way to the park recreation center on the Parlatuvier Road.

The Spring Trail starts near a water pipe where the clean spring water comes gushing out. After about 20 minutes, the Spring Trail connects with the mile-long Blue Copper Trail, named after the very tough and hard wood known as blue copper. The Spring Trail may be the best bird walk in the entire reserve: common are yellow-legged thrush, hummingbirds, rufus-tail jacamar, colored trogans, and more. Considerable nesting activity occurs on this trail, more than you'll probably see on the Gilpin Trail. The forest is not as thick because of some selective cutting.

3. SEVRETTE TRAIL

Length: 0.3 mile (0.5 km). | **Time:** 15 minutes. | **Difficulty:** 1. | **Trailhead:** Near the park's interpretive center.

This short trail is designed primarily as an educational trail for visiting school children, with interpretive/name signs for the different flora.

ELSEWHERE ON TOBAGO

4. ARGYLE FALLS

Time: 15 minutes each way. | **Difficulty:** 1. | **Trailhead:** On the windward coast main road. Admission fee. Guides will descend on you.

One of the easiest and most scenic spots on Tobago, it's about a 15-minute walk to the falls from the main road. Because the series of four falls are at different levels, you can choose from several different pools to bathe in. The largest is at the bottom. This is cool spring water, so be prepared for the shock. Also a popular tourist attraction, you're charged a fee according to how high up you go. The higher, the prettier (naturally!). At 177 feet (54 m), these are the island's highest falls.

5. Bay Walks

Time: Up to 4 hours. | **Difficulty:** 3. | **Trailhead:** Begin at Batteaux Bay and follow the coastline to Belmont Bay.

This walk goes by a series of three bays with a rugged hill climb at the end. Lowland sections can be quite hot; take water. Starwood Bay, the real object of this walk, is about 45 to 60 minutes from the outset. There is absolutely nothing there except a grand beach. It's so rarely frequented that it's often used for skinny-dipping. The walk is quite easy for the first three-quarters, but the last section is a steep incline normally kept clear by the government. Once you reach Belmont Bay you'll have a lovely view even though most of the trees have been cut down and the beach washed away.

You have an option for the return walk. Between Belmont and Starwood Bays is an unmarked trail climbing rugged Flagstaff Hill. Unless you want to retrace your same steps, make the climb. Eventually you will come out on a road that is half asphalt and half stones. This will take you out to the main road, which will take you to Speyside or Charlotteville. This circuit takes four hours.

6. Murcheson Trace

Time: 30 minutes. | **Difficulty:** 2. | **Trailhead:** A sign on King's Bay Road points to the road leading to Murcheson Trace.

Just before reaching the house atop the hill, a trail off to the right will bring you back down to King's Bay beach and its facilities. After you descend, you're only a few hundred feet from what was one of Tobago's prettiest waterfalls, its flow now greatly reduced because of a dam built to provide drinking water.

7. Rainbow Waterfall

Time: 20 minutes. | **Difficulty:** 1. | **Trailhead:** From the Rainbow Nature Resort, located on a dirt road about a mile from Goldsborough on the windward coast.

The waterfall is based on the "rainbow people" phrase coined by Archbishop Desmond Tutu of South Africa when he visited the Caribbean. Trinidad and Tobago currently have adopted the slogan, "The Rainbow Is Real." Although Trinidad has a very diverse heritage with a strong Indian influence, most Tobagonians are of African descent. The short walk is under a canopy of bamboo, banana leaves, and forest and involves walking in and out of a small stream.

8. Hillsborough Dam

Length: Up to 5 miles. | **Time:** 1–2 hours. | **Difficulty:** 2. | **Trailhead:** At Mount St. George, located a few miles from Scarborough off the Windward Road headed toward Speyside.

The road heading inland at Mount St. George is identified on maps as the Mount St. George–Castara Road. For a longer hike, you can use it as a walking trail that leads to the reservoir. Greebs, anhingas, herons, and martins reside in the reservoir area, filled by stream runoff from the Main Ridge in the rain forest. Some locals claim caimans also live here.

Take the old road beyond the damn to climb to the top of the Main Ridge. Depending on how far you care to walk, this can total as much as five miles. The views of Scarborough and Mount St. George are especially panoramic.

9. FORT KING GEORGE

Time: 30–45 minutes. | **Difficulty:** 1. | **Trailhead:** Overlooking the city of Scarborough.

Historical sites don't play a major part in walking/hiking around Tobago, but this magnificently restored fort 400 feet above the capital city of Scarborough has beautifully kept walking paths and excellent panoramic views. Built in 1777, Fort King George consists of a lighthouse, powder magazine and officer's mess. One building has been converted into an art gallery. Lots of cannon on display, and either these or their ancestors were put to good use. After a prolonged battle, the French took the fort, renamed it Fort Castries, and occupied it from 1781 to 1793. Recaptured by the British, it changed hands in battle several more times, so it's amazing anything at all is left. It was abandoned in 1854.

Locals will tell you that Tobago changed hands politically 31 times in 200 years, making their island one of the most traded/fought for landfalls in the Caribbean. Tobagonians are kind of proud for having been so highly prized.

LITTLE TOBAGO

Little Tobago is a 243-acre uninhabited island about 1.4 miles off the east coast of Tobago proper, a 20-minute boat ride from Speyside.

I rate this one of the Caribbean's best hikes (No. 5) for its bird-watching and sheer spectacle; it reminded me of the Galápagos Islands off the coast of Ecuador. This island is also the easiest place in the Caribbean to view the sleek and majestic red-billed tropic birds in vast numbers.

Little Tobago receives only about 2,000 visitors a year. Because so few visit, the government hasn't yet had to enact quota restrictions, even during the nesting season when sea birds are so plentiful you have to step around the nests that contain boisterous fledglings.

The main nesting season is from April to August. At least 23 species breed on Little Tobago, including frigate birds, laughing gulls, bridled and sooty terns, and brown boobies. Year-round residents include Audubon's shearwaters.

Spring is excellent for hummingbirds, too, when the trees are flowering. Forestry officials says it's possible to see as many as 17 different hummingbird species, more than enough to tire the eyeballs of even the most avid bird-watcher.

For decades, Little Tobago was advertised as the only place to see the Bird of Paradise outside of its New Guinea homeland. However, that's not been true for a good number of years. The last of the introduced birds disappeared in the early 1980s, probably blown away/killed by a hurricane. The government tried negotiating for a new batch of birds from New Guinea and even built an enclosed aviary in anticipation of their arrival, which has yet to occur.

Caution: Trails on Little Tobago can be slick and slippery immediately following a rain. It's recommended you wait at least two or three hours for the sun and wind to dry out the ground. Otherwise, some sections will be like a water slide. Tree roots criss-cross the path at many points, so the ride will be bumpy and unpleasant. However, because most of the trails are well inland; at least you don't have the danger of falling off the side of a mountain.

Little Tobago offers more than 20 different trails. Following are the most frequently visited and most scenic trails. Expect to spend three or four hours on this fascinating preserve to explore it unhurriedly and take pictures. The trails are well laid out and easy to follow. Again, interpretive signs for plants and trees do not exist yet; this is why a guide would be helpful.

10. Trails of Little Tobago

A. Main Ascent (Beach) Trail

Length: Time: 10–15 minutes. | **Difficulty:** 1–2 depending on how recently it's rained. | **Trailhead:** The jetty/picnic shelter where most boats land.

The trail climbs steadily to what will one day be an active interpretive center. The trail is well shaded much of the way with a canopy consisting mainly of sabal thatch palm.

Because of the poor nature of the soil, trail erosion is very much a problem on Little Tobago. On this main ascent trail, concrete steps were selectively placed in 1990 to prevent runoff from sweeping away the path. Only the main trail has these occasional steps; the rest of the island is still in a natural state.

Just as sometimes too much water falls on Little Tobago, drought can also be a problem. On this ascent, you'll pass bamboo water troughs about two feet long that the Forest Service has to keep filled during the dry season. When cisterns on Little Tobago run dry, water is hauled in by boat from Tobago, an impressive indication of how dedicated the government is to maintaining Little Tobago as a permanent, year-round bird sanctuary.

The interpretive center at the top of the hill dates back to the early 1960s. Lack of funding has prevented its full completion. At present it has both inside and outside toilets (the latter always work). Plans call for outfitting a kitchen and sleeping quarters for as many as 20 people. Ventilation at night could be an interesting problem because the building currently has to be kept sealed after dark to keep out bats. A fruit garden of cashew, banana, guava, and soursop is cultivated near the house for the benefit of birds, not people.

B. Bird of Paradise I

Length: 0.3 mile (0.5 km). | **Time:** 20 minutes, one way. | **Difficulty:** 1–2. The trail ascends at the beginning, then winds around part of the cliff. | **Trailhead:** First path you encounter after leaving the interpretive center. Located on the left, 100 yards, this also connects with Bird of Paradise II.

After an initial moderate ascent, the trail winds along the hillside, taking you on the route where the bird of paradise was most commonly seen. Good luck on spotting one here today;

the sign is as much a tombstone as a trail marker. The last sighting of a bird of paradise in the wild on Little Tobago was November, 1981.

According to local accounts, 48 pairs of these colorful birds were introduced to the island in 1909 and another pair added in 1912. What happened to the birds is unclear. They apparently fell victim to predators and storms. Because of their limited ability to fly, it's not believed they simply flapped off to South America.

The birds of paradise may have flown the coop, but in this area you can see the blue-crowned mot mot (also known as the king-of-the-woods), which grows to 18 inches and is noted for its racquet-shaped tail; the tiny yellow and black bananaquit; mockingbirds; and the crested oropendola, commonly called yellowtails.

C. Bird of Paradise II

Length: About 1.2 miles (2 km). | **Time:** 1 hour. | **Difficulty:** 2. | **Trailhead:** This walk is a continuation of Bird of Paradise I.

Not much to say except it goes up a hill and then across the mountain.

D. Yellowtail Trail

Length: 0.8 mile (1.3 km). | **Time:** 45 minutes round-trip. | **Difficulty:** 2. | **Trailhead:** Located just beyond the entrance of Bird of Paradise I.

The trail is named for the impressive number of the unique and distinctive yellowtail nests hanging from the trees. These yellowtails have an unusual characteristic. Although the birds of paradise disappeared years ago, some yellowtails apparently copied their call and adopted it as their own.

E. Seabird View I

Time: 3–5 minutes. | **Difficulty:** 1. | **Trailhead:** Located only about 100 meters from the interpretive center.

The view from Seabird View I comes as an astonishing, surprising sight. You walk up to it unaware that suddenly right before you is an outlook that dramatically reveals the windward side of the island, the rolling Atlantic, and a cove of sheer cliffs peppered with birds. Most magnificent of all are the red-billed tropic birds continually circling over the bay, a major fishing ground. Below you are some of the most turbulent waters in all Trinidad or Tobago, and the vista is an incredibly impressive one. This is the spot that reminds me so much of the Galápagos.

In the distance are the St. Giles Islands, a clump of rocks that are another thriving nesting area. Boat tours are available around St. Giles in good weather (that is the feisty Atlantic out there, remember), but landing at the preserve is prohibited.

If you feel active, you can take a branch trail down to the rocks to observe sea bird nests close up. Noddy and sooty terns, laughing gulls and brown boobies all nest this coastline. Tropic birds, which build right at the cliff edge, are said to do so because they have short legs and need an easy landing site. This branch trail takes only about five minutes going down; a tough ten minutes scrambling to get back up. It may be closed off at the peak nesting times.

F. Mockingbird Trail

Length: 0.3 mile (0.4 km). | **Time:** 10 minutes. | **Difficulty:** 2. | **Trailhead:** Continues beyond Seabird I.

Named for one of the local birds commonly found in this area, the trail borders some West Indian cherry trees planted to attract/feed the birds. It also passes an old building once used by naturalists studying here. The hill climbs steadily and moderately, then flattens out a little at the end. The brief walk leads to a crossroads (Hike H, p. 339).

G. Seabird View II

Length: 0.5 mile (0.86 km). | **Time:** 15 minutes. | **Difficulty:** 2. May be muddy and requires a slight ascent. | **Trailhead:** This marked path is on the left on the Mockingbird Trail (above) just before you reach the ruins of the old naturalist house.

Seabird II is another panoramic platform for observing major sea bird nesting colonies. The trail passes under a palm canopy and by a fair amount of bamboo. If you hear something rustling through the ground cover, it may be one of the huge hermit crabs. The crabs, which wear mostly whelk shells, are very inquisitive and if you hold the shell long enough, the crab will come out.

The brown "cold snake" is sometimes found in this region; it feeds on the young nestlings of species that lay their eggs on the ground. Locals say the snake, which grows between 18 and 24 inches, seems to love the smell of rank things, hence its name. Of course the rustling noise might also be a green iguana, sometimes seen on this trail.

If you notice a pronounced ammonia smell, you're not crazy; it's the pronounced presence of the bats that reside in this section.

The Seabird View II isn't quite as dramatic as Seabird I, but it is still impressive. The coastline is fringed with cactus, especially prickly pear and Turk's Head. Boobies, terns, and laughing gulls all inhabit here. Birds sometimes build their nests closer to this site than at Seabird I. However, the drop is so sheer it's not possible to see what's directly below you at the shoreline on Alexander Bay.

The opposite shore is a finger of land that leads to a light beacon. Thousands of birds lay their eggs here in nesting season. Except for the workers who service the beacon, few people make the ridge walk, a scorcher in dry season.

H. George Ride Trail

Time: 10 minutes. | **Difficulty:** 1. | **Trailhead:** Access starts at Seabird View II.

This trail, named after one of the island's first custodians, passes through one of the island's oldest fruit gardens. You may also spot evidence of cotton, because sea island cotton was grown here for several years. Feral fowl are also on the island, further indication of earlier inhabitation.

I. CAMPBELL'S WALK

Length: 1.5 miles (2.4 km). | **Time:** 1.5 hours. | **Difficulty:** 3. | **Trailhead:** It branches left off the George Ride Trail.

Campbell's Walk leads to the light beacon. At first, you descend a rugged and bushy area before the path smoothes out. This is one of the longest and most rugged trails on the island.

Between a third and halfway along Campbell's you'll encounter a difficult stretch with dense undergrowth. When it clears out, look for a rugged branch trail (about 100 yards long) that leads down to the nesting tropic birds and laughing gulls. This is not an easy descent because of the thick undergrowth. If you continue to the light beacon at the end of the point, you'll need to scramble to actually reach the marker due to the rugged nature of the trail

J. CROSSROADS

Time: 5 minutes. | **Difficulty:** 1. | **Trailhead:** Coming back from the light beacon on Campbell's Walk, turn left when you reconnect with the George Ride Trail. In a few minutes you will be at a major crossroads where George Ride intersects with three other trails: Mockingbird Trail (p. 338), Ingram's Walk (below), and the Waljack Dam walk (below).

At this point, you are only 0.3 mile (0.5 km) from the second Seabird overlook and 0.24 mile (0.4 km) from the beginning of the Mockingbird Trail. To return to the beach, take Mockingbird Trail which takes you back to the interpretive center.

K. WALJACK DAM

Length: 0.3 mile (0.5 km). | **Time:** 7 minutes descent, 15 minutes ascent. | **Difficulty:** 2–3 depending on how slippery the conditions. | **Trailhead:** Access is from the Crossroads (above).

This is a water catchment area, a natural spring named after two naturalists, Wallace and Jack. Built in 1990, the dam is four to five feet high and about ten feet long. The all-season watering hole is an excellent bird attracter for white-tipped doves, yellowtails, pigeons, king-of-the-woods, bananaquit, the Caribbean martin, and even hummingbirds. The dam, located near the coastline, is a dead end walk.

L. INGRAM'S WALK

Length: 0.2 mile (0.34 km). | **Time:** 10 minutes. | **Difficulty:** 3. | **Trailhead:** Access is at the Crossroads.

This trail leads to the highest point on Little Tobago, regrettably not nearly as scenic as the Seabird overlooks. Ingram's Walk takes about ten minutes because it is a steep climb.

M. Dinsmoor/Shearwater Trails

Length: About 0.6 miles (1 km). | **Time:** 5 minute descent, 10–15-minute return ascent. | **Difficulty:** 2–3. | **Trailhead:** At the end of Ingram's Walk, continue along the short 70-yard Dinsmoor Trail, which connects with Shearwater.

The whole purpose for having such short trails as Ingram's and Dinsmoor seems to honor naturalists who've worked here. These just as easily could have been a single trail.

Shearwater is one of the more rugged trails because it is not kept as clear as the others; shrubs and vines clog the trail, which is steep in some parts. Shearwater leads to a seasonal nesting area for yellow-crown night herons.

20   TRINIDAD

Trinidadian Saying: "*Okra don't bear peas.*"
Translation: "*Children inherit traits.*"

The southernmost of all Caribbean islands, Trinidad has a greater diversity of bird and animal species than any other island in the Caribbean. The reason: Trinidad is an extension of the Venezuelan mainland, an annex of South America instead of part of the West Indies. Situated just seven miles off the coast, Trinidad is all that remains of an eastern spur of the Andes that was probably joined to South America as recently as 10,000 years ago.

Because of its proximity to South America, Trinidad has evolved into a huge animal and plant reserve, a microcosm of South American flora and fauna. Plants and animals thrive profusely here, not just due to Trinidad's continental origins, but because its terrain is so diverse. Roughly rectangular in shape and still about 50 percent forested, Trinidad is crossed by three mountain ranges separated by savannahs, undulating plains, and brackish and fresh water swamps. Elfin forest, montane rain forest, and lowland rain forest, along with the fresh- and saltwater swamps, all contribute to vital habitat.

Trinidad boasts 108 different mammals (most of which are bats), compared to the handful found on most Caribbean islands. Ocelots, capuchin, howler monkeys, and wild hogs are just a few of the animals Trinidadians refer to as "moving scenery." As for reptiles, Trinidad has 55 different kinds, 25 of them amphibians. Trinidad is also a butterfly heaven: 620 different species of extremely colorful "flutterbys" call this island home. The variety of orchids—700 types—is unbelievably diverse.

The bird population here contrasts so greatly from that of the Northern Caribbean that it's not unusual for experienced birders to add as many as 120 to 150 new species to their "life list" on a single visit. Like most of the 430 different avian species found on Trinidad (and Tobago, too), the 17 different species of hummingbirds are primarily South American birds. You just about need a computer and calculator to keep an accurate bird count at the Asa Wright Nature Centre, a haven for 200 low- and high-elevation avian species; that's half of Trinidad's total species in just one spot.

That's just the fauna. At least 2,300 species of flowering plants are known to exist, including 700 varieties of orchids. Undoubtedly, more will be identified. For sheer natural spectacle, the shaded, foliage-rich trails of Asa Wright deserve to be on anyone's list of the Caribbean's Top 10 walks. I rank it No. 6.; an avid birder might place it No. 1. If you see no other spot on Trinidad, let it be Asa Wright.

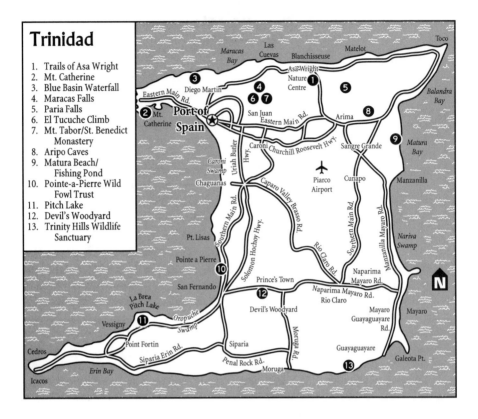

Trinidad

1. Trails of Asa Wright
2. Mt. Catherine
3. Blue Basin Waterfall
4. Maracas Falls
5. Paria Falls
6. El Tucuche Climb
7. Mt. Tabor/St. Benedict Monastery
8. Aripo Caves
9. Matura Beach/ Fishing Pond
10. Pointe-a-Pierre Wild Fowl Trust
11. Pitch Lake
12. Devil's Woodyard
13. Trinity Hills Wildlife Sanctuary

BACKGROUND

Until the 1980s, Trinidad prospered far more than most islands. Where did the wealth come from? Right out of the ground, in the island's oil wells. Because the government co-owned all of the local drilling operations, most of the oil money remained right in the country, giving the island a standard of living that was the envy of many of its sister states. Unfortunately, when the price of oil decreased dramatically in the 1980s, so did the local economy. Today, tourism occupies an increasingly important role. Port-of-Spain wouldn't look so much like an industrial center if tourism had been vital from the start.

Legend suggests that before embarking on his third journey to the New World, Christopher Columbus dedicated his expedition to the Holy Trinity and vowed to name the first landfall he spied "La Trinite." Either that or he named Trinidad, which he discovered in 1498, after its three mountain ranges. Whatever the reason, Trinidad replaced the Arawak Indian name for the island—"Iere," land of the hummingbird. And it was an Arawak name, not a Carib. The Caribs, who were in the process of decimating (and supposedly eating) the Arawaks elsewhere in the Caribbean, never were able to take much of a bite out of Trinidad's Arawaks.

The Spanish established their first outpost on Trinidad in 1532, which stood until 1595, when the English under Sir Walter Raleigh destroyed it. Raleigh was drawn to Trinidad because of an unusual natural resource found there—the asphalt at Pitch Lake that provided excellent caulking for ships. Trinidad remained in Spanish hands until the British fleet came calling in 1797 and the local governor quickly surrendered the island.

Trinidad was officially ceded to Britain in 1802, and in 1877 Tobago was turned over to Trinidad as a ward. In 1888, the British politically lumped together Trinidad and Tobago, which never really had much in common before or since. The islands are now an independent republic within the British Commonwealth.

THE BIRTH PLACE OF PAN (STEEL BAND)

Although you may never have visited Trinidad, you probably are already familiar with part of its culture. The island's influence on music heard around the world has been tremendous.

Calypso, limbo and steel band, the unique, lively music and dancing that have come to characterize the islands, all originated in Trinidad as enthusiastic expressions of everyday life. These musical forms were so instantly popular that many other tourist-seeking islands adopted them and attempted to pass them off as their own. This plagiarism was so successful that most people probably believe calypso and steel bands started in the Bahamas or Jamaica. But no, Trinidad is the birthplace of the Caribbean's most lively musical spirit.

Every February to early March, this artistic vigor is displayed in one gigantic celebration known as Carnival, a huge revelry that combines the world's best calypso and soca music with elaborate and original masquerade costumes. Trinidad's Carnival for years has been known as the Caribbean's largest and loudest celebration. Carnival began when early French settlers would march in masked processions from one house to another (thus the local name "Mas"), a custom slaves adopted after emancipation in 1834. Wary authorities attempted to discourage this new Carnival, but obviously without success.

From the beginning, pounding drums have led the Mas processions. After World War II, steel bands added a whole new dimension when local musicians discovered they could get as many as 32 different notes from something as ordinary as the top of an oil drum. From such an unlikely beginning, the steel bands formed and the loudly thumping heart of modern day Carnival was born.

Carnival lasts for weeks, but the revelry explodes the weekend just before Lent. Costume and band competitions are capped off by the incredible walk (or shuffle or stagger depending on your condition). It is the J'ouvert (pronounced "jouvay"), a jump-up or dawn dance that parades through the streets of Port-of-Spain from about 4 a.m. until 10 a.m. With many thousands of people taking part, J'ouvert is deafening, intoxicating, crushing, unforgettable, a true celebration (and testing) of the senses. For tourists, it generally is a safer celebration than the only other comparable spectacle, Rio de Janeiro at Carnival time. (Mardi Gras is small-town compared to Carnival.)

Outsiders are invited to party throughout it all. In fact, to be authentic, you can even buy your own Carnival costume at a Mas Camp. Trinidad, long a melting pot of many ethnic groups, is accustomed to welcoming newcomers. It is home to more than 40 different nationalities, including East Indians, Chinese, Portuguese, Syrians, Jews, Latin Americans, as well as the black population. No other Caribbean island has a population as diverse as these "rainbow people."

It may take as long as a year to complete a costume for Carnival

PAN AND CARNIVAL

Amazing but true: The oil drum tops that create all the sounds of a steel band are considered the only new musical instrument of modern times. Known locally as "pan," steel band beating is an outgrowth of the religious drumming traditions of both Africa and India. Steel band competitions are equivalent to national football and soccer league championship clashes. The Super Bowl occurs at Carnival, where the steel bands are like nowhere else. They are enormous, with 300 to 500 players. You may sometimes even hear classical music mixed with the soca and calypso. Common carnival lingo: "Make ah mash Mas," to thoroughly get into the party spirit. "Fete" is the same as party. "Wine": not something to drink but a suggestive motion of the hips. If someone wants to "wine" with you, they may want to simulate sex with you with a rapid flurry of hip grinds (but never touching).

Exploring Trinidad's remarkable diversity, it may seem that no matter where you go, you're continually discovering something unique, colorful and exotic. Trinidad definitely is the best place in all the Caribbean to view wildlife, and lots of it (especially during Carnival).

TRAVEL TIPS

Area: Trinidad is roughly rectangular in shape, 37 miles wide and 50 miles long, a total of 1,864 square miles.

Language: English with some French and Spanish occasionally spoken.

Population: Approximately 1.3 million, one of the most heavily populated in the Caribbean.

Time Zone: Atlantic Time, one hour ahead of Eastern Standard Time.

Rainy Season: June through December. Showers can be torrential—real frog stranglers—but usually clear quickly. Both Trinidad and Tobago are well south of the normal hurricane belt, but powerful storms don't respect any man-made boundaries and hurricanes still clobber the region periodically.

Getting There: Trinidad's Piarco Airport is the main entry for visitors to Trinidad or Tobago. U.S. visitors have a choice of American Airlines or BWIA . Canadians can take Air Canada . The airport is 16 miles from Port-of-Spain, so allow plenty of time when leaving.

Documents: U.S. and Canadian citizens need a birth certificate with some form of photo ID that is valid for two months. For everyone else, passports are required of anyone above age 16. Visas are required of some citizens. Entry permits are good for one month. If you plan to stay longer, ask for up to three months on arrival because extensions can be a time-consuming process. An ongoing, dated ticket (not open-ended) may also be required at immigration, plus proof you are able to support yourself during your stay. A specific address for your stay will also be requested.

Getting Around: The official taxis have an "H" as the first letter on their license plate. Negotiate ahead of time and know whether the price is in TT$ or US$. Other taxis that have the "P" registration of a private car on the license are known as pirate taxis. You may be able to negotiate a better rate with them. In time you will discover route taxis with the "H" initial; these are far cheaper but drive only a specified route, like a bus. They stop and pickup wherever you wish along that route. The only way to tell a "regular" from a "route" taxi is ask the driver. Some taxis also charge 50% more after midnight.

Rental cars just for weekends are difficult to find because many locals, who cannot afford the exorbitant price of a car, lease on a long-term basis. Make sure the rental company accepts credit cards. If it requires a cash deposit, be aware your money may be returned to you in TT$, which you then have to change back. A foreign or international drivers license is good for 90 days.

Where to Stay: Finding a reasonably comfortable place to stay near animal and bird preserves can be a challenge. To overnight in the heart of a bird-rich rain forest, contact the **Asa Wright Nature Centre and Lodge,** (800) 426-7781; fax (868) 667-0493. The lodge can accommodate up to 50 guests in its 25 twin-bedded rooms, each with private bath and hot and cold water. This is hardly roughing it. Meals are Trinidad style, featuring fresh fruit, vegetables, baked bread and pastries, and homemade jams and jellies.

Port-of-Spain has several large hotels, including the **Hilton,** the **Normandie,** and the **Bel Air Piarco** at the airport. Guesthouses are an excellent alternative. **Monique's Guest House** in Maravel, (868) 628-3334, is on the road to Maracas Bay; the people are very friendly, the food excellent, the rooms large. The **Bed and Breakfast Association of Trinidad & Tobago** also has an office in the Trinidad airport before immigration; Diego Martin Post Office, Box 3231; (868) 637-9329; fax (868) 627-0856. This is the best way to get out and see the country.

Camping: None.

Currency: The Trinidad and Tobago or TT dollar is worth about TT$6.24 = US$1. This is a floating rate that has steadily been declining in value since 1985. Banks are open 9 a.m. to 1 p.m. Monday through Thursday and 9 a.m. to noon, 3 p.m. to 5 p.m. on Friday. U.S. currency is readily accepted everywhere. Banks may charge a fee for cashing traveler's checks.

Taxes & Tips: The hotel room tax is 10% and the service charge (tacked on to about everything) is also 10%. There's also a 15% value added tax on all goods and services. An exit tax is required on leaving: TT$100 and it must be paid in the local currency, a real annoyance.

Electrical Current: Either 110 or 220 volts, 60 cycle on both Trinidad and Tobago.

Safety & Health Warnings: Stray from the marked trails and marijuana farmers with their trap guns could pose a problem, particularly in the Northern Range. Due to increased crime, Port-of-Spain, including the Queen's Park Savannah, is not considered safe to walk at night. In fact, be watchful and careful anywhere after dark. The Trinidadians, who for the most part are very friendly and a joy to be around, have also been called the "Trickidanians" because their manner is sometimes a little rough and direct.

Snakes & Other Venomous Creatures: Trinidad has a total of about 47 different snake species, of which only 4 are poisonous: they are the bushmaster, fer-de-lance, and 2 species of coral snake. Trinidad apparently takes top prize in the Caribbean for the variety of vipers because of its one-time link to the mainland and/or its close proximity to the Orinoco River, whose seasonal flooding seems to be the source for most animal dispersion throughout the Caribbean. No island is closer to the Orinoco than Trinidad. Exercise proper caution and snakes should be no more a problem here than elsewhere.

Hiking & Walking Services: The **Trinidad Field Naturalists Club,** 1 Errol Park Road, Port-of-Spain, has monthly field trips which tourists are welcome to join. These include visits to caves as well as long distance walks. Call (868) 625-3386 or 645-2132. Taxi drivers and other guides know the way to most of the places mentioned, which you should also be able to find on your own.

The **Asa Wright Nature Centre** also can arrange guides for field trips to the various birding hot spots on both Trinidad and Tobago. Contact the Lodge directly at (868) 667-4655; fax (868) 667-0493. Or Caligo Ventures, Inc., 387 Main St., Armonk, NY 10504-0021; toll-free in the United States and Canada (800) 426-7781; fax (914) 273-6370.

Additional Information: Trinidad and Tobago Tourism Office, 350 Fifth Ave., Suite 6316, New York, NY 10118; phone (800) 748-4224 or call the Tourism Hotline at (888) 595-4tnt. Web site: www.visittnt.com. In Canada: Taurus House, 512 Duplex Ave., Toronto, Ontario, M4R 2E3; call (800) 267-7600. In England: International House, 47 Chase Side, Enfield, Middlesex, EN2 6NB2; (0181) 367-3752.

Dining Out: You could probably spend an entire lifetime in Trinidad and never get bored by the diverse cuisine. The mixture of cultures offers just about every sort of food imaginable. The Indian curries are particularly good, as are rotis, an East Indian version of a burrito with meat, potatoes, and curry. You'll probably need to wash one down with large amounts of Carib, the favorite local beer that advertises "every bottle tastes different." Locals seem to think that a plus, not a problem with quality control.

A popular local drink is mauby, made from a tree bark soaked in sugar and spices. It tastes like a sweet ginger beer. Angostura bitters originated on Trinidad; a dash of it to any drink—cola or beer—dramatically changes and usually improves the taste. Be careful, as this stuff (full of unspecified secret ingredients) may be addictive; there are worse vices.

PORT-OF-SPAIN AFOOT!

Time: 2–3 hours. | **Difficulty:** 1. | **Trailhead:** Woodford Square.

At first glance, your reaction to Port-of-Spain may be one of disappointment. The coastal waters are muddy thanks to the Orinoco River, and Port-of-Spain itself is a big, commercial port with high-rise skyscrapers, totally devoid of any charming tropical island look. You could almost be in crowded Miami or San Juan.

Take heart: the real beauty of Trinidad is in its lush countryside and in its people. Still, there are a few parts of even industrialized Port-of-Spain that should pleasantly surprise you.

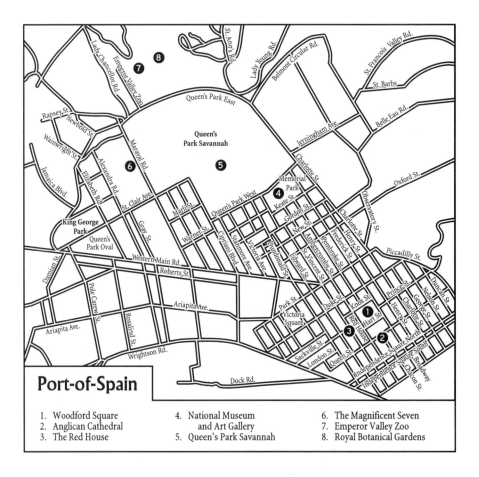

Port-of-Spain

1. Woodford Square
2. Anglican Cathedral
3. The Red House
4. National Museum
   and Art Gallery
5. Queen's Park Savannah
6. The Magnificent Seven
7. Emperor Valley Zoo
8. Royal Botanical Gardens

1. Woodford Square: The square is named after governor Sir Ralph Woodford (in office from 1813–28) who was responsible for importing a landscape architect in 1820 to create the country's beautiful Botanical Gardens (see later in this chapter).

2. Anglican Cathedral: On the south side of the square is the Anglican Cathedral of the Holy Trinity noted for its hammer-beam roof decorated with many carvings. The church was consecrated in 1823.

3. The Red House: Across from Woodford Square is the Red House. This is where the parliament meets. The huge building was built in 1907 on the site of its predecessor, which was destroyed by a 1903 fire/riot caused by increased water rates. The Red House has to be the most conspicuous building in the entire city because of its color and size. Why was it painted red in the first place? To mark Queen Victoria's Diamond Jubilee in 1897. Even though there was a chance to change it when the new Red House was built, by then people had kind of grown fond of the garish color.

The Red House gained international publicity in 1990 when the prime minister and several Cabinet members were held captive by Muslim rebels for five days. The rebels finally surrendered to the army. That's Trinidadian politics: Sometimes violent but nearly always loud.

4. **National Museum and Art Gallery:** Everything from Amerindian archaeology, historic artifacts and documents, local painters and carnival costumes. Open 10 a.m. to 6 p.m. Tuesday through Saturday. No admission fee. Call (868) 623-5941.

5. **Queen's Park Savannah:** Port-of-Spain's most picturesque section is just a little north of the town center, at the 200-acre Queen's Park Savannah situated in the foothills of the Northern Range. Once used to graze cattle, Trinidadians claim that the road circling the park forms the world's largest roundabout; at 2.5 miles, they may be correct.

In the dry season (January to May), Queen's Park Savannah boasts a striking display of flowering trees, including pink and yellow poui, purple and white petria, and the brilliant "shower of gold." This big open field has cricket and soccer fields and a racecourse with stands.

The Rock Gardens, locally called the "hollows," are part of the Savannah but below the regular level. These are two well-maintained lily ponds with many rustic rocks set in a beautiful flower garden. Picnicking here is popular with locals.

6. **The Magnificent Seven:** Flanking the entire western edge of the Savannah are several old, elaborately decorated buildings known as the "Magnificent Seven." These are all European-styled mansions that represent some of the finest surviving European architecture anywhere. They do deserve the title "magnificent," though some are becoming a little run-down. All but one was built in 1904. They are best photographed in the early morning sun before the area becomes crowded. Be safe; do not walk here at night.

Starting at the corner of St. Clair and Maraval and going northward along the Savannah, the first building reached is Queen's Royal College, a German renaissance design. Next is Hayes Court, residence of the Anglican bishop, built in 1910. Ambar's House, built in the French baroque style with marble imported from Italy, appears next.

Fourth is "Mille Fleurs" or Prada's House, a townhouse typical of the turn of the century with impressive iron fretwork. Fifth is the Roman Catholic archbishop's home, built in 1904. Next to it is the opulent Moorish-style mansion known as White Hall, which is the prime minister's office.

The last of the Magnificent Seven is Killarney, a brick and turreted residence also called the Stollmeyer house after the family who built this miniature Rhine castle.

7. **Emperor Valley Zoo:** North of the Savannah but still within walking distance is the Emperor Valley Zoo. The zoo, which covers eight acres, has a good representation of Trinidad's different mammals, reptiles, and birds; it also contains a number of imported species. Ironically, the name comes from the emperor butterfly, which was common to this valley before development.

8. **Royal Botanical Gardens:** Adjacent to the zoo is the 70-acre Botanical Gardens, which have the best single display of orchids on the island. The Botanical Garden displays its most colorful foliage between April and June when plants like the scarlet

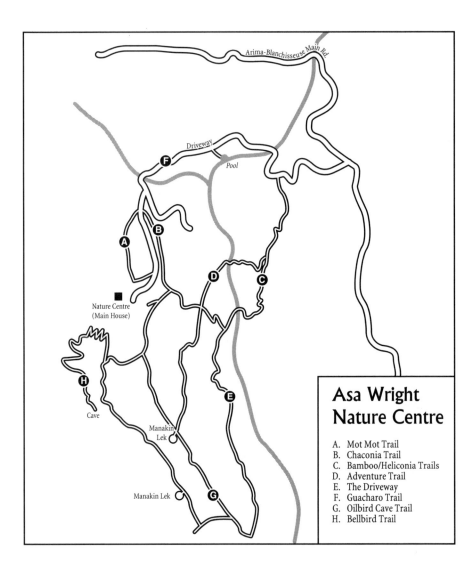

Asa Wright
Nature Centre

A. Mot Mot Trail
B. Chaconia Trail
C. Bamboo/Heliconia Trails
D. Adventure Trail
E. The Driveway
F. Guacharo Trail
G. Oilbird Cave Trail
H. Bellbird Trail

Isora, bougainvillaea, oleander, jacaranda, and the pink poui are in flower. The gardens with their meticulously designed walkways were laid out in 1820. Besides local plants and shrubs, the gardens have a good variety of tropical and subtropical trees and shrubs from South America and Southeast Asia. The former Governor's House, built on the grounds between 1873–75, is now the residence of Trinidad and Tobago's president. The gardens are open daily from 6 a.m. to 6 p.m.

Asa Wright Nature Centre

1. Trails of Asa Wright

Time: 1–3 hours | **Difficulty:** 1–4.

The Asa Wright Nature Centre, founded in 1967, is located in the Northern Range on Spring Hill Estate (a coffee-cocoa-citrus plantation partly reclaimed by secondary forest) ten miles north of the town of Arima on the Blanchisseuse Road. The climate is tropical and humid, in mid-montane rain forest. A light sweater or jacket is often necessary in the evenings, not for dining but to ward off the cold. Temps vary from 65° to a maximum of 86° F. Dress is informal at all times. Sneakers, cotton slacks, long-sleeved shirts, and a hat are all recommended. So are a lightweight rain coat and flashlight.

Summer seminars are offered in nature photography, entomology, ornithology, tropical ecology, and drawing and painting. Vegetation is at its most striking in the dry season, January to May.

Nowhere else in the Caribbean compares to Asa Wright for observing such a huge diversity of bird, animal, and plant life, all of it concentrated in just 200 acres of rain forest in the Northern Range, near the town of Arima. A series of nine trails meander through a good portion of the preserve, all intended to provide the best possible introduction to South American birding.

This is a popular spot for day tours that it's wise not to simply show up but to call ahead at least 24 to 48 hours to arrange for a guide.

However, you need never move out of a rocking chair to see scores of different birds: The main building has a huge front porch with numerous bird feeders just a few feet away. It's the Caribbean version of Kenya's Treetops or the Ark, except your species count here will be far higher than in Africa. You won't believe the numbers of hummingbirds.

Expect to spend a minimum of two to three days to fully avail yourself of this wonderful habitat. Walk quietly, talk in quiet whispers to avoid scaring off the critters you have come to see. Nothing is caged; everything roams free.

Asa Wright has what is considered the world's most accessible colony of oilbirds *(Steatornis caripensis)*, the only nocturnal fruit-eating bird on the planet. Oilbirds were given their name in 1799 by scientist Alexander von Humboldt, who observed Venezuelan Indians and monks rendering the very fat young chicks into oil for cooking and torches. The Amerindians called oilbirds "Guacharos," meaning the ones that wail and mourn, and Trinidadians refer to it as the "Diablotin." Both names refer to the sounds oilbirds make when disturbed; they scream, snarl, and chuck incredibly weird and unforgettable sounds from your worst nightmare.

Normally limited to the South American continent, the oilbird measures 18 inches in length and has a wingspan of 3 to 3.5 feet. It has short legs, is rich brown in color with white spots, and has a large hooked beak with conspicuous rictal bristles. The young develop slowly, staying on the nest for up to 120 days. They are also incredibly fat: at 70 days they may be 50 percent heavier than an adult. Trinidad has at least five oilbird colonies, all protected by law. The one at Asa Wright has a population of about 130 birds.

The life of an oilbird probably appears dull, unless you are one. They stay on their nests (with or without young) in dark caves all during daylight. The nests, made mostly of regurgitated matter, are used year after year and eventually form into low cylindrical mounds. A clutch typically has two to four white oval eggs, pointed at one end.

At dusk, oilbirds depart to dine on the fruit of palms, laurels, incenses, and camphor, traveling as far as 70 miles away to feed. Oilbirds are similar to bats not only in lifestyle but in their ability to employ echo-sonar for finding their way around obstacles in the dark. They are able to detect an object eight inches in diameter in total blackness. Oilbirds apparently see quite well, too, as they use sight whenever light is adequate.

A. MOT MOT TRAIL

Time: 30 minutes. | **Difficulty:** 1–2.

An easy trail from the main house through the plantation offers an excellent opportunity to photograph plants, butterflies, and hummingbirds.

B. CHACONIA TRAIL

Time: 1 hour, 1 way. | **Difficulty:** 2–3.

This trail passes below the main lodge. Look for butterflies in the wet sections, for woodpeckers in the forest.

C. BAMBOO/HELICONIA TRAILS

Time: 2 hours, 1 way. | **Difficulty:** 3–4. Steep climbing required on both

The longer Bamboo Valley Trail has the remains of the hydroelectric station that once supplied the power for the preserve. Both trails have stream crossings and openings in the forest canopy along the river, so many blossoming flowers are as close as eye level, not a hundred feet off the ground. Many birds are also attracted to these flowers from the canopy.

D. ADVENTURE TRAIL

Time: 3 hours, 1 way. | **Difficulty:** 3–4. A vigorous walk with steep slopes.

This is the longest and most difficult trail at the nature center. Plan on a good half-day to complete it. Large ant nests and the haunting cry of the mot mot are among the features.

E. THE DRIVEWAY

Time: 30 minutes. | **Difficulty:** 1–2.

Not the most likely place to look, but the entrance driveway is an excellent walk. Besides having good solid footing, it cuts through the rain forest and thereby provides the opportunity to see birds and animals normally found only on deep forest walks. Several bridges offer a grand overlook.

F. GUACHARO TRAIL

Time: 1 hour, 1 way. | **Difficulty:** 2–3 if you don't make the descent; considerably harder (and longer) if you do.

One of the most popular forest paths, this is an old trail that burros used to pull their carts along and then over the pass. Beyond the nature center boundary the path drops sharply with no easy return. Most visitors stop before the descent. A short side trail leads to the display courts of the male white-bearded manakins. Each male clears and defends his own court, where he attempts to dazzle females by a variety of sounds with his wings, including loud snaps, buzzes, and rattles that sometimes sound like firecrackers. Besides being notable for all the noise he makes, the male is colored black with a gray lower back and a wide priest's collar that encircles his neck below the beak; the female is olive green. Locals call him "Casse Noisette."

G. OILBIRD CAVE TRAIL

Time: 1 hour, 1 way. | **Difficulty:** 2–3.

This trail is open only by arrangement with the nature center. Although all other trails are self-guided, you must take an escort to the oilbird cave. This is done to keep the birds from being needlessly disturbed. The birds nest in Dunstan Cave, actually a chasm cut out of rock by a stream that still flows through the deeply shaded rock valley. Oilbirds don't appear bothered by flash photography; flash is the only way you will be able to take pictures.

H. BELLBIRD TRAIL

Time: 1 hour, 1 way. | **Difficulty:** 2–3.

The male bearded bellbird is another notorious showoff, best described as a ventriloquist whose "bock" sounds like a hammer striking an anvil. However, the male can also emit musical sounds that sound like bells, hence his name. Bellbird Trail follows the mountain contour to offer the unusual opportunity to see another unique South American bird living in the Caribbean.

CHAGUARAMAS NATIONAL PARK

Everything from mountain climbing to caving to snorkeling is available in this one park which encompasses the entire Chaguaramas Peninsula. Named by the Amerindians for the royal palms that flourished here, this is one of the most arid areas in Trinidad, so be watchful of your liquid intake to prevent dehydration. This scrubby area was leased to the United States during World War II, and some of the old buildings remain. The presence of so many well-paid Americans inspired the calypso song "Working for the Yankee Dollar" as a complaint about the way the local girls were deserting their men for greenback-loaded sailors.

Chaguaramas is home to the red howler monkey, so keep a sharp eye for him at all times. These monkeys, which usually travel in troops of 4 to 20 individuals, generally stay at the tops of taller trees. Other good places to see them on the peninsula include Tucker Valley, Govine Valley, Macqueripe, Golf Course Cabazon, Scotland Bay, and Mt. Catherine.

Ocelots are another possibility, though they usually sleep during the day. Their marbled coats of brown, black, and cream allow them to blend in with the shadows. They range from 36 to 54 inches long, including a tail that makes up about one-third of their total length.

A 20-minute boat ride from the Crews Inn Marina will take you to the Gasparee Caves located on Gaspar Grande Island, one of five islands located off the Chaguaramas Peninsula. On Chacachacare Island, about 30 minutes offshore, you can hike to the Salt Pond that has the unusual campecho tree, also called the bread and cheese tree. From Perruquier Bay, you can hike to the old wooden lighthouse built in 1896, still in operation.

2. Mt. Catherine

Length: 6 miles, one way. | **Time:** 2 hours, one way. | **Difficulty:** 3. | **Trailhead:** The northwesternmost point of Trinidad.

The six-mile-long hike up Mt. Catherine (1,768 feet) begins at Carenage Bay. The track passes through dry scrub woodlands and eventually overlooks the Tucker Valley on the east. The secondary montane rain forest offers good birding: squirrel cuckoo, turquoise and blue-headed tanagers, blue dacnis, and more. In addition, from the Chaguaramas Public Golf Course you can walk to 180-meter-high Edith Falls. On the way you'll pass through a tonka bean plantation and rain forest. A 1.6-mile (2.5-km) trail from the cove at Macqueripe to the golf course provides good views of Tucker Valley and the North Coast.

ELSEWHERE ON TRINIDAD

3. Blue Basin Waterfall

Time: 5 minutes. | **Difficulty:** 1. | **Trailhead:** The town of Diego Martin.

It's only a five-minute walk down a bridle path from the trailhead in the town of Diego Martin to Blue Basin Waterfalls, which was a popular tourist spot long before there were nature centers. A tropical pool at the end of the waterfall was once hidden by the Blue Basin village and used only by locals for bathing. Do not leave anything of value in the car.

4. Maracas Falls

Length: About 2 miles. | **Time:** 2 hours. | **Difficulty:** 2. | **Trailhead:** Maracas Falls is not anywhere near the famous beach but in the mountains above the Maracas Valley near the town of St. Joseph, just 6 miles east of Port-of-Spain. Take the Maracas Royal Road and look for the marked road to the right leading to the waterfall trail. This secondary road goes for about a mile before depositing you at the trailhead.

The trail, which leads off to the right, goes for less than a mile before arriving at the first cascade and its three mini-waterfalls. There are also two natural pools here, but the water is cold. It's another 20 minutes to reach the spectacular, 270-foot-high main falls. Not surprisingly, the waterfall is considered a sacred place, which is why some of the rocks have candle stubs or pools of candle wax left here by Hindus and other religious groups. Colored flags in the trees also indicate its special significance. You can also climb to the top of the falls, but you'll need to rock hop and scramble up a slippery path. You can swim here, too, in a stream pool up from the falls.

Although the falls are considered sacred by some, people have been robbed; that's less likely to happen if you're in the company of a local guide. So if a resident guide flags you down while you're still driving to the trailhead, you might want to negotiate a fee. He may also suggest that you park at the bottom of a hill about a 15-minute walk from the trailhead because it's a more secure location for your vehicle. In any case, a guide knows the easiest way to reach the top of the falls.

5. Paria Falls

Time: 6–7 hours. | **Difficulty:** 3. Take snacks and water. | **Trailhead:** From Blanchisseuse, take the Arima-Blanchisseuse Road south 4 miles (6.4 km) to Brasso Seco and turn left onto the Paria Morne Blue Road. You'll have to leave your car near a house and make the short walk to mile post 4.75, where there's a house on the left just after a bridge. The trail starts here, but there's no parking.

The Paria River begins in the foothills of the Northern Range. This is a goodly hike of several hours through the forest that eventually brings you to the clear, natural bathing pool of Paria Waterfall. The trail winds north for the first 1.5 hours until you cross a stream flowing east. Then, 35 minutes later, you'll reach the Jordan River, which you cross. After another hour's climb over the hill, arrive at a beach where you turn right, walk for two minutes to reach the wooden bridge crossing the Paria River. Walk another five minutes up the right bank to reach the waterfall.

6. El Tucuche Climb

Length: 7 miles. | **Time:** 6–7 hours. | **Difficulty:** 3. | **Trailhead:** From Port-of-Spain, go east along the Maracas Royal Road, then turn right onto Acona Road (well before the turn to Maracas Falls). Follow Acona Road to some old cocoa sheds at a farm where the climb begins.

A guide is highly recommended because the first part of the trail wanders through old plantations, old abandoned roads, river beds, and over two mountain passes before you reach the trail that ascends the summit. It's easy to make a wrong turn and end up passing the day in strange but wondrous places.

This ascent of the island's second highest peak is best reserved for the dry season, but true die-hards may ignore the weather. During your climb, you'll pass through a forest reserve that is also an animal sanctuary, so you may be able to spot deer, armadillos, and agoutis as well as numerous birds. The El Naranjo Tropical Gardens on the side of El Tucuche is particularly beautiful: streams, flowers of many kinds, silk cotton trees, and primary forest are well worth the effort to see.

The climb up is steep, but the last two hours will keep you comfortably shaded in high-canopied tropical forest above 1,600 feet. Expect to see tree ferns, plenty of epiphytes, ground ferns, and mosses. The view from the summit can be spectacular.

7. MT. TABOR/ST. BENEDICT MONASTERY

Time: 1–3 hours, depending on trail. | **Difficulty:** 2–3. | **Trailhead:** At the St. Benedict Monastery. From Port-of-Spain go east on the Eastern Main Road through Tunapuna then turn left onto St. John's Road and drive to the end.

At 1,800 feet, Mt. Tabor supplies some impressive views of Port-of-Spain on the west, El Tucuche to the north and the Caroni Plains to the south.

Hiking trails begin at the Mount St. Benedict monastery, which has a public guesthouse; the rates are a bargain at US$40 a day for lodging, breakfast, and dinner.

The guesthouse grounds, located at 800 feet elevation, are filled with birds at daybreak and twilight. Trails lead to the top of the peak and to various parts of the mountain. All tend to be steep but not too difficult to climb. Photography seminars are held here periodically.

8. ARIPO CAVES

Length: 18 miles. | **Time:** 10 hours. | **Difficulty:** 4. | **Trailhead:** About 4 miles east of Arima, a steep road follows the Aripo River to Dandrade Trace, a distance of about 10 miles.

Trinidad's highest peak is El Cerreo del Aripo (3,083 feet), a noteworthy climb of nine miles that also leads to the Aripo Caves, Trinidad's largest cave system, which also contains oilbirds (often seen from the entrance) and stalagmites and stalactites. You pass through Aripo village on the way, and it wouldn't be a bad idea to arrange a guide for the ascent trail, which is sometimes difficult to discern. The undulating path crosses streams, goes up and down limestone cliffs and through upper montane rain forest. All in all, it's an excellent variety.

9. MATURA BEACH/FISHING POND

Time: Variable | **Difficulty:** 1 if you're well rested; 5+ if you need sleep. | **Trailhead:** Located on the east coast.

These two sites are prime turtle-watching spots from about mid-April to July when the world's largest marine turtles come ashore at night to deposit their eggs. These are the giant leatherbacks, which may weigh as much as 1,200 pounds. The carapace, often more than six feet in length, is distinguished by its longitudinally ridged shell, which looks like leather stretched tight over a frame. It is colored a dark bluish gray and spotted with white.

At night during the nesting season, leatherbacks come ashore and lay their eggs just above the high water mark. After digging a hole about three feet deep, the female deposits between 70 and 120 billiard-sized eggs, which she then covers and conceals. The female returns to the sea, but her nesting is far from over. Leatherbacks may nest up to eight times in a season, at intervals of about every ten days. The turtles hatch in about 60 days and head straight for the sea. For many years it wasn't known where baby leatherbacks went, but recent research shows many find their way to the Sargasso Sea.

Turtle eggs are protected by law, although they are occasionally still poached. Asa Wright conducts turtle watching tours in season.

10. Pointe-a-Pierre Wild Fowl Trust

Time: Plan on at least 2 hours. | **Difficulty:** 1. | **Trailhead:** At Point Cumana near the city of San Fernando on the southwest coast.

This former Texaco Oil operation, the largest refinery in the island, was bought by the government in 1984. Volunteers have created a 26-acre wild fowl preserve on the two lakes for breeding endangered species of fowl and birds and reintroducing them to natural wildlife areas. About 100 different birds nest here during a year, many visible from the forest trail and walkways around the lakes. Although a pest on many lakes in North America, Moscovy ducks were eaten to extinction and are part of the repopulation program, as are black-bellied, fulvous, and white-faced whistling ducks. More exotic species are the blue and yellow macaw and the blue-headed parrots. Gallinules, herons, cormorants, flycatchers, and tanagers are among the birds usually found year-round. An Environmental Learning Center with library, audiovisual room, a small museum of Amerindian artifacts, and a souvenir shop is open daily from 10 a.m to 5 p.m. Bird-watchers only will be admitted as early as 7 a.m. and may stay as late as 6 p.m. Because this is a volunteer operation, reservations need to be made in advance; call (868) 658-4230, ext. 2512. A small admission fee includes a guide. Visitors are welcome to bring a picnic.

11. Pitch Lake

Time: Variable. A 120-mile tour around the entire lake takes 5 hours. | **Difficulty:** 1. | **Trailhead:** From Port-of-Spain, take the Solomon Hocoy Highway south to San Fernando, then follow the South Trunk road to La Brea; it's about a 2-hour drive to the village of La Brea, which is on the lake's north shore.

The Pitch Lake at La Brea (Spanish for "pitch") on the southwest coast is the largest deposit of asphalt in the world, measuring 300 feet deep at the center and covering a surface area of 89 acres. Like most parking lots—and that is what it most looks like—you can actually walk on the goo, but it is springy underfoot. Avoid air holes bubbling up from the pressure. You leave an imprint walking, and if you stand still, you'll start to sink. They say it takes between one to two hours for someone to totally disappear, becoming a preserved tar baby that may one day reappear. The lake is continually being stirred, so everything from prehistoric tree trunks to fast food garbage occasionally surfaces.

Several theories abound about how this remarkable phenomenon was created. One story says an Arawak chief once killed a sacred hummingbird, and the angry gods got even by glopping the whole village with pitch. Another variation claims an entire tribe of Chaima Indians were punished for eating sacred hummingbirds containing the souls of their ancestors. The village sank into the ground, replaced by the tar pit that continually refills itself.

The most mundane theory suggests it was formed millions of years ago when asphaltic oil flowed into a mud volcano. The oil and mud were mixed by underground gases that resulted in the big asphalt pool. Many locals will tell you the lake is self-replenishing, but that is not true. The level is dropping steadily as the asphalt is shipped around the world for road construction projects. One estimate says that at the removal of 300 tons per day, the current level, will deplete the lake within a half century.

Official tours are no longer given around the lake, but many former guides are always present to haggle over a tour. Set a fee in advance and make certain whether it's TT$ or US$. It's the history and lore of the lake that makes it fascinating more than the actual sight of it.

Sir Walter Raleigh is credited with discovering the lake in 1595. He found it to be excellent ship's caulking because it did not appear to melt in the sun. He was wrong. After carrying pitch back to England and asphalting Westminster Bridge for the opening of Parliament, the asphalt did melt and clogged the coach wheels and horses' hooves. Since then, it has worked successfully covering streets not only in Port-of-Spain but Cairo, Singapore, and London.

Trinidadians also tried covering weeds with the stuff, but apparently the mud/oil combination was such an ideal fertilizer that weeds were worse than ever. Attempts were also made to burn it for street lighting, but the foul stench and smoke was more than anyone could tolerate. However, it was used to fumigate Port-of-Spain in 1920 after a smallpox epidemic. These and many other tales are readily supplied by the guides.

The lake has supplied many of the island's most valuable Amerindian artifacts that are displayed at several museums around the island. Still no sign of the swallowed village.

12. DEVIL'S WOODYARD

Time: 30 minutes. | **Difficulty:** 1. | **Trailhead:** Located at Princes's Town.

The Devil's Woodyard contains an active mud volcano emitting warm, bubbling mud through surface cracks that forms into a cone as it cools. Some local Hindus hold this to be a sacred spot and worship here. The Devil's Woodyard first erupted in 1852 and, until the discovery of another mud volcano in 1964 at Moruga, it was thought to be the only one on the island. Since 1964, 18 other mud volcanoes have also been located, usually in places where oil is produced.

13. TRINITY HILLS WILDLIFE SANCTUARY

Length: 2 miles. | **Time:** 1 hour each way. | **Difficulty:** 2-3. Advance permission may be necessary from the Trinidad and Tobago Oil Co. (TRINTOC) at Pointe-a-Pierre. Call (868) 658-4230. | **Trailhead:** In the Southern Range, reached by going west of Guayaguayare.

This 16,000-acre sanctuary dates from 1934. It is one of the oldest preserves, giving sanctuary to monkeys, deer, opossums, bellbirds, parrots, toucans, and pigeons.

21

U.S. Virgin Islands

With all the shops, traffic, and people, it's sometimes hard to remember that the U.S. Virgin Islands are part of the Caribbean and not an annex of New York, Atlanta, or Miami. But the colorful names of plants will remind you that you're in the West Indies. "Catch and Keep" is the thorny vine that sticks to everything. The trunk of the "Monkey Don't Climb Tree" bristles with thorns. "Jump Up and Kiss Me" is a beautiful scarlet blossom. And the "Nothing Nut" is just that, good for nothing.

Christopher Columbus discovered the Virgin Islands on his second voyage, in 1493. His choice of names has long puzzled historians. While sailing among the lushly fertile, gently rounded, warm and welcoming islets after a long, hard voyage, Columbus apparently was reminded of St. Ursula, who undertook a long voyage of her own, accompanied by 11,000 virgins.

All well and good, but historians—who have obviously never spent prolonged celibate periods at sea—cannot figure out why Columbus didn't name the new land St. Ursula. It would go nicely with the other saintly names, John, Thomas, and Croix. Perhaps it was the virgins Columbus fixated on. Columbus singled out one voluptuous landmass—obviously a favorite—as his "Fat Virgin" (Virgin Gorda in the British Virgin Islands).

Columbus apparently found the islands more warmly compelling than did later visitors. The British and Dutch came, saw, and split. The French took control in 1650, laying out town sites, plantations, and forts, but left by the end of that century. (However, they did start one curious custom on St. Croix: dying newborn babies' hands and feet blue with indigo as an indication of wealth and to attract good fortune.)

By 1733, the Danes controlled the islands, with the intent of turning sugar into gold, and lots of it. St. Croix, the largest and flattest island, was a natural for cultivation and became the leading sugar cane producer by 1750. Slaves were imported to work the fields in 1763. Sugar brought St. Thomas and St. Croix great wealth, and the planters commissioned the elaborate great houses you still see standing today. Few other islands can boast such attractive and durable structures.

With the fall of the sugar economy, the Danish West Indies became a financial drain instead of a valuable asset. The United States first became interested in buying St. Thomas and St. John in 1867, shortly after the Civil War. Denmark was agreeable, but then the U.S. Congress was not. The United States made another offer for all three islands in 1902, but that attempt also failed.

A marine iguana, St. Thomas

After World War I broke out, the United States feared that Germany might capture the area and turn St. Thomas into a submarine base, so the government offered $25 million for the islands. The Danes accepted in 1917. It was an expensive sale for its time, coming out to about $300 per acre. Through this purchase, the U.S. Virgin Islands became the first territory under the U.S. flag actually discovered by Columbus.

The U.S. Navy administered the islands until 1932. St. Thomas was further developed as a military facility during World War II, with the addition of a submarine base and airfield.

With so much else to do, most visitors don't come to the U.S. Virgin Islands for the hiking and walking. If you're traveling with a nonhiking partner, they'll have plenty of opportunity—but afterward their credit cards may complain it was too much opportunity—to shop until they drop in what is probably the Caribbean's best duty-free area.

After the shopping gets old, the gentle hikes of St. John are a good way to introduce novice walkers to the fun and adventure of hiking in the tropics. St. John offers magnificent views and trails on par with many other islands, and it's not necessary to bust a gut getting to the best sites. Hiking in the U.S. Virgin Islands is total pleasure, never an ordeal.

While in the countryside, keep a sharp eye out for what look like extremely fast, skinny, brown squirrels. This is the mongoose, a weasel-like mammal from the Indian subcontinent originally introduced by cane growers to kill poisonous snakes and rats.

TRAVEL TIPS

Area: St. Thomas: 32 square miles; St. John: 28 square miles; St. Croix: 84 square miles. Approximately 70 cays, islets, and rocks form the entire U.S. Virgin Island chain.

Language: English.

Population: St. Thomas: 50,000; St. John: 2,500; St. Croix: 50,000.

Time Zone: Atlantic Time, one hour ahead of Eastern Standard Time.

Getting There: American Airlines has direct flights from many parts of the United States to St. Thomas and St. Croix; St. John does not have an airport. American Eagle flies in more than a dozen times daily from San Juan. Delta has nonstop flights to St. Thomas in winter.

    To reach St. John, the easiest and fastest way is to take the ferry, (340) 776-6282, from Red Hook at the eastern tip of St. Thomas to Cruz Bay. Except for 6:30 a.m. and 7:30 a.m. departures from Red Hook, the ferry runs hourly from 6 a.m. to midnight. The trip takes about 20 minutes. It's also possible to take a 45-minute boat from the Charlotte Amalie waterfront but this schedule is not as regular.

    To reach St. Croix from St. Thomas, American Eagle departs from the airport several times daily. It's also possible to take the Seaborne Seaplane, (340) 773-6442, from the Charlotte Amalie waterfront. A hydrofoil, (340) 776-7417, also makes the one-hour trip twice daily. It's the slowest as well as most expensive way to travel but also one of the more interesting.

Documents: A passport is necessary for all except U.S. citizens, who can get by with either a voter's card or certified birth certificate (although a passport will speed things up). Although the U.S. Virgin Islands are an unincorporated territory and all residents are citizens of the United States, everyone—regardless of nationality—has to clear Customs upon departure. When several flights are departing at the same time, customs can get very backed up, so allow yourself plenty of time.

Getting Around: Taxis and rental cars are available everywhere. In exploring St. Thomas, it's probably a good idea to take a taxi tour first to get a feel for the island. Road signs are almost nonexistent and traveling on your own can get confusing. In taking a taxi, make certain the vehicle has a TP on its license plate and a dome light above it. Otherwise it is not a licensed cab and things could get messy because the cabs are unmetered. Drivers are supposed to carry a rate card with fares approved by the Taxi Commission; (340) 776-8294. Driving is on the left.

Where to Stay: The U.S. Virgin Islands have more hotels per square inch of land than anywhere else in the Caribbean. The best hiking is on St. John. Both St. Thomas and St. Croix have interesting city tours and picturesque countryside. St. John, alone, has everything you come to the Virgin Islands for. For an interesting St. Thomas stay, try **Blackbeard's Castle,** a five-story, 16-room, tower-shaped inn overlooking Charlotte Amalie, (800) 524-6599. Built in 1678 by a local resident, it's doubtful Blackbeard (who did anchor here occasionally) ever slept in it.

Camping: Three campgrounds available. See the St. John section.

Currency: The U.S. dollar is standard. Credit cards are taken almost everywhere. Banking hours are 9 a.m. to 2:30 p.m. Monday through Friday and 3:30 p.m. to 5 p.m. Friday afternoon.

Taxes & Tips: A government tax of 8% is added to all hotel bills. In addition, some resorts add a 15% service charge, plus another $5 per night as an energy surcharge. For taxis and restaurants, tips of 10–15% are expected. There is no sales tax.

Electrical Current: Same as for most of North America, 110 volts, 60 cycles.

Safety & Health Warnings: You could suffer harm if you don't watch where you go after dark, especially in Charlotte Amalie on St. Thomas, which has a crime rate that would make any American city proud. Never leave anything unattended anywhere, especially on the beaches. Prowling land sharks are far more bothersome than the ones cruising in the Caribbean waters.

Snakes & Other Venomous Creatures: No poisonous snakes. You may be fortunate enough to see a three- to four-foot-long marine iguana meandering along one of the beaches. Though fierce and prehistoric-looking, marine iguanas are totally harmless. Some plants do look attractive enough to make you want to touch, but they should be bypassed. One is the **Christmasbush** that resembles a form of holly. But festive this plant is not. It's in the same family as poison ivy, and if the spiny leaves scratch you, the irritating agent may not only cause blisters around the scratches, it may also be absorbed into the bloodstream and travel to other parts of the body, where additional sores could erupt. Christmasbush is common all over the U.S.V.I., growing as a single plant, in clusters of plants or as a tree. It reaches 10 to 20 feet high. The spines are on the underside of the leaf.

Hiking and Walking Services: See specific islands for information.

Additional Information: U.S. Virgin Islands Division of Tourism, call (800) 372-USVI. In the United Kingdom, 2 Cinnamon Row, Plantation Wharf, York Place, London SW11 3TW; call (071) 924-3171.

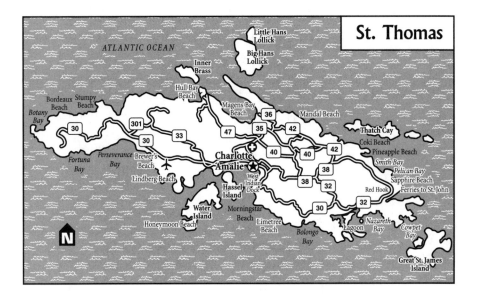

St. Thomas

St. Thomas

Although St. Croix is the largest island of the group, St. Thomas is the capital and the most developed island. It is an island of contrasts. The harbor area is like any large American city with its attendant hustle and bustle. But up in the hills, where you can even find cattle grazing in emerald fields, a more tranquil pace prevails. The countryside reminds many travelers of France. In fact, just outside the busy downtown is a place called Frenchtown.

St. Thomas has eight beaches, most of them ideal for short walks as well as for snorkeling. Heart-shaped Magens Bay was named one of the world's ten most beautiful beaches by

Charlotte Amalie Afoot!

Time: 2–3 hours. | **Difficulty:** 1. | **Trailhead:** At the Government House.

National Geographic. I'll take St. John's Trunk Bay or Cinnamon Bay over Magens Bay anytime. If you prefer development on a small scale, you may agree.

At some point, you should enjoy an overview of Charlotte Amalie, St. Thomas's capital and the seat of government, either from the mountains or the water. Only then will you appreciate the dazzling checkerboard roofs of silver and red. Motor traffic is congested because the streets, built by the Danes for horse and carriage, are too narrow to easily accommodate today's traffic. Walking is the easiest and most pleasant way to tour Charlotte Amalie.

The majority of the midtown buildings are of thick masonry, originally old warehouses, built to replace burned-out wooden structures. Living by candlelight may appear romantic to us, but in the 1600s and 1700s it was extremely dangerous. The dried, weathered buildings

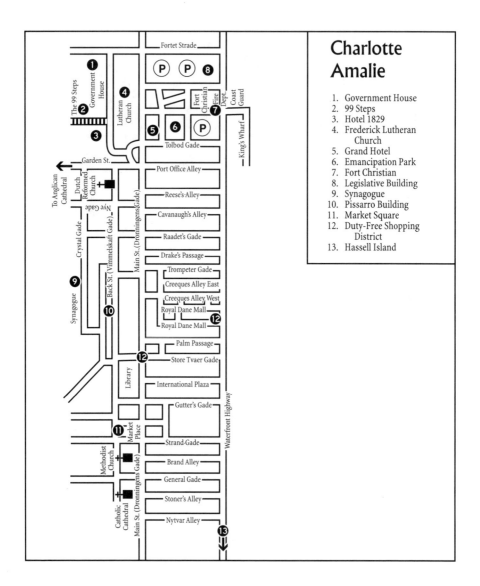

Charlotte Amalie

1. Government House
2. 99 Steps
3. Hotel 1829
4. Frederick Lutheran Church
5. Grand Hotel
6. Emancipation Park
7. Fort Christian
8. Legislative Building
9. Synagogue
10. Pissarro Building
11. Market Square
12. Duty-Free Shopping District
13. Hassell Island

were piles of kindling, waiting for a flame. Most of the old warehouses have been totally remodeled into colorful stores bursting with duty-free goods from all over the world.

Charlotte Amalie's original name was Tap Hus, Danish for "rum shop," in honor of its most popular product. St. Thomas has always been appreciated by people who liked a good time, and never more appreciated than by pirates who used it as an R&R stop, right under the nose of the Danish authorities. The Danes were canny enough not to drive off their best customers, as long as they behaved while in port. Honest pirates who paid their bills in gold were always welcome.

In fact, it was through the pirates and the plunder they offloaded in St. Thomas that the harbor city was turned into a great port. The Danes declared it a freeport in 1724, and nothing has changed except today things are imported legally. You can still find a "steal"—that is, a bargain—compared to the price-plus-tax elsewhere.

As a freeport, Tap Hus under the Danes became a very rich city. As such, the place required a more respectable name than Rum Shop, so in 1730, Tap Hus was renamed Charlotte Amalie, after the wife of Danish King Christian V.

A small fortification called Fort Skytsborg has been turned into a landmark hotel, Blackbeard's Castle. The five-story tower supposedly is the "oldest extant historical structure in the Virgin Islands." Pirates, including the infamous Blackbeard, reputedly used it for a lookout tower.

If the stories about Blackbeard are to be believed, he was as much a freak show as a swashbuckler. He's said to have gone into battle after these preparations: braiding his long black beard, tying the tails of it around his ears, and putting lighted candles in his hair. Another version has him wearing lighted fuses, not candles.

Blackbeard is said to have married (very formal, for a pirate) 14 different women, killing them when he tired of their charms. What message does that imply for the bridal suite of Blackbeard's Castle?

1. **Government House:** On Government Hill on Kongen's Gade. This is the residence of the governor of the U.S. Virgin Islands. Visitors are allowed on the first two floors of the three-story building. The floors are made of wood and the walls are decorated with paintings and murals by Camille Pissarro, the impressionist painter who was born here and whose house you will see later on this tour.

2. **99 Steps:** Located next door to the Government House, these steps date to the 1700s and go from Government Hill to Lille Tarne Garde (Danish for "Little Tower Street"), a shortcut up the hill. If you climb them, count and see how many you come up with.* Many such staircases were built to get up and down the steep hills here.

3. **Hotel 1829:** Also on Kongen's Gade, this nineteenth-century, Spanish-style building with its narrow passages, dark bar, and picturesque open courtyard is one of the island's better restaurants. It also still functions as a hotel. You are welcome to look around.

4. **Frederick Lutheran Church:** At the head of the street leading to Fort Christian, the building went up in 1793, replacing two earlier structures lost to fire (1750 and 1789). It's still the second-oldest Lutheran church in the Western Hemisphere. Refurbished in 1826, this was the official church of the Danish West Indies.

5. **Grand Hotel:** Built in the nineteenth century, it now houses offices and gift shops. This can be a good stop for T-shirts, seashells, and Haitian wood carvings. It opened in 1840 as a hotel and coffeehouse. The Greek Revival building had a third story but lost it to hurricane damage around 1896.

6. **Emancipation Park:** Containing a gazebo and a replica of Philadelphia's Liberty Bell, the park commemorates the freeing of the slaves in 1848. Official ceremonies are still held here occasionally. Grab a bench, relax, and watch the local children at play.

---

* The author counted 103 steps.

7. **Fort Christian:** The dark red walls of this fort were begun in 1672, as soon as the Danes arrived. That first colony was so small everyone could fit inside the fort, which later served as a jail, governor's residence, courthouse, and church. A museum of local history is located in the former dungeons. Along with Blackbeard's Tower, it also claims to be the oldest standing structure in the U.S. Virgin Islands. Which to believe—pirates or government? It's a tough call.

8. **Legislative Building:** This lime-green building with the beautiful flower gardens is where the Virgin Islands Senate meets. The building, dating from 1874, was built as barracks for Danish troops.

9. **Synagogue:** On Crystal Gade. Rebuilt several times, this is the second-oldest Jewish temple in the Western Hemisphere. (The oldest is in Curaçao.) The sand on the temple floor is a reference to the exodus from Egypt.

10. **Pissarro Building:** On Main Street between Store Tvaer and Trompeter Gades, this is where impressionist painter Camille Pissarro was born. He lived upstairs in what is now a perfume shop. A plaque marking his birth is around the block on Back Street. There is no museum here; the best exhibition of his paintings is at Government House (see p. 365).

11. **Market Square:** On Strand Gade, where fruits and vegetables from all over the island are sold. This was one of the most active slave markets in the eighteenth century. The roof shelter was purchased from a European railway company in the early 1900s.

12. **Duty-Free Shopping Districts:** This couldn't be easier. All the stores lining both Main and Back Streets are duty-free. In case you can only find Danish street signs, Main Street is Dronnigens Gade; Back Street is Vimmelskaft Gade. For 300 years, these have been some of the world's greatest shopping streets. Arguably, they could be the birthplace of the strip mall. Remember, the Stateside duty-free allowance is higher for the U.S. Virgin Islands than for most other islands.

13. **Hassel Island:** Part of the Virgin Islands National Park system and located just in front of Charlotte Amalie, with plenty of old ruins to explore, from military sites of the 1700s to an old marine yard. Go by water ferry.

WATER ISLAND HIKE

Length: Time: 2–3 hours. | **Difficulty:** 2–3, depending on heat.

At 491 acres, Water Island is the fourth largest of the U.S. Virgin Islands. It can be reached from the Crown Bay Dock on the west side of Charlotte Amalie. In its earliest incarnation as Fort Segarra in World War II, it underwent an amazing metamorphosis to become a one-time exclusive resort. It is such a unique tale that it helped inspire Herman Wouk's *Don't Stop the Carnival*, a classic novel describing the pitfalls and heartaches of Caribbean hotel ownership. Once you read this book, you'll better understand why things so often go wrong at tropical resorts.

After World War II troops pulled out of Water Island, the Chemical Warfare Division laid claim to it for experiments with poison gas. The program was discontinued in 1950, and the army did nothing more with the island.

In 1951, retired New York stockbroker Walter H. Phillips and his wife visited Water Island in search of a likely home site. Although the land was deserted and desolate, Phillips decided the island had resort potential. He enlisted the help of local officials who wanted to see the island developed, and a bill was passed through Congress that transferred ownership of Water Island from the army to the Interior Department.

Phillips then leased the entire island—without charge—from the government for a period of 40 years in return for developing it. In essence, Water Island became a separate principality: exempt from all taxes, it was up to Phillips to supply all roads, garbage collection, and other services.

In addition to constructing a hotel (now closed), Phillips was also leasing individual land plots for $2,500, and many of his leaseholders were converting old gun turrets, concrete latrines, and soldiers' barracks into small homes and apartments. The island's rugged terrain has several roads crisscrossing it. There are still a few remains of old Fort Segarra to see. Iguanas and hummingbirds are also commonly spotted on Water Island treks.

St. John

It's just four miles east and a 15-minute ferry ride from Red Hook on St. Thomas to St. John, an island nearly as big as St. Thomas but without its big-city ways. Most of St. John is a national park, and consequently, both the land and waters surrounding it are well protected. Cruz Bay, the main town, is a tiny backwater village compared to thriving Charlotte Amalie. For those who like to feel they're in the uncrowded Caribbean, St. John is the place to be.

Like St. Thomas, St. John has some spectacular beaches. The best-known is at Trunk Bay, whose underwater snorkeling trail with its red, white, and blue markers isn't nearly as well known (or crowded) as the Buck Island Trail at St. Croix.

St. John remains green and natural—a stark contrast to intensely developed St. Croix and St. Thomas—thanks to developer Laurance Rockefeller. In 1956, Rockefeller and his Jackson Hole Preserve Corporation donated two-thirds of St. John to the U.S. National Park system, which has allowed approximately 10,000 acres of landscape to evolve naturally into second-generation forest including seagrape, kapok trees, cactus, and century plants.

The Park Service has opened the forest to visitors with 20 different walking/hiking trails, among the easiest and most scenic paths in the Caribbean. Some paths are actually old donkey-cart trails, in use as late as the 1940s.

It's hard to believe that today's quiet, laid-back St. John was like other prosperous islands in the 1700s; most of the hillsides were clean-cut and terraced to grow the sweet green gold—sugarcane. St. John is the site of one of the most successful slave rebellions, when African workers took control of the island for nine months in 1733. The Danes, who owned St. John at the time, were unable to quell the revolt alone and had to call in both British and French forces to finally subdue the slaves. Rather than return to servitude, many Africans committed suicide by jumping off the Mary's Point cliffs.

Because most of St. John is only slightly above sea level, it is one of the Caribbean's few major hiking islands where you'll be concerned about mosquitoes, usually early and late in the day, or during rainy periods. It's also drenchingly hot much of the time because of the low altitude, so water bottles are essential. You won't find much in the way of supplies outside of Cruz Bay or Coral Bay.

Getting Around: Your best bet is to rent a car or jeep at about $50 per day. Cabs are too expensive to keep one waiting while you explore. Most of the major car rental agencies have offices right at the Cruz Bay ferry dock. Shop several for the best price. St. John is so compact it is quite easy to explore, although driving short stretches will probably take far longer than you anticipate. Most rental car agencies are small and locally owned. They include C&C Car Rental, (340) 693-8164; Hospitality Rent-A-Car, (340) 693-9160; Lionel Jeep Rental,(340) 693-8764; Conrad Sutton Car Rental, (340) 776-6479; Paris Car Rental, (340) 776-6171; Cool Breeze Car Rental, (340) 776-6588; Courtesy Car Rental, (340) 776-6650; St. John Car Rental, (340) 776-6171. Hertz and Avis also have local branches.

The Park Service information center is just left of the ferry dock in Cruz Bay; after disembarking, follow the road to the left for five to ten minutes. You can't miss the building on the left, almost directly across from Mongoose Junction, a small mall that is Cruz Bay's main shopping district.

Where to Stay: Choices are few, compared to St. Thomas or St. Croix. The massive **Westin Resort St. John** is the island's most expensive and luxurious hotel; phone (800) 808-5020. On St. John, you may want to keep in touch with the environment at **Harmony Studios,** which overlooks the tent cottages at Maho Bay Camp. The two-story buildings are world-famous for their pioneering efforts in sustainable resort development, conservation, recycling, and restoration. They are solar powered. The Bedroom Suites have twin beds, kitchenette with microwave, kitchen appliances, cooking utensils, all linens, private tiled bath, and deck with furniture. Living Room Studios have a queen sofa bed, two twin beds, and all the amenities listed above. Rates are $105–135 in summer for double occupancy, $165–195 in winter. A sister property, **Estate Concord Studios,** is located on the secluded southeast shore overlooking Salt Pond Bay and Ram Head. With a hillside swimming pool, the nine units are available as a three-person studio or six-person loft duplex. Rates are $95–150 double occupancy in summer, $135–155 in winter.

In Cruz Bay, **Battery Hill's** fully equipped condos overlooking the harbor make it easy for hikers to dine whenever they wish. From $99–239 per night. Call (800) 416-1205; www.batteryhill.com.

Hiking groups with a four-wheel-drive vehicle will find it a bargain to stay at the **V.I. Environmental Resource Station (VIERS)** at the south end of the island. A bunk in a tent and three meals a day is just $60. However, the four-wheel-drive is essential because of the steep, washed-out terrain. Call (340) 776-6721. This is a really remote area, and the phones sometimes don't work well in bad weather.

Camping: Campgrounds on St. John are very popular, so reservations need to be made well in advance. Tenting at the **Cinnamon Bay Campground** in the national park is one of the Caribbean's great bargains. It costs about $25 per night for a bare site, but there are only about a dozen of them. Forty ready-pitched tents and 40 one-room cottages rent for $40–90 per night for two people in summer, $60–135 in winter. Tents and cottages come with cots, two-burner propane stove, charcoal grill, ice chest, and linens (twice weekly). A restaurant is on site, and there is a full gamut of water sports. Contact Cinnamon Bay Campgrounds; phone (800) 539-9998; www.cinnamonbay.com.

Maho Bay Campground is slightly larger, with 113 tent cottages that sleep one to four persons. These fully furnished units, $70 per couple in summer, $105–115 in winter with 7-night minimum stay, are mostly concealed in hillside vegetation. Linens, blankets, towels, cooking utensils, propane stove, cooler, and five-gallon water tank are included. Available water sports include kayaking, wind surfing, snorkeling, and sailing. Contact Maho Bay Campground at (800) 392-9004; www.maho.org.

Concordia Eco-Tents may be the most luxurious of all the tent cottages and certainly the most remote. Overlooking Salt Pond Bay and Ram Head on the south end, they feature private baths, running water, kitchen facilities, and solar and wind energy. Separate dining areas offer views of the Caribbean. No restaurant is on the property. Double occupancy rates are $70–80 in summer, $110–130 in winter with a 7-night minimum stay. For information, call (800) 392-9004; www.maho.org.

Guided Walks: The Virgin Islands National Park Visitor Center located near the Cruz Bay ferry dock is open daily from 8 a.m. to 4:30 p.m. Guided walks are conducted several times weekly by park service guides, who are very familiar with the island's history and resident wildlife, including the wild donkeys, mangrove cuckoos, gallinules, and pelicans. A walking schedule is posted at the interpretive center, an excellent place to stock up on books describing the native vegetation if you decide to take self-guided hikes, which is what most people do. The guided walks include the Reef Bay, Cinnamon Bay, and Leinster Bay hikes, plus a walk through the Annaberg Sugar Mill. Although there is no fee to enter the park, some guided hikes do have a charge. For instance, on the Reef Bay walk, there is a $15 transportation fee for boat pickup at the bottom of the trail. In all cases, hikers need to provide transportation to the trailheads. For more information call the National Park Service at (340) 776-6330. Scott McDowell's **Thunder Hawk Trail Guides** can take you hiking whenever you wish. McDowell, a half Cherokee from South Carolina, is St. John's only licensed hiking guide. He has a good knowledge of local history and bush medicine, which makes every hike highly entertaining. Hikes are about $20 per person. Contact him through his booking office on St. Thomas, Aquamarine Tours, phone (340) 774-1112, or through Connections on St. John, phone (340) 776-6922.

HIKING AROUND THE ISLAND

The precise distance of all these trails has been measured by the Park Service, a rare service in the Caribbean, where hikes are normally measured by walking time. Always carry water and bug spray. The low altitude makes these some of the Caribbean's hottest trails to walk. The paths are well marked, but if you do get lost, head downhill where you'll eventually reach water. The sun sets suddenly here, usually by 6:30 p.m. in winter and by 7:30 p.m. in summer, so don't linger on the trails near sunset or you could find yourself stumbling around in the dark. And it *will* be dark because there are so few lights around.

1. LIND POINT TRAIL

Length: 1.1 miles, one way. | **Time:** 45 minutes to 1 hour. | **Difficulty:** 1. | **Trailhead:** Starts at the National Park Visitor Center and connects with Honeymoon Beach and Caneel Bay Beach

The easiest-to-reach trail in the park, it begins less than a half mile from the Cruz Bay ferryboat landing and combines the two things people seek in St. John: a hike and a beach.

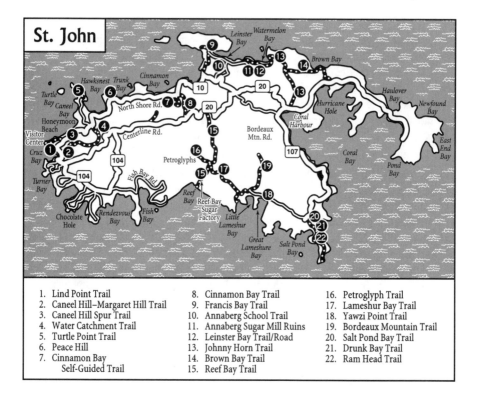

St. John

1. Lind Point Trail
2. Caneel Hill–Margaret Hill Trail
3. Caneel Hill Spur Trail
4. Water Catchment Trail
5. Turtle Point Trail
6. Peace Hill
7. Cinnamon Bay
   Self-Guided Trail
8. Cinnamon Bay Trail
9. Francis Bay Trail
10. Annaberg School Trail
11. Annaberg Sugar Mill Ruins
12. Leinster Bay Trail/Road
13. Johnny Horn Trail
14. Brown Bay Trail
15. Reef Bay Trail
16. Petroglyph Trail
17. Lameshur Bay Trail
18. Yawzi Point Trail
19. Bordeaux Mountain Trail
20. Salt Pond Bay Trail
21. Drunk Bay Trail
22. Ram Head Trail

The trail begins behind the National Park Visitor Center at Cruz Bay. Because of its convenient location, it's one of the park's most popular trails. It's a bit of a scramble at the start but the path soon widens and it's an easy 0.4-mile climb up to the scenic view at Lind Point (elevation: a dizzying 160 feet). You'll have a great view of Pillsbury Sound, the ferries coming and going and the sailboats at anchor. At 0.7 mile, a spur trail leads to Salomon Beach. Tiny Salomon Beach, which is only 100 yards long, has become the island's nude beach, though sunbathing nude technically is illegal. This appears to be one of those instances where, if authorities don't see and no one complains, nobody cares.

To reach Salomon Beach, take the left spur 0.3 mile northeast of Lind Point overlook, where you pass through mostly dry forest and cactus scrub. Continue on the main path another 0.2 mile, turn right and you'll connect with the North Shore Road and the Caneel Hill Trail.

2. Caneel Hill–Margaret Hill Trail

Length: 2.4 miles, one way. | **Time:** 2 hours. | **Difficulty:** 2. | **Trailhead:**
The Caneel Hill Trail begins in Cruz Bay about 20 yards past the Mongoose Junction parking lot. It ends at the entrance to the Caneel Bay resort. *Note:* This hike can be made in reverse, leaving from Caneel Bay. The uphill climb isn't quite as rugged coming from Caneel Bay.

This hike, mostly a steep ascent, is one of St. John's few loop trails. It's 0.9 mile to the overlook tower on Caneel Hill (elevation: 719 feet). At 0.3 mile you'll intersect with the Caneel Hill Spur Trail, which will be on the left. The spur trail descends to the North Shore Road and eventually connects with the Lind Point Trail. Continue to the right, up Caneel Hill. Just before reaching the peak you'll find a bench and a terrific scenic view over the north coast. At the top the panoramic view is even more impressive.

From Caneel Hill, it's 0.5 mile to reach Margaret Hill. Descend steeply and then begin climbing again as you walk the ridge connecting the two mountains. The park service has been kind enough to place a bench at the bottom of this descent.

Near the summit of Margaret Hill is a large, flat rock offering fine panoramic views of the part of St. John known as the Pastory. It's one of the finest viewpoints on the island.

Heading downhill (840 feet down) to Caneel Bay, look for a large triangular-shaped rock covered with orchids. This section of the path is well shaded. **Shortcut to Margaret Hill:** You can reach the Margaret Hill overlook by starting at the Water Catchment Trail on Centerline Road (see p.372) and taking the spur to Margaret Hill.

3. CANEEL HILL SPUR TRAIL

Length: 0.3 mile, one way. | **Time:** 10 minutes. | **Difficulty:** 1. | **Trailhead:** Located on the left side of the North Shore Road (Route 20) near the Caneel Bay Resort entrance—almost directly across from the Caneel Hill Trail— this path is next to the big brown Virgin Islands National Park sign.

Take this short trail to the beach at Caneel Bay and cool off in the water. All beaches in the Virgin Islands are public beaches, so everyone has the right to swim and sun. However, you probably won't be allowed to use resort amenities, such as beach chairs, or be allowed to enter the resort grounds.

4. WATER CATCHMENT TRAIL

Length: 1 mile, one way. | **Time:** 30 minutes. | **Difficulty:** 2. | **Trailhead:** Starts on Centerline Road (Route 10). The trailhead is marked with a sign.

Not often used, this forest-canopied road runs between Centerline Road and the North Shore Road. The trail descends an old gut (drainage channel) leading to the reservoir that once served as the main water source before the Caneel Bay resort installed its reverse osmosis plant. At the reservoir is a sign pointing to the Margaret Hill and Caneel Hill Trails. If you take that route, expect some long uphill hiking and about a 90-minute walk to Cruz Bay. But if you continue straight, the path will continue to descend until it reaches the North Shore Road near the Caneel Bay entrance. Now it's time to turn around and go back uphill to your vehicle.

5. TURTLE POINT TRAIL

Length: 0.6-mile loop. | **Time:** 30 minutes. | **Difficulty:** 1–2. | **Trailhead:** This circular trail begins at the north end of Caneel Bay Plantation, inside the resort grounds. Take the North Shore Road (Route 20) to the resort.

To make this short walk, you'll need to enter the Caneel Bay resort and register at the front desk as a day guest. A resort shuttle will take you to the trailhead. The path follows the shoreline around the Caneel peninsula, through a forest and out to a rocky cliff with good views of the offshore islands and cays. The trail continues to Turtle Point Beach where you can catch a resort shuttle back to the parking lot.

6. PEACE HILL

Length: 0.1 mile, one way. | **Time:** 5 minutes, one way. | **Difficulty:** 1.
| **Trailhead:** 2.8 miles from Cruz Bay on the North Shore Road (Route 20). Start looking for the parking lot about 100 yards past a huge boulder (called Easter Rock) on the left shoulder of the road. Easter Rock gets its name from the legend that every Easter it rolls down the hill and then somehow climbs back up.

The main attractions here are the scenic overlook of Hawksbill Bay and an old windmill tower. The trail starts at the parking lot on the hill near Hawksbill Bay. The path goes uphill and past some night-blooming cereus cactus on the right. It's worth coming back to see after dark. You'll reach the sugar mill tower first, then the plateau that offers a wonderfully scenic overlook. For many decades a large statue of Christ stood on the hill, but it was destroyed by a hurricane. The statue was an interesting if not very artistic endeavor. The huge figure looked like it was sculpted out of modeling clay by an elementary school class. Still, the old landmark is sorely missed. With the statue gone, Peace Hill isn't as popular a stop for the bus/cab tours.

7. CINNAMON BAY SELF-GUIDED TRAIL

Length: 0.5-mile loop. | **Time:** 30–45 minutes. | **Difficulty:** 1. | **Trailhead:** The trail begins on the right, just a few yards past the Cinnamon Bay campground and on the opposite side of the road. The ruins are easily visible from North Shore Road (Route 20).

One of the park's most popular trails, this loop tours the ruins of an old Cinnamon Bay sugar plantation. Park in the campground parking lot. The well-shaded walk has plenty of signs explaining the parts of the old factory and identifying many of the trees. At the horse mill, horses once turned the rollers to crush the cane. The huge copper pots held boiling cane juice. The trail also goes past a number of old Danish graves.

8. CINNAMON BAY TRAIL

Length: 1.1 miles, one way. | **Time:** 1 hour. | **Difficulty:** 2–3. | **Trailhead:** The trail starts from North Shore Road (Route 20) just to the left of the Cinnamon Bay plantation ruins, about 100 yards beyond the campground. It connects with Centerline Road (Route 10).

Another popular trail, but unlike the neighboring self-guided path with virtually the same name, this is a true hike.

The moderately steep ascent follows an old Danish plantation road through a moist shady forest. It comes out on Centerline Road, requiring a return descent or a pickup.

The first few minutes of the walk are the worst. The old plantation road is steep and fairly open to the sun at the start, but then the climb moderates and remains steady all the way to the top. You'll soon cross an old drainage gut and encounter an old iron post. The post marks a turn to the America Hill Trail (a spur trail) leading uphill to an old crumbling estate house, once used as a guesthouse. An old metal pot for boiling sugar is near the decrepit house; it is dangerous to enter.

Continuing on the Cinnamon Bay Trail to Centerline Road, you'll encounter a number of switchbacks and a couple of good overlook points. At Centerline Road, if you're brimming with excess energy you can walk another 0.9 mile east to reach the Reef Bay trailhead (see p. 375), the park's most popular trail. However, because the round-trip Reef Bay hike is a steep 4.4 miles, most people never combine the two. If you do, climb Cinnamon Bay Trail, walk to the Reef Bay trail, make the Reef Bay hike and return to your vehicle on North Shore Road, you will have traveled a total of 8.4 miles, which will take most of a day. And you will be tired!

9. FRANCIS BAY TRAIL

Length: 0.5 mile. | **Time:** 30 minutes. | **Difficulty:** 1. | **Trailhead:** At the intersection of the Leinster Bay and Maho Bay Roads, near the stone building.

An especially good trail for viewing bird life, particularly during winter months. First, the path goes through dry scrub forest and past the ruins of the Francis Bay Estate House. Note the old floor tiles, but don't try to enter the rickety ruins. This must have been a very popular place: The kitchen had five ovens.

After climbing a small hill, you'll enter a mangrove forest and cross a brackish pond by boardwalk. This where you're apt to see birds, such as mangrove cuckoo, white-cheeked pintail, and smooth-billed ani. The trail then takes you out to Francis Bay Beach, a popular snorkeling spot.

10. ANNABERG SCHOOL TRAIL

Length: 0.2 mile. | **Time:** 15 minutes. | **Difficulty:** 1. | **Trailhead:** The trail is on the left just before the North Shore Road (Route 20) intersects with the Leinster Bay Road. Be careful of the traffic.

This leads to one of the oldest public schoolhouse in the Caribbean. Dating to the 1800s, the schoolhouse is just a shell and not really worth visiting unless you have a real affinity for ruins. The school site offers good views of Mary Point, Leinster Bay, and Tortola. Interestingly, schools like this were built after the Danes passed a law mandating education for all children, including slaves. The government paid for construction of the schools, Moravian missionaries staffed them, and classes were taught in English. English was the chosen language because the area was occupied twice by British troops after 1800 and newspapers were published in English.

11. ANNABERG SUGAR MILL RUINS

Length: 0.25 mile. | **Time:** 30 minutes. | **Difficulty:** 1. | **Trailhead:** The buildings are just off the paved road to the right of the Leinster Bay Trail. Use the parking lot and either walk up the road to the ruins or take the boardwalk through the forest. Small admission fee.

These are the finest sugar plantation ruins on St. John and should not be missed. During the tour of the old plantation, you'll also enjoy a terrific view of Tortola and Jost Van Dyke in the British Virgin Islands.

The eighteenth-century Annaberg estate exhibits its windmill tower and slave quarters made of stone, ballast brick, and coral, although nothing is fully restored or in working order. Great vats once used to turn the sugarcane into molasses are still present.

Established in 1718, the plantation was named Anna for the daughter of absentee owner. Annaberg mean's Anna's Hill. The park service provides an excellent brochure describing the ruins in detail.

LEINSTER BAY–JOHNNY HORN–BROWN BAY TRAILS

12. LEINSTER BAY TRAIL/ROAD

Length: 0.8 mile, one way. | **Time:** 30 minutes. | **Difficulty:** 1. | **Trailhead:** Begins on the shore east of the Annaberg picnic site (Hike 11).

You'll still find cobblestone remnants along this old Danish road that leads to the ruins of the Leinster Bay Estate and Watermelon Bay. The road borders a popular boat anchorage and swimming and snorkeling area. Marine turtles come ashore at night to bury their eggs on the beach during summer, something worth staying up late to see. If you walk the seashore of Leinster Bay, you may hear what sounds like the laughter of a psychopathic maniac. It's the cry of the duck-like bird known as a coot and apparently the source of the phrase "crazy as a coot."

13. JOHNNY HORN TRAIL

Length: 1.8 miles. | **Time:** 2 hours, one way. | **Difficulty:** 2. | **Trailhead:** The northern end begins where the Leinster Bay Trail ends at Watermelon Bay. The southern trailhead can be accessed on the left, off the East End Road (Route 10) at the Emmaus Moravian Church in Coral Harbor, just past the turnoff to Route 107.

The trail was named after Johan Horn, commandant on St. John during the 1733 slave rebellion. From the northern end, the hike ascends steeply to an upland dry forest and scrub, following the ridges southward to Emmaus Moravian Church at Coral Bay on the south shore. Near the trailhead, a short spur leads to Watermelon Bay and provides the closest access to offshore Watermelon Cay.

Continuing on the main trail, in less than 100 yards you'll come to a second spur that veers to the left. This spur goes to the ruins of a Danish guardhouse at Leinster Point. The guardhouse was intended to block slaves trying to escape to nearby Tortola in the B.V.I.

Climbing the main trail, you'll ascend a hill where the trail forks. The Johnny Horn proceeds to the right. The left spur leads to the Windy Hill estate ruins about 100 yards down the trail. It later became a popular boarding house but was destroyed during the hurricane of 1916.

Continuing on the last leg of the Johnny Horn Trail, you'll cross a gut and then climb a 400-foot-hill with a good view of picturesque Coral Bay Harbor. Descend to Emmaus Moravian Church, one of the oldest sites on the island. The first church here was built in 1782, but it was destroyed three times. The last one, which has thick concrete walls that should withstand almost anything, is from 1919.

14. BROWN BAY TRAIL

Length: 1.6 miles, one way. | **Time:** About 2 hours. | **Difficulty:** 2–3. | **Trailhead:** This spur turns off to the east 0.7 mile from the beginning of the Johnny Horn Trail. The eastern trailhead can be accessed on the left of East End Road (Route 10). Go 1.2 miles east of Emmaus Moravian Church, pass Estate Zootenvaal, and then cross a concrete bridge. Take an immediate left after the bridge and park. The dirt road soon forks; the trail on the right will take you to Brown Bay.

Seeing even less traffic than Johnny Horn, this pathway is not maintained. It descends through a hot, dry valley, borders Brown Bay for a time and then ascends to overlook Hurricane Hole. It comes out on East End Road 1.2 miles east of the Emmaus Moravian Church at Coral Bay on the south shore.

Brown Bay contains the ruins of an estate house dating from 1872. Look for the concrete plaque with the date. Also present are extensive ruins of a sugar mill from an earlier period. These include two horse mills, an old well, copper boiling pot, and cisterns for distilling rum. You're almost guaranteed to see wild donkeys somewhere along this trail. The ruins are just 0.8 mile from the Brown Bay trailhead at East End.

SOUTH SHORE TRAILS

15. REEF BAY TRAIL

Length: 2.2 miles. | **Time:** 2 hours, each way. | **Difficulty:** 2, descending; 3, ascending. Carry insect repellent and water. | **Trailhead:** The trail begins 4.9 miles east of Cruz Bay on Centerline Road. A stone barrier on the side of the road marks the trail beginning. There is a small pull-off area on the opposite side of the road for a handful of cars.

This is one of park's best hikes because it is representative of the island's vegetation. Longer than most, it is the trail on which the Park Service provides scheduled tours down the trail to

Reef Bay. Along the way, you'll pass the visible ruins of four old sugar estates and have the chance to see petroglyphs.

On the park outings, a boat picks you up at Reef Bay for return to Cruz Bay, eliminating the return ascent.

Start by descending a flight of stone steps to reach the sign marking the trailhead. Most of the vegetation here is second- and third-growth, as most of the trees were cut down during plantation days to clear cane fields and to make charcoal. However, the high, steep valley at the beginning was never completely cut, so you can get a sense of what the original subtropical forest was like. This upper stretch also gets more rainfall, so parts of the path can be quite slippery.

The Reef Bay Trail follows the course of the **Reef Bay Gut;** *gut* is the local name for a streambed or drainage ditch. This trail is a microcosm of the entire island. Species you'll pass at the outset are the bay rum tree, whose oil-laden leaves were used to make bay rum cologne popular from the 1890s to the 1940s; the West Indian locust; and the kapok tree. The locust tree, once used for shipbuilding, fence posts, and furniture, contains seeds with a strong-smelling yellow pulp that originally gave it the name of "stinkin' toe." Actually, this pulp is quite edible and sweet. The kapok (silkwood) tree's seed pods contain a fluffy cotton-like fiber that planters once used to stuff mattresses.

You'll pass several drainage gullies, but watch for the pockets of shale; they can be icy-slick even when dry. These drainage gutters, centuries old, keep the trail in good condition. The Danes built the stone gutters to carry water across—not down—the road, preventing washouts, despite the steep terrain. At one time, the path was paved with volcanic rock and ox carts loaded with heavy loads of sugar-filled hogsheads used it regularly.

Note how several of the trees beside the path are bound with strangler figs, so named because the fig may overrun and kill the host tree. The latex of the bark and the fruit of the strangler fig were once used for caulking boats. The broad green leaves have even served as writing paper and playing cards.

Wild donkeys, wild hogs, huge termite mounds, and striking, beautiful golden orb spiders may all be seen along the trail. In the fall you may witness a hermit crab migration of sorts when the crabs go to sea to reproduce and find new, larger shells.

About 30 minutes along the trail, you'll reach the **Jossie Gut Sugar Estate.** Ruins include a circular sugarcane grinding platform from the eighteenth century. The sugar boiling room and several other parts of the factory still stand. The walls are a mosaic of stone, coral, and red and yellow brick. Mortar was made of a mixture of lime from the seashells, sand, and sweet sugarcane molasses. The entire exterior once was covered with a reddish plaster, so it must have been quite a sight.

You'll also see a thorny lime tree, imported from Southeast Asia and cultivated as an export crop on St. John. Sailors ate them to prevent scurvy (a vitamin C deficiency) on long voyages. Other good uses for lime juice you may not know: The juice helps dissolve sea urchin spines, should you step on one. It also helps heal sand fly bites.

After another 15 minutes, you'll arrive at the **Par Force Village,** the foundations of a plantation workers' village. Although sugarcane was no longer cultivated after 1916, some workers tried to stay on by raising cattle and farming. They finally abandoned the land in the 1940s. Old bottles, pots, and glass shards are displayed on the foundation to be admired, not taken.

Walk just five minutes more and you'll reach both the halfway point and the right turnoff for the **Petroglyph Trail,** described below. The Petroglyph Trail is 1.2 miles from the **Reef Bay sugar plantation ruins.**

Continuing to the beach, you'll enter a much drier forest. Eventually you'll reach a small picnic area and pit toilets near the Reef Bay sugar factory ruins. The plantation, one of four on this route, produced sugar and molasses from the 1860s until 1916. The ruins are in good condition and well worth exploring.

At the end of the trail near the beach are pit toilets and a picnic site.

Alternate approach to the ruins and petroglyphs via Reef Bay Beach: From Cruz Bay, go to the right of the Texaco station, proceed downhill and turn right onto the South Shore Road (Route 104). Go just under two miles on South Shore Road to the intersection of Marina Drive and Reef Bay Road. Turn left on Reef Bay Road for about 0.2 mile and, staying on Reef Bay Road, go left up a steep hill. Go for 0.2 mile until on the left you see a house with wooden shingles. Park in the small pull-off (for three or four vehicles) opposite it.

The trail starts at the utility pole. It's a steep descent to the beach, and someone has kindly placed a number of knotted ropes to make the climb down (and back up) much easier. But be careful; the rocks can be slick and slippery.

The path comes out on the beach at Parrot Bay, a part of Reef Bay. Go left along the beach until you reach a cliff of red rocks you must climb around. The 20 to 30-yard trail is obvious, and at high tide you might get your feet wet. Here you'll enjoy a spectacular panorama of Reef Bay that most visitors never see. However, this route does require some tricky scrambling along a seaside cliff where your hands need to be free.

From the rocks you'll step down onto Little Reef Bay Beach, a nice secluded spot that even locals rarely see. Follow the beach, detouring into the woods to skirt around fallen trees blocking the way. At the end of the beach you'll see a trail leading up a cliff. This trail skirts the water and brings you out at the Reef Bay sugar mill ruins. The marked route to the Petroglyph Trail is to your left, just 1.2 miles away.

16. PETROGLYPH TRAIL

Length: 0.2 mile, one way. | **Time:** 7 minutes. | **Difficulty:** 1. | **Trailhead:** This trail starts 1.5 miles, or about 50 minutes, from the beginning of the Reef Bay Trail on Centerline Road. The trailhead is marked and much of the path borders an old stone wall.

After a five-minute walk from the main Reef Bay Trail, the path leads to a small freshwater pool formed by a gut, or streambed, known as the Living Gut. In the rainy season, you can sometimes enjoy the view of a waterfall. Crayfish and shrimp live in the pool, but they may be difficult to see because of algae or the water's dark color. Because this is a rare supply of fresh water, you'll hear lots of birds; near dark, also lots of insects humming overhead, waiting to descend.

The petroglyphs are difficult to see, only faint impressions in the rock at the pool water line. They vary in shape, style, and location and it's likely that each new group of inhabitants left their own graffiti. Most of the drawings, some of which are attributed to the Taino

Indians, are located at the far right end of the pool. However, at the opposite corner are a very obvious cross and several faces. This watering spot is an interesting cultural crossroad of those who've lived on St. John.

The first inhabitants lived in the Reef Bay Valley around 3,000 years ago. They were hunter-gatherers who were replaced by an agricultural group that arrived about 1,000 years later. Columbus reported the island was deserted when he sailed by. The Danes arrived in 1718 and by 1726 Reef Bay Valley was the site of 12 plantations.

Petroglyph Pool may hold a bombshell secret. It's something called the **Fat God,** an eerie, overweight figure carved into the hard rock wall, and one man thinks it was drawn by settlers from Teotihuacan, the pre-Aztec civilization that built the huge pyramids to the sun and the moon near Mexico City.

Robert McCartor, a former history professor at Texas Tech who's made proving his theory a lifelong project, explains his theory about the Fat God. "No one seems to know what he's the god of, but his fat face, fancy vestments, and strange pointed hat are ubiquitous to Mesoamerica."

McCartor says the great Teotihuacan empire had trading posts up to 600 miles away from their base outside Mexico City. He theorizes that they may have set up an outpost on St. John because of its varieties of rock and mined here for greenstone, gold, and other precious metals. St. John, he says, is also at the apex of a possible trading route from South America to Mesoamerica—the pre-Spanish civilization that extended from Mexico to Central America. McCartor points out that the ancient ball court on nearby St. Croix is clearly another remnant of that culture.

When McCartor took me to the pool to show me his proof, he guided me down a precarious shortcut that involved lowering ourselves down a rope fastened to a telephone pole. (He'd warned me he is an expert on shortcuts—especially the ones not to try. He once disappeared for two days in the thick forest of the Virgin Islands National Park, a modern day record for accidental wandering around here. "While I was waiting to be rescued, the National Park Service went hunting for me in all the bars," grumbles McCartor, who still bristles about the 1994 incident. "I got lost only because I tried a shortcut one of their people told me about. Turns out it didn't exist.")

McCartor handed me a blowup of a photo he took at the Petroglyph Pool. The picture shows what thousands see each year at the basin: a seemingly random collection of rock carvings just above the water line. But when I turned the photo on its side, a strange figure emerged from the reflection of the petroglyphs in the water. Once I knew what to look for, I sat back in a crude rock chair a few yards from the pool and there he was in person: the enigmatic fat man.

McCartor is not the first to recognize that the pool has a remarkable mirror image. When he placed an image of the Teotihuacan Fat God (from Michael D. Coe's *The Maya*) next to his own photo from St. John, the similarity was astounding. Another print showing a hefty holy man is in the Royal Danish Library, Copenhagen, and reproduced in *Conquest of Eden* by Michael Paiewonsky. The book identifies the figure as an Arawak god.

Another possible Teotihuacan connection is a peculiar petroglyph at the same pool, near the foot of the Fat God. This one has googly eyes and three threads of droplets drooling from its mouth. McCartor believes they are drops of rain and that the face belongs to Tlaloc, the Mexican rain god.

But are the possible connections between the pool's stone faces and the god's of relatively far-off civilizations enough to rewrite history? Not yet. McCartor visits St. John several times a year searching for Teotihuacan ruins to confirm his theory. "The chances of finding any buildings are remote," he admits. "They'd be several thousand years old." But what keeps McCartor going is the knowledge that discovering them would set off perhaps the biggest scientific explosion since the volcanic eruption that formed St. John.

17. LAMESHUR BAY TRAIL

Length: 1.5 miles. | **Time:** 1.25 hours, round trip. | **Difficulty:** 2–3. There's a steep 467-foot-high hill in your way. | **Trailhead:** You absolutely need a four-wheel-drive vehicle for this road. Starts at Great Lameshur Bay, which is reached by taking Centerline Road (Route 10) to Coral Bay and turning right onto Route 107 at the harbor. Shortly after passing Salt Pond Bay the road turns gnarly, becoming mostly rubble and there is a steep hill to descend shortly before reaching Lameshur Bay. The trailhead is well marked and there's plenty of parking space. Also some ruins on the left.

This hike connects Lameshur Bay with the Reef Bay Trail. From the Lameshur Bay trailhead, it's 2.6 miles to the Reef Bay sugar mill ruins and 1.2 miles to the petroglyphs. Going through open dry forest, it is a much tougher walk to the sugar mill ruins and the petroglyphs than coming in via Reef Bay Beach (described above). Within sight of the trailhead (unless it's been removed) is a sign that says "No Crab Hunting." The large land crabs are considered a great delicacy on many islands, including this one, but hunting them is prohibited inside park boundaries.

You'll pass two spur trails. One spur of 0.3 mile leads off to a small salt pond and Europa Bay, which is mostly a coral rubble beach.

Near the end of the hike as you're descending into Reef Bay Valley is another fork in the trail. The left path goes to the Reef Bay Trail. The right leads to the Reef Bay Great House. At one time the national park was attempting to restore the house and did manage to replace the roof before funds ran out. It is unlikely the house will be restored anytime in the near future. Too bad—the architecture is worth preserving and the view is good. The last resident of the house, Anna Marsh, was killed here and her jewelry stolen. The murderer was caught when he attempted to sell the jewelry in St. Thomas.

18. YAWZI POINT TRAIL

Length: 0.3 mile, one way. | **Time:** 20 minutes. | **Difficulty:** 1. | **Trailhead:** Starts at the end of the beach at Little Lameshur Bay. From Route 10, turn south on Route 107 to just past Salt Pond Bay.

This very short trail is named for outcasts infected with yaws, the West Indian version of leprosy who were forced to live in isolation on this narrow peninsula. Yaws, which is confined almost exclusively to the warm moist tropics, causes eruptions on the skin and is highly contagious, transmitted either by flies or by direct contact with an open sore. Once considered a tropical form of syphilis, yaws can appear on any part of the body. Sexual contact is the least likely way it is spread. It is easily treated today. Consider what it must have been like to be exiled in this region of thorny scrub vegetation and isolated coves.

The trail ends at a rocky point with a good view to the east of Great Lameshur Bay and, to the west, St. John's southern coast.

19. BORDEAUX MOUNTAIN TRAIL

Length: 1.2 miles, one way. | **Time:** 1 hour down, 2 hours up. | **Difficulty:** 3–4. There is a 1,200-foot difference in elevation from top to bottom. | **Trailhead:** To walk down, start on Bordeaux Mountain Road 1.7 miles southeast of Centerline Road. To climb up, the path begins to the right of the Lameshur Bay trail (Hike 17). Follow the directions of the stone wall upwards.

As a practical matter, it makes more sense to climb up, rest, and walk back down. Yes, it is a tough walk, but the trail follows an old plantation road that oxen with heavy loads had to climb from the Lameshur Bay estate to the Bordeaux estate at the top. The grade is steady but not overly steep.

The first 0.2 mile of the walk is part of a four-wheel-drive road leading to a ranger's house off to the right. Soon you'll come to a one-person stone seat, the first of several built along the trail. You'll also pass from dry forest to moist forest, spending a lot of time in the sun.

The trail emerges at Bordeaux Mountain Road across from the Bordeaux sugar plantation, built between 1790 and 1820. Part of it was demolished during the construction of the road, which links Centerline Road with Coral Bay.

SALT POND BAY–DRUNK BAY–RAM HEAD TRAILS

20. SALT POND BAY TRAIL

Length: 0.2 mile, one way. | **Time:** 7 minutes. | **Difficulty:** 1–2. | **Trailhead:** Driving east on Centerline Road, turn right at Coral Bay onto Route 107 (Bordeaux Mountain Road). Go 3.9 miles to Salt Pond Bay to the parking area on your left. The road down to Salt Pond Bay is usually gated off, which does not mean the trails are closed. Walk around the gate and follow the road down.

This graded, open roadbed descends through cactus scrub to Salt Pond Beach, which has some of the best snorkeling on the south coast. There is a picnic area and a chemical toilet. Some families bring a picnic and spend the day swimming and sunning here. It never seems very crowded. In May and June you may see locals harvesting salt from Salt Pond. The bay is a popular sailboat anchorage.

21. DRUNK BAY TRAIL

Length: 0.3 mile, one way. | **Time:** 10 minutes. | **Difficulty:** 1. | **Trailhead:** At the south end of Salt Pond Bay Beach.

From Salt Pond Bay Beach, turn east to follow the Drunk Bay Trail. A sign points the way. The vegetation here is stunted and windswept near the rocky bay, where swimming is dangerous. Interesting to speculate about how this place received its name.

22. RAM HEAD TRAIL

Length: 1 mile, one way. | **Time:** 45 minutes. | **Difficulty:** 2–3. Wear shoes, not sandals, because of all the loose cactus spines on the trail. | **Trailhead:** This rocky, exposed trail also starts at the southern end of Salt Pond Bay Beach.

I consider this the best hike on all of St. John. The trail eventually leads to Ram Head Point, that striking hump of green landscape off in the distance to your right. The views from the point are spectacular, and the deeply cut shoreline is impressive. Geologically, Ram Head Point is composed of the oldest rock found on St. John. Take plenty of water and sun protection. A sunrise hike is the most pleasant. Go too close to sunset and you'll come home in the dark. This is not a trail to walk for the first time in pitch black, even with the best flashlight.

Runaway slaves apparently lived at Ram Head Point in the 1700s. Although the ground is rocky and thorny, living would have been relatively easy. Whelks could easily be taken from Salt Pond Bay, and the point is always cooled by the tradewinds. During the slave rebellion of 1733 a number of slaves (somewhere between 8 and 12) committed suicide at the point. Legend says they leaped to their deaths on the rocks below rather than face recapture. (Other accounts relate that they committed suicide with firearms.)

This can be a very confusing hike because the trail is not well marked. Furthermore, many different false trails have been made by people trying to reach the point. This is *the* one hike on the island where you need to pay close attention to the accompanying directions to avoid getting lost. If you do wander afield, you won't come to any harm; the hike will just take a lot longer. Possibly hours longer.

To find the trail, walk along Salt Pond Bay to the end of the beach and turn right. Walk along the rocky shoreline for about 0.25 mile. In some spots you'll be able to discern a trail of sorts among the rocks, but for many yards there is no indication anyone has ever passed this way before. Have faith.

After about 0.25 mile you'll find an obvious, identifiable trail that begins to climb above Salt Pond Bay. The path follows the top of a ridge and then descends to Blue Rock Beach. Avoid the trail going off to the left that appears to skirt the ridge. You'll come down to Blue Rock Beach near a tree with an aged, very thick rope hanging in the branches. Remember this sight: it's your trail marker coming back.

You'll walk the rocky shoreline for about 0.25 mile. However, unlike at the first rocky beach, there are many indications of previous hikers. Some have even built small stone cairns. Most of the cairns are meaningless construction but one of them will signal that it's time to leave the beach and start climbing upward. If you're lucky, an arrow will be pointing to the path; unless it's been blown away.

Avoid the many side trails. Follow the path and its several switchbacks along the ridge. The trail will come almost to the edge of the east shore at a truly striking ravine where the wind can blow at gale force. To the east, there's nothing but open ocean between you and the nearest coastline: Africa. Walk carefully because of all the hundreds (thousands?) of barrel cactus.

You'll probably see wild goats and envy their agility on this uneven terrain. Standing on the peak of Ram Head Point, you'll be almost 200 feet above sea level.

Returning, find the white arrow of stones that points to the return trail from Blue Rock Beach. Look for that hanging rope. Turn left at the tree and you'll be back on the trail. If you stay on the beach and go past the rope, you should encounter the trail once you're forced to start climbing uphill.

St. Croix

The largest of the U.S. Virgins, St. Croix (pronounced "Saint Croy") covers a total of 84 square miles, compared to St. Thomas's 32 square miles and St. John's 24 square miles. Its name is the French version of the name Columbus gave it, Santa Cruz ("Holy Cross"). The Danes bought the island from the French in 1733, after establishing themselves on St. Thomas.

St. Croix has at times been preeminent among the U.S Virgin Islands, particularly during the days of sugarcane. Just how important sugar was to the local economy is still clearly evident: the island is dotted with the ruins and restorations of more than 100 old sugar mills and great houses. The islands were so wealthy mere militiamen wore epaulets of gold, an ostentation forbidden in Denmark because such elaborate ornamentation might drain the country's treasury.

After the slaves were emancipated, labor costs made growing cane unprofitable. Owners of the big sugar plantations began abandoning their estates, the island's population dwindled, and the economy went into a severe slump. It has never kept up with the far more prosperous St. Thomas.

St. Croix is separated into two distinct regions marked by the cities of Christiansted and Frederiksted. Both cities are characteristically Danish, adapting eighteenth-century European styles to the West Indies. Strict building codes kept the towns from becoming shoddily built tinderboxes. Unlike some of the more ramshackle British-ruled outposts, these cities were never leveled by fire. By law, the first floor had to be constructed of brick and stone, so a lot of yellow brick was shipped as ballast from Denmark for this purpose. Wood could be used only in the second floor, normally the living quarters. The first floor usually contained the shops and retail stores. It was common to build long galleries across the front on the second floor and support them with stone arches, leaving the sidewalks well shaded.

Although the Danes owned St. Croix and offered tax concessions to anyone who would come to raise sugarcane or cotton, mostly British, Dutch, and Portuguese took up the offer. By 1800, 375 different estates were growing sugarcane, cotton, tobacco, and indigo. Because the English controlled the economy by producing most of the sugarcane and rum, English became the everyday language on this Danish island. That helps explain why some of the old estate names still used today—Good Hope, Judith's Fancy—are in English, not Danish. (I can't help wondering what the owner of Slob Estate was really like. Was that his name or his manner?)

Getting Around: St. Croix needs more road signs. Because things are so spread out, a rental car is only way to move around the island; taxi fares will eat you alive. But if you drive, remember: drive on the *left*. True, you're on American soil, but these American territories have used the "English" side of the road since they were under Danish rule.

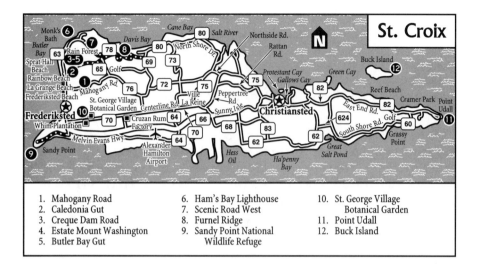

St. Croix

1. Mahogany Road
2. Caledonia Gut
3. Creque Dam Road
4. Estate Mount Washington
5. Butler Bay Gut
6. Ham's Bay Lighthouse
7. Scenic Road West
8. Furnel Ridge
9. Sandy Point National
   Wildlife Refuge
10. St. George Village
    Botanical Garden
11. Point Udall
12. Buck Island

Where to Stay: The Hotel Caravelle is located on the Christiansted waterfront just a few steps away from the seaplane landing and the Caravelle Arcade. The 43 newly furnished rooms include air conditioning, private bath, refrigerator, cable TV, and direct-dial phones. For information, call (800) 524-0410.

Hiking & Walking Services: Unlike St. John, where the trails and distances are clearly marked with a system of signs, St. Croix's hikes tend to be hidden treasures, and so visitors often hike in guided groups. However, it is easy to walk the roads at the western end, such as Mahogany Road and Creque (pronounced "creaky") Dam Road, which provide an obvious path into the rain forest. **The St. Croix Environmental Association (SEA)** offers hikes into the Caledonia rain forest and in the Salt River National Park on a demand basis. SEA rates its rain forest hike as strenuous because of the boulders and fallen trees. For more information, call (340) 773-1989. The charge is $20 for adults and $12 for children age 12 and under.

Environmentalist **Olasee Davis** conducts group hikes (30-person maximum) on Sundays and holidays for a charge of $15 per person. The itinerary changes regularly and he sometimes can be persuaded to do individualized hikes. Contact him at (340) 778-9491 or (340) 772-0325.

St. Croix Heritage Tours offers weekly walking tours of Christiansted and Frederiksted. Each walk lasts about 1.5 hours. The Christiansted tour starts at 9:30 a.m. on Tuesdays at the gazebo on the grounds of Fort Christiansvaern. It costs $12, which covers all admission fees and includes a cold drink; half-price for children under age 10. The Frederiksted walk, beginning at 9:30 a.m. on Wednesdays, starts at the end of the cruise-ship dock. The cost is $8. Tours also are offered of Estate Mount Washington, the St. Croix

Leap wood-carving operation, and Estate Little Princess, which is owned by the Nature Conservancy. For more information, call (340) 778-6997.

CHRISTIANSTED AFOOT!

Time: 1.5 hours. | **Difficulty:** 1. | **Trailhead:** Visitor's Bureau.

Most of the hotels and shopping are located in Christiansted, considered one of the Caribbean's prettiest ports, with a lingering Danish influence. Several blocks along the waterfront are part of a 27-acre Christiansted National Historic District, including 6 historic buildings operated by the U.S. National Park Service. With its colonial buildings and open-air restaurants, Christiansted is a joy to explore on foot.

1. **Visitor's Bureau:** Built in 1856 as the Old Scalehouse, this was the site of the huge scale that weighed all merchandise being imported into Christiansted. It was also where exports were inspected and where troops attached to the Customs Service were garrisoned. The scale is still present.

2. **Old Danish Customs House:** This is the first place the Danish captains would report to pay their Customs fees. Part of the first floor was built in 1751, but most of the building was constructed between 1828 and 1830.

3. **Fort Christiansvaern:** This is the most outstanding building in town. Sailors entering port would see this wall of bright yellow, a color the Danes seemed to favor. Begun in 1733 with yellow ballast-brick, the fort was partially destroyed by a hurricane and then rebuilt in 1837. It saw its last use by the military in 1878, then became a police station and courthouse. Fort Christiansvaern, the best preserved of the five Danish forts in the U.S. Virgin Islands, is restored to its 1830s incarnation and contains an exhibit of local military history. Dungeons, ramparts, and old cannon are but a few of its features.

4. **Old Danish West India and Guinea Company Warehouse:** This is the company that purchased St. Croix from France and turned it into a sugarcane factory. The building's history traces back to 1749 when it first housed provisions, offices, and personnel. Slave auctions were held in the courtyard. After 1833, the Danish military used it as a depot, later a telegraph office. Now the post office, it is located across Company Street.

5. **The Steeple Building:** Built as a Lutheran Church by the Danes in 1753, the steeple was added around 1794. After 1831, the Danish government turned the church into a military bakery, a hospital, and a school. This prominent landmark is now a National Park Museum with archaeological, historical, and architectural exhibits.

6. **Government House:** Located on King Street beyond the Steeple Building, it is considered one of the finest examples of Danish architecture remaining in the islands. It was built in 1747 as a home for a wealthy Danish merchant. The Danish government purchased the house in 1771 and connected it to a house on the corner of Queen Cross Street. It became the seat of Danish government. The building still houses government offices and a court. Its most striking feature is the elegant eighteenth-century staircase rising from the street into the building.

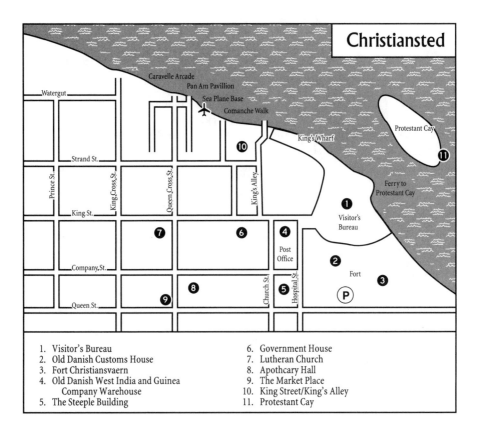

Christiansted

1. Visitor's Bureau
2. Old Danish Customs House
3. Fort Christiansvaern
4. Old Danish West India and Guinea Company Warehouse
5. The Steeple Building
6. Government House
7. Lutheran Church
8. Apothcary Hall
9. The Market Place
10. King Street/King's Alley
11. Protestant Cay

7. Lutheran Church: Built in the 1740s as the Dutch Reformed Church, it became the Lutheran Church in 1834.

8. Apothecary Hall: On Company Street, this was an eighteenth-century pharmacy and a private residence. It has been carved up into offices, a restaurant, and boutiques.

9. The Market Place: Another half-block beyond Apothecary Hall on Company Street. It is not nearly as colorful or as interesting as the markets on some other islands. Since 1735, this has been the place to buy fresh, locally grown vegetables and fruits.

10. King Street/King's Alley: A prime waterfront shopping area housed in what were once old trading houses. This section features boutiques and open-air restaurants; an enjoyable place to window-shop.

11. Protestant Cay: This small island-hotel at the harbor entrance is typically called the Hotel on the Cay. Its original name comes from the era of French ownership, when only Catholics could be buried on St. Croix. Protestants were buried on this tiny spit of land. When the French left St. Croix around 1696, pirates turned it into a favorite meeting point.

FREDERIKSTED AFOOT!

Time: 1 hour. | **Difficulty:** 1. | **Trailhead:** Fort Frederik, near the cruise ship pier.

Frederiksted is located at the western end of St. Croix, a 45-minute drive from Christiansted. Since its founding in 1751, it has been St. Croix's main deepwater harbor; all cruise ships dock here. Visitors are then transported by bus to Christiansted and other points of interest. Compared to Christiansted, however, this is a ghost town with little happening, except at the fort when the cruise ships are in. Unfortunately, the elaborate West Indian gingerbread trim on buildings, such as the Lacy Victoria House, which was built before 1803, has largely fallen victim to time and hurricanes. If you are arriving by cruise ship, my advice is take the first taxi out of town and leave Frederiksted for last. The fort is really the only thing worth seeing.

1. **Old Town Pier:** Now underwater, this is one of the finest night dives in the Caribbean. Lots of sea horses! See one of the dive shops along the waterfront.

2. **Fort Frederik:** Where the Governor General in 1848 announced the emancipation of all Danish-owned slaves; for this reason, the town today is still sometimes called "Freedom City" by locals. The fort, begun in 1752, is where the flag of the 13 rebelling U.S. colonies was first saluted by a foreign flag, in 1776. The fort is now a museum, restored to the way it looked in 1820. Adjacent to it is Buddhoe Park with a bronze statue of the slave rebellion leader.

3. **Old Custom's House:** Built in the late 1800s with a twentieth-century addition.

4. **Victoria House:** Built in 1803, fire destroyed it in 1878. Rebuilt, it is noted for its gingerbread trim and Victorian architecture.

5. **The Market Place:** On Queen Street, this is a lively place for fresh fruit and vegetables.

6. **Apothecary Hall:** On King Cross Street, is another example of the architecture popular in the mid-1800s.

7. **Old Public Library:** Built in 1803. In 1888 the staircase was decorated with bells by an owner named, well, Bell.

ELSEWHERE ON ST. CROIX

THE WEST END

1. MAHOGANY ROAD

Length: 2.5 miles. | **Time:** 1–2 hours. | **Difficulty:** 1–2. | **Trailhead:** At the beginning of Mahogany Road (Highway 76) where it turns inland from Highway 63 between Frederiksted and Spratt Hall Beach. Look for the sign pointing to St. Croix's Leap, which produces mahogany handicrafts. Park on the side of the road, well off the pavement.

Despite the "rain forest" name, St. Croix does not have true rain forest; it doesn't receive nearly enough precipitation. However, the vegetation is definitely moist and luxuriant, and the

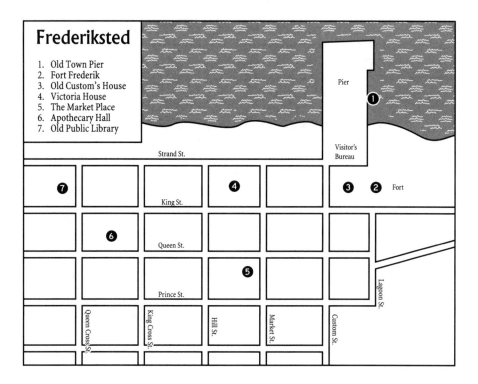

Frederiksted

1. Old Town Pier
2. Fort Frederik
3. Old Custom's House
4. Victoria House
5. The Market Place
6. Apothecary Hall
7. Old Public Library

Pier

Strand St.

Visitor's Bureau

King St.

Fort

Queen St.

Prince St.

Lagoon St.

Queen Cross St.

King Cross St.

Hill St.

Market St.

Custom St.

tree canopy, which towers 100 feet overhead, contains orchids and ferns, just as you would expect to find in a genuine rain forest. The farther inland you go, the cooler it becomes, making this an exceptionally nice walk.

The striking giant 200- to 300-year-old mahogany trees lining the start of the road are becoming fewer, and unfortunately they are not being replanted. The greathouse on the left is **Estate Prosperity,** which is private. The road makes a gradual ascent. At about 1.5 miles on the right is the Carl & Marie Lawaetz Museum at **Little LaGrange Estate.** It's open 10 a.m. to 4 p.m. Tuesday to Saturday; $5 admission fee to enter the house. You're allowed to walk the grounds free. Its concrete aqueduct was built in the early 1900s to provide water to the estate. It was St. Croix's first irrigation project. Another 0.6 mile along Mahogany Road is the turnoff to **St. Croix Leap,** at the end of the 0.3-mile dirt road on the right. At St. Croix Leap artisans fashion carvings from a variety of local woods, including mahogany that was felled by storms. Return to the car.

2. CALEDONIA GUT

Length: 3 miles, round trip. | **Time:** 1.5 hours. | **Difficulty:** 2–4. This walk involves rock hopping in some sections of the dry streambed. | **Trailhead:** At the foot of the Caledonia Valley coming up the gut and in from the beach on Route 63. It's the same location as the quarry.

In the U.S.V.I., gut is the term of a stream bed, and that's what this walk involves, a walk up a normally dry stream bed to a 50-foot-high waterfall. The gut usually flows only after rains and even then the water level is low; the waterfall runs only after a recent rainfall. If you happen to be here in March and August you could see throngs of soldier crabs moving through the gut as they travel to the ocean to lay their eggs. There is a road beside the gut that offer an alternative passage, but it may be fenced off; if so, you'll have to walk up the gut the entire way. Unfortunately, the walk is a lot more open than it used to be. Many of the trees along the gut were burned in 1995; before that you couldn't see the sky.

Soon after starting, you'll reach a dam built in the 1950s. You'll have to scramble up a tree to get to the top. The tall shining kapok tree on the left is like a lighthouse; a tree this big would have made several canoes. You'll also pass a slave wall from an old cocoa plantation as well as cocoa trees. The gut will become narrower and the rocks larger and slicker as you continue. You'll have to scramble up some of those rocks to reach the base of the waterfall at a confluence about 1.5 miles from the beach.

3. Creque Dam Road

Length: 6.4 miles. | **Time:** 3 hours, round trip. | **Difficulty:** 2. | **Trailhead:** Where Route 58 splits off from Spratt Hall Road (Highway 63) north of Frederiksted.

Pronounced "Creaky" Dam Road, it first passes through Spratt Hall Plantation, which accepts overnight guests. It enters another section of moist forest and ends at the Western Scenic Drive.

Badly washed out by several hurricanes, the road was paved and widened in 1997. It parallels a watercourse and was once famous for its tall trees, some over 100 feet high. But as part of the paving process, the thick tree canopy was pruned for the power lines and many of the bush medicine plants were removed. Today, there is much more open sky over the road but the surrounding forest remains just as thick.

After 1.3 miles, you'll encounter Creque Dam itself, a 45-foot-high arch dam built in 1926 to store water for Frederiksted. The dam sometimes runs low because it has a leak. It's possible to walk across the spillway to the opposite bank. If you do, you'll certainly notice how the dam is silting up. Designed to hold 9 million gallons of water, it may be storing nothing but silt in another quarter century.

The large tree here with trunk spines is the native sandbox tree. Flowering winter through summer, its name comes from its fruit, which once was hollowed out while still green to hold sand that would be sprinkled over letters and documents to blot the ink. A bird commonly heard here is the pearly-eyed thrasher.

Continuing on Creque Dam Road, you will pass another kapok tree that is buttressed, one way of telling it apart from the sandbox tree. Kapok thorns also tend to be less densely packed and its leaves are shaped like a fan while the sandbox has a simple two-inch-long leaf.

At 1.95 miles are the ruins of the estate Mount Victory greathouse, which was turned into a school in the 1840s. Shortly you will pass kapok, sandbox, and spreading raintrees introduced from Brazil and Mexico.

At 2.95 miles Creque Dam Road junctions with Route 765 (which joins Mahogany Road [Route 76] 1.2 miles later, headed south). At 3.2 miles Creque Dam Road ends at the junction with the Western Scenic Drive (Route 78). Going west (left) from here, it's 3.4 miles to Ham Bay (see below).

4. Estate Mount Washington

Length: About 3 miles. | **Time:** 1.5 hours. | **Difficulty:** 2. | **Trailhead:** The dirt road begins off Route 63 almost 4 miles north of Frederiksted.

This road has so many interesting plants that cruise ship passengers are sometimes brought here on hikes. It's shady much of the way. First, pass an old village cemetery on the left and at about 0.8 mile you'll reach ruins the sugar factory and animal mill on the left. A self-guided walk with interpretive signs explores the ruins.

To reach the top of Mount Washington (also called Frenchman Hill), return to the road. Almost immediately you'll come to a three-way fork. Continue straight ahead. In less than 0.25 mile there is another three-way fork. Once again take the middle road. You'll follow the ridge line through moist forest, ending with a good panoramic view of the area.

5. Butler Bay Gut

Length: 1 mile, one way. | **Time:** 45 minutes. | **Difficulty:** 2–3. Some rock hopping up the dry stream bed. | **Trailhead:** On Route 63, about 5 miles north of Frederiksted. The dirt road leading to the gut is across from the popular swimming and picnic beach at Butler Bay.

Walk a couple of hundred yards up the dirt road until it forks. Go right, down to and across the streambed. Go left for about 100 yards, following a trail that stays close to the gut. In about another 100 yards the gut clears of vegetation, and you should find it easier walking.

You'll pass strap ferns with long unbranched fronds, as well as strangler figs that literally do strangle the life out of a tree with their powerful roots. You'll have ascended about 300 vertical feet when you reach the gut's 80-foot-high waterfall. It's not likely to be running unless it has rained. Without a guide, it can be risky going up and beyond the falls. Most people turn back at this point.

6. Ham's Bay Lighthouse

Time: 1 hour. | **Difficulty:** 3. A good uphill climb in places. | **Trailhead:** Follow Route 63 north until the hard surface ends at concrete pillars marking the Scenic Road West, a dirt road.

To reach the lighthouse, take the paved road uphill until you reach a fence. Stay on the outside of it until you can cross a footbridge and begin the steep walk to the lighthouse. The coastal view is worth the effort. The big tidal pool down below is called Maroon Hole. You might want to visit the beach after you descend because the shelling can be interesting.

7. SCENIC ROAD WEST

Length: 7.5 miles, one way. | **Time:** 5 hours. | **Difficulty:** 3. | **Trailhead:** Follow Route 63 north until the hard surface ends at concrete pillars marking the Scenic Road West, a dirt road. (The same as for the Ham's Bay Lighthouse hike.)

The Scenic Road West is a dirt road best traveled on foot or with a four-wheel-drive vehicle. This is a very isolated stretch where you probably won't see anyone else, so provision yourself well: It takes five hours to walk just one way, and it's occasionally strenuous terrain. You'll ascend a ridgeline populated with kapok and mahogany trees and long trailing vines. Stay left at the next intersection. At 3.4 miles, you'll intersect Creque Dam Road (see above), and at 4 miles you'll come to a superb view of Davis Bay to the north, Blue Mountain to the east and the rolling fairways of the Fountain Valley Golf Club off to the south. Another 1.5 miles will put you at the end of the Scenic Road West and place you on paved Route 69. This is perhaps the best panoramic view on the entire island.

8. FURNEL RIDGE

Time: 10–12 hours. | **Difficulty:** 3. | **Trailhead:** Going west on the Scenic Road West is an obvious pull-off for an overview of the north coast; it's the first such pull-off.. The trail down begins here, not an obvious starting point.

As you'll notice from the overlook, the valley below is incredibly lush and green, a complete wilderness of nothing but treetops. Along the trail you'll have options to visit many bays and coves, starting with Annaly Cove, then Annaly Bay, Annaly Notch, Willis Bay, Wells Bay, and on to Davis Beach. Or you can stick to the main Furnel Ridge path, which comes out on the Scenic Road West several miles farther east.

To really do this right, it's a strenuous hike, an all-day endeavor that requires 10 to 12 hours of occasionally steep ascents and descents. And you start out with a very steep descent down to the coast, dropping over 600 feet in under a half-mile. Wear long pants, take plenty of water and snacks, and start early.

9. SANDY POINT NATIONAL WILDLIFE REFUGE

Length: 3 miles. | **Time:** 3 hours. | **Difficulty:** 2–3, depending on heat. | **Trailhead:** You have two choices. The simplest is to start at Frederiksted and walk southeast along the shore toward Sandy Point. Signs will tell you when the beach becomes part of the NWR.

If you're interested in birding, the following route will take you closer to the salt pond near the point. Take Route 70 from Frederiksted. Where it turns left at a 90° angle for Christiansted, go straight ahead on Route 661 to where it makes a 90° turn left onto Route 66. Do not take

Route 66 but go right onto a dirt road. At the first intersection on the dirt road, bear left. Go straight at the next intersection to the gate marking the NWR boundary. *Note:* The beach may be closed during the leatherback nesting period from March through July. Call (340) 775-6762 for information.

The 380-acre Sandy Point peninsula is a protected reserve for the leatherback and other sea turtles. The leatherback is the largest of all sea turtles, weighing from 700 to 2,000 pounds. However, it starts life as a mere two-ounce egg. Leatherbacks may live as long as 80 years. This is one of the 13 most important leatherback nesting grounds in the world and the most important in U.S. possession. It's been said that at one time a person could walk the beach to Frederiksted on the backs of nesting turtles without touching the sand. The leatherback turtles favor this beach because the water around it is deep, providing easy access.

A salt pond here usually has plovers feeding in it. The stunted plant community bordering the gorgeous, flat beach is a marked contrast to the dark green hills of the moist forest that dominate the northern horizon.

10. St. George Village Botanical Garden

Time: 1–2 hours. | **Difficulty:** 1. | **Trailhead:** Located just off Centerline Road, 3.5 miles east of Frederiksted in Estate St. George. For information on fees and hours, call (340) 772-3874.

With 16 acres of various gardens, this is considered one of the finest botanical collections in the Caribbean. In addition, you'll find the ruins and restorations of a nineteenth-century Danish sugar plantation workers' village. A map takes you on a self-guided tour through sites identified as the Rain Forest, Laura's Garden, the Cactus Garden, the original sugar factory, a cemetery, and the largest Arawak Indian settlement on St. Croix. Some of the trees/plants identified are worthy of special mention. The dildo cactus is shaped just as you would expect but slightly more thorny than the (un)real thing. The pods of the prickly barked sandbox tree were popular in the 1700s for holding sand for blotting ink. You can write on the leaves of the autograph tree, but please, go easy on the drawings of anatomic parts. The dildo cactus itself is shocking enough for some people.

The East End

11. Point Udall Hikes

Length: About 1 mile. | **Time:** 45 minutes to Jack's Bay. | **Difficulty:** 2–3. | **Trailhead:** Follow Route 82 east to the very end, the easternmost point of the United States.

Point Udall is a dry, fairly barren area that most people visit only because of its unique geographic location. But it also is the jumping-off point to quite a good hike. You can park at Cramer Beach Park and walk for about an hour to reach Point Udall, or you can drive along the paved road leading right to it.

The best way to appreciate this place is close to the point, down by the sea where you can hear it and truly feel the wind. The path going over the guardrail is obvious. The barrel cactus growing red Shriner-like hats are called Turk's head cactus. Don't get too close to the waves.

You can also take the trail down to Isaac Bay, which is fairly secluded because most people don't take the time to make the short walk down to the half-mile of white sand beach. Below and to the right, you'll see more Turk's head cactus; the tall ones are called dildo cactus.

From Isaac Bay you can visit the secluded white sand beach at Jack's Bay by climbing and following the natural gullies in the rocks at Isaac Point. There's also an old trail, but it's sometimes difficult to find and follow.

12. BUCK ISLAND

Time: Excursions last either a half or full day. | **Difficulty:** 2. | **Trailhead:** Offshore, 2 miles north of St. Croix.

Buck Island Reef National Monument is probably the most-visited and best-known snorkeling/diving site anywhere in the Virgin Islands. Under the protection of the U.S. National Park Service since 1962, it has 700 acres of protected coral reef.

You also can hike into the interior of 180-acre Buck Island. Once a major grazing location for goats, Buck Island was stripped of its trees to create pasture. Now free of domestic animals and humans, the land is returning to a more natural state. It is a dry place, particularly the eastern and southern sections, where the vegetation is mostly cactus and low thorny bushes. Trees are found in some moist areas, on the western slopes and in ravines.

Buck Island walks have become increasingly popular. The Park Service has installed two picnic areas, and the 45-minute hike to the 300-foot high summit has an observation tower for better views of Buck Island and St. Croix. This trail is rocky, so wear shoes. A combination snorkel/hike excursion from St. Croix will take anywhere between a half and a full day.

ST. CROIX PLANTATIONS

When sugarcane was king, St. Croix had 250 plantations working the island. Today, many of the old greathouses have been restored and turned into private homes. The few estates open to the public provide interesting walks.

Estate Whim Plantation Museum: The Whim Estate, just west of Frederiksted, is the finest plantation greathouse still surviving. The oval-shaped, high-ceilinged great house made of rock and coral and banded together with a mortar of sugar molasses and seashells has been carefully restored and is furnished with period antiques throughout. Architecturally unique, it even has a small dry moat around the base, used not for defense but to help ventilate and light the basement where the provisions for slaves were once held. Besides the restored cook house (where you can snack on a johnnycake), mills, and a gift shop, the Whim Estate has the island's most photogenic windmill, complete with giant white blades, something you rarely see on any of the islands. Open Monday to Saturday 10 a.m. to 4 p.m. Call (340) 772-0598.

Estate Little Princess: A 24-acre plantation belonging to the Nature Conservancy that overlooks Christiansted harbor. It contains eighteenth- and nineteenth-century greathouses, water well towers, sugar mills, and walking trails through native plants. Call (340) 773-5575 or (340) 774-7633 for opening times.

Estate Mount Washington: Cruise ship passengers use the dirt road leading to the greathouse for a nature walk. Located near Frederiksted, the estate was only rediscovered in 1984. Ruins of the old stone buildings are open to the public, but the greathouse is not. Visitors are invited to drive here as well as walk. The great house at neighboring Estate Butler Bay is privately owned and being remodeled; it is not open to the public.

I N D E X

Index

Index

A B O U T   T H E   A U T H O R

Old Caribbean Saying: "*You catch cows by their horns, men by their words.*"

M. Timothy O'Keefe specializes in travel and outdoor activities. His magazine articles and photography have won more than 50 regional and national awards. A former president of the Florida Outdoor Writers Association, he has been a regular contributor to *Caribbean Travel & Life* magazine since its inception.

His books include *The Spicy Camp Cook Book* (1997, Menasha Ridge Press); *Great Adventures in Florida* (1996, second edition 2000, Menasha Ridge Press); *Seasonal Guide to the Natural Year: Florida and the Alabama and Georgia Coasts* (1996, Fulcrum Publishing); *The Hiker's Guide to Florida* (Falcon Press, 1993, second edition 2000); *Sea Turtles, The Watcher's Guide* (1995, Larsen's Outdoor Publishing); *Manatees, Our Vanishing Mermaids* (1993, revised 1995, Larsen's Outdoor Publishing); *Diving to Adventure* (1992, Larsen's Outdoor Publishing); and *Fish and Dive the Caribbean* (1991) and *Fish and Dive Florida & The Keys* (1992, Larsen's Outdoor Publishing), both of which were co-authored with Larry Larsen; and *AAA Photo Journey to Central Florida* (1991).

The Florida Outdoor Writers Association named the *Seasonal Guide to the Natural Year* "Best Book" of 1996 and *The Spicy Camp Cook Book* the "Best Book" of 1997. *Fish and Dive the Caribbean* was a finalist for "Best Content" in the annual competition of the National Association of Independent Publishers.

Tim holds a Ph.D. from the University of North Carolina at Chapel Hill and is head of the journalism division in the Nicholson School of Communication at the University of Central Florida.